For reference
Not to be taken from the room.

D1767567

Poetry
for Students

National Advisory Board

Susan Allison: Head Librarian, Lewiston High School, Lewiston, Maine. Standards Committee Chairperson for Maine School Library (MASL) Programs. Board member, Julia Adams Morse Memorial Library, Greene, Maine. Advisor to Lewiston Public Library Planning Process.

Jennifer Hood: Young Adult/Reference Librarian, Cumberland Public Library, Cumberland, Rhode Island. Certified teacher, Rhode Island. Member of the New England Library Association, Rhode Island Library Association, and the Rhode Island Educational Media Association.

Ann Kearney: Head Librarian and Media Specialist, Christopher Columbus High School, Miami, Florida, 1982–2002. Thirty-two years as Librarian in various educational institutions ranging from grade schools through graduate programs. Library positions at Miami-Dade Community College, the University of Miami's Medical School Library, and Carrollton School in Coconut Grove, Florida. B.A. from University of Detroit, 1967 (magna cum laude); M.L.S., University of Missouri–Columbia, 1974. Volunteer Project Leader for a school in rural Jamaica; volunteer with Adult Literacy programs.

Laurie St. Laurent: Head of Adult and Children's Services, East Lansing Public Library, East Lansing, Michigan, 1994–. M.L.S. from Western Michigan University. Chair of Michigan Library Association's 1998 Michigan Summer Reading Program; Chair of the Children's Services Division in 2000–2001; and Vice-President of the Association in 2002–2003. Board member of several regional early childhood literacy organizations and member of the Library of Michigan Youth Services Advisory Committee.

Heidi Stohs: Instructor in Language Arts, grades 10–12, Solomon High School, Solomon, Kansas. Received B.S. from Kansas State University; M.A. from Fort Hays State University.

Poetry for Students

Presenting Analysis, Context, and Criticism on Commonly Studied Poetry

Volume 25

Ira Mark Milne, Project Editor

Foreword by David Kelly

THOMSON
GALE

Detroit • New York • San Francisco • New Haven, Conn. • Waterville, Maine • London

Poetry for Students, Volume 25

Project Editor
Ira Mark Milne

Editorial
Anne Marie Hacht

Rights Acquisition and Management
Edna Hedblad, Lisa Kincade, Timothy Sisler

Manufacturing
Drew Kalasky

Image Research & Acquisition
Dean Dauphinais, Kelly Quin

Imaging and Multimedia
Lezlie Light, Mike Logusz

Product Design
Pamela A. E. Galbreath

Vendor Administration
Civie Green

Product Manager
Meggin Condino

© 2007 Thomson Gale, a part of The Thomson Corporation.

Thomson and Star Logo are trademarks and Gale is a registered trademark used herein under license.

For more information, contact
Thomson Gale
27500 Drake Rd.
Farmington Hills, MI 48331-3535
Or you can visit our Internet site at
http://www.gale.com

ALL RIGHTS RESERVED
No part of this work covered by the copyright hereon may be reproduced or used in any form or by any means—graphic, electronic, or mechanical, including photocopying, recording, taping, Web distribution, or information storage retrieval systems—without the written permission of the publisher.

For permission to use material from this product, submit your request via Web at http://www.gale-edit.com/permissions, or you may download our Permissions Request form and submit your request by fax or mail to:

Permissions Department
Thomson Gale
27500 Drake Rd.
Farmington Hills, MI 48331-3535

Permissions Hotline:
248-699-8006 or 800-877-4253, ext. 8006
Fax: 248-699-8074 or 800-762-4058

Since this page cannot legibly accommodate all copyright notices, the acknowledgments constitute an extension of the copyright notice.

While every effort has been made to ensure the reliability of the information presented in this publication, Thomson Gale does not guarantee the accuracy of the data contained herein. Thomson Gale accepts no payment for listing; and inclusion in the publication of any organization, agency, institution, publication, service, or individual does not imply endorsement of the editors or publisher. Errors brought to the attention of the publisher and verified to the satisfaction of the publisher will be corrected in future editions.

ISBN-13: 978-0-7876-8715-1
ISBN-10: 0-7876-8715-4
ISSN 1094-7019

Printed in the United States of America
10 9 8 7 6 5 4 3 2 1

Table of Contents

Guest Foreword
  "Just a Few Lines on a Page"
  by David J. Kelly ix
Introduction xi
Literary Chronology xv
Acknowledgments xvii
Contributors xxi

Art Thou the Thing I Wanted
(by Alice Fulton) 1
  Author Biography 1
  Poem Text 2
  Poem Summary 3
  Themes 5
  Style 6
  Historical Context 7
  Critical Overview 9
  Criticism 9
  Further Reading 30

Bonnard's Garden
(by Rick Barot) 32
  Author Biography 33
  Poem Text 33
  Poem Summary 34
  Themes 35
  Style 36
  Historical Context 36
  Critical Overview 37
  Criticism 38
  Further Reading 49

Chorale
(by Kevin Young) 50
- Author Biography 51
- Poem Text 51
- Poem Summary 51
- Themes 53
- Style 53
- Historical Context 55
- Critical Overview 56
- Criticism 56
- Further Reading 67

The Cossacks
(by Linda Pastan) 68
- Author Biography 69
- Poem Text 70
- Poem Summary 70
- Themes 71
- Style 72
- Historical Context 73
- Critical Overview 74
- Criticism 75
- Further Reading 81

Daughter-Mother-Maya-Seeta
(by Reetika Vazirani) 82
- Author Biography 83
- Poem Text 83
- Poem Summary 83
- Themes 85
- Style 86
- Historical Context 87
- Critical Overview 88
- Criticism 89
- Further Reading 96

Hum
(by Ann Lauterbach) 97
- Author Biography 98
- Poem Summary 98
- Themes 99
- Style 101
- Historical Context 102
- Critical Overview 103
- Criticism 103
- Further Reading 110

Knowledge
(by Kim Addonizio) 112
- Author Biography 113
- Poem Text 113
- Poem Summary 113
- Themes 115
- Style 117
- Historical Context 117
- Critical Overview 118
- Criticism 118
- Further Reading 126

The Legend
(by Garrett Hongo) 127
- Author Biography 128
- Poem Summary 128
- Themes 129
- Style 131
- Historical Context 131
- Critical Overview 133
- Criticism 134
- Further Reading 143

Originally
(by Carol Ann Duffy) 145
- Author Biography 146
- Poem Text 146
- Poem Summary 147
- Themes 148
- Style 150
- Historical Context 150
- Critical Overview 152
- Criticism 152
- Further Reading 162

Rent
(by Jane Cooper) 163
- Author Biography 163
- Poem Text 164
- Poem Summary 164
- Themes 164
- Style 166
- Historical Context 166
- Critical Overview 168
- Criticism 169
- Further Reading 189

The River Mumma Wants Out
(by Lorna Goodison) 190
- Author Biography 191
- Poem Text 191
- Poem Summary 192
- Themes 193
- Style 195
- Historical Context 196
- Critical Overview 197
- Criticism 198
- Further Reading 207

Self-Portrait
(by Adam Zagajewski) 208
- Author Biography 209

Poem Summary 209	Critical Overview 251
Themes 210	Criticism 252
Style 211	Further Reading 260
Historical Context 212	
Critical Overview 213	
Criticism 214	
Further Reading 226	

Virtue
(by George Herbert) 261
   Author Biography 262
   Poem Text 263
   Poem Summary 263
   Themes 264
   Style 265
   Historical Context 266
   Critical Overview 267
   Criticism 267
   Further Reading 283

Supernatural Love
(by Gjertrud Schnackenberg) 227
   Author Biography 227
   Poem Summary 228
   Themes 229
   Style 230
   Historical Context 231
   Critical Overview 233
   Criticism 233
   Further Reading 243

Whoso List to Hunt
(by Thomas Wyatt) 284
   Author Biography 285
   Poem Text 286
   Poem Summary 286
   Themes 286
   Style 288
   Historical Context 289
   Critical Overview 290
   Criticism 291
   Further Reading 309

View
(by Marvin Bell) 245
   Author Biography 246
   Poem Text 246
   Poem Summary 247
   Themes 248
   Style 250
   Historical Context 250

Glossary 311

Cumulative Author/Title Index 331

Cumulative Nationality/Ethnicity Index 341

Subject/Theme Index 349

Cumulative Index of First Lines 355

Cumulative Index of Last Lines 363

Just a Few Lines on a Page

I have often thought that poets have the easiest job in the world. A poem, after all, is just a few lines on a page, usually not even extending margin to margin—how long would that take to write, about five minutes? Maybe ten at the most, if you wanted it to rhyme or have a repeating meter. Why, I could start in the morning and produce a book of poetry by dinnertime. But we all know that it isn't that easy. Anyone can come up with enough words, but the poet's job is about writing the *right* ones. The right words will change lives, making people see the world somewhat differently than they saw it just a few minutes earlier. The right words can make a reader who relies on the dictionary for meanings take a greater responsibility for his or her own personal understanding. A poem that is put on the page correctly can bear any amount of analysis, probing, defining, explaining, and interrogating, and something about it will still feel new the next time you read it.

It would be fine with me if I could talk about poetry without using the word "magical," because that word is overused these days to imply "a really good time," often with a certain sweetness about it, and a lot of poetry is neither of these. But if you stop and think about magic—whether it brings to mind sorcery, witchcraft, or bunnies pulled from top hats—it always seems to involve stretching reality to produce a result greater than the sum of its parts and pulling unexpected results out of thin air. This book provides ample cases where a few simple words conjure up whole worlds. We do not actually travel to different times and different cultures, but the poems get into our minds, they find what little we know about the places they are talking about, and then they make that little bit blossom into a bouquet of someone else's life. Poets make us think we are following simple, specific events, but then they leave ideas in our heads that cannot be found on the printed page. Abracadabra.

Sometimes when you finish a poem it doesn't feel as if it has left any supernatural effect on you, like it did not have any more to say beyond the actual words that it used. This happens to everybody, but most often to inexperienced readers: regardless of what is often said about young people's infinite capacity to be amazed, you have to understand what usually does happen, and what could have happened instead, if you are going to be moved by what someone has accomplished. In those cases in which you finish a poem with a "So what?" attitude, the information provided in *Poetry for Students* comes in handy. Readers can feel assured that the poems included here actually are potent magic, not just because a few (or a hundred or ten thousand) professors of literature say they are: they're significant because they can withstand close inspection and still amaze the very same people who have just finished taking them apart and seeing how they work. Turn them inside out, and they will still be able to come alive, again and again. *Poetry for Students* gives readers of any age good practice in feeling the ways poems relate to both the reality of the time and place the poet lived in and the reality of our emotions. Practice is just another word for being a student. The information given here helps you understand the way to read poetry; what to look for, what to expect.

With all of this in mind, I really don't think I would actually like to have a poet's job at all. There are too many skills involved, including precision, honesty, taste, courage, linguistics, passion, compassion, and the ability to keep all sorts of people entertained at once. And that is just what they do with one hand, while the other hand pulls some sort of trick that most of us will never fully understand. I can't even pack all that I need for a weekend into one suitcase, so what would be my chances of stuffing so much life into a few lines? With all that *Poetry for Students* tells us about each poem, I am impressed that any poet can finish three or four poems a year. Read the inside stories of these poems, and you won't be able to approach any poem in the same way you did before.

David J. Kelly
College of Lake County

Introduction

Purpose of the Book

The purpose of *Poetry for Students* (*PfS*) is to provide readers with a guide to understanding, enjoying, and studying poems by giving them easy access to information about the work. Part of Gale's "For Students" Literature line, *PfS* is specifically designed to meet the curricular needs of high school and undergraduate college students and their teachers, as well as the interests of general readers and researchers considering specific poems. While each volume contains entries on "classic" poems frequently studied in classrooms, there are also entries containing hard-to-find information on contemporary poems, including works by multicultural, international, and women poets.

The information covered in each entry includes an introduction to the poem and the poem's author; the actual poem text (if possible); a poem summary, to help readers unravel and understand the meaning of the poem; analysis of important themes in the poem; and an explanation of important literary techniques and movements as they are demonstrated in the poem.

In addition to this material, which helps the readers analyze the poem itself, students are also provided with important information on the literary and historical background informing each work. This includes a historical context essay, a box comparing the time or place the poem was written to modern Western culture, a critical overview essay, and excerpts from critical essays on the poem. A unique feature of *PfS* is a specially commissioned critical essay on each poem, targeted toward the student reader.

To further aid the student in studying and enjoying each poem, information on media adaptations is provided (if available), as well as reading suggestions for works of fiction and nonfiction on similar themes and topics. Classroom aids include ideas for research papers and lists of critical sources that provide additional material on the poem.

Selection Criteria

The titles for each volume of *PfS* were selected by surveying numerous sources on teaching literature and analyzing course curricula for various school districts. Some of the sources surveyed included: literature anthologies; *Reading Lists for College-Bound Students: The Books Most Recommended by America's Top Colleges*; textbooks on teaching the poem; a College Board survey of poems commonly studied in high schools; and a National Council of Teachers of English (NCTE) survey of poems commonly studied in high schools.

Input was also solicited from our advisory board, as well as educators from various areas. From these discussions, it was determined that each volume should have a mix of "classic" poems (those works commonly taught in literature classes) and contemporary poems for which information is often hard to find. Because of the interest in expanding the canon of literature, an emphasis was also placed on including works by international, multicultural, and women poets. Our advisory board members—educational professionals—helped pare down the list for each volume. If a work was not selected for the present volume, it was often noted as a possibility for a future volume. As always, the editor welcomes suggestions for titles to be included in future volumes.

How Each Entry Is Organized

Each entry, or chapter, in *PfS* focuses on one poem. Each entry heading lists the full name of the poem, the author's name, and the date of the poem's publication. The following elements are contained in each entry:

- **Introduction:** a brief overview of the poem which provides information about its first appearance, its literary standing, any controversies surrounding the work, and major conflicts or themes within the work.

- **Author Biography:** this section includes basic facts about the poet's life, and focuses on events and times in the author's life that inspired the poem in question.

- **Poem Text:** when permission has been granted, the poem is reprinted, allowing for quick reference when reading the explication of the following section.

- **Poem Summary:** a description of the major events in the poem. Summaries are broken down with subheads that indicate the lines being discussed.

- **Themes:** a thorough overview of how the major topics, themes, and issues are addressed within the poem. Each theme discussed appears in a separate subhead and is easily accessed through the boldface entries in the Subject/Theme Index.

- **Style:** this section addresses important style elements of the poem, such as form, meter, and rhyme scheme; important literary devices used, such as imagery, foreshadowing, and symbolism; and, if applicable, genres to which the work might have belonged, such as Gothicism or Romanticism. Literary terms are explained within the entry, but can also be found in the Glossary.

- **Historical Context:** this section outlines the social, political, and cultural climate *in which the author lived and the poem was created*. This section may include descriptions of related historical events, pertinent aspects of daily life in the culture, and the artistic and literary sensibilities of the time in which the work was written. If the poem is a historical work, information regarding the time in which the poem is set is also included. Each section is broken down with helpful subheads.

- **Critical Overview:** this section provides background on the critical reputation of the poem, including bannings or any other public controversies surrounding the work. For older works, this section includes a history of how the poem was first received and how perceptions of it may have changed over the years; for more recent poems, direct quotes from early reviews may also be included.

- **Criticism:** an essay commissioned by *PfS* which specifically deals with the poem and is written specifically for the student audience, as well as excerpts from previously published criticism on the work (if available).

- **Sources:** an alphabetical list of critical material used in compiling the entry, with full bibliographical information.

- **Further Reading:** an alphabetical list of other critical sources which may prove useful for the student. It includes full bibliographical information and a brief annotation.

In addition, each entry contains the following highlighted sections, set apart from the main text as sidebars:

- **Media Adaptations:** if available, a list of audio recordings as well as any film or television adaptations of the poem, including source information.

- **Topics for Further Study:** a list of potential study questions or research topics dealing with the poem. This section includes questions related to other disciplines the student may be studying, such as American history, world history, science, math, government, business, geography, economics, psychology, etc.

- **Compare and Contrast:** an "at-a-glance" comparison of the cultural and historical differences between the author's time and culture and late twentieth century or early twenty-first century Western culture. This box includes pertinent parallels between the major scientific, political, and cultural movements of the time or place the poem was written, the time or place the poem was set (if a historical work), and modern Western culture. Works written after 1990 may not have this box.

- **What Do I Read Next?:** a list of works that might complement the featured poem or serve as a contrast to it. This includes works by the same author and others, works of fiction and nonfiction, and works from various genres, cultures, and eras.

Other Features

PfS includes "Just a Few Lines on a Page," a foreword by David J. Kelly, an adjunct professor of English, College of Lake County, Illinois. This essay provides a straightforward, unpretentious explanation of why poetry should be marveled at and how *Poetry for Students* can help teachers show students how to enrich their own reading experiences.

A Cumulative Author/Title Index lists the authors and titles covered in each volume of the *PfS* series.

A Cumulative Nationality/Ethnicity Index breaks down the authors and titles covered in each volume of the *PfS* series by nationality and ethnicity.

A Subject/Theme Index, specific to each volume, provides easy reference for users who may be studying a particular subject or theme rather than a single work. Significant subjects from events to broad themes are included, and the entries pointing to the specific theme discussions in each entry are indicated in **boldface**.

A Cumulative Index of First Lines (beginning in Vol. 10) provides easy reference for users who may be familiar with the first line of a poem but may not remember the actual title.

A Cumulative Index of Last Lines (beginning in Vol. 10) provides easy reference for users who may be familiar with the last line of a poem but may not remember the actual title.

Each entry may include illustrations, including a photo of the author and other graphics related to the poem.

Citing Poetry for Students

When writing papers, students who quote directly from any volume of *Poetry for Students* may use the following general forms. These examples are based on MLA style; teachers may request that students adhere to a different style, so the following examples may be adapted as needed.

When citing text from *PfS* that is not attributed to a particular author (i.e., the Themes, Style, Historical Context sections, etc.), the following format should be used in the bibliography section:

"Angle of Geese." *Poetry for Students*. Eds. Marie Napierkowski and Mary Ruby. Vol. 2. Detroit: Gale, 1998. 5–7.

When quoting the specially commissioned essay from *PfS* (usually the first piece under the "Criticism" subhead), the following format should be used:

Velie, Alan. Critical Essay on "Angle of Geese." *Poetry for Students*. Eds. Marie Napierkowski and Mary Ruby. Vol. 2. Detroit: Gale, 1998. 7–10.

When quoting a journal or newspaper essay that is reprinted in a volume of *PfS*, the following form may be used:

Luscher, Robert M. "An Emersonian Context of Dickinson's 'The Soul Selects Her Own Society.'" *ESQ: A Journal of American Renaissance* Vol. 30, No. 2 (Second Quarter, 1984), 111–16; excerpted and reprinted in *Poetry for Students*, Vol. 1, eds. Marie Napierkowski and Mary Ruby (Detroit: Gale, 1998), pp. 266–69.

When quoting material reprinted from a book that appears in a volume of *PfS*, the following form may be used:

Mootry, Maria K. "'Tell It Slant': Disguise and Discovery as Revisionist Poetic Discourse in 'The Bean Eaters,'" in *A Life Distilled: Gwendolyn Brooks, Her Poetry and Fiction*. Edited by Maria K. Mootry and Gary Smith. University of Illinois Press, 1987. 177–80, 191; excerpted and reprinted in *Poetry for Students*, Vol. 2, eds. Marie Napierkowski and Mary Ruby (Detroit: Gale, 1998), pp. 22–24.

We Welcome Your Suggestions

The editor of *Poetry for Students* welcomes your comments and ideas. Readers who wish to suggest poems to appear in future volumes, or who have other suggestions, are cordially invited to contact the editor. You may contact the editor via E-mail at: *ForStudentsEditors@thomson.com*. Or write to the editor at:

Editor, *Poetry for Students*
Thomson Gale
27500 Drake Rd.
Farmington Hills, MI 48331–3535

Literary Chronology

1503: Thomas Wyatt is thought to have been born in about 1503 at Allington Castle, in Kent, England.

1542: Thomas Wyatt dies in the fall in Sherborne, England.

1557: Thomas Wyatt's "Whoso List to Hunt" is published.

1593: George Herbert is born on April 3 into a wealthy and titled family at Montgomery Castle in Wales.

1633: George Herbert's "Virtue" is published.

1633: George Herbert dies of tuberculosis on March 1.

1924: Jane Cooper is born on October 9 in Atlantic City, New Jersey.

1932: Linda Olenik Pastan is born on May 27 in New York City.

1937: Marvin Bell is born on August 3 in New York City, to a Jewish family that had emigrated from the Ukraine, and he grows up in a rural section of Long Island, New York.

1942: Ann Lauterbach is born on September 28 in New York City.

1945: Adam Zagajewski is born on June 21 in Lwów, Ukraine, a city that is occupied by and integrated that year into the Soviet Union.

1947: Lorna Goodison is born in Kingston, Jamaica.

1951: Garrett Kaoru Hongo is born on May 30 in Volcano, Hawaii.

1952: Alice Fulton is born on January 25 in Troy, New York.

1953: Gjertrud Schnackenberg is born on August 27 in Tacoma, Washington.

1954: Kim Addonizio is born on July 31 in Washington, D.C.

1955: Carol Ann Duffy is born on December 23 in Glasgow, Scotland.

1962: Reetika Vazirani is born on August 9 in Patiala, Punjab, India.

1970: Kevin Young is born on November 8 in Lincoln, Nebraska.

1984: Jane Cooper's "Rent" is published.

1985: Gjertrud Schnackenberg's "Supernatural Love" is published.

1988: Garrett Hongo's "The Legend" is published.

1990: Alice Fulton's "Art Thou the Thing I Wanted" is published.

1990: Carol Ann Duffy's "Originally" is published.

1997: Adam Zagajewski's "Self-Portrait" is published.

1998: Reetika Vazirani's "Daughter-Mother-Maya-Seeta" is published.

2001: Rick Barot's "Bonnard's Garden" is published.

2002: Linda Pastan's "The Cossacks" is published.

2003: Kevin Young's "Chorale" is published.

2003: Reetika Vazirani commits suicide.

2004: Kim Addonizio's "Knowledge" is published.

2004: Marvin Bell's "View" is published.

2005: Ann Lauterbach's "Hum" is published.

2005: Lorna Goodison's "The River Mumma Wants Out" is published.

Acknowledgments

The editors wish to thank the copyright holders of the excerpted criticism included in this volume and the permissions managers of many book and magazine publishing companies for assisting us in securing reproduction rights. We are also grateful to the staffs of the Detroit Public Library, the Library of Congress, the University of Detroit Mercy Library, Wayne State University Purdy/Kresge Library Complex, and the University of Michigan Libraries for making their resources available to us. Following is a list of the copyright holders who have granted us permission to reproduce material in this volume of *PFS*. Every effort has been made to trace copyright, but if omissions have been made, please let us know.

COPYRIGHTED EXCERPTS IN *PFS*, VOLUME 25, WERE REPRODUCED FROM THE FOLLOWING PERIODICALS:

Ariel, v. 1, 1970 for "George Herbert's 'Vertue,'" by Helen Vendler. Copyright 1970 The Board of Governors, The University of Calgary. Reproduced by permission of the publisher and the author.—*Blackbird*, v. 2, fall, 2003 for "An Interview with Rick Barot," by Rick Barot and Craig Beaven. Reproduced by permission of the publisher, http://www.blackbird.vcu.edu, and the authors.—*Booklist*, v. 100, December 15, 2003; v. 101, May 15, 2005. Copyright © 2003, 2005 by the American Library Association. Both reproduced by permission.—*Comparative Literature*, v. 40, spring, 1988 for "Wyatt's Transformation of Petrarch," by Reed Way Dasenbrock. Reproduced by permission of the author.—*English Review*, v. 15, November, 2004. Copyright 2004 Philip Allan Updates. Reproduced by permission.—*George Herbert Journal*, v. 6, fall, 1982; v. 17, fall, 1993. Both reproduced by permission.—*Harvard Review*, v. 29, December, 2005. Copyright © 2005 by the President and Fellows of Harvard College. Reproduced by permission.—*Iowa Review*, v. 25, winter, 1995 for "An Interview with Jane Cooper," by Jane Cooper and Eric Gudas. Reproduced by permission of the authors.—*Lambda Book Report*, v. 13, November–December, 2004 for "Critical Mass: A New Generation of Gay Poets," by Christopher Hennessy. Copyright 2004 Lamda Literary Foundation. Reproduced by permission of the author.—*Library Journal*, v. 127, February 1, 2002; v. 128, January, 2003; v. 129, January, 2004. Copyright © 2002, 2003, 2004 by Reed Elsevier, USA. All reprinted by permission of the publisher.—*Michigan Quarterly Review*, v. 34, spring, 1995 for "Distortion, Explosion, Embrace: The Poetry of Alice Fulton," by Emily Grosholz. Copyright © The University of Michigan, 1995. All rights reserved. Reproduced by permission of the author.—*The Nation*, v. 241, December 7, 1985; v. 280, May 9, 2005. Copyright © 1985, 2005 by *The Nation* Magazine/The Nation Company, Inc. Both reproduced by permission.—*The New Leader*, v. 68, September 23, 1985; v. 71, June 13, 1988. Copyright © 1985, 1988 by The American Labor Conference on International Affairs, Inc. All rights reserved. Both reproduced by permission.—*The New Republic*, v. 218, March 23, 1998; v. 225, November 12, 2001. Copyright © 1998, 2001 by The New Republic, Inc. Both reproduced by permission of *The New Republic*.—*Parnassus*, v. 15, 1989 for "An Ecstasy of Space," by Rachel Hadas. Copyright © 1989 Poetry in Review Foundation, NY. Reproduced by permission of the publisher and the author.—*Poetry*, v. 173, December, 1998 for a review by John Taylor of *Mysticism for Beginners*; v. 183, February, 2004 for a review by Brian Phillips of *Jelly Roll: A Blues*. Copyright 1998, 2004 Modern Poetry Association. Both reproduced by permission of the respective authors.—*Prairie Schooner*, v. 79, summer, 2005. Copyright © 2005 by University of Nebraska Press. Reproduced from *Prairie Schooner* by permission of the University of Nebraska Press.—*Publishers Weekly*, v. 240, October 11, 1993; v. 249, November 25, 2002; v. 250, January 20, 2003; v. 250, December 22, 2003; v. 251, March 22, 2004; v. 252, April 18, 2005. Copyright © 1993, 2002, 2003, 2004, 2005 by Reed Publishing USA. All reproduced from *Publishers Weekly*, published by the Bowker Magazine Group of Cahners Publishing Co., a division of Reed Publishing USA, by permission.—*Research in African Literatures*, v. 36, summer, 2005. Copyright © Indiana University Press. Reproduced by permission.—*TriQuarterly*, winter, 1996-1997 for "A Conversation with Alice Fulton," by Alice Fulton with P. Alec Marsh. Copyright © 1997 by Alec Marsh and Alice Fulton. All rights reserved. Reproduced by permission of Alice Fulton and P. Alec Marsh.—*Virginia Quarterly Review*, v. 67, spring, 1991; v. 77, autumn, 2001. Copyright 1991, 2001 by *The Virginia Quarterly Review*, The University of Virginia. Both reproduced by permission of the publisher.—*Washingtonian*, v. 31, May, 1996 for "Word Perfect: For Linda Pastan, Revision Is the Purest Form of Love," by Ken Adelman. Copyright 1996 Washington Magazine, Inc. Reproduced by permission of the author.—*World Literature Today*, v. 74, autumn, 2000; v. 79, May–August, 2005. Copyright © 2000, 2005 by *World Literature Today*. Both reproduced by permission of the publisher.—*Writer's Digest*, v. 83, March, 2003 for "Marvin Bell: Professor of Poetry and Poet Laureate," by Julianne Hill. Reproduced by permission of the author.

COPYRIGHTED EXCERPTS IN *PFS*, VOLUME 25, WERE REPRODUCED FROM THE FOLLOWING BOOKS:

Addonizio, Kim. From ***What Is This Thing Called Love: Poems***. W. W. Norton & Company, 2004. Copyright © 2004 by Kim Addonizio. Used by permission of W. W. Norton & Company, Inc.—Arakawa, Suzanne K. From "Garrett Hongo," in ***Encyclopedia of American Literature***. Edited by Steven R. Serafin. Continuum Publishing Co., 1999. Copyright © 1999 by The Continuum Publishing Company. Republished with permission of Continuum, conveyed through Copyright Clearance Center, Inc.—Barot, Rick. From ***The Darker Fall: Poems***. Sarabande Books, 2002. Copyright © 2002 by Rick Barot. All rights reserved. Reproduced by permission.—Bell, Marvin. From ***Rampant (Poems)***. Copper Canyon Press, 2004. Copyright 2004 by Marvin Bell. All rights reserved. Reproduced by permission.—Caldwell, Ellen C. From "Thomas Wyatt," in ***Dictionary of Literary Biography***, Vol. 132, ***Sixteenth-Century British Nondramatic Writers, First Series***. Edited by David A. Richardson, Gale Research, 1993. Reproduced by permission of Thomson Gale.—Cooper, Jane. From ***The Flashboat: Poems Collected and Reclaimed***. W. W. Norton & Company, 2000. Copyright © 2000 by Jane Cooper. Used by permission of W. W. Norton & Company, Inc.—Duffy, Carol Ann. From ***The Other Country***. Anvil Press Poetry, 1990. Copyright © Carol Ann Duffy 1990. Reproduced by permission.—Fulton, Alice. From ***Powers of Congress***. Sarabande Books, 2001. Copyright © 1990, 2001 by Alice Fulton. All rights reserved. Reproduced by permission.—Goodison, Lorna. From ***Controlling the Silver: Poems***. University of Illinois Press, 2005. Copyright 2004 by Lorna Goodison. Used with permission of the poet and the University of Illinois Press.—Herbert, George. From "Virtue," in ***Seventeenth-Century Prose and Poetry, Second Edition***. Edited and translated by Alexander M. Witherspoon and Frank J. Warnke. Harcourt, Brace & World, Inc., 1963. Copyright © 1929, 1946, 1957, 1963 by Harcourt Brace & World Inc.—Lobanov-Rostovsky, Sergei. From "Alice Fulton," in ***Dictionary of Literary Biography***, Vol. 193, ***American Poets Since World War II, Sixth Series***. Edited by Joseph Conte, Gale Research, 1998. Reproduced by permission of Thomson Gale.—Michelis, Angelica, and Antony Rowland. From an Introduction to ***The Poetry of Carol Ann Duffy: "Choosing Tough Words."*** Edited by Angelica Michelis and Antony Rowland. Manchester University Press, Manchester, UK, 2003. Copyright © Manchester University Press 2003. Reproduced by permission of the publisher and authors.—Moyers, Bill. From ***The Language of Life: A Festival of Poets***. Doubleday, 1995. Copyright © 1995 by Public Affairs Television, Inc., and David Grubin Productions, Inc. Used by permission of Doubleday, a division of Random House, Inc.—Parameswaran, Uma. From "World Hotel," in *South Asian Women's Network (SAWNET)*. Reproduced by permission of the author.—Pastan, Linda. From *The Last Uncle*. W. W. Norton & Company, 2002. Copyright © 2002 by Linda Pastan. Used by permission of W. W. Norton & Company, Inc.—Vazirani, Reetika. From *World Hotel*. Copper Canyon Press, 2002. Copyright 2002 Reetika Vazirani. All rights reserved. Reproduced by permission.—Wyatt, Thomas. From "VII," in *Sir Thomas Wyatt: Collected Poems*. Edited and translated by Joost Daalder. Oxford University Press, 1975. Copyright © 1975 Oxford University Press. Reproduced by permission of Oxford University Press.—Young, Kevin. From *Jelly Roll: A Blues*. Alfred A. Knopf, 2003 Copyright © 2003 by Kevin Young. Used by permission of Alfred A. Knopf, a division of Random House, Inc.

COPYRIGHTED EXCERPTS IN *PFS*, VOLUME 25, WERE REPRODUCED FROM THE FOLLOWING WEBSITES OR OTHER SOURCES:

From *Contemporary Authors Online*. "Carol Ann Duffy," www.gale.com, Thomson Gale, 2006. Reproduced by permission of Thomson Gale.—From *Contemporary Authors Online*. "Lorna Goodison," www.gale.com, Thomson Gale, 2005. Reproduced by permission of Thomson Gale.

Contributors

Bryan Aubrey: Aubrey holds a Ph.D. in English and has published many articles on twentieth-century poetry. Entry on *Supernatural Love*. Critical essays on *Daughter-Mother-Maya-Seeta* and *Supernatural Love*.

Jennifer Bussey: Bussey is an independent writer specializing in literature. Entries on *The Cossacks* and *Rent*. Critical essays on *Chorale*, *The Cossacks*, and *Rent*.

Douglas Dupler: Dupler is a writer and college English teacher. Entry on *The Legend*. Critical essay on *The Legend*.

Sheldon Goldfarb: Goldfarb is a published writer with a Ph.D. in English. Critical essay on *The Legend*.

Joyce Hart: Hart is a published writer and former teacher. Entries on *Art Thou the Thing I Wanted*, *Bonnard's Garden*, *Daughter-Mother-Maya-Seeta*, and *The River Mumma Wants Out*. Critical essays on *Art Thou the Thing I Wanted*, *Bonnard's Garden*, *Chorale*, *Daughter-Mother-Maya-Seeta*, and *The River Mumma Wants Out*.

Neil Heims: Heims is a writer and teacher living in Paris. Entry on *Virtue*. Critical essay on *Virtue*.

Pamela Steed Hill: Hill is the author of a poetry collection and an editor for a university publications department. Entry on *Originally*. Critical essay on *Originally*.

Michael Allen Holmes: Holmes is a freelance writer and editor. Entry on *Chorale*. Critical essays on *Chorale*, *Daughter-Mother-Maya-Seeta*, *Knowledge*, and *View*.

Sheri Metzger Karmiol: Metzger Karmiol has a doctorate in English Renaissance literature and teaches literature and drama at the University of New Mexico. Entries on *Knowledge* and *Whoso List to Hunt*. Critical essays on *Knowledge* and *Whoso List to Hunt*.

David Kelly: Kelly is an instructor of creative writing and literature. Entry on *View*. Critical essays on *Knowledge*, *The Legend*, and *View*.

Wendy Perkins: Perkins is a professor of American and English literature and film. Entry on *Self-Portrait*. Critical essay on *Self-Portrait*.

Kathy Wilson Peacock: Wilson Peacock is a writer and editor of articles about literature. Entry on *Hum*. Critical essay on *Hum*.

Art Thou the Thing I Wanted

Alice Fulton
1990

"Art Thou the Thing I Wanted," by Alice Fulton, was first published in 1990 in her collection *Powers of Congress* (reprinted in 2001) and was also published in 2004 in her larger collection *Cascade Experiment: Selected Poems*. "Art Thou the Thing I Wanted" is a poem about longing, among many other things; one particular overtone focuses on how one accepts one's lot in life, and this acceptance in fact stands in opposition to longing. Each of these two opposing forces is subtly apparent in the poem's title, which suggests as well as questions that longing, as if the speaker is sure of neither her desire nor the object of her desire.

Fulton has stated that her writing revolves around words, and indeed, "Art Thou the Thing I Wanted" provides a good example of how much fun Fulton has with language. She appears to like employing obscure vocabulary, often using words that might push her readers in surprising directions, as if she is enjoying a private joke. Her poems are playful—but the message underneath may be more serious. The emotions are hidden, waiting to be discovered, much like the "solutions" that Fulton refers to in the poem. "Problems," one line asserts, are "more interesting than solutions." The situation may be similar for the poem itself: the wordplay and twists in meaning may be at least as interesting as the emotions they describe.

Author Biography

Alice Fulton was born on January 25, 1952, in Troy, New York. She majored in creative writing

Alice Fulton Photograph by Hank De Leo. Courtesy of Alice Fulton

as an undergraduate at Empire State College, in Saratoga Springs, New York, and then attended Cornell University in Ithaca, New York, where she gained a master of fine arts in 1982. Since then, Fulton has taught writing at various schools, completing a long tenure at the University of Michigan and a year each at the University of California, Los Angeles, and at the University of California, Berkeley. In 2004, she was asked to join her alma mater Cornell, where she was given the Ann S. Bowers chair as distinguished professor of English.

Fulton has published several books of poetry, including *Palladium* (1982), winner of the 1985 National Poetry Series and the 1987 Society of Midland Authors Award; *Dance Script with Electric Ballerina* (1982), winner of the 1982 Associated Writing Programs Award; *Powers of Congress* (1990), in which the poem "Art Thou the Thing I Wanted" first appeared; *Sensual Math* (1995); *Felt* (2001), her most famous work, for which she received the Rebekah Johnson Bobbitt National Prize for Poetry from the Library of Congress in 2003; and *Cascade Experiment* (2004), a compilation encompassing works from each of her first five collections. She also has published a collection of prose essays about poetry called *Feeling as a Foreign Language: The Good Strangeness of Poetry* (1999). In addition, Fulton's work has been honored by inclusion in five editions of the annual series *The Best American Poetry* and was also published in the 1988–1997 edition of *The Best of the Best American Poetry*. Fulton has won what is colloquially referred to as the "genius" award, a fellowship given by the John D. and Catherine T. MacArthur Foundation to people who have shown extraordinary originality in their creative pursuits. Fulton also has won awards for the quality of her teaching.

Poem Text

These unprepossessing sunsets
and aluminum-sided acres
retain us like problems
more interesting than solutions,
solutions being perfect   5

lots of condos, the groomed weather
of elsewhere. Well, we must love
what we're given, which is why
we get stuck
on the steel-wool firmament   10

of home. Since it's the nearest
partition between us and what,
we choose to find it peerless.
And maybe why we wish
to lean our heads on the dense rocking   15

in a particular chest, as if the only
ocean lives there or a singular wind
swarms where that heart begins.
Sometimes a passing friend
becomes a mascot in our lives,   20

day in, day out. The thought of this anybody
affects us like a high
pollen count, inspiring a suffering
not unto death, but petty.
Having a crush is the expression.   25

And we do feel pushed over, compressed
by chaperones we half-asked for.
Take me, take you. Say someone quips
"Your favorite so-and-so got drunk
and said to say hello," I accept it   30

as a secular blessing. I glow.
Glorious things of thee are spoken!
There should be a word for you
muses of unreason, like "vector"
since vectors have magnitude   35

and direction without a physical presence.
And the second meaning is "carrier
of infection." Don't we resent
the way our minds circle
unfavorable terrain for easement,   40

like jets above imagined runways?
Yet we like to be immersed, no sweat, in solutions
cooler than 98.6 degrees,
which explains the lure of fantasy.
"You never wanted," people say accusingly,   45

as if glut were gladness
rather than a bargain struck.
But what comes to live here—burrs
through clay, brown negligence—
comes to live without   50

certain fertile perqs. High-tension
wires droop their rules
between harsh Eiffels in our yards.
Eyesores at first, they quickly become
backdrops whose presence nests.   55

in every residence unseen.
And when a line falls, the field sizzles
for a million inches without a sign
of flinch. Yesterday the elder
out back up and tumbled.   60

It wasn't hit by wind or lightning,
which made the sight of it—suddenly
half hanging on the barn
like a besotted lover on the arm—
more frightening. The trunk was hollow,   65

devoured by some tree disease.
In a few hours the limbed fluttering
looked normal on the lawn,
and its jagged profile fit
this make-do neighborhood of farms   70

run in the ground by agri-biz:
The three wilted pickups
in the yard, the tire of rusty geraniums
and sign that reads Beware
of Dog where there's no dog—   75

the tree looked right
at home among them, metaphorically
on its knees. Like others,
I mistake whatever is
for what is natural.   80

You know the commonplaces. How people think
women are good
at detail work when that's the only work
they're given. Or how
the city's invisible   85

engines jiggled our coffee
till we believed quivering a constant
property of liquid.
Everything happens to me, I think,
as anything reminds me of you: the real estate   90

most local, most removed.
As on the remains of prairie
the curving earth becomes a plinth—
from which we rise, towers
of blood and ignorance.   95

Poem Summary

Stanzas 1–2

"Art Thou the Thing I Wanted" begins with the line "These unprepossessing sunsets." The soft, sibilant *s*, constituting noteworthy consonance here, is used heavily throughout the poem. "Unprepossessing," one of Fulton's many uncommon word choices, means "unattractive," or "not noteworthy," a perhaps unexpected descriptor for "sunsets." Next come "aluminum-sided acres," which, together with the sunsets, "retain us like problems / more interesting than solutions." A restatement of these lines may be that worrying about and solving problems can sometimes be more fascinating than the actual solutions.

The second stanza continues the thought (and sentence) of the first stanza: the solutions are likened to "perfect / lots of condos," where "lot" is used as a noun; modern condominiums, one should note, typically have outer shells of aluminum siding. Here, the reader realizes that the solutions are not simply "perfect," as the last line of the first stanza might seem to say; rather, the lots of condos are "perfect," as in, perhaps, perfectly arranged. The "groomed weather / of elsewhere" may refer to the artificially heated or cooled rooms inside the condos. The clause, "we must love / what we're given," may mean that one learns to appreciate one's environment, however unattractive it may be. Indeed, "home" (referred to at the beginning of stanza 3), one's original environment, is described as a "steel-wool firmament." Steel wool, an abrasive, is used to scrape things clean, while the word "firmament" is typically used in reference to the sky or the heavens; thus, "home" is perhaps framed as an idealized but in truth abrasive place.

Stanzas 3–5

"Home" is next described as "the nearest / partition between us and what," where "what" perhaps refers to all that is unknown. That is, one's house is one's primary protection from the outside world. As such, the home is a sort of sanctuary, and, naturally, "we choose to find it peerless," or one comes to believe in one's home as an ideal place, whatever it truly is. The next sentence, beginning with "And maybe why," may be read as an addition to the remark in stanza 2 that begins "which is why." Thus, in the same way that "we get stuck / on the steel-wool firmament / of home," we also "wish / to lean our heads on the dense rocking / in a particular chest." The narrator implies that both home and a particular person can come to be seen as partitions from the outside world. The "rocking" is presumably a reference to the sound of the heart, which, in turn, is compared to the sound of ocean waves as well as to "a singular wind." That "singular wind," which "swarms where that heart begins," is the source of a type of power or attraction, drawing two people together—the one listening to the sound of the heart and the one who possesses that heart.

The person who owns that heart is then likened to "a passing friend" who "becomes a mascot in our lives," where a mascot may perhaps be considered an artificial source of inspiration. Indeed, continuously thinking about this friend comes to affect one "like a high pollen count." That is, these thoughts act as a mild irritant, causing a discomforting reaction. The fifth stanza ends "*Having a crush* is the expression," confirming that the narrator is referring to infatuation with another person, which, like allergens in the air, can cause a sense of suffocation of the self. One's mind is filled only with thoughts of the other.

Stanzas 6–9

In stanza 6, the speaker continues to explore the feeling of being infatuated. She adds that one becomes constrained by "chaperones," or people watching over. That is, a friend ("chaperone") might note that the object of one's affection has, in an inebriated state, passed along a greeting. This greeting is then accepted by the person with the crush as "a secular blessing"; she even glows at the news. The next line, "Glorious things of thee are spoken!" may be ironically self-referential, as one might refer to oneself in the second person, perhaps mockingly, while looking in a mirror. The next lines read, "There should be a word for you / muses of unreason," where the narrator is presumably referring to the objects of crushes, who can foster irrationality in those who are infatuated with them. The narrator then compares the object of a crush to a "vector," which is first defined, in its mathematical sense, as something that gives direction but does not truly exist. The word is then defined as a "carrier / of infection," such as an insect or a virus, again denoting the negative aspects of having a crush on someone.

The speaker then further investigates the workings of her mind, again referring to the obsessive nature of thoughts about a crush. The territory that her mind is circling, like a jet above an imagined runway, is "unfavorable terrain." The circling itself is done in search of "easement," which can mean "the release of tension" or also "the limited use of another's property"; both of these meanings may have relevance here. The next lines read, "Yet we like to be immersed, no sweat, in solutions / cooler than 98.6 degrees." The term "solutions" likely refers back to the problem-and-solution puzzle of the first stanza as well as to liquids, like chemical solutions; the normal temperature of a healthy human body, of course, is 98.6 degrees. That is, perhaps, one might often choose to immerse oneself in situations that are not realistically sustainable; thus, one submits oneself to "the lure of fantasy" and harbors thoughts about a situation that may never come to pass, such as being united with one's crush.

Stanzas 10–12

The last line of stanza 9, " 'You never wanted,' people say accusingly," invokes one of the words from the title of the poem. To "want" may mean to "desire" or to "be in need"; that is, others may be upset in believing that the narrator had found satisfaction in abundance, while, perhaps, the narrator herself realizes that in striking a "bargain" to obtain whatever abundance she has obtained, she has sacrificed something. She then remarks that whatever, or whoever, comes to live "here" learns to "live without / certain fertile perqs." "Perqs" is likely a respelling of "perks," which originally comes from the word "perquisites." "Burrs," meanwhile, are prickly growths that attach to the fur of animals so as to transport seeds to new locations, allowing the plant whence the burr originated to produce a sort of "offspring" elsewhere. Thus, if a burr is embedded in infertile "clay," its existence has come to naught.

At the "here" mentioned in stanza 10, where the narrator herself presumably lives, can be found "high-tension wires," such as electric wires, which bear "rules," perhaps referring to both "straight lines" and "regulations." The poles that hold those wires are referred to as "Eiffels," where the Eiffel Tower, in Paris, in fact itself serves as a radio tower; many may have originally seen the crude, metallic design of the Eiffel Tower to be "harsh." Yet the residents eventually become used to these "eyesores," as the utility poles "become / backdrops" and are later "unseen." That is, these originally objectionably intrusive poles are accepted, however insidious they might remain. Even when one tower topples to the ground and scorches "the field," it does so "without a sign / of flinch," denoting the desensitizing/desensitized nature of the poles' presence. Then the reader is told that "the elder / out back up and tumbled." That is, an older something that could be found, say, in the backyard, perhaps, fell over.

Stanzas 13–16

As described in stanza 13, the elder from the preceding stanza is understood to be a tree that tumbled of its own accord. In that the tree fell as if willingly—just as a lover who is "besotted" or "infatuated" or "made dull" would willingly drape herself on the arm of one who cares little about her—its appearance is all the "more frightening." However, by the fourteenth stanza, the fallen tree, "devoured by some tree disease," is barely even noticed, just like the utility poles. In fact, in its state of suspended death, the tree is seen to fit in with its surroundings, that is, small farms, defeated by big agricultural businesses, that are themselves likewise held in a state of suspended death. Indeed, several other images, for example, the decrepit trucks, the unused tire swing, and the sign referring to a dog that no longer exists, all harmonize with the image of the fallen tree, which is then said to be "on its knees," perhaps as if begging for mercy. The final lines of the sixteenth stanza read, "Like others, / I mistake whatever is / for what is natural." In other words, the narrator accepts her present surroundings, however insidious or decrepit, as what she is meant to be surrounded by; the narrator perhaps has a strong acceptance of what she sees as her fate. If people simply accept their surroundings, the narrator suggests here, they are settling for a reality that is, in fact, not "natural."

Stanzas 17–19

In stanzas 17 and 18, the narrator gives examples of how people come to expect whatever the present reality happens to be. The "invisible / engines" may be any of the various vibrations that exist in city life. In the closing lines of stanza 18, the speaker turns to a personal address, as if talking to the object of her own infatuation. Even the land reminds her of this person, whether the land around her or someplace else. She then refers to the prairie, which is often a symbol of the infancy of America, before farms took over the vast heartland. She states that "on the remains of prairie," the earth becomes a "plinth," a "base" or "foundation." On that plinth, "we rise, towers / of blood and ignorance."

Themes

Wanting

The theme of wanting is introduced in the title of the poem, as the narrator questions whether she truly desires the poem's "thou." In the second stanza, the narrator states, "we must love / what we're given," where love can be seen as another aspect of want; that is, one comes to want whatever one is given. This theme is pursued further in the third stanza, where the wanting of a particular something develops into a kind of "partition between us and what." This partition could be likened to a form of protection between a person and the outside world or between a person and his or her inner conflicts. This wanting, this expecting to find "solutions" in this partition, makes one feel eminently protected. The object of one's wanting might be compared to a drug, which might provide a false sense of satisfaction. In fact, three lines of the poem read, "The thought of this anybody / affects us like a high / pollen count, inspiring a suffering"; in ending the second of those lines on the word "high," the poet suggests the "state of elation" most typically associated with drugs as well as with athletic endeavors and spiritual euphoria. Thus the person who *wants* becomes addicted to the object of a crush, who he or she comes to believe is the solution to life's problems. This thought was developed earlier with the image of a person leaning his or her head against another person's chest "as if the only / ocean lives there." Indeed, the wanting of fulfillment from the object of one's desires makes one falsely believe that the entire world revolves around this object, producing a "petty" sort of "suffering."

Conversely, in stanza 9, people accuse the narrator of having "never wanted." The precise meaning of this passage is debatable, as this particular wanting may or may not be the same as the wanting alluded to throughout the poem. Here, people may be accusing the narrator of having never been in need of anything, materially speaking, as suggested by the "glut" of stanza 10. At this point, the narrator refers to the place where she lives: "what comes to live here," she says, "comes to live without / certain fertile perqs." That is, she talks about living in a world in which one learns to adjust to what is given, a world in which people believe that they can do what they are doing only at that moment, without considering what they may have done in the past or might do in the future. She speaks of a world without the sort of wanting that can be motivational rather than detrimental, and this world is certainly portrayed in a negative light.

Acceptance

In many ways, acceptance is the opposite of wanting, and indeed, the opposite of wanting is itself a major theme in Fulton's poem. With wanting, one desires something. One dreams about having more of something good or less of something negative. With acceptance, one simply takes what one is given. The narrator introduces the theme of acceptance in referring to "glut," which some people equate with "gladness." She continues by describing the ugliness

Topics For Further Study

- Read two other poems of Fulton's from her collection *Powers of Congress*; find and list all the examples of wordplay in the poems. Then write a short poem of your own using similar wordplay.

- Using any part of "Art Thou the Thing I Wanted" as inspiration, complete a sketch or painting. For example, paint a picture of what you think the fallen tree from stanza 13 might look like.

- Research the effect of large agricultural businesses on small family farms in the United States. How has the agriculture industry changed in the past two or three decades? If you live in a farming community, interview local farmers to personalize your research; alternatively, find and interview large-scale gardeners in your city. Present your findings to your class.

- Find examples of postmodernist thought in various fields, such as art, literature, philosophy, science, religion, or political science. Can consensus be found on a definition of postmodernism? How do you see the effects of postmodernism represented in culture, in news stories, on television, and in music? Present your findings to your class.

(or at least lack of beauty) where she lives, with "harsh Eiffels" (or utility poles or tension-wire towers), which she calls "eyesores," eventually blurring into the background of the residents' view. Even when the grass sizzles from fallen electrical lines or when an old tree collapses onto a barn, the eye quickly forgets that these eyesores exist; the scene is soon regarded as "normal." The narrator mentions the rundown farms, the broken machinery, the old tire in which "rusty geraniums" are growing, and a dog who is no longer there. All of these things, perhaps, are in part the result of big "agri-biz" coming into town and taking over the economy, leading to poverty and possibly a loss of livelihood. The tree rests "metaphorically / on its knees," the speaker says, as if in supplication. People believe that women can only perform "detail work" because that is the only kind of work they are ever given. The poem notes an absence of a sense of fight. Things happen, and people just accept them.

Discomfort

Fulton's poem conveys a sense of discomfort, sometimes through implication and at other times through metaphor. The opening phrase features the word "unprepossessing," which refers to something making an unfavorable impression. The phrase "aluminum-sided acres" conjures an image of being surrounded by metal. The narrator notes that "we get stuck / on the steel-wool firmament," referring to metal, once again, as well as to abrasiveness. The effects of infatuation are likened to the inhaling of pollen and the allergic reaction produced. The narrator mentions "brown negligence," suggesting decay; "high-tension / wires," implying frustration; and "quivering" that is "constant," as with irritation. That is, perhaps, the narrator is feeling discomfort and therefore sees it wherever she looks and points it out so that the reader will understand what she is going through.

Style

Alliteration

Someone interested in language often has sensitivity to the sounds of words. Fulton makes notable use of alliteration, the repetition of a sound at the beginnings of consecutive words, and consonance, the repetition of a sound throughout words. The title features the phrase "thou the thing." In the first line of the poem, the sibilant *s* is present in each of the three words. In the second line of the second stanza, "of elsewhere. Well, we must love," the letter *w* is repeated three times. In the lines that follow, the letter is repeated six more times at the beginnings of words. Reading the stanza aloud, one can feel the emphasis produced by the repetition of this sound and realize its power. The letter *w* is again employed in repetition in stanza 3, with "why we wish." Other examples of alliteration and consonance can be found throughout the poem.

Similes

Similes provide images for the mind in comparing two different things, specifically using the words "like" and "as" (whereas metaphors do not use those words), thus allowing the reader a greater degree of understanding. In Fulton's poem, in the first stanza, she writes that "aluminum-sided acres / retain us like problems." That is, the "aluminum-sided acres" can hold on to a person the way a problem can hold on to a person; the phrase is fairly simple, but its meaning can be long pondered. Indeed, the poet has left the comparison somewhat open-ended, leaving the reader to conjure his or her own interpretation. In stanza 5, the poem reads, "The thought of this anybody / affects us like a high / pollen count." This unique comparison aptly denotes the feeling that the poet is attempting to share, especially for those who have experienced allergies. In stanzas 8 and 9, the poem reads, "Don't we resent / the way our minds circle / unfavorable terrain for easement, / like jets above imagined runways?" Once this complicated simile is grasped, the image is quite effective. One can imagine those times when a thought is so worrisome that one simply cannot stop thinking about it. One can then imagine a pilot circling a dangerous field, looking for a runway that exists only in his or her mind. Thus, the poet paints a picture for the reader, allowing a deeper understanding of her pattern of thought.

Wordplay

One common element of postmodernist writing is wordplay. Fulton often employs words in ways that allow for multiple interpretations, often where one connotation is first understood, to be supplanted by a second connotation that can be understood only upon the reading of a subsequent line. In the first stanza, for instance, the last line reads as if it is complete: "solutions being perfect." In the context, the poem seems to be saying that problems are more interesting than solutions, as solutions are simply perfect. Yet no punctuation is placed after the word "perfect," such that the second stanza must be read as a continuation of that thought. The phrase in its entirety then reads, "solutions being perfect / lots of condos." As such, the phrase bears a substantially different meaning.

A similar play on words occurs in the fifth stanza: "The thought of this anybody / affects us like a high." The word "high" ends the second line, and the phrase sounds complete until the reader continues to the third line, where the words "pollen count" complete the phrase. The idea of thoughts acting "like a high" is much different from that of thoughts acting "like a high / pollen count." Still, both connotations are relevant to the overall meaning of the poem.

In stanza 9, the reader again finds the word "solutions," which was used in the first stanza strictly to refer to the solving of a problem; in its later usage, both this first meaning and a second, "liquids," are implied. "High-tension" can refer both to the "tightness" of the wires and to emotional tension. In stanza 15, the narrator refers to the pickup trucks as "wilted" and the geraniums as "rusty," reversing the placement of adjectives that the reader might otherwise expect. In stanza 16, the first line, "the tree looked right," bears a different meaning alone than it does in conjunction with the second line: "the tree looked right / at home." The next line concludes that the tree is "on its knees." Although the following words, "Like others," are part of a separate sentence, their placement after the previous phrase leads the reader's mind to connect them. That is, perhaps, the reader is left with the image that "others," maybe trees or neighbors, also are on their knees. In such ways, the poet plays with her readers, twisting and contorting the meanings of her words through their minds.

Historical Context

Postmodernism

Postmodernism, a movement that has influenced literature in the latter part of the twentieth century, has been defined as both a reaction against and a refinement of modernism. Some of the key elements of modernism in literature have been identified as experimentation, an emphasis on the individual and his or her perceptions, and a focus on rational thinking as opposed to the emotions. (Emotional writing was one focal point in literature during the Romantic period, a precursor to modernism.) The modernism movement is said to fall roughly between the 1860s and the 1970s. In the United States, the period is often limited to the first part of the twentieth century, up to about 1970. The British author Virginia Woolf is considered a modernist. She tended to write in a stream-of-consciousness mode (as in

Compare & Contrast

- **1980s:** According to U.S. Census reports, the number of small farms (of 1 to 9 acres) is about 187,000; middle-sized farms (50 to 179 acres), 712,000; and large farms (2,000 acres or more), 64,000.

  Today: According to U.S. Census reports, the number of small farms is about 179,000; middle-sized farms, 659,000; and large farms, 78,000.

- **1980s:** According to the USDA Forest Service, the majority of the land in the Midwest is devoted to agriculture.

  Today: Although the majority of land in the Midwest is still devoted to agriculture, the amount of urban space has increased by 23.4 percent since the 1980s.

- **1980s:** According to U.S. statistics, the percentage of the population that is divorced rises from 6 percent at the start of the decade to 8 percent by the end of the decade.

  Today: According to U.S. statistics, by the turn of the century, 10 percent of the population is divorced.

To the Lighthouse, published in 1927) in which the reader was privileged to the characters' interior monologues as they reacted to events around them. The American E. E. Cummings, who delivered a commencement address on modernism upon graduating from Harvard, broke many conventions of traditional poetry, as exemplified by his poem "n(o)w." Modernists tended to challenge tradition.

Postmodernism began as early as the 1920s, gaining momentum in the United States especially after World War II. One of the key elements of postmodernism is a sense of play, as opposed to seriousness. This can be seen in Fulton's poem and her play with words. A sense of play is also typically evident in postmodernist writing in the forms of irony, textual manipulation, and paradox, accentuating the concept that meaning is not simply rooted in words. Indeed, postmodernists tend to believe that truth, ethics, and beauty are rooted in individual perception. Since postmodernism is sometimes defined as a furthering of modernism, characteristics of modernist literature are also found in postmodernist literature, and distinguishing between the two movements is sometimes difficult. Writers associated with the postmodern movement include the novelists Don DeLillo, author of *White Noise* (1991); Toni Morrison, author of *Beloved* (1994); and Salman Rushdie, author of *Midnight's Children* (1995). Various poems often classified as postmodernist include Amy Gerstler's "Bzzzzzzz," John Ashbery's "Paradoxes and Oxymorons," and Allen Ginsberg's "Howl."

Emily Dickinson

Fulton has stated that Emily Dickinson, one of her favorite poets, has had a profound effect on her life as well as on her writing. She began reading Dickinson as an adolescent and found much comfort in her poetry; she was especially impressed by the emotions displayed by Dickinson in her poems. Dickinson made unusual use of punctuation, especially the dash, and capitalization. The subject matter of "Art Thou the Thing I Wanted" can be likened to Dickinson's "Proud of My Broken Heart," "To Lose Thee," and "It's Such a Little Thing," all of which focus on love gained and love lost.

Above all, Fulton certainly drew upon a poem by Dickinson titled, almost identically, "Art Thou the Thing I Wanted?" Another primary aspect of postmodernism is the reconstruction of established works. (For example, Jane Smiley's *A Thousand Acres* is in effect a retelling of William Shakespeare's *King Lear*.) Dickinson's work essentially consists of two drafts of a single eight-line poem, with many words and phrases identical in both drafts; in changing certain words, however, the second draft is given a meaning drastically different from that of the first. Together, the drafts can be seen as constituting a meditation on the positive and negative aspects of the state of wanting. Thus, Fulton's poem can be seen as a revisitation of concepts introduced by Dickinson more than a century earlier.

Critical Overview

Fulton's "Art Thou the Thing I Wanted" was originally published in the collection *Powers of Congress*, which was reviewed by several publications with mixed reception. A critic for *Publishers Weekly* states, "Although Fulton . . . possesses a keen sense of the pliability of language, her imagery is often incoherent or heavy-handed." Indeed, many reviewers have referred to Fulton's ability to deftly handle and have fun with language, and not all have liked the effect. The *Publishers Weekly* reviewer finds that she has "sacrificed the emotionality of her subject to the bravado of wordplay."

Another critic, Eavan Boland, writing for *Partisan Review*, finds Fulton to be "an ambitious, powerful poet." Boland goes on to say that Fulton's poems "are daring and broad. She will try anything; and the latest thing she has tried is neither proof nor promise of the next." Boland adds, "Her language is not always certain and her tone is occasionally too much the same from poem to poem, making for an occasional lack of freshness and variety." She concludes, "These flaws need not disguise her considerable skill and the real pleasures of *Powers of Congress*."

Mutlu Konuk Blasing, writing for the *Michigan Quarterly Review*, finds fault with Fulton's lack of connection with the reader: "Fulton's voice is never intimate: her volume is turned just a notch too high and tends, at times, to overshoot the inner ear." Blasing further describes the nature of Fulton's expression thus:

> Her voice is public, and she usually speaks as 'we'; even when she uses 'I,' her experience is either representative or meant to instruct or illustrate some larger truth—about how 'we' experience, feel, behave, or should behave.

Blasing also mentions Fulton's use of wordplay:

> Fulton is polished in what she does, and her flash hooks the reader. On the down side, she can be breezy and even facile. Her language has very little undertow; her accomplished verbal play, for example, is on display and never gives a sense of making a connection that might have taken the speaker herself by surprise as well as the reader.

Finally, in a review for the *Library Journal*, Kathleen Norris notes, "These are intense, fast-moving but oddly abstracted poems" that suffer from "overwrought language."

Criticism

Joyce Hart

Hart is a published writer and former teacher. In this essay, she explores the emotions that are carefully hidden in Fulton's playful poem.

Fulton's poem "Art Thou the Thing I Wanted" contains many playful images and poetic wordplay, while seldom approaching overt emotional expression. Still, as with the work of one of the poet's favorite writers, Emily Dickinson, Fulton's poem is indeed inspired by deep sentiments. Hidden beneath the clever wordplay and somewhat lighthearted similes is a heart that has been hurt and is longing to heal. Indeed, from the title, the reader might suspect that the speaker of this poem is in a quandary. The verb in the title is in the past tense, so the narrator can be understood to be looking back on a situation, recollecting and sorting through her feelings, and reflecting on the overall experience. At one time, the speaker thought she wanted something or someone; now, she is pondering those emotions, trying to determine whether they were real.

If by the word "unprepossessing" in the poem's first stanza the narrator means "unattractive" or "unappealing," she could be perceiving what she once considered romantic (as sunsets often are) as a source of sadness. The sunsets might have once made her feel as if she were experiencing love; yet in looking back on the situation, she believes that she was merely experiencing an infatuation. This concept of mistaken love is underscored in the artificial environments described in the second stanza. The feelings she had for the person, who is given no more identity than the "thou" of the title, may have been as unreal as "the groomed weather / of elsewhere" that is pumped artificially into the condos of the poem.

Love is first mentioned in the second stanza, in a statement that reveals some of the negative sentiments that the narrator might have about love. First, she uses the imperative "must," as in, "Well, we must love." The second clue that her emotions might be amiss is the fact that she states that this imperative love is being applied to something "given," not something that she has chosen—and that "is why / we get

> *The narrator seems to be saying that when she found herself in a state of infatuation that was mentally harmful to her, she nevertheless grew accustomed to the associated sentiments and came to believe that that sort of desperate, irrational wanting was somehow positive.*

stuck." She then examines that love more closely, likening it to a "partition between us and what." Her love, or perhaps the object of her love, feels like protection from everything that the "what" in this phrase represents—perhaps the outside world, perhaps her interior world. Regardless, in her involvement in loving, she feels more secure, and this sense of security glosses over everything else that might reveal the flaws inherent in both her love and her beloved. "We choose to find it peerless" nonetheless, the narrator states, probably referring to the notion that if one feels comfortable with something, one may fail to examine it too closely for fear of finding something wrong with it.

The speaker then focuses more specifically on the beloved, whom she represents first as "a particular chest," then as "a passing friend," and then as "a mascot." None of these representations is very substantial. A chest is just a body part; "a passing friend" implies a surface relationship; and a mascot, merely a symbol, is essentially as superfluous as a superstition or a lucky charm. In the fifth stanza, the lover becomes "this anybody," another phrase suggesting insignificance. The inconsequentiality of the whole affair that the speaker is exploring is further played with in the fifth stanza: "this anybody / affects us like a high / pollen count." The poet has written this phrase quite mischievously, first suggesting that the relationship provides some kind of "high" in ending the line after that word and then completing the phrase and shifting the meaning; even with the alternately negative connotation of the high pollen count, the speaker dismisses the "suffering" by calling it not lethal but "petty."

At the end of stanza 5, the narrator finally describes the relationship in question as a "crush"—an infatuation that leads her to "glow" when someone tells her, "Your favorite so-and-so got drunk / and said to say hello." The fact that the object of the narrator's crush was inebriated implies that he may have lost his inhibition as well as a sense of doing the right thing, such as, perhaps, by not leading the narrator on. Here, for the first time, the narrator adopts a tone of facetiousness, exclaiming, "Glorious things of thee are spoken!" Whether the "thee" is the narrator herself or the object of her crush, she seems to be mocking the gravity with which one's attention for the other was regarded. She then uses the word "resent" in reference to the way her mind circles "unfavorable terrain," implying that she is tired of allowing herself to always harbor thoughts about the object of her crush.

In stanza 9, "people" accuse the speaker of never wanting. She refutes this indirectly by stating that the fact that she does not have a lot of things does not mean she has no desires. The reference to "a bargain struck" implies compromise, which the speaker likewise perhaps regrets. Continuing to see pitiable reflections of herself in her surroundings, she projects the image of a "besotted lover" onto the fallen tree. Indeed, the image is frightening to her, as she may be reminded of what she once was: a woman completely obsessed with another person. The last lines in stanza 16 read, "Like others, / I mistake whatever is / for what is natural." This statement is made following the description of the rundown neighborhood of small farms, which agricultural corporations have essentially ruined. The wrecked trucks and "make-do neighborhood," then, look natural because the people have grown accustomed to their state of want. The narrator seems to be saying that when she found herself in a state of infatuation that was mentally harmful to her, she nevertheless grew accustomed to the associated sentiments and came to believe that that sort of desperate, irrational wanting was somehow positive.

In reflecting, the narrator may or may not have truly moved on from her crush. Residual emotions are certainly evident, and the title of this poem is a question, but that question lacks the closing punctuation that would make it a true question. The

What Do I Read Next?

- Fulton's *Cascade Experiment: Selected Poems* (2004) is a compilation of poems from her first five collections, including *Powers of Congress* (1990) and the award-winning *Felt* (2002). The book offers a great overview of the author's progression from the more simple poems of her early years to the newer and more complex; throughout the collection, Fulton becomes more experimental with language as she digs deeper into her emotional world.

- Besides writing poetry, Fulton teaches and writes essays. In *Feeling as a Foreign Language: The Good Strangeness of Poetry* (1999), she writes about the poetic process and the various forms of postmodern poetry, and she also examines Emily Dickinson's work. Fulton devotes a section of this book to reflections on her own work.

- Emily Dickinson, one of the most celebrated of American poets, is often mentioned in discussions about Fulton. The two poets' works indeed feature similarities, which Fulton has herself pointed out. To discover these similarities, *Collected Poems of Emily Dickinson* (1988) is a good place to start.

- *I Never Came to You in White* (1996) is Judith Farr's fictionalized account of Emily Dickinson's life, focusing on some of the poet's idiosyncrasies. Farr tells her story through letters and poetry that she imagines Dickinson might have written.

- B. H. Fairchild was the 2004 winner of the Rebekah Johnson Bobbitt National Prize for Poetry, which Fulton won in 2003. Fairchild's collection *Early Occult Memory Systems of the Lower Midwest* (2003) has a midwestern flavor not unlike that found in Fulton's work.

---

narrator states in the eighteenth stanza, "anything reminds me of you: the real estate / most local, most removed." Thus, perhaps, no matter where she goes, she thinks of the lost, or abandoned, crush. She refers to herself and others as towers, leading the reader's mind back to the "harsh Eiffels" of stanza 11. The utility towers were held together by "high-tension / wires," just as the narrator and her crush are connected by the wires of emotion. They are, she continues, "towers / of blood and ignorance." The reader then wonders what, precisely, these people are ignorant about. Did they not understand each other? Or did they not comprehend their own emotions? In the title, the speaker suggests that she remains uncertain as to whether she wanted the "thou" in question, yet she equates the "thou" to a "thing," or an object. If the person is reduced to an object, the poem may indeed be more about the wanting, or about her specific emotions, than about the object that inspired them. Therefore, the ignorance might indeed relate mostly to the feelings that the speaker is trying to sort through, as might the poem as a whole.

Source: Joyce Hart, Critical Essay on "Art Thou the Thing I Wanted," in *Poetry for Students*, Thomson Gale, 2007.

Sergei Lobanov-Rostovsky

In the following essay, Lobanov-Rostovsky gives a critical analysis of Alice Fulton's work.

In her essay "To Organize a Waterfall" Alice Fulton describes the central concern of her poetry as "an exploration of mind." The phrase hints at the paradox of Fulton's work: her poems are at once deeply personal and defiantly abstract. Her implicit subject is the workings of the poetic imagination, the way poetry emerges from the mind's web of associations, stimulated by memory, experience, and the seductions of popular culture. She notes the central role of random associations in her compositional method: "The quirk, the oddity, the extreme, the line where the language tilts, can be the most valuable facet of a poem. They are the linguistic equivalents of genetic 'point mutations': variants produced by small changes in an organism's chromosomes." As the poem emerges from the imagination,

> *This conflict between the role of science as metaphor and its power to expose the limits of metaphoric consciousness lies at the heart of Fulton's work. In Powers of Congress Fulton reflects on the fragility of this impulse to reason in several poems.*

it resembles a waterfall in which each idea incites the next and the form of the poem "is based on the continuous chain of a cascade." This metaphor, with its origin in the scientific theory of "cascade experiments," reflects the complex relationship between content and form in Fulton's poems. Ideas are crucial to her poetry, yet she rarely writes about science or philosophy in any real sense. Instead Fulton's poems explore the way ideas are transformed by their inclusion in the poem and the power such ideas possess to reshape the more traditional lyric subjects of the poem: family history, landscape, erotic love. She celebrates the power of the poetic imagination to transform the most mundane experience into a beauty defined by abstraction; as she said in a 1988 interview with Karen Clark: "My poetry asks people to think, to become more conscious. It asks the same of me. The greatest thing about writing poetry has been the way it's made the world more interesting: every facet of the world. I can sit in a fast food restaurant and become interested in a grove of streetlights across the road, the way they cast veils through the trash and hard horizontals."

In a similar manner Fulton's poetry regards the objects of memory as the substructure on which metaphor can be shaped. She was born in Troy, New York, 25 January 1952 into a Catholic family. Her early poems, such as "Another Troy" in *Palladium* (1986), reimagine the battered industrial city of her childhood as the material for parodic myth:

> In the seismic hiss of the Volcano
> Restaurant I invented Armageddons
> guaranteed to free us: fires coasting down from heaven,
> spumes of air pollutants hurled into the stratosphere
> and we, the *damnificados*, fleeing.
> An erupting Italian restaurant—
> that would put us on the map!

Yet this urge to see her native city's "rough edges / . . . buffed by the crumbled palladium / of ash" gives way to Fulton's perception of how memory—and poetry itself—transforms by the simple act of description:

> Oh, if I sing of icicles
> dangling like syringes from friezes
> "neo-grec" or French,
> of roses battened down with sackcloth, trees
> lumbagoed under lumpen winters,
> I'm minting an insignia. Take this, "Troy—
> the City without Glibness,"
> for your spartan tribute.

Such gestures of memory evoke the traditions of mainstream American poetry only to defy them: the insistent play of language and parodic tone of Fulton's memory poems suggest her darker purpose. When she writes memory poems, as in "On the Charms of Absentee Gardens," also from *Palladium*, they are about the ambiguous process of memory rather than its banal products:

> Leaving meant commencement.
> Legend says an angel banished us
> with a sword of flame, though rumor
> claims the owners torched
> our hangouts for insurance.
> In any case, we preened with self-
> congratulations as though our origins were ruinous
> accidents from which we'd walked away.
>
> Fire fixes the magnetic alignment
> of clay, and wooden beams remember
> weather in their rings. But what Cortez will come
> in search of tambourines and beads? We'd like a past
> that won't decay with distance or yield
> to interference. Failing that,
> we want what we've abandoned
> to wear: that is to crumble
> and to last. We want a ruin: uselessness
> permitted the luxury of existence.

Her poems devoted to family history are in many respects her most accessible, yet Fulton is insistent in regarding the autobiographical detail as only the raw material for the mind's habit of metaphor. As she noted, with some irritation, in her interview with Clark two years after the publication of *Palladium*, "I've written as many, if not more, poems on the ontological struggle between engagement and estrangement as I have on 'family,' but only one critic has commented on the former topic. It's a more subtle topic than 'family,' and like most subtleties it can be completely overlooked." Indeed, the memory work of Fulton's poetry affirms the relationship of these two themes: engagement with a past that retains its power to shape the poet's consciousness becomes a process of estrangement. Family history, while the subject of many of her early poems, is only visible through the distorting lens of the imagination. What memory excavates from her own life proves to be the influence of this same quicksilver substance, "imagination, kicking like a worm in a jumping bean." Fulton adopts voices in many of her poems, or she regards her own experience from the distance of an analytical third-person ("From Our Mary to Me"), deploying it as evidence of a profound mistrust for the ideology that memory carries with it ("Cherry Bombs," "All Night Shivering").

Fulton graduated from Empire State College in Albany, New York, with a B.A. in creative writing in 1978. She completed her M.F.A. at Cornell in 1982, where she studied with A. R. Ammons. Since 1983 she has taught at the University of Michigan, where she is currently a professor of English. She was Visiting Professor of Creative Writing at Vermont College in 1987 and at the University of California, Los Angeles, in 1991. She is currently a fellow of the MacArthur Foundation and has received many fellowships and awards, including MacDowell Colony fellowships in 1978 and 1979; a Millay Colony fellowship, 1980; the Emily Dickinson Award, 1980; the Academy of American Poets prize, 1982; the Rainer Maria Rilke Award, 1984; Michigan Council for the Arts grants, 1986 and 1991; Yaddo Colony fellowship, 1987; Guggenheim fellowship, 1986-1987; the Bess Hokin prize from Poetry, 1989; and an Ingram Merrill Foundation award, 1990. In 1980 she married the painter Hank De Leo, with whom she lives in Ypsilanti, Michigan.

In her interview with Clark, Fulton credits Ammons with helping her "regard a poem less as a product, a neatly packaged, finished thing, and more as a reflection of mind." In Ammons's work Fulton found a model of poetry presenting "the course of the mind as continual high points, continually interesting travel, though part of his method is to allow the mundane to accompany the complex." This variation of tones is crucial to her own poetics as well. Fulton delights in allowing her language "to have a will of its own . . . wily, duplicitous," refusing "to be subdued into an orderly, simple form." W. D. Snodgrass began his introduction to Fulton's first book, *Dance Script with Electric Ballerina* (1983), by christening her "the veritable Lady of Logopoeia," celebrating the "constant delight and dazzle in language textures, the ever-shifting shock and jolt of an electric surface."

Her poems draw the language of science, advertising, and pop culture into an uneasy juxtaposition. In doing so, her poems celebrate the protean nature of such language. Scientific terms acquire multiple meanings through the shifting contexts of the poem, as in the "slant truths" of the word *palladium* that organize her second major volume or the "lexicon of recurring words and images" that give shape to *Powers of Congress* (1990). Yet, as she notes in "To Organize a Waterfall," the inclusion of scientific language has a deeper metaphoric significance for Fulton; wrenched out of its traditional context, scientific language illuminates "the poem's real investments: the way our present beliefs affect or distort our future knowledge; the unreliability of human perception; the old-fashioned question of whether consciousness might in any way continue after death." The implicit subject of Fulton's poems, then, is faith, which she defines as "the suppositions and convictions that allow us to live in the world." Science proves a crucial source for Fulton's poetry because it represents a mode of discourse which "strains our capacity to imagine, let alone believe."

This conflict between the role of science as metaphor and its power to expose the limits of metaphoric consciousness lies at the heart of Fulton's work. In *Powers of Congress* Fulton reflects on the fragility of this impulse to reason in several poems. "Behavioral Geography" considers the desire "to make the world / look one way to us all" by invoking reason free of "ecstasy":

> I cling to wishful visions
> like someone clinging to a tree, complaining
> that the tree won't leave.
> Hope springs up in me.
> Lost, found, bewildered,
> when will I learn
> to like unsettling transits,
>
> to use the universal
> corrective of the sky,
> a continental drift
> with nothing fixed about it?
> Once a woman dressed in wood
> lunged down the falls,
> as if her flesh were not
>
> irreparable, and lived.
> The beauty's the impossibility. Proving?
> All views are seasoned
> subjectivities, beds
> carved by freshets,
> warps of the heart.
> Ecstasy has its reasons.

In the final poem of the book, "Art Thou The Thing I Wanted," Fulton rejects the seductions of reason, preferring instead "problems / more interesting than solutions, / solutions being perfect...." The poem offers a meditation on its own metaphoric consciousness, how the mind naturalizes the unfamiliar into a landscape that fits its assumptions:

> Like others,
> I mistake whatever is
> for what is natural.
>
> You know the commonplaces. How people think
> women are good
> at detail work when that's the only work
> they're given. Or how
> the city's invisible
>
> engines jiggled our coffee
> till we believed quivering a constant
> property of liquid.

Reason, in these terms, is simply one more metaphor by which the mind describes for itself a world it nervously takes on faith. Viewed in this context, Fulton's taste for oxymoron and dramatic variations in tone reflects the mind's struggle to imagine itself as distinct from what it perceives:

> Everything happens to me, I think,
> as anything reminds me of you: the real estate
>
> most local, most removed.
> As on the remains of prairie
> the curving earth becomes a plinth—
> from which we rise, towers
> of blood and ignorance.

The self is an oxymoron, a work in progress, as the mind struggles to assemble itself from conflicting shards of memory, perception, and popular culture. The poetic imagination embodies this dissonance, drawing upon multiple discourses—pop culture, advertising, science—juxtaposed in a style that celebrates oxymoron, tonal variation, and the tension between lyric tradition and the chaotic movements of mind.

Fulton foregrounds this conflict within her poetry by such "perverse" strategies as acrostic lines (constructing the phrase "BOWLING DEVELOPS THE RIGHT ARM" along the left margin of "The Fractal Lanes") and her insistence upon the interplay of structure and chaos in her compositional method. In her essay titled "Of Formal, Free, and Fractal Verse: Singing the Body Eclectic" in *Conversant Essays: Contemporary Poets on Poetry* (1990), she argues for an understanding of the implicit structure within apparently chaotic forms. Drawing upon the mathematician Benoit Mandelbrot's theories of "self-similar fractal form," in which "each part of a fractal form replicates the form of the entire structure," Fulton offers the following precepts for "fractal" verse:

> Any line when examined closely (or magnified) will reveal itself to be as richly detailed as was the larger poem from which it was taken: the poem will contain an infinite regression of details, a nesting of pattern within pattern (an endless imbedding of the shape into itself, recalling Tennyson's idea of the inner infinity); digression, interruption, fragmentation, and lack of continuity will be regarded as formal functions rather than lapses into formlessness; all directions of motion and rhythm will be equally probable (isotropy); the past positions of motion, or the preceding metrical pattern, will not necessarily affect the poem's future evolution (independence).

While the mathematical origin of this central thesis of Fulton's poetics reflects her interest in such "nonpoetic" discourses as the language of science, it also suggests the range of her poetic resources. With her delight in juxtapositions of tone and voice, Fulton challenges the privileged language of emotional experience that is the legacy of lyric tradition. Her style is dialogic, contrasting multiple voices and perspectives, including all that poetry traditionally excludes; as she says in her interview with Clark:

> Most broadly, my poems try to question assumptions. I like to juggle cultural notions of centrality and sneak in what we consign to the periphery. I try to bring hidden relationships to the fore, disrupt assumptions surrounding gender, muddle in the fuzziness of ethics. The poems' language, including syntax and grammar, can provide a means of unhinging complacency and cliche.... I like my poetry to be insidious, rather than didactic; multiplistic, rather than singular in meaning.

What poetry traditionally excludes is not the prospect of multiple meanings, but the unheroic voice: the everyday, the commonplace, the feminine. Fulton's "inclusions" subvert this dominant tradition, creating a style that she describes as "more disjunctive than contiguous, more discursive than linear."

In her earliest work Fulton's feminism appeared to take second place to her interest in creating a poetic style that could accommodate her sense of the poetic imagination as a cascade of associations. Yet this concern with the exclusion of female voices, as she notes in "To Organize a Waterfall," this concern was always implicit in her poetry:

> The feminist strategies of my work are embedded because I believe linguistic structures are most powerful when least evident.... Whereas concealed meanings usually enforce the status quo, I use recondite structures to say subversive things. Few readers have noticed the preoccupation with gender in my work because it's eclipsed by the poems' starring subjects. The unnoticed female lizards [in "Cascade Experiment"] suggest that many "facts" about females are obscured or influenced by our existing notions.

In "Cherry Bombs" (*Powers of Congress*) Fulton associates the culture's gendering of childhood expectation with a game of false choices: "Would you rather be liquidated / or boiled in oil?" The binarisms that define gender in the poem—"Out/in. Girl/boy. Truth/lies."—are the *opposite* of the oxymoron by which Fulton imagines consciousness: instead, the culture demands that the speaker give in, choose between each pair of terms, become complicit in her own reduction to the "compulsory unsung heroics" that define a woman's life.

In her fourth book, *Sensual Math* (1995), Fulton articulates more explicitly the feminist implications of her poetics. In almost every poem she reflects on the urge to comprehend—to define, to contain—as a metaphorical violence, an act of repression that poetry must contest. Yet the book is impressive for its coherence, less a traditional book of poems than variations on a single theme: the conflict between this urge to comprehend and a style of response that she calls "immersion." In Fulton's vocabulary these are opposite terms; she rejects the mode of reading enacted daily by the checkout scanner in favor of the "treason" of immersion, which demands real presence, the dissolution of self into the poem's dark matter. As she says in "Fuzzy Feelings":

> Metaphor is pure immersion. Pure sinking
> one into another and the more
> difference that's dissolved the more = =
>
> often I'll sink
> into a book that swimless way.

In return for this immersion Fulton offers her readers wonder. If the poems resist her readers at times—and they do—that only serves to draw the readers in, to demand that they dissolve their difference in the poem's fluid meanings, to be—at once—both "rapt" and "wrapped."

Fulton anchors the book with two set pieces. In "My Last TV Campaign: A Sequence" an advertising man comes out of retirement to sell one final product—"the beauty of dissolving / boundaries." "Give: A Sequence Reimagining Daphne and Apollo" envisions Apollo as Frank Sinatra, in "snap-brim hats, // alligator shoes and sharkskin / suits from Sy Devore's Hollywood men's store"; Cupid as the young Elvis, "gyrating / primitive / and part of nature"; and Daphne as the poem's "dark matter," the vinyl on which the Voice is pressed. In "A New Release," from that sequence, she describes:

> Easing the new release from its sleeve, I saw
> myself
> bent
> out of shape in its reflections: a night whirlpool or a
> geisha's

> sleek chignon, an obsidian never reached by skin
> since skin
> always has a warmth of blood beneath. It was a
> synthetic
> Goodyear black,
> like all records, pressed with a tread the needle
> traced,
> threading
> sound through ear and nerves and marrow. I
> touched its
> subtle
> grain sometimes wondering how music lurked in
> negative
> space
> that looked so unassuming. The marvel was—the
> missing
> had volition.

If "the missing had volition," it has voice in Fulton's poem. Both sequences use the language of pop culture not only to articulate Fulton's ideal of immersion but also to enact it. In "The Profit in the Sell" the adman's Madison Avenue sales pitch echoes the postmodern aesthetic that makes such language the vehicle for poetry:

> I'd rather be emerging than retiring. I came out
>
> to sell a big account
> that needs to keep its identity
> hidden. They're deep
> into everything it seems.
> A job so sweet you'd do it
> for free. Career candy.
> I couldn't wish away the rush I felt
> once I grasped what they were after:
> A campaign that demonstrated the beauty of
> dissolving
> boundaries between yourself and the Martian
> at the heart of every war.
> An ad that pushed viewers to incorporate-embrace
> rather than debase-slash-erase the other
> gal-slash-guy. A commercial saying blend,
> bend, and blur, folks. It works!

Fulton's taste for paradox becomes, in "Fuzzy Feelings," a metaphor in its own right—the binding of contradictory terms and tones to produce a visible seam in her text, a flaw that perfects:

>   Simulants
>
> tend to be flawless, while natural
> emeralds have defects
> known as inclusions, imperfections
> with a value all their own.

Like Daphne, she refuses Apollo, but she pays homage to Elvis Presley. Indeed, it is Elvis who serves as the book's patron spirit in the poem "About Face," embodying both its poetics ("the mixed metaphor of his jumpsuit that flared to wedding / bells white / as a pitcher plant's") and its vision of a self betrayed by its own defenses:

I do not suffer
from the excess of taste
that spells embarrassment:
mothers who find their kids unseemly
in their condom earrings,
girls cringing to think
they could be frumpish as their mothers.
Though the late nonerotic Elvis
in his studded gut of jumpsuit
made everybody squeamish, I admit.
Rule one: the King must not elicit pity.
Was the audience afraid of being tainted
—this might rub off on me—
or were they—surrendering—
what a femme word—feeling
solicitous—glimpsing their fragility
in his reversible purples
and unwholesome goldish chains?

Such embarrassment, for Fulton, is desire's reverse image, "intimacy for beginners, the orgasm no one cares to fake." In the late Elvis she finds an image of strange authenticity, an image with the power to negate the daily repressions ("Elvis from the waist up") by which the self struggles to affirm its separateness.

To this same end Fulton creates her own punctuation ("=="), a sign that she calls "a bride / after the recessive threads in lace." She deploys this symbol in the poem titled simply "= =" to compel the readers' attention to "the unconsidered / mortar between the silo's bricks":

It might make visible the acoustic signals
of things about to flame. It might

    let thermal expansion be syntactical. Let it
add stretch

    while staying reticent, unspoken
as a comma. Don't get angry = = protest = = but a
comma seems so natural, you don't see it
when you read: it's gone to pure
transparency. Yet but.
    The natural is what
poetry contests. Why else the line = = why stanza
= = why
    meter and the rest. Like wheels on snow

Fulton offers this improvised sign as a symbol for immersion, "a seam made to show," which compels our attention to what our reading ignores, "the white between the ink." Yet this symbol also serves as a summary device that draws together Fulton's complex themes. It embodies, at once, horizon, immersion, lace, and suture, Fulton's images for what the mind embraces—and represses—as it contends with the world. She explains in "Immersion":

Let it be horizon levitating on horizon
with sunrise at the center = =
the double equal that means more
than equal to = = within.

It's sensual math
and untied railroad tracks = =
the ladder of gaps and lace
unlatched. It's staples
in the page and the swimmer's liquid lane.
Those sutures that dissolve into the self.

These images are multiple in their meaning. Lace, in particular, appears most often as Fulton's image for the acts of repression by which a culture naturalizes its concealed violence, as in this meditation in the dentist's chair from "Fuzzy Feelings":

Lace
is a form of filth I hate.
As for the dying moan and gush

of the deer killed by hunters down the road—
I'd find it more tasteful
done in plastic or an acrylic
venison Christmas sweater.
I'd rather wear vinyl than hide.

I didn't mean what I said about lace.
Lace in a vacuum would be okay.
Even beige would have its place. It's context,
culture makes them = = wait, I'll take the novocaine.

In "The Lines are Wound on Wooden Bobbins, Formerly Bones," the third poem in Fulton's Daphne and Apollo sequence, this image of lace evolves into a metaphor for the woman's role as sexual prey:

A daughter like the openwork of lace = = between
    the raised motif

    the field, formed by lines
of thread called brides, shies back

    in order to let shine.

The image hints at the complexity of Fulton's metaphor, its doubleness: the bride "shies back," but in this act of receding, she shines. Fulton summons the repressed into the foreground, displays what the culture habitually conceals:

    = = the dense
omissions crystallize the lack

that's lace. She is to be that
    yin of linen

    that dissolves
under vision's dominion = = be the ground

of silk that's burned away with lye = =
    the bride.

Daphne, in "Splice: A Grotesque," embodies all that male desire negates, "the lack / that's lace," a fabric that both entices the male gaze and demands to be torn. The object of Apollo's desire, she is "neither-nor," "nevergreen"—the antimatter that is destroyed by contact with Apollo's maleness:

Given the heavens, he's the stellar,
not the black bridle between stars. He's the type

on white, he's text. He's monarch, please,
he's god. The impressive = = living end.
Though luminous matter is less than one percent
    of the whole
required for closure, though foreground
was an afterthought, he's the great attractor the
field falls
    on its knees before. Go figure.

Yet Fulton's imagery subverts this easy opposition, even as she constructs it: Daphne, by implication, is the page that makes the type visible, the unseen matter "required for closure." She is the desire that defines him, the repressed that Fulton's poem brings into view.

Daphne's transformation into the laurel in "Turn: A Version" becomes for Fulton an image of immersion, an "engagement" with nature that offers refuge from Apollo's predatory desire:

    People get a kick
out of ambivalent
betrothals and collisions full of give. Flowers that
remodel
themselves to look like bees are nice, but the scientist whose
atoms get commingled
with a fly's might be my favorite. "Help me! Help
me!"
I can identify.

Fulton reclaims the laurel ("Tree of completion—presence—and immersion") from Apollo and transforms it into an image of poetry that demands engagement. Where poets have traditionally taken the laurel, Fulton's imagery makes it a figure for the dissolution of self that poetry demands of us ("collisions full of give"). Daphne escapes into the laurel's embrace, as if heeding the admonition in Fulton's earlier sequence to "blend, / bend, and blur, folks. It works!"

One implication of this revision of the iconography of Apollo's laurel wreath is Fulton's more profound "re-imagining" of the poet's craft. She identifies Daphne closely with her own poetic method, "the deep / meanders of her / mind" through the culture's multiple languages, navigated in "Mail" by the associative pattern she calls "echolocation":

    she'd bounce
sound
off distant objects to predict their motion, shape,
and place.
Echolocation
is what she used to navigate, traveling up to one
hundred
    miles
a day.
Her sonar let her see right through opacities: read
the entrails
coiled inside the trees....

    But her gift for visualizing the inner
chambers
of words was most impressive. She'd tell of *wedlock's* wall
that was a shroud
of pink, its wall that was a picket fence, the one of
chainlink
and one
that was all strings.
....

This idea of echolocation—the ability to navigate, like a bat, by reflected sound—is central to Fulton's method: her poems strike the reader like the echo bouncing off the visible objects of culture. Yet what those echoes reveal most clearly is all that remains hidden. In "Some Cool" Fulton associates the pig ornaments she hangs on her tree with the memory of pigs hauled to slaughter; she describes this movement of mind as a form of "cultural incorrectness," the insistent presence in her poetry of thoughts that the culture tries to repress:

Now when people ask what kind of poetry I write
I say the poetry of cultural incorrectness—
out of step and—does that help?

I use my head
voice and my chest voice.
I forget voice
and think syntax, trying to add
so many tones to words that words
become a world all by themselves.
become a world all by themselves.
I forget syntax
and put some street in it. I write

for the born-again infidels
whose skepticism begins at the soles
of the feet and climbs the body,
nerve by nerve.

Fulton offers her readers a handy critical phrase here—"the poetry of cultural incorrectness"—but the more revealing moment of this brief *ars poetica* is the inclusive compositional method she confesses to in the second stanza. The inspired tonal variations that characterize her best work reflect a kind of immersion in her own writing process ("trying to add / so many tones to words / that words / become a world all by themselves"). In these terms her claim on our skepticism extends to our own process of reading. Like the students in the summer immersion course in "Drills," who "must speak the language they're learning / in brittle artificial dialogues," readers are prompted to confront the limits of their comprehension:

    ... the teacher plucked me from the chorus
with a question out of sync with all our drills:

"Does suffering help one understand
the suffering of others? What do you think, *Alice?*"
I wanted to describe an essay I'd received—
    I also was a teacher—
from a former Marine
who wrote of the wounds, humiliation,
        he'd endured in the war
        and how he'd held up well
until a medic touched him gently.
I wanted to build complex sentences,
    quivering with clauses that reveal
        the meaning sheath by sheath
        and lead to, or perhaps enact, the fact
that understanding is itself unbearable.
    Sentences beyond the depth
of my thin French. So I just said yes.

This is not agreement, but surrender. The poem emerges as an elegy for her niece ("Laura: Latin feminine of *laurus*, bay laurel"), linking the abstractions that govern Fulton's poetics to the most personal of griefs. No language can express—or allow readers to comprehend—such suffering. At best, as in Fulton's intricate riffs, it can dare readers to wonder. That's no small thing, but as Fulton notes: "What causes less comfort / than wonder?"

Fulton's self-awareness in these poems tempts her readers to the conclusion that such meditations on her own poetic imagination must be read as statements of aesthetic intent—an ongoing ars poetica that commences in the aspirations to a dangerous grace in "Dance Script with Electric Ballerina" and reappears in such poems as "The Wreckage Entrepreneur," with its description of a woman who rescues beauty from what the culture casts aside. Yet Fulton's poetics resist such attempts to impose coherence on the movements of the poetic imagination. Her poems demand from her readers nothing less than immersion, a process in which they share the creation of meaning by allowing the poem to shape—but not dictate—their own consciousness. Her meanings are multiple, fluid, and provisional; reading her work reveals our minds to be the same. As she celebrates the transformative power of poetic language, it becomes clear that it is her *reader* that is transformed, made aware by these "explorations of mind" that the poet simply sketches a horizon, displaying for her readers—as she notes in *Palladium*—"this reliable frame / that lets color be // color and light light." The rest she leaves to imagination.

Source: Sergei Lobanov-Rostovsky, "Alice Fulton," in *Dictionary of Literary Biography*, Vol. 193, *American Poets Since World War II, Sixth Series*, edited by Joseph Conte, Gale Research, 1998, pp. 138–147.

Alice Fulton and Alec Marsh

In the following interview conducted November 29, 1995, Fulton discusses the influence of television on poetry; her own use of dramatic monologue, dialogue, and "multi-logue"; and the nature of writing in the voice of the opposite gender.

This early morning interview took place on November 29, 1995, in the recording studio of WMUH, Muhlenberg College's tiny radio station; it has been edited and Fulton has taken the opportunity to expand on some of her responses. The studio setting is one reason we got to talking about popular music and television and its influence on poets. But Fulton's new book, *Sensual Math*, contains a sequence called "My Last TV Campaign," which raises the issue of the poet's relationship to the electronically mediated world.

[Marsh:] *One of the things we have been talking about this morning is the influence of television on poetry. You are of a generation, as I am, that grew up within the world of television. One of the opening lines of one of your poems in* Sensual Math, *"Vanishing Cream," begins "TV rules." I wonder if you could talk about what that means to you.*

[Fulton:] In that particular poem, it's an advertising executive who's speaking. The first line is "TV rules: it must be visual velcro . . ." There's a double meaning on "TV rules," one implication being that it rules in the sense of dominates. But the poem also is listing various rules for the production of a TV commercial, such as ". . . it must be visual velcro / at four grand per second." What does "TV rules" mean to me? Let's see . . . I grew up watching it, but I never liked it very much truthfully. As a kid there were certain shows I watched. I can't really remember what they were, but by the time I grew old enough to think—at twelve or so—I wasn't watching much TV anymore. My parents would have it on, and I would be up in my room listening to records or reading.

What was happening to music in the sixties was more powerful to me than anything I saw on TV. I always found TV kind of vacuous and boring, in fact. Other people seemed to find it mesmerizing, but at that time and I guess even today, I don't find it very engaging. I can walk away from it, turn it off. My husband, for instance, says that he can't do that. He gets sucked in; he's a visual person, a painter, and he finds it much more engaging than I do.

I tend to disagree with many of the values encouraged by TV. In "My Last TV Campaign," the ad executive, after a life of selling dish soap, et cetera, is given the chance—finally—to create a campaign for something she or he believes in, a big idea that could have a positive social impact. The poem considers the difficulties of presenting or "selling" ideas that are not already part of culture. At least, that's one thing the poem does.

I wonder if "TV rules" dictate, or give you a structure from which the quick cuts of your poetry are derived. Is there an influence there?

Well, in "Vanishing Cream" there might be an influence. That poem quotes from ad copy the speaker is trying to write. It is a little disjunctive, at times. But the disjunctiveness in other poems of mine probably comes more from what I've read and from postmodern ideas that question continuity and unity. Shifts of viewpoint and diction are a means of disrupting the poem's surface. I'm interested in dismantling the single, firm, unified speaking voice. Rather than the continuity and smoothness and polish of a steady subject, I'm interested in plurality of voices and registers of diction. My notion of poetry itself suggests quick cuts—those moves that used to be called poetics leaps. They allow the reader to fill in the gaps and participate by recreating the poem's meaning in their own minds. Poetry, to a greater degree than prose, depends on what happens between the lines. The gap between meanings is wider in poetry. My concept of poetry depends upon deletion and non sequiturs that the reader can reconstruct into meaning. To me, this is a component of poetry. It has nothing to do with TV.

I noticed when you were reading last night that some of the poems that I took to be monologic, actually seemed to have a couple of voices coming in. It suggests to me that often lines that are taken off the left-hand margin indicate another speaker. Am I making that up?

In one poem, "Some Cool," I used indentation to show shifts in thought. When I read that poem, it has the effect of being in different voices because the poem's speaker—me, in this case—is remembering the various voices. She's putting a string of pig lights—those lights they make now in the shape of animals—on the Christmas tree. While doing this, she's remembering two voices: her neighbor and the text of the Elvis cookbook she's received as a gift. But these various languages take place in the speaker's mind and in that sense are part of her shifting sense of self.

In this poem and other ones there's counterpoint—so I think you're right to pick up on

> *Poems of "desire" or loss are the safest, least vulnerable poems imaginable these days. It is far riskier, more vulnerable, to allow contrarian feelings—humiliation, vulgarity, perversity, humor, et cetera—into the poem than to express loss."*

that. To make it easier for people to hear them when I'm reading them, I'll say, for instance, "This poem is in the voice of an ad executive." But you don't have to read it that way; it can be read as parts of a sensibility, rather than parts of a single steady speaking subject. There are various polyphonic ways to look at the poems.

The first time I picked up the book, I cracked it open to one of the poems in "My Last TV Campaign," it was the Valentino poem, "Passport," and I thought, "Oh I'm not sure about this." When I realized it was a dramatic poem I felt much better. It made sense as the mind of this TV person. But at first I took it as sincere: this is Alice Fulton speaking.

You used the word "sincere," just as I might use it. But I wonder—what do we mean by "sincere?" Are autobiographical poems necessarily "sincere?" It seems to me that lyric poems often assume the pose of sincerity, and I find that posture off-putting, sometimes even offensive. I don't like it when manipulation insists upon its innocence or tries to pass itself off as guilelessness. All writing is manipulative, but writing that admits to its manipulations—by use of surface effects, tone, disjunction, what have you—seems more honest, perversely, and therefore has a better chance of convincing—or moving—me.

Even in lyrics, where it seems I'm the poem's speaker, that sense of self and voice is something of a fiction. I'm wary of being completely identified with the words being said because that way of reading fails to account for the mediation—those screening, selection, censorship—that inflects all writing. On the other hand, I have to admit that whenever I create a persona some of my own beliefs come through.

Basically, I think that autobiographical poetry needs to be viewed as a construct rather than as a "sincere," unmediated slice of life. At the same time, poetry in voices—or poetry that creates characters—can be read as mediated autobiography, mediated sincerity, if you will. During the late seventies, I worked for a brief time as an advertising copywriter in New York City, and there's a part of me in "My Last TV Campaign." I sympathize with the intentions of the speaker and the outrageously benign ad campaign she or he is trying to devise. But unlike the persona of the poem, I knew I couldn't stand advertising right from the start. I used to come home, go into the bedroom, and cry. I couldn't have lived the life of the ad executive in my poem. For me, that job was a horror. Yet to write that character, I had to have some area of sympathy or congruency.

Some readers have mistaken "My Last TV Campaign" for a satire on advertising, but that wasn't my intention at all. Advertising is a satire on itself already. The poem is much more "sincere" than people might think.

Dramatic monologues or dramatic multi-logues, as some of your poems are, do seem to give a poet a lot of freedom about hiding and coming forth.

"Multi-logues" is a good term. It describes contrapuntal poems very well. I began writing them because I got so tired of writing from my own experience, writing about my own life; it didn't include everything in a certain way. There were areas of human experience and thought that I wanted to experience vicariously; I wanted to go deeper into otherness. One of the ways of going more deeply into otherness is to write from the perspective of someone who's not you, of course. So that was how I began doing it, just trying to stretch that lyric sensibility a little bit. Now I'm going back more toward my own life and experience and away from other personas.

"My Last TV Campaign" seems to have one speaker—although it's difficult to say just who that speaker is.

People read my sequences, like "My Last TV Campaign," and sometimes don't know if it's one speaker. I have no objection to reading the poem as polyphony, but when I wrote it, I thought of it in terms of a single character.

The poem's speaker is deliberately androgynous. When I started reading the sequence I just took it to be a woman, because you're a woman. Very naive. As I got halfway through I thought that maybe it was a male speaker, but it's actually deliberately left fuzzy.

Right, the speaker's sex and gender are left open. But people always inscribe it. I think that's because the mind has trouble seeing two things at the same time. You could envision a transvestite or someone who is androgynous, but to envision both a gendered male and gendered female together is, perhaps, impossible. The poem is meant to oscillate between them. Some people inscribe it as male and will tell me about the man in my poem; others will say the woman. But it can be both; it can be either. The two overlap, switching back and forth, shuffling and flexing.

Have you ever written dramatic monologues with a male speaker?

Yes, yes. Several times. A sequence in *Powers of Congress* called "OVERLORD" is spoken in part by a soldier who's landing in Normandy on D-Day. That was definitely a male speaker. And in a recent issue of *TriQuarterly*, I published a poem called *"World Wrap"* that was in the voice of a man I'd describe as a feminist.

When you write a poem and the speaker is the other gender (if there is just one other gender) it makes one think about the role of gender, or the role that gender is. What's that like for you?

Before I answer let me be clear—when I say "sex" I'm referring to biology, while "gender" refers to the social and cultural construction of the self. Now that we've cleared that up—I think gender is a great inconvenience. I'd like to get rid of it. I don't mean the word "gender," which is very useful, but gender in action. For women, it's terribly constricting. The female gender role involves much more artificiality and contrivance than the male—though neither role is "natural."

When I was writing "OVERLORD," I tried to imagine my way into the consciousness of a soldier in World War II, who found himself in that particular historical predicament. I thought about what his background might be, and I thought of how he regarded women—that was one of the interesting things for me in the poem. When he's at war, he's remembering sex and the woman waiting for him back home.

More deeply, the poem's concerns had nothing to do with character. It thinks about the connection between childbirth and warfare as triumphant spheres of endeavor. Since antiquity, childbirth has been woman's means of transcendence and heroic endeavor, and war has been man's. "OVERLORD" is a means of meditating on that deep structure. There's a childbirth poem, in the voice of a woman, too, in that sequence. It gave me a chance to engage with sensibilities and thoughts that I wouldn't have encountered otherwise, and become more of a "chameleon poet," as Keats said.

You obviously believe, as most poets of consequence do, that "the poet thinks with the poem" as William Carlos Williams said. You mentioned meditation. How do poems begin for you? How does meditation happen?

It depends on whether it's a commission or whether it's something I choose to do on my own. Writing without an assignment is in some ways ideal because you're free to follow the deepest passions and interests. With commissions, the challenge lies in finding a connection between the assigned theme and your own urgencies. When I'm writing on my own, I look into notebooks I keep. And look at what I have written and see where I was, where I left off, where I was deeply engaged last.

And then, what I *haven't* said is of interest to me. Have I neglected anything? Was I shortchanging some aspect of a subject that interests me? Have I shied away from it? Have I been uncourageous or have I been wimpy about something?

In a way, that's how I got interested in writing more about emotion. Language has always attracted me in poetry. When I read poetry, it's the way things are said that appeals to me. So as a poet, that's very much where I began. That was the praxis or center for me. It still is. But as I thought about it, I realized that I'm also very drawn to poems because of their emotive qualities, because of what they make me feel. That's very hard for the poet to guess, to do, to control. I don't think you can control it really. But by not thinking about emotion at all and just letting it happen if it did, I felt that I was not taking on something that was finally important to me and important to poetry.

On the other hand, it seems to me that too many poets cultivate emotion at the expense of language. There's a lot of sappy poetry being written and published. The language in the poems might be plain—monochromatic, beige language—but the content is florid and gushy as cabbage roses. I have a horror of writing that way. When it comes to emotion, I prefer poems that err on the side of austerity. Most contemporary poems want to move the reader. But the emotions I feel when reading them are not the ones the poet intended. I might feel anger or disgust because I sense that the poet is trying to manipulate me with sincerity. All language is manipulative, but the poems that move me are those that seem somewhat surprised, taken aback, by their own emotional developments. I believe that can happen when feeling seeps into the poem without calculation on the poet's part. That's why I've allowed emotion into my work as an accidental (not an accident, but a fortuitous, unforeseen chromatic alteration), and maybe that's why the emotion in my poetry tends to go unnoticed.

With emotion, you can't only think, because then you're back where you were before, with the analytical. But it's possible to be analytical at first and then to allow spontaneity and feeling. To think and then let the poem rip, in both senses of the phrase. Let it be more vulnerable. Poems of "desire" or loss are the safest, least vulnerable poems imaginable these days. It is far riskier, more vulnerable, to allow contrarian feelings—humiliation, vulgarity, perversity, humor, et cetera—into the poem than to express loss. The emotional range of contemporary poetry seems far too limited. When I think of the poetry of emotion I think of surfaces that tear. Things are exposed that maybe you didn't intend to show. Those can be the most powerful points in writing.

Did those moments happen in your notebooks or only when you move from the notebook to the poem? I'm trying to imagine your notebooks now.

I have so many notebooks. Some are just collections of words and phrases that I like. But in them I'll put things I notice, things that I might feel. They are full of observations, aphorisms, about emotions or things that I've noticed about how people are acting—little things that I could work out and develop in a more nuanced and complex way in a poem.

I have a friend I talk to who's a scientist, John Holland, who's a colleague at Michigan, and we have wonderful conversations about science and literature, and I keep notes on that. So I have many different kinds of notebooks.

Do you carry them all around with you?

Never, no. That wasn't why my suitcase was so heavy! I don't because I'm afraid I'll lose them if I travel with them. I keep them at home. I have one small one that I carry with me sometimes, one where I might just jot something down, like a diary, if something happened. I also keep language in it that strikes me—bits of phrasing and words. There's nothing to notebook-keeping that's a "should-do." And I like that.

I was wondering if you feel you need a subject to bounce off of to begin the poem, or do you sit down and wait for the poem to say itself to you?

I usually have something in mind. Very often what I have in mind isn't where I end up. But at least it's something to start from, something to meditate on, to think about, and something that interests me. If the poem is a commission, of course, I'm given that start. Then the difficulty is connecting it to my own deep interests. But I don't start with absolutely nothing. The blank slate is off-putting, while words give rise to words.

Do you meditate on words or images?

I always look at entries in my notebooks. I've occasionally stared at visual images—such as photographs. This morning I was thinking of book titles, and I came up with the word "vinyl." To me it's an interesting word. And not a "poetic" word, not "desire," not "angels." A poem name that came to me was "dirt." I'm interested in the word "failure" as a poem title. America is so much about success. The idea of admitting failure, of admitting weakness, is interesting to me at the moment. I'm very interested in the connotations and the feeling and the taste and the texture of particular words. Sometimes I'll copy down a beautiful sentence from someone I'm reading.

There's so much energy and tension in a good sentence. I think of prose writers as people who write great sentences. With poets you think great lines. What's the difference between a sentence and a line?

Well, for me, the line is still the unit of composition, which might be a little bit old-fashioned at this point. It's a shame that the possibilities of the line are being neglected. It's a linguistic structure that I'm not keen on giving up, though writing in lines is certainly a lot of trouble. The line is something that poetry gives us that prose doesn't, a little sculptural thing on the page, a unit of thought with a brief rest at the end.

A line should be interesting in and of itself, and then it has to work within the context of the sentence. The line provides an opportunity for syntactic doubling—a wonderful term I learned from Cristanne Miller, a scholar who writes brilliantly about poetry. It is possible to create one meaning when the line is decontextualized and read as a thing unto itself, and another meaning when the line is connected to what follows. This sort of syntactic doubling depends upon the multiplicity of the last word in the line. But a word within the line can also act as a syntactic door, opening and closing on meaning, changing from noun to verb, for instance. "TV rules: it must be visual velcro," the line you cited earlier, is an example. "Rules" can be read as a noun or a verb. It isn't something poets want to overdo, but it can add to the richness and ambiguity of the poem. This particular linguistic effect is not possible in prose.

The line makes poets and readers think about language very closely. The end word in a line receives a great deal of pressure and attention. It's interesting to try to move the weight toward the beginning of a line. Enjambments that end the line on function words like articles, little words like "a" or "the," the seam stitching of language, are less teleological or end-driven. They lighten up the right side of the poem. Beginning with a noun or verb places more weight to the left, frontloading the line.

The most common way to lineate is to simply write lines that follow the syntactical pauses of the sentence. Poets who support this lineation sometimes call it naturalistic and say that it mimics speech. But if you listen to people talk, they pause in ragged places, leaving the prepositions in midair.

The line adds multiplicity and depth to poetry, while asking the reader to slow down. The wide margins of poetry should be read, just as much as the text. The white space and the silent rest at the end of every line conduct the music of the poem.

But When I quote poems, I probably remember phrases rather than lines. I think in terms of the phrase. Last night I was quoting Dickinson, "I like a look of agony, because I know it's true." I don't know how that sentence is lineated. I'd have to look it up.

What about those dashes in Dickinson? You use them too, and then you also have invented a new form of punctuation, the double equal sign, which is a kind of double dash and must at some level has something to do with the effect of Emily Dickinson on you.

Yes, oh absolutely. Her dashes are so mysterious. In her work, I feel the dash has been done to perfection. And that's partly why I made up another sign that could be something to think about in terms of punctuation. It wouldn't be the dash because I just can't imagine anyone using it as well as Dickinson. She uses it in ways that let you become more involved with the poem's syntax, you can fill it in, inscribe it. The dash is an empty space, but Dickinson's syntactical deletions often ask to be filled in; they exist to be recovered. Recovering the deletions makes reading her a very active, reciprocal experience. You feel like you're building the poem with her as you read. Sometimes you can't recover the deletions. The phrases on either side of the dash remain non sequiturs. Again, I have to credit Cristanne Miller, whose marvelous book on Dickinson, *A Poet's Grammar*, articulates these effects.

I also love the way the dash looks like . . . well, sewing. It suggests the way Dickinson sewed her manuscripts together. For me, it has a feminist aspect: it looks like thread, it looks like sewing, holding the lines together. But mostly I love it because it allows multiplicity. And I like the story of Dickinson's reception. I love the way that they tidied her up and put the periods in, and by regulating her punctuation, removed the single best thing, for us, that she did.

It seems to me that one of the reasons that her reception was so belated was that readers had to have already been trained with a little bit of modernism, by Marianne Moore perhaps, to understand those dashes as dashes and not as little Emily's mistakes.

I think that's true. She seems postmodern in fact. We needed indeterminacy, we needed all these twentieth-century ideas about turbulence before we could really appreciate what she had done.

Now your revision of a dash into this double thing. It's a sign that's not voiced when you read the poems so it's a form of punctuation . . .

Uh-huh.

—and therefore it's a visual sign—

Uh-huh.

—and you just mentioned that good lines of poetry reminded you of sculpture, which makes me think that you see your lines before you hear them. Always tricky to make a judgment about that, but maybe you could talk about the relationship between sound and sight in your double dash, or "bride" as you call it.

Although the sign is visual, as you say, when I'm writing a poem the sound comes first, the music. Again I think I'm old-fashioned that way. Not that the poems have a steady meter, but I hear the music of the words and rhythm. The bride sign is silent and it's mostly for readers of the page, because when I read the poems, you hear a rest or pause, but you don't know what the punctuation mark looks like. There's so much going on, I think, not only in my poetry, but in most poetry, that it's very hard for listeners to hear it and take it in if they haven't read the poem on the page. So, that's the kind of writer I am, the book kind, not the performance kind.

Well, having seen you perform last night, I want to qualify that. You read your poems beautifully and you do make the poems complex in a different way, by revealing a play of voices or slight shifts of inflection which give the impression that there is more than one voice.

Oh good, it's nice that there's a reason to read them. Thank you.

You were talking last night about your "Daphne and Apollo" poem, and you used a wonderful image about how Daphne had been "stirred into" a tree at the moment of metamorphosis. This curling image reminded me again of a word you like a lot: "turbulence." I began to wonder if the bride sign [==] is silenced because it's also a bride—perhaps a woman who has been silenced and who is full of turbulence—it marks a moment of transformation.

Oh that's really lovely. I think it is a moment of transformation; I'd like it to be that. It could also be a hinge; I see it that way too—the hinge that allows the door to open onto another realm. That threshold moment is transformative. Actually, one title I considered for *Sensual Math* was *Transformer*.

I also think of the double equal as the sign of immersion. The single equal sign retains the separation of whatever is on either side. We know that separate is not equal. The double equal, as I said in one defining poem, "means more / than equal to == within." It signals an absence of boundary, that two things are immersed in one another, as in metaphor. A simile is separated by "like" while a metaphor is transformative; one thing actually becomes the other. So, I think of the double equal as a metaphorical sign and a feminist sign, imbued with the qualities of the background, of negative space, of reticence. Yet, it's also very visible. It calls attention to itself because it's a mark that no one has ever seen in a poem before. I like the fact that it both recalls the reticence of women, the way that women have been in the background historically, and it also brings them visibly to the fore.

I also think it's a turbulent sign. To make up your own sign is probably in some ways not a good idea. It could cause some anxiety and hostility. I was aware of that, but I think poetry should be a bit turbulent and should raise arguments. It should have people saying "Why are you making me notice this?" Those are valid things for poetry to do that it hasn't been doing. It's been disappearing and being decorous. It's been behaving itself. In making that sign I wanted to take a bit of a risk, the risk of being called gimmicky and contrived and all that. That's part of the turbulence for me, that's the risk of it.

It will be interesting to see if this sign will proliferate.

Well, that would be the ultimate compliment. That would be an honor to me, because if you wrote a poem with that sign in it, you'd be saying to me that you weren't ashamed of being associated with the ideas that we've been talking about, that you were a fellow traveller. If others were to use the sign, they'd be supporting a world view. I have to add that I don't expect to see this.

It's amazing how conservative poetry is. Many people who get involved with poetry seem to be fearful, easily threatened. Maybe that's just human nature. But I do wish the world of poetry weren't so small and mean. If you change a tiny aspect of poetics it's "Off with her head! Off with his head!" It's as if you've done something very rude and conceited, calling attention to yourself and so on.

It sounds like you've caught some flak about the sign already.

No, in fact I've been lucky. I've just been counting my blessings. I'm waiting for it, it might happen next week. There's a book review coming out next week, and it might be in that, I don't know.

It's always in the next review.

In the next one, sure.

You'll get slammed—

Yeah, you're just waiting for it.

Insofar as the sign does have this sense of the feminine, we can interpret the term feminine very broadly to suggest all that is disorderly, contaminated, seductive and therefore problematic in an ordered, male, analytical, philosophical world. The sign seems to remind us that the silence of the silenced is always turbulent, must necessarily be turbulent.

Yes, under the surface there's writhing.

It reminds me of your Daphne, stuck in a tree and looking out through the cracks in the bark.

Waiting for her chance to be seen. She's a figure for what's happened to women historically. I didn't just think of her as a woman in American culture, because women in this country have a much more comfortable way of living than women do world-wide. I was thinking of her in terms of what has happened to women in the biggest ways. At the end of "Turn: A Version," she peers out of a tree waiting to see and be seen. Apollo had installed mirrors in the tree, so that Daphne's reflection of herself is his construction, his idea of her. All she could see was the image of herself that was given to her by the male god. She's trying to open the tree to see the world from her own point of view, and to have someone see her as she is.

If there were such a someone, who would it be?

I think it happens when women become more culturally dominant. It occurs when women are empowered (if it ever happens. I don't know that it ever will.) If women came to the fore of culture and were more visible, everyone would start to see what women can do. Women's image might not be limited to stereotypical or essentialist notions that define women as part of nature because of their association with child-bearing and child-rearing. Women could redefine themselves through opportunity, showing that they could do science, they could do math, they could be analytical. The world gaze would be their gaze.

I'm beginning to see that the person looking through the crack on the other side might first be a woman poet, or a woman philosopher.

Yes, she could be in any number of fields as long as she's a pioneer.

Because you mentioned vinyl earlier, because we were talking about growing up in the 1960s, has the poetry of rock 'n' roll influenced your work? I mean, you said that when you were twelve, you were upstairs listening to records.

Yes, Dylan, The Beatles, Joni Mitchell and all those sixties people.

I don't actually hear them in your work as I've read it, but—

No, not really. I think they wrote wonderful songs, but I'm sure you've noticed if you write down those lyrics, they don't do very much. It's the music, it's the phrasing, the production that gives them life.

It's the particular sneering way they get sung.

Dylan certainly sneered. The difference between song lyrics and poetry is that, with poetry, the music has to be in the language itself. The language of the poem has to do everything. Musicians have instruments behind them and they have their singing voices and so on. If I wrote words like theirs, the words would fall flat without the tunes and chords.

The pretend book called Vinyl sounds like it might have to do with records. Records are a big image for you. I know you were a DJ once. What is it about records? Say something about vinyl.

O.K. Vinyl is a highly artificial, human-made substance with associations of resiliency, longevity, cheapness and sleaziness. I'm thinking of vinyl car seats, now, not only records. Vinyl is much tougher than natural substances. It doesn't biodegrade, which is very bad from an ecological point of view. Vinyl is forever. It's a petroleum product, and it looks like solid oil. Vinyl is used in place of leather, but considered declasse, less lovely. However, vinyl is less cruel than leather, a material that evokes suffering—the suffering of slaughterhouses. Leather is fetishistic because it evokes the living and the dead. It's a fabric of domination—evoking not only sexual domination, but the human domination of the natural world. Leather is much more expensive than vinyl, and displaying leather is a means of asserting wealth, taste, class. Vinyl, on the other hand, is a subject of jokes and dismissal. Yet, as I've said, vinyl is more eternal than leather. Vinyl is kinder. The vinyl used in records is a repository that looks unassuming—dark, uninteresting—but within its negative space are sonic complexities, beautiful, invisible harmonics.

You reminded me of something else with your question, actually, about the effect of rock lyrics. (They were all on vinyl, for me.) I think one thing they did for me was not make sense. In those days, the sixties, seventies, lyrics were things that you puzzled over. You heard them again and again, appreciating them for everything that they didn't say clearly. You appreciated the mystery of them. Who is "the Walrus" in the Beatles' song? And Dylan was terrific for lines that had resonance but couldn't be pinned down. I think today's popular music is clearer. I don't mean the sort of marginal music that is played on college radio stations but the mainstream. I've asked students, "Don't you listen to music this way anymore?" A way of listening that appreciates something for what it retains and conceals, so that you had to hear it again and again. That is the appreciation I took to literature. The need to read that poem again and again was part of the pleasure. The places where the poem interested me most were those places that retained a residue I couldn't completely excavate. One of the deepest pleasures of literature for me was the sense that a work had no bottom: it was infinitely understandable because it couldn't be completely understood. It couldn't be seized back from connotation into denotation. There would always be a layer of meaning that I couldn't retrieve.

Where did that happen for you? Do you remember a time when you picked up a poem and couldn't get to the bottom of it?

All the time in high school. My sister was an English major, and her books were up in the attic. Around the time I was listening to records, I was also reading poetry anthologies. I'd write out Keats and Shakespeare's monologues in my own hand as a way of appropriating them. I was doing that with the song lyrics, too. It was the same appreciation. They both were mysterious and wonderful things made of words that I wanted to memorize and internalize, but even at the time, I recognized that the rock lyrics were not as good as the language of the poems. When you took away the music, the song lyrics fell flat, while the poems didn't need any music, outside of the music they made themselves. Since I'm not musically talented, I had to write poems rather than music. I would have probably become a musician if I could have.

Who wouldn't?

Right, who wouldn't? But I couldn't. If you could sing! To me, that's the best. Many poets really want to sing, especially lyric poets. But since I couldn't, I came to poetry.

Who was the first poet who grabbed you with the same intensity as, say, the Beatles must have grabbed you?

Gosh, I read so many, but probably Dickinson, from way back. I loved her work when I was in high school and then, of course, you just go on and find out that there's a lot more than those pocket-sized, gift shop volumes of her love poems. That was where I started, and then I realized that it didn't have to end there. Dickinson had this big body of work, and so she carried me through. I became fascinated with her biography. Of course, the legend of Emily Dickinson seems so romantic when you are in high school, you buy into it. You believe all that, the romantic mythology—

—her lowering the little basket out the window—

[Fulton:]—exactly, the white dress.

Who was the first contemporary poet whose next book you would wait for with the same eagerness?

Probably Adrienne Rich. Denise Levertov, Elizabeth Bishop, Anne Sexton and Maxine Kumin. I didn't start to read contemporary poetry till the mid seventies, when I was an undergraduate in college. The first course I took was "Women Poets" at Empire State College. It was a very small seminar, with only about four people, and our teacher, Carolyn

Broadaway, was outstanding. She took us to a feminist poetry conference at U Mass., Amherst, where Adrienne Rich was reading and speaking, along with other poets of the day, feminist poets. So I actually was sitting, literally sitting, at Adrienne Rich's feet in this informal meeting. Hearing her speak, hearing her read, and I'd already read all of her books to date, in the course, along with all of Denise Levertov. Rich is one poet who made me think this is the kind of thing I wish I could do. She was an inspiration.

Is she still that inspiration for you?

She'll always be a wonderful poet for me.

A final question. Where do you think poetry's going? Which is just another way of saying where do you think the culture's going?

Oh, it's so hard to say where poetry is going. I don't think it's going to become more popular because electronic media are on the rise, our lives are changing. Maybe not mine, I'm very old-fashioned and I don't have much to do with television or computers, but I think electronic media are increasingly important within world culture. I also think books and poetry will always have their place. Books offer a particular kind of intense, complex, imaginative experience that can't be found electronically or through visual images. Reading requires a more active reimagining than viewing a screen. TV and film do a lot of the work for the viewer. That's one reason they're popular. But for those who learn to read as children—I mean those who learn to love books—reading is a kind of deep intoxication, a means of experiencing otherness deeply. That, nothing can replace. As long as kids still learn to read that way, I believe some of them will value books and want them around. As long as there's a written language, I think people—centain small groups of people—will prize poetry as the best example of an elegant, and thrilling, linguistic structure.

Source: Alice Fulton and Alec Marsh, "A Conversation with Alice Fulton," in *Triquarterly*, No. 98, Winter 1996–1997, pp. 22–40.

Emily Grosholz

In the following essay excerpt, Grosholz discusses the language distortion and the influences of love in Alice Fulton's poetry.

All poetry distorts language. Formal patterns wrench it from its everyday cadences, and figures from its accustomed ways of referring. Alice Fulton's poetry puts especially intense pressure on English. But she understands very well that in art, distortion is expressive as well as inescapable. Indeed, the studied distortions of art are not only meaningful, they play an essential role in the way we make the world mean, which is often how we make the world *tout court*. In fact, undistorted representation is just as impossible as meaningless experience.

Recognizing that distortion must be consciously studied and also made intelligible, Fulton is distinguished among poets of her generation for language that is at once radically inventive and communicative. She escapes both the hermetic incoherence of the Language poets and the prosiness of the new formalists, perhaps because she has taken as her guides two poets (one nineteenth century and one contemporary) who also elude those traps, Emily Dickinson and A. R. Ammons. The study of Dickinson led Fulton to pay careful attention to poetic surface, its compressions and amplifications, its oddities, even its visible deletions. Yet Dickinson's inspired mannerism, that draws so much attention to the way her words work, never obscures her vision; her poems sing as clearly as the hymns whose metrical patterns they borrow. Likewise, Ammons's generous inclusion of the more obvious realms of science and philosophy into the more mysterious, conventionally literary realms of his poems is never prosaic, for it is balanced by a series of wonderfully inventive combinations of the discursive and lyric by which poetry is not impoverished but enriched. Ammons was in fact Fulton's teacher at Cornell University, and his influence, strong but not anxious, is still apparent in her work.

In her earliest book, *Dance Script with Electric Ballerina* (1983), Fulton writes about the art of painting, and the curious distortions involved in representing the three-dimensional world on a two-dimensional plane of canvas in the poem "Picture Planes." What the poet observes about the distortions of painting holds all the more true of poetry. For there is at least a partial morphism, describable by projective geometry, between a painted image and what visual perception yields; the link between experience and words is even more indirect and mediated by convention. The poet distorts not only what experience presents, but linguistic patterns and poetic conventions.

> For instance, painters
> resent a form's excursions
> in the third dimension, live to smear
>
> slithery light and branching
> shapes onto solid sheets, pillage
> the world in a war so contained
>
> it goes unnoticed. They'll take
> a sea monster, say, and force its image
> to a picture plane, intact. To do it

they must slice the thing in half.
A profile expels a hissing double
on the world, while a front view sets free

the flickering hinderparts. That's why
artists seek extremes: only the scaliest
dragon, snowiest angel will do.

Thinking of its dimensional soul, condemned
to wander, they leave cowed
monsters, fleeced seraphim.

Some of Fulton's most characteristic distortions are visible here. Like many post-modernist poets, she plays with enjambment, ending lines and even stanzas in unexpected ways. But her play is never careless; she gives close attention to the ambiguities and resonances those suspensions of sense, in the thin air around the printed word, create. The reader must think, and feel, her way over the abysses crossed by Fulton's invisible threads: "painters ... live to smear / slithery light and branching / shapes onto solid sheets." The small nothing between "smear" and "slithery" echoes the formal, white margin of the canvas, and the gestural pause the artist's hand waits in, before moving on to illuminate and shape the picture....

II

Who are the loves that anchor Alice Fulton's poetry, that keep it dense, well-formed, grounded, and substantial? One set of loves is the originally working-class family she grew up with in an Irish-Catholic, middle-class neighborhood in Troy, New York. (Her father owned and ran a hotel, affectionately recalled in "A Union House.") Fulton explores the landscape of her youth in a mode that is monochromatic (curious in a poet so interested in painting) and wintry. In most of her poems of home, snow is falling, evening is lowering. Winter takes its time in upstate New York, and does in fact dominate the rest of the year, and one's memories. Winters so long and harsh impose their own telling distortions on human life; so do the constraints of petty bourgeois life. Harsh weather is an overriding figure in Fulton's poetry, true and false to the conditions of her childhood....

In the poem "Perpetual Light" in *Dance Script* (a poem about visiting a cemetery with her mother, and dedicated to her), Fulton gives her mother a kind of originary, funerary speech evoking the people who populate so many of her poems:

Later you studied the glitter

in the dull or rosy stones, wondering
was it smidgins of the perpetual
light you prayed to shine upon them.
"The things we survived

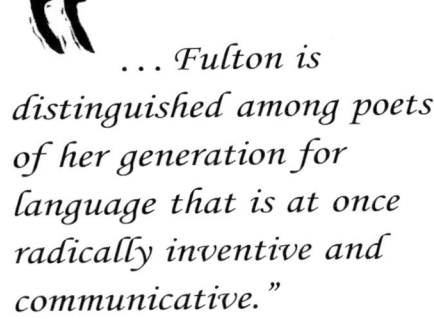

"... Fulton is distinguished among poets of her generation for language that is at once radically inventive and communicative."

or died from!" you exclaim.
"James to pneumonia, as you know.
Fran lay huddled on the sofa
for months with typhoid.

Her hair fell out in hanks
and she never touched milk again.
Mother said it was skunk oil
cured her. Sickness, I remember,

had a different smell then. After Azalea's
scarlet fever they fumigated the house...."

And mumps brought Fulton's mother hallucinations about the return of her dead siblings, tapping on the window to call her out to play. With an imagination overheated not by fever but by poetry, Fulton too almost believes in revenants, "the mysterious / half-world we know exists / if only we could find it," though unlike her mother she hopes they're not much entangled in the intentions of the living. Invoking her lost loves abroad in the universe, Fulton gives the last stanza of the poem a twist of diction that is like a teenager's, spinning the poem suddenly away from her mother's mode of speech. Let the dead, she writes in her own, younger voice, "hotfoot it through the universe / like supple disco stars: their glamor sifting / into our rare, breathtaking dreams, our rarer prayers / mere twinges in their unimaginable limbs." In these lines, the voice that echoes is not her mother's but Rilke's, nuanced by the phantasms of MTV.

The poem "Everyone Knows the World is Ending," from *Palladium*, includes the observation, "But in the love, the grief, under and above / the mother tongue, a permanence hums." Her mother uses remembering, as Fulton uses poetry, to consider and counter the impermanence of things. Confronted by the title's claim,

my mother speaks in memories,
each thought a focused mote in the apocalypse's
iridescent fizz. She is trying to restore a world
to glory, but the facts shift with each telling

of her probable gospel. Some stories have been
trinkets in my mind since childhood, yet what
clings is not
how she couldn't go near the sink
for months without tears when her mother died,
or how she feared she wouldn't get her own
beribboned kindergarten chair, but the grief
in the skull like radium
in lead, and the visible dumb love like water
in crystal, at one with what holds it.

The price of the artful constructions that hold things fast, is that they distort as well as secure: "She is trying to restore a world / to glory, but the facts shift with each telling / of her probable gospel." There is no narrative without distortion, for we must reorganize experience so that it has a tellable beginning, middle, and end. But then again, there is no experience without the organizing narratives we construct to make it memorable. The other price we pay for memory, or poetry, is grief, for by calling up the departed, we revive our love for them and our sorrow at their passing. Indeed, the perpetual grief of the cemetery or poem casts its shadow everywhere, since all that we love is mortal. In reviving her mother's childhood grief at losing her mother, Fulton mourns her own mother, a little, in advance. As in "Perpetual Light," the two strange and powerful images of this poem quoted above wrest the diction away from mother to daughter, so that the daughter can express her own proper grief. The analogy between mother and daughter, condition for the possibility of Fulton's remembering in her poems, is also fraught with difference.

III

Two other loves figure centrally in the romance of Fulton's poetry, playing analogous but obviously distinct roles: her father and her husband. The importance of these two people is especially clear in the book *Palladium*, which of all her first three books has the most obvious narrative structure. It is a structure articulated in terms of place, though the opening sections are very strangely located.

In a sense, the book opens in nowheresville. The initial three poems of the first section hover, outside of space and time; the final three treat hell and rather hellish, phantasmagoric cityscapes. Throughout the first section, the poet's persona seems lost and disoriented. Of course, the confusion is studied and carefully structured; all the same, the poems are hard to place. In this context, Fulton's poem for her father, "Nugget and Dust," is a sheer lament, a regret, despite its wit and self-consciousness. How could I? she asks, the question hovering without a question mark at the end of the first stanza.

How could I

admit I withdrew from him
as from a too-gentle thing I wanted to live
forever? I couldn't stand the forthcoming
sadness. Love, if true, is tacit.
It accumulates, nugget and dust, arcade of sweet
exchange. I argued the self-
evidence of all enhancements.
Yet we were camouflaged. I told lies
in order to tell the truth,
something I still do.

Camouflage, and silence, serve their purposes in life, as in poetry. If there were such a thing as the whole truth, we would not tell it to anyone we love; love is too strong a mixture of aggression and devotion to be served up straight.

The loss of her father leaves Fulton's world unregulated: he had always dispensed remedies for illness, unwavering moral dicta, and advice about how to maintain a car, that indispensable vehicle for getting into and out of the scary, confusing grids of American cities. It was hard, she observes,

to imagine a world in tune
without his attention
to its bewildering filters, emergency
brakes, without his measured tread. Diligent world,
silly world! where keys turn and idiot lights
signal numinous privations.

The pages that follow are full of idiot lights and numinous privations, some of them shaped like language, as in these lines from "The Body Opulent": "Outside, the night was laced with bright fillips / of pidgin English: Glassbenders, / in bins among transformers, standing / burners, the din and smell of lightning, / formed these Lifesavers and double helices of neon. . . ." Here and in the following section, Fulton's love of mixing up different vocabularies goes wild, as if she were "The Wreckage Entrepreneur" she writes of, dealing in old words instead of keystones and gargoyles.

Just at this point, Fulton introduces "My Second Marriage To My First Husband," and "Fables From The Random: to Hank." In the first, the ordinary American wedding looks phantasmagoric; its rituals keep the lovers apart just at the moment of marriage, recorded forever in the photograph album, *de rigueur*.

Bring squeeze boxes, gardenias,
a hybrid of the two. Congratulate us,
chums. Smile and freeze: our dimples stiffen
to resolute framed stares. How adult
we look! Our eyes burn
stoplights in the Instamatic squares.

The problem, summed up in Fulton's ironic instamatic of a poem, is an excess of order and external scaffolding. Love needs spontaneity and inwardness. Thus in the second poem, she contemplates the accidents at the heart of love, from which it constructs its own necessities. All true creation, and love itself, she argues, have to involve the random.

> When I tossed bouquets through the open
> window of your high and empty room,
> some weedy flowers drifting
> on the bed, some dangling
> from the sill,
> you returned to wonder
> how I'd managed without a key—
> the daisies were so sweetly placed.

With this act of random caress, Fulton begins to believe that she can manage without a key, that the world without her father's ordering can still make sense. And here, the book starts to go back home, to a real place: Troy, New York.

In the next sections, the figure of father recedes behind a flurry of mostly female relatives, and the figure of husband flickers into congeries of imaginary and remembered boyfriends. Trying out varieties of love is propadeutic to finding the Friend, the Person, the Other; experience on the whole is a likelier way to arrive at marriage than innocence. These poems are especially tactile, even when they talk about the suspension of touch in fantasy, or fear. In "Fugitive," Fulton's younger self learns to play a rock star's songs on her guitar to bring him near, even sacrificing her long nails to the new skill: "The strings left pink / incisions backed by fugitive / strings, surprising / after years of not touching." In "Scumbling," she writes with a ghostly, glancing touch that transposes some of Emily Dickinson's more spiritual invocations of mood into the realm of eros.

> So I watched feelings hover
> over like the undersides
> of waterlilies: long serpentines
> topped by nervous almost—
> sunny undulations. I had to learn
> largo. I had to trust
> that two bodies scumbling
> could soften one another.

All these amours, deeply and superficially felt, rush together and announce their worldly station in the poem "Another Troy," where Fulton seems finally to live through and down into her birthplace. This city really is where I come from, she announces. It's not so pretty, and in some ways it's moribund and icy. And now, a woman of letters, I can't even say its name without referring to that other Troy. But it didn't imprison me after all, and in many ways those cold winter mornings got me started, and saved me from the laxity that easier climates tolerate.

> In time, I escaped the ruinous romances,
> but Troy remains. Today the eccentricity
> of its willful brick begins
> to look like character.
> Oh, if I sing of icicles
> dangling like syringes from friezes
> "neo-grec" or French,
> of roses battened down with sackcloth, trees
> lumbagoed under lumpen winters,
> I'm minting an insignia. Take this, "Troy—
> the City without Glibness,"
> for your spartan tribute.

So it's just at this point in the *Palladium* process where Fulton is ready to move on. The place she moves on to is Provincetown, in the book's two final poems, "Semaphores and Hemispheres" (dedicated to her husband) and "Traveling Light" (written for and about her father). Provincetown is home to an artist's colony, the Fine Arts Work Center, where Fulton and her husband Hank De Leo lived for many months, plying their arts as poet and painter, protected and rewarded for doing what they want to do. When this happy confluence of need and desire happens for the first time, it seems like a miracle: the external world actually acknowledges one's secret art! The poet goes so far as to add a splash of color: "crocuses poked up like palette / knives thick with yellow / oils."

Fulton's happiness (can a poet dare to be happy? why yes) finds expression in her specialty, a series of brilliantly incongruous images that conjoin the natural and artificial by compressing disparate levels of diction.

> the ocean, too, forms
>
> coigns more restless than the set
> coigns of a crystal, and turbulence
> in the air makes the stars
> glimmer. Somehow
> everything squares. The lighthouse oars the night
> as if its white trunk could go soaring
> up, concentric and outgoing
> as a helicopter, unhurried
> as a ceiling fan in old movies
> of the tropics. . . .
> Some days we're simply happy
>
> to be just where we are,
> where the lighthouse strokes
> the hemispheres, a cane for the voyaging
> blind, who chart their lives
> by a star of the 19th magnitude
> that shines unseen tonight but shines.

"Somehow everything squares," even the amorphous ocean. The lighthouse is a helicopter, a fan, a cane; the poem generates all those bizarre associations, threatening to explode, and yet holds them together by the force of linguistic attraction and the logic of beauty. Fulton manages to hold the protean shape of her life in her arms, despite so much estrangement, and it becomes a book.

The act of integration should not be underestimated. The life in Troy that sent Aunt Fran to work forever in the cafeterias of Troy High and the Daughters of Sarah did not encourage Alice Fulton to become a poet or enter the academy. Even her father, had he lived longer, would not have understood Fulton's wish to write poetry. In "Traveling Light," looking around at the ramshackle paradise of Provincetown, Fulton wonders of her father, "What would he have made of this off-season / resort? Though he never lived to see it / I can hear him say, "Don't worry, / Al, if the poetry don't go / I'll buy you your own beauty shop." The love and incomprehension in those lines is very touching.

So too is the last poetic gesture in the book, at the end of this poem, where Fulton brings her father back on the tenth anniversary of his death, rising above the surface of the wintry Atlantic "rip[ping] itself / out sideways, thoughtless as a torn seam," beyond the dunes blanched to the color of seashells.

> I'm half-prepared to see my father,
> to whom the world gave nothing
> without struggle, rise up beaming
> anyway upon it, as if he never meant
> to let it go. Saltboxes appear and disappear
> in the slurry fog. Gulls open
> against the sky like books
> with blank, beautifully demanding pages,
> and behind me the stolid ocean
> slams itself on earth
> as if to say *that's final*
> though it isn't. Behind me the ocean
> stares down the clouds, the little last remaining
> light, as if to remind me of the nothing
> I will always have
> to fall back on.

Postscript

Nothingness, cast in the image of a horizon where earth and sky may no longer be distinguished, recurs at the end of all of Fulton's first three books. Two kinds of nothing interest artists. One is the white blankness of the page when it is used to frame and order. Then the white surround isolates the image, bringing attention to it as an image, individuating it and calling attention to its beauty. Any multiplicity in the image is presented in series, according to conventions of spatial and temporal sequence. But in the contrasting second kind, images seem to boil up from the white page, melt into and interfere with each other, and threaten to recede back into it. Then the blankness of the page is like a plenum, a womb-grave that ceaselessly spawns and devours.

To use Nietzsche's well-worn vocabulary, the first is Apollonian, the second Dionysian. The first exhibits the distortions of art, which mask with order the chaos of underlying being. The second exhibits the distortions of being, which disturb the smooth homogeneity of nonbeing. Fulton's poetic nothing in "Traveling Light," by means of which she closes the poem and her book, has both the pathos and roil of Dionysus, and the stability and articulation of Apollo. Her poetry, playful and wise, anarchic and restrained, inhabits a middle ground that the philosopher, in love with his distinctions, did not imagine.

Source: Emily Grosholz, "Distortion, Explosion, Embrace: The Poetry of Alice Fulton," in *Michigan Quarterly Review*, Vol. 34, No. 2, Spring 1995, pp. 213–29.

Sources

Blasing, Mutlu Konuk, "The American Sublime, c. 1992: What Clothes Does One Wear?" in the *Michigan Quarterly Review*, Vol. 31, No. 3, Summer 1992, pp. 431, 432.

Boland, Eavan, "In Perspective," in *Partisan Review*, Vol. 60, No. 2, Spring 1993, pp. 317–18.

"Contents of Agriculture Table," U.S. Census Bureau, http://www.census.gov/statab/USA98/dd-ag.txt (February 24, 2006).

Fulton, Alice, "Art Thou the Thing I Wanted," in *Powers of Congress*, Sarabande Books, 2001, pp. 105–108.

Norris, Kathleen, Review of *Powers of Congress*, in *Library Journal*, Vol. 116, No. 2, February 1, 1991, p. 80.

Review of *Powers of Congress*, in *Publishers Weekly*, Vol. 237, No. 40, October 5, 1990, pp. 94–95.

"U.S. Divorce Statistics," *Divorce Magazine*, http://www.divorcemag.com/statistics/statsUS.shtml (February 21, 2006).

Further Reading

Addonizio, Kim, and Dorianne Laux, *The Poet's Companion: A Guide to the Pleasures of Writing Poetry*, W. W. Norton, 1997.

> This book, written by two published poets, comes highly recommended for students who want to explore their own abilities to write poetry. The authors' advice addresses subjects about which to write, the craft of writing, and the things that might distract one from writing.

Butler, Christopher, *Postmodernism: A Very Short Introduction*, Oxford University Press, 2003.

> This is a very readable, accessible, and short introduction to the basic tenets of postmodernism, with a particular focus on how the movement is defined in art, philosophy, politics, and ethics.

Henry, Brian, and Andrew Zawacki, eds., *The Verse Book of Interviews: 27 Poets on Language, Craft & Culture*, Verse Press, 2005.

> This volume contains interviews with working poets collected by the publication *Verse* over the years. American as well as international poets offer their insights on their art.

Mayes, Frances, *The Discovery of Poetry: A Field Guide to Reading and Writing Poems*, Harvest Books, 2001.

> This book can help readers understand the nature of poetry. Mayes, best known for her novel *Under the Tuscan Sun*, which was made into a movie, also teaches creative writing; in this volume are several essays taken from her teaching experience.

Paz, Octavio, *The Other Voice: Essays on Modern Poetry*, Harvest Books, 1992.

> The Nobel Prize–winning Mexican poet Octavio Paz is highly praised for his analysis of modern poetry. In this collection, he helps readers understand poetry's political, social, and cultural roles.

Bonnard's Garden

Rick Barot

2001

Rick Barot's poem "Bonnard's Garden," like a Romantic painting, is filled with images of nature, such as flowers, vines, clouds, shrubs, birds, and deer. The meaning of the poem is obscure, and the language only hints at its subjects, as if the speaker is in a dreamlike trance—or, more accurately, as if the speaker were like the "sleepwalking girl" who wanders, unexpectedly, in and out of the poem. The work first appeared in the literary magazine *Ploughshares* in the Winter 2001–2002 issue and was then included in Barot's prize-winning first collection, *The Darker Fall*, published in 2002.

Like a majority of the other poems in Barot's collection, "Bonnard's Garden" is focused on a specific place. The place in this particular poem is described through beautiful imagery, depicting flora and fauna, mysterious intruders, and even a startling scream. In examining such places as gardens, street corners, and other outdoor scenes, Barot, as he has explicitly stated, better perceives himself. Although he often employs elements characteristic of Romantic poetry—such as the emphasis on nature and one's surroundings—and has stated that he is indeed drawn to poetry of the Romantic era, Barot refers to himself as a post-Romantic poet. His influences include William Wordsworth, the great eighteenth-century English Romantic poet; the Nobel Prize–winning Irish poet Seamus Heaney, who also emphasizes setting; and the novelist Virginia Woolf, whom Barot admires most for her acuity, especially as found in her diaries. Indeed, in "Bonnard's Garden," Barot has produced an exercise in the construction of poetic language.

Rick Barot Photograph by Karim Logue. Courtesy of Rick Barot

Author Biography

Rick Barot, the author of "Bonnard's Garden," was born in the Philippines but grew up near San Francisco, California. He attended Wesleyan University, in Connecticut; the coveted Writers' Workshop at the University of Iowa; and Stanford University, in California. Upon graduating, he began teaching poetry at Stanford, where he was a Wallace E. Stegner fellow. He next moved to the Pacific Northwest; in the early 2000s, he was working as an assistant professor of English at Pacific Lutheran University, in Tacoma, Washington.

When he first started college, Barot thought that he wanted to become a lawyer. Although he had been encouraged by teachers to follow a writing career, he thought that he needed to tackle something more academically challenging; passing English classes had always been easy, but he did not see that as a reason to make writing his life's work. However, in taking several literature classes as an undergraduate, he started to recognize an underlying passion. After he received encouragement from the author Annie Dillard, who taught one of his English classes, Barot finally took his first poetry-writing class, during his senior year. In graduate school, he began writing some of the poems that eventually were published in his first poetry collection, *The Darker Fall*, which contains "Bonnard's Garden."

In 2001, Barot received a poetry fellowship from the National Endowment for the Arts. The next year, *The Darker Fall* was published and won the Kathryn A. Morton Prize in poetry. Barot noted in an interview with Craig Beaven for the online literary journal *Blackbird* that writing *The Darker Fall* was like an apprenticeship for him: through the writing of the poems collected in that book, he learned the art of poetry. As of early 2006, Barot was working on a second poetry collection, which was to have an overall theme based on the mythological character Echo, who loved the sound of her own voice.

Poem Text

As in an illuminated page, whose busy edges
have taken over. As in jasmine starred
onto the vine-dense walls, stands of phlox,
and oranges, the flesh of each chilled turgid.

By herself the sleepwalking girl arranged   5
them: the paper airplanes now wrecked
on the vines, sodden, crumpled into blooms
which are mistaken all morning for blooms.

The paint curls out of the tubes like ointments.
In his first looking there is too much hurry.   10
Dandelions, irises smelling of candles.
Two clouds like legs on the bathwater sky.

Drawn out of the background green, getting
the light before everything else, the almond
tree comes forward in a white cumulus,   15
as though the spring had not allowed leaves.

Last night she asked what temperature arctic
water could be that beings remained in it.
Then the question brought to the blood
inside her cat, the pillow of heat on a chair.   20

His glimpse smudged. As in: it's about time
I made you dizzy. Here are pink grasses,
shrubs incandesced to lace, tapestry
slopes absorbing figures and birds and deer.
                                                   25
Nothing is lean. The lilacs have prospered
into bundles, the tulips fattened hearts.
Pelts of nasturtiums, the thicket the color of
pigeon: gray netted over the blueberry lodes.

Then the girl's scream, her finger stirring
the emerald tadpole-water, the sound   30
breaking into his glimpse for an instant
then subsiding to become a part of the picture.

Not the icy killing water. But the lives there,
persisting aloft. Like the wasps held in
by a shut flower at dusk, by morning released,   35
dusty as miners, into the restored volumes.

Poem Summary

Stanza 1

The first four-line stanza of "Bonnard's Garden" contains two punctuated phrases: each ends in a period, but neither is a complete sentence. The ornate language describes fragmented images, leaving the reader's imagination to fill in the empty spaces. The word "illuminated" could mean "lit up" or perhaps "made clearly understood." Jasmine and phlox are types of flowers; *turgid* means "swollen with fluid."

Stanza 2

The second stanza is a complete sentence. A "sleepwalking girl" has apparently placed a number of paper airplanes "on the vines," that is, presumably, on the "vine-dense walls" referred to in stanza 1. The planes are "wrecked" and "sodden," suggesting, perhaps, the presence of dew. The word "blooms" is repeated at the end of the stanza's third and fourth lines; no other rhyme structure is present.

Stanza 3

The third stanza, two complete sentences followed by two phrases, begins with paint curling out of tubes, implying the presence of an artist; the paint itself is compared to medication. In the stanza's second line, a male appears. Perhaps it is the artist in question, "In his first looking." This artist may be the one mistaking the paper airplanes for blooms, especially in that he looks with "too much hurry." This phrase may be connected with the first stanza's "illuminated page" with "busy edges," as the words "busy" and "hurry" both suggest rapid movements or clutter. In more peaceful images, on the other hand, additional flowers are compared to "candles," and the sky is compared to "bathwater."

Stanza 4

The fourth stanza is one complete sentence. An almond tree is perhaps blooming, with the blossoms lending the tree the appearance of a fluffy white cumulus cloud. The narrator wonders whether the "spring had not allowed leaves," assigning a sort of personified power to the season. As the tree is "getting the light before everything else" and as "morning" was mentioned in the second stanza, the reader may infer that the scene is taking place at dawn.

Stanza 5

The fifth stanza contains one clear complete sentence and one somewhat confusing one. The "she" in question is likely the sleepwalking girl, the only female yet mentioned. This "she" asks how "beings" could survive in arctic waters. The inferred coldness of the arctic water is then juxtaposed with the phrase, "the pillow of heat on a chair," where the "pillow of heat" seems to refer to the cat. The second sentence suggests that the girl may have asked another question, regarding the temperature of the cat's blood; that is, "the question brought to" might be restated as "the girl next asked about."

Stanza 6

In the sixth stanza, the male returns. The first sentence, "His glimpse smudged," may be another reference to his being an artist, as if his perception of something might be made unclear in the same way that an image on a page might be made unclear. In the stanza's second line, one of the characters, seemingly the male artist, is given a voice; he is speaking to someone, perhaps the sleepwalking girl. The words "dizzy" and "smudged" both indicate a lack of clarity. Next come "pink grasses" and "shrubs incandesced to lace," that is, perhaps, grasses and shrubs whose dewy tips are glowing in various ways in the morning light. Given the narrator's attention to the texture of the scene, the word "tapestry" is perhaps used to indicate the fabric-like quality of a hillside, on which birds and deer can be found.

Stanza 7

In the seventh stanza, the sense of spring bounty is deepened. The flowers are in full bloom. The narrator associates being "fattened" and not "lean" with "prospering."

Stanza 8

In the eighth stanza, the girl screams, with no reason given. At the same time, more calmly, she stirs with her finger the green water, perhaps of a pond. The sound of the scream is described as "breaking into his glimpse," where the word "glimpse" is used for the second time in reference, seemingly, to the artist's surveying of the scene before him. The scream has a permanent effect on the artist, "subsiding to become a part of the picture" that he would seem to be then painting.

Stanza 9

The first line in the last stanza ties previous stanzas together: "Not the icy killing water" harks back to the "arctic water" mentioned in stanza 5 as well as to the "tadpole-water" of stanza 8. Thus, pond water teeming with life is set in opposition to arctic water, which would seem to be too cold for most life. The next phrase, "But the lives there, / persisting aloft," may refer to either of those bodies of

Topics For Further Study

- Sit in a garden—yours or a public one—and write sketches of what you see as if you were painting still-life portraits. Do not worry about creating a story, instead concentrating on the images that you are creating with words. Give life to your sketches, so that when you read them in front of your class, your classmates will be able to envision what you saw.

- Choose one of the stanzas in Barot's poem and paint or draw a picture to illustrate it.

- Choose a poem from Seamus Heaney's *Death of a Naturalist* and compare it to Barot's "Bonnard's Garden." In an essay, consider how they are alike and how they differ. Which poem presents a more unified meaning? Which poet creates more realistic images? Present your findings to your class.

- Lead a class discussion regarding the significance of the "sleepwalking girl" in Barot's poem. Consider the following questions: Why do you think he included her in the poem? Is she the person who is said to have asked about the arctic water? How might she be related to the artist? What is the connection that she and the wrecked paper airplanes have to the rest of the poem? What is the significance of her scream? Finally, does the presence of the girl add to or detract from the overall quality of the poem?

---

water. The last statement of the poem is an elaborate one: "Like the wasps held in / by a shut flower at dusk, by morning released, / dusty as miners, into the restored volumes." The wasps, trapped in flowers overnight, are perhaps being compared to the tadpoles, which spend the first part of their lives in water before growing to travel on land. "Volumes" could be a reference to books, which would connect with the initial mention of an "illuminated page."

Themes

Nature

Nature is prevalent in Barot's poem, in the title itself and throughout the piece. The garden is richly imagined, with phrases such as "jasmine starred / onto the vine-dense walls" and "pink grasses." Barot's narrator wanders in and out of descriptions of the garden, ever returning to the blossoms and wild creatures inhabiting the landscape. As the precise meaning of the poem is somewhat obscure, due to the vagueness of the fragmented statements, the theme of nature most securely ties the pieces of the poem together; if nothing else, the reader will take from the poem a picture of Bonnard's garden. As such, the poem generally communicates soft emotions, as the reader contemplates spring warmth, perfumed air, and the abundance of colors and textures. Natural prosperity abounds; "nothing is lean," as everything is bursting out of the wraps and confines of winter, much like the release of the "wasps held in / by a shut flower at dusk." Nature calms the spirit of the poem, despite references to "busy edges" that "have taken over," "wrecked" airplanes, and "too much hurry." Much like the scream that breaks into the artist's "glimpse," all the jagged corners of distraction eventually subside "to become a part of the picture" because of the soothing garden.

Spring

Barot's poem presents not just nature but a specific time in nature: spring, a time of rebirth and emergence, when flowers and trees are blossoming. Tadpoles are evolving, wasps are escaping, and paint "curls out of the tubes." The sun is rising, and the feeling of cold arctic temperatures is quickly replaced with the warmth of a cat. There is a sense of prosperity in the lilacs, and the tulips are endowed with love in the image of "fattened hearts." Life is brilliant and restored. The theme of spring weaves through the theme of nature, emphasizing the natural world at its grandest moment.

Art

The theme of art is most obviously presented through the image of the painter. Given that he has tubes of paint, the reader can logically assume that he also has an easel, paintbrushes, and a palette. The artist is seeking to capture on the canvas all the riotous colors and forms that are speaking to him, as well as his own emotions. The poet, of course, is engaging in the same exercise when creating his poem. The medium is different, but the poet likewise uses his tools—words, language, and syntax—to create images. He, too, is searching for objects outside himself that reflect the emotions he holds inside. This pattern might also be recognized in nature itself, which can be seen as another form of art: mere seeds and buds are transformed into works of flora and fauna. Poem, painting, and nature can all be seen as creative works of great imagining.

Style

Free Verse

"Bonnard's Garden" is written in free verse, meaning that no regular meter is present; that is, the poet has not arranged his words in such a way as to produce a rhythmic flow. For coherence of form, the lines are all of similar length, with each stanza consisting of four lines, but no other structure exists. Similarly, the lines do not rhyme. If the poet were to read the work aloud, he would most likely allow the lines to flow subtly into one another, perhaps as if reading delicate, well-crafted prose.

Language as Art

In the foreword to Barot's collection *The Darker Fall*, the poet Stanley Plumly describes Barot's skill at creating art through his use of language, whereby a given portion of one of his poems is in essence an "implicative, animated still life." That is, his work consists of small portraits of scenes featuring clusters of various elements. The lines of "Bonnard's Garden" can therefore be looked upon as sketches, such that the reader should not necessarily dig too far into the words, looking for meaning everywhere. Rather, the meaning of the poem more likely lies somewhere in the poem's greater picture—the sum of the collage of small sketches. Using his skill with language, Barot creates images that readers can visualize; his brushstrokes are words and phrases. His paint is his well-tuned vocabulary and his keen understanding of exactly which word will make an image appear best. Plumly also refers to Barot's musicality, in that each line of the poem has similar weight, just as each measure of a song, to which the listener must pay attention for the same amount of time, has similar weight.

Softening Metaphors

The metaphorical descriptions within this poem begin with the paper airplanes, which are seen as blooms, and the artist's paint, which is seen as ointment. Both of these metaphors turn the original objects into things that carry with them a sense of healing. From the minor tragedy of the destroyed paper airplanes comes something beautiful and pleasant; from the chemicals and water or oil that constitute the paint comes an ointment, a salve or balm that is used to heal. Further, the sky is like "bathwater," where a soak in warm water is certainly restful and relaxing. The cat changes from an animal into a soft "pillow of heat." Finally, the sound of the girl's scream first becomes something that can be seen, "breaking into his glimpse," and then subsides "to become a part of the picture." That is, the sound is transformed into something that the artist paints into his picture, subduing it. These various metaphors soften the poem's edges of harshness, much like an impressionist painter typically softens the edges of real objects, obscuring flaws in order to emphasize beauty.

Place

The poem has a firm sense of place: Bonnard's garden. Readers are never told who Bonnard is, but Barot is undoubtedly referring to the French painter Pierre Bonnard (1867–1947), who thus may also be the man present in the poem. Bonnard's garden, like every garden, with flowers and weeds, bushes and trees, animals and insects, is a place in which one revels in the beauty of the season, losing oneself in the elements. The garden is captured on canvas by the painter and through words by the poet. Indeed, like a painter, the narrator of the poem concentrates on the place, watching what is happening, paying attention to whatever demands his focus, and filling his images with emotion.

Historical Context

Romanticism

The Romantic movement originated in the late eighteenth century in Germany and England. Whether in art, literature, music, or philosophy, emphasis was placed on the imagination, the natural world, the emotions, and simplicity. In literature,

Romantic authors are noted for their subjectivity and individualism; the solitary life reigns over society life as subject matter, and freedom from rules is very important. As such, Romanticism contrasts with the classical and neoclassical eras, which stressed more formalized language filled with classical allusions that only the elite could understand. Romantic influences can indeed be seen in Barot's poem, with its emphases on the natural environment, simple images, and private life.

Barot has himself specifically referred to the influence of the English Romantic poet William Wordsworth (1770–1850). Wordsworth's "To the Cuckoo" features images from nature similar to those in "Bonnard's Garden." In general, Wordsworth's main focus in writing was on nature, children, and the poor. Unlike his predecessors, he believed in using common language in poetry rather than an obscure vocabulary that only poetic scholars would understand. He also believed that poetry should be infused with the poet's emotions. In his time, Wordsworth was known as a nature poet, deriving so much poetic imagery from the local landscape that tourists were known to flock to the Lake District to see the area's beauty for themselves.

Other Literary Influences

Barot's poem is focused on a particular place, which is fully and lushly described. The poet has mentioned that this emphasis on place was in part inspired by the writing of Seamus Heaney (1939–). A Nobel Prize–winning poet from Northern Ireland, Heaney writes poems that deal with his surroundings. The Nobel Foundation cited his "works of lyrical beauty and ethical depth, which exalt everyday miracles and the living past." In his Nobel lecture, Heaney stated that he found poetry most exciting when it offered a direct representation of the world.

Barot has also cited the insights of Virginia Woolf (1882–1941), one of the foremost writers of the twentieth century, as a source of inspiration. Woolf's work is labeled both modernist and feminist, and her style of writing was considered experimental in her day. Her thoughts on writing and the writing life are elucidated in the extended essay *A Room of One's Own* (1929), in which she examines the difficulties presented to women of her generation when they attempted to develop their skills as writers.

Pierre Bonnard

"Bonnard's Garden" was undoubtedly inspired by the French artist Pierre Bonnard, who is known for his love of color, especially as exemplified in his landscape paintings—which often featured private spaces such as gardens. Bonnard began his painting career in Paris in the 1890s, joining a group of artists who referred to themselves as the Nabis, which in Hebrew means "prophets." Bonnard's work, which included paintings, illustrations, stained-glass windows, and posters, is said to have been heavily influenced by the French painters Paul Gauguin and Claude Monet. Gauguin's influence is particularly noticeable in the bright colors favored by Bonnard, while Monet's impact can been seen in the brushstrokes used by Bonnard in his later years. Indeed, toward the end of his career, Bonnard's intense colors took over his subjects, with his works becoming more and more abstract. One of his most important works is *Dining Room on the Garden*.

Critical Overview

Neither Barot's poem "Bonnard's Garden" nor his collection *The Darker Fall* has received much critical attention. One reviewer, Brian Phillips, writing for *Poetry*, compliments Barot's competence as a writer but believes that something is lacking in his work. While he finds no "bad" poems in Barot's collection, he also fails to find a "really good one." Indeed, Phillips finds that Barot's expertise in writing "a certain kind of poem" cannot be challenged, but he sees an absence of risk taking, as the poems feature "steady retreats from the desperate and uncharted." Phillips concludes that Barot might have been seeking approval in presenting this first collection of poems, a "condition" that does not give birth to good poetry.

In his foreword to Barot's first collection, Stanley Plumly praises the poet's relationship with language. Plumly observes,

> The first responsibility of poetry is, of course, language.... Those who believe in language as an end see language as the end of the experience. Others, like myself and Rick Barot, who believe in language as a means, understand it to be the means to another end, perhaps meaning, perhaps the language of the experience.

Plumly calls Barot's first collection "a brilliant example of language as means, as an art nearly flawless in its transformation of emotional and actual sources," adding that Barot "never permits the anxiety of the content to out speak the scrutiny of his

A visitor at the Musee d'Art moderne de la Ville de Paris, in January 2006 views a painting by Pierre Bonnard called The Bathroom with Pink Sofa *(1908)* © Pascal Pavani/AFP/Getty Images

form." Plumly finally discusses the inherent weight of Barot's writing:

> Gravity is what gives Barot's poems their quiet beauty. Gravity of the elegy and the love poem, the meditation and celebration, is what secures the lines of the interconnections, the weaves, the overlappings, and the leaps this poet is so fond of.

Criticism

Joyce Hart

Hart is a published writer and former teacher. In this essay, she closely examines the language of Barot's poem, which appears to be the author's dominant focus.

Barot's poem "Bonnard's Garden" was published in his first collection, which he once described as a type of apprenticeship; that is, the poems were exercises in which he practiced the language and form of poetry. In the collection's foreword, the poet Stanley Plumly states that the "first responsibility of poetry is, of course, language."

Plumly goes on to say that Barot's poems are prime examples of the use of language "as a means" in itself. He also refers to Barot's "linguistic skills" as demonstrative of his "metaphorical and musical intelligence." Barot has mentioned that he sometimes writes a stanza and then puts it away; after time has passed, he might write another stanza, possibly matching it to one previously written. In this way, a poem will come together. Considering these notions of how Barot writes, one can examine "Bonnard's Garden" to determine how these elements work and whether certain passages exist where they do not.

In the first stanza of Barot's poem, the reader arguably encounters the musicality of improvisational jazz—as if walking into a concert performance by the trumpeter Miles Davis or the saxophonist John Coltrane that is already under way. In traditional jazz, a melody, or head, is provided before the musicians start improvising. This not only gives the players a base from which to build their improvisations but also allows the audience to hear that base, which in turn helps them follow the improvisations. If a person were to walk in on a concert without hearing the original melody, the mind would have difficulty grasping that original form; the notes might seem entirely random. The first stanza of Barot's poem feels much the same: rather than a base of complete sentences, the reader finds only fragments. One wants to ask, What is this "illuminated page," with its "busy edges?" What are the roles of the jasmine, phlox, and oranges? The reader might feel as if the phrases are being carelessly thrown out; the phrases are beautiful, the collections of words are creative, and the flow of the beat is smooth, but what do the lines mean?

The question might then be, Must a poem have meaning? Is "metaphorical and musical intelligence" enough? The first stanza might be read as a sketch. The aural and visual resonance of the language is clearly poetic; can the rational mind be content with that fact? An "illuminated page" with "busy edges" is a playful image, and "The flesh of each chilled turgid" is interesting to pronounce. Thus, the reader may view the first stanza as an abstract painting. The image might be abnormal, but the colors and forms are intriguing. When a professional artist paints an abstract picture, the skill is evident, and the feat could not be easily reproduced by a layperson. Perhaps further analysis is unnecessary; the audience can appreciate the work and move on.

The second stanza of "Bonnard's Garden" makes more sense, allowing the reader to more easily visualize the scene and understand what is occurring. A sleepwalking girl made paper airplanes, which were eventually somehow wrecked and lodged on vines; after a rainfall, perhaps, or a dewy evening, the soaked paper airplanes were mistaken for the blooms of flowers. Those images are easy to grasp, and with its steady flow and carefully placed words, the passage certainly sounds like poetry. Yet nothing bridges the first and second stanzas—or the second and third. All that ties the various images together is the garden: the reader finds flowers and fruit in the first stanza, vines and blooms in the second, and dandelions and irises in the third. The setting is secured—and perhaps no more is necessary.

Nevertheless, the third and fourth stanzas have an additional bridge: the artist, who stands and looks around in the third stanza as he squeezes out his paint. In the fourth stanza, he sees a blossoming almond tree capturing the first light. The fifth stanza, however, breaks the established connections, as it can only truly be linked to the sleepwalking girl and the artist, the two people mentioned in this poem. The girl asks a question, with someone—presumably the artist—present to answer. If this stanza features a theme, it is temperature, as both cold and heat are mentioned. This stanza alone feels as though it does not take place in the garden; the setting is night, a time usually not reserved for gardens, and no depictions of nature are offered. Arctic water and the cat's blood are discussed, but they are distant, not forcefully present, as with the flowers in previous and subsequent stanzas.

The sixth stanza is also somewhat removed, but nature again offers a link. The artist also returns, in the form of the pronoun "his." The artist's presence is not very clear. In fact, something about his look is smudged, and the word "dizzy" is used; the artist appears to be either seeing things that are not there or painting a scene that leans toward the fantastic. He sees pink grasses, glowing shrubs, and animals disappearing into the landscape. The words are twisted in this stanza more than anywhere else, especially with the remark, "His glimpse smudged," and with the fragmented statement "As in: it's about time / I made you dizzy." The feelings that arise are similar to those stirred by the first stanza.

The seventh stanza is deep into the garden again, with beautiful words that conjure springtime images so real that the reader can touch them. Indeed, when the poem is deep in the garden—that

> "The aural and visual resonance of the language is clearly poetic; can the rational mind be content with that fact?"

is, when it returns to the melody that serves as the base for improvisation—no bridge is necessary, as the occasional gaps are not so worrisome. The phrases portray wonderful sketches of garden patches, and that is enough. They are grounded, rather than floating around half-finished; they are planted firmly in the focused place around which the poem revolves.

The girl and the artist return in stanzas 8 and 9, though with little added clarity. Indeed, the eighth stanza begins with a mystery: the girl screams, with no explanation given as to why. Is the water cold? Was she bitten by a tadpole when she stirred her finger in the pond? No one runs to her rescue. She does not scream again. Readers might hear the scream, and it might send a chill down the spine, but it does not appear to bother the artist, who incorporates the sound into his painting. Or does he? The sound subsides "to become a part of the picture." The word "picture" here calls to mind the canvas, paints, and brushes, but the reference could be to the whole garden and everyone in it. Then, the reader might ask again, must clear meaning be present? Imagining the sound of the scream being absorbed into the picture is in many ways pleasing and familiar. The natural world around the girl and man is perhaps so full that the sound is simply swallowed. So much is happening within the scene that the noise is just one more small element—one tiny fraction of a very large picture.

Finally, in the last stanza, the narrator mentions "icy killing water." Each of these three words has connections to other parts of the poem. "Icy" refers back to the arctic waters; the "killing" can abstractly suggest the wrecked airplanes; and "water" is mentioned in stanza 5, when temperature is discussed, and in stanza 8, in which the girl stirs the pond water. Thus, overall, the poem contains several bridges. Some are stronger and more

What Do I Read Next?

- Virginia Woolf's diaries, which were published in four volumes after her death, have been a particular inspiration to Barot. Woolf's husband, Leonard, culled extracts from her diaries and collected them in *A Writer's Diary* (1936).

- Seamus Heaney, winner of the 1995 Nobel Prize for Literature, is another of Barot's favorites. As with Barot, language and place are important elements in Heaney's work. To compare the two, read one of Heaney's first collections, *Death of a Naturalist* (1966).

- William Wordsworth has been a third influence on Barot's writing. Like "Bonnard's Garden," Wordsworth's "Upon Westminster Bridge" focuses on a specific place. This poem as well as works by Wordsworth's contemporaries can be found in *The Oxford Book of English Verse* (1939).

- Barot's writing is often compared to that of Elizabeth Bishop, who was independently wealthy as an adult and spent most of her time traveling around the world and writing about what she saw. Her first collection, *North and South* (1946), focuses on her time spent in Florida.

- *Introducing Romanticism* (2000), by Duncan Heath, offers insight into all aspects of the Romantic movement, focusing on the end of the eighteenth century and the first half of the nineteenth century.

---

obvious than others—but none, in fact, truly clarify the poem's meaning. The poem is ruled by the language, not by the bridges, as the language creates the images imposed on the reader's mind. Indeed, Barot's poem can be most fully enjoyed in emphasizing those images, even if they sometimes float around with no strings attached to the rest of the poem. Trying to muster a unified meaning, on the other hand, might take a leap of intellectual faith.

Source: Joyce Hart, Critical Essay on "Bonnard's Garden," in *Poetry for Students*, Thomson Gale, 2007.

Christopher Hennessy

In the following interview-essay, Hennessy interviews four new gay poets, including Barot, to discover the unique elements of their poetry and to elicit their insight into issues and themes in gay poetry.

All poets—or at least, surely, the best—react to and learn from their predecessors, the ancestors that both taught them and inspired them. Perhaps, then, one way to guage the health of any poetry scene is to take the pulse of poets who are emerging from their apprenticeships, who are staking their claim as the next generation. If one uses this as the measure for gay men's poetry, then the news is encouraging.

I came to this conclusion as I researched for a selected bibliography of new gay poets for my forthcoming book *Outside the Lines: Talking with Contemporary Gay Poets*. I found what seemed a critical mass of new queer poets who had recently produced debut volumes, many of which had won first-book prizes. Their poems were electric, eccentric, challenging, disconcerting, lush and a host of other adjectives. What's more, the new work suggested this next generation had its own ambitions and its own obsessions, both of which draw from past traditions but search for new mediums, myths and structures. Several of these new voices were heartily recommended to me from some of the most established, accomplished gay poets currently writing.

So, to offer a taste of some of the more intriguing and challenging verse being written, included here are brief interviews with four emerging gay voices, all with first books published since 2002. Three of the four won first-book prizes.

> "The Darker Fall is a young writer's book. In it I was trying to learn the hand-eye coordination you need to bring the world to words. Wittgenstein and company were the grown-ups I went to for advice."

They include: Randall Mann, a poet adept at crafting traditional poetic forms but with a brashness that imagines, for example, Dante—on a gay beach in the Seventh Circle of hell wearing a thong; Brian Blanchfield, who produces an oftentimes rich (albeit confounding) poem, charged by a convulsed syntax, frustrated expectations and devious wordplay; Brian Teare, a poet of haunting verse—about myth, sexual awakening and surviving abuse, among other themes—who mixes a breathy lyric impulse with a desire to understand one's origins through narrative's grammar; and Rick Barot, who crafts a complex, elegant verse that is as much about artists and philosophers as it is about desire and understanding the self.

The four poets answer questions about what makes their poetry unique and explore the queer element (whether explicit or implied) in their work. And grouped at the end of the interviews are their insightful (and varied!) thoughts on what issues and themes they see recurring in gay poetry.

Randall Mann, *Complaint in the Garden*
(Zoo Press, 2004) (2003 Kenyon Prize)

[*Christopher Hennessy:*] *Your book contains forms like settings, villanelles, pantoums, sonnets, etc. Your subjects include porn stars, drag queens, AIDS, sexual awakenings and homophobia. Is it energizing to write about contemporary gay subjects in traditional forms?*

[Randall Mann:] Yes, just as it's energizing to write a formal piece about, say, the landscape of the American South. (My hope—I suppose this is every formal poet's hope—is that the form of a poem both deepens and complemets its content, no matter the subject matter.) I don't think a traditional form and "titillating" queer contemporary subjects are at cross-purposes; real trailblazers, brave formal poets—Thom Gunn, Marilyn Hacker—have allowed me this luxury.

[*Christopher Hennessy:*] *You write about Florida (where you grew up) in a sensuous but knowing view: e.g. "A shock of pink, the sky / went on forever . . . the moon / creeping into its corner" and yet "men go here to die." Are beauty and sadness linked for you as a poet?*

[Randall Mann:] Inextricably. The sadness of beauty—of the land, of men—lies not only in its mutability, but also in the artist's inability to represent beauty, truly. "A word is elegy to what it signifies," wrote Robert Hass in his great poem "Meditation at Lagunitas": once beauty has been considered carefully, then written, the word, even the best word, cannot help but diminish things in the naming. Something already has fallen.

[*Christopher Hennessy:*] *You write, "I have not forgotten the place from which I come" but there's also "the buried world" and things under the surface in your work. Is it important for poets to both confront and embrace origins, identity?*

[Randall Mann:] Not necessarily. I think it might make me a bad party guest were I to dictate the ideas that other poets should confront or embrace. I can say this: My interest lies in the things below the surface—the man who paints his face and slips on pumps not only to change but deepen identity; the porn star who seems perfect on tape but already is succumbing to AIDS—because identity and origins are never simply about one's history, and are never simple. "This is the past, and so it must be true," I repeat in one villanelle in the book, the repetition reinforcing the inescapable irony of this line.

Brian Blanchfield, *Not Even Then*
(University of California Press, 2004)

[*Christopher Hennessy:*] *Your very first poem in the book contains "the raw desire to articulate." I recall that Crane once wrote, "Thou canst read nothing except through appetite." Does that resonate for you?*

[Brian Blanchfield:] That poem of Hart Crane's is a choice example of the lover-as-reader theme everywhere in his work, most memorably in "Voyages," in which a tumultuous affair is set on a sheet of ocean where sunlight on waves resembles script and seems literally to underwrite the ecstatic connection between the poem's two lovers. The subtext is that the two are writing their own script, as it were, and when they realize there is no sanction greater that their "appetite" for sanction, their shared language becomes illegible at sea. The often neglected brilliance is in the final section, when the model of transcendence is discarded and we are landed on an island, first place we come to, where the Word is never discarnate or unrevealed; the Word, in the Beginning and as ever, is with Man, let's be clear. I set that hopeful island smack in the middle of my book, and wash despair repeatedly ashore.

I like that your questions conflate reading and writing, which are anyway, like smell and taste, continuous. Nor canst thou, after all, write without likewise being hungry for the word to come. I'm with Roland Barthes who relishes a word for its potential to be put in play.

[*Christopher Hennessy:*] *You have a very playful side, sometimes with a very queer wink: (e.g. "Boy, have you predilections? / Sir, for predicaments."). Is the idea of "play" important to you? With language?*

[Brian Blanchfield:] We'll never know whether Frank O'Hara would have been flattered by Ginsberg's eulogizing him as a practitioner of "deep gossip," but if because of my poems I were known as a "profound flirt" or some such, I could live with that. Once I'm dead.

[*Christopher Hennessy:*] *Tarzan, Cujo, a sestina on Scooby-Doo's Velma. References to Freud, Wilde, Auden, Kant. Drawing from obscure films, texts, people. The popular, intellectual, obscure—are they all the same to you when you write?*

[Brian Blanchfield:] I suppose they are equally available as potential elements of a poem, as is, I hope, anything that interest and impacts me. But I'm not a writer who decorates or ornaments a poem with multiple and sundry cultural references merely to signal distress in the busy information age or what have you. Generally—or specifically—I'll use a figure such as Moses or Stephen Jay Gould or Godzilla only to activate or motivate the poem's implicit logic. The book contains several monster or specters, and together perhaps they populate the pandemonium I mean to suggest by the book's first part title, "Weremen," a species of creature half-man, half-man [the derivation of "were" is "man"]. I'm interested in examining self-sameness as a sort (perhaps a queer sort) of monstrosity. In "The Same Question," the only question is one that Jane asks Tarzan, making his acquaintance as they mirror each other palm to palm on the bank of a stream: Do you like the difference? Difference? Tarzan, unlike any beast he'd ever seen until Jane, had surely been studying their similarity.

Brian Teare, *The Room Where I Was Born* (University of Wisconsin Press, 2003) (2003 Brittingham Prize)

[*Christopher Hennessy:*] *Two of your book's subjects are sexual childhood abuse and teenage sexual encounters. What do you hope you bring to these subjects that is new, unique?*

[Brian Teare:] In writing about these subjects, I'd hoped for so much, but I'll focus here on narration. Many of the poems feature a first- or third-person narrator observing his own—my own—experience. I hoped this cinematic disembodiment wound allow me, especially in the case of incest, both to capture a struggle to articulate identity in the face of violation, and to explore an extremity of desire.

I'd also hoped using a technique associated with fiction to render autobiographical experience would allow for the reader a certain intellectual dispassion while leaving room for an emotional reaction. As eerily voyeuristic as it can seem, it's a combination I think of as intrinsic to the experience of trauma. Especially in the first half of the book, I wanted the reding experience to mimic a traumatized consciousness.

[*Christopher Hennessy:*] *Your book contains a new take on the myth of Sleeping Beauty and a myth about a figure called the "Milk Father" (who lures young boys to feed from "a row of swollen, hairless teats"). Does being gay help to re-imagine myths or how to use myth in poetry?*

[Brian Teare:] I love this question! Being gay doesn't just help me to re-imagine myths, it makes re-imagining myths necessary. Myths—both local and universal—are the genetic code of our consciousnesses. They create us as much as our parents, our own genes. And when I say "myths," I mean Freud and the Bible as much as Zeus and Little Red Riding Hood; I mean the archetypes, stereotypes and ideologies through which we read our identities. So few of these are queer, or even vaguely queer-positive, that to re-imagine them is to re-imagine the basic building blocks of cultural reality, and I want to tamper with the source!

[*Christopher Hennessy:*] *Your poetry uses a longer line and highlights an inherent strangeness of language (and grammar specifically), among other traits. Is this part of a desire to test the boundaries of what poetry can do?*

[Brian Teare:] Yes. I want all my poems to test the boundaries of what I think poetry can do linguistically and thematically. An impatience with, or refusal of, what is known is where art and politics meet.

For me, linguistic experiment is tied to knowledge: to try new forms, new ways of using syntax, is to learn about how language, and the mind, work. The harder I push against words, the closer the poem gets to what I don't know, the mysteries at the core of being.

But this is true of writing about new subject matter: It's an uncovering, a discovery. Though we often speak of experimentation exclusively in terms of what a poem does with syntax, the line or the page, there are as many conventions about subject matter—and how we feel about certain subjects—to be tested. For instance, writing a good lyric poem about enjoying anal sex: That too is a resistance, a test of what poetry can do.

Rick Barot, *The Darker Fall* (Sarabande, 2002) (2001 Kathryn A. Morton Prize)

[*Christopher Hennessy:*] Plato, Wittgenstein, Walter Benjamin, painters Miro, Bronzino and Bonnard, are some of the figures who appear in your book. Beyond the interest as subjects, what do you seek from philosophers and artists?

[Rick Barot:] In many ways, the book is about how to really look at things, how to make art of the world you experience, and, maybe most importantly, how to make a life as an artist. Those figures were muses to me. By their difficulties, and also their accomplishment, they helped me to approach the problems of my own thinking and writing. *The Darker Fall* is a young writer's book. In it I was trying to learn the hand-eye coordination you need to bring the world to words. Wittgenstein and company were the grown-ups I went to for advice.

[*Christopher Hennessy:*] *In "Riffing," the world is made of "Just one thing and then / another, Tom says, his tongue here and then here. / Each kiss different and yet somehow the same." Is desire its own special language for you?*

[Rick Barot:] Those lines are about how the world's multiplicity can sometimes make the world blur into chaos or sameness. It's the artist's job to isolate the specific dazzling "kiss" that gives order to that blurring. About desire—I think of it as the Duracell bunny in the heart and head that makes a person live. Of course it's not something special to me. Everyone has that bunny, that appetite, clamoring hotly inside. But as poet I do try to be more attuned to how that appetite works, the complex ways it can be talked about, as opposed to the perhaps oversimple ways it's rendered in "popular" media.

[*Christopher Hennessy:*] *Does being gay and having been born in the Philippines give you an outsider's perspective, specifically on Beauty? Does this influence what I see as your painterly descriptions of the body, the scenery of the world, landscape?*

[Rick Barot:] Wallace Stevens said that "The greatest poverty is / not to live in a physical world." I agree with that, which probably accounts for my "painterly" style. An artist's style, though, is a separate thing from his "identities." I don't have a painterly style just because I'm gay or Filipino. As for being an outsider, all artists are already that. Every artist is born with a kind of queerness. One of the things art does is help the artist process the terms of his distance from the world. At one level that process is just therapy, but at the most ambitious level the art becomes a true, complicated rendering of what the world is about, a rendering only an outsider could supply.

[*Christopher Hennessy:*] *When you read or encounter other living poets who happen to also be gay, are there issues/themes you find that come up again and again?*

[Mann:] I'm not certain I am widely and deeply read enough to answer. I can tell you what I like in two living queer poets I admire: the frank, beautiful, unapologetic eroticism of Marilyn Hacker; and the dark, uncomfortable, self-lashing eroticism of the last three books by Henri Cole. (Both poets can also be quite funny.) And though he just passed away, I think my model queer poet is Thom Gunn, who was as comfortable scribbling an epigram about Henry James as he was, say, writing about gnawing a man's armpits. I think queer poetry could use a bit more armpit gnawing.

[Teare:] Sex. Gender. Race. Desire. Embodiment. AIDS. Time. Death. Nature. Beauty. Politics. Injustice. Passion. Loneliness. Though our attitudes toward language and our points-of-view concerning these subjects often differ radically from those of straight writers—and therein lies our necessary and often difficult differences, both within our community and without—we tend to use poetry as it has always been used: to touch each others' lives as deeply as possible.

[Blanchfield:] Poets who happen also to be gay (and alive): a subset at least as varied as all of contemporary poetry, to mind. Isn't it a truism that gay literature is given to the second-person point of view, that in it a "you" character is addressed as if by a watchful angel or by oneself later in life? Consider Jim Grimsley novels. This is developed most interestingly by transgressive writers, often queer, like Eileen Myles in poetry, for whom the "you" (the reader) is someone to oblige and implicate in transactions of control and vulnerability. The reader I want to be is both menaced and blessed.

[Barot:] You used the word "desire," so I'll invoke that here. Desire, its ravishing and costly nature, seems to be the theme that runs through a lot of contemporary gay writing. We're now in an amazing moment where artists can describe gay desire without having to camouflage it as something else. That desire can finally be an open subject matter, and this freedom has given us some recent writing that is scary, truthful, beautiful, and profoundly new.

Source: Christopher Hennessy, "Critical Mass: A New Generation of Gay Poets," in *Lambda Book Report*, Vol. 13, No. 4–5, November–December 2004, pp. 6–9.

Rick Barot and Craig Beavan

In the following interview conducted January 25, 2003, Barot discusses the journey of the "I," the interior self, through the exterior landscape of the poems in The Darker Fall *and goes on to talk about the relatedness and sequence of the poems.*

[*Craig Beaven:*] *This is Craig Beaven. It's January 25th, and I'm in Washington D.C. on the campus of George Washington University talking with poet Rick Barot for* Blackbird.

Thanks for meeting with us, Rick. I really appreciate it.

I guess I wanted to begin by responding to something you wrote to one of the editors of Blackbird *in an email. But before that, I wanted to just give our readers a little bit of history. Your first book is* The Darker Fall. *It won the Kathryn Morton Prize. It was published by a highly reputable press, Sarabande Books. It was selected by the esteemed Stanley Plumly, and you've held the Stegner Fellowship at Stanford. But when the review came out in* Blackbird*, you expressed surprise at seeing the review, and you said something to the extent that you thought that it had been published and then disappeared. And I was wondering if you could talk about that because it seems to be a pretty common thing in the art form. There's this anticlimactic . . . there's this build-up of years of toiling, and then publishing sometimes can just be like dropping it in the Grand Canyon or something. It just disappears.*

[Rick Barot:] Right, and you don't get the echo. I think it's become a trend that a lot of books, whether first books or second books or third books, don't get reviewed anymore, and so you wonder, how are these books getting out there? I know that the book is selling well enough, and so it makes me wonder, how's it doing that if it's not being reviewed? So in many ways, in terms of the usual reviewing channels, the book hasn't had much of a life. But it . . . what I said was perhaps a little bit facetious because the book *has* had a life in terms of a readership, but that readership hasn't been accessed or they haven't accessed the book through reviews. That's interesting to me. I don't know what that means, necessarily, about how the life of a book proceeds without the review.

So the book is out there living and breathing and having a life, you think.

I think so.

That's good. That's reassuring because often you hear poets lamenting there's no readership.

It is out there. I think part of the reason why it has, it's had a life of its own[,] is because I've been giving a lot of readings in the last year. That's one of the things that Sarabande is so great about. They help their [*writers*] get out there and do readings and promote the book. And so . . . I would say that I've given at least twenty-five readings all over the country in the last year, and so that has really helped.

I was reading through the book and I was thinking that the most pronounced motif in the book is the evocation of, not landscape, but something much more specific, like street corners, rooms, apartments. And the listing of place names becomes almost incantatory by the end of the book. If you read it all the way through you get all this geography. I was wondering if you could talk about that as a poet, like what about landscape, or what about these places that seems to hold kind of a mythic power, if it's mythic at all.

Maybe this is a high-minded answer, but this is something I've been thinking about. The idea of the romantic lyric has to do with an "I" that's situated in a landscape of some kind, whether that's urban or natural. And so in many ways, the "I" of the book is undergoing some sort of post-romantic journey through the poems of that book. Therefore, the staging is very important and very foregrounded in terms of the urban spaces or the natural spaces or even those in-between spaces. I'm not really sure why I've been enamored of those places, but perhaps it's one way of thinking about it, that in the lineage that I find myself it's a post-romantic world.

So it's sort of like how the self of the poet gets expressed is going to be via this landscape or via this . . .

A lot of it gets displaced onto the landscape. If you're trying to figure out or imagine an interior place, the coordinates of your interior life, what do you have? How do you map that? You go out there and see what the world has to offer you as mirror for those things. It is a narcissistic activity, looking at these things. But what happens is that the self becomes effaced in the delineation of objects which are outside of itself.

There's a line in your book from the poem "Battersea Bridge," and I think this sort of sums up where you write, and I'm paraphrasing: "Is there a more human habit than this, to stand here looking out, letting our natures yield to all we see, so that the streets . . . begin to stand for our longings?" So it's the landscape and self relationship?

Absolutely. That poem, which is a sonnet, has two [...] ghosts behind it. One of course is Whistler and his nocturnes, but the other one of course is Wordsworth. I'm forgetting the title of the poem, but he's got a wonderful poem, a sonnet, about standing on one of the bridges in London and looking at it [*"Composed Upon Westminster Bridge"*]. He's got that other great sonnet, "The world is too much with us; late and soon." I'm not thinking about that one, but it's another vision by him, standing on another bridge. That was in my mind somewhere when I was writing that sonnet. Wordsworth was in there, and that line seems to me . . . it's a romantic line.

You seem to be using the word romantic quite a bit already in the interview and . . .

I should stop.

One of the questions I was going to ask you about, who you see as your models, or who you read or how you conceive, what you've read that has sort of informed your conception of poetry? In Plumly's introduction he says—I think of the poem "Battersea Bridge"—he says, "postmodern but romantic," and I was wondering, do you see yourself situated in that way as a romantic or in the vein of?

You know what? I would love to say yes, but attached to my saying yes, I am a post-romantic poet, attached to that is a whole lot of baggage that I would be uncomfortable with.

Right.

> *The book is basically a sort of transcription of my apprenticeship as a writer. And the reason why so many of those poems are in sections is because I didn't know, or I didn't think I knew, how to write a poem by itself in the sense that it could stand by itself.*

Which is the baggage that you're a strictly conservative, traditional, un-ironic writer or perceiver of the world.

Right. That's certainly not the case with the poems in The Darker Fall. *I guess getting back to the idea of place, obviously you're here in Washington, D.C., as a visiting writer, and that's a long way from home. One of the poems in the book is called "The Exile" and the stance of the speaker is of the exile. Can you talk a little bit about that, your relationship to place and its . . . the idea of loss or desire of place? That seems to be the driving emotion.*

You know, Anne Carson has that great book, *Eros the Bittersweet*, where she talks about the triangulation that happens between the beloved, the lover, and then the third leg being the thing that keeps those two people apart. For me, I wonder if place has some part of that, that idea of triangulation where it's the self and then there's a perceived ideal of the self and then there's the issue of place having to act as a kind of fulcrum for those two things. Once again it's that romantic thing where the place becomes the source of difficulty, and yet because it's an objective barrier perhaps between you the earthly person and you the ideal, perhaps platonic person slash poet, and place gets in the way of that because you have to navigate through the objectivity of that . . . I feel that I've gotten away from the question.

I was going to ask about place, and then you sent me some of your new work, and you have poems titled ["West 16th Street" and "Iowa,"] and it's like place is coming back, and again it doesn't go away. So it seemed to be such a resonant part of the book or of your work, so I wanted to...

I'd never thought about that, the idea of place. Maybe place is just another word for reality. You know, it's one way of putting a frame on a particular reality that I'm trying to describe in my poems, whether it's Iowa or New York City.

Moving along, I guess I wanted to respond again to something you'd written in an email to me. You said that you're "trying desperately to finish a new manuscript." And I was wondering about that, when the composition becomes desperation or something. where it becomes like it's no longer fun or inspired? Like I'm putting a thesis together, and it seems more mechanical than contacting the muse or anything. How does that work? Does it become a job, does it become business or...?

No, it's never a job because when I write a poem it never arrives when I want it to. It always comes unexpectedly. It is always sort of like being visited by the weather—you don't [know what's] going to come. When I wrote you that, I was basically talking about the fact that the second book is predicated on a theme, the Echo and Narcissus story, and I'm writing a lot of the poems with Echo as a muse behind the poems. And I've been writing this book for more than two years now. And I'm getting impatient with the theme. Not with the work, because it's not finished yet. The reason why I said I'm desperately trying to finish it is because I want to finish it before I get really tired of it, the work and the theme. And I don't want to be repeating myself. That's why I just want to finish it and move on to something else.

Something fresh... I was wondering if you could take us through the process of a poem, from the moment the idea is received to completion. How long does that usually take you? Is this a long process? Do you take years on poems or do they come quickly? How does that work?

It really depends. I'll give you an example of both. The poem in the first book that took the longest to write was a poem called "The Gecko," in which I describe a friend getting a tattoo. And the poem is in three stanzas, and altogether I would say the poem took about five years to write. I wrote the first stanza and then I put it away. And then a couple of years went by and I wrote the second stanza, and then I put it away again. I knew what the poem was going to be about, but the issue I had there did not have to do with not knowing what it was going to be. It was more I was grappling with the issue of narrative. How do you write a narrative poem? That poem taught me a lot about how to... just the issue of information. How do you give information in a poem and still have it be partaking of a lyrical aura? In a lot of the poems that I had written before that poem, the lyric stance had always sort of taken care of the writing. I wasn't interested in doing a narration that was A plus B equals C, but in that poem I was describing a scene in a tattoo parlor, and so the issues of narration were very important to me and very difficult. So that's one poem that took a long time. It's not quite "The Moose," but it's my moose. It took about five years. On the other hand, there's a poem in the book... the last poem I wrote in the book is a poem called "Aubade," which is a pantoum, and that poem literally wrote itself in five minutes. I had all of these lines written down already on a bulletin board that I have over my desk. And these lines, which were discrete from each other, suddenly cohered into this pantoum form. They all just funneled into this poem in one go, and I didn't have to change anything. I think that all poets would recognize those two extremes, the poem that takes you forever and the poem that comes, you know...

So did you really celebrate when you finally finished "The Gecko"? Did you charge through the streets cheering?

No, because I had already lost so much blood along the way I didn't have the energy for that celebration. And the fact is it's not even that good of a poem. You write these poems even if they take forever, learning something from them as processes. And that's something that I learned from that poem: How do you write a poem that's narrative, that has a real narrative grid underneath it, and make the lyrical push out of the narrative instead of the lyrical constructing a shadow narrative out of the stance that it's created for itself.

More of an overt narrative.

Yes, an overt narrative.

Something also noticeable about the work in The Darker Fall, *beyond just place, the evocation of place, is the use of sequence. Half the poems... of the twenty-four poems, exactly half are comprised of numbered sequences, and I was wondering if you could talk about the poems' need for that kind of space and the poems' need to just go on thinking and speaking, even when sections seem full and finished?*

Right. The book is basically a sort of transcription of my apprenticeship as a writer. And the reason why so many of those poems are in sections is because I didn't know, or I didn't think I knew, how to write a poem by itself in the sense that it could stand by itself. And so a lot of these . . . some of these, a good number of those poems in sequences were written individually without the thought of the sequence, and what would happen is that I would write a short poem and think that it wasn't good enough to stand on its own. Therefore, I would play around with putting it with two or three other poems, just to see if the accumulation in the sequence would somehow give these poems a weightiness that they didn't have on their own. That's true of a sequence like, let's say, "Passage Work" or "Blue Hours." Those are two sequences where those poems were written years apart from each other, in very different moods, and yet they had enough of the same, perhaps atmosphere, that I could put them in a sequence and call the whole thing a sequence. And then there are other poems of course where the sequencing was very deliberate, like "Eight Elegies."

Yeah, I was going to ask you about that one.

Or "Bird Notes," where I knew I was working with a lot of material that I couldn't encompass into one poem, and I needed the sequencing as a kind of . . . as an aid to myself.

"Eight Elegies" seems like it really riffs. They're not overt elegies, or they don't seem to be overt elegies, but you have that kind of echoing in the title when you go through and read. It almost seems like the speaker is . . . the use of sequence there seems almost like the speaker's just trying to say all this stuff to get it out and be released from a burden. That seemed different than the way some of the others, some of the other sequences work together.

Well, "Eight Elegies" was written very late in the manuscript, and at that point I knew exactly what I was doing in terms of the sequencing. All the sequencing I'd done before then was just me fumbling around trying to fill a canvas with very different things. "Eight Elegies" was a very deliberate canvas that I knew I couldn't fill just in one go, and so I made these little pieces and patched it together.

When you're composing, are there certain things you look for, certain conscious places you want to take your poems? The book seems so unified, like such a coherent whole, that I wondered if you sought out things, and are there poems that maybe you love, that didn't make it into The Darker Fall? *Does that happen, you leave a lot out?*

Yeah. By the time I put the book together it had gone through about three or four permutations, and I would always take things out, even stuff that I had just written very recently, before I had finished the manuscript, because I was thinking of the book as a whole at that point. I wasn't thinking of individual poems anymore. So if a poem, even though it was okay, didn't quite fit the flow that I had in mind, I would . . . I got rid of it. But it's interesting because the earliest poems in the book were written when I was an undergrad, and so there is a full range of poems in there from the eight or so years of my life when I was writing that book. Then there are a lot of poems from the middle period [I didn't include].

So when you say eight or so years, do you mean from when you began writing or from when you began sort of consciously sitting down to think of a manuscript, or how does that work?

I'm talking about from the very first poems I wrote.

From the first poem you ever wrote.

Which were in an undergrad class I took with Annie Dillard when I was a senior. Those were some of the very first poems I wrote.

What drew you to poetry suddenly your senior year? Were you always an English major or. . . ?

I was conflicted. I started college wanting to be a lawyer. I took a lot of poli sci classes my first few years, and then I started taking more English classes. At some point, I started to understand that just because I was good at something and it was something that I enjoyed didn't mean that I could take it for granted as being, you know, mere pleasure. Because I was always good in English all through high school, I was always told that I should be . . . I should pursue or think about writing. But it just came so naturally and easily that I didn't think, so why should I therefore study that? But the minute that writing and literature started to speak to my emotional life as a person and not just something that I could do skillfully, where it did seem to mirror what was happening inside, that's when I started to take it seriously as something I could perhaps do and study more seriously. Annie Dillard was very crucial in that. I took a creative writing class with her when I was a sophomore, and as a sophomore, who's a good writer? No one probably is. But she was so encouraging, and also forceful, that she had me beginning to think that perhaps I could do something with that. At that point I was just writing prose, but the encouragement was everything.

So when do you start thinking of a manuscript? I mean, you're writing poetry, and then when do individual poems, I guess, become a collection? Do you know like at what point in the process?

For *The Darker Fall* it happened, I would say, three or four years after I started writing poems. What happened was that I got a title for myself, a book title, and it seemed to galvanize all of the elements which were already there and helped me, gave me a sort of prescription for how to proceed. And the working title of the book for about three or four years was "City Entries," which is the title of one of the poems in one of the sections. I think it's "Blue Hours." Having that phrase in mind for years on end helped me to write the latter half of the book. The idea of the notational quality of the poems, having all of the sectioning, I got permission for that from the idea of "City Entries," writing a diary. The idea of the city itself became a big informant in the writing of the poems. You had asked earlier about urban spaces. Having the caption before the picture, it helps you to construct the picture. Eventually, of course, I understood that the title wasn't the best title. "City Entries" wasn't the best title, so I got rid of it. But it had helped me move through the journey of the book as a sort of scaffolding.

How did you come up with The Darker Fall, *then? Was it sad to let go of "City Entries"?*

It wasn't sad because it was like a marriage that was very old and very boring, and to somebody else it might have sounded good, but I was just tired of it at that point. *The Darker Fall* was suggested to me by a friend who read through the manuscript after it had been accepted by Sarabande and by Stanley Plumly. I had an intermediary title. I had submitted the manuscript as "Night and Hydrangea," which is a very florid title, and Plumly wasn't too happy with that title. And once he started not being happy with it, I started not being happy with it. And so I gave the manuscript to a few friends, and a friend of mine, Brian Teare, who's also a poet, picked out the phrase from the book, from one of the poems in the book. And that's how it came about. I have to say that if I had more time, and more guts, frankly, I would have stuck with the title that I had then, which was "Night and Hydrangea."

"Night and Hydrangea," you like that better than The Darker Fall?

I do like it. It was mine. One thing that I have learned, actually, having published that first book and working [on] a second book now [...] that's coming along fairly well, is that you need these necessary illusions to finish the book, but the minute that [...] I saw *The Darker Fall* in between covers, I stopped understanding why I had put things the way they were in terms of the sequence of the poems, the ordering, or even the title of the book itself—it stopped being material. What became important to me was the fact that I had these three or four or five poems in the book that I thought had really spoken truthfully about particular emotional and aesthetic and formal problems that I'd been having, and so you know what, I'm writing poems, but during the time that I'm trying to finish a book, I'm writing a book. But the minute the book is finished, I forget that the book exists. I only care about the four or five poems that I love. And it's always surprising to me—well, it's surprising to other people—that my favorite poems in my first book are not necessarily the poems that people would think of as being, let's say, the most ambitious or being the big poems. It's never about that. It's usually the smaller poem where I felt as though I had totally captured what was in my mind and in my eye.

So it's the few, as you see them, the purest expressions . . .

The happy few.

Yeah, those are the ones we have to hold on to, right?

But you do need the illusion. For those five or six years when "City Entries" was the title, I had it all in my head. The title was "City Entries" . . .

Yeah, you're like getting shirts printed up, right?

Absolutely. And the cover art was going to be one of those Ocean Park paintings by Richard Diebenkorn.

Yeah, those are great paintings.

But it didn't happen that way, and I feel no loss.

I was noticing that there's really little personal autobiography revealed, and I was wondering if that's a conscious decision or if that's . . . or if that comes out of just sort of a theory of poetry, or if that comes out of just hitting the delete button sometimes and just taking personal things out? Was that a conscious decision, or how does that work?

You're talking about the first book. The fact is, I, you know, I'm an Asian American person. I was born in the Philippines. And anybody reading that book is not going to find anything of that in there. The way I've been able to explain that to myself has to do with the fact that it's a very important content, [...] the issue of this Asian American identity, and I didn't feel worthy of addressing that as yet. I feel as though my work is going to move into that content a little bit more as I begin to be more confident of my skills as a writer. But the first book, it's really just an exercise book in formal issues and in issues of visual and descriptive acuity. That's the way I think about it. This is not to belittle the book, but it's a book where I'm learning how to write a line, how to write a stanza, how to write sentences which are long or short, how to do those formal things. And so I wasn't interested, frankly, in content in that book. I was interested in exercising the writing muscle in as many ways [as] I could. It was not a conscious pushing away of content by any means. I was just more interested in the gestures that you could do with language, with the writing. The issue of content had to do with form in that first book for me. There are all kinds of things happening in that book that have to do with long lines and short lines, and couplets and quatrains and tercets, because that's what I was discovering when I was starting, when I was teaching myself how to write poems. I would read, let's say Seamus Heaney, his book *North*, and I suddenly understood what it meant to write a short line. He was working with, I think, trimeters in a lot of those shorter poems, and I started to ask myself: What does it mean for you, Rick, to write a short line? And so I would write a poem in a short line. Or I went through a phase where I was reading a lot of Wolcott, and all of these wonderful pentameters were happening in his work, and so I became interested in writing these pentameter lines. Virginia Woolf [had] a huge influence [on] me, and she has this wonderful thing in her diaries where she talks about how writing is putting words on the backs of rhythms. I really lived by that when I was writing that first book. I was interested in the formal aspects, in the visual aspects. The liability, of course, is that there's a lot of sensibility in the book, and in my 3 a.m. moments I wonder, where's the content?

Well, thanks for doing this with us. I really appreciate it.

Sure. My pleasure.

Source: Rick Barot and Craig Beavan, "An Interview with Rick Barot," in *Blackbird* (online), Vol. 2, No. 2, Fall 2003.

Sources

Barot, Rick, "Bonnard's Garden," in *The Darker Fall*, Sarabande Books, 2002, pp. 16–17.

Barot, Rick, and Craig Beaven, "An Interview with Rick Barot," in *Blackbird*, Vol. 2, No. 2, Fall 2003, http://www.blackbird.vcu.edu/v2n2/features/barot_r_040104/barot_r.htm.

"The Nobel Prize in Literature 1995," *Nobelprize.org*, http://nobelprize.org/literature/laureates/1995 (February 17, 2006).

Phillips, Brian, Review of *The Darker Fall*, in *Poetry*, Vol. 183, No. 5, February 2004, p. 293.

Plumly, Stanley, "Foreword," in *The Darker Fall*, Sarabande Books, 2002, pp. xi–xiv.

Further Reading

Auden, W. H., ed., *The Portable Romantic Poets: Blake to Poe*, Penguin, 1977.

    This collection provides ample material for an overview of English and American Romantic poets.

Hagedorn, Jessica, *Burning Heat: A Portrait of the Philippines*, Rizzoli, 1999.

    Rick Barot was born in the Philippines. Addressing the topics of religion, culture, food, and lifestyles, Hagedorn, a published novelist also from the Philippines, takes her readers on an intimate trip through the country, exposing its contradictions as well as its beauty.

Kooser, Ted, *The Poetry Home Repair Manual: Practical Advice for Beginning Poets*, University of Nebraska Press, 2005.

    The Pulitzer Prize–winning poet and U.S. poet laureate (2004–2005) Kooser draws from the classes he was teaching at the University of Nebraska. His advice tends to be practical, suggesting that poetry should, above all, make sense. He takes his readers through poetic devices and forms and makes the writing of poetry enjoyable.

Lowy, Michael, Robert Sayre, and Catherine Porter, *Romanticism against the Tide of Modernity*, Duke University Press, 2002.

    For students of literature, this book contains a unique exploration of what the authors see as a protest of the modern industrial era through the basic tenets of Romanticism. They follow a trail from the eighteenth to the twenty-first century, exploring the prominent writings of each era therein.

Chorale

Kevin Young

2003

In his third collection of poetry, *Jelly Roll: A Blues* (2003), Kevin Young presents the reader with verses drawing first and foremost on the musical genre of the title and also on a wide variety of other historical genres. The titles of the poems themselves are the first indication of his inspirations: "Rhythm & Blues," "Early Blues," "Blues," and "Late Blues" affirm the collection's foundation; "Dixieland," "Ragtime," and "Boogie-Woogie" indicate that Young is wandering further afield while nevertheless remaining rooted in the blues tradition; and "Etude" (a composition with both technical and artistic merit), "Cantata" (a composition employing voices in various forms), and "Rhapsody" (an irregular, improvisational composition) offer evidence of the author's widespread understanding of the essence of music. Indeed, nearly all of the more than one hundred poems in the collection reverberate with musicality, with fifteen titles including the word *song*. The work's opening epigraph consists of fourteen lines of lyrics written by the blues guitarist Robert Johnson.

"Chorale" fits neatly into this musical framework. According to *Merriam-Webster's Collegiate Dictionary*, a *chorale* is "a hymn or psalm sung to a traditional or composed melody in church." In appearing directly after the extended ruminations of "Sleepwalking Psalms" and a few poems before "Jubilee"—where the word *jubilee* has religious connotations both within the Roman Catholic Church and among African Americans regardless of denomination—"Chorale" can be seen as providing

something of a core of spirituality within the collection as a whole.

Outside the literal context of its title, "Chorale" can be read as a lamentation of uncertainty. The narrator seems to question what the world has thus far given him and what he can reasonably expect from it in the future. The reader, in turn, wonders along with him. The poem is brief; it consists of eight couplets, or two-line stanzas, and a solitary closing line. In all, the poet uses only sixty-four words to communicate the essence of his train of thought, such that the reader must approach the poem with the utmost attention in attempting to grasp that essence.

Author Biography

Kevin Young was born in Lincoln, Nebraska, on November 8, 1970, although his family's roots lie in Louisiana, where his forefathers were preachers, musicians, and storytellers. His family moved six times before he reached the age of ten. After attending middle school and high school in Kansas, he earned admission to Harvard University, where he studied under the Nobel Prize–winning poet Seamus Heaney. While he was in Cambridge, Massachusetts, he joined a group called the Dark Room Collective, which offered support for black artists in various fields. After graduation, Young spent two years at Stanford University, in California, as a Stegner Fellow and then earned a master of fine arts degree from Brown University, in Providence, Rhode Island.

Young's first book of poetry, *Most Way Home* (1995), was selected and published as part of the National Poetry Series and won the Zacharis First Book Award, presented by the literary journal *Ploughshares* and Emerson College. His second collection, *To Repel Ghosts: Five Sides in B Minor*, which he musically dubbed a "double album," was inspired by the art of the late Jean-Michel Basquiat, an African American. In association with this collection, Young contributed to an installation called *Two Cents*, featuring both Basquiat's art and his poetry, which toured across the nation. Young next produced the collections *Jelly Roll: A Blues* (2003), in which "Chorale" appears, and *Black Maria* (2005), his poetic interpretation of film noir. Young also has edited *Giant Steps: The New Generation of African American Writers* (2001), *Blues Poems* (2003), and *John Berryman: Selected Poems* (2004) and has written a number

Kevin Young Photograph by Tod Martens. Reproduced by permission

of essays. He has served as professor at the University of Georgia, Indiana University, and Emory University.

Poem Text

Quite difficult, belief.
Quite terrible, faith

that the night, again,
will nominate

you a running mate— 5
that we are of the elect

& have not yet
found out. That the tide

still might toss us up
another—what eyes 10

& stars, what teeth!
such arms, alive—

someone we will, all
night, keep. Not 15

just these spiders
that skitter & cobweb,

share my shivering bed.

Media Adaptations

- Video clips of Young reading several poems from *Jelly Roll* can be found on the Random House website, at http://www.randomhouse.com/knopf/authors/young/desktop.html.

- In an interview conducted by Renée Montagne, aired on National Public Radio's *Morning Edition* on March 3, 2005, and found online at http://www.npr.org/templates/story/story.php?storyId=4520872, Young can be heard commenting on and reading from his 2005 collection, *Black Maria*.

Poem Summary

Lines 1–5

Beyond the significance of the title, the first two lines of "Chorale" seem to make clear that it can be read in a religious context. The first line mentions "belief," while the second mentions "faith." Further, the reader can understand that this context has conflicting connotations for the narrator, as the "belief" is described as "difficult," the "faith" as "terrible." Still, while "terrible" is most commonly used in a strictly negative sense, the word can also be read, more neutrally, as indicating that something is "formidable," "awesome," or "great." Thus, the reader cannot necessarily conclude that the narrator has a negative opinion of faith. Notably, the first two lines feature the repetition of the opening word "quite."

Line 3, as a continuation of line 2, indicates that the narrator is not, after all, speaking of "faith" in a wholly generic sense, and indeed, the reader may need to move beyond a spiritual context in order to understand the poem. Lines 2 through 5, in their entirety, read as follows: "Quite terrible, faith / that the night, again, / will nominate / you a running mate." (Note that when reading the poem as a whole, so as to fully reveal its aesthetic, or artistic, value, substantial pauses might be given between lines and stanzas, in accordance with the format. In the course of interpretation, on the other hand, lines may be better read with attention given only to punctuation; as such, the meanings of individual phrases may be easier to determine.) In literal terms, this sentence has evident political overtones, endowing the thought with a certain dryness. Temporarily setting aside the word "again," the reader may understand that when the narrator refers to "faith / that the night ... / will nominate / you a running mate," he may be referring to a romantic context. As such, instead of actually choosing his or her own "running mate," the person addressed by the narrator has that complementary person chosen by "the night," or by fate, or chance, alone. In that the poem's addressee may be convinced that this will happen "again," the reader may understand, perhaps, that the addressee has allowed random romantic pairings to occur on more than one occasion.

Lines 6–12

As indicated by the hyphen closing line 5, the phrase begun in line 6 is a second ending for the sentence started in line 2. As such, the lines might together read, "Quite terrible, faith / ... / that we are of the elect / & have not yet / found out." Here again the narrator uses a word with political overtones, "elect." Within a religious context, on the other hand, the phrase "of the elect" can mean "chosen for salvation through divine mercy." Thus, the narrator is likely pointing out the "terribleness" of the conviction that two people, that is, the two people whom the night may choose as running mates, might be destined to be together, in a sort of heaven. These two people "have not yet / found out," of course, because they have not yet met each other. Throughout *Jelly Roll*, Young employs an ampersand in place of the word *and*, most likely simply to reduce the attention that would otherwise be given to the insignificant word. In recordings of his readings, Young indeed pronounces the ampersand more like "an" than "and."

The second half of line 8 again takes up the thread of the same phrase, although this time beginning a new sentence, one that will not turn out to be a complete sentence, confirming that this is another continuation of line 2. Here, the narrator once more uses a first-person plural pronoun; earlier he employed "we," and now he employs "us." He seems to be universalizing his meditations; that is, he is aware that many people may share his sentiments regarding the hope that a "running mate" might one day be fortuitously found. He indicates again the role that fate may play in this search, as we may hope that "the tide / still might toss us up / another," where the tide, as a force of nature, is certainly beyond any human being's control.

The second half of line 10, together with lines 11 and 12, seems to constitute a series of vague proclamations of the beauty of the "running mate" who might one day appear. Indeed, this unknown person is essentially featureless. The narrator refers to "eyes / & stars," perhaps juxtaposing the glowing orbs of a person's countenance with those of the sky, again invoking a grand image of nature. Also, as astrologers "read" the stars in considering the future, this reference may rouse further thoughts of fatefulness in the reader. In that the person in question consists only of eyes, teeth—both of which are white—and arms that are "alive," the reader may imagine this person in a shadowed context, such as, perhaps, a nightclub.

Lines 13–17

Lines 13 and 14 make further reference to the idealized future seen between these two people who have been brought together by chance, as the found person is described as "someone we will, all / night, keep." The final lines depart from the dreamy tone maintained by the majority of the poem, in a sense returning to the more negative connotations of the first two lines. The narrator makes reference to "spiders / that skitter," or move in a jerky way. These spiders, in addition to some unnamed thing, share his "shivering bed," which may be understood to be so, perhaps, because the narrator is usually cold there in his solitude. Whether the unnamed thing sharing the bed is another person—a person who does little to make it any warmer—the narrator's own fantasies, or some other object or idea entirely is unclear. Regardless, in that the spiders "cobweb," or make webs that lie unused and accumulate dust, the reader may attribute a certain stagnancy to the narrator's general state of existence.

Themes

Spirituality

While the title of this poem, "Chorale," can refer more generally to a chorus or choir, the word's origins are distinctly religious, and the scholarly Young, who attended several prestigious institutions of higher education, would certainly have given due consideration to this fact. Indeed, his opening references to "belief" and "faith" would seem to leave little doubt that the poem has a religious aspect. Beyond these opening lines, however, the only phrase with direct association with religion is "of the elect," which has connotations concerning the salvation of the soul. The reader might then consider the poem's spiritual aspects in a more general sense. The narrator certainly makes subtle references to fate, or predestination, which is often thought of in spiritual terms. Many religions hold that God has preordained all that will occur within his creation, and the narrator may be alluding to the presence of such a religious attitude in those who nevertheless imagine that "the night" may provide them with their predestined mates.

Sadness

While a certain hope is evident throughout the poem, most pointedly in lines 10 through 12, with line 11 containing the poem's one exclamation point, the underlying sentiment seems to be one of sadness. The first two lines refer to this hope, or "faith," as "terrible," perhaps in that the narrator understands to a certain extent that his hopes, and indeed the hopes of many, are unfounded, unbearable, or unrealistic. After wandering through his hopeful ruminations, the narrator concludes with references to cobwebs, reflecting a reality undisturbed by mere hopes, and his "shivering" bed. In that the reader has no reason to believe that the narrator is incapable of retaining his physical warmth with, say, blankets, she can understand the implied coldness to be mental or emotional, such as the coldness caused by solitude, or, perhaps, by physical closeness to one with whom no emotional closeness exists.

Style

Anaphora

Anaphora is the repetition of a word or phrase at the beginning of multiple lines or clauses. In this poem, anaphora is used but twice. First, each of the first two lines begins with the word "quite." In that the construction appears at the beginning of this short poem, it helps set a tone that is maintained throughout. The words "difficult" and "terrible" are given

Topics For Further Study

- Young based his second collection of poetry, *To Repel Ghosts*, on the life and art of Jean-Michel Basquiat. Base your own work of art on Young's "Chorale." This work could be a painting of a scene from the poem (such as the narrator's "shivering bed"), a collage of the images found in the poem, or some other artistic presentation. As Young does not offer a wide variety of physical description, feel free to produce a work of art that provides an abstract interpretation of the poem.

- Write a poem of at least twenty lines in the style of "Chorale" on the subject of destiny. You may want to answer questions such as the following: Where do you think your life or the lives of others might lead, romantically or perhaps professionally? How much control will you have over the course of events that you will experience? Use metaphors to communicate your thoughts. Write your poem in couplets, with short lines, occasionally employing rhyme and rhythm. Read your poem aloud to the class, identifying afterward several locations where you believe the flow of your poem was musical.

- Choose and read two other poems from Young's collection *Jelly Roll* and two poems from one of his other collections. (All of these poems should be at least ten lines long.) In an essay, for each pair of poems consider the following questions: How are the two poems similar, and how are they different? How do the poems reflect the overall theme of the collection? Do you think that the presence of the theme makes the poems stronger or weaker? Then, for the two pairs of poems together, answer the following questions: What aspects of the poems suggest that they were all written by the same author? Do you prefer the poems from one collection over the poems from the other? Why or why not? Within your essay, comment on any other aspects of the poems you find deserving of comment.

- Research the history of the blues, focusing on its original development and also addressing its development throughout the twentieth century. Present your findings in an essay. At the conclusion of your essay, discuss how well you think Young has contributed to the history of the blues, through both his own collection *Jelly Roll* and the collection *Blues Poems*, which he edited.

---

particular attention and stress, and wherever the poem wanders thence, the reader does not forget that everything being described can essentially be modified with those two words. Indeed, the second example of anaphora is connected to the first: line 3, line 6, and the second half of line 8 all begin with the word "that," specifically because they are all describing things in which a certain "terrible" "faith" is held.

Rhythm and Rhyme

As Young's collection is subtitled "A Blues," the reader would expect his poems to demonstrate a certain musicality. Here, this musicality is evident not in a structured meter maintained throughout the poem but in isolated incidences of rhythmicity and rhyme. The first two lines each open with a one-syllable word followed by a three-syllable word. In lines 4 and 5, the word "nominate" and the term "running mate" have the same pattern of syllable stress, in addition to rhyming. In lines 7 and 8, on the other hand, the phrase "have not yet / found out" demands that the reader slow to a staccato thumping. Much of the following verse meanders without musicality, featuring only the distant rhymes of "teeth" and "keep," perhaps indicating the arrhythmic nature of the distant hopes being described. In the end, the reader is left with the mournful tapping out of the phrases "skitter & cobweb" and "shivering bed," featuring the double rhymes of "skitter" and "shiver" alongside "web" and "bed."

Deemphasized Structure

The structure of "Chorale" seems to be fairly unimportant with respect to the poem's overall meaning. The lines are presented in couplets, but beyond the first two lines, no couplet presents a single coherent thought. Punctuation appears at the ends of lines as often as in the middles. Further, the reader might consider that most of the poems in *Jelly Roll* feature precisely the same general format, with couplets running into one another and lines rarely longer than five words. As such, one might conclude that Young does not intend for the structure to have a substantial impact on the meaning of the poem. Indeed, in recordings of Young reading his poetry aloud, sometimes he pauses significantly between lines and stanzas and sometimes he does not. As such, he tends to place greater emphasis on each individual word, as one might expect in such a brief poem. His use of ampersands in place of the word *and* would seem to be further indication of his desire to waste as little space in his verse as possible.

Historical Context

The Blues

The blues are considered by many to be the ultimate source of virtually all modern genres of music. From blues came jazz; from jazz came rock and roll. Hip-hop, rap, alternative rock, and so on can all be seen as sprouting from these original genres. The blues themselves originated in African American spirituals sung on plantations by laboring slaves, with the call-and-response format, employed both vocally and instrumentally, evincing the genre's roots in West African music in particular. The blues, specifically, are held to have come into existence in the early twentieth century, with W. C. Handy playing one of the most significant roles. Robert Johnson, who is quoted in the opening epigraph of Young's collection, is generally credited with standardizing the twelve-bar blues, a term that refers to a certain style of chord progression.

In an interview for *Bold Type*, Young remarks, "The blues aren't just important musically, their attitude I think tells us so much about how black folks viewed the world and remade it, made it swing." With respect to his own appreciation for the blues, he adds, "I listen to the blues to feel better, not worse—it transforms us as listeners, takes our troubles away not by pretending they don't exist (like much other early pop music) but by naming them."

Finally, with respect to his collection *Jelly Roll: A Blues*—where Jelly Roll Morton was a pioneer jazz musician, with one of his tunes titled "Jelly Roll Blues"—Young notes, "I was trying to get at not strictly the repeating form of the blues (though sometimes that too) but its tragicomic spirit." On *PoetryNet*, he further comments, "You could say the poems seek to 'finger the jagged grain' (as [the novelist] Ralph Ellison described the blues), turning pain into performance and danger into humor." Thus, Young has attempted to translate the musical form of the blues into a poetic form, much in the way that artists like Langston Hughes wrote poems meant to convey the feel and spirit of jazz.

The Black Arts Movement

The Black Arts movement is considered the cultural extension of the Black Power movement of the 1960s and 1970s. During this time period, a number of publishing houses and periodicals, under black ownership, assisted in the greatly increased production of literature and poetry by black authors. In association with the often militant Black Power movement, which opposed many forms of integration as disguised methods of assimilating blacks into white culture, Black Arts writers did not feel compelled to produce work that harmonized with the preexisting canon of works by white writers. Similarly, writers of this era did not shy away from making political statements that might otherwise have been seen as detrimental, in preventing the authors in question from being fully accepted by white society. In this cultural context arose the proliferation of poetry that drew on the distinctly African American musical form of jazz. In fully embracing his own cultural context, as well as that of his ancestors, Young can be seen as echoing the heralding cries of his literary predecessors.

Post-Soul

In his introduction to the anthology *Giant Steps: The New Generation of African American Writers* (2000), which he edited, Young makes reference to "the post-soul writer." The term *post-soul* was coined by the writer and filmmaker Nelson George to describe the black world that came into existence after the "soul power" advances of the 1960s. Young writes, "Just as previous generations made a way of no way, forging not just themselves but a brilliant array of opportunities for us to occupy, we are taking culture, both black and popular, and attempting to make it sing." In summing up the significance of various African American movements, Young notes, "Soul, another parallel to Black Arts, for me also parallels, if not creates, the rise of a black popular culture." Thus, post-soul writers are sustaining the outspoken tradition fostered by their foremothers and forefathers, asserting that black literature and arts constitute not just an extension of American cultural traditions but a permanent cultural tradition in and of themselves.

Critical Overview

With respect to *Jelly Roll*, critics have almost universally lauded Young's ability to absorb the reader in the rhythmic flow of his writing. In the *Hudson Review*, Mark Jarman declares, "Young makes a supple, changeable music out of the marriage of dialect and standard English." Jarman presents a sample of Young's verse and then adds, "You can hear the sound of this voice alive on the vivid page. That's poetry." In classifying the verse in *Jelly Roll* as among the best poetry of 2003 in *Library Journal*, Barbara Hoffert notes, "Young struts his stuff with verve, tossing us off-kilter lines with a sort of insouciant melancholy. He'll get under your skin." In *Black Issues Book Review*, Dike Okoro observes, "The jazzy swagger and the quirky syntax (and the omnipresent long dash) marry to produce a dizzying flow."

Still, some reviewers have found Young's linguistic presentation disagreeable. In *Poetry*, Brian Phillips makes reference to the fact that Young was educated at Harvard and questions the veracity of his poetic voice. He contends that, at times, "dialect simply pinch-hits for poetic effort." Phillips presents lines from "Disaster Movie Theme Music," found in *Jelly Roll*, which include the phrases "mom'n thems" and "Heard tell you / were a-ready lost" and remarks, "Surely this is imitation, mere strategic typography: this is not Young's voice." Interestingly, with respect to the same passage, Mark Jarman remarks, "I may have been living in the South too long, but to my ear 'mom'n thems' is just right." Thus, perhaps each individual reader must decide for herself whether Young's use of dialect is effective.

Okoro and Phillips question whether Young's blues framework is used successfully. Okoro states, "His wit, an essential ingredient in the blues, is at times awkwardly employed," such that "the reader's faith in the authentic sentiment of the poems might be undermined." Phillips notes,

> The need to engraft an approved cultural paradigm onto the expression of one's experience in art is dangerous to a lyric poet. The danger is that it will excuse the kind of aesthetic laziness . . . in which one writes down to the "authenticity" of a tradition one is intellectually or experientially beyond.

Indeed, Phillips believes that Young can fulfill his amply evident promise as a poet only by forgoing his reliance, however intellectually sound, on established African American forms.

Overall, regardless of their opinions of Young's use of dialect and his overarching construct, reviewers have tended to see and admire the sizable heart from which his poems have issued forth. In *Library Journal*, Fred Muratori asserts that Young manages "to explore the hazardous dimensions of emotional commitment with gritty grace and disarming candor." Similarly, a *Publishers Weekly* reviewer states, "The verse here shows Young to be not only a terrific love poet but one of real emotional variety." In closing, the reviewer notes, "Young has daringly likened himself in earlier poems and prose to Langston Hughes: this versatile tour de force may well justify the ambitious comparison."

Criticism

Michael Allen Holmes

Holmes is a freelance writer and editor. In this essay, he considers the intersection of romance and religion in "Chorale" and other poems in Young's Jelly Roll: A Blues.

The opening lines of "Chorale"—"Quite difficult, belief / Quite terrible, faith"—are undeniably striking. The anaphoric use of the adverb "quite" immediately focuses the reader's attention on the seemingly negative adjectives that follow, "difficult" and "terrible," and throughout the rest of the brief poem the echo of those words is felt, if not actually heard, in the mind of the reader. As for the nouns that close these two lines, "belief" and "faith," either alone might bear various meanings, but in concert they certainly conjure thoughts of religiousness and spirituality. Indeed, a *chorale* is a churchly hymn or song; thus, the theme of the poem would seem to be concretized. Yet, beyond a later mention of "the elect," which can be understood as referring to "those divinely chosen for salvation," the theme of religion seems to be thence cast aside in favor of meditations on the possibility of predestined romance. Rather than dismissing the originally understood theme, however, the reader might consider what can be found at the intersection of the two substantial issues of religion and romance.

In fact, that intersection is prominent in a number of poems in Young's *Jelly Roll*. In "Sleepwalking Psalms," an extended lamentation on the departure of a loved one (which immediately precedes "Chorale"), Young offers the following: "There are no more saints—/ only people with pain / who want someone to blame. / Or praise." Here he may be contending that religion, particularly Christianity, is no longer primarily a moral system in which people transcend worldly concerns and disseminate positive energy through acts of benevolence, such as with, say, Mother Teresa. Instead, religion has evolved into a framework of authority that allows individuals to absolve themselves of responsibility for whatever adversity, or even fortune, they have encountered by holding some god accountable instead. After commenting on these "people with pain," Young affirms, "I am one of them, of course." Two stanzas later, he refers to the woman who left him as being a "hairshirt," an uncomfortable garment worn by some Catholics to signify their penance. That is, perhaps he retains his torturous remembrances of this woman as a way of asserting to himself that God, or, essentially, the woman herself, has forsaken him; he, of course, cannot be blamed for this misfortune.

Similarly couched references to the religious aspect of romance are made in succeeding poems, beginning with "Torch Song" (which immediately follows "Chorale"): "The heaven of her / hips—over me, such sway—/ She got some saint / standing at the gate / keeping the crowds away." Thus, the woman in question is herself both heaven and the chief resident of heaven. The narrator then declares that he would build a church and "slave" away in his "Sunday best" just to see this woman, further equating her with God. The first lines of the next poem, "Fish Story," read, "For you I would give up / God—repeal / once & for all, unkneel." Thus, he is turning away from God and toward the woman. In "Jubilee," Young opens with "Sister, you are a late-night / preacher" and closes with "just don't leave me lone / like God / done, promising return."

Indeed, Young seems to have been, to a certain extent, abandoned by God. Illuminating thoughts on the fading importance of religion, especially among intellectuals—which Young should certainly be considered, as his multiple volumes of poetry and degrees from Harvard and Brown attest—can be found in *The Future of an Illusion*, by Sigmund Freud. Therein, Freud asserts that rational evidence for the existence of God is, in truth, utterly absent; all that can lead a rational person to believe in God,

> "'Chorale' epitomizes Young's worship of the woman. 'Quite terrible' is his 'faith' in finding this idealized woman, perhaps because he is on some level aware of the inauspicious nature of his idolatry."

then, are the assertions of other persons, none of whom have had any more verifiable proof of God's existence than can be found in modern times. For the rationally grounded person, God must cease to exist. The closing lines of "Jubilee," cited earlier, would seem ample evidence that Young has found himself in this state of mind.

In *Future*, Freud also posits the reason that God was invented in the first place: "When the growing individual finds that he is destined to remain a child for ever, that he can never do without protection against strange superior powers, he lends those powers the features belonging to the figure of his father." Indeed, in ancient times, people had much to fear from nature, including droughts, deluges, and pestilence. In modern times, on the other hand, civilization, at least in America, has essentially subdued nature, to the extent that for most people fear of nature's power is not a driving psychological concern. Apart from such catastrophes as hurricanes and earthquakes, Americans, particularly those with ample wealth, are well insulated from the worst effects of weather, sickness, and other natural forces. Thus, protection is no longer an essential trait for a divine being. What, then, might God become? Freud reminds us who the original iconic figure is for all humans: "The mother, who satisfies the child's hunger, becomes its first love-object and certainly also its first protection against all the undefined dangers which threaten it in the external world." Only with the heightening of these external threats is the mother "replaced by the stronger father."

As such, for the modern male, who is quite possibly never confronted with external threats that

What Do I Read Next?

- Kevin Young's first collection, *Most Way Home* (1995), won the Zacharis First Book Award from the literary magazine *Ploughshares* and features a somewhat wider variety of form than is found in *Jelly Roll*.

- One of Young's favorite poetry collections is *Ask Your Mama: 12 Moods for Jazz* (1961), by the groundbreaking African American intellectual Langston Hughes.

- Another collection of poems admired by Young, especially in that it originally brought him to the realization that poetry could speak of the profoundly personal, is Rita Dove's *Thomas and Beulah* (1986).

- Young has been compared to the poet Yusef Komunyakaa. Komunyakaa's collection *Neon Vernacular: New and Selected Poems* (1993) includes samplings from earlier works as well as original material and earned him the Pulitzer Prize for Poetry in 1994.

- Young has cited "Blues People: Negro Music in White America" (1963), by Imamu Amiri Baraka, who was originally named LeRoi Jones, as offering a good account of the social relevance of the blues.

---

can be warded off only by a powerful father figure, the mother retains her position of supremacy. In adulthood, of course, any male must inevitably renounce the worship of his own mother. Taking the mother's place, then, will be the object of his romantic affection, who may be a particular woman (considering heterosexuality in this argument, where a similar argument might be made regarding homosexuality), with whom he may or may not have already had a relationship or a romantic encounter, or perhaps in time an idealized woman, whom he will marry and with whom he will start a family.

Young leaves little doubt that he has often engaged in this type of romantic worship. In "Threnody," he remarks, presumably of a romantic interest, "Without you I got no one / to say *sorry* to." That is, he yearns for someone to bless him with forgiveness, as with Catholic confession. Freud asserts, "The superior wisdom which directs this course of things, the infinite goodness that expresses itself in it, the justice that achieves its aim in it—these are the attributes of the divine beings who also created us and the world as a whole." Young seems to hope that he will find this wisdom, goodness, and justice not in God, in whom he no longer believes, but in the woman who can forgive his sins.

"Chorale" epitomizes Young's worship of the woman. "Quite terrible" is his "faith" in finding this idealized woman, perhaps because he is on some level aware of the inauspicious nature of his idolatry. Indeed, in an ideal relationship, neither of the two individuals can have an idealized view of the other; rather, they must be equals. In "Chorale," the very forces of nature from which a father-figure god might have once offered Young protection have transformed into forces that he hopes will one day bring him his idealized other. These forces are represented here by "the night," or the unknown, and "the tide," or the elements. In his description of the future object of his affection, he can only vaguely state, "what eyes / & stars, what teeth! / such arms, alive," and indeed, one rarely assigns distinct physical features to an imagined god; rather, one will simply know this god when one sees him or her. Also, in mentioning "stars," Young again invokes the heavens in reference to a woman.

Based on the contents of "Chorale," Young's state of mind is still in the course of a certain evolution. He recognizes that his trust in fate, and particularly in the coming of that one messianic woman who will prove to be his own personal object of worship, is "difficult"; he may prove able to bear his reliance on this essentially spiritual construct for only so long. It is unclear the degree to which his worship has progressed beyond that of a particular individual with whom he desires immediate physical contact to that of a woman, known or unknown, with whom he would wish to spend the rest of his life. The lines "someone we will, all / night, keep" might seem to suggest relatively shallow desires, but the tone of the poem appears to indicate that "all / night" is here intended to represent the rest of his life, that is, all night for every night to come. Having established himself as "a terrific love poet," as described by a *Publishers Weekly* reviewer, Young may find himself further conflicted when he next produces a volume of personal poetry. (His collection *Black Maria*, which followed *Jelly Roll*, is an interpretation of film noir and as such constitutes a more fictional approach to poetry.) Will he be true to whatever further mental and spiritual development he will have undergone, as one would expect such an intelligent man to undergo, or will he seek to recreate, or perhaps rechannel, the palpable heartache he once felt? The reader can only await.

Source: Michael Allen Holmes, Critical Essay on "Chorale," in *Poetry for Students*, Thomson Gale, 2007.

Joyce Hart

Hart is a published writer and former teacher. In this essay, she explores the mixture of religion, nature, politics, and the blues in Young's poem.

In the seventeen short lines of Young's poem "Chorale," the poet hints at several diverse topics, as he wends his way from beginning to end. In the first few lines, one might be led to believe that the poem is about religion or spirituality. The last line of the poem conjures up the emotional image of loneliness. Between the beginning and the end are allusions to politics and nature. In addition, the poem resonates with lyrics from a blues song, with its reference to lost or elusive love. It is as if the reader is traveling down an unknown waterway. Just when the reader thinks that he or she has grasped the intent of the poet, the poem rounds yet another bend in the river.

Young's poem begins, in its very title, with a sense of religion. A chorale is a religious hymn sung to a melody. The religious rebel Martin Luther is credited with creating the first chorales, which were sung by his congregations. Later, Johann Sebastian Bach added harmonies to the simple musical lines of religious chorales. Basically, however, chorales were written in uncomplicated, rhyming lines for ordinary people to sing. Although there is no rhyming in Young's "Chorale," the surface simplicity of the stanzas are reflective of the original Lutheran church songs.

> *Just when the reader thinks that he or she has grasped the intent of the poet, the poem rounds yet another bend in the river."*

In the first two lines of the poem, Young mentions both "belief" and "faith." Although these words can be used in a secular context, it is quite common for most people to first react to them with the understanding that they are imbued with either a spiritual or a religious connotation. If someone were to ask a person, "What is your faith?" most people would reply by naming their affiliation with a church or a spiritual practice. Young sets his readers up to assume this religious attitude by combining a religiously inclined title with a spiritually inclined first two lines. So begins a somewhat bewildering journey through Young's poem.

If the reader looks back at the first two lines, after realizing that this is not really a poem about spirituality, the words take on a different meaning. "Belief" and "faith" could, after all, be references to something more generic, as one would find in such aphorisms as "love conquers all." These types of beliefs can indeed be "quite difficult" if circumstances prove that all is not conquered by love after all. Having faith in someone who is not worthy of one's trust can be "quite terrible." With the opening lines, then, the poet could be reflecting on a sad ending to a relationship, one in which he had, at some time, great faith and belief. Remembering his faith and belief in his former lover could very well now be extremely difficult and terrible to bear.

In the third line, the poet continues with his thoughts on faith. The speaker of this poem refers to faith in reference to "the night," which is imbued with a sense of power: "the night, again, / will nominate." One might question whether the word "night" suggests a god or some other strong spiritual influence. There is also an overtone of religion in the third stanza (line 6) with the term "elect."

Those of the Puritan faith used the term *elect* to differentiate people who had been predestined for salvation from those who were not so chosen and could never receive God's grace. At the same time that the poet hints at religion with the word "elect," he also begins to lean toward more political language with the phrase "will nominate / you a running mate." In this context, "elect" sounds more like a reference to a political campaign. Here the poem takes on simultaneous religious and political overtones. The word "again" indicates repetition, as if the night has done this before or will continue to do this later. The use of the word "again" becomes more significant in the context of lines 13 and 14: "someone we will, all / night, keep." In these later lines, another "running mate" has entered the picture, one tossed up by the tide and one that will be kept through the night.

It is important to dwell on what the poet means with his statement that the "night" nominates "a running mate." Perhaps this "you" has been nominated as the speaker's running mate. Or perhaps the night nominated someone else to be the running mate for the person who is referred to as "you." "You" might be the speaker or the friend or lover of the speaker. In line 6, the speaker uses the first-person plural pronoun "we." "We" suggests unity, which could mean that the "you" is the running mate of the speaker. "We are of the elect," the speaker says. Since this poem is about love, the speaker could be trying to describe what it feels like when two people fall in love. When connections are made between two people through love, the lovers might feel that they have become two of God's chosen people (thus, the elect). They are so happy that they might believe that they have been blessed, or anointed.

None of this is entirely clear, not even for the speaker of this poem. There is confusion in lines 7 and 8. Although there is the possibility, as the speaker states, that these two lovers have been nominated to the elect, they "have not yet / found out." They are as yet unaware of this blessing. From this point in the poem, things seem to fall apart, as if the lovers' lack of awareness implies an impairment of their vision. This is where nature makes a strong appearance in the poem. Like "the night" before it (in line 3), "the tide" (in line 8) now has power over the lovers. The tide "might toss us up / another." It is not until lines 13 and 14, however, that the reader knows what the tide has tossed up: "someone we will, all / night, keep." It is curious to note that the poet again uses the first-person plural pronoun (we) in these lines, but this time the feeling of unity is not as strong. Rather, it seems as if the lovers are no longer together or else that their previous union is beginning to crumble—someone has come between them. The tide is challenging the lovers. There is someone new in their midst that one of them will "all / night, keep." The last line implies that the speaker has been left out in the cold.

It is in the last lines of this poem that a true sense of the blues comes in. The speaker is lonely and sad, a typical theme of the blues. The running mate is not present. The speaker is left to ruminate about the past, as he looks around his room and notices only the spiders and the cobwebs. Spiders, like the tide, are part of nature, but there are few people who can think of spiders without feeling skittish. The image of spiders might have been chosen as a metaphor for the speaker's discomfort. Spiders in one's bed do not conjure up images of a good night's sleep. The presence of cobwebs indicates a space that has accumulated dust and dirt, a place that has not seen much movement. The untidy bed in what seems to be a close room not entered by anyone but the speaker might portray a sense of the speaker's depression. If spiders and cobwebs were not enough to make readers grasp the speaker's emotions, the last line of the poem makes matters clear. The spiders share the speaker's "shivering bed." He might be pleading for some unknown person to share his lonely bed as well, but a shivering bed is not very inviting.

These last images accurately portray the distraught feelings and loneliness of the speaker. They are also capable of eliciting the sympathy of readers. But they do not beckon; they do not entice. They fend off, as if the speaker is mournfully singing his blues while signaling that he does not want anyone to come too close. The speaker might be so lost in his journey that he is not yet ready to step out of the boat that is carrying him down the river of the blues.

Source: Joyce Hart, Critical Essay on "Chorale," in *Poetry for Students*, Thomson Gale, 2007.

Jennifer Bussey

Bussey is an independent writer specializing in literature. In this essay, she explores the relevance of musical form and content in Young's "Chorale."

Young's 2003 poetry collection, *Jelly Roll: A Blues*, showcases the poet's particular expertise in music as it relates to poetry. Although the poems include a wide range of subjects and tones, they are held together by the influence of American music. Young's comfort with the form is evident in the intimacy of his poems and his willingness to explore personal and sometimes painful musings. In "Chorale," he expresses loneliness and hope within the twin contexts of blues music and the chorale. These two musical forms are very different, yet the poem is cohesive and the voice sympathetic. Somehow, Young draws on these disparate musical influences in a way that works for the poem. The collection *Jelly Roll* bears the subtitle *A Blues*. It is fair, then, to read the poems Young chose to include in the collection with the blues in mind. Young is known for his deep interest in African American history and music (especially the blues) and for finding poetic inspiration in those studies. His writing participates in and continues the history, tradition, and culture of African Americans, but he brings to his work contemporary style and settings. Young's expertise in blues lyrics qualified him to edit *Blues Poems*, an anthology of poetry by great blues musicians, such as Robert Johnson and Muddy Waters, alongside the poetry of poets inspired by blues music, such as Langston Hughes and W. H. Auden. All of this biographical context points to how deeply blues music influences Young's individual voice and how natural it is that he should use it as a context for an entire collection of poetry.

Blues, like jazz, is a distinctly American style of music. A shortened version of the "blue devils," *blues* refers to experiencing hard times and feeling low. The music grew out of African American spirituals, chants, and work songs. It is characterized by "blue notes," specific musical notes that set an emotional tone, and "call-and-response" patterns in the lyrics. Call-and-response is intended to mirror everyday communication in that it uses phrases that seem to suggest a dialogue and build a narrative. This type of communication is common in West African communities that use call-and-response formally in everything from political participation to religion and music. The roots of call-and-response run deep, and Young knows very well how significant this pattern is to African American culture. In "Chorale," Young suggests this pattern in the particular way he uses anastrophe, or the inversion of the usual order of words in a sentence to build a particular effect. Anastrophe is evident in the first two lines of the poem and again in line 12. Young takes unified thoughts and breaks them into two separate utterances. In the first line, for example, instead of writing, "Belief is quite difficult," he writes, "Quite difficult, belief." The word

> *In many ways, the chorale stands in stark contrast to blues music, yet Young's poem joins the two in a unified and meaningful way. Despite the disparate influences of the chorale and blues, the poem is better for having them both."*

"belief" seems to answer the question of what is difficult. It is a subtle form of call-and-response.

The first two lines also demonstrate how "Chorale" is consistent with blues from a content perspective. Blues is often about struggles, love problems, oppression and hopelessness, and feeling vulnerable to greater or more powerful forces. Blues music also carries a strong narrative element, so that a blues song tells a story that often explains the singer's plight. The song itself seems to arise from the singer's need to tell his or her sad story, and the listener is moved to sympathize with the singer. In "Chorale," Young borrows heavily from the tradition of blues content. The poem is about loneliness, as the speaker describes in the last three lines, "just these spiders / that skitter & cobweb, / share my shivering bed." He is alone with spiders and cobwebs, and his bed is both literally and figuratively cold. Although the crux of the poem is that the "tide" will probably "toss up" someone whom the speaker can keep "all night," he does not speak of true love, and the notion of hope is both difficult and terrifying (according to the first two lines of the poem). The little hope the speaker has seems to be merely for a respite from his loneliness, but not a love relationship that would actually banish it.

The speaker's sense of powerlessness is also consistent with the blues point of view. He does not feel the least bit in control of his love life but is instead subject to the whims of "the night" that will choose a "running mate" for him. His only choice is seemingly to wait and see who this person will be. He writes that "we are of the elect / & have not yet / found out." The tide, without his agency, might "toss up / another." This is a very fatalistic view of love, in which the speaker is really nothing but a pawn of fate; he never even considers claiming authority over his own love relationships. Blues often laments powerlessness and oppression, and here Young borrows that theme to describe the speaker's view of love.

Still, Young named the poem "Chorale." In many ways, the chorale stands in stark contrast to blues music, yet Young's poem joins the two in a unified and meaningful way. Despite the disparate influences of the chorale and blues, the poem is better for having them both. While blues is distinctly American and secular, the chorale has its roots in European religious music. Traditionally, a chorale was a hymn sung by an entire Lutheran congregation. That it was a hymn means it was intended to be a form of worship or to teach theological truths. What is important for Young's poem, however, is that it was sung by the entire congregation. It was intended as a group, or universal, expression. Thus, the feelings described by the poem's speaker are part of the common human experience. The speaker becomes not just a single person alone in bed at night but, in fact, anyone who has ever felt alone. Indeed, the speaker becomes the reader, and the reader identifies with the struggles the speaker faces.

In form, the chorale is very different from Young's poem. Traditional chorales were subject to rather specific criteria, such as rhyming lines, simple melodies, and certain stanzaic conventions. Young's poem is written in free-verse couplets with heavy use of enjambment. In enjambment, a phrase or sentence runs over from one line of verse to the next, splitting closely related words and sometimes forming two distinct thoughts. While chorales were formal, "Chorale" is very natural and loose in its rhythms. It is fair to draw the conclusion, then, that Young wants the reader to focus more on the collective nature of the chorale's presentation than on the rigors of the form.

Combing the different forms of the blues and the chorale, Young creates a poem that holds together well. Both forms—blues and the chorale—arose from human experience and the need for self-expression. Whether in Europe hundreds of years ago or in America in the early twentieth century, people have always felt drawn to music as an outlet for expression. While the chorale and blues are very different musical forms, they both encompass a wide range of expression that can overlap. In "Chorale," Young finds the area where the forms converge, without forcing them to work together. Ultimately, the poem works because the speaker's feelings and language patterns arise from blues and the universality of experience arises from the chorale. The poem is a sophisticated blend of styles, but the style does not detract from the speaker's central expression of loneliness with slight hope in fate.

Source: Jennifer Bussey, Critical Essay on "Chorale," in *Poetry for Students*, Thomson Gale, 2007.

John Palattella

In the following review, Palattella examines Jelly Roll *in the context of several of Young's books, calling his language "clunky" and "careless" and faulting his bad puns.*

Five years ago an enterprising poet named Kevin Young edited an anthology called *Giant Steps: The New Generation of African American Writers*, which he packed with impressive work by writers such as Hilton Als, Edwidge Danticat and Joe Wood. Young wanted to update The New Negro anthology, that touchstone of the Harlem Renaissance, for the hip-hop generation, and he undertook the project in a spirit of reverence. "I see it as the writer's job, especially the African-American writer's job, not to 'kill the literary father' but rather to celebrate our ancestry," he explained in the book's introduction. It's understandable that Young would not want to look back to the past in anger since, for African-American writers, killing the literary father has often meant getting tangled up in fights over the proper way to "represent the race" (think of James Baldwin's attacks on Richard Wright in "Everybody's Protest Novel" and "Many Thousands Gone"). Young's decision to avoid the zero-sum game of patricide, then, is as much political as aesthetic. In a "post-soul society," Young explains in *Giant Steps*, "the essentialist and often easy answers to questions of race—which have never been easy; just ask Bert Williams or Paul Robeson or Josephine Baker or Muhammad (Ali, that is)—are as complicated as ever. In recognizing the diversity of 'the black experience,' the poets here ask: Where do Shaft and Langston Hughes meet?"

That's a good question, and it raises another: Can Shaft and Langston Hughes be made to meet? In other words, how can Young talk about celebrating one's entire ancestry—let alone knowing it—without resorting to empty provocation? That's not an unreasonable question, especially since

Young knows better. His first book of poems, *Most Way Home*, is an unsentimental portrait of postwar life in the Deep South. A key poem is "The Preserving," and while it concerns the seasonal ritual of canning, it also delicately evokes the complex chemistry involved in any act of preservation:

> One Thanksgiving, while saying grace
> we heard what sounded like a gunshot
> ran to the back porch to see
> peach glass everywhere. Reckon
> someone didn't give the jar enough
> room to breathe.

Young's work as a preservationist has garnered much critical acclaim. In 1993 *Most Way Home* was selected by Lucille Clifton for publication as part of the National Poetry Series. *To Repel Ghosts*, a manic epic about the painter Jean-Michel Basquiat, appeared in 2001 and was named a finalist for the James McLaughlin Prize from the Academy of American Poets. Two years later Young published *Jelly Roll*, a blues-tinged breakup book that was a finalist for the National Book Award—and his first book with a big trade press. It also landed Young on the cover of *Poets & Writers*, which published a profile of him by Colson Whitehead, a contributor to *Giant Steps*.

Young's new book, *Black Maria*, tells another breakup story in verse, this time by reverentially drawing on the wiseguy tones and bleak settings of film noir. But Young's homage to film noir doesn't translate into good poetry. *Black Maria* is a bland mannerist exercise—a remade ready-made. Reading the book, one can't help but wonder if Young's preservationist impulse has spoiled his poetry, and whether the only way for him to reinvigorate his art would be to pack his jars so they explode.

Young's first two books revealed a poet of talent and ambition, though not in the same proportion. *Most Way Home*, which Young wrote when he was an undergraduate, is a short, sturdy collection of lyric poems loosely based on stories passed along by Young's Louisiana relatives. First books by young poets can be dreary, especially if they focus on deceased kin. Usually the poet zeroes in on a fetish object (such as Grandpa's photo album), swaddling it in layers of ambivalent nostalgia and relinquishing it after experiencing a tiny epiphany. Young mostly avoided this trap by writing a personal history that is not explicitly autobiographical. Inspired by Rita Dove's Pulitzer Prize–winning collection of poems *Thomas and Beulah* (1986), in which Dove uses the lives of her grandparents to dramatize the midcentury northern migration of American blacks, Young uses family anecdotes to flesh out a history of deprivation and endurance in the Jim Crow South. Like Dove, Young focuses on the underside of history, the dramas of everyday people circumscribed by big events. The subjects of *Most Way Home* are generic—the seasons, sickness, death—and Young kindles them to life by using the elliptical resources of lyric poetry to score the clipped rhythms of vernacular speech:

> Broke as we were, we didn't need
> fixing. But that autumn the men
> weighed down our porch, sweating
> in their suits, hats-in-hand,
> we answered.

To Repel Ghosts seems like an entirely different kind of book. More than 300 pages long and comprising five sections organized as "album sides," it left behind the shotgun houses and mason jars of the postwar Louisiana countryside for the grubby lofts and cocaine-fueled parties of the New York City art world of the 1980s. The inspiration of *To Repel Ghosts* is Jean-Michel Basquiat, a protean figure of that era's downtown punk and art scenes. Born in Brooklyn in 1960 to a Haitian father and a Puerto Rican mother and dubbed "The Radiant Child" by Rene Ricard in Artforum in 1981, Basquiat painted huge, color-drenched canvases that, at their best, blended contradictory styles and elements—primitive and urbane, image and text—to generate an insouciant pop energy. That energy continues to mesmerize young artists, especially black ones. In his profile of Young, Colson Whitehead recalls lifting some text from a Basquiat painting—PAY FOR SOUP/BUILD A FORT/ SET THAT ON FIRE,—and putting it in his first attempt at a novel "as some graffiti on a wall, but it was so much better than anything else in the book

> "The kind of lackluster wordplay that mars parts of *To Repel Ghosts* is very prominent in *Jelly Roll*, and instead of focusing on the face of disaster, this sloppy language obscures it."

that I had to take it out." Young and Whitehead share more than admiration for Basquiat. Like John Henry, the nineteenth-century steel driver whose legend is the center of Whitehead's novel *John Henry Days*, Basquiat functions not as a character as much as a medium, one through which Young draws the lives of other African-American artists (Billie Holiday, Charlie Parker, Lester Young, Robert Johnson) into a shattered mural of twentieth-century American life.

Yet for all its narrative sprawl, *To Repel Ghosts* closely follows the plot of *Most Way Home*, telling the story of fugitives trying to wrest a sense of place and dignity from a hostile world. The up-from-Jim-Crow story told in *Most Way Home* is framed by the lyric "Reward," a description of two runaway slaves. In the opening pages of *To Repel Ghosts*, we find Jean-Michel Basquiat moving out of his parents' Brooklyn apartment, wallpapering lower Manhattan with graffiti and painting in a dingy basement, which, as Young writes in the book's first poem, Andy Warhol called "a nigger's loft—/not The Factory." Elsewhere Young lambastes art-world glitterati for romanticizing Basquiat as a black primitive: "Intro'd/from the dark/continent—African//Killer B—deadly—" begins "The Pictures," an attack on Julian Schnabel's biopic *Basquiat*.

Young, however, has no qualms about romanticizing Basquiat himself. The second "album side" features a profile of Jack Johnson, the first black heavyweight champion of the world and one of several famous black athletes painted by Basquiat. Young uses the Johnson profile to suggest that the painter admired the boxer because he too was a black man who fought epic battles on canvas. Curiously, while Young portrays Johnson with a series of vivid monologues that convey the boxer's wit, tenderness and pride, none of the poems that focus on Basquiat are monologues; they are all third-person affairs. This could be construed as a commentary on Basquiat's elusiveness, but Young's representation of the painter suggests otherwise. As *To Repel Ghosts* wears on, Basquiat is depicted as a victim of menacing forces (the white, decadent art world) and toxic habits (heroin), and in their grip his life becomes a slow-motion death. Young's Basquiat has no inner demons, let alone interiority, which allows Young to install Basquiat in a romantic pantheon of doped-up hipster superheroes. With Young's reverence of Basquiat comes a lack of curiosity that sometimes reduces the painter to a cliché of degradation.

Still, Young has a keen appreciation of Basquiat's chatty, wry and even cynically neo-primitivist style. Young abandons the colloquial rhythms of *Most Way Home* for tercets made from very short, unrhymed lines that gain an elastic power from being heavily enjambed. Each tercet is a cluster of syncopated phrases that snap past the reader, and as the sounds and images of the tercets tumble together and fly apart, it's as though Young had become locked in a battle royal with Basquiat's busy paintings. From "Defacement (1983)":

> Basquiat scrawls
> & scribbles, clots
> paint across
> the back
> wall of Keith Haring's
> Cable Building studio—
> two cops, keystoned,
> pounding a beat,
> pummel
> a black face-scape
> goat, sarcophagus—
> uniform-blue
> with sticks

Young's tercets aren't consistently lively. Some of his poems have monotonous rhythms, while others are overstuffed with details of Basquiat's life. More debilitating are Young's strained attempts to be witty: "Put out/to pasteur—/Quart cartons//of lost children." This is the sound of a poet growing too pleased with his own words.

"There's always something a little funny in all our disasters," James Baldwin once said, "if one can face the disaster." In *To Repel Ghosts*, Young's romanticization of Basquiat short-circuits a serious reckoning with the wreckage of the painter's life. The kind of lackluster wordplay that mars parts of *To Repel Ghosts* is very prominent in *Jelly Roll*, and instead of focusing on the face of disaster, this sloppy language obscures it. The book is filled with lukewarm puns—"Hottentot to trot//you are not"— and clunky metaphors: "You burn me/at both ends, send//the geese bumping/within my skin."

Even when Young is not trying to be cunning, his language is often careless. "Intermezzo" begins: "Lately I head down/to the river//& watch what washes/past: garbage//boats, tugs, occasional/sail." To say that boats and tugs wash by is not an impossible usage, but in "Intermezzo" it is not apt. The image of garbage washing past makes sense, but how, in that context, can a boat wash past? It's unclear whether this peculiar usage reflects the state of mind of the speaker, who is sorting through a breakup. If the word choice is a sign of the speaker's emotional confusion, then why is the language in the rest of the poem unambiguous?

The blues aren't existential in *Jelly Roll*. Instead of plumbing the tension between the sting of disaster and its solace, many poems in *Jelly Roll* play vamp at the blues. Here's "Cheer," which appears just after the speaker has thrown himself into a passionate affair with a woman:

> I am
> a stadium!
> your cheerleader
> sans underwear
> half-
> time lover
> back door man
> leave your
> little porch light on

Like the poem's speaker, Young's language cries, Look at me, look at me.

Black Maria is an even more disappointing production than *Jelly Roll*. In five sections of lyric poems called "reels," Young tells the noir-inflected saga of A.K.A. Jones, a private dick who drinks and smokes his way through the mazes of a city called Shadowtown in pursuit of an ingenue named Delilah Redbone, a country girl who has moved to the city to sing her way to fame and fortune. As Jones and Redbone elude, seduce and betray each other, they cross paths with a cast of noir types: the Killer, the Boss, the Snitch, the McGuffin.

It's no surprise that Young has gravitated to noir, since the genre can accommodate his passion for pop culture and the blues story of romance and betrayal. But by choosing noir Young has also set himself a tough challenge. Whether they are pop songs or detective flicks, genre productions stand or fall on their style. Because its plot twists, situations and character types are terribly familiar, a genre piece is engrossing only if its style has pungency and vitality, evidence that the writer has temporarily transmuted a genre into his or her own way of thinking.

Young doesn't meet that challenge, and one stumbling point is the plot of *Black Maria*. Filled with wild tangents and shifts in point of view, the narrative is fractured and confusing, a state of affairs meant to echo a bewildering noir story such as *The Big Sleep*. But unlike that film, Black Maria isn't intriguing. Young tries to repair this problem by beginning each "reel" with an epigraph and voiceover that summarize the section's plot, but that device only compounds the book's fractures.

Another weakness is the book's language. Jones's and Redbone's fast-talking monologues are derailed by the same kind of bad puns that fill *Jelly Roll*. "Slant hat, broad/back, my entrenched coat//of fog" is how Jones describes himself when Redbone first saunters into his office. *Black Maria* isn't without a few cutting lines—at one point a jealous Jones mutters, "She made her bed/now everyone lies in it"—but such witty moments can't carry the book.

As with *Jelly Roll*, the longueurs of *Black Maria* aren't necessarily the result of carelessness. Rather, they signal that Young's preoccupation with looking back in reverence has become paralyzing instead of fructifying. In a sense, each of Young's four poetry collections has been a debut book, with the poet venerating a genre (family melodrama, the blues, film noir) or an iconic personality (Basquiat) steeped in cultural history. Basquiat himself painted tributes to jazz musicians and other black figures, but in those portraits he also treated his subjects ironically. He knew that the difference between reference and reverence amounts to more than one consonant, which is why his romps through various styles and genres were more antic than innocuous. Kevin Young grasped that lesson in *To Repel Ghosts*, even if he didn't perfect it. The only mystery left unsolved in *Black Maria* is why he has forgotten it.

Source: John Palattella, Review of *Jelly Roll: A Blues*, in *Nation*, Vol. 280, No. 18, May 9, 2005, pp. 28–31.

Brian Phillips

In the following review, Phillips calls into question Young's easy, fanlike devotion to blues music in these poems and faults him for overuse of slang but praises his "gift for wordplay" and ear for sound.

The subtitle of this plump and play-acting new book declares it *A Blues*, "composed and arranged" (as we learn on the title page) "by Kevin Young." There is a long epigraph from Robert Johnson's "Kind-Hearted Woman Blues," next to which a picture of Johnson's head has been left jauntily floating, a piece of unhallowed clip-art. Thus the book declares its fidelity to the tradition of the blues. But through 190 pages, these poems are rarely more than a fan's eager notes, a sophisticate's predilections.

On the page Young's poems look minimal, thin couplets in a field of white space, but this long book is a surfeit of its own technique; Young seems to have left nothing out. Even in its many poems on heartbreak, this work flashes the easy grin of a writer being generous with himself:

Young often reverts to an affected dialect ("everythang," "Dear, I needs") when he wants to be winning; here, the clownishness is used to forestall any judgment of his famine metaphor's questionable taste. Elsewhere in the book dialect simply pinch-hits for poetic effort, as in these lines from "Disaster Movie Theme Music":

> By the time I got
> to mom'n thems
> Heard tell you
> were a-ready lost

But surely this is imitation, mere strategic typography: this is not Young's voice. Any book subtitled *A Blues* is likely to include blues slang; but when the Harvard-educated Young calls a sexual partner "Rider," the effect is decidedly uncomfortable. The word sounds more natural coming from the Rolling Stones.

Young is a talented writer, with a poet's gift for wordplay and an ear for the sounds words make, and when he leaves behind his blues mimicry he is capable of genuinely affecting work—when he describes being pulled over by the police at night, "their bright // lights making me / mole" ; or in the opening lines of "Busking," in which a chilly urban sunset is described as money falling in the case of a street musician:

> The day folds up like money
> if you're lucky. Mostly
> sun a cold coin
> drumming into the blue
> of a guitar case.

This is striking, and suggests that Young is capable of better work than the soft indulgence of most of his present collection. Successful poets, as Yeats assured Joyce, have had worse beginnings.

To achieve his promise, I suspect that Young will have to give up a certain theoretical attitude he has taken up toward "African-American experience"—specifically, that it can only be addressed in terms of popular music and archetypes from the past. Young has made this argument at some length in his prose work, and it is central to the project of these poems. But the need to engraft an approved cultural paradigm onto the expression of one's experience in art is dangerous to a lyric poet. The danger is that it will excuse the kind of aesthetic laziness also visible in some of Langsten Hughes's blues-inspired verse, and sometimes risked by Yeats, in which one writes down to the "authenticity" of a tradition one is intellectually or experientially beyond. Young has based his last three books on the pretense that they are really records. It may be time for him to look to a literary past, and to his own experience, and admit to writing poetry. After all, the blues depend on adapting a set of sung lyrics to a highly formal musical pattern that has no poetic equivalent. Lyric poetry depends on finding a means of written expression in language which is equal to one's mind.

Source: Brian Phillips, Review of *Jelly Roll: A Blues*, in *Poetry*, Vol. 183, No. 5, February 2004, pp. 299–301.

Fred Muratori

In the following review, Muratori notes the musical rhythms and references, coupled with a "literary sensibility," in Young's third book of poetry.

Though you won't find any musical notation in Young's third poetry collection, it's clear that the rhythms of traditional Delta and urban blues form the lattice against which these tightly spun lyrics, most written in couplets, are set. Young understands the blues as an effective medium for seduction and praise, yearning and loss, and while *Jelly Roll* pays homage to the traditional stylings of Robert Johnson and other seminal blues artists, its wry sense of humor ("Hottentot to trot/you are not"), elliptically paced rhymes (past/path, air/stares), and associative freedom, ("You are some sort/ of September// I look for your red car everywhere") evince a sophisticated, contemporary literary sensibility that never compromises the characteristic directness of the form. Young minimizes sexual swagger, preferring instead to explore the hazardous dimensions of emotional commitment with gritty grace and disarming candor ("Woman, knock me down,/ out, anoint—// just don't leave me lone// like God/done, promising return"). While the collection's extended length might work against the economy of its individual poems, Young's achievement is nonetheless admirable, attesting to both the resilience of the blues and the skill of its talented practitioner.

Source: Fred Muratori, Review of *Jelly Roll: A Blues*, in *Library Journal*, Vol. 128, No. 1, January 2003, p. 116.

Bowker Magazine Group

In the following review, the writer points to the vast range of musical genres from which Young has borrowed—from Dixieland to calypso to classical—and shows how Young matches his poems' subject and words with his musical choices.

The careful, colloquial, lyrical *Most Way Home* (1995) established Young among the best-known poets of his emerging generation; this third book will satisfy many readers' long-held hopes. Despite the title, Young's new work relies not just on blues but on a plethora of musical genres; poems (almost all in short, two-line stanzas) take their titles and sometimes their sounds from older popular genres ("Dixieland" "Ragtime" and "Calypso") and classical forms ("Scherzo," "Nocturne"), bringing things up to date with "Disaster Movie Theme Music." Young matches these various models with a unity of subject: like an old-fashioned sonnet sequence writ large, the book chronicles the start, progress, and catastrophic end of a love affair. Early on, poems like "Shimmy" describe the birth of passion: "You are, lady,/admired—secret//something kept/afar." In "Riff," Young comes up with a precise, slow-motion polyphony: "I am all itch,/total, since you done//been gone-zero/sum, empty set." Despite the self-imposed, consistent limit of short lines, the verse here shows Young to be not only a terrific love poet but one of real emotional variety: after a sonnet sequence (called "Sleepwalking Psalms") Young turns from excitement and romance to disillusion, breakups and regrets ("Joy is the mile-/high ledge"), concluding with poems addressed to landscapes, and with an elegy for a dead male friend. Young has daringly likened himself in earlier poems and prose to Langston Hughes: this versatile lyric tour de force may well justify the ambitious comparison.

Forecast:While Young gained a reputation with poems in journals (and with his anthology *Giant Steps*), his sophomore effort *To Repel Ghosts*, a narrative poem about Jean-Michel Basquiat, was not quite a breakthrough, especially as its publisher went under. This long but reader-friendly third collection should do far better; expect strong reviews nationwide.

Source: Bowker Magazine Group, Review of *Jelly Roll: A Blues*, in *Publishers Weekly*, Vol. 249, No. 47, November 25, 2002, p. 58.

Sources

Freud, Sigmund, *The Future of an Illusion*, W. W. Norton, 1961, pp. 24, 30.

Hoffert, Barbara, "Best Poetry of 2003: Ten Titles, Four Collections from Major Poets, and Four Anthologies," in *Library Journal*, Vol. 129, No. 7, April 15, 2004, pp. 88–89.

Jarman, Mark, "A Life on the Page," in the *Hudson Review*, Vol. 56, No. 2, Summer 2003, pp. 367–68.

Muratori, Fred, Review of *Jelly Roll: A Blues*, in *Library Journal*, Vol. 128, No. 1, January 2003, p. 116.

Okoro, Dike, "Healing Mother Africa: Contemporary African Poets Explore New Rhythms and Themes," in *Black Issues Book Review*, Vol. 5, No. 5, September–October 2003, pp. 32–34.

Phillips, Brian, "Ten Takes," in *Poetry*, Vol. 183, No. 5, February 2004, pp. 290–302.

Review of *Jelly Roll: A Blues*, in *Publishers Weekly*, Vol. 249, No. 47, November 25, 2002, pp. 58–59.

Young, Kevin, "The Black Psychic Hotline, or The Future of African American Writing," in *Giant Steps: The New Generation of African American Writers*, edited by Kevin Young, Perennial, 2000, pp. 7–8.

———, "Chorale," in *Jelly Roll: A Blues*, Alfred A. Knopf, 2003, p. 114.

———, *Jelly Roll: A Blues*, Alfred A. Knopf, 2003, pp. 111, 115, 116, 118, 177.

———, "Poet of the Month: Kevin Young," on *PoetryNet*, May 2003, available online at http://members.aol.com/poetrynet/month/archive/young/index.html.

Young, Kevin, and Ernest Hilbert, "A Conversation with Kevin Young," in *Bold Type*, Vol. 6, No. 11, available online at http://www.randomhouse.com/boldtype/0403/poetry/young_interview.html.

Further Reading

George, Nelson, *Post-Soul Nation: The Explosive, Contradictory, Triumphant, and Tragic 1980s as Experienced by African Americans (Previously Known as Blacks and before That Negroes)*, Viking, 2004.
   George characterizes the era that was the 1980s in terms of the African American experience, with extensive reference to a wide variety of aspects of popular culture, including music, television, and literature.

Komunyakaa, Yusef, *Blue Notes: Essays, Interviews, and Commentaries*, University of Michigan Press, 2000.
   This text offers a sampling of writings by Komunyakaa (to whom Young has been compared) with respect to his influences, his own poetry, and his artistic sensibilities.

Wald, Elijah, *Escaping the Delta: Robert Johnson and the Invention of Blues*, Amistad, 2004.
   This historical work examines in extensive detail the inception of the blues and offers a short biography of Robert Johnson, one of the genre's most influential figures.

Young, Kevin, ed., *Blues Poems*, Knopf, 2003.
   This collection offers a variety of poems, selected by Young, that can be considered influential to or exemplary of blues poetry, by such authors as Langston Hughes, Gwendolyn Brooks, and Allen Ginsberg.

The Cossacks

Linda Pastan

2002

Linda Pastan's poem "The Cossacks" appears in her 2002 collection titled *The Last Uncle*. Although Pastan is generally associated with poetry related to domesticity and personal experience, her later poetry often considers themes of aging, mortality, and the reality of death. "The Cossacks" contains these themes, but the poem is somewhat unusual in her canon of work because it is presented as a poem about her Jewish heritage. In the poem, she gives voice to what she describes as an aspect of Jewish thinking. She describes the tendency to focus on the negative or to assume that the worst is ahead, admitting a fear and deep pessimism in her own thinking. In contrast, her mother and F. (to whom the poem is dedicated) handle crises with serenity. Pastan touches on the theme of social masks to explain the difference between the two figures facing their own mortality; her mother pretended to be calm, but F. was genuinely calm. Ultimately, the speaker longs for the latter, but her own nature resists it.

Historically, the Cossacks to whom Pastan refers were groups of mercenaries who lived along the Russian border. Cossacks first appeared as a people in the fifteenth century, in the form of loosely organized, but related communities. By the sixteenth century, these groups had coalesced into two major groupings, one in the Ukraine and the other on the river Don bordering the Grand Duchy of Moscow. In the late nineteenth century, the Cossack men who served the czar had become active in suppressing rebellion and massacring Jews.

Because of their violence and aggression toward Jews, Pastan uses them as figures of hostility and danger in "The Cossacks." The poem opens with the statement that they are always coming, and it ends with the sound of horses approaching, which the reader can imagine are those of the Cossacks. It is an effective image that infuses the poem with a sense of impending danger. Pastan is known for her affinity for metaphor and imagery, and both of those devices are in full force in this poem. The danger associated with the Cossacks is brought to life with imagery, but the Cossacks are actually a metaphor for death.

Author Biography

Linda Olenik Pastan was born on May 27, 1932, in New York City. Her interest in writing poetry emerged when she was only ten or eleven years old, but she did not anticipate pursuing a career as a writer. In 1953, she married Ira Pastan, a molecular biologist, and the couple had two sons and a daughter. Pastan graduated in 1954 with a bachelor of arts from Radcliffe College. In 1955, she earned a master of library science from Simmons College, and in 1957 she received a master of arts from Brandeis University. Although she did not study writing formally, she continued to work at it and to seek improvement of her writing skills. She won the first of many poetry awards in 1958, when at age twenty-six she received the *Mademoiselle* Dylan Thomas Poetry Award. The noted American poet Sylvia Plath came in second. Among Pastan's other awards and honors are a National Endowment for the Arts fellowship (1972), a Bread Loaf Writers Conference fellowship (1974), the Poetry Society of America's De Castagnola Award (1978), the Ruth Lilly Poetry Prize (2003), and a Pushcart Prize. She held the position of poet laureate of Maryland from 1991 to 1995. Her first book, *A Perfect Circle of Sun*, was published in 1971. From 1971 to 2005, she published fourteen more volumes. Two of her books, *PM/AM: New and Selected Poems* (1983) and *Carnival Evening: New and Selected Poems, 1968–1998* (1998), were nominated for the National Book Award. Pastan's 2002 collection, *The Last Uncle*, contains the poem "The Cossacks."

Despite her interest in and talent for writing poetry and the early recognition of her work, Pastan set aside any career ambitions to fulfill

Linda Pastan © Photograph by Oliver Pastan. Reproduced by permission

her roles as a wife and mother, accepting the traditional duties of housekeeper consistent with the expectations of women in the 1950s. Still, her poetic voice remained active, and Pastan wrote poetry about domesticity, motherhood, children, seasons, and marital struggle. She is known for her spare and accessible style, and she often introduces metaphors and imagery that add depth to her treatment of her subjects. Although Pastan's themes generally center on domestic life and on her personal experiences, her poetry explores family relationships, maternal musings, and domestic frustration without becoming overly emotional or sentimental. While Pastan writes about the balance of power and dependence in marriage, she does so without a feminist agenda. In her early poetry, she presents an honest portrayal of her domestic life, defending it as difficult and challenging. In her later poetry, Pastan focuses on the themes of aging and mortality. Her poetry has been compared to that of Emily Dickinson, Edgar Allan Poe, and Walt Whitman. Such comparisons point to her strong poetic voice, her consistent vision, and her distinctly American point of view.

Poem Text

For Jews, the Cossacks are always coming.
Therefore I think the sun spot on my arm
is melanoma. Therefore I celebrate
New Year's Eve by counting
my annual dead.   5

My mother, when she was dying,
spoke to her visitors of books
and travel, displaying serenity
as a form of manners, though
I could tell the difference.   10

But when I watched you planning
for a life you knew
you'd never have, I couldn't explain
your genuine smile in the face
of disaster. Was it denial   15

laced with acceptance? Or was it
generations of being English—
Brontë's Lucy, in *Villette*
living as if no fire raged
beneath her dun-colored dress.   20

I want to live the way you did,
preparing for next year's famine with wine
and music as if it were a ten-course banquet.
But listen: those hoofbeats
on the frosty autumn air.   25

Poem Summary

Lines 1–5

"The Cossacks" is composed of five five-line stanzas (cinquains) written in free verse, or verse without a set rhyme pattern or meter. The first stanza opens with the statement that to Jews, hostility and danger are always around the corner. The speaker asserts that "the Cossacks are always coming," referring to the mercenary group that massacred Russian Jews in the nineteenth century. She generalizes her own fear and pessimism by claiming that her mind-set is common among Jews. Because of that tendency to assume the worst, she assumes that a spot on her arm is cancer. Also because of that tendency, she spends the last evening before the new year listing everyone who has died in that year, rather than reflecting on the promise and excitement of what is ahead of her. This first stanza introduces the themes of pessimism and death. The speaker's backward thinking is evident in Pastan's use of oxymoron when she writes that she "celebrate[s]" by "counting / my annual dead."

Lines 6–10

In the second stanza, the speaker recalls her mother's final days. Knowing that she was going to die, her mother entertained visitors with small talk. Pastan paints a picture of social awkwardness through the image of visitors coming to see a dying woman, perhaps to say their last goodbyes and ask if they can do anything at all to give her peace and instead finding themselves engaged in talk about books and past travels. The speaker interprets her mother's behavior as showing "serenity" and "manners." She suspects, however, that her mother was just pretending to be serene and was looking for security in artificial manners rather than choosing to be genuine and honest with her visitors. Because the speaker knew her mother so well, she says that she "could tell the difference."

Lines 11–15

The third stanza opens with a telling "But," which indicates a turn in the speaker's thought process. In this stanza, she recalls the way someone else handles herself in the face of her own mortality. Interestingly, the speaker addresses this person directly, even though the poem indicates that the person has died. The speaker does not give a name or relationship, referring to the person only as F., to whom the poem is dedicated. What is striking to the speaker is how F. conducted herself, planning for the future despite her knowledge that she had no future. She remained optimistic and hopeful to the very end, but with calm instead of desperation. When the speaker says, "I couldn't explain / your genuine smile in the face / of disaster," she reveals the fundamental difference between herself and F. While F. has a genuine smile, the speaker sees only the disaster. Clearly, F. did not view her situation as one of disaster. The stanza ends with an incomplete question that is finished in the next stanza. This break suggests a pause in the speaker's thinking. She ends one stanza with "Was it denial" (her first assumption), and begins the next with "laced with acceptance?" (her thoughtful conclusion).

Lines 16–20

The fourth stanza explores more deeply the theme of social masks. The speaker wonders whether F.'s ability to remain peaceful can be attributed to her English heritage, with the idea that the English are very reserved. Pastan draws in a literary allusion to Charlotte Brontë's novel *Villette*, in which a young woman, Lucy, hides her strong emotions. Pastan reinforces the theme of social masks in the contrast she sets up between the emotional "fire" and the "dun-colored dress." The brightness of Lucy's emotions remains completely hidden by the dull neutrality of her outer appearance. Similarly, the speaker wonders whether F.'s emotional turmoil was hidden by a calm appearance.

Lines 21–25

As is evident in the final stanza, the speaker concludes that F.'s peaceful countenance was genuine. The speaker tells F., "I want to live the way you did," meaning that she wants to find a way to be genuinely optimistic and peaceful about whatever happens in her life. She likens F. in her final days to someone who disregards next year's famine and lays out a lavish banquet of food and wine. The speaker, however, cannot change her nature. Even as she describes the banquet, she is interrupted by the perception of hearing the Cossacks coming. In the last two lines, she writes, "But listen: those are hoofbeats / on the frosty autumn air." Again, the poem turns on the word "but," and the tone changes completely. The hoofbeats might be those of the Cossacks' horses, indicating that the speaker is unable to surrender fully to the fantasy of living as F. lived. The danger, real or perceived, is always a few steps behind her.

Themes

Pessimism

The speaker in "The Cossacks" is a pessimistic person, a fact she reveals in the first stanza. The first line describes her feeling that demise is always on the way. While she makes this statement as a comment about the Jewish community from which she comes, the poem is really about her own feeling that the worst awaits her. Perhaps she feels comfort or justification in her feelings by being part of a collective mind-set, which is why she claims that her pessimism is part of her culture. Regardless of why she feels the way she does, her grim outlook on life shapes her experience of life. Most of the first stanza describes that experience; she assumes that a spot on her own arm is the beginning of cancer, and she chooses to spend New Year's Eve totaling up the people who died that year instead of planning for a wonderful new year ahead. Thoughts of death pervade her thinking, and she sees death as a menacing and violent hunter.

The speaker's pessimism also shapes the way she sees other people. In the second stanza, she discusses her mother's final days as death approached. Because she knew her mother so well, she feels confident in saying that the manners her mother exhibited to visitors were merely covering her real feelings. In the third stanza, she wonders whether her friend adopted the same strategy. She wonders whether her friend's serenity in her final days was denial or repressed feelings. Because the speaker holds such a pessimistic view of death, she interprets other people's experience through that lens. Even at the end of the poem, when she claims to want to embrace optimism and hope, she cannot help but feel the impending doom of death.

Social Masks

In describing her mother's death, the speaker recalls visitors coming and being greeted by superficial chat about books and vacation destinations. The speaker says her mother displayed "serenity / as a form of manners." Rather than engage visitors in meaningful ways that might give them closure and peace, her mother prefers the safety of small talk. She does not want to show the emotions—fear, regret, uncertainty, or sadness—that would be expected at such a time. What is particularly interesting about her mother is that she has nothing to lose in being honest with her friends and family at this time. She is facing death, so there would be no consequences of sharing her true feelings with them, yet she chooses to remain confined within the comfort and familiarity of idle chat. Her social mask seems to be such a part of her personality that, even in her final hours, she cannot remove it.

In contrast, F. has no use for a social mask because, in her final hours, she has genuine peace. She makes plans for a future that will include her, perhaps for the benefit of those who will carry on without her. F. chooses to spend her time engaged in something meaningful, even if her plans will not be fulfilled. Perhaps F. is playing out important "what if" scenarios, or perhaps she is letting her friends and family know that she expects them to continue living satisfying lives without her. Whatever her reasons, she occupies her final days with something more meaningful than shallow discussions of books and travel, as the speaker's mother chose to do. The speaker can tell the difference between her mother and F., even though they both show serenity in their times of crises. The reader can assume that the speaker has this insight because

Topics For Further Study

- In "The Cossacks," Pastan uses Cossacks as an effective metaphor for death. What would you choose as a metaphor for death? Think of something that is specific to your experience, background, or feelings so that the metaphor will be uniquely yours. Write a poem developing your metaphor.

- In "The Cossacks," the speaker refers to denial and acceptance, two of the five stages of grief. One of Pastan's previous collections, *The Five Stages of Grief* (1978), is arranged to parallel the five stages of grief described by Elisabeth Kübler-Ross in *On Death and Dying*. Research *On Death and Dying* or Kübler-Ross's *On Grief and Grieving* to better understand the five stages a person goes through when faced with death. Take into account not just the person who is dying but also the loved ones who are preparing for their own loss. Write an essay about what you have learned.

- Everyone has worn a social mask at some time, whether to get through a life-and-death crisis, to deal with peer pressure, or to fulfill someone else's set of expectations. Recall a time when you felt it necessary to wear a social mask. Write a brief script in which you retell the experience of that time, putting your true thoughts and feelings in italics or as asides in parentheses to the audience.

- Based on your reading and interpretation of "The Cossacks," how do you think the speaker will handle her own death when her time comes? In the poem, her feelings are conflicted as she struggles against her own nature. Do you think she will be like her mother, like F., or different from both of them? Lead a group discussion on the topic, and be sure to support your arguments with excerpts from the poem.

- Find a plot summary and character profile for Charlotte Brontë's novel *Villette*. Which of the three women in "The Cossacks" (the mother, F., or the speaker) do you think is most like Brontë's Lucy? Which do you think is least like her? Is there any commonality among the four? Write up your conclusions in an essay, or create a chart or poster showing the similarities and differences you have found among the characters.

---

she, too, struggles with her own social mask, but her awareness of it (as evident in the poem) indicates her desire to live without it.

Style

Metaphor

Known for her use of metaphor, Pastan uses powerful images in "The Cossacks" to portray death. The dominant metaphor in the poem is the representation of the Cossacks as death itself. It is a particularly strong metaphor because it reveals precisely how the speaker views death. Death has been portrayed in numerous ways by poets, and while others may see it variously as a peaceful figure, a welcome figure, or even a worthy adversary, Pastan's speaker views death as a ruthless mercenary who actively pursues her. Because Pastan refers to her own Judaic background in the first line, the image of the Cossacks adds an element of terror. The Cossacks massacred Russian Jews in the nineteenth century, so they represent cruelty and persecution to Pastan and her speaker. In the first line, the speaker states, "For Jews, the Cossacks are always coming." She immediately describes assuming that she has melanoma and her activity of counting the dead. Both of these are, in the speaker's mind, examples of the Cossacks who are coming or have already come. Pastan brings the poem full circle when, in the last two lines, she writes, "But listen: those are hoofbeats / on the frosty autumn air." This essentially restates the first line and gives the metaphor another level of panic. By demanding that the reader listen and feel the cold air, using the senses to reinforce the metaphor, Pastan adds drama to the reader's experience of the poem. The final lines have an ominous feel, and the speaker seems to be warning the reader against deadly danger.

In the last stanza, Pastan introduces another metaphor in which she describes death as an imminent famine. She admires F. for the way she planned for the famine by having a sumptuous banquet, complete with wine and music. It is an image of celebration and carefree delight, rather than sorrow and dread. The metaphor of death as a famine is effective, as it portrays the nothingness of death and the emptiness felt by the surviving loved ones. The counterbalance of that metaphor with one of a banquet gives the reader a concise illustration of F.'s response to the realization of her own death. She chose to live fully the rest of the time she had left, and that is what the speaker struggles to be able to do.

Symbolism

Just as Pastan uses imagery to reinforce metaphor, she uses imagery to give dimension to symbolism in "The Cossacks." The dark spot on her skin brings the speaker to assume that she has cancer, which provides important insight into the speaker's thinking. These spots, made by the sun, stand for the everyday occurrences that seem harmless to many people but represent death to the speaker. When her mother lies dying, she speaks of "books / and travel" with her visitors. Books symbolize secondhand knowledge or escapist experience, and travel represents firsthand knowledge through experience. In her final days, the mother discusses on a superficial level things that are knowable, rather than revealing her emotions or sharing reflections on her life. In the fourth stanza, Pastan alludes to Charlotte Brontë's novel *Villette* and the main character, Lucy, who could control the expression of her own strong feelings. Lucy makes the choice to wear a social mask and to control feelings rather than be controlled by feelings, and her character represents this choice. Pastan ends her poem with a line rich in symbolism. She writes that the "hoofbeats / on the frosty autumn air" can be heard. Cold often signifies harshness and lack of emotion, and autumn is highly symbolic as a season when living things lose their color and lushness and seem to die.

Historical Context

Jewish American Literature

The field of Jewish American literature as an area of academic study began to take shape in the twentieth century. Literary scholars who study the work of Jewish writers have focused more on the careers of playwrights such as Arthur Miller and novelists such as J. D. Salinger (whose father was Jewish), Norman Mailer, Saul Bellow, and Philip Roth. To a more limited extent, poets (most notably, Allen Ginsberg and Karl Shapiro) have received a degree of critical and scholarly attention in this field. There is no doubt that the contributions of Jewish writers have shaped American literature in important ways. Among the best-known writers are Woody Allen, Isaac Asimov, Paul Auster, Judy Blume, Betty Friedan, Joseph Heller, E. L. Doctorow, and Harold Bloom.

Many scholars of Jewish American literature examine questions of Jewish identity as it pertains to living in America and look at the ways in which the long-standing traditions of the faith and culture survive in this country. As the field grows, scholars are also exploring such aspects of the culture as linguistics, religion, politics, and social issues. In looking at the works of Jewish writers across genres and circumstances, scholars note certain themes that seem to characterize this body of work, including violence, intergenerational struggle, and guilt.

Cossacks

Derived from the Turkic word *kazak*, the word *Cossack* means "free-booter" or "vagabond." The original Cossacks formed settlements in the Don region of Russia during the fifteenth century as groups of mercenaries and fugitives looking for a place to escape the reach of authority. The largest group was always the Don Cossacks, but other groups (Zaporozhian Cossacks, Terek Cossacks, and others) formed as well. Most of the Cossacks were of Russian descent, with some having Turkic or Kalmyk roots.

Although the Cossacks retained territorial and political autonomy, they eventually forged a relationship with the Russian government to act as a military group in exchange for needed goods and money. In this capacity, they helped defend the Russian border and carry out various military objectives. During the seventeenth century, the government tried to tighten control and even asked that fugitives be returned. The Cossacks saw these attempts to assert authority over them as an affront. This event put distance in the relationship between the government and the Cossacks until 1738, when the Don Cossacks' chief commander was no longer elected but was appointed by the Russian government. This led to a series of events that ultimately

Dancers with the Russian Cossack State Song and Dance Ensemble rehearse on February 27, 2002, in the Peacock Theatre in London © Sion Touhig/Getty Images

resulted in the Cossacks' becoming part of the Russian military proper. By the turn of the century, Cossacks had equal military ranking within the Russian army. Military service was a way of life; enlisted Cossacks served a thirty-year term until 1875, when the term was reduced to twenty years. Young Cossack men were sworn into service as a group, and discipline was harsh.

The Cossacks were notorious for their willingness to wield power to its fullest extent. The Russian government assigned them to crush rebellion and slaughter Jews during pogroms. Fifty-seven regiments served in World War I, but the twentieth century saw the relationship between the government and the Cossacks deteriorate. By World War II, they were outdated and disbanded.

As a people, the Cossacks were rugged and strict. They originally supported themselves through fishing, hunting, animal husbandry, and collecting loot from their raids. Their relationship with the government enabled them to earn cash, grain, liquor, and weaponry. In the eighteenth century, they added agriculture to their economy. While their religion was Russian Orthodoxy, they incorporated folklore and superstition into religious tradition. Military heroics were very important to the Cossacks, and they kept the stories of heroism alive through the oral tradition. When they celebrated with singing and dancing, they usually sang about battles.

Critical Overview

Over the course of her lengthy career, which began in the late 1950s, Pastan has earned a loyal following of readers and critics alike. For her exalting of domestic subjects and her spare style, she has been compared to Emily Dickinson. For her appreciation of nature, its character, and its relationship to people, she has been compared to Walt Whitman. And for her psychological insights, she has been compared to Edgar Allan Poe. In *Contemporary Poets*, Jay S. Paul remarks, "Like Poe, Pastan has been conscious of the limits of the mind and the impossibility of exceeding them." Paul also notes that Pastan's perspective is of someone who is very aware of her own human fallibility. He writes that she "has long seen herself as Eve—one of the fallen." Paul praises the fact that Pastan's "vision has been consistent throughout her books." In *Dictionary of Literary Biography*, Benjamin Franklin V notes that Pastan's "ability to create memorable images and her penchant for examining life's unpleasant emotions" have been characteristic of her poetry since her first collection, *A Perfect Circle of Sun*. When Pastan won the 2003 Ruth Lilly Poetry Prize, one of the most lucrative prizes awarded to American poets, the staff of *Poetry* extended its congratulations to her, "thanking her for her consistently excellent contributions to American poetry over four decades."

Critics praise *The Last Uncle*, in which "The Cossacks" appears. A *Publishers Weekly* reviewer commends her "fluent, accessible lyric seriousness, finding in seasonal and domestic properties . . . signs of mortality, gratitude, and wonder." *Library Journal*'s Louis McKee writes, "Pastan has done a good job of turning our attention to what really matters. . . . Pastan's poems are always worthy of our attention." The themes portrayed in "The Cossacks" are among those that critics have long appreciated in Pastan's work. Franklin comments, "Pastan frequently observes that pleasing exteriors conceal death's roots," a prevailing message in "The Cossacks." In his concluding comments on Pastan's career, Franklin writes, "Pastan deserves serious attention for her finely wrought dark comments on the human condition. Not spectacular, she is a solid poet whose work speaks to all of mankind. Her verse will endure."

Criticism

Jennifer Bussey

Bussey is an independent writer specializing in literature. In the following essay, she discusses Pastan's poem "The Cossacks" with emphasis on the speaker's preoccupation with death.

Pastan's poem "The Cossacks" conveys images of mercenaries, small talk, manners, final days, strong emotions, a plain dress, a banquet, and a crisp autumn day. It is evidence of Pastan's skill as a poet that these wide-ranging images and ideas converge to give unified insight into the speaker's preoccupation with death. The speaker sees death not as the peaceful and inevitable end of a person's life but as a cruel enemy constantly on the hunt for her. Because the speaker's voice has such depth and is so well developed, the various images form

> *It is evidence of Pastan's skill as a poet that these wide-ranging images and ideas converge to form a unified insight into the speaker's preoccupation with death."*

a unified message of fear. In less accomplished hands, such differing thoughts and images would result in confusion, but in Pastan's hands, each line creates a voice that is consistent, believable, and sympathy-evoking. In fact, the voice is so consistent that even when the speaker tries to embrace a new way of relating to death, her deep-seated fear resurfaces.

The speaker addresses F. (to whom the poem is dedicated) directly, as if she were still alive, yet the reader knows by the end of the poem that F. has died. So, from the beginning of the poem, the speaker is grappling with death; she is addressing someone she has already grieved. Perhaps this expression as poetry is part of her grieving process. Her motivation for expressing these thoughts is never made clear, nor is it at all apparent how much time has passed since she lost F. The speaker's matter-of-fact tone indicates that she has gone through the most immediate, painful stages of grief, so it is reasonable to assume that she has arrived at a point where she can analyze F.'s death. It is clear from the progression of the poem that the speaker wants to learn from F.'s graceful acceptance of death. She does not understand F.'s fearless and peaceful response to what she herself sees as terror and tragedy, but she sees clearly enough to understand that she wants to change this aspect of herself. She wants to be able to disarm death with a genuine smile, as F. did.

The speaker opens the poem with an ominous statement: "For Jews, the Cossacks are always coming." The Cossacks the speaker refers to were a military group of Russian mercenaries who asserted their power by putting down rebellion, massacring Jews, and carrying out other acts of extreme force. Given the history of the Cossacks and the

Jews, the poem's opening statement reveals the speaker's sense of powerlessness and terror. It soon becomes apparent that the Cossacks are a metaphor for death, which makes the first line even more revealing. The speaker feels that she is constantly being sought by death, and she sees death as an active force that is cruel and emotionless. While the speaker claims that Jews in general are treated this way by death, or at least feel that they are, what is really at stake in the poem is the speaker's individual preoccupation. She might not need to question her preoccupation if she can convince herself that it is merely a cultural inheritance, but regardless of its origins it haunts her.

By the second line, the speaker is talking about herself directly. Her preoccupation with death is evident in that she mentions death on every other line of the first stanza. "Cossacks" refers to death itself, "melanoma" refers to a possible carrier of death, and "annual dead" refers to those who have already succumbed to death in the preceding year. In the speaker's mind, death is all around her. It is as far away as the spirits of those who have died, and it is as near as her own arm. The speaker's twisted thinking about death is expressed in the oxymoron of celebrating a holiday by counting how many people she knows who have died over the course of the preceding year. Either she means this sarcastically, or she means it as celebration of the fact that they were the ones who died, not her.

In the second stanza, the speaker recalls the way her mother handled her crisis of death and contrasts it with the way F. did. Both women knew they were dying, and both seemed to accept death with grace and serenity. Because the speaker was close to both of them, however, she knows that the truths of the two women were very different. She knows that her mother only pretended to be peaceful and accepting, preferring manners and niceties to moments of intensity and honesty with the people she loved. Her mother seems to have chosen to behave according to a code of manners as much for the comfort of her visitors as for herself. The reader cannot help but wonder, however, whether the visitors would not have preferred to connect at a deeper level than the speaker's mother allowed. In her mother, the speaker sees the same fear she herself feels. Why would her mother put on such an artificial countenance if the truth were not too terrifying to accept? The speaker sees through her mother's act, but she does not judge her for it.

In contrast to her mother, the speaker recalls, in the third stanza, the genuine peacefulness that F. displayed during her time of crisis. She remembers watching F. plan for a future that would never come and embrace life fully to the very end. The speaker admits that this response to death confused her: "I couldn't explain / your genuine smile in the face / of disaster." Her lack of understanding derives from the fact that "disaster" is in the eye of the beholder. The speaker sees everything related to death as the ultimate disaster, but F. clearly did not see it in the same way. Although it was F.'s death, it was actually the speaker's disaster. This is why she could not explain the genuine smile or the planning for the future. The speaker cannot help but wonder if the smile might not have been an outward sign of some kind of denial, but, as she moves into the fourth stanza, she entertains the idea that F. may have reached acceptance. When she wonders whether F. was actually hiding strong feelings, like Lucy in Charlotte Brontë's *Villette*, she knows better. What is unsaid is that the social mask she remembers from *Villette* is actually the type worn by her mother.

The speaker seems to have a sense that people understand crisis as their ancestors did. She aligns her fear of death with her Judaism, and in the fourth stanza she considers F.'s controlled emotion as a possible result of her "generations of being English." This provides an important insight into the speaker, because it suggests that she does not feel responsible for her own feelings about death but believes that they are an inescapable part of her culture. She clearly feels a strong connection to her heritage, but in the fifth stanza, she seems prepared to forge her own path.

In the fifth and last stanza, the speaker decides that she would rather face death as F. did rather than as her own mother did. This will not be an easy task, given that the speaker identifies with her mother's fear of death so readily. She has a high level of self-knowledge that includes cultural self-knowledge, but she wants to choose better for herself so that she can approach death with contentment and genuine serenity. She sees death as an inevitable famine (another disaster image), but she deeply admires the way F. disregarded disaster and held the metaphorical equivalent of a lavish banquet. This is an actual celebratory image that overpowers the false celebration of New Year's Eve in the first stanza. The banquet is almost tangible to the speaker; she can see that there is wine, music, and ten courses. It is an inviting image in which the speaker longs to participate. But equally tangible to her is the threatening sound of hoofbeats. Are these the Cossacks approaching? The thumping of the hoofbeats could very well be the speaker's own heartbeat quickening again at the thought of actually facing death. She knows death is coming, and her pessimism drives her to assume that it is coming soon. She is not prepared for it, and she is not ready to accept or embrace it. This is a pivotal moment for the speaker. Her conflict has peaked. She has to choose whether to surrender to her own nature and continue to live in fear, looking over her shoulder for death, or to fight her nature, assert her will, and strive to be like F. The poem ends here, and Pastan leaves the reader to speculate on the speaker's choice.

Source: Jennifer Bussey, Critical Essay on "The Cossacks," in *Poetry for Students*, Thomson Gale, 2007.

Louis McKee

In the following review, McKee notes Pastan's focus in these poems on time and passages, especially aging, loss, and death.

"The pills I take to postpone death/ are killing me," writes Pastan in her new collection of poems, her 11th in about 35 years. Here she deals with loss, with death and other passings, and with the often curious journey through the stages of aging. However, in these careful, insightful considerations of time and its occasional rough edges, the poet finds much to celebrate: the hard-won beauty of her son's piano playing; the "love and/disobedience" of her dog, who is given to sit regardless of the command; a tree surrounded by "a dozen monarchs/ and swallowtails . . . as if they were/its second crop of blossoms." These are the things to remember, to praise: a branch outside the window, soon to be kindling; an old car going to rust; "the 8th dog of my life;/the 10th scribbled book./And love turning its back on endings/one more time." Pastan has done a good job of turning our attention to what really matters. "If death is everywhere we look,/at least let's marry it to beauty." Pastan's poems are always worth our attention.

Source: Louis McKee, Review of *The Last Uncle*, in *Library Journal*, Vol. 127, No. 2, February 1, 2002, p. 106.

Linda Pastan and Ken Adelman

In the following interview, Pastan discusses what she has learned as a poet and, in turn, what she can impart to others. She notes that poetry is more about "emotional experience" than "knowledge."

Above her desk, poet Linda Pastan has posted a quote from Tennessee Williams: "The only honor you can confer upon a writer is a good morning's work."

> "To me all poetry is, in a sense, political. Evil acts generally grow out of a failure of imagination, and poetry, by exercising the imagination as if it were a muscle, can ultimately help influence decisions made out in the real world."

Pastan is one of the lucky poets for whom many good mornings' work have yielded tangible honors, including nine published books, the Dylan Thomas Award, the Di Castagnola Award, a Pushcart Prize, and a recent four-year stint as Maryland's poet laureate. *The Gettysburg Review* said of her latest book, *An Early Afterlife*, that it "reaffirms her place among the finest contemporary poets in America."

Born in New York City, Pastan began submitting poems to the *New Yorker* at the age of 12. (The magazine did not publish its first Pastan poem until almost 30 years later.) She graduated from Radcliffe and later received a master's degree in English literature from Brandeis.

After a ten-year break to raise her three children, she resumed writing. Her poems soon began appearing in the *Atlantic Monthly*, the *New Yorker*, the *New Republic*, the *Paris Review*, and the *Georgia Review*. She has read her works at Harvard, Yale, Princeton, the Folger Shakespeare Library, the Library of Congress, and other institutions.

Pastan lives with her husband, Ira, head of the Laboratory of Molecular Biology at the National Cancer Institute. They have three grown children: Stephen, a nephrologist with Emory Medical School in Atlanta; Peter, a chef who owns two restaurants, Obelisk and Pizzeria Paradiso, in downtown DC; and Rachel, who writes fiction in Madison, Wisconsin.

It was in the study of her Potomac home, filled with books and with a vista of the surrounding forest, that we discussed what she's learned.

What Do I Read Next?

- Edited by Taryn Benbow-Pfalzgraf, *American Women Writers: A Critical Reference Guide from Colonial Times to the Present* (2000) profiles thirteen hundred writers spanning the full history of the United States and including all genres.

- Edited by Barbara Charlesworth Gelpi and Albert Gelpi, *Adrienne Rich's Poetry and Prose: Poems, Prose, Reviews, and Criticism* (1993) gives readers the best of Rich's poetry and essays. Although Rich's background is very similar to Pastan's and both women are respected writers, their bodies of work are very different.

- Mary Oliver's *New and Selected Poems: Volume Two* (2005) is hailed as a fitting companion to Oliver's National Book Award–winning first volume. Here, she offers her readers the Robert Frost–like poetry they have come to love, coupled with the perspective of wisdom and age.

- Pastan's first book of poetry, *A Perfect Circle of Sun* (1971), takes the reader through a different season in each of the four sections of the book. Pastan is concerned less with commenting on how the seasons relate to nature and more on how they affect people's feelings and experiences.

- Nominated for the National Book Award, Pastan's *PM/AM: New and Selected Poems* (1982) prompted many critics to comment on how she had matured as a poet. These poems reflect the passing of a day from the morning to the night, with special attention to poems drawn from dream fragments.

- In the nineteenth-century novel *The Cossacks* (originally published in 1862), the master Russian writer Leo Tolstoy tells a story about a young aristocrat, Dmitri Olenin, and his quest for happiness and purpose. When he joins the military, he falls in love with a Cossack girl who is betrothed to a fierce Cossack soldier.

[Ken Adelman:] What does one do as poet laureate of Maryland?

[Linda Pastan:] Six years ago, someone in the governor's office approached me about becoming poet laureate and asked if I'd be willing to write poems for state occasions. "Absolutely not," I replied. "You'll have to find somebody else." Then she asked what I would be willing to do if I took the post. I said I'd be happy to read poems and talk about poetry to people around Maryland who usually had no contact with poetry or poets. I'd like to help those who think they don't know anything about poetry, and are therefore afraid of it, learn that there isn't that much to "know."

Not much to know about poetry?

No. Poetry is not a matter of knowledge but of emotional experience. It's there to be enjoyed, to be used for celebration and for consolation. I find that people ask me if they can use a certain poem of mine for a funeral or a wedding. They sense they need poetry in their lives, especially on these important occasions, but they don't always know how to find it.

So, as poet laureate, I traveled around the state a lot, to a prison, an old-age home, hospitals, schools, talking to people about poetry and reading some of my own poems aloud to them.

Do you read your poems differently than other people do?

Yes. Every writer has a unique way of viewing his or her own work, and that comes out in the way she reads it aloud. I go to many public readings by poets I like, mainly to hear their voices. Then, when I read their poems to myself, I can still hear that voice in my head.

Should a reader care what you intended to put in a poem?

Only to some degree. All readers bring to each poem their own experiences and emotions and interpret and enjoy the poem in their own ways. Personally, I am interested in knowing a writer's specific intent, but only later and more professionally—that is, from a craft point of view.

Suppose I can find different meaning in your poem than you intended?

That does happen, and it's all right with me, at least up to a point. I mean, if you come to an opposite conclusion—if I were praising something you thought I was denigrating—that would upset me. I certainly don't want to be completely misconstrued.

But if you find meanings in one of my poems that I hadn't realized were there, that would be fine. I've often learned about my own work from hearing other peoples' interpretations of it. There can be things that perhaps I knew in my subconscious that I hadn't realized I knew and that someone else helped me to see.

For instance, the title poem of my first book, *A Perfect Circle of Sun*, has a layer of meaning I hadn't consciously intended. In that poem I described the experience of looking at the world through a skylight. In fact, the poem is called "Skylight." Some critic wrote that the poem was really about looking at the world through the lens of poetry. Once I read that I thought, "Yes. That really is one of the things the poem is about." I must have known it on some level but hadn't known I knew it. And that's good. Because though writing poetry certainly doesn't bring you fame or fortune, it can bring you—as William Stafford, a poet I very much loved and admired, pointed out—a way of discovering things you didn't know you knew. And so the act of writing a poem can become an act of exploration and discovery.

Why did you choose poetry over fiction?

It seems to me that most writers have an impulse to expand or to condense language and experience, and in general the first path leads to fiction, the other to poetry. Of course there are some poets like Walt Whitman who are very expansive and some fiction writers who write small, jewel-like stories. And a few writers, like Thomas Hardy or, in our time, Margaret Atwood, can do both well. But my impulse to condense is very strong.

What drove you into poetry?

I've always written, at least I have from the time I was 12 or 13. As an only child, books were my main companions, and writing became my way of talking to the characters in those books and to the authors of those poems. But I stopped writing after I got married and started having children. That was in the '50s, and I didn't think, then, that I could be the right kind of wife and mother and keep pursuing something as important to me as poetry always has been. I think now that I was wrong. And a young woman probably wouldn't make that mistake today. Anyway, when I returned to writing, almost ten years later, I did try a novel, but I soon found I wasn't interested in the plot or the characters. I was interested in the descriptive passages, and particularly in the metaphoric language. And my novel kept getting shorter and shorter, becoming almost a short story. Before long I realized that what it really wanted was to become a poem.

Your poems deal with nature and art.

Whatever is in my life seems to end up in my poems. I do go to a lot of museums and galleries, and some of my poems are about what I see there. And living here in the middle of the woods, I watch the leaves changing and the snow falling, and I write about that too. But I don't consider myself primarily a nature poet. I use the natural world for metaphoric material rather than trying to simply describe it.

Do you need a burst of creativity to write a poem?

No; there aren't that many bursts. If I waited to be inspired, I'd write maybe one or two poems a year.

But I make myself sit at my desk each morning, whether I feel like it or not, and when I get bored enough, I always start writing something. Inspiration, I find, can be coaxed. And if things get really desperate, I do allow myself to read other people's poems, and that may get me started, may trigger my own imagination.

It's always the getting started that's so hard. I often wish I were a novelist so I could work on one thing for three or four years at a time, but a poet has to keep starting from scratch, over and over again. I finish one or two poems a month, if I'm lucky.

Do you revise a lot?

Oh yes. One of my poems, "The Myth of Perfectibility," even deals with revision as a subject. In it I try to say that a poet must be in love with revision in order to write. The original ideas and metaphors may take only a few hours to get on paper. Then the revision may take a couple of months, years even. I go through maybe 100 revisions for nearly every poem.

Do you finally say, "That's it. I've had it!"

Sure, I say that. But I don't necessarily stick to it. Between a poem's publication in a magazine and later in a book, I often make changes. Then when I put together a collection of selected poems from various books, as I'm doing again now, I may change a few more things, particularly titles. It's called fear of closure, I guess.

In my latest book I have a poem called "Vermilion." It's about the painter Pierre Bonnard, who would never feel that his paintings were finished. He'd even walk into museums where his pictures were hanging and take a paintbrush to them there. In my poem I try to show how life, as well as art, entails constant revision. The poem ends: "As if revision were the purest form of love," and I think it is.

What's your advice to a young poet?

Read, read, read! Revise, revise, revise!

What's the purpose of poetry?

For the writer it's an act of discovery and of letting out, and onto the page, what's deep within. It doesn't cure the pain of feelings but it expresses it through intense language, and if the poet gets it right, it can help the reader to see the world in new ways. To me all poetry is, in a sense, political. Evil acts generally grow out of a failure of imagination, and poetry, by exercising the imagination as if it were a muscle, can ultimately help influence decisions made out in the real world.

Is judging poetry subjective?

To some degree, yes. It is usually clear when poetry is really bad, but it is harder to agree on what's really good.

After time, though, a few poets are still read and most are forgotten.

I guess so. But many are forgotten because of accident or bad luck. The great poems handed down to us usually are great, but I bet there are a lot of wonderful poems we've never had the chance to see or hear.

How do you deal with rejection?

Quite well, actually. That's probably because I started writing poems seriously when I was in my thirties and isolated from any writing community. I didn't know even one other writer. So for me, sending out my poems and getting them back was exciting. I liked the action. A note from an editor, even a form rejection slip, made me feel as if something more were happening in my life than just changing diapers.

In any case, all poets get rejected, even the most famous and honored. I tell young poets one trick I've learned. For each group of poems you send out, have an envelope ready on your desk to resubmit those poems. Then, when they come back, don't leave them sitting around on your desk; send them right back out into the world.

Do you learn from other poets?

I certainly try to. In fact I can't read poems anymore simply for pleasure, the way I read fiction. I always feel I have to try to learn something.

What have you learned?

Different things from different poets. From William Stafford I learned to trust myself, to start quietly and be willing to stay quiet within the poem. From Charles Simic I learned to try strange and daring metaphors. From Ann Sexton and Sylvia Plath, I learned that no subject matter was really off limits. That lesson was very liberating, especially when I first began writing poems again.

Is your poetry autobiographical?

Some of it is, but only up to a point. I think of the "I" in my poems as my fraternal, not identical twin. And though I may use my own children's names, for instances, I am inventing some of what I have them do or say. I am after emotional truth, not literal fact.

How should an amateur begin to read poetry?

Don't be afraid. Don't think about what the poem "means." Read it for the joy of language and for the way it moves you. Later you can go back and read it again and perhaps find new things in it you didn't notice right away. Too many people have had poetry ruined for them in school by bad teachers. Read a poem for pleasure, and if it's a really good poem, it will draw you back again and again.

How does a poet make a living?

A poet doesn't make a living. Most poets I know teach, since that leaves them some time at least for their own writing. But poets have supported themselves many ways—for instance, Wallace Stevens was an insurance executive, and William Carlos Williams was a doctor.

What have you learned from writing poetry?

I've learned more about myself than I would have known otherwise, since writing is such an introspective act. To do it well, you must examine your deepest feelings honestly and somehow articulate them on the page.

I've also learned that my family is the most important thing to me and will always come first. If one of my kids was in a play and I was invited to something that might help my career, I'd always go to the play. When my daughter gets a short story published, I'm much more excited than when I get a poem published.

I've learned to tolerate some loneliness living out here in the woods. I'd probably be happier living in town where things are more lively, but I've learned that I have to accept some isolation to gain the space to think and to write. I've learned that an artist and a scientist can have a good life together.

Lessons of life?

Commit yourself to your work and to your family and friends. Try to actually enjoy the too-brief time we all have here.

Source: Linda Pastan and Ken Adelman, "Word Perfect: For Linda Pastan, Revision Is the Purest Form of Love," in *Washingtonian*, Vol. 31, No. 8, May 1996, pp. 29–31.

Sources

Franklin, Benjamin, V, "Linda Pastan," in *Dictionary of Literary Biography*, Vol. 5, *American Poets since World War II, First Edition*, edited by Donald J. Greiner, Gale Research, 1980, pp. 158–63.

McKee, Louis, Review of *The Last Uncle*, in *Library Journal*, Vol. 127, No. 2, February 1, 2002, p. 106.

"News Notes," in *Poetry*, Vol. 182, No. 3, June 2003, p. 181.

Pastan, Linda, "The Cossacks," in *The Last Uncle*, W. W. Norton, 2004, p. 15.

Paul, Jay S., "Linda Pastan: Overview," in *Contemporary Poets*, 6th ed., edited by Thomas Riggs, St. James Press, 1996.

Review of *The Last Uncle*, in *Publishers Weekly*, Vol. 249, No. 3, January 21, 2002, p. 85.

Further Reading

Berenbaum, Michael, *After Tragedy and Triumph: Modern Jewish Thought and the American Experience*, Cambridge University Press, 1990.

As the project director for the U.S. Holocaust Memorial Museum, Berenbaum has unique expertise on how this and other important chapters in Jewish history figure into modern American Jewish thought. This book compiles thirteen essays that give insight into the complexities of the topic.

Chametzky, Jules, John Felstiner, Hilene Flanzbaum, and Kathryn Hellerstein, eds., *Jewish American Literature: A Norton Anthology*, Norton, 2000.

This comprehensive anthology includes biographical sketches and work samples of 145 writers from all genres. The editors give a full picture, from the seventeenth century to the present, of the literary contributions made by Jewish Americans.

Kooser, Ted, *The Poetry Home Repair Manual: Practical Advice for Beginning Poets*, University of Nebraska Press, 2005.

Known for his accessible writing style, Kooser has earned a reputation as a poet of stature and, as of 2006, has served two terms as poet laureate of the United States. In this book, he draws from his many years of experience as a poet to offer easy-to-follow advice for beginners.

Nelson, Deborah, ed., "Gender and Culture in the 1950s: Special Issue," *Women's Quarterly Review*, Vol. 33, Nos. 3 and 4, 2005.

In this double issue, Nelson brings together writers on a variety of topics to give an overview of what life was like for women in the 1950s. The pressures and expectations women faced are discussed, along with articles about women who made their own ways in a world that promoted conformity.

O'Rourke, Shane, *Warriors and Peasants: The Don Cossacks in Late Imperial Russia*, Macmillan, 2000.

O'Rourke provides a thorough look at the history, culture, politics, and family lives of the largest group of Cossacks, the Don Cossacks.

Daughter-Mother-Maya-Seeta

Reetika Vazirani

1998

Reetika Vazirani's poem "Daughter-Mother-Maya-Seeta" focuses on a mother figure, very possibly the poet's own mother. Indeed, Vazirani used the name Maya to denote her mother in previous poems. This poem was written before the poet conceived her son, which supports the assumption that she describes her own mother, who had given birth to a son and several daughters and was a widow, as is the speaker in the poem. No matter to whom the poet refers, the speaker is a mother, recounting her life experiences.

The poem makes allusions to Indian culture that are easily related to any society. Motherhood, after all, is a human condition. The love shown for the mother and the mother's reciprocal pride in her offspring can be understood no matter what part of the world the reader is from. Sadness underlies the images, such as mention of prejudice brought on by the dark skin color of the mother and her children. The sadness is concealed, however, by a happiness expressed through love, gifts given, and the bright colors of the silken sarongs.

"Daughter-Mother-Maya-Seeta" was first published in *Prairie Schooner* in 1998. It was reprinted in *The 2000 Pushcart Prize Anthology*, *The New American Poets* (2000), and Vazirani's second book of poetry, *World Hotel* (2002).

Author Biography

Reetika Vazirani was a prize-winning poet who died tragically at the age of forty. In 2003, the year Vazirani died, the second of her two collections, *World Hotel* (2002), in which the poem "Daughter-Mother-Maya-Seeta" appears, received the Anisfield-Wolf Book Award. Vazirani was born in Patiala, Punjab, India on August 9, 1962, but her parents immigrated to the United States in 1968. She grew up in Maryland and, as a child, took ballet lessons and ran on her high school track team. Vazirani attended Wellesley College for her undergraduate degree and then the University of Virginia, where she earned a master of fine arts degree. After graduate school, Vazirani taught creative writing at various schools, including the University of Virginia, Sweet Briar College, and the University of Oregon.

Vazirani's father had wanted his daughter to become a physician, but Vazirani found that her passions pulled her toward the written word. Once she latched on to poetry, Vazirani focused on improving her skills, getting her work published, and gaining the notice of a literary audience. She began to realize her goals and supported herself through teaching. Vazirani's first poetry collection, *White Elephants* (1996), was honored with the Barnard New Women Poets Prize. Vazirani led a somewhat typical middle-class life, but she seemed troubled. Many of her poems deal with the topic of otherness, as if she felt that she was part of no particular group with which she could identify, either in her adopted land or the country of her parents.

When Vazirani was eleven years old, her father committed suicide. Paula Span notes in "The Failing Light" that in 2003, Vazirani wrote a letter to the poet Rita Dove, her former teacher, telling Dove: "I have been desperate, silent, silenced, alone, hungry, angry, and crushed." Vazirani used these words to describe her experiences of pregnancy and motherhood and her relationship with the father of her son, the poet Yusef Komunyakaa. Although Komunyakaa supported the boy, he and Vazirani never married and lived together only a short time. They were estranged at the time of Vazirani's death, but it is unclear whether the estrangement was the cause of Vazirani's depression. On July 18, 2003, a friend found the bodies of Vazirani and her two-year-old son on the dining room floor of the house in Washington, D.C., in which Vazirani was temporarily living. Both the child and the poet had stab wounds. Telephone messages and notes were later found, indicating that Vazirani had killed her son and herself.

Poem Text

To replay errors
the revolving door of days
Now it's over
There's no one point thank god in the turning
    world
I was always moving   5
tired too but laughing
To be a widow is an old
freedom I have known
Vidua paradisea a bird
Singly I flew   10
and happiness was my giraffe
in the face of Africa
me among daughters
and my son at work
me pregnant with them   15
taking in the glamour days
town and country mirabella elle vogue
cosmopolitan We have made this world
brown women
laughing till we cleared the dining table   20
In hotels men asked my girls to fetch them towels
In restaurants they asked us for bread
Today I'm a civil servant on the Hill

From the mall what colorful sarongs
my children bring to drape my ankles   25
the gifts we give
to Mina pearls
Tara a Paloma purse for cosmetics
Lata a pair of lime shoes for the miles
Devi gives me her eclectic lit eyes   30
the glamour of our wilder regions
Bombay weavers on the twenty-four-hour looms
shocking pink is the navy of India

Listen I am listening
my mind is a trip   35
I took its English ships
I flew over oceans
I flew in the face of skies
orienting my loss of caste in a molting nation
my dark complexion   40
the folly of envy
wishing all my life to be fair
My jealous god leaves
Hello son this is your mother
Here daughters take these maroon saris   45
these maroon bras
I am proud to have borne you
When you gather around me
newness comes into the world

Poem Summary

Stanza 1

"Daughter-Mother-Maya-Seeta" begins by making reference to a pattern in which one's mind can become stuck, in this instance, repeating the scenes of mistakes. The first line moves, without punctuation, into the second, "the revolving door of days." The imagined door turns around and around, replaying and cycling through errors over and over again. The feeling is not pleasant, but line 3 announces, "Now it's over," suggesting relief. In line 4, the speaker says, "There's no one point thank god in the turning world." Perhaps the speaker has not been caught in the trap of revolving doors, or errors. She was not stuck; she was "always moving." "Always moving" was sometimes tiring but also pleasant; the speaker says that she was also "laughing."

Despite the laughter, the circumstances of the speaker's life have been difficult: she is a "widow." The word "widow" is associated in the next line with the word "freedom," which is an unusual interpretation of matters. After mentioning her freedom, the speaker brings in the image of *Vidua paradisea,* a small bird. The Latin name of this brownish finch translates to "paradise widow." This particular bird is often used as a pet, a caged bird, so the image is perhaps contradictory. It seems as though the speaker, as a widow, experiences a thwarted or restricted freedom. Perhaps in this metaphor the speaker is pointing out that the loss of a husband is difficult to endure but that there is a measure of freedom to be found in her new life and even pleasures to be enjoyed. Maybe the speaker felt like a caged bird when she was married but has been released in her widowhood. In lines 10 and 11, the speaker is flying free and happy "singly."

The speaker states that happiness was her "giraffe," an animal native to Africa. Happiness is linked here to the "face of Africa." The speaker may be remembering an experience of visiting Africa, a place where she found happiness. In lines 13 through 15, the mother ponders her children, remembering being pregnant with them, and speaks of "glamour days." This indicates a time of ease, when the mother had time to think of herself as a woman, to relax and read women's fashion magazines, such as *Vogue* and *Cosmopolitan.* In line 18, the speaker states, "We have made this world"; she follows with the word "brown" in line 19. Stopping at "world" suggests that the speaker feels that she and her children have made this world, possibly her personal world. Connecting "world" to "brown" in the sentence "We have made this world / brown" may be a reference to brown skin, linking back to Africa. A third interpretation could be that beautiful brown women have made the world or, more specifically, that they have made the world of glamour magazines "brown." As the stanza continues, these women are both "laughing" and crying as they share their chores as well as their emotions. There is a sense of a closely knit family of "brown women."

The location of the references in lines 21 through 23 of the poem is unclear: "In hotels men asked my girls to fetch them towels / In restaurants they asked us for bread." In any case, the speaker's "girls" are described as servants. There is irony in the last line of the stanza: "Today I'm a civil servant on the Hill," perhaps a reference to Capitol Hill, where the affairs of government are conducted. The speaker works for the government but is still called a servant, albeit a civil servant. There seems to be an implied correspondence of race and the servant class. A servant is typically a lowly position, relegated to those who lack status. Servants are often immigrants and people of color.

Stanza 2

"From the mall" at the beginning of stanza 2 may be a play on words. "Mall" could mean a shopping mall or the National Mall, which is the strip of land between the U.S. Capitol and the Washington Monument, in Washington, D.C. From the "mall," the speaker's children bring her "colorful sarongs," or Asian garments. A list follows of gifts given to certain females, perhaps the speaker's children. Someone named Mina receives pearls, Tara a purse, and Lata "lime shoes." These are not ordinary gifts; they are of exquisite and unusual quality. Mikimoto pearls are world renowned, and "Paloma" could imply that the purse is one from the collection of the designer Paloma Picasso. "Devi" does not receive a gift but rather gives the speaker "her eclectic lit eyes / the glamour of our wilder regions." The coupling of "eclectic" with "glamour" suggests that Devi is a heterogeneous and exotic blend of foreign elements. Perhaps Devi herself is the richest gift.

The last two lines of stanza 2 take the reader to India. The line "Bombay weavers on the twenty-four-hour looms" conjures images of long, tedious hours spent laboring. The next line suggests a comparison between India and the United States: "Shocking pink is the navy of India." In India, shocking pink may be as ordinary as navy blue is in the United States, especially on Capitol Hill. "Shocking pink" also may refer to the "wilder regions" of line 31 of the poem. The United States can be seen as dull and confined compared with India.

Stanza 3

The beginning of stanza 3 is similar to that of stanza 1 in that the speaker is inside her mind again, listening. She may be listening to memories: "my mind is a trip / . . . I flew over oceans / I flew in the face of skies." It is as if the speaker is remembering leaving India, "orienting my loss of caste in a molting nation / my dark complexion." In Hindu India, dark-complexioned people tend to be of the lower castes. The speaker may be thinking that her dark skin will no longer make a difference in her new home. In the lines "The folly of envy / wishing all my life to be fair," the word "fair" may mean light coloring as opposed to dark coloring, but it also may suggest the unfairness of caste systems and discrimination. The line "My jealous god leaves" may imply that in leaving India behind, along with her envy of those with lighter skin, the speaker has also left behind her jealousy.

The end of stanza 3 returns to the theme of motherhood. The speaker says: "*Hello son this is your mother*" as if she has been separated from him for a while and is now returning. Lines 45 and 46 read as if the speaker has brought gifts of "*maroon saris*" and "*maroon bras*" for her daughters. The speaker then seems to look around and take in the beauty and blessedness of her children. She is proud of them, and when she is with them ("*When you gather around me*"), the speaker feels as if the world has renewed itself.

Themes

Discrimination

The theme of discrimination is clear in "Daughter-Mother-Maya-Seeta." The speaker and her daughters are mistaken for, or assumed to be, servants in the restaurants and hotels they visit, rather than being acknowledged as equals of the other patrons. It is because of their brown skin, the poem implies, that this discrimination occurs. Another undercurrent of discrimination occurs in line 23 of stanza 1, which immediately follows the telling of the hotel and restaurant experiences: "Today I'm a civil servant on the Hill." Although discrimination is not overtly stated in this line, its association with the previous statements of discrimination suggests that the speaker is giving another example of being perceived as having a lower status. The word "servant" is closely related to what the men in the hotels assume the women to be. There is also irony in the last line of stanza 1. A civil servant earns a good living and is respected. Nonetheless, a servant is a servant, especially on Capitol Hill, where the power is retained by the senators, representatives, lawyers, and lobbyists. A civil servant is fairly low on the ladder of success in that environment. A servant's role is to serve, much as the workers who bring bread in a restaurant and towels in a hotel.

Discrimination is also present in the mention of caste, the strict categorization of status according to one's birth in Hindu India. Dark complexions are discriminated against both in India and in the United States, two locations implied in this poem. Emphasizing discrimination based on skin color comes through in the speaker's comment that she is "wishing all my life to be fair" and the mention of her jealousy, which is assumed to be roused by lighter-skinned women. The theme of discrimination is played against the mother's love. Discrimination would seem to make one's life miserable, but the speaker has days of laughing and happiness, which appear to be based on her love of her children.

Mother's Love

The love of the speaker for her children is the dominant theme of "Daughter-Mother-Maya-Seeta." Despite hardship, such as discrimination and the loss of her husband, the speaker has found joy in life. When the speaker mentions her children, as adults, as children, or even still in her womb, the images are filled with a sense of completion and pride. "I am proud to have borne you," the speaker says. Despite all her trials, the moving, and the insults, no one can take away from her the love of her children. She shares laughing with them, the giving and receiving of gifts. When they "gather around me," the speaker states, "newness comes into the world." Her world is made fresh in simply looking at her children and being in their presence.

In writing of mother's love, the poet is showing her own love of her mother. The reader can feel this love come through the speaker, even though the speaker represents the poet's mother. That is why the title of the poem includes a reference to "daughter." The daughter, the poet, pays tribute to her mother's strengths and unselfish compassion for her children through the poem.

Freedom

Images of freedom are woven through "Daughter-Mother-Maya-Seeta" in subtle ways. "Now it's over," the speaker states in line 3 of stanza 1. There is a release of some kind, possibly

Topics For Further Study

- Compare the poetry of Vazirani with the poetry of Sylvia Plath. Choose two poems by each poet that express similar feelings, topics, or themes. Specify the similarities. Look for evidence of depression that may indicate the poets' states of mind. Present your findings to your class.

- Gather statistics on suicide rates among poets and other artists. Look for studies that have linked creativity to an inclination to depression. What other professions, if any, are associated with a high rate of suicide? Compare these rates with the rate in the general population. Note the age groups that have the highest rates of suicide. Create a chart delineating your findings.

- Research the caste system of Hindu India. Examine the religious and social aspects. How do Hindus rationalize the caste system? What did Mahatma Gandhi have to say about it? What are politicians in India doing to alleviate the discrimination that continues there? Gather your findings in a research paper.

- Talk to people who have emigrated from other countries to your city or state. What have been some of the changes in their lives? How does the original culture differ from the adopted culture? What, if any, forms of discrimination did these people feel in their homeland? What kinds of discrimination do they feel in the United States? What, if any, differences do they perceive in the way they raise their children and the way people who are naturalized U.S. citizens raise their families? Summarize your findings in a report. Invite one of your interviewees to your class and lead a question-and-answer session.

---

from the replaying of errors mentioned in line 1. In line 4, the speaker thanks god, not as a prayer but as an interjection. It is an appeal or an announcement of gratitude. The verb "flew" in line 10 of stanza 1 is another symbol of freedom. The speaker flies like the "*Vidua paradisea*," the widow of paradise. Despite her difficulties, the speaker states that she "was always moving," another symbol of freedom. Even though the terrain was restricted, the speaker was not trapped. There is also mention of "glamour days." To be able to dwell on glamour, a woman has to have an excess of time, which is related to freedom. The woman is not tied to drudgery. The word "glamour" is repeated in "the glamour of our wilder regions," which gives the sense of freedom in the wild, an untying from the strings of society. In stanza 3, the speaker states, "My jealous god leaves." With this subtle reference to a type of freedom, the speaker has no need for envy. Her mind is free of this disabling emotion. The theme of freedom, like the theme of mother's love, plays in opposition to the theme of discrimination. One sets off the other, making each stand out more emphatically.

Style

Metaphor

In "Daughter-Mother-Maya-Seeta," the poet makes consistent use of metaphor, a comparison of two unlike things in which the essence of one is identified with the qualities of the other. In stanza 1, she refers to "the revolving door of days." A revolving door has a circular motion, similar to the circling of the rising and setting sun. The metaphor suggests an element of sameness. One day resembles another, as a revolving door passes again and again through the same space. In the same stanza, the poet writes, "To be a widow is an old / freedom." This is not the usual interpretation of widowhood. Rather than coloring widowhood as completely sorrowful, the poet suggests that there is something liberating about it. Metaphors offer readers images that enhance the meaning of words and give the imagination a picture with which to work in trying to understand the meaning or the emotions that underlie a poem.

Free Verse

In free verse, the poet is not restricted to traditional rules of poetry that dictate that lines must have a rhyme scheme or meter or be of a consistent length. "Daughter-Mother-Maya-Seeta" has lines and stanzas of varying lengths, and there are no apparent rhymes. The poetic devices of metaphor and enjambment are used, however, and attention is paid to the overall rhythmic beat of syllables. Although the beat is not consistent throughout the poem, there are lines that mimic one another in the number of beats. These techniques distinguish a free-verse poem from prose.

Enjambment

The term *enjambment* can be traced to a French word meaning "to straddle." Some poetic lines purposely do just that: their sense straddles two lines. A poet might use enjambment for emphasis, for ambiguity, or to maintain an established rhythm. In "Daughter-Mother-Maya-Seeta," enjambment occurs in lines 18 and 19, "We have made this world / brown women." Enjambment leaves room for interpretation. Readers might ask whether the poet means "We have made this world brown, women." Or perhaps she means "We have made this world, brown women." The enjambment makes readers stop and contemplate the various possible meanings, taking from the poem a meaning of their own.

Italicized Words

In several spots, the poet has used italics. In line 9, for instance, the speaker mentions a certain type of finch, giving its Latin (or scientific) name. The name, *Vidua paradisea*, recalls her mother's widowed state, suggesting that perhaps the caged bird has been freed. In lines 17 and 18, the poet lists the names of certain fashion magazines that she read in her "glamour days," making those days come alive again. The final lines of the poem are also italicized, implying that the mother is talking aloud to her children. Previously the mother seems to have been speaking to herself or to the reader. In these last lines, there is a heightened sense of the human voice, one filled with love and pride for the children.

Punctuation

There is no punctuation in this poem, although the poet occasionally uses capitalization to suggest where new sentences begin. This gives the poem a feeling of freedom, like flowing water or moving air. The technique also places importance on the ends of each line, as that is the only clear definition of some kind of stop. This lack of punctuation, especially when combined with the dashes used in the title, lends a sense of unity or a connectedness to all the words and to all the lines of the poem, as if the poem were one long sentence, a sentence that never ends.

Historical Context

Multicultural Poetry

Being immersed in a new culture can give immigrants important and distinct points of view, especially if the language of their home differs from that of their adopted country. Learning a new language often forces a person to think in different ways, because language is more than just words. Language helps shape the way a person sees, understands, and explains the world. Having come to live in a new culture, an immigrant also has the advantage of comparison. What does the new culture have that the original culture does not and vice versa? In the assimilation process, immigrants decide, either consciously or subconsciously, how to change to fit in and what elements of their heritage to retain.

Since the 1960s, a growing awareness of multiculturalism (which was brought to the forefront of intellectual discussions through the Civil Rights movement) has resulted in a demand for a wider selection of published works by ethnically diverse authors. Publishers have responded with works by individual authors as well as collections of the works of immigrant poets, telling of their challenges and celebrations in assimilating to a new life. The voices of Asian Americans, Hispanic Americans, and others from the original immigrant generation through second and third generations are being heard in all genres, including poetry. Courses on multicultural poetry are abundant on most college campuses, as are websites devoted to promoting multicultural poetry and literature.

Indian Castes and Culture

In "Daughter-Mother-Maya-Seeta," the poet uses the phrase "orienting my loss of caste," referring to the caste system prevalent in the Hindu communities of India. Some people in India believe that the caste system is for the best because it helps maintain social order, but the caste system also can be experienced as extreme segregation and discrimination, with which many people in the United States are familiar.

There are thousands of castes in Hindu India, which fall into four main categories. The Brahmin caste consists of priests and spiritual teachers. The Kshatriya includes rulers, warriors, and landowners. The Vaishya caste is made up of merchants. The Shudra caste comprises artisans and farmers. Persons belonging to the Dalit group, a fifth category, typically work in jobs that are considered disgusting, such as those that deal with the dead or with bodily wastes. They were once considered outside the caste system and called "untouchables," but this category has been officially abolished in modern India (though it still exists in social practice in some areas). In an attempt to raise the status of the untouchables, the Indian political and spiritual leader Mahatma Gandhi referred to them as Harijans, or "people of Vishnu" (which is essentially the same as saying "the people of God"). Gandhi, a member of the Vaishya caste, also went against society's rules and adopted a Harijan child.

Being born into a specific caste determines such factors as wealth and opportunity. The higher castes have the most potential for living a comfortable life. The Dalit usually work at menial jobs and are at risk of being harmed physically, psychologically, and financially if they try to rise above their predetermined status. The Indian constitution makes caste discrimination illegal, but that has not completely changed the social attitude, especially in the countryside, where most people live. In urban centers, discrimination is less prevalent. Scholarships, for example, have been provided to people in the Dalit group in an attempt to better their traditional educational level and allow them a chance to advance in life.

Immigration

In 2003, 33.5 million foreign-born people accounted for approximately 12 percent of the U.S. population. Of that number, one million persons (or 3 percent of the foreign-born population) were from India, the third-largest immigrant group (behind Mexican Americans and Filipino Americans). Immigrants from India tend to be highly educated and often receive visas based on their educational training and the need of U.S. businesses to fill specialized positions. States with large Indian populations include California, New Jersey, and New York. Between 1990 and 2000, the number of immigrants from India more than doubled, increasing from slightly more than 450,000 in 1990 to a just over one million in 2000. In 2003, fifty thousand immigrants from India arrived in the United States.

Students who come to the United States to go to school have great influence on the U.S. economy. Estimates of the amount of money fed into the economy reach twelve billion dollars. Making the transition to the United States goes more smoothly for students from India than for students from some other countries, mainly because most students from India learn English before their arrival. In 2003, more than 74,000 persons from India were granted student visas to attend U.S. schools.

Critical Overview

World Hotel, Vazirani's second collection, in which "Daughter-Mother-Maya-Seeta" appears, was brought to the attention of readers of the *Washington Post* by the poet and columnist Rita Dove, who begins her review of the book by stating that it had been her policy not to feature works by her friends, colleagues, or former students. In the case of Vazirani, who was once a student of Dove's, the columnist writes, "I feel compelled to make an exception in the case of Reetika Vazirani. After all, she was an exception as a student." The collection, Dove concludes, offers "penetrating portraits from and keen glimpses into a world which—for all its unfamiliar place names and vivid accessories—we recognize as strikingly similar to our own."

"Daughter-Mother-Maya-Seeta" won the 1999 Pushcart Prize and thus was published in the Pushcart anthology the following year. It also was anthologized in *New American Poets*. The collection *World Hotel* has not received any awards, but Michael Scharf writes in *Publishers Weekly*, "This book's style and substance should get it nominated for one or another prize." Scharf considers the poems in the collection a "blend of tersely bittersweet lyricism and biographical data." Vazirani's strengths, according to Scharf, include "clarity, geographical detail, and a way with short, unpunctuated lines."

A reviewer for the *Virginia Quarterly Review* finds that Vazirani's "poems have always concerned themselves with one place: the colonized and colonizing human heart." The reviewer also refers to *World Hotel* as an extension of Vazirani's first book, as she further explores "the stylistic and thematic range of her" earlier poems. Vazirani does so, according to the writer, "in daring ways." Paula Span's memorial to Vazirani in the *Washington Post* states that Vazirani's poetry is distinguished because of the poet's skill: "She was known for continual revisions, for chipping at each line, sanding down every couplet."

Criticism

Joyce Hart

Hart is a published writer and former teacher. In this essay, she examines the contradictory emotions in "Daughter-Mother-Maya-Seeta" to show how the poet uses the emotions to accentuate one another.

"Daughter-Mother-Maya-Seeta" is full of conflicting emotions, which are at the same time often understated. Perhaps *conflicting* does not fully describe their mission. It is possible that the poet uses oppositional emotions to highlight one another or to emphasize one over another, much in the way a painter uses dark colors to make the lighter hues stand out. Pairing emotions in this way demonstrates how one feeling can work as shadow, making the other stand out as if lit by a blazing sun.

The exact meaning of the first four lines of stanza 1 of Vazirani's poem is not clear. The underlying feelings are, in order, frustration, release, and celebration. It is as if these emotions were being expressed in a rising scale, the most negative emotion being offered and then its betterment replacing it twofold. To begin, the speaker states, "To replay errors / the revolving door of days." These lines suggest how one might feel in the throes of depression. No matter what one does, the mistakes keep repeating, whether in real-life experiences or in the mind. A person makes an embarrassing error, and the mind tends to replay it, trying to make it right or learn from the mistake so as not to repeat it. The process of replaying takes a great deal of mental energy. While the mind is stuck on the errors, not much else is accomplished. People who think in these terms may be constantly denigrating themselves. Their confidence and their focus may suffer. In lines 3 and 4, the speaker then states, "Now it's over / There's no one point thank god in the turning world." The frustration and agony are finished, at least for a time. "Thank god," the speaker states, for making the world in such a way that there is "no one point." Time moves on, things change, and people learn and grow. The speaker appears to be celebrating those facts.

In line 6, there is another apparent comparison of differing emotions. The speaker states that she was "tired too but laughing." Life has been wearing

> *It is possible that the poet uses oppositional emotions to highlight one another or to emphasize one over another, much in the way a painter uses dark colors to make the lighter hues stand out."*

her out, but she is not too tired to find happiness. She does not say that she has been tired *and* laughing, which would imply two possibly different situations. Rather, she implies that she has been laughing despite her exertions. No matter what life experiences have been thrown her way, the speaker has been able to handle them. She sees both sides of each situation, or, possibly, she sees beyond the situation. Whatever the difficulty, the speaker has handled it in an objective manner, never abandoning her sense of humor. Sometimes people find that laughing at their pain helps them to step back from it. The replacement of an emotion on the more negative end of the spectrum with one on the positive end is a strategy that optimistic people, people with faith that everything works out for the best, use to propel them through life. The poet must have seen this attribute in her mother and chooses to honor her mother for the strength she used in moving through life. It seems, for example, that the poet's mother has demonstrated courage in her widowhood. Her mother could have succumbed to depression and the pressures of raising her children on her own. Instead, she has taken from her situation the positive aspects, or so the speaker suggests. The mother describes herself in widowhood as a bird that finds freedom.

In lines 15 through 18, the speaker refers to her pregnancies and then immediately speaks of "glamour days." Many women do not equate pregnancy with glamour. Although pregnancy is a beautiful state, most people do not naturally associate it with the type of feminine beauty and allure found in such women's magazines as *Vogue* and *Cosmopolitan*. Pregnancy is not typically considered fashionable in that sense. Some women become

What Do I Read Next?

- Vazirani's first award-winning collection, *White Elephants* (1996), pays special attention to the challenges of assimilation in a new country. The theme of "other" is prevalent in these poems. The writer recalls memories and stories of her homeland and transfers them to her experiences in the United States.

- *Mother Love* (1995), by Rita Dove, gives insight into how Dove's poetry and instruction influenced Vazirani.

- *Neon Vernacular* (1993), by Yusef Komunyakaa —an award-winning poet and the winner of the Pulitzer Prize, addresses themes such as the Vietnam War and the loneliness of growing up as an African American in the Deep South.

- Vazirani was influenced by the work of the poet Seamus Heaney. Heaney's eleventh book of poems, *Electric Light* (2001), brings together reflections on Ireland, the poet's family, and the art of poetry. Heaney's sense of the importance of place is also a theme important to Vazirani.

- Immigrant poets' voices can be read in collections such as *Unsettling America: An Anthology of Contemporary Multicultural Poetry* (1994), edited by Maria Mazziotti Gillan and Jennifer Gillan.

- Sylvia Plath, another American poet who suffered from depression and committed suicide, wrote journals collected in *The Unabridged Journals of Sylvia Plath, 1950–1962* (2000). Plath's husband, the poet Ted Hughes, published his edited versions of Plath's journals in 1982. The 2000 edition, however, collected by Karen V. Kukil, adds material left out by Hughes.

- Arundhati Roy's *The God of Small Things* (1997) is a novel about life in India in the late 1960s told through the eyes of the female member of a set of twins. Part of the story is recounted from the child's point of view and the rest from the adult perspective. The language of the novel is almost as fascinating as the complicated story itself.

---

distraught with their bulk during pregnancy, and bulk is certainly not represented in the thin models who grace the pages of these magazines. The speaker does not seem bothered by the changes in her body during pregnancy. Instead, she seems to be rejoicing in them. Whether or not she would be called glamorous by the editors of the magazines she is reading, she herself is feeling glamorous.

At the end of stanza 1 is another juxtaposition: "brown women / laughing." Are they laughing so hard that they clear away everyone else who has been sitting near them? Are they laughing while they work through the chore of clearing the table of the dirty dishes? The image is open-ended. The reader can choose the interpretation. The main point is that the women are together and they are laughing, despite the "brown" skins that sometimes bring ridicule. The women are demeaned despite their laughter. Others try to put them in a significantly lower place. The women's brown faces may laugh, but the indignation of being discriminated against still hurts. The poet has taken her speaker from laughter to pain. In the face of laughter, the pain of prejudice hurts all the more.

In stanza 2, the speaker is honored by her children as they bring "colorful sarongs" to "drape" her ankles. One can almost picture the mother sitting in a chair, with her children nestled around her as she opens the gifts. The bright colors bring memories of home. The speaker recalls "Bombay weavers on the twenty-four-hour looms." These bright colors are the result of the dreadful conditions endured by the weavers of the fabric. The never-ending grind of the weavers' labor is an integral part of the bright fabric. The speaker cannot separate the two images. She can enjoy and feel pleasure in the gifts, but she cannot forget how fortunate she is compared with those who must work long, debilitating hours for poor pay. The "shocking pink" can have a hidden meaning. It may refer to the brightness of the color, but it also may be an allusion to shocking working conditions. The speaker has escaped the caste system and the discrimination that she experienced in her homeland and found freedom, but many others are still suffering.

In stanza 3, the speaker returns in her mind to her homeland, the place she refers to as "a molting nation." She has left behind her "caste," "the folly of envy," and a "jealous god," though she remembers them. She recalls "wishing all my life to be fair." Here, "fair" could be construed in two ways, as light-complexioned or as just and nondiscriminatory. It could be that she envisions her new life as one in which she is not viewed and judged by her complexion or her caste. The speaker's thoughts turn to her children, as if she has suddenly spotted them, and her mood becomes happier. She sees her children and salutes her son: "*Hello son this is your mother.*" The speaker then hands her daughters positive reminders of her homeland. "*Here daughters take these maroon saris*," she tells them. The saris are not "shocking pink." The tones are more somber but also more regal. The speaker is restored. She feels happy again, and she passes this feeling on to her children. "*I am proud to have borne you*," she tells them. Children cannot expect or want to hear their mothers say words that are more positive. The poem comes to a place in the emotional spectrum opposite to the one at which it begins. It starts with replayed errors and ends with a world reborn. "*When you gather around me / newness comes into the world*," the speaker tells her children. There is hope.

Source: Joyce Hart, Critical Essay on "Daughter-Mother-Maya-Seeta," in *Poetry for Students*, Thomson Gale, 2007.

Bryan Aubrey

Aubrey holds a Ph.D. in English and has published many articles on twentieth-century poetry. In this essay, he discusses "Daughter-Mother-Maya-Seeta" in the context of the experience of Indian immigrants to the United States.

As a poet of the Indian diaspora until her tragic death in 2003, Vazirani was a lively contributor to the outpouring of writings by South Asian immigrants to the United States that has made its mark on American literature over the last quarter of the twentieth century and the beginning of the twenty-first. The essential task of this new Indian American literature is to come to terms with the immigrant experience in all its variety. As Craig Tapping puts it in his essay "South Asia/North America: New Dwellings and the Past," "Like other ethnic literatures in North America, writing by immigrants from the Indian subcontinent is concerned with personal and communal identity, recollection of the homeland, and the active response to this 'new' world."

Bharati Mukherjee, an Indian-born writer who immigrated to the United States and fully embraced American culture, had this to say about the contribution made by such immigrants to American literature:

> We immigrants have fascinating tales to relate.... We have experienced rapid changes in the history of the nations in which we lived. When we uproot ourselves from those countries and come here, either by choice or out of necessity, we suddenly must absorb 200 years of American history and learn to adapt to American society. Our lives are remarkable, often heroic.

The theme of the poem is acceptance in the face of constant change; it tells a story of a progression from self-denial and even self-shame to an affirmation and celebration of Maya-Seeta's Indian culture even though she has spent many years in the new world of America. (*Maya* and *Seeta* are names that the poet gives to her mother in other poems in her "Inventing Maya" section.) The poem also affirms the blessings of family, in particular, Maya-Seeta's son and her daughters, through whom continuity is expressed in the midst of cultural transformation.

The poem is a little more complex than it might first appear. As Marilyn Hacker commented in her introduction to Vazirani's first collection, *White Elephants*, Vazirani's poems often involve "shifts in scene, time, focus, point of view, [and they] demand an approach more akin to a verbal equivalent of cinema than to 'straightforward' narrative prose." Thus "Daughter-Mother-Maya-Seeta" shifts scenes rapidly as the speaker recalls her peripatetic, restless life, which involved travel by ship and air around the world, and records her own changing attitudes to it. The note of acceptance, as if it is something newly found, is heard in the first four lines:

> To replay errors
> the revolving door of days
> Now it's over
> There's no one point thank god in the turning world

The last line quoted is an allusion to T. S. Eliot's poem "Burnt Norton," which contains the line "At the still point of the turning world," a stillness that the speaker of Vazirani's poem has learned not to seek. For her, everything is movement, flux, change, and, she appears to be saying, it is now time to cease dwelling on past mistakes, even if they were seemingly endlessly repeated. Now is the time, as the poem will go on to state, to embrace and celebrate change as well as the permanent nature of her self-identity.

It was not always so, as the poem makes clear. Looking back, Maya-Seeta acknowledges what she lost when she left her native India, a strictly stratified society in which she had her own place, determined by tradition and culture. She exchanged this "loss of caste" for a "molting nation," the United States. The word "molting" carries connotations of self-renewal by shedding of the old (as an animal may shed fur or skin), and also of "melting," as in the common expression that America is a melting pot in which new immigrants gradually lose their ethnic and cultural differences and form a new identity as part of the American mainstream. At first in the United States, it would appear that Maya-Seeta was overwhelmed by the dominance of the white culture she encountered there. Like the young black girl in Toni Morrison's novel *The Bluest Eye* (1970), who is so bombarded with images of beauty by white culture that she can conceive beauty only in terms of possessing blue eyes, Maya-Seta internalized a kind of self-negating racism in which she regarded being brown-skinned ("my dark complexion") as unfortunate, and "wish[ed] all [her] life to be fair." Vazirani the poet once mentioned that her mother used to use Porcelana skin cream, which to her daughter was a sign of her desire for whiteness, a desire to erase who she really was.

The problems Maya-Seeta and her family faced in an alien culture and how she made her response are clear from these lines:

> In hotels men asked my girls to fetch them towels
> In restaurants they asked us for bread
> Today I'm a civil servant on the Hill

In addition to pride in achievement is the note of affirmation, celebration, and joy that is heard in the poem and that will finally become its dominant voice:

> ... We have made this world
> Brown women
> Laughing till we cleared the dining table

The joyful affirmation of an exotic (to American eyes) culture is sounded again in the following lines.

> Devi gives me her eclectic lit eyes
> the glamour of our wilder regions
> Bombay weavers on the twenty-four-hour looms
> shocking pink is the navy of India

> *Here daughters take these maroon saris*
> *these maroon bras*
> *I am proud to have borne you*
> *When you gather around me*
> *newness comes into the world*

The last line develops the idea hinted at earlier. The newness that the mother celebrates is neither entirely Indian nor entirely American but rather a unique product of the interaction of two cultures in the experience of Indian immigrants and those of Indian heritage born in America. As many immigrants know, this can be a delicate balancing act, but Maya-Seeta in this poem seems to be able to straddle two cultural worlds and to uphold the value of both of them. Her position, which by implication may also be that of the poet, is unlike that adopted by such Indian writers as V. S. Naipaul (to expand the discussion to an expatriate writing in Britain), whose work expresses a constant sense of exile, as if there is no possibility of finding a real home. Nor does it resemble the opposite position of a writer such as Bharati Mukherjee, who took American citizenship, embraced the new culture, and identified herself not as Indian American but as American. If in "Daughter-Mother-Maya-Seeta," America is the headquarters of a multicultural "world hotel," the poem suggests that all guests, Western and Eastern, are welcome, and each has a contribution to make as "newness" is perpetually born into a constantly changing world.

Source: Bryan Aubrey, Critical Essay on "Daughter-Mother-Maya-Seeta," in *Poetry for Students*, Thomson Gale, 2007.

Michael Allen Holmes

Holmes is a freelance writer and editor. In this essay, he interprets Vazirani's poem as so highly artful as to defy academic analysis.

One might contend that all forms of art draw to some extent on the emotions of their audience, whether they are readers, listeners, viewers, or appreciators of other kinds. *Merriam-Webster's Collegiate Dictionary* gives the relevant definition of art as "the conscious use of skill and creative imagination especially in the production of aesthetic objects," where an object that might be labeled *aesthetically pleasing* could in most cases be described as in some way *beautiful*. With respect to written work, a range of artfulness can be found in the various forms: a classification might hold technical writing and textbooks as entirely artless, nonfiction prose as somewhat artful (as limited by the intent to convey information), fictional prose as generally artful (as limited by intellectualization), and poetry perhaps as the most artful use of the written word. Of course, some poems are more artful than others.

Arguably, the presence of any sort of established structure, whereby the poet is guided not by his or her own "creative imagination" but by formulaic convention, detracts from artfulness. The least artful poetry, then, lends itself well to analysis, as a keen critic might find conventionally formulaic elements with regard to meter, rhyme scheme, construction, and so on. ("Unartful" poetry, as defined for the purpose of this essay, may certainly still be deemed *good* poetry, as long as one finds it pleasing.) The most artful poetry, which might be expected to rely more heavily on emotional impact than on intellectual relevance, will likely have little if anything for a critic to "analyze." That is, if a poet has written verse from a purely self-directed imaginative, emotional standpoint, one would search in vain for the intentional use of constructions so as to elicit certain responses in readers, because in being guided by her emotion the poet would not have consciously constructed the poem with any reader in mind but herself. The poet may certainly reread and revise her poem so as to hone the wording with the utmost care, but if she does so only to please her own eyes and ears, the critic has no genuine manner of approaching the poem other than to simply enjoy it or not. Vazirani's verse would seem to be precisely such truly artful work.

Vazirani has been widely recognized as both an emotional person and an emotional poet. Sadly, her father committed suicide when she was an adolescent, and her mother took pains to prevent her and her siblings from learning of the circumstances surrounding his death, perhaps ultimately heightening the confusion and trauma they experienced. In "The Failing Light," a posthumous biographical appreciation of the poet written for the *Washington Post*, Paula Span states, "She knew suffering, even despair. Her father's death haunted her." With regard to her life experience, Vazirani was born in India but moved to the United States at a very young age and professed to feel profound cultural displacement. Span cites a letter that Vazirani wrote to her poetic mentor, Rita Dove, in which she remarked, "I have been desperate, silent, silenced, alone, hungry, angry, and crushed." Span quotes Kendra Hamilton, a friend of the poet, as saying, "She had a longing for a home of her own that was overwhelming." In truth, perhaps no evidence need

> *In distilling her emotions and presenting them in poetic form with the utmost artfulness, Vazirani manages to inspire in her readers the sorts of visceral surges of emotion of their own that can arise only in the absence of unartistic, formulaic structure and intellectualization."*

be given regarding the degree to which Vazirani was guided by her emotions other than the fact that she committed suicide after first taking the life of her beloved two-year-old son—acts that could have been perpetrated only by a person truly overwhelmed by her own sentiments.

The poem "Daughter-Mother-Maya-Seeta" would seem to very well represent Vazirani's virtual indifference toward structural elements. (Much "free verse" does follow poetic conventions, simply in less obvious ways.) The three stanzas are of no particular length. Lines are typically short, but the poet is not constrained by artificial attempts at brevity, as evinced by the fourth line, "There's no one point thank god in the turning world," as well as the last several lines of the first stanza. Vazirani uses no punctuation, yet a semblance of sentence structure is provided by the occasional lines that begin with capital letters. Interestingly, lines 9 and 17–18 begin with italicized terms and then feature lengthy spaces before romanized words; a poet explicitly concerned with the appearance of her poem would have likely presented the romanized characters on the following line, without losing much in the way of meaning. (Of course, the association between the magazine title "*cosmopolitan*" and the statement "We have made this world" is a very strong one.)

Further, Vazirani is not afraid to include elements that are somewhat esoteric, in that the depth of their relevance cannot be understood by a reader unaware of the poet's life circumstances. Lines 7 and 8, "To be a widow is an old / freedom I have known," are given no explication and as such may come across as quite mysterious. Lines 11 and 12, "and happiness was my giraffe / in the face of Africa," do little more for the reader than tie together the notions inherent in those four nouns. The gifts enumerated in lines 27 to 31, while colorful, also seem to bear relevance that is mostly unexplained; in fact, this passage perhaps more than any other indicates to the reader that he is not *expected* to fully grasp everything. If Vazirani had been seeking to provide full understanding to a specific audience, she might have explained why, for example, a "Paloma purse," in particular, is worth mentioning—but she does not.

Line 34, "Listen I am listening," may offer the surest evidence that Vazirani wrote "Daughter-Mother-Maya-Seeta" not *for* anyone but herself (and, of course, her family). As indicated by biographical information, the poem is understood to be written from the point of view of the poet's mother, and the title certainly stresses the interplay between the identities of daughter and mother. Here, Vazirani seems to be concluding her maternal ruminations by inhabiting both mother and daughter at once; she is both speaker—commanding someone to listen—and listener herself. At this point in the poem, the reader may almost feel as though he is intruding on a private conversation between mother and daughter. Thus, the world depicted in this poem was not created *for* the reader; the reader is merely allowed to look into that world and so to understand for himself whatever he is able to understand. The last six lines, a direct address from mother to son and daughters, seem to solidify the notion that the poet has all along been guided only by her emotions; she did not "construct" the poem but instead allowed it to flow forth from her mind, with the fluidity of stream of consciousness or spontaneously spoken words.

In her article, Paula Span quotes Charles Rowell, editor of the African diaspora literary magazine *Callaloo*, in which Vazirani was published, as saying with respect to the poet's work, "This is devotion to language, devotion to craft, the assumption that a poem is a piece of art, not just an assertion of an emotion or some sort of divine inspiration." Here, Rowell has almost presented "art" and "emotion" as contradictory; at the very least he seems to be saying that art is more than mere emotion. Yet he is more specifically stating that art is necessarily more than "an assertion of an emotion." That is, Vazirani does not simply gush forth with the kind of emotional release one might find in electronic mail correspondence between close friends. Rather, she has so fully refined the *expression* of her emotions as to be able to convey them through images and loosely connected statements that reach the reader only on the most subtle, sublime level. Indeed, if the emotion inherent in "Daughter-Mother-Maya-Seeta" were to be explicated in prose form, many pages would have been needed. In distilling her emotions and presenting them in poetic form with the utmost artfulness, Vazirani manages to inspire in her readers the sorts of visceral surges of emotion of their own that can arise only in the absence of unartistic, formulaic structure and intellectualization.

Source: Michael Allen Holmes, Critical Essay on "Daughter-Mother-Maya-Seeta," in *Poetry for Students*, Thomson Gale, 2007.

Bowker Magazine Group

In the following review, the writer describes Vazirani's poems as a many-voiced exploration of multicultural "heritage, geography, and language."

Eight years after her well-received debut, *White Elephants*, Vazirani returns with a skillful, inviting sophomore effort, exploring South Asian, North American and Caribbean heritage, geography and language through a variety of masks and voices. Foremost among those voices is the articulate woman (apparently based on Vazirani's mother) who tells her own complex life story in "Inventing Maya," a careful sequence that forms the first half of this book: its detailed short poems follow Maya through her north Indian childhood ("In the Himalayas, I ran faster than any girl"), overseas to Washington, D.C., and then through an eventful adult life (spent mostly in the U.S.), where she remembers "those who had/ no books to brace/ them in the havoc." With its blend of tersely bittersweet lyricism and biographical data, "Inventing" might be a South Asian–American answer to Rita Dove's famous sequence Thomas and Beulah (which chronicled Dove's grandparents): Vazirani's sequence stands up very well beside that imposing model. The book's second half occupies quite other territory, pursuing in villanelle, sestina, semighazal, Cavafy-esque narrative and other, more compressed forms the poet's own contemporary concerns. Though Vazirani's light verse can fall flat the serious poems toward the close of the volume return to her strengths, among them clarity, geographical detail, and a way with short, unpunctuated lines: "Dedicated to You" (about posthumous fame) begins spry and ends with remarkable gravity, while "It's a Young Country" ties America's troubles convincingly to the poet's own.

Forecast: A recent profile in *Poets & Writers* should raise awareness of Vazirani's work among her fellow writers, and this book's style and substance should get it nominated for one or another prize. With *Copper Canyon* riding high on its two NBA nominations (and Ruth Stone's winning of the award), interest in this title will be further bolstered.

Source: Bowker Magazine Group, Review of *World Hotel*, in *Publishers Weekly*, Vol. 250, No. 3, January 20, 2003, p. 78.

Sudeep Sen

In the following review excerpt, Sen speaks of the fast-paced narrative style of Vazirani and her almost photographic visual imagery.

Another Indian American poet, Reetika Vazirani, launched herself into the poetry world by winning the Barnard New Women Poets Prize, which resulted in the publication of her debut collection, *White Elephants*. The competition judge, the well-known feminist poet Marilyn Hacker, noted that this is "a young writer's book about richness and confusion, the music, the flavors, the constant questioning of a genuinely multicultural existence." Vazirani is at her strongest when using the long poem sequence form. My personal favorite—"White Elephants," forty-two linked sonnets under different subheadings—has an immensely strong narrative drive, taut use of language (especially everyday speech), and a fine sense of pace and movement. Another poem, "The Rajdhani Express," uses the freeze-frame technique with good effect. The next-to-last section, "VI. Lotana Station," reads: "Coconut palms shoot branchlessly up / with tiny tufted tops; some bend sideways, strain, / frozen where the wind went. / The citrus sun flashes on window panes, / and a few early risers see / a coconut palm growing out of a hardwood tree." and in "VII: Vadodra Station," the concluding section, recollection, food, attire, and landscape mingle in unusual ways: "I have lived here before. / Kulfi melts across the sky. / Plains, longer than a sari's hem, / stretch northward, cropless and rich."

Reetika Vazirani, born of Bengali and Sindhi parentage, moved from India to the United States at age seven. She grew up learning English (and French) under the influence of the American education system. She could have, like so many others, been tainted by the systematic, homogeneous university creative-writing workshop regimentation. But in her case she was not, and the experience was an added side benefit. Vazirani is blessed with very personal, individual powers of poetic skill, imagination, and language that are all her own.

Source: Sudeep Sen, "Recent Indian English Poetry," in *World Literature Today*, Vol. 74, No. 4, Autumn 2000, p. 783.

Uma Parameswaran

In the following review, Parameswaran discusses the biographical background to Vazirani's poetry, focusing on the story of her mother, a child of the Indian diaspora.

This is Reetika Vazirani's second book of poems. She was born in India and raised in Maryland.

"I am your mother. Invent me," says the mother, Maya, to her daughter. And the daughter does. She culls memories not her own, seeking to resurrect, relive and record her mother's childhood in India and her teens in Maryland, her early married life in U.S., return to India, and a re-return to U.S. The narrative is chronological, and plays like a musical interlude, with soft strings and poignant pauses.

Born in 1937, Maya is the daughter of an army officer, and is educated at a boarding school in Mussoorie by teachers born in England. She remembers the barracks outside Lucknow, and being told about the island from where other officers came:

> "And when I said island, it was a mint leaf
> on my tongue, almond slice, a moon
> with its thin rays on the windowpane."

At about age nine, her mother leaves her father. Brother Ved and she "are stick people forever/climbing up the brown hill." They come to Washington D.C., and get a stepmother.

Many of the memories are common to the Diaspora. There is the British accent of mission schools, colloquialisms and rhymes typical of the 1960s: "Wish for me, I wish for you, ship's in, we have to run." There is the Indian mindset of new immigrants: father's mind converts all price tags into rupees, so that "When I bought my first lipstick/it was as if I bought a cow in India."

William Stratford appears in her life, and with it the wish to be white:

> I am nineteen years . . . and I'm left churning *if I were*
> But I kept hearing us laugh *were white* as I dreamt.
> . . ."

Back in India, there are friends and visits to palaces and to the Taj, where Maya can only view

Mumtaz Mahal with pity, imagining her dressing like her handmaid so she could sneak away to the bazaar and buy beads. Then marriage to Kiran, and two daughters; then a single poem about an extra marital affair that is intriguing in its mystery, but also somewhat disturbing in that he seems rather cavalier. "He asked would you, and I said I would" and after the one-week stand, he goes away. I suppose one should see it as an act of self affirmation. She had always seen herself as dark and small and married to a dark talent from a small world because of "The parent who. The British voices who. I became those who bent me. I am dark and small." This act liberates her in some way.

Then there are servants who domineer and cheat her, and the runaround at Kiran's workplace, "for those who studied abroad nowhere to go." So back to the United States, a familiar ending for those of us who left India a second time, in search of job satisfaction.

I have dwelt long on the first part, because it is closer to me. The second part is the daughter's story, "It's me, I'm not home." The lilting syllables of the first part are replaced by a kaleidoscope of harsher tempo, shorter words, references to fast cars and designer clothes, series of lovers, the whole kit and kaboodle of living in this "young country":

> through orange portals lit tunnels
> over bridges Brooklyn Golden Gate
> weather be bright wheels turn yes
> pack lightly we move so fast.

Source: Uma Parameswaran, Review of *World Hotel*, http://www.sawnet.org/books/reviews.php?World+Hotel.

Sources

Carb, Alison B., "An Interview with Bharati Mukherjee," *Massachusetts Review*, Vol. 29, No. 4, 1988, pp. 653–54.

Department of Homeland Security, Office of Immigration Statistics, *2004 Yearbook of Immigration Statistics*, January 2006, available online at http://uscis.gov/graphics/shared/statistics/yearbook/Yearbook2004.pdf.

Dove, Rita, "Poet's Choice," in the *Washington Post*, November 25, 2001, sect. T, p. 12.

Eliot, T. S., "Burnt Norton," in *T. S. Eliot: Collected Poems, 1909–1962*, Faber and Faber, 1974, p. 194.

Hacker, Marilyn, "Introduction," in *White Elephants*, by Reetika Vazirani, Beacon Press, 1996, p. xiv.

Review of *World Hotel*, in *Virginia Quarterly Review*, Vol. 79, No. 3, Summer 2003, p. 98.

Scharf, Michael, Review of *World Hotel*, in *Publishers Weekly*, Vol. 250, No. 3, January 20, 2003, p. 78.

Span, Paula, "The Failing Light," in the *Washington Post*, February 15, 2004, sect. W, p. 16, available online at http://www.washingtonpost.com/ac2/wp-dyn/A30475–2004Feb10?language=printer.

Tapping, Craig, "South Asia / North America: New Dwellings and the Past," in *Reworlding: The Literature of the Indian Diaspora*, edited by Emmanuel S. Nelson, Greenwood Press, 1992, p. 35.

Vazirani, Reetika, "Daughter-Mother-Maya-Seeta," in *World Hotel*, Copper Canyon Press, 2002, pp. 68–69.

Further Reading

Jamison, Kay Redfield, *Night Falls Fast: Understanding Suicide*, Vintage, 2000.
> Jamison, a professor of psychiatry at Johns Hopkins University who once contemplated her own suicide, provides insight into the mind of those who consider or commit suicide.

Kolanad, Gitanjali, *Culture Shock! India*, Time Books International, 2003.
> Vazirani went through her own version of cultural shock in the United States. This book is a guide to the culture and etiquette of the various regions of India.

Oliver, Mary, *A Poetry Handbook*, Harcourt, 1995.
> Oliver, the recipient of a Pulitzer Prize and National Book Award, provides insider information on how to write poetry. She never says that writing poetry is easy, but she equips students with poetic tools and insights.

Yapko, Michael D., *Breaking the Patterns of Depression*, Main Street Books, 1998.
> Yapko, a clinical psychologist and expert on depression, articulates the clinical definitions of depression in accessible language and offers exercises and treatments that complement the use of medications.

Hum

Ann Lauterbach
2005

"Hum" is the title work of Ann Lauterbach's 2005 poetry collection published by Penguin. The poem is deceptively simple; it is composed of short lines, everyday words, and seemingly innocuous images of the sky and weather. Through its circuitous framework and tangible sense of bewilderment, however, "Hum" presents a visceral eyewitness reaction to the terrorist attacks on September 11, 2001, on the World Trade Center, in New York City, where Lauterbach then lived and worked.

The poem is composed of twenty-seven couplets, or two-line stanzas, full of repeated words and phrases. "Beautiful," "tomorrow," "weep," "weather," "yesterday," and "here" are all echoed multiple times, giving the poem a tone of sorrow and a theme of temporal dislocation. "Hum" is written in free-verse style, meaning that its lines do not rhyme and do not have a consistent meter, or rhythm. In a postmodernist style, the images and phrases are fragmentary and often not meant to be taken literally. In a work such as this, the poet relies on the reader to fill in details based on his or her own experiences.

Lauterbach is often considered a member of the New York School of poets, a loose-knit group working primarily in Manhattan after 1950, whose work is influenced by the visual arts, especially abstract expressionism. This group includes such poets as John Ashbery, Barbara Guest, and James Schuyler, and their work is often as much about the process of writing as about the result. Like many abstract expressionist paintings, whose meanings can be difficult to decipher on the basis of their titles and images alone, "Hum" does not refer to the tragedy of the terrorist attacks directly, nor does it seek to explain or even mention the "hum" of the title.

Author Biography

Ann Lauterbach was born on September 28, 1942, in New York City. Both of her parents were active in leftist politics. Her father was a reporter for *Life* magazine and head of the Moscow bureau of *Time* magazine during World War II. He died of polio when Lauterbach was eight, after which her mother retreated into alcoholism. These early events profoundly affected Lauterbach; she came to see poetry and art as ways of lending meaning to her life and connecting with other people. Toward that end, she attended the High School of Music and Art in New York City, from which she graduated in 1960. After earning an English degree from the University of Wisconsin and spending a year as a graduate student at Columbia University, she moved to London, where she immersed herself in the vibrant art scene of the late 1960s. There, her crowning triumph was organizing a poetry conference featuring John Ashbery, who even then was considered a titan of the poetry world, as the keynote speaker. Lauterbach credits Ashbery as being a major influence on her work.

After seven years in England, Lauterbach returned to the United States in 1974 and worked at a series of art galleries in New York's up-and-coming Soho district. In those days, artists, poets, and musicians populated the same countercultural milieu. Lauterbach's poetry was especially influenced by visual artists, particularly the abstract expressionists, whose nonrepresentational paintings often became the inspiration for her poems. In 1979, she published her first significant book of poetry, *Many Times, but Then*, which was well received by critics.

In addition to three residencies at the prestigious Yaddo writers' community in the 1980s, Lauterbach also received a Guggenheim Fellowship and grants from the Ingram Merrill Foundation and the New York State Council for the Arts. In 1989, she became the Theodore Goodman Professor of Creative Writing at City College at the City University of New York, and in 1993 she was awarded a MacArthur Fellowship. Her other poetry collections include *Sacred Weather* (1984), *Before Recollection* (1987), *Clamor* (1991), and *On a Stair* (1997). In 2005, she published *The Night Sky: Writings on the Poetics of Experience*, a collection of essays on contemporary poetry that she wrote in the late 1990s for the *American Poetry Review*. The same year, she also published *Hum*, a collection of poems inspired by art, music, and the terrorist attacks of September 11, 2001, which a critic for *Publishers Weekly* said reads like "a chorus of angels."

Poem Summary

Lines 1–18

The first line of the poem, "The days are beautiful," is immediately repeated as the second line—and, in fact, the line appears a total of nine times; five of those repetitions come within the first fourteen lines. This type of repetition is called *anaphora* and usually serves to underscore a point the narrator wants to make. In the most literal sense, "The days are beautiful" could refer to the weather in New York on September 11, 2001, which was unusually warm and sunny.

In the second stanza, the narrator's framework becomes circuitous. She states, "I know what days are," perhaps calling the word "beautiful" to the mind of the reader, but then states, "The other is weather," and the reader is given no clue as to what "the other" is referring. At this point, the reader is required to bring his or her own imagination into the poem. Also, the third line, "I know what days are," sets up another anaphoric parallel, with the fifth line, "I know what weather is."

The fourth stanza introduces new words and images: "Things are incidental. / Someone is weeping." "Things," like "other," is entirely nonspecific and represents another opportunity for the reader to overlay his or her own ideas onto the poem. Similarly, the reader is not told who is weeping. As such, the precise "things" and "someone" may be seen as of secondary importance. The next line, on the other hand, reveals that the narrator is herself weeping "for the incidental." Then, the first line of the poem is repeated.

The sixth stanza introduces the theme of time with the question, "Where is tomorrow?" The next line is, "Everyone will weep." Thus, in three successive stanzas the narrator has related that someone is weeping, she herself is weeping, and everyone will be weeping. That is, the act of weeping is to a certain extent universal. The seventh and eighth stanzas begin with the same line: "Tomorrow was yesterday." Here, the narrator sustains her puzzlelike framework with even more anaphora. In the eighth stanza, in fact, the narrator refers to yesterday, tomorrow, and today, deepening the focus on shifting perceptions of time. With the ninth stanza, "The sound of the weather / is everyone weeping"—the first stanza in which the two lines of the couplet constitute a single sentence—the previously introduced ideas and sorrowful tone of the poem are more firmly established.

Lines 19–38

The universality of the unnamed cause of the weeping is indicated in the tenth stanza: "Everyone is incidental. / Everyone weeps." The first of those lines could be literally understood to mean that every individual is subject to the forces of chance, while the second may indicate that these forces can cause great sadness. The next stanza returns to the issue of passing time, asserting that today's tears will extinguish tomorrow, conveying a certain hopelessness.

The twelfth stanza returns to weather imagery: "The rain is ashes. / The days are beautiful." The two lines create a dissonant image. Raining ashes would seem to be at odds with beautiful days. With the next lines, "The rain falls down. / The sound is falling," the imagery becomes more complex. Rain, ashes, and sound are all falling. More ominously, line 27 states, "The sky is a cloud." Together, these lines create an image of a cloud filled with rain, ashes, and sound. The narrator then becomes more specific, stating in line 29, "The sky is dust." The image of a sky filled with dust, ashes, rain, and the sound of mass weeping undoubtedly stirs negative feelings in the reader. The narrator, meanwhile, still refrains from directly naming what she sees, instead presenting only fragmentary images.

Lines 30 and 31 are the same: "The weather is yesterday." This is something of an inversion of line 16, "Today is weather." Line 32 returns to the sound of weeping, briefly, before the narrator asks her second question in line 33, as if underscoring a certain confusion: "What is this dust?" Stanza 18 provides the first concrete clue to the subject of the poem: "The days are beautiful. / The towers are yesterday." That second line may be read as another way of stating that the towers, which are given no physical description, no longer exist.

The narrator then declares in line 37, "The towers are incidental," harking back to lines 7 and 19, in which "things" and "everyone" are also described as incidental, and line 9, "I weep for the incidental." The next line is another question, a companion to line 33: "What are these ashes?" The repetition of the words "ashes" and "dust" is reminiscent of the common incantation of Christian burial rites, as written in the Book of Common Prayer, "ashes to ashes, dust to dust," which in turn was inspired by Genesis 3:19: "Dust thou art, and unto dust thou shalt return." As such, the notion of death, not explicitly mentioned, may also be called to mind.

Lines 39–54

In the last section of the poem, the narrator abruptly switches focus. Gone is concern with time, as the words "yesterday," "today," and "tomorrow" do not again appear. Instead, each stanza, in a continuation of the poem's reliance on anaphora for dramatic effect, begins with the word "here." These last eight stanzas present a catalog of images that are abstract and expressionist in their randomness. The narrator speaks of a robe, books, and stones, and in the context of the poem, all of these objects have undergone some transformation, even as they are still "here." The words are "retired to their books," while the stones are "loosed from their settings."

The last three stanzas present three final ambiguous images. "Here is the place / where the sun came up" gives particular importance to the sun's coming up on one particular occasion in one particular place. Stanza 26, "Here is a season / dry in the fireplace," implies the burning up of an entire season. In view of earlier references, the final lines call to mind burning and death on the one hand, light and beauty on the other: "Here are the ashes. / The days are beautiful."

Themes

Passage of Time

Lauterbach's repetition of the words "yesterday," "today," and "tomorrow" make the passage of time a major theme in "Hum." The puzzlelike framework in which the terms are placed underscores the sense of dislocation the narrator must be feeling. At various points, she states, "Tomorrow was yesterday" and "The towers are yesterday." The first statement implies that the day before had been a fateful "tomorrow"—a day whose events had been long in coming. Yesterday, also, the towers existed. Yesterday things were different and perhaps more

Topics For Further Study

- In the front matter of *Hum*, Lauterbach includes a quote from Shakespeare's play *King Lear*: "What, art mad? A man may see how this world goes with no eyes. Look with thine ears" (act 4, scene 6). Go to a busy place and "look with your ears"; that is, close your eyes and listen to the surrounding sounds for at least ten minutes (or take a tape recorder and listen later). Did you hear anything that you might not have heard had your eyes been open? Write a short essay on what you "saw" when you were listening and relate your experience to Lauterbach's "Hum."

- If you did not know that "Hum" was about the tragedy of September 11, do you think you would have deduced as much? Using pictures from magazines and newspapers, assemble a collage based on the images Lauterbach evokes in her poem. Present your collage to the class and lead a discussion about the kinds of feelings your collage brings to mind, noting whether they are similar to or different from Lauterbach's themes in "Hum."

- Many of Lauterbach's poems are inspired by specific paintings or musical compositions. Pick one of your favorite songs or works of art and write a poem about it. Then write a companion essay on how your words were influenced by the subject you chose.

- Read other poems inspired by the terrorist attacks of September 11. Write an essay describing the images and language of these poems and compare and contrast them with Lauterbach's "Hum."

- Lauterbach gave a speech on February 12, 2003, at a symposium called "Poems Not Fit for the White House," which was organized to protest the cancellation of a White House poetry event because many of the guests opposed the war in Iraq and had written protest poems to present at the event. "Perhaps poets come to the fore at such times," Lauterbach said in her speech, which was reprinted in an article by Joshua Clover in the *Village Voice*, "because we already live at the margins, we represent a kind of powerless power, and maybe people become interested in this." Research news articles of this event and use them as the basis for a classroom debate. Prepare and deliver a short speech explaining whether or not you believe the poets were right to foster such controversy.

---

hopeful. Furthermore, "The tears of today / will put out tomorrow." That is, the future that once existed for many—including those who perished in the September 11 terrorist attacks as well as their family and friends—has been replaced by grief. Also, the statement "Today is weather" is something of a neutral revision of the repeated statement "The days are beautiful." The sense of beauty has been replaced by the valueless term "weather." In effect, yesterday held hope, today holds only weeping, and tomorrow has been extinguished.

Air and Sky

Many of the narrator's words in "Hum" relate either directly or indirectly to the air and sky. The word "weather" itself appears seven times; also appearing multiple times are the words "rain," "sky," and "cloud." Lauterbach states directly that the weather is, variously, "other," "today," "the sound of . . . weeping," "yesterday," and "nothing." The "towers" themselves indirectly reference air and sky; the World Trade Center's twin towers, at 110 stories each, were the tallest buildings in the world when they opened in 1973. They were an integral part of the New York skyline, visible from myriad locations both inside and outside Manhattan. Through the narrator's free association of ideas, the reader gets the sense that the towers were in fact part of the sky. The ominous sense of tragedy in "Hum" comes, in part, from the narrator's observations that sounds, ashes, and dust are all falling from the sky.

Beauty

"The days are beautiful" is one of the most enigmatic lines of "Hum," in addition to being its most frequent, appearing as both the first and last lines and seven other times in between. Its juxtaposition with the foreboding images of ashes, dust, and the sounds of everyone weeping create a stark discordance, which further results in a mood of a world off-kilter and out of synchronization. The narrator seems to be in a state of incomprehension, as if she cannot make sense of what is happening. Her insistence that "the days are beautiful," which is reinforced by her declaration "I know what days are," is upended by the sounds of weeping. The narrator herself is weeping "for the incidental," which, though unstated, might refer to the beautiful days; beauty is as fleeting and elusive as time in "Hum."

Disintegration

"Ashes" and "dust," by definition, conjure images of disintegration. The falling rain, the falling sound, and the statement that "the towers are yesterday" all further contribute to that theme. "The sky is dust" and "Here are the ashes," along with the narrator's concern with weeping, tears, and the loss of tomorrow, indicate that the disintegration is both physical and metaphorical.

Lamentation

A *lamentation* is a song or poem expressing sorrow over a loss, particularly the death of a loved one. Although Lauterbach does not directly address the loss of any one person, her choice of words and the concatenation of images lend to the eulogizing effects of the poem. The narrator mentions that she weeps and that "everyone will weep." She weeps, in particular, for the incidental, which, as defined in the poem, includes "things," "everyone," and "the towers."

The narrator's use of the words "ashes" and "dust" in the questions, "What is this dust?" and "What are these ashes?" indicate her incomprehension of the tragedy. Those familiar with the images of the World Trade Center's collapse will recognize Lauterbach's words as literal; the sky over Manhattan was indeed filled with ash and debris for days, as the rubble smoldered in the aftermath of the attacks. As a lamentation, the terms bring to mind the words of the Christian burial rite, as written in the Book of Common Prayer: "earth to earth, ashes to ashes, dust to dust." These words conjure images of solemn ceremony and the memorializing of the dead. Many of those who died in the World Trade Center literally became the dust and ashes that fell from the sky.

Style

Abstract Imagery

Abstract imagery is a literary device favored by the New York School of poets, who, again, were influenced by the visual arts, especially the abstract expressionism of such artists as Jackson Pollock and Willem de Kooning. Their poems incorporate fragmentary, or incomplete, images to achieve a "painterly" style. Indeed, with their phrases and disparate words, they emulate the way artists can use color and brushstrokes, rather than representational depictions of objects, to evoke meaning. *Abstract* images are those that do not overtly appear to make sense or relate to the subject at hand. "Here is the robe / that smells of the night" presents such an image in "Hum." These words have little apparent relation to the poem's topic and represent an invitation for readers to bring their own ideas and interpretations to a work. In such a way, the artist creates a sort of dialogue between the poet and the reader. By using cryptic language and nonlinear frameworks, Lauterbach, like many other poets of the New York School, seeks to actively engage readers in endowing her poems with meaning.

Language Poetry

Language poetry, sometimes written as "L=A=N=G=U=A=G=E" poetry, in reference to the magazine that bore that name, evolved in the 1970s, when many poets became more concerned with the process of arranging words than with the meanings of the words themselves. As influenced by the modernist prose of Gertrude Stein, the objectivist poet Louis Zukofsky, and the philosopher Ludwig Wittgenstein (who proposed that language was itself a game), the Language poets spread their influence through such journals as *This* magazine and *L=A=N=G=U=A=G=E Magazine*. In "Hum," the stanza "I know what days are. / The other is weather" both follows and precedes lines with the words "days" and "weather." This focus on simple words is reminiscent of Stein's famous line "Rose is a rose is a rose" and serves to break down the reader's expectations based on literal interpretations of the words "days" and "weather."

Repetition

The most notable feature of "Hum" is its repetition. Like a painter who chooses a palette made up of only a few colors, Lauterbach establishes the mood of "Hum" by choosing a palette of words that she arranges in different combinations in order to achieve a particular mood. "Days" appears ten times, "beautiful" nine times, and "here" eight times. Other words repeated multiple times include "tomorrow," "today," "yesterday," "sky," "rain," "weep," "ashes," and "dust." In addition, several lines are repeated in their entirety. "The days are beautiful" appears nine times; "Tomorrow was yesterday" appears twice. This repetition emphasizes words that the author deems important. The repetitions fall mainly into two categories: words representing time and place ("here," "yesterday," "today," and "tomorrow") and words evoking imagery of nature and destruction ("weep," "ashes," "dust," "rain," "sky," and "fall"). Collectively, these repeated words create images that are at once ethereal, ominous, and transient, suggesting the narrator's sense of unease and sadness and her shifting perceptions of reality. Ultimately, the line "The days are beautiful" may serve as an example of irony, as if the narrator repeats the phrase in order to reassure herself of something she wishes to be true, despite the evidence of destruction that surrounds her; also, in ending the poem, the line may be meant to evoke the sense of rebirth and renewal that, however distant, might follow any loss.

Anaphora

Anaphora refers to the practice of repeating the same word or phrase at the beginning of several lines of a poem. The repetition of "The days are beautiful" is an example of anaphora, even though the words constitute an entire line. "The sky is a cloud" is echoed two lines later in "The sky is dust," and "The rain is ashes" is followed by "The rain falls down." This repetition serves to alert the reader that the sky and rain in question are of great importance. As a cloud, the sky becomes part of the poem's weather imagery; as dust, it becomes part of the poem's imagery of destruction. The narrator's sense of shifting time is signaled in the repeated lines "Tomorrow was yesterday" and "The weather is yesterday." The poem's third section is notable for its sharp diversion to anaphora that concerns the present place, "here," which is repeated at the beginning of each of the final eight stanzas, rather than "tomorrow" or "yesterday." This anaphora suggests that the narrator is taking stock of her surroundings in order to make sense of what has happened.

Historical Context

Postmodernism

Lauterbach's writing, including "Hum," is firmly grounded in the postmodern tradition. Postmodernism evolved primarily after World War II, when writers and artists declined to restrict themselves to the confines of form and structure that had defined artistic expression in previous generations. By definition, postmodernism is a continuation of modernism, which was itself a primarily twentieth-century artistic movement that influenced music, literature, and the visual arts by challenging accepted cultural norms. In terms of poetry, modernism was marked by the work of W. H. Auden, one of Lauterbach's acknowledged influences. The postmodernists continued to develop the avant garde in the arts by becoming even more experimental in their work.

Many postmodernists created works of music, poetry, and painting that were deemed "minimalist" because of their stripped-down, elemental style. In music, the postmodernist composer John Cage created a composition that does not require any instrument to play a single note. "Color field" painters such as Mark Rothko created large canvases made up of solid squares of single colors, and writers such as Raymond Carver penned stories in which meaning is derived from what does not happen or from what happens in multiple ways. Lauterbach's poems, including "Hum," can be considered postmodernist because of her frequent use of repetition, short lines, simple language, and fragmentary images.

The Impact of September 11

On the morning of September 11, 2001, almost three thousand people died in near-simultaneous terrorist attacks in which four domestic passenger airplanes were hijacked and crashed into the World Trade Center, in New York; the Pentagon, in Arlington, Virginia; and a field in Somerset County, Pennsylvania. The country, and indeed the world, was stunned by the events, which marked the first time the United States had been attacked on its home soil since Pearl Harbor was bombed on December 7, 1941. Unlike Pearl Harbor, however, millions of people saw much of the events of September 11 on live television, thus themselves witnessing the enormity and severity of the attacks and the loss of innocent lives. Collectively, the raw emotions evoked by the attacks engendered an unprecedented feeling of national mourning. This feeling of overwhelming disquietude is what

Lauterbach explores in "Hum," wherein "everyone weeps," and "the towers are incidental."

Lauterbach, who was then living and working in New York City, first published "Hum" in 2005, four years after the terrorist attacks took place and the subsequent so-called war on terror, as led by the United States, had become mired in political controversy. However, "Hum" is not concerned with the perpetrators of the attacks or with how the nation responded; rather, Lauterbach focuses solely on an individual's visceral reaction to a sky filled with ashes. Many artists and poets created works in response to these attacks. The philosopher Arthur C. Danto, in an essay published in *ArtNet* magazine, writes of the possibility of the art world's responding to the tragedy:

> By day's end the city was transformed into a ritual precinct, dense with improvised sites of mourning. I thought at the time that artists, had they tried to do something in response to 9/11, could not have done better than the anonymous shrine-makers who found ways of expressing the common mood and feeling of those days, in ways that everyone instantly understood.

In the years that followed, the images and memory of September 11, 2001, became part of the American consciousness and permeated all aspects of society. One year later, *An Eye for an Eye Makes the Whole World Blind: Poets on 9/11*, an anthology of poems inspired by the disaster, was published by Regent Press, while *Poetry after 9/11: An Anthology of New York Poets* was published by Melville House.

Critical Overview

Lauterbach's "Hum," like most of her work, is considered by critics to exhibit a love of abstraction and language that is typical of postmodernism. Lauterbach's language is not difficult; both her words and most of her images are simple. Still, this simplicity belies the highly evolved nature of her work. As the poet James McCorkle wrote in the *Dictionary of Literary Biography*, Lauterbach's poems "explore the most central of lyric and human conditions—eros, mortality, the coil of time, and the material of language." Other critics, however, have taken issue with her reliance on the tools of the New York School poets. D. H. Tracy, reviewing the collection *Hum* in the journal *Poetry*, first notes that the "New York School's approach, with its offhand radicalism . . . has intense appeal," but he then avers that this type of "urbanity, taken too far, can become absurdity." Conversely, Shrode Hargis, writing of *Hum* in the *Harvard Review*, states that "Lauterbach thrives when . . . she leads the reader through the catalogue of worlds that language makes possible."

Lauterbach herself states that "although I teach poetry all the time I have no idea how I would teach my own," as Eric Goldscheider of the *Boston Globe* quoted her as saying during a 1999 symposium at Bard College. She did, however, invite her readers "to participate in the making of meaning as an act of pleasure in the materiality of language." That is, Lauterbach expects readers to bring their own interpretation to her work; for her, a poem is a dialogue between reader and writer. Such a definition liberates critical response from being overly formal or concerned with traditional forms of explication.

Criticism

Kathy Wilson Peacock

Wilson Peacock is a writer and editor of articles about literature. In this essay, she discusses the role of the poet in times of national crises, focusing on Lauterbach's "Hum" and Robert Pinsky's "9/11."

One of the poet's main responsibilities is to deliver us from clichés in moments when words threaten to fail us. "It is so hard to know what to say" is what so many *do* say when confronted with grieving friends or loved ones. Rare is the eulogy that does not include the words of a poet, be that poet contemporary or biblical, as part of ritual's salve. This phenomenon was writ large after the terrorist attacks of September 11, 2001, when the United States cohered as a single community united by grief. The nation's poets, masters and novices alike, moved to the forefront during this time, their collectivity of words creating a liturgy like none other. Lauterbach's "Hum" stands out as one of the least literal yet most effective of these poems. Its power is derived from the use of ordinary means—simple words and images—to express extraordinary thoughts.

As in so much minimalist art, "Hum" is as notable for what it says as for what it does not say. It does not even "say" its title; a "hum" is in essence the opposite of spoken words. Beginning with the title and the repetition of the first verse, "The days are beautiful," the poem appears at first glance as

> *With its musical attributes of repetition and refrain, Lauterbach's poem is a stirring dirge that is elegant in its universality and unprocessed rawness of feeling.*

innocuous as that bright September morning in 2001. In a series of twenty-seven fleeting stanzas, many only seven or eight words in their entirety, Lauterbach launches into a deceptively breezy lamentation that cycles through the concepts of shifting time, the beauty of weather, a shower of ash and dust, and a catalog of material objects that have nothing to do with airplanes, terrorists, heroism, freedom, or any of the other knee-jerk signifiers that permeate so many 9/11-inspired poems. In direct reference to the tragedy at hand, she says only, "The towers are incidental" and "The towers are yesterday." Hers is a poem that expresses the unbearable lightness of being in a moment of incomprehensible madness.

"Hum" is different from other 9/11-inspired poems because it is not what we might expect. "The days are beautiful" is repeated again and again, nine times total, in a poem essentially about mass bloodshed. The statement is too important to be taken as an example of irony and perhaps too opaque to be taken literally. A contrasting poem is the one that the *Washington Post* commissioned the U.S. poet laureate Robert Pinsky to write in commemoration of the first anniversary of 9/11, which he titled, simply enough, "9/11." Pinsky's words are full of images that soothe rather than challenge; the work's three-line stanzas are a litany of easily grasped references to Emily Dickinson, Will Rogers, and Marianne Moore. It includes the occasional high-school vocabulary word ("expropriation"), pedestrian phrases such as "terrible spectacle" and "doomed firefighters," and the requisite splash of patriotism via references to the "Eagle's head" and the Statue of Liberty. Pinsky hits all the notes a poet laureate is expected to hit, corralling a population of nearly three hundred million people into a single-minded "collective we" that wrings its hands over a self-conscious desire for titillating televised disaster. In doing his job, Pinsky delivers a belated eulogy that stirs up just enough discomfort to be neatly swept away with phrases borrowed from "America the Beautiful."

Perhaps, however, a comparison is unfair. After all, the poems "Hum" and "9/11" were written for different reasons. Lauterbach's lamentation is a visceral reaction to a tragedy still under way, while Pinsky's poem is a reflection of events a year in the past. Lauterbach's narrator is concerned with the images at hand: images of dust, ash, a feeling that tomorrow is gone. She writes of a sky subsumed by sound and debris, of weather that is nothing, and of weeping, all of which serves to upset her sense of equilibrium, her sense that "the days are beautiful." Hers is the reaction of a camera's lens, unfiltered by politics, raw in its questions ("What is this dust?"). Moreover, she presents the voice of a single narrator, one of a million witnesses, whose experience is unique. Her narrator alone is the one who notices the robe "that smells of the night" and the stones "loosed from their settings."

Conversely, Pinsky's purpose is not to put forth a singular vision but to act as the spokesman of our collective response; hence the recitations regarding donated blood, box cutters, and Ray Charles. As a minimalist work, "Hum" does not need to focus on the images of crushed fire engines or the doctors and nurses who had nothing to do because there were no walking wounded to be saved. Lauterbach's intent as a poet is to create an unusually variegated collage based on snatches of thoughts, much as Picasso's painting *Guernica* achieved the power of a thousand-page manifesto through a single mural in black and white that starkly and simply depicted the devastation from the bombing of Guernica, Spain, and its civilian population during the Spanish Civil War.

Several generations ago, Wilfred Owen, a soldier who ultimately died in battle, alerted the world to the first killing fields of the modern age in his poem "Dulce Et Decorum Est," which presented the indelible image of a soldier suffocating in the "thick green light" of a mustard gas attack. His words were graphic; they needed to be, in order to convey the horror of World War I to those who still espoused outdated romantic notions of warfare from the insulated confines of their Edwardian-era parlors. Almost a century later, on 9/11, there was no insulated parlor; millions upon millions saw the

What Do I Read Next?

- *Poetry after 9/11: An Anthology of New York Poets* (2002), edited by Dennis Loy Johnson and Valerie Merians, presents forty-five poems written in response to the terrorist tragedies. Featured poets include Stephen Dunn, Hal Sirowitz, Molly Peacock, and Alicia Ostriker.

- The poem "9/11," by Robert Pinsky, a former U.S. poet laureate, was commissioned by the *Washington Post* for the first anniversary of the attacks and was published on September 12, 2002. It is available at http://www.pbs.org/newshour/bb/poems/july-dec02/9-11_9-11.html from *Online Newshour*.

- Frank O'Hara's "Why I Am Not a Painter," from his 1965 collection *Lunch Poems*, is a breezy response to all of his admirers who wondered why he became a poet. As a founding member of the New York School of poets, O'Hara was greatly influenced by the contemporary art scene of the 1950s.

- W. H. Auden's "September 1, 1939," published in his *Selected Poems* (1940), was written to commemorate the day the Nazis invaded Poland at the beginning of World War II. Written in the first person, it recounts Auden's reaction to hearing the news as he sat in a Manhattan diner.

- John Ashbery, considered one of the greatest American poets of the twentieth century, was a leading voice of the New York School of poets. His 1986 collection *Selected Poems* offers an overview of his work.

- Jorie Graham's *Overlord* (2005) tackles many of the same themes that interest Lauterbach with a style that is also influenced by abstract art. While Graham's work is infused with more religious imagery than Lauterbach's, this collection, like *Hum*, is a post-9/11 meditation.

- Lauterbach's *If in Time: Selected Poems, 1975–2000* (2001) offers readers an overview of the poet's career.

- *The Night Sky: Writings on the Poetics of Experience* (2005) is a collection of essays written by Lauterbach for the *American Poetry Review* between 1996 and 1999. Subjects include the impact of her father's early death on her work and ruminations about poetry's role in popular culture.

- The comic novel *A Nest of Ninnies*, written by the New York School poets John Ashbery and James Schuyler and originally published in 1969, is a satirical look at the follies of middle-class and upper-class suburbanites. The work was written in a slightly experimental "dialogue" format.

---

horror firsthand. Television collapsed the physical distance between the site of the World Trade Center and the places where the nation's people stood and sat, whether Manhattan or Montana.

Thus, the twenty-first-century poet's language of tragedy need not be gruesome to be effective. Whereas Owen described blood "gargling from the froth-corrupted lungs" of the dying soldier, Lauterbach wrote, "The sound is falling," and both achieved much the same effect. The horror of 9/11 was already seared into the nation's collective mind. Owen, in a world not yet saturated with mass media, served as a literary war correspondent with literal images. His was a poem of admonition; his way of saying, "Tomorrow was yesterday," was to call the battle cry "It is sweet and proper to die for one's country" ("Dulce et decorum est / Pro patria mori") a lie. Both Owen and Lauterbach bore witness to the greatest horrors of their generations and responded with eulogies that burst free from the clichés of their respective days.

The narrator of "Hum," in the midst of horror's confusion, seeks to reassure herself of what she knows. She knows the days are (supposed to be) beautiful; she knows what is (supposed to be) incidental; she knows that the ash falling from the sky is *not* weather. She knows the towers are gone; she knows tomorrow is gone—at least the tomorrow that she had imagined yesterday. These are the unfiltered, unedited thoughts that occur in the suspended moment of time between perception and understanding.

Conversely, Pinsky's narrator has had a year to consider the tragedy. Instead of focusing on the action in slow motion, he gathers together images of popular culture in order to create touch points that soothe. Who is more effective, one then asks, Lauterbach or Pinsky? The answer depends on what one seeks from poems. With more universal words (everyone knows of yesterday, tomorrow, dust, and weather, but not everyone knows of social security numbers, Frederick Douglass, and Ray Charles's charity recording), Lauterbach's "Hum" comes closer to evoking the primal aspects of sorrow aroused by 9/11 than Pinsky's poem. Pinsky writes for the part of the popular consciousness that is American; Lauterbach writes for the part of the American consciousness that is human. With respect to the universal need for words to ameliorate tragedy, and with respect to finding the "right thing to say" without descending into standard funereal clichés, "Hum" demonstrates that less can be more. With its musical attributes of repetition and refrain, Lauterbach's poem is a stirring dirge that is elegant in its universality and unprocessed rawness of feeling.

Source: Kathy Wilson Peacock, Critical Essay on "Hum," in *Poetry for Students*, Thomson Gale, 2007.

Donna Seaman

In the following review excerpt, Seaman notes Lauterbach's ability to address both the physical and the intellectual aspects of consciousness.

A new book of poems and an essay collection showcase the subtle and philosophical work of a rarefied yet captivating poet.

In *Hum*, Lauterbach taps into both the sensual and the cerebral aspects of consciousness. Her exquisite lyric poems are like lacework, netting feeling and thought, and embodying the inner flickering of light and dark, presence and absence. As Lauterbach gambols between sense and sensibility, elusiveness and lucidity, she sketches a poetic universe similar in topography and weather to that of Stevens and Ashbery. She meditates on the music of Mahler and the art of Botticelli and Gerhard Richter, and, like a particle accelerator, her whirling poems atomize experience. In her most focused and moving poems, Lauterbach, like so many writers, including Jorie Graham in *Overlord* (2005), traces the concussive emotional effects of 9/11.

Source: Donna Seaman, Review of *Hum*, in *Booklist*, Vol. 101, No. 18, May 15, 2005, p. 1630.

Bowker Magazine Group

In the following review, the writer puts Lauterbach's poems in a space between an abstract ideal and the real world as we see and know it, and says that their meanings are revealed with grace.

"Maybe what is interesting will also be beautiful," writes Lauterbach at the opening of her seventh collection of poems, knowingly marking out a world that exists after beauty, after emotion, after nature—after everything that traditionally makes poetry. Her speaker is determined to make the absence of beauty beautiful without being postmodern; the poems are abstract and slippery, and yield their meanings with reluctant late modernist grace. The book is organized into three sections, the first attending chiefly to sound, the second to visual art, the third to 9/11. The poems limn a space somewhere between the world-as-given and the ideal, concentrating on language's dual relationship to experience, "[a]s if 'life' could touch its metaphors." The rifle poem addresses 9/11 in a series of simple declarative sentences, which repeat at intervals: "The days are beautiful./ The towers are yesterday." A poem about a Malevich painting argues for abstraction always derived from the concrete: "the square was only/ a boy with his knapsack/ a woman crossing his path." When her speaker, at intervals, simply gives it up ("I'm lonely for the integrity of sacred life, not religion, but love's/ trove, its coil around sex"), the hum of this book becomes a chorus of angels.

Source: Bowker Magazine Group, Review of *Hum*, in *Publishers Weekly*, Vol. 252, No. 16, April 18, 2005, p. 58.

Shrode Hargis

In the following review, Hargis concentrates on Lauterbach's use of anaphora and catalogues as linguistic devices.

In his essay "Poetry and Happiness," Richard Wilbur writes of the poet's "primitive desire ... to lay claim to as much of the world as possible," a desire which manifests itself in what he calls "cataloguing": a poetic mode that allows the poet to both "name the world ... and embody the self." Eric Pankey, in his six previous books, has specialized in a particular blend of cataloguing which one might characterize as "psychological pastoral," wherein the aim is to take stock of the outer world (nature, in particular) in order to comment on and create an aperture to the inner. Indeed, Pankey writes in the tradition of Wallace Stevens and has confirmed as much himself.

Reliquaries, his new book, is a departure from this on two levels. For one, Pankey's cataloguing, though still imbued with the fodder of the pastoral, resides mainly in the realm of the heroic "I"; and two, Pankey abandons the compressed and predominately formal metrics of his previous work for a longer, more prosaic line:

> If only I were fluent in another language, I might
> be fluent at last and at least in this one.
> When I hear an angel rustle in the matrix of vines
> and hedges amid a thousand thorn spurs,
> When the screw-head is stripped and no tool I own
> can turn it,
> When I find a pale blue egg fallen, unbroken, in
> the green shade of the shriveled irises,
> It is my own wordlessness by which I set down the
> moment and its abracadabra.

The entire book reads this way, with each line acting as its own grammatical entity and each poem sounding like an engaging litany of Whitmanesque oratorios. Where the roll calls of Pankey's previous books succeeded, however, by granting flora and fauna the starring roles, *Reliquaries* sometimes verges on long-windedness when the poet too volubly rears his head:

> I want to wake and find myself awake amid the
> fog, Venice veiled in drizzle.
> I want to sleep so that I might wake to muted bells
> and the water's echoed slosh.
> I don't want to lament the duration nor the flux of
> hours as they're spent.
> I drop a coin into the poor-box, another coin to illumine the fresco.
> I stand in the light until the light clicks off, then
> fumble for another coin.

Most of the successes of *Reliquaries* come at the level of specific lines (or, as it were, particular elements of his many lists). One comes across gestures that are both beautiful and impressionistically affective—"The water, full of light, pulled from the well's depth, spilled in cold thick braids," or "Then as now, the road rolls behind like a winding sheet into a forest with Spanish Moss." But too often Pankey follows with a line that seems sophomoric and flat: "Then as now, the moon, my one companion, drifts beside me on a current of stars."

The form might be to blame for this. Each poem consists of four sections, and each section consists of five lines, but how these sections relate to one another is often unclear. In fact, without the poems' titles—which Pankey apparently intends as the lens through which each poem is to be interpreted—the interrelation of their sections would often be indecipherable. It's as if he sat down with conceptual cues ("Lessons in Art" or "Inertia" or "The Suspension of Disbelief"), constructed four litanies of self-contained reactions to them, then called it a poem. As a consequence, the book comes off feeling like a protracted Rorschach test, and many of the poems fail to culminate in satisfying endings.

Ann Lauterbach's new book, *Hum* (her first since the publication of her *Selected Poems*), reads like a post-structuralist inversion of *Reliquaries*. Whereas Pankey catalogues his different responses to the same word or concept, Lauterbach often attempts to create a catalogue of responses using the same word or concept:

> Is this a lyric? Can you tell me if this is a lyric?
> It is about a doll, which is a thing and also an image, one
> kind of thing image. Anyway, there is a doll.
> A "female," or else a cross-dresser, doubtful, but
> an interesting idea for an image.
> You would have to lift up her petticoats.
> Is this the same doll? Is it archival?
> Is it part of a collection, people have collections of
> dolls,
> they are serial doll lovers.
> I have had many dolls, and many lovers.
> Does this make me a lyric poet?
> Am I singing now, the way the doll might have
> sung
> something from "Guys and Dolls," a musical,
> in which there were lyrics I once knew by heart.
> If I know things by heart, does this make me a
> lyric poet?

Of course, this is more than just modernist anaphora—a rose is a rose is a rose—for a doll is no longer just a doll and a rose is no longer just a rose. As Lauterbach writes in "Trianges and Squares (Guston, Malevich)," one of the many successful poems in *Hum*. "The roses are desolate in their insufficient arrangement./The subject grows old. The subject may or may not be roses." Self-conscious word-play such as this is hard to pull off, and sometimes in *Hum* one feels battered over the head with it: "A doll, let's say again a doll . . ." But Lauterbach has been perfecting this approach to poetry ever since the release of her third book, *Clamor*, and in this new collection she is at the top of her game.

The best poems in *Hum* are those in which Lauterbach stages a fusion of the musical narratives representative of her early work and the "vocabulary of displacement" that runs throughout her most recent. Many of these poems consist of, as she puts it in her poem "Topos," a "plural wandering" that is reminiscent of Wallace Stevens (the same Stevens whom Pankey abandons in *Reliquaries*). "There is no span," she writes in "Event Horizon,"

> all arguments blur
> and lower life mildews along the riverbank
> and a figure goes on a rampage in the exhausted vocabulary of displacement
>
> the arc of the bridge has collapsed
> things remain under their masks
> there is neither the one nor the other with whom
> to flirt. This is what occurs, less than a horizon.

This is Ann Lauterbach at her best and provides a small taste of just one of the many mesmerizing journeys that can be found in *Hum*. Indeed, Lauterbach thrives when, rather than cataloguing the many possibilities of language, she leads the reader through the catalogue of worlds that language makes possible and therefore provides alternative perspectives "into" poetry and art and (why not?) life:

> Maybe what is interesting will also be beautiful
> although that is—
> that is:
> not to look out or at, but into.

Source: Shrode Hargis, Review of *Hum*, in *Harvard Review*, Vol. 29, December 2005, pp. 232–35.

Susan M. Schultz

In the following essay excerpt, Schultz discusses Lauterbach's debt to John Ashbery in her use of houses as a metaphor for poetry and for community.

Critics have written much about John Ashbery's relation to the poets who precede him but little about his influence on poets who follow him. I will argue here that two of the finest of the poets who have gone to school to Ashbery, namely Ann Lauterbach and Donald Revell, are now revising his vision to fit a more social context. I am especially interested in their use of houses as metaphors for poetry and for community. Where Ashbery abdicates the traditional metaphor of the house (associated as it is with community) as a location for poetic creation, Revell and Lauterbach in different ways reclaim the trope as the site for their poetry. Where Ashbery elides the problematic tension between confinement and freedom, form and the drive toward transcendence, Revell and Lauterbach both reinstall the problem and fail—or refuse—to go around it. Revell investigates the site of marriage, and marries Ashbery's distrust of language's instability with a more earnest desire for the confinements of poetic form. Lauterbach considers the house as the home of female creativity and wants the comfort of that tradition even as she means to get past its tyranny. . . .

Lauterbach's use of the house is complicated by her gender, for limitations—and poems—have been historically male constructions:

> Garden, hedge, pool,
> Planned to guard the old line, define
> And compose the imagination's brown capacity.
> Our extent is more than memory
> Or the text of a poem willed to the wall
> Although our tenacious forebears whisper
> Collections, passed from father to son to son
> While mother prunes.

That the "old line" is poetic as well as social is especially worrisome for a female poet; that the poem, like the "will," enforces limits means that her poems must resist those same kinds of limitation. "It is not the dark that scares me, but the limit / which places the house in the field, the horse in its stall." Hers will not be the "garden, hedge, pool"—the Eden of social memory—but the house itself. For Lauterbach, to be at home is both a blessing and a curse, for it metaphorically represents a feminine line of creation at the same time as it closes her out of Whitman's open road. She attempts to get past this impasse by opening her house to infinitude, as Dickinson did. In "Naming the House," she posits the conflict between a "longing for dispersal" and the "joy of naming it this, and this is mine":

> And I think also of how women, toward evening,
> Watch as the buoyant dim slowly depletes
> Terrain, and frees the illuminated house
> So we begin to move about, reaching for potholders
> And lids, while all the while noting
> That the metaphor of the house is ours to keep
> And the dark exterior only another room
> Waiting for its literature.

This poem is an apt response to Dickinson's poem about the differences between prose and poetry, confinement and freedom, which is built on the metaphor of a house:

> I dwell in Possibility—
> A fairer House than Prose—
> More numerous of Windows—
> Superior—for Doors—

where it becomes clear that Dickinson is describing a house not circumscribed by walls, but by the sky:

> Of Chambers as the Cedars—
> Impregnable of Eye—
> And for an Everlasting Roof
> The Cambrels of the Sky—

Just so Lauterbach sees the outside as "only another room" and the poet as someone who "dallies now in plots / But feels a longing for dispersal." We can read "plots" as plots of ground, as graveplots, or as the prose that represents for Dickinson and for her the genre of confinement, the woman's genre. The word "household" tells the story nicely.

Where Ashbery seems content to evade the question, posed so incessantly by Stevens, of the relation between reality and imagination, between place and the thoughts we have about it, Lauterbach is not: she personifies this dualism as "Bishop" and "Beckett" in "St. Lucia." "Elizabeth Bishop" she uses to mean a reverence for the place itself; "Samuel Beckett" to mean the allegorization of place. The dualism does not, of course, bear too much scrutiny, something that Lauterbach doubtless knows well enough as she places herself between them:

> The sea, solitary or not,
> Implies the confines of a dream.
> I'm between Beckett and Bishop,
> The one entirely in, the other there
> Civilizing Brazil, clarity to clarity.

Lauterbach's conversation with Stevens is ongoing, but nowhere so compelling as in "Carousel," where she takes on Stevens's "Idea of Order at Key West" and Ashbery's early poem, "The Painter," from *Some Trees*. This poem, like so many of Revell's, works by repetitions of key images, the working of language apart from human agency. Stevens' woman/artist, we recall, ordered the sea through her song:

> She sang beyond the genius of the sea.
> The water never formed to mind or voice,
> Like a body wholly body, fluttering
> Its empty sleeves

Where Stevens gives us an image of a woman walking beside the sea, Ashbery, in his sestina "The Painter," gives us an image of the artist as the sea—an image that he comes to acknowledge is dangerous. The mechanical working of the poem reflects the inhuman machinations of the painter's scene:

> Imagine a painter crucified by his subject! . . .
> Others declared it a self-portrait.
> Finally all indications of a subject
> Began to fade, leaving the canvas
> Perfectly white. He put down the brush.
> At once a howl, that was also a prayer,
> Arose from the overcrowed [sic] buildings.

Both the painter and his painting are thrown off the tallest building, and are devoured by the sea, which had been his subject.

Lauterbach presents herself as both the agent of order and as someone who distrusts order. It is she, seemingly, who sets Ashbery's painter right, In "Carousel," where she wears the sea's sleeves:

> *Lauterbach considers the house as the home of female creativity and wants the comfort of that tradition even as she means to get past its tyranny.*

> I like masks, deeper shades of blue,
> How it concludes black.
> A swimmer is adorned with one arm
> Rising out of the blue.
> A man in the sea.
> A painting of a man in the sea.

> I like the way it comes out of the blue.
> The horse rises and falls; my sleeves are waving.
> It is not dark that scares me, but the limit
> Which places the house in the field, the horse in its stall.

The man in the sea is again the same as a painting of the man in the sea, but without the chaos portended in Ashbery's poem. Instead, what frightens this poet is precisely the opposite, the limits that Ashbery had so blithely erased in his poem. The image with which she ends the poem preserves the contrast between limit and limitlessness:

> Over her shoulder, the painting depicts will.
> Staring at the view, she has a sense of place
> And of omission. The ways in which we live
> Are earmarked for letting go, and so
> She makes her descent, plucks it, rises into the blue.

Lauterbach's resolution of the problem, then, is its revaluation; the poet's job is to trace, "The syntax of solitude . . ./ To witness versions that clock and petal, / Enfolding instances." This clocking (mechanical) and petaling (organic) are the edges of the liminal space in which Lauterbach operates; it is a house, but one that perishes before her eyes. "The soul's haphazard sanctuary" is more like Stevens' dump than like Dickinson's house, but the final chamber promises, even if it does not deliver, revelation:

> We might think of this as a blessing
> As we thrash in the nocturnal waste:
> Rubble of doors, fat layers of fiber
> Drooping under eaves, weeds
> Leaning in lassitude after heavy rain
> Has surged from a whitened sky.

> Thunder blooms unevenly in unknowable places
> Breaking distance into startling new chambers
> We cannot enter; potentially, a revelation.

This comes from the first poem in the book, "Still." The last poem, "Sacred Weather," describes "a gathered dispersal"—rather like Hart Crane's "slip of pebbles" in his last poem, "The Broken Tower." This is an elegy for her father, "whose sleeve was last seen bound to a wing," in that liminal space he shares with Stevens' last philosopher in Rome. The moment of transcendence she describes as a place, a landscape:

> Nevertheless a balance forms, its crest
> The start of radiance like that grassy limit
> Or shore. Certain early episodes rub,
> Curiously nearby, poised to ensue.
> A pale linearity hangs a new surface in the air
> Like a mute plow stretching the light.

In the poem's final section, Lauterbach uses puns (pine and pain is one) to show how language itself becomes "a new surface in the air." But more telling is her use of the word "refrain" in what follows, the final lines in *Beyond Recollection*:

> May have ceased to pine.
> Stasis is an attribute, domain of the lily.
> Even the sky gives color up,
> An ecstasy too slight, less than free.
> I myself long to refrain
> But would bleed and bless
> Robe opening on slowly mounted stair.

That she longs to refrain bespeaks a double, and contradictory, desire; to read the word as a verb indicates a desire to cease, even to die. Yet poetic refrains are precisely those passages that repeat themselves, and the poetic act is itself one of repetition. Her final image, likewise, speaks both of death and of eroticism, of enclosure and of opening.

Are Revell and Lauterbach, then, mere backpedalers in the literary history now creating itself around us? Have they quailed at the radicalism of Ashbery's project, which seems in so many ways both late Romantic and postmodernist? This is perhaps not for any of us to say—yet. But, if Ashbery seems the darling of deconstructionists, his poems (like "Houseboat Days") undoing themselves as purposefully as Penelope's tapestry, then Lauterbach and Revell will surely appeal more to critics wanting to stop the gaps in deconstruction's logic. Certainly they will not be the darlings of New Historicists—they are too Ashberyan for that—but they may show us how Ashbery's model can be revised to include social, even political, contexts. For, even if Revell and Lauterbach trade more in metaphor than in fact (Revell's Gaza is *not* that of the PLO, to one reviewer's chagrin), their metaphors are grounded more consistently in the social and political realm than are his. If these two poets do not give us the radical wealth we are accustomed to in Ashbery, they at least give us hope that we can, still, make coherent selves for ourselves.

Source: Susan M. Schultz, "Houses of Poetry after Ashbery: The Poetry of Ann Lauterbach and Donald Revell," in *Virginia Quarterly Review*, Vol. 67, No. 2, Spring 1991.

Sources

"Burial of the Dead: Rite Two," in *The Book of Common Prayer*, Seabury Press, 1977, p. 501.

Clover, Joshua, "American Ink: Why Poetry? Why Now?" in the *Village Voice*, February 19–25, 2003, available online at http://www.villagevoice.com/news/0308,clover,41980,1.html.

Danto, Arthur C., "9/11 Art as a Gloss on Wittgenstein," in *artnet Magazine*, September 9, 2005, available online at http://www.artnet.com/magazineus/features/danto/danto9-9-05.asp?p.

Goldscheider, Eric, "Meeting Takes on Challenge of Teaching Contemporary Poetry: 'It's Hard to Explain,' Writers Concede at Conference," in the *Boston Globe*, August 22, 1999.

Hargis, Shrode, Review of *Hum*, in *Harvard Review*, Vol. 29, December 2005, pp. 232–35.

Lauterbach, Ann, "Hum," in *Hum*, Penguin Books, 2005, pp. xiii, 76–78.

McCorkle, James, "Ann Lauterbach," in *Dictionary of Literary Biography*, Vol. 193, *American Poets since World War II, Sixth Series*, edited by Joseph Conte, Gale Research, 1998, pp. 180–92.

Owen, Wilfred, "Dulce et Decorum Est," in *The Collected Poems of Wilfred Owen*, edited by C. Day Lewis, New Directions, 1963, p. 55.

Pinsky, Robert, "9/11," *Online Newshour*, September 12, 2002, http://www.pbs.org/newshour/bb/poems/july-dec02/9-11_9-11.html.

Review of *Hum*, in *Publishers Weekly*, Vol. 252, No. 16, April 18, 2005, p. 58.

Tracy, D. H., Review of *Hum*, in *Poetry*, Vol. 187, No. 4, January 2006, pp. 338–39.

Further Reading

Altieri, Charles, *The Art of Twentieth-Century American Poetry: Modernism and After*, Blackwell, 2006.
    Altieri, a leading poetry critic, offers a comprehensive overview of modernism in poetry, with emphases on Wallace Stevens and W. H. Auden, both of whom have influenced Lauterbach. Altieri

concentrates on explaining how modernism arose and how poetry has been influenced by the other arts.

Lauterbach, Ann, "Links without Links: The Voice of the Turtle," in *American Poetry Review*, Vol. 21, No. 1, January–February 1992, p. 37.

Lauterbach discusses contemporary poetry, touching on the subject of the Persian Gulf War. She believes that poetry represents a distaste for power and states that poets need to reject literalism in their work in order to convey truth and create a new perception of the world.

———, "2001 Lenore Marshall Poetry Prize," in *Nation*, February 4, 2002, pp. 33–34.

Lauterbach gave this speech several months after the 9/11 attacks. In it, she discusses her reaction to the tragedy and provides context for how other poets have responded to this and other disasters.

Lauterbach, Ann, and Tim Peterson, "Rootless Elegiac: An Interview with Ann Lauterbach," in *Rain Taxi*, Vol. 7, No. 2, Summer 2002.

Lauterbach discusses Wallace Stevens, the influence of music on her poetry, and her sensory "synesthesia," in which sounds, images, place, and time meld into each other during the creative process.

Yezzi, David, Review of *On a Stair*, in *Poetry*, Vol. 21, No. 5, August 1998, p. 292.

In a brief review of Lauterbach's collection, Yezzi comments (not altogether favorably) about the tension in Lauterbach's work and her many artistic references.

Knowledge

Kim Addonizio

2004

Kim Addonizio's poem "Knowledge" is a twenty-line free-form poem, with no rhyme scheme. Indeed, free verse has no distinct limits or rules and so does not restrict the poet to a particular format. In "Knowledge," Addonizio's narrator asks the reader to consider whether the horrors of modern life are limited in some way to the tragedies to which one has already been exposed. "Knowledge" appears in Addonizio's fourth book of poetry, *What Is This Thing Called Love*, published in 2004. The collection is divided into five sections, with the first devoted to love, the second to death, the third to the world, the fourth to drinking, and the fifth to no topic in particular. "Knowledge" is found in the third section.

The poem focuses on the most horrific things that take place in the world, although it does not mention any horrors in particular. Addonizio begins the poem with a lengthy dependent clause that allows the reader to slowly come to an understanding of the assertion that even though one might think one knows the depth of human cruelty and the extremes of barbarity, some events can still prove utterly appalling. As she suggests in the last line, one might remain frightened that even worse acts are yet to come. Addonizio uses the second-person "you" throughout the poem, inviting the reader in as a participant in her very personal exploration of the horrors that continue to shock the world.

Kim Addonizio Courtesy of Kim Addonizio

Author Biography

Kim Addonizio was born in Washington, D.C., on July 31, 1954, as one of five children of Pauline Betz Addie, a U.S. tennis champion in the 1940s, and Bob Addie, a sportswriter for the *Washington Post*. Addonizio moved to San Francisco, California, in 1976, where she worked in a succession of jobs as secretary, waitress, and office clerk. She began writing poetry in her twenties. She earned a bachelor of arts degree from San Francisco State University when she was twenty-eight years old, in the same year that her daughter was born. In 1986, after another four years of part-time classes, Addonizio earned a master's degree in fine arts.

In 1987, Addonizio published several poems in collaboration with two other poets in a book of poetry called *Three West Coast Women*. She received her first National Endowment for the Arts (NEA) grant in 1990, which gave her the economic freedom to focus on her poetry. At the age of forty, she published her first book of her own poetry, *The Philosopher's Club* (1994). Subsequently, she won a second NEA grant in 1995 and published *Jimmy & Rita*, a verse novel, in 1997. She won a Pushcart Prize and the Chelsea Poetry Award in 1998 and was a finalist for the 2000 National Book Award for Poetry for her third collection, *Tell Me* (2000). She was awarded the James Dickey Prize for poetry in 2001 and the John Ciardi Lifetime Achievement Award in 2003.

"Knowledge" is from Addonizio's 2004 collection, *What Is This Thing Called Love*. She was awarded a Guggenheim Fellowship and published her first novel, *Little Beauties*, in 2005. She has spent most of her adult life living and working in the San Francisco Bay Area, where she has also occasionally taught classes on poetry at regional colleges.

Poem Text

Even when you know what people are capable of,
even when you pride yourself on knowing,
on not evading history, or the news,
or any of the quotidian, minor, but still endlessly
    apparent
and relevant examples of human cruelty—even   5
    now
there are times it strikes you anew, as though
you'd spent your whole life believing that
    humanity
was fundamentally good, as though you'd never
    thought,
like Schopenhauer, that it was all blind, impersonal
    will,
never chanted perversely, almost gleefully,   10
the clear-sighted adjectives learned from Hobbes—
solitary, poor, nasty, brutal, and short—
even now you're sometimes stunned to hear
of some terrible act that sends you reeling off, too
    overwhelmed
even to weep, and then you realize that your   15
    innocence,
which you had thought no longer existed,
did, in fact, exist—that somewhere underneath your
    cynicism
you still held out hope. But that hope has been
    shattered now,
irreparably, or so it seems, and you have to go on,
    afraid
that there is more to know, that one day you will   20
    know it.

Poem Summary

Lines 1–6

The first several lines of "Knowledge" contain a dependent clause that forces the reader to continue reading without understanding the intent of the rumination until the middle of line 6. The first line suggests that the poem will explore events or

Media Adaptations

- *Swearing, Smoking, Drinking, & Kissing* (2004) is an audio CD of poems read by Addonizio and Susan Browne, with musical accompaniment, produced by Dan Brown and available from Speakeasy Literary Audio.

---

behaviors that are outside the ordinary events of daily life. The words "Even when you know" imply that one can still be surprised, that not everything can be understood or anticipated. The second line continues in this mode, with the addition of "even when you pride yourself." The inclusion of the word "pride" clarifies how fully the poem's addressee, "you," claims to understand the world, in that this person is proud of this knowledge. Thus, the reader may anticipate that the narrator is asserting that even those who understand the cruelty and arbitrariness of the world can still be surprised by the level of cruelty that is inflicted on innocent people. She expands on this point in line 3 when she points out that unflinchingly studying history or watching the news still may not prepare one for the barbarities to which some people can subject others. That is, no history book, newspaper, or newscast can prepare a reader or viewer for the horrors that will be committed. This line makes clear that, for example, forcing people to study the Nazi Holocaust does not mean that they can be ready to objectively understand the situation when such an event occurs again.

In line 4, Addonizio continues the topic of line 3, explaining that even when one is aware of the "quotidian," or everyday, examples of human cruelty, this awareness provides no immunity. The poet uses the word "minor" in this line to reinforce how ordinary these events have become, how unimportant they seem; that is, she stresses the theme of how accustomed people can become to other people's meanness. She labels these incidents "endless" and in the first part of line 5 refers to them as "relevant examples" of how cruel human beings can be to one another. The ideas of the first five lines culminate in line 6, where the narrator provides an independent clause to which the preceding dependent clause can be linked. (The end of line 5, "even now," is in essence an abbreviated restatement of all that appears in lines 1–5.) She proposes that no amount of study or awareness of cruelty can fully prepare one for the reality of what some human beings will do to others. This cruelty still occasionally "strikes you anew."

Lines 7–9

Once the independent clause has been provided, the thought continues at the end of line 6 and the beginning of line 7. The narrator suggests that this renewed shock might lead those who feel that shock to think that they must have previously believed "that humanity / was fundamentally good." That is, if they had truly understood the extent to which men could be evil, they would not have been shocked at all. Thus, lines 7 and 8 together suggest that a belief in the fundamental goodness of humankind is perhaps a core part of most people's ideology, whether they realize it or not—again, otherwise, they would not be shocked by the manifestation of evil. The narrator suggests that this fundamental belief in the goodness of human beings has not generally been influenced by more pessimistic views of humankind. Line 9 refers to the nineteenth-century German philosopher Arthur Schopenhauer, a pessimist who believed that people do not have individual free will but instead are subject to a vast and wicked will that is inclusive of everyone. Schopenhauer does not refer to this collective will as a god figure; rather, the source of this negative will is cosmic in origin, such that humankind is simply at the mercy of the surrounding world. In line 9, Addonizio summarizes Schopenhauer's philosophy as holding that humanity is "all blind, impersonal will."

Lines 10–12

The narrator proceeds to suggest in line 10 that people have generally been positive enough not to accept the similar contentions of Thomas Hobbes, an early-seventeenth-century philosopher who also dismissed humankind's ability to control itself. In line 10, the narrator refers to followers of Hobbes as people who might "perversely" and "gleefully" accept a pessimistic view of life. These followers would find joy in being pessimistic about the future of humankind and its ability to govern itself. The five italicized adjectives presented in line 11 illustrate the "clear-sighted" ideas put forth by

Hobbes, who thought that each person should embrace determinism and do exactly as he or she desires. For Hobbes, this was freedom. Indeed, Hobbes thought that people are essentially self-serving, leading the narrator to mention the adjective "solitary." Hobbes also believed that in their natural state, people live in a state of chaos and incessant war. This is the "nasty" and "brutal" nature of humankind, which is thus often "short," or brief, in its existence. All of the words in line 12, "*solitary, poor, nasty, brutal, and short*," are devoid of hope for the future. These words contradict the optimism with which most people struggle to understand the world.

Lines 13–18

The first words of line 13 echo the last two words of line 5: "even now." Even now, the narrator again asserts, people can be shocked by terrible cruelty, even after having witnessed so many examples of humans being cruel to other humans. Line 14 refers to this new "terrible act" that can be so horrible that we hear of it with disbelief. People are thus sent "reeling off," perhaps dizzy and unable to feel secure, as well as "overwhelmed." This feeling of helplessness leaves people unable to weep. Indeed, the "innocence" that people did not know they still possess has been with them all along, as made evident by that horror too terrible to contemplate. At the end of line 17 and the beginning of line 18—where the sentence that has constituted the entire poem to this point finally comes to a close—the narrator asserts that even when one has become too cynical, too aware of horror to believe in the goodness of human beings, the desire to *want* to believe still exists.

Lines 19–20

In the continuation of line 18, the narrator suggests that the desire to want to believe in the goodness of humanity has been defeated. Addonizio uses the words "shattered" and "irreparably," or beyond repair, stating that this hope might "seem" to be gone completely. Yet human beings continue to exist, despite the horror of the world and their awareness of events too terrible to easily accept or understand. The acknowledgment of this horrible reality leaves human beings "afraid." In the final lines of the poem, the narrator contends that people will remain with this devastating fear that more surprising horrors, more terrible events to "know," will come about. That is the "knowledge" of the title: the awareness that worse things may yet happen.

Themes

Fear

Addonizio's poem ends with an awareness of fear and an acknowledgment that the horrors of the past might well presage worse events in the future. She holds that one indeed has reason to be afraid, as the future will hold more to "know," more to grasp that will remind humankind that not all people are "fundamentally good," as is perhaps too often believed. Fear about what might still happen is prevalent throughout the poem; indeed, that fear is the central focus underlying the text. In spite of people's innate willingness to believe in the goodness of humankind, ample evidence of evil exists. The poet uses the word "afraid" prominently, at the end of line 19, as she brings the poem to a close. Thus, the image that she leaves with her readers is a depressing reminder that while one may believe that no event could be worse than what has already taken place, the possibility of worse horror remains. This possibility is what creates so much fear.

Hope

Much of Addonizio's poem reminds her readers that hopefulness is a natural human condition. She acknowledges that despite the evidence of "human cruelty," people spend their whole lives "believing that humanity / was fundamentally good." This is an observation that cannot be supported by the events of the past, and yet hope perseveres. Addonizio cites the most pessimistic of philosophers, Arthur Schopenhauer and Thomas Hobbes, as examples of pessimism that people ignore as they continue to view life optimistically. Because of this natural inclination toward hope, humankind is "stunned" when terrible events unfold. As such, when reality intrudes, people are "overwhelmed" by the events that they are unprepared to accept. Yet in the face of horrific tragedies, people need hope in order to maintain a positive existence. Without hope, despair would overtake people's lives and diminish their ability to happily exist.

Innocence

Another theme in "Knowledge" highlights the ability of human beings to maintain their basic innocence in the face of terrible tragedy. She devotes the first eight lines of the poem to an extended discussion of this innocence, inserting frequent repetitions of the word "even." "Even when" and "even now" imply that even in the face of so much evidence of humankind's cruelty, people retain an unwarranted innocence with respect to the world.

Topics For Further Study

- Take the first line of Addonizio's poem "Knowledge" and use it as the first line of your own poem. Your poem should contain at least twenty lines and should continue Addonizio's line to whatever conclusion fits your own subject or ideas. Your poem may mirror Addonizio's technique, in that it can be free verse, without a specific rhyme scheme. Your poem should also incorporate a similar style. For instance, try to create a lengthy dependent clause that leads into the main point of the poem.

- Research the history of al Qaeda and its relationship to the Taliban. Write an essay in which you discuss your research and the roles that the United States and the former Soviet Union played in the creation of the conflict in Afghanistan. Be sure to include information about how the Taliban became associated with al Qaeda and the role of Islamic extremism in Afghanistan's history.

- Write a report in which you compare the philosophical ideas of Arthur Schopenhauer and Thomas Hobbes. Then create a poster that details the differences and similarities of these two men's ideas and present the poster and your report to your class.

- Nelly Sachs also wrote poems about the horrors that men inflict upon one another, such as in her book *The Seeker and Other Poems*, published in 1970. Select at least two poems written by Sachs and compare them to Addonizio's poem. Consider the similarities and differences found in the verse of these two women. Write an essay in which you discuss the different ways in which they give voice to death and fear. Be sure to include quotations from the authors' poems in your essay.

Addonizio indeed uses the word "innocence" to classify this ability to shift focus from horror, from "what people are capable of," to hope, despite the occurrence of tragedies that cannot be rationally justified or understood.

Love

The inclusion of "Knowledge" in Addonizio's collection of poems *What Is This Thing Called Love* illustrates the complexities of that sentiment. One of love's greatest assets is its ability to endure, even when death or tragedy intervenes. In a way, love cannot exist without fear—fear that the object of that love will be injured or die. In the final lines of "Knowledge," Addonizio focuses on the awareness that terrible evil can occur, leaving people afraid that even more danger exists. The fear of losing those who are loved motivates much of that worry, and yet love is what turns people away from the pessimism of Schopenhauer and Hobbes and toward a fundamental belief in the goodness of humankind. Love connects us all and allows us to endure.

Understanding

Understanding is a theme in Addonizio's poem that unites the many other themes regarding love, hope, and innocence. Understanding requires an acknowledgment and an acceptance of the realities of the world. Horror and "relevant examples of human cruelty" exist—but so does a belief in the goodness of humanity. The awareness of these differing elements of human existence fosters understanding of the complexity of human beings. Addonizio's poem points out that humankind remains innocent even in the face of its past experiences. This does not necessitate the ignoring of reality; indeed, several lines of the poem maintain that people are not "evading history" or ignoring the news. That is, a willingness to accept evil while still maintaining hope does not suggest ignorance. Rather, humankind understands that evil exists, and while people may fear it, they must still find ways to live, love, and nurture themselves in a world filled with risk. Understanding that evil exists does not entail succumbing to fear. Addonizio suggest this very notion in line 19, when she writes that "you have to go on." Being afraid of danger is an important part of understanding the risks of living.

Style

Free Verse

Free verse is verse with no discernible structure, rhyme scheme, or meter. Free verse allows the poet to fit the poetic line to the content of the poem. Thus, the poet is not restricted by the need to shape the poem to a particular meter but can instead create complex rhythm and syntax. Free verse is not the same as blank verse, which also does not use a rhyme scheme. Blank verse almost always adheres to iambic pentameter, where each line contains ten syllables in the form of five iambic feet, each of which is composed of an unstressed syllable followed by an accented syllable. By contrast, free verse relies on line breaks to create a rhythm. Free verse is most often associated with modern poetry, such as with Addonizio's poem. Indeed, no pattern of rhyme or meter can be found in "Knowledge"; instead, the irregular line breaks give the poem a rhythm that is best appreciated in hearing it read aloud.

Line Breaks

Line breaks are a defining element of poetry. They can be used to impart varied meaning to lines, to focus the reader on certain ideas, to create rhyme or rhythm, or to lend a specific appearance to the poem on the page. Addonizio most pointedly uses line breaks to impart meaning and to emphasize ideas. The use of a dash at the end of line 11, as followed by the list of words in line 12 ("*solitary, poor, nasty, brutal, and short*"), emphasizes the importance of these words. Addonizio also uses the line break to build tension at the end of line 5, putting more emphasis on the words "even now." Placing the conclusion of the clause on the next line helps to sustain that tension.

Narrative Poetry

Narrative poetry is a form in which the author tells a story. Like a short story, a narrative poem generally has a beginning, middle, and clear ending or resolution. Not all narrative poems follow this formula, however; some narrative poems reflect the author's artistic interpretation of events. In these cases, the narration is less structured. Addonizio might have chosen to write a poem that recounted a specific frightening moment and then explained that this event left her frightened for the future. Had she done so, her poem may have been less powerful. Instead, she begins her poem with the disillusionment that she felt when she realized that the world in which she trusted had seemingly disappeared. No actual events are mentioned, but the fact that the narration concerns a certain event is implied. This approach allows Addonizio to universalize her artistic vision, which ends with the prophecy that worse events (also undescribed) are possible, such that the poem becomes more powerful to the reader.

Parallelism

Parallelism refers to a repetition in style or words within a poem. This device is one way to express several ideas of comparable importance in a similar manner or to establish the importance of a particular idea. Addonizio uses parallelism to set the tone of the poem and to create tension. For example, the opening words of line 1, "even when," are balanced with the closing words of line 5, "even now." Also, the opening words in line 1 are repeated as the opening words in line 2. Another example of this device occurs when the closing words of line 5, "even now," are repeated at the beginning of line 13. This use of parallelism focuses the reader's attention on these lines and signifies that they are important elements of the poem.

Historical Context

Addonizio's poem tells her readers about "some terrible act that sends you reeling off." Many such acts occurred during Addonizio's lifetime as well as in the years before her birth. As she observes in her poem, some events are so shocking that "even when you know" what people are capable of doing to one another, these appalling acts defy belief. In many ways, the twentieth century was defined by a succession of genocides, including that of the Armenians in Turkey (1915–1918), Stalin's crushing of the Ukrainian revolt (1932–1933), the Japanese murder of Chinese in Nanking (1937–1938), the Nazi Holocaust (1938–1945), the Khmer Rouge's slaughter of Cambodians (1975–1979), the Rwandan slaughter of Tutsis (1994), and the massacre of Muslims in Bosnia (1992–1995). Through these events, upward of seventeen million people were killed simply because they were of a particular race or ethnic group or because they practiced a particular religion. Many acts of individual terrorism also occurred. The Palestine Liberation Organization was responsible for the murder of eleven Israeli athletes at the 1972 Olympics in Munich, as well as many attacks in the Middle East. Also, the Irish Republican Army carried out various attacks in Great Britain. By 1995, terror was no longer limited to areas outside the United States. That year an American terrorist blew up the Alfred P. Murrah Federal Building in Oklahoma City, killing 168 people.

The first several years of the twenty-first century were also characterized by death and terrorism. On the morning of September 11, 2001, nearly three thousand people died in attacks on the World Trade Center, in New York City, and the Pentagon, in Washington, D.C., along with the crash of a hijacked plane in Pennsylvania. These incidents of terrorism seemed more shocking than those of previous centuries, and as Addonizio suggests in the final lines of her poem, such events leave people frightened that "there is more to know." The September 11 attacks led to the U.S. involvement in a war in Afghanistan against the Taliban, who were at the time that nation's ruling faction. The Taliban, a name derived from an Arabic word for "religious students," was originally composed of revolutionaries who fought the Soviet occupation of Afghanistan (1979–1989). Once they gained control of most of their nation, the Taliban instituted strict Islamic rule, even while a civil war continued against the Northern Alliance, who also controlled part of Afghanistan. The Taliban was closely aligned with the militant organization al Qaeda and allowed that group's religious fundamentalist leader, Osama bin Laden, to establish training camps for terrorists. Al Qaeda was responsible for the events of September 11, 2001.

Although the Taliban eventually was ousted from Afghanistan, many members remained in hiding and continued to plan terrorist activities. Indeed, attacks took place in Istanbul, Turkey, and Casablanca, Morocco, in 2003; in Madrid, Spain, in 2004; and in London, England, in 2005. Other attacks were executed throughout the world, and although no additional terrorist attacks were launched in the United States after 2001, warnings of possible attacks have sporadically arisen. These warnings have heightened public awareness, but they also have fostered feelings of vulnerability and fear. As Addonizio tells her readers, examples of human cruelty are "endlessly apparent" and serve to remind people that they have reason to be afraid. The final line of her poem leaves readers with what is almost a warning—that "one day" people will witness even worse examples of human cruelty.

Critical Overview

Critical reviews of Addonizio's fourth collection of poetry, *What Is This Thing Called Love*, were mixed. In *Publishers Weekly*, an anonymous reviewer states that the collection is written in a style that is "two parts confessional, one part standup comedy, and one part talking blues." The reviewer also notes that "Addonizio's in-your-face persona and her avoidance of technical difficulty should help her attract the wide audience she explicitly invites." A more favorable review of Addonizio's book was published in *Booklist*. The reviewer, Donna Seaman, claims that "Addonizio's poems are like swallows of cold, grassy white wine" in that they "go down easy and then, moments later, you feel the full weight of their impact." Seaman also observes that Addonizio's poems are "finely crafted and irreverent" as well as "timeless in their inquiries into love and mortality." According to Seaman, the poems are "rife with mystery and ambivalence, and [are] achingly eloquent in their study of the conflictful union of body and soul."

Diane Scharper's review of *Love* for *Library Journal* was less enthusiastic. Scharper compares Addonizio's collection to Anne Sexton's collection *Love Poems* (1969) and declares that Addonizio is "neither as sharpedged nor as passionate as Sexton." Rather, Addonizio's poems are "lukewarm and 'cool' at their best" and are best suited "for larger public libraries." William Logan's review in *New Criterion* was even more negative. In an article that is largely an attack on modern poetry, Logan begins by referring to Addonizio as "a hot babe who can bang out a sonnet on demand." This comment is not meant to be flattering, as the remainder of the review makes clear. Logan claims that Addonizio's poetry is "part of the latest contemporary manner—ha! ha! poetry can be just as dumb as television, too!" Logan continues his review with the comment that "too many of Addonizio's poems are made in Betty Crocker style, all helpful hints and ingredients whipped in a jiffy for a dish tasteless as a stuffed pillow." Logan concludes by suggesting that the problem with modern poetry is that too often the poet does not have anything to say. None of these reviews mention "Knowledge" specifically, instead focusing on the collection of poems as a whole.

Criticism

Sheri Metzger Karmiol

Metzger Karmiol has a doctorate in English Renaissance literature and teaches literature and drama at the University of New Mexico. In this essay, she discusses Addonizio's poem as a conduit to understanding the common sentiment of fear and the emotional toll exacted when the illusion of safety no longer exists.

One of the ways in which poetry speaks to its reader is through its ability to reach deep inside that reader and stir memories, and sometimes fears, of an event or time already past. Film does this, of course. Sitting in a darkened theater also gives filmgoers the opportunity to immerse themselves in a world they might otherwise never experience. For the film audience, however, the experience will be the same, or at least similar, for each person viewing the film. That is, unless a film is extremely abstract, most viewers will respond with similar emotions. Most people will react to the villain and identify with the heroic lead in the same manner, or perhaps the plot will be familiar in some universal way and thus instantly recognizable to the audience. Regardless of the content, a connection, a common experience, is fostered among the members of the audience. Poetry creates a connection between art and audience as well, yet a difference exists with respect to the commonality of experience. With poetry, each reader's experience will be unique, as a poem can suggest various images or realities, depending entirely on each reader's individual experiences.

Addonizio's poem "Knowledge" is a prime example of a poem that can mean different things to different people. Is the poem about terrorism as mass murder, or could it be about the particularly cruel murder of just one innocent victim? It might also be about the random murder of office workers by a deranged individual. Regardless of the specific intent of the poem, which only Addonizio can address, the knowledge that a new danger has emerged in the world, even when that world is strictly a personal one, will have an impact on every person who reads the poem.

For some people, "Knowledge" may bring forth images of the many genocides of the past fifty years—the Holocaust, Rwanda, Bosnia—all of which left legacies of hate and horror in the late twentieth century. For others, the poem will suggest a more immediate, personal tragedy, such as the death of a child or spouse as a result of the actions of another person. Interviews with Addonizio suggest that the poem was possibly inspired by terrorism. For those who have lived under the threat of terrorism since 2001, Addonizio's poem recalls the devastating destruction of the World Trade Center complex on September 11 of that year. Her opening line, "Even when you know what people are capable of," may leave readers recalling the shock they felt as they watched and then rewatched the collapse of the twin towers on that sunny morning. That tragedy was clearly not an accident but the deliberate murder of thousands of innocent people. The resulting shock was profound in large part because of the absolute evil of the event.

> "*The commonality of experience is what appeals to Addonizio; as such, she wants her poetry to be accessible, which is why so many people can find meaning in her poem 'Knowledge.'*"

Indeed, evil speaks to Addonizio. In a November 2000 interview for the literary newspaper *Poetry Flash*, she explained to Leza Lowitz that evil is "one of the things I obsess about. Evil and suffering and power—all of that." She further noted that the "whole question of good and evil" is a theme she pursued ever since she became aware that, eventually, innocence "is going to be crushed, somehow." According to Addonizio, people have to come to an understanding of the cruelty of the world "in order to survive." This is an important theme in "Knowledge," which ends with the suggestion that everyone will soon know that innocence has no place in this world. Although this interview predated the terrorism of 2001, Addonizio's words suggest the kind of response that she might have had to that attack.

Throughout "Knowledge," Addonizio sustains a dialogue that explores feelings of disbelief in the face of events so horrific that innocence must surely be eradicated. She ends her poem with the warning that although "there is more to know," there is also reason to be afraid. The fear that "one day you will know it" is what many people experience each time another terror alert is announced, each time a new message from terrorists is released, and each time

What Do I Read Next?

- *The Philosopher's Club* (1993) is Addonizio's first collection of poetry. This small book of fewer than eighty pages is filled with a diverse collection of poems on topics ranging from death to teenage drinking to the world of Anne Frank, a victim of the Holocaust. Here, too, are poems about aspects of women's lives, including the love a mother feels in carrying her daughter to bed and the realization that as daughters grow up, they also grow away.

- *Jimmy & Rita* (1996) is a verse narrative by Addonizio, focusing on the lives of a young boxer and a prostitute.

- Addonizio's collection *Tell Me* (2000) was nominated for a National Book Award. It is similar to her other collections in that the poems are sometimes based on her own experiences and are very realistic in their subject content, ranging from divorce to love to spending too much time in a bar.

- Addonizio cowrote *The Poet's Companion: A Guide to the Pleasures of Writing Poetry* (1997) with Dorianne Laux. This book is designed as a textbook for writing poetry, with topics such as choosing a subject and crafting an actual poem.

- *What We Carry* (1994), by Dorianne Laux, is a collection of poems covering topics as varied as the innocence of childhood and life at forty. Like Addonizio, Laux writes poems about real women and their experiences, and her work is equally accessible. She does not rely on poetic devices that might confuse readers, instead using her poetry to tell stories about ordinary people in such a way that everyone can understand her messages.

- In his novel *September 11 from the Inside* (2003), Rubram Fernandez presents a fictional account of what experiencing the terrorist attacks on September 11, 2001, might have been like. Fernandez tries to recreate the stories of those who were on the hijacked planes as well as those who were in the attacked buildings, blending historical details with fictional characters.

- *Dear Zoe* (2005), by Philip Beard, is the story of a young girl whose sister dies in an automobile accident on September 11, 2001. While the rest of the world focuses on the attacks against the United States, Zoe's older sister tries to separate her grief at her sister's death from the larger grief of the nation. This book specifically targets young adult readers.

---

another bombing occurs, even in some far-off country. In a fall 2001 interview with Tod Marshall for his book *Range of the Possible: Conversations with Contemporary Poets*, Addonizio related that a month after the September 11 attacks, she went to see a museum exhibit on torture. This exhibit and the World Trade Center destruction combined to throw her "into complete despair about the innate evil of our species." She became aware that the modern world has brought about new risks; she told Marshall, "Here we are at war again, and there are real dangers to our survival." This fear of not surviving is projected in line 18 of "Knowledge," where Addonizio writes that "hope has been shattered now." In line 19 she asserts that once that hope is gone, people have very good reason to be "afraid."

In a profile published in the *San Francisco Reader*, Jerry Karp claims that Addonizio "has an uncanny ability to apply fresh and urgently personal perspectives to recognizable moments of crisis and calm." This is precisely what she has done with "Knowledge." In referring to an incident so horrible that people find it difficult to comprehend, she has articulated—whether intentionally or not—the grief, disbelief, and fear that gripped the United States in the years following September 11, 2001. Karp quotes Addonizio as remarking that she is "interested in communication, and in talking about things that are common to people's experience," such as "love and loss and death and time and feeling afraid." The emotions of hope and fear are also part of love; thus, the appearance of a poem about the loss of innocence in a collection of poetry titled *What Is This Thing Called Love* is perhaps appropriate. Falling in love and sharing someone else's life puts a lover at risk of heartache and loss. Terrorists do not care about the loves of those whom they kill, but empathy for those who lost loved ones in the terrorist attacks is part of the common emotional experience of that day.

The commonality of experience is what appeals to Addonizio; as such, she wants her poetry to be accessible, which is why so many people can find meaning in "Knowledge." In the interview with Marshall, she states that she is not interested in creating poetry that does not effectively communicate a message. She believes "in narrative, in story" and not "in destroying meaning." In telling Marshall that she believes that "language was developed over millions of years as a way to communicate," Addonizio clarifies why a poem like "Knowledge" works so well to capture the emotions of her readers. Readers understand the disbelief and the feeling that although "endlessly apparent / and relevant examples of human cruelty" have come to pass, people can still be sent "reeling off, too overwhelmed / even to weep." The experience of horror on September 11, 2001, was shared by everyone who could turn on a television set and watch the events replayed endlessly. Even after witnessing the towers fall a dozen or more times, one could still be shocked at "what people are capable of."

Addonizio's poem reminds her readers of this shock because of its clarity. The poet makes no effort to deliberately obscure meaning or create a level of complexity that only literary critics might comprehend. Instead, the poem and the emotions articulated are easily accessible. This is what Addonizio told Ryan G. Van Cleave she wants her poetry to accomplish in an interview published in the *Iowa Review*. Van Cleave titled this interview "Kim Addonizio: A Poet with Duende." Something with *duende*, a word with Spanish origins, is irresistibly attractive. That label would please Addonizio, who tells Van Cleave that while there is "nothing wrong with difficult poetry," she "can't write that kind of thing." She wants her poetry to be easy to understand, though not simple; she wants to write well, and she wants her poetry to be complex "where life is complex." She accomplishes this with "Knowledge," which captures not just an event but also the emotional toll of that event.

The ability to tell a story that speaks to readers and perhaps changes the world is a rare gift. In an interview with Jalina Mhyana for the online literary magazine *Rock Salt Plum Poetry Review*, Addonizio discusses the importance of writing political poems, stating that "it's everyone's responsibility to tackle injustice, one way or another." She believes that poetry is one way to illuminate and perhaps bring an end to injustice. Whether a poem like "Knowledge" can bring an end to the horrors of terrorism cannot be predicted. But it is clear that poetry such as Addonizio's can help readers understand the commonality of experience. A poem can help a reader contemplate the emotions of the moment, the fears that transport people when they are reminded of the risks they face, and the possibility that certain types of innocence will never again exist—and indeed, "Knowledge" fits that description quite well.

Source: Sheri Metzger Karmiol, Critical Essay on "Knowledge," in *Poetry for Students*, Thomson Gale, 2007.

David Kelly

Kelly is an instructor of creative writing and literature. In this essay, he explains that "Knowledge" breaks from the common poetic practice of using direct experience to convey thoughts and emotions, managing to be powerful even while filled with abstract concepts.

Throughout the twentieth and now the twenty-first centuries, poets, critics, and teachers have held the position that sensory experience is the standard by which to judge effective poetry. Beginning writers, in search of the techniques that will make it possible for them to communicate effectively with their audiences, are continuously exhorted to "show, don't tell." Beginning readers, who are not trained in the skills needed to extract meaning from the raw situations presented, end up confused and wishing someone would explain to them the mysteries of a poem that refuses to make clear its point.

This emphasis on physical imagery derives principally from the theoretical scaffold built by the poet T. S. Eliot, who, in his 1919 critique of Shakespeare's *Hamlet* (quoted in Wayne Booth's *Rhetoric of Fiction*), proposed that effective writing relies on an "objective correlative": that is, he suggested, a specific object or sequence of events must be used, instead of generalized and vague language, to evoke consistent responses from all readers, regardless of their personal histories. Eliot's point, which has since his time become almost universally accepted, is that it does no good to write with words that talk about ideas or emotions, because they mean different things from one person to the next. For example, one reader might imagine that the phrase "I hate this" to mean a burning, seething

> "The words that make up the poem may not be the jarring physical experiences that Eliot required, but they are indeed evocative of a certain kind of intellectualism that people use to avoid thinking of reality's horrors."

animosity toward whatever the object is, while another reader might take the phrase to imply just a mildly strong dislike. To convey the desired message, the writer would be better off showing an action toward the hated object, such as glaring, striking, or destroying. Abstract terms are too removed from actual human experience to make readers feel emotions deeply: a poet trying to communicate on a level that strikes readers emotionally would do better to write in terms of things that can be seen, heard, felt, smelled, and tasted. These are the ways all people, regardless of their intellectual practices, know the world.

While this is standard practice in modern poetry, there are, of course, exceptions: rules are made to be broken. One particularly successful exception to the rule about showing and not telling is Addonizio's "Knowledge." Readers who have a general familiarity with Addonizio's work know that she is best known as a sensualist, a writer not afraid to address her poetry to the basic, less-refined aspects of human behavior, particularly erotic behavior. As such, she might be expected to use physical imagery even more than the average poet in relating to the audience. But there is a social aspect to behavior that erotic poetry must address, and to the degree that this is her subject matter, Addonizio is something of a sociologist. She concerns herself with objective reality, of course, but there is also a strong vein of the theoretical throughout her poetry. This is taken to an extreme in "Knowledge," where the subject matter is the process of abstract intellectualization itself: despite the basic tenant of the objective correlative, this is a poem that cannot reach out to readers by bringing them to a common ground in the physical world.

The poem concerns the acquisition of abstract knowledge: the kind that is not gained from immediate personal experience but is instead brewed within an individual's mind, developed by musing on implications echoing from previous experiences. Over the course of twenty lines, Addonizio discusses the capacity of humans to arrive at shocking realizations, so shocking that they can change a person's view of the world. But the poem itself does not contain anything shocking. Instead of hitting readers hard with the direct experience of the sort of "terrible act" that can remind one of long-lost innocence, move one to tears, and make one reconsider one's deepest cynicism, she merely refers to an act and tells readers to accept that the act is indeed terrible. Each reader is free to imagine what that terrible act might be. When Addonizio gives a list of "clear-sighted adjectives" cribbed from the English philosopher Thomas Hobbes, it contains words that are not comfortable, but that does not mean that they are powerful, either. "*Solitary, poor, nasty, brutal, and short*" may bring to mind the unwanted facts of life, but they are not words that force readers to take life's horrors to heart.

The benefit of this is that readers can fill in the poem with their own sense of what is shocking. The drawback is that the poet loses control of the meanings that readers take from it. Abstract language raises the likelihood that the different possible readings will produce interpretations of the poem that are not within the range of the poet's intention. Because the poem is built on abstractions, it can mean different things in different circumstances. Addonizio seems to welcome this span of meaning, taking the risk of diverse feelings about the poem as a price that has to be paid if one is to explore the topic of abstract thought at all.

One reason "Knowledge" is able to operate without giving any of the specific "endlessly apparent / and relevant examples of human cruelty" that it talks about is that it is carefully, meticulously structured. The words that make up the poem may not be the jarring physical experiences that Eliot required, but they are indeed evocative of a certain kind of intellectualism that people use to avoid thinking of reality's horrors. When Addonizio refers to the German philosopher Arthur Schopenhauer's phrase about "blind, impersonal will," she uses words that sound as if they should mean more but end up hollow. All of her references to philosophy, in fact, serve to establish the world of this particular poem as being far removed from experience. Other words that

Addonizio has chosen, including "terrible," "overwhelmed," "innocence," "hope," and especially "quotidian," are so abstract that they do not even pretend to come close to hands-on experience. If the poem were trying to follow Eliot's theory, it might be deemed a failure, but Addonizio makes it clear with her word choices that she has no interest in being held to such a basic rule.

While the words used in "Knowledge" might be overly intellectual, Addonizio gives the poem a musical cast that makes art of them. For one thing, the use of "even" throughout the first half of the poem makes the poet's controlling hand obvious. It acts as a sort of musical refrain, clarifying the distinction between art and thought. Addonizio also makes strong use of the second-person "you" voice. Common enough in poetry, the second-person form of address is seldom as necessary as it is in this poem, where the poet needs to do all she can to make readers connect personally with the presented ideas. Finally, there is the poem's unmistakable, undeniable sense of rhythm: Addonizio does not deal here with any standard pattern of stressed and unstressed syllables, but the frequent caesuras, or pauses, give the words a lyrical cadence that abstract language about an abstract subject generally lacks. Addonizio makes use of anything that can slow the reader down—commas, dashes, periods, and line breaks—to make readers feel her verbal artistry even if they are not aware of feeling it.

After so many decades have passed by with writers being told to "show, don't tell," it is only right that a talented poet should feel free to flout that rule. In a poem like "Knowledge," in which the subject matter is itself abstract thought, Addonizio is practically obliged to tell and not show. Stripped of the techniques that give poetry its immediacy and make it a moving experience—that is, unable to appeal directly to the senses—Addonizio uses other poetic devices that subtly remind readers that this is, after all, a poem and not an essay. The fact that she does not feel the need to show, and is successful without doing so, is a clear indicator that in art rules are made to be broken.

Source: David Kelly, Critical Essay on "Knowledge," in *Poetry for Students*, Thomson Gale, 2007.

Michael Allen Holmes

Holmes is a freelance writer and editor. In this essay, he considers the contrast between the tone and content of Addonizio's poem.

One of the advantages of the poetic format, in relation to standard prose, is that it generally allows

> "Given the scope of understanding of both history and philosophy that the reader may reasonably expect Addonizio to have, the breathless, enthusiastic narrator originally envisioned, in light of the grammatical structure of the poem, would seem to be a fiction."

for a greater range of expression in fewer words. Many novelists have certainly defied the conventions of syntax so as to communicate their ideas most effectively. In *Lonesome Traveler*, Jack Kerouac, the icon of the beat generation, crafted sentences spanning entire paragraphs and characterized by indifference to proper grammar and the widespread use of hyphens to reflect the digressive rhythm of his thoughts and actions. In *The Autumn of the Patriarch*, the Nobel Prize–winning Colombian Gabriel García Marquez concludes with a forty-nine-page chapter that consists of a single sentence punctuated almost exclusively with commas, as indicative of the manner in which the main character gets swept up in his own life. With poems, meanwhile, a reader may expect to need to spend considerable time with the text in order to grasp nuances of form and language. Addonizio's twenty-line poem "Knowledge" consists of only two sentences, the first of which is seventeen and a half lines long. As such, the reader may expect that unconventional structure to serve a particular purpose, and the contemplation of that purpose may prove enlightening.

Indeed, given the length of that first sentence, "Knowledge" has an undeniable breathless quality about it. Addonizio repeats a number of words and phrases, perhaps less to specifically emphasize those phrases than to impart a certain emotional enthusiasm. The first and second lines both begin with "even when," while "even now" appears in lines 5 and 13, "even" in line 15, and "now" in line 18.

The term "as though" appears in lines 6 and 8, and "thought" appears in lines 8 and 16. Apart from the title, the word "know" appears in lines 1 and 2 and twice in the last line. Meanwhile, readers cannot forget that they are being addressed by the narrator of the poem, as "you," in some form, appears sixteen times. Thus, the reader may imagine the narrator to be delivering the poem with particular effusiveness, as if unable, or unwilling, to separate her thoughts into smaller, more coherent units; in interviews, Addonizio has professed her fascination with the social setting of the bar, and one might imagine her passionately addressing a friend at length over a drink in the manner of this poem.

Yet the content of the poem seems to belie that impression regarding the tone. The "you" of the poem is assigned a fair degree of personality. This subject is understood to be socially aware, being familiar with the "endlessly apparent / and relevant examples of human cruelty" from both historic and current events. The subject is also versed in philosophy, having studied the German Arthur Schopenhauer and the Englishman Thomas Hobbes. The narrator initially suggests that the "you" has spent his or her "whole life believing that humanity / was fundamentally good"; however, in further suggesting that this subject has "never chanted perversely, almost gleefully" the list of negative adjectives associated with Hobbes, the reader has no choice but to believe that the "you" has, in fact, chanted those adjectives just so. That is, the adverbs "perversely" and "gleefully" seem to have been chosen to reveal that the "you" did once sink into such a pessimistic state of mind. The remainder of the poem suggests that despite the worldly knowledge already possessed by the subject, she may still find innocence she did not know she still possessed to be "shattered" by some additional revelation.

Given the intricacy of character assigned to this "you," the reader may understand the person in question to be the narrator herself, in the sense that one may address another as "you" merely to universalize one's own experiences. Indeed, in an interview with the *Rock Plum Salt Poetry Review*, regarding a poem found in one of her earlier collections, Addonizio remarked, "If you take the 'you' as a second-person narrator, then it's potentially the writer." She further stated, on the other hand, that she hoped that the reader would "start to feel like the 'you' is you . . . on some level." Thus, she establishes here that she has been inclined to employ the second person as a way of depicting herself while also connecting with the reader.

From there, however, the reader may notice inconsistencies regarding the subject. As noted earlier, the "you" is said to be versed in the cruelties of history and the work of at least two renowned intellectuals. Addonizio herself was born in 1954, making her fifty years of age at the time of the poem's publication. Thus, not only did she live through the politically disgraceful and widely inhumane Vietnam War, but she also would most certainly be familiar with the unspeakable horrors of the Holocaust of World War II. While one could be aware that these wars took place without realizing the extent of the atrocities therein, the reader may have difficulty believing that the macabre Addonizio would lack that knowledge. (In "One Nation under God," also from *What Is This Thing Called Love*, one stanza, presumably with heavy sarcasm, reads, "And speaking of executions. How many / have there been lately? Not nearly enough.") With respect to the philosophers, understanding the scope of their work necessarily requires a certain distancing from the emotional trials of humanity, which makes their being mentioned in this poem somewhat counterintuitive. In an interview with the *San Francisco Reader*, Addonizio remarked, "I'm interested in communication, and in talking about things that are common to people's experience." In "Knowledge," if she means to speak of innocence and to connect to people with lingering innocence, the two philosophers are likely to be entirely unknown, weakening whatever connection she is seeking—unless, of course, she is seeking merely to impress her readers by mentioning such names.

Given the scope of understanding of both history and philosophy that the reader may reasonably expect Addonizio to have, the breathless, enthusiastic narrator originally envisioned, in light of the grammatical structure of the poem, would seem to be a fiction. No one familiar with the Holocaust, beyond the factual circumstances, could be genuinely "stunned" by any modern-day atrocity, unless he or she lacks the imagination to truly understand the extent of the horrors of World War II. Given Addonizio's age and poetic and intellectual experience, one may be unable to imagine her being at all naive.

Different readers may draw different conclusions from the evident contrast between the tone and content of "Knowledge." The more skeptical reader may simply perceive Addonizio as disingenuous, indirectly portraying herself, through the ambiguous "you" of the poem, as more emotionally innocent than she actually is. Another reader may interpret the tone of the poem to be substantially more complex than can be understood from the text alone.

That is, if Addonizio were to read the poem aloud, she would perhaps employ inflection that the reader could not have anticipated; instead of emphatic, her reading might be understated, or melancholy, with pauses and pacing more protracted than the absence of terminal punctuation would indicate.

Yet another reader, perhaps favorably considering the poet's professed desire to communicate as effectively as possible with her readers, may conclude that she has adopted the perspective of the poem's narrator precisely because she believes that that sense of breathlessness will heighten the average reader's emotional response. In an interview with *Poetry Flash*, Addonizio stated, "I'm very attracted to formal verse because it's a way to put the brakes on the material; it's very comforting and ordered. Actually, I think it fits my personality very well, since I'm somewhat schizophrenic. I have a lot of chaos in me as well as a great need for order and structure. Using set forms can be a way to address that." Thus, while "Knowledge" is not an exceptionally formal poem, Addonizio perhaps envisioned its extended-sentence structure as most reflective of the sentiments she wished to convey, whether the sentiments are genuinely hers or not.

In the same interview, she commented with respect to her work, "There's a kind of tension between the impossible and the desire for something." That tension may be evident here, in that while she indeed already knows enough about the world to no longer be "stunned" by "some terrible act," she still idealizes the notion of innocence. The first sentence, spanning almost the entire poem, ends with the word "hope," which is then repeated three words later. Perhaps in her own sustained yearning for the state of innocence that all people pass through in the early years of their lives, Addonizio simply wishes to connect with those who are still especially innocent. She may wish to do this not only for her own sake but also to warn such people that one day they, too, will know better than to expect all human beings to deem life as sacred as they do.

Source: Michael Allen Holmes, Critical Essay on "Knowledge," in *Poetry for Students*, Thomson Gale, 2007.

Diane Scharper

In the following review of What Is This Thing Called Love, *Scharper compares Addonizio's work to that of Anne Sexton in her focus on the theme of love, noting a cooler and less passionate tone in Addonizio's work.*

One could say that Addonizio (whose *Tell Me* was a National Book Award nominee) celebrates love as "a side trip./ It wasn't love for eternity, or any such crap," whereas Anne Sexton celebrated love as a grand passion. Otherwise, their work contains many similarities. Addonizio's most recent collection looks at love in all its guises, especially those concerned with a disappointing love affair, as did Sexton's 1969 book, *Love Poems*. Mourning the loss of love as well as the loss of sexual attractiveness that comes with aging, both collections use slang, eroticisms, and the details of contemporary urban life as a source of imagery and a way into the mostly freeverse poems. Both poets also share a tone that is simultaneously angry, sad, and brittle, although Addonizio is neither as sharpedged nor as passionate as Sexton. Sexton cared about everything, perhaps too much, and her life and poems tended to boil over—tragically. These poems, however, are lukewarm and "cool" at their best. Suitable for larger public libraries.

Source: Diane Scharper, Review of *What Is This Thing Called Love*, in *Library Journal*, Vol. 129, No. 1, January 2004, p. 118.

Bowker Magazine Group

In the following review of What Is This Thing Called Love, *the writer speaks of Addonizio's poems as part intimate and candid autobiography and part "standup comedy," and notes their blues-like quality and references.*

Unashamedly populist, and often charming, Addonizio's fourth book of verse explores the pleasures of sex, the pains of mourning, the efforts of raising a daughter and the difficulties of minor celebrity, setting all her musings and recollections in a style two parts confessional, one part standup comedy, and one part talking blues. Addonizio (*Tell Me*) makes reference both to famous bluesmen (Robert Johnson) and to their repetition-based forms. The first two parts of this five-part collection repeat single subjects as well: first the erotic life (a "31-year-old lover" "stands naked in my bedroom and nothing/has harmed him yet"), and then the dead ("no real grief left/for the man who was my father"). Exploring "the way of the world—/the sorrowful versus the happy," the rest of Addonizio's book takes up lighter, more varied subjects, often with a defter hand: "Tiffs Poem Wants to Be a Rock and Roll Song So Bad" self-mockingly "captures the essence of today's youth," while "This Poem Is in Recovery" promises "I'm not going to get drunk and take off my clothes/to sign my book for you." One poem adapts a form from Billy Collins, another responds (by name) to Sharon Olds: others recall the candid representations of (for example) Molly Peacock. Addonizio's in-your-face persona and her avoidance of technical difficulty should help her attract the wide audience she explicitly invites.

Source: Bowker Magazine Group, Review of *What Is This Thing Called Love*, in *Publishers Weekly*, Vol. 250, No. 51, December 22, 2003, p. 54.

Donna Seaman

In the following review of What Is This Thing Called Love, *Seaman calls attention to the "resonance" and "panache" of Addonizio's wide-ranging and ambivalent poems on love and mortality.*

Addonizio's poems are like swallows of cold, grassy white wine. They go down easy and then, moments later, you feel the full weight of their impact. Her first collection, *Tell Me* (2000) was a National Book Award finalist, and any reader who enjoyed her candor and sexiness will find her writing here with even more panache and greater resonance. A smoky-voiced chanteuse, she sings the blues of lost youth and past wildness, protesting the assaults of age, the void left by a grown child and a deceased father, and the sorrows of loved ones battling disease. High heels and hangovers, horror movies and empty hotel rooms, regrets and resignation, elements all in Addonizio's articulation of lust, the quest for oblivion, and the body's unrelenting archiving of every pleasure and pain. For all their fleshiness, stiletto stylishness, and rock-and-roll swagger, Addonizio's finely crafted and irreverent poems are timeless in their inquiries into love and mortality, rife with mystery and ambivalence, and achingly eloquent in their study of the conflictful union of body and soul.

Source: Donna Seaman, Review of *What Is This Thing Called Love*, in *Booklist*, Vol. 100, No. 8, December 15, 2003, pp. 720–21.

Sources

Addonizio, Kim, "Knowledge," in *What Is This Thing Called Love*, W. W. Norton, 2004, p. 71.

Addonizio, Kim, and Jalina Mhyana, "Interview with Kim Addonizio," in *Rock Salt Plum Poetry Review*, Spring 2004, available online at http://www.rocksaltplum.com/RockSaltPlumSpring2004/KinAddonizioInterview.html.

Addonizio, Kim, and Leza Lowitz, "Coming Out the Other Side: Talking with Kim Addonizio," in *Poetry Flash*, No. 289, January–March 2002, available online at http://www.Poetryflash.org/archive.289.Lowitz.html.

Addonizio, Kim, and Tod Marshall, "Kim Addonizio," in *Range of the Possible: Conversations with Contemporary Poets*, Eastern Washington University Press, 2002, pp. 3–15.

Booth, Wayne C., *The Rhetoric of Fiction*, 2d ed., University of Chicago Press, 1983, p. 97.

Karp, Jerry, "Kim Addonizio Tells Us," in the *San Francisco Reader*, No. 1, July 2002, available online at http://www.sanfranciscoreader.com/profiles/addonizio%20profile.html.

Logan, William, "Jumping the Shark," in *New Criterion*, Vol. 24, No. 4, December 2005, pp. 75–76.

Review of *What Is This Thing Called Love*, in *Publishers Weekly*, Vol. 250, No. 51, December 22, 2003, p. 54.

Scharper, Diane, Review of *What Is This Thing Called Love*, in *Library Review*, Vol. 129, No. 1, January 2004, p. 118.

Seaman, Donna, Review of *What Is This Thing Called Love*, in *Booklist*, Vol. 100, No. 8, December 15, 2003, p. 720.

Van Cleave, Ryan G., "Kim Addonizio: A Poet with Duende," in *Iowa Review*, Vol. 32, No. 3, 2002, p. 126.

Further Reading

Behn, Robin, *The Practice of Poetry: Writing Exercises from Poets Who Teach*, Collins, 1992.
This book is ideal for anyone who wants to learn to write poetry. The book consists of a series of exercises designed to help would-be poets find their own poetic voices and begin writing.

Germin, Pamela, *Sweeping Beauty: Contemporary Women Poets Do Housework*, University of Iowa Press, 2005.
This appropriately titled collection focuses on what women most often do in the home: housework. Many of the poems will make readers laugh, but many more will cause readers to sit up and take notice of the exceptional women poets who have written them, turning even housework into art.

Giunta, Edvige, *Writing with an Accent: Contemporary Italian American Women Writers*, Palgrave, 2002.
This book examines the ways in which Italian American women poets use their poetry as a way to identify and explore their Italian heritage. Although the author mentions Addonizio several times, none of her poems is discussed in depth.

Mullaney, Janet Palmer, ed., *Truthtellers of the Times: Interviews with Contemporary Women Poets*, University of Michigan Press, 1999.
This collection of fifteen interviews includes a broad spectrum of women's voices, with diversity of race, ethnicity, and age. Although Addonizio is not among them, the poets speak of topics that interest all women poets, such as women's stories and women's survival as writers.

National Commission on Terrorist Attacks upon the United States, *The 9/11 Commission Report: Final Report of the National Commission on Terrorist Attacks upon the United States*, W. W. Norton, 2004.
This book presents an unbiased, well-researched study of these terrorist attacks by a foreign entity on U.S. soil. The work is very readable, is written in easy-to-understand prose, and provides one context for understanding the fear that Addonizio mentions in her poem.

The Legend

Garrett Hongo

1988

"The Legend" is the concluding poem in Garrett Hongo's award-winning book of poetry *The River of Heaven*, published in 1988. In an interview with Bill Moyers in *The Language of Life*, Hongo recalled that the poem was written during an unhappy period in his life, when he was struggling to find direction in his work as a graduate student in literature. On a trip to Chicago, Hongo found himself alone in a hotel room watching a television program on random street violence, which included a segment on an Asian man who was accidentally shot on the street. According to Hongo, the program treated the man as virtually anonymous, vaguely identifying him as Asian. Hongo claimed that the next morning, when he sat down to write, the poem "The Legend" came flowing out of him spontaneously. In addition to portraying images of incidental street violence, the poem contains a reference to an old Asian legend that Hongo had been told as a child. Hongo regards the writing of the poem as an influential moment for him; in fact, he then decided to leave his graduate studies and instead write a book of poems. This poem in particular guided him in his efforts.

"The Legend" is a narrative poem with a contemporary, readable style. Although it is not a long poem, it touches upon many ideas important to Hongo, including the alienation and violence of the streets, the difficulties faced by immigrants in America, the poet's own questioning of his ethnic identity, and the mixing of Asian and Western cultures. The poem is dedicated to the memory of Jay

Kashiwamura, who may be assumed to be the man featured on the television program seen by Hongo, who perhaps made an effort to seek out the deceased man's identity so as to pay him respect.

Author Biography

Garrett Kaoru Hongo was born on May 30, 1951, in Volcano, Hawaii. His parents were third-generation Japanese Americans. When Hongo was six years old, his father moved the family to California. Hongo attended a working-class, racially mixed high school in Los Angeles, where he was exposed to urban street life and racial divisions that he would later describe in his poetry. Hongo earned a scholarship and attended Pomona College, in California, where he majored in English. At college, he cultivated his interest in poetry and writing and in Asian American culture in general, graduating in 1973. He then moved to Japan for a year, where he worked and studied at a Buddhist monastery in Kyoto. In 1975, Hongo founded a theater group in Seattle called the Asian Exclusion Act, named after laws that had discriminated against Asian immigrants in America. He received attention for a play he wrote and accepted a job in Hollywood as a television writer, which he quickly left. He then enrolled in the University of California, Irvine, to pursue a master's degree in poetry, graduating in 1980.

In 1982, Hongo published his first book of poetry, *Yellow Light*. That same year, he married Cynthia Thiessen, a violinist and musicologist. A year later, Hongo visited Hawaii for the first time since leaving as a child. In 1988, he published another book of poems, *The River of Heaven*, which contains the poem "The Legend." Hongo was nominated for the Pulitzer Prize for Poetry for this second book and won the Lamont Poetry Prize from the Academy of American Poets.

Hongo has taught writing and literature at several universities, including the University of Missouri and the University of Oregon, where he was the director of the creative writing program from 1989 to 1993. In addition to teaching, Hongo has been very active in the field of Asian American literature, compiling and editing several anthologies. In 1994, Hongo edited *Songs My Mother Taught Me: Stories, Plays and Memoir*, the work of the Japanese American woman Wakako Yamauchi. In 1993, he compiled *The Open Boat: Poems from Asian America*, and in 1995 he edited *Under Western Eyes: Personal Essays from Asian America*.

Also in 1995, Hongo published a book of prose nonfiction, *Volcano: A Memoir of Hawai'i*. Hongo's literary honors include fellowships from the Guggenheim Foundation, the National Endowment for the Arts, and the Rockefeller Foundation. As of 2006, Hongo was teaching in the writing program at the University of Oregon in Eugene.

Poem Summary

Stanza 1

Hongo begins "The Legend" by quickly establishing the setting of the poem: the streets of Chicago during a soft snowfall, in the "twilight of early evening." The narrator uses detailed images to convey a story, with the language focusing on external events. The first image is that of a man carrying a load of laundry, neatly folded within a crumpled shopping bag; the narrator states that the man enjoys the feel of the warm laundry in his hands. Thus, the narrator is one who can make assumptions about the internal state of the character. The narrator then compares the color of the man's face to a Rembrandt painting, alluding to the Dutch painter Rembrandt van Rijn (1606–1669), of the European baroque school of painting. This description reveals not only the color of the man's cheeks but also the character of the narrator: he has knowledge and cultural sophistication. As such, the poet is revealing complexity beyond his simple images. At the end of the first stanza comes an instant of foreshadowing, as the last flash of sunset lends an orange glow to the scene.

Stanza 2

In the second stanza, the narrator describes the man. He is Asian, and the narrator estimates him to be either Thai or Vietnamese. Thus, although the narrator has insight into the character's internal state, he is not omniscient. The man is described as frail and poorly dressed, in a working-class jacket and wrinkled pants. The poem continues to show movement, as the man negotiates the icy sidewalk, opens the back door of his car, and puts his laundry inside. Then, although the man remains nameless, the car is identified as a Ford Fairlane. This is, after all, America, where automobiles have names but people in the streets are anonymous. At the end of the second stanza, the action suddenly intensifies. The narrator mentions a flurry of footsteps and commotion. The Asian man hears shouts from pedestrians, as an armed boy has just robbed the corner package store. The boy fires a pistol and hits the Asian man in the chest, and the man slumps over, surprised.

Stanza 3

The storytelling mode continues into the third stanza, with images of a crowd gathering and a wounded man struggling to speak. The man makes noises that none of the bystanders can understand; in fact, the narrator remarks that the man's noises mean "nothing" to the crowd, endowing the man with a sense of alienation and inconsequentiality. The boy who shot him disappears into the snowy evening, leaving behind only footsteps in the snow. The reader may get the sense that justice will not be served.

Stanza 4

In the fourth stanza, the setting and tone of the poem abruptly change, as the reader enters the narrator's mind. The narrator states that he has been reading about René Descartes (1596–1650), a French philosopher associated with the European Enlightenment. Descartes theoretically doubted everything in his world except himself, thus elevating thought as the most important function of his being. He is perhaps most widely remembered for the statement "I think, therefore I am." Individuals such as Descartes helped free science and philosophy from religious dogma. The narrator considers the "grand courage" that Descartes possessed with respect to his intellectualization, all of which is extraordinarily remote from the random shooting he has just described. The narrator asserts that he feels "distinct" from the Asian man; in fact, he feels "ashamed." The narrator may be ashamed of his privilege; he is safe and reading philosophy, while a man going about his working-class life is randomly shot and dies in the streets. Implicit in this passage is the connection that the narrator must feel to the dying man; he cannot merely withdraw back into his thoughts about philosophy.

Stanza 5

In the final stanza of the poem, the narrator again changes tone, moving away from thoughts of himself and speaking to the heavens. He offers both a prayer and a eulogy for the dying man, asking the night sky to cover him and provide his final comforts. He then prays that "the weaver girl cross the bridge of heaven" and take the dying man's hands. The mention of the weaver girl is an allusion to an old legend told in some Asian and Native American cultures on the Pacific Rim. In Japan, this legend is celebrated in an annual festival called Tanabata, which is held on the seventh day of the seventh lunar month of the lunisolar calendar. According to the legend, as explained by Hongo to the interviewer Bill Moyers, the Milky Way is seen as a river of stars in the sky, the River of Heaven. Two young sweethearts, a weaver girl and a goatherd boy, are separated from each other by this river of stars. The weaver girl must remain separated from her true love because she has a huge responsibility: to weave together the fabric of the universe that gives everything existence. The legend is a story of sad separation, except that once a year the heavens take pity on the young couple and provide a way for them to come together, such as by having a flock of birds serve as a bridge over the river of stars so that they can meet. The poem concludes with its reference to this Asian legend.

Media Adaptations

- Hongo reads his poetry aloud and is interviewed by Bill Moyers on *The Power of the Word with Bill Moyers*. This six-part television series, broadcast on public television in 1989, features a variety of contemporary poets and their poetry. Produced and directed by David Grubin, the video recording was published by Films for the Humanities and Sciences in 1994.

Themes

Alienation

Alienation is the state of feeling unwelcome in the world, or of experiencing the world as inhospitable, empty, or meaningless. Large, modern cities are a common setting in literary works treating the theme of alienation. In "The Legend," the narrator evokes this theme by presenting the Asian man as alone and lacking in friendship or human contact. The cityscape is described as cold and becoming dark. The crowd that gathers after the man is shot is faceless, and no individuals are described as coming forward to help or to provide human

Topics For Further Study

- Research the Tanabata festival of Japan and other Asian countries. Create a presentation that discusses the customs and ceremonies surrounding the festival. Provide photographs, if possible, and show how various countries celebrate the festival differently. In your presentation, compare the story of the weaver girl to the Western idea of heaven, noting the differences and similarities between the two stories.

- In "The Legend," the author refers to two figures from European history, Rembrandt and Descartes. Research each figure and write an essay for each, describing the time and place in which they lived, summarizing the contributions that each made to their cultures, and explaining why these contributions are important.

- Think of an event that you heard about on the news that affected you emotionally. Write a poem in which you tell the story of this event with photographic detail and, within the poem, also try to relate that event to your own life, describing the emotions that the story brought out in you.

- Hold a group discussion on the issue of teenagers, street violence, and firearms. Compile a list of incidents that have involved these elements and then compile a list of specific factors that contribute to the problem of teenage violence. Finally, list various courses of action that might help prevent such incidents in the future and discuss and debate the positives and negatives of these courses of action.

---

warmth to the suffering man. The man is also unable to communicate to the crowd. When the narrator enters the poem, he, too, seems isolated from the world, watching from a distance and likewise failing to share in human contact.

Anonymity

Anonymity is the quality of being nameless and lacking individuality within a crowd. Whereas alienation is generally a negative emotional response to the inhumanity or emptiness of the world, anonymity is simply the condition one can have within society. The condition is not necessarily a negative one; some people prefer it. The man in "The Legend" is essentially anonymous. He is referred to as a nameless Asian man, without any further depth of description. His appearance is plain, his clothing common. As he lies wounded in the street, the sounds he makes are not understood by the people around him. The narrator of the poem is emotionally affected in witnessing the man's anonymity, eventually registering the feeling of shame.

Identity

Identity is the concept that a person has about himself. Identity can be influenced both individually and culturally; that is, identity stems both from who a person truly is when cultural influences are stripped away and from how these cultural influences affect how a person is perceived. In "The Legend," the narrator questions the identity of the Asian man he is describing. He examines external markers, such as appearance, clothing, and actions, in order to identify the man. To establish his own identity, on the other hand, the narrator refers to his feelings, to the philosophy that he reads, and to an Asian legend.

Mixing of Eastern and Western Cultures

The poem contains elements of two cultures. The language of the poem might be described as common American speech, and the poem is set in a typically American city. The main character in the poem is Asian, while the poet is Japanese American. An American brand name, a Ford Fairlane car, appears in the poem, exemplifying Western commercialism. An Eastern man owns the car and is presumably living a Western lifestyle, judging from his mode of dress. The narrator makes references to figures from Western history, Rembrandt and Descartes, specifically comparing the Asian man to a Rembrandt painting and himself, in a sense, to the philosopher.

The poem also contains two stories that might be seen as representative of Eastern and Western cultures. The first story is typically American, featuring robbery, gunshots, violence on the street, and a fleeing criminal. The second story is an old Asian legend that mentions the existence of the heavens and a compassionate weaver girl in the sky. In certain ways, the poet has attempted to "bridge" these two stories.

Shame

Shame is a complex emotion. When a person feels shame, a fundamental devaluing or loss of belief in the self is implied. The narrator of the poem notes that he feels shame upon recounting the story of the innocent man's shooting. This shame may relate to his distance from the man on the streets, from his own sense of privilege, or from his observation of the devaluing treatment of the man by the crowd. The shame might also relate to the simple witnessing of a senseless, unjust act. The narrator is unable or unwilling to specify the cause of his shame; because he did nothing to cause the event he witnessed, the shame he feels must have already lain within him.

Style

Allusion

In "The Legend," the poet employs allusion several times. An *allusion* is a reference within a story to related people, things, events, or stories. Here, the narrator alludes to a painter, a philosopher, and an old legend. These allusions add meaning to the poem, pointing to deeper meanings and enhancing the descriptions.

Straightforward Diction

The diction, or the poet's choice of words, is simple and straightforward in Hongo's poem. The types of words used by the narrator reveal the kind of person he is and the way he sees the world. The Asian man, meanwhile, is poor and plain in appearance, and the poet uses language that is simple and nonornamental to describe him. In this way, the diction aligns with the meanings of the poem.

Visual Imagery and Plot

Through precise descriptions, the narrator evokes images in the reader's mind. Indeed, Hongo relies on a series of images to tell the poem's story. The poem is organized as a series of verbal photographs, making the poem a highly visual experience for the reader.

Subjective Narration

The poem is told as a story by a narrator who is recounting events. A story's narrator may be a neutral, objective presence, or he may be subjective, presenting a particular point of view. The narrator in "The Legend" speaks in the first person; he is the poem's "I." This narrator comments upon and speculates about the Asian man and is also specific in detailing his own feelings. In relating this story through a subjective narrator, Hongo allows the reader to understand that narrator's particular impressions and sentiments.

Varying Tone

Tone relates to the feelings and moods conveyed by a poem. Hongo twice changes the tone of the poem for effect. In the beginning, when description and images are relied upon, the tone of the poem is detailed and primarily objective. In the fourth stanza, when the narrator is given an identity, the tone changes to become personal and emotional. In the fifth stanza, the tone becomes formal and even reverent, as the poem's final lines serve as a prayer or eulogy for the wounded man.

Historical Context

Discrimination and Asian American History

Hongo's work is grounded in his deep awareness of Asian peoples' history in America, including the struggle of Asian immigrants to gain respect and equality in society. As such, his work has also served to memorialize the various injustices suffered by Asian Americans. For instance, Hongo has written about the Asian Exclusion Laws of the early 1900s, which prohibited Asian Americans from owning property and marrying whites and also barred single Asian women from moving to the United States. In California, the Alien Land Law prohibited Japanese people from owning real estate.

In 1941, the Japanese bombed Pearl Harbor, in Hawaii, bringing the United States into World War II. In 1942, President Franklin Delano Roosevelt issued Executive Order 9066, requiring the 120,000 Japanese Americans living on the West Coast to be

Compare & Contrast

- **1980s:** The United States sees a wave of immigration from Asia and the Pacific Islands. According to the 1990 U.S. census, the number of persons of Asian and Pacific Islander descent increased from 3.7 million to 7.2 million between 1980 and 1990, nearly doubling.

   Today: The fastest-growing ethnic minority in the United States is Asian Pacific Americans. The population of this group is projected to grow to more than forty million by the year 2050. The largest group of Asian Pacific Americans is formed by those of Chinese descent (23 percent), followed by Filipinos (19 percent), Japanese (12 percent), Koreans (11 percent), and Indians (11 percent).

- **1980s:** The U.S. Congress issues a formal apology to the Japanese Americans who were relocated and confined to internment camps during World War II and also creates a reimbursement fund for those who were detained.

   Today: The sixtieth anniversary of the atomic bombing of the Japanese cities of Nagasaki and Hiroshima by U.S. armed forces during World War II is observed in 2005. There is public debate as to whether the United States should issue an apology over the bombings and the deaths of Japanese civilians in those cities, but no formal apology is forthcoming.

- **1980s:** Gun-related deaths in the United States reach epidemic proportions, averaging more than thirty thousand per year throughout the 1980s, according to the U.S. Centers for Disease Control and Prevention.

   Today: The rate of gun deaths in the United States is decreasing slightly, after peaking in the early 1990s, but gun deaths still claim about thirty thousand lives per year, according to the U.S. Centers for Disease Control and Prevention.

---

relocated to ten internment camps throughout the nation. Indeed, Japanese Americans faced widespread prejudice and bitterness in society due to wartime tensions. During this time, Hongo's grandfather was taken into custody in Hawaii and questioned by the FBI. Hongo has noted that his parents' generation refused to talk about the relocation camps after the war, preferring to try to forget that episode of history. This aspect of Japanese American history has been an important context for Hongo.

Stereotypes

Hongo has written about how Asians have faced stereotyping in American society. Movies, television shows, and newspaper cartoons portrayed Asians in caricature or in disempowering, voiceless roles during and after the tensions of World War II. Hongo writes in his introduction to the multi-author collection *The Open Boat: Poems from Asian America* (1993) that he has been "forever fighting the stereotype, the dehumanized image of Asians in America, the *invisibility* of our historical, social, and cultural presence in this country." "The Legend" relates to this context because it portrays the relative invisibility of an Asian man in American society.

Cultural Denial

Hongo has noted that many of his Japanese American classmates in high school would not talk about the World War II relocation camps, maintaining the cultural taboo set by their parents. As a writer, Hongo has felt impelled to address the suffering endured by Japanese Americans who lost their homes and jobs during that period. Some of Hongo's poems, including "The Legend," can be seen as transgressing this cultural denial concerning discrimination and injustice.

The 1980s

By the 1980s, second-, third-, and fourth-generation Asian Americans were contributing to

The Chicago skyline silhouetted by winter trees © Richard Hamilton Smith/Corbis

American society. A new generation of Asian American students had attended college and had helped establish Asian American studies departments in many universities. Young Asian American writers were creating literature that addressed their individual and cultural issues, and they were also finding outlets for their work. Dozens of new Asian American poets and writers, including Hongo, published works in literary journals, magazines, and books. In the 1980s, Amy Tan's novel *The Joy Luck Club* and David Henry Hwang's play *M. Butterfly* were especially prominent Asian American works. In 1989, the U.S. Congress finally made a formal apology to the Japanese Americans who had been held in camps during World War II. Congress also created a permanent entitlement program to financially reimburse those who had endured life in the internment camps.

Critical Overview

The River of Heaven was nominated for the Pulitzer Prize for Poetry and won the Lamont Poetry Prize from the Academy of American Poets. Indeed, the poems were well received by the critical establishment and established Hongo as an important voice in Asian American poetry. Robert Schultz, writing in the *Hudson Review*, notes that Hongo's poems show "care to those excluded from whatever the American Dream has become in the 1980s."

Hongo's rich and versatile style has been especially noted by critics. Schultz comments that his "rich vocabulary and undulant syntax hold his stories of loss and remembrance in a secure, distinctive music." A reviewer for *Publishers Weekly* states that Hongo skillfully uses language that "ranges from the lyric and elegant to the earthy and everyday" and that the "poet's song is built on a keen sense of history and purpose." Fred Muratori, writing in *Library Journal*, comments that Hongo's "character studies and first-person narratives that speak of life in non-white America attain an authority unobscured by imagistic mannerisms." Reflecting Hongo's substantial stature as a poet, Muratori compares him to the renowned poets William Wordsworth and Walt Whitman.

"The Legend" is considered by critics to be one of the most outstanding poems in Hongo's second collection. Laurie Filipelli writes in her book *Garrett Hongo*, "The poem functions to bestow dignity and intimacy upon a story of anonymous street violence, providing, through legend, an afterlife consolation for unexplainable suffering."

Criticism

Douglas Dupler

Dupler is a writer and college English teacher. In this essay, he discusses the effectiveness of Hongo's poetic style in expressing the themes that are important to the poet.

Hongo's poem "The Legend" shows the power of well-intentioned brevity, as therein a few incidents drawn from common life reveal meanings beyond their specific time and place. The poet efficiently endows this poem with several levels of meaning, conveying genuine emotion and insight with the use of simple language and a few images economically evoked. Indeed, Hongo has stated his dedication to conciseness of expression and his firm belief in the power of the written word. In *Volcano: A Memoir of Hawai'i*, he expresses this artistic credo in contemplating time spent with a mentor:

> I learned that a generation has an emotional note which can be captured in a song, that entire lifetimes of experience . . . could be figured forth in a story of only a few words so long as those were the *right* words, in the right order.

In the first stanzas of the poem, the focus is on the setting, on the exterior qualities of the world as the poet sees it. The narrator begins telling the brief and tragic story of one man's evening on the cold streets. The setting is Chicago, in the heartland, far from the poet's place of birth, in the Pacific. The man being described is alone; instead of human contact, he has only the "warm laundry and crinkled paper" that he is carrying as a tactile connection to the world. The sun is going down, and the waning light brings a "Rembrandt glow" to the man's cheek. In the second stanza, this man is identified further, though ambiguously, as "Asian, Thai or Vietnamese." He is also identified as poor and shabbily dressed, as any man on the street might be, regardless of nationality or race. Thus, this man represents to the narrator both an Asian man and an everyman, different from the crowd by virtue of his race yet anonymous and alone.

The end of the first stanza and beginning of the second stanza effectively highlight the distance between the narrator and the Asian man. First, the narrator reveals his knowledge of centuries-old European paintings in comparing the light on the Asian man's face to a Rembrandt canvas. In this efficient description, layers of depth can be found. The choice of comparison evokes the issue of class difference. The narrator is educated, almost flippantly revealing his difference from the other man, who in reality probably has little in common with a character in an old European painting. The uncertainty regarding the Asian man's nationality further confuses the issue of identity for the narrator. If the poet is Asian as well, how exactly does he share in identity with the character in his poem? This is a common theme with Hongo; in another poem in the same collection, "The Pier," the narrator notes,

> I'd see Vietnamese in small, family groups,
> or they were Cambodians—Asians as foreign to me
> as my grandfathers might have been
> to the Yank seaman who stared, stopped

Having established the setting and the subject of "The Legend," the narration quickly moves along in images. The Asian man is hit by a random gunshot from an adolescent robber, a crowd gathers, and the Asian man struggles over his last breaths. In death, the man remains anonymous and not understood by the crowd. His words are "a babbling no one understands," and the people who surround him are "bewildered at his speech." In the next line, the narrator subtly reveals his own anger with and alienation from this uncaring society in concluding, "The noises he makes are nothing to them." The killer escapes, hinting that justice may not be served.

In the fourth stanza, the poem introduces a major shift in perspective. The narrator personally enters the poem for the first time, stating, "Tonight, I read about Descartes' / grand courage to doubt everything / except his own miraculous existence." Again, the narrator is both distancing himself from the subject and identifying himself, with the reference to Descartes bearing several layers of meaning. The narrator is portraying himself as an intellectual. He also seems as lacking in compassion as the people on the street who have witnessed the shooting, jumping into scholarly references as opposed to compassionate plaints. On another level, the reader may be aware that Descartes was a figure of the Enlightenment. Descartes' work is associated with the strengthening of individual intellectual thought and the weakening of the power of religious myth in the Western mind. These ideas further identify the perspective of the narrator.

The narrator quickly recovers the faith of the reader when he acknowledges the distance he feels from the wounded man, admitting to feeling "distinct" from him. The narrator then becomes emotionally deep and honest, claiming that shame lies beneath his sentiments, pervading his perceptions. The reaction is interesting, as the narrator could have then revealed many emotions, including compassion, anger, fear, sadness, or guilt. Yet shame overshadows all of these responses. The narrator explains no further, saying only, "I am ashamed." Once again, the narrator's statement contains various layers. He is a member of a society where adolescents commit murder and innocent people die, regardless of race, while his own life has lifted him above these troubles on the streets; he has become insulated in a world of ideas. The narrator also ethnically identifies with the wounded man suffering on the street, his words neither heard nor understood by the crowd.

Perhaps the silencing of the dying man is the greatest source of shame for the narrator. A recurring theme in Hongo's work has been ethnic Americans' lack of voice in greater society; indeed, he has personally struggled to claim that voice. In *Volcano*, he discusses shame as it relates to his people:

> I learned that what mainstream society perceived as "shame" and we younger Japanese Americans called "silence" or "passivity" was actually a great burden of pain and disappointment.... After the dispossession of the war, after the loss of farms, businesses, and homes and half a lifetime of building a life, the Issei [first-generation Japanese Americans] who'd translated themselves over into becoming Americans were simply heartbroken and exhausted.... Perhaps detachment, a Buddhist recommendation, was the most they could muster.

Had the poet ended the poem after this admission of shame, it would have been a very different poem—one of grieving and emotional damage. Instead, in the three concluding lines of the final stanza, the poet achieves an outcome of redemptive emotional expression. Rather than succumbing to shame and defeat, the poet reaches as deep inside himself as possible. He appeals to the sacred and to forces that are beyond himself and the dying man; he appeals to the heavens, assuming a tone of prayer. He asks the night sky to the cover the dying man, recognizing a force of nature that is beyond culture and race and that will cover everything equally in due time.

When the narrator prays for the "weaver girl" to "cross the bridge of heaven" to comfort the dying man, he moves beyond his shame to affirm his own existence. He does this by giving words to one of the oldest legends of his ancestors, thus honoring his cultural past and his ethnicity and more deeply accepting himself. He also moves beyond his Western rationality, which was exemplified by the reference to Descartes a few lines earlier. That is, the rational questioning and individualism of Western tradition is no solace for him in that moment. By appealing to an old Asian creation

> " *Like the Romantic poets to whom he has been compared, Hongo affirms the power of the word to make peace with, and even transcend, human prejudice, suffering, and limitation.*"

legend, the narrator appeals to the realm of the transpersonal and the mythic. The legend referred to by the poet is a story that upholds a compassionate universe. This legend is an antidote to the despair the poet has just witnessed and to the shame that he feels. Like the Romantic poets to whom he has been compared, Hongo affirms the power of the word to make peace with, and even transcend, human prejudice, suffering, and limitation.

Source: Douglas Dupler, Critical Essay on "The Legend," in *Poetry for Students*, Thomson Gale, 2007.

David Kelly

Kelly is an instructor of creative writing and literature. In this essay, he examines how Hongo avoids sentimentalizing the situation in this poem by openly admitting his own shortcomings.

Poetry is based on the practice of observation. Poets tend to view the world in greater detail than the average person, in an effort to render it in a few words that might match the intensity of living. When poetry carefully reconstructs the physical world, the things that are considered commonplace or even ugly reveal their inherent beauty. Poets create their most convincing statements on the nature of the universe not by theorizing but by looking at things carefully and accurately reporting what they see.

The same dynamic applies when poets want to address social situations. While it might be tempting for a poet to discuss rather than unveil—to proclaim theories about the way things are instead of giving readers evidence with which to reach their own conclusions—this only leads to weak poetry. Literary works that try to force a particular religious, political, or moral perspective on their readers are labeled "didactic" and often put aside and ignored. Still, poets will always try to control

What Do I Read Next?

- *The Floating World* (1989) is a novel by Cynthia Kadohata. Set during World War II, it tells the adventures of a Japanese American family in search of a home.

- *The Open Boat: Poems from Asian America* (1993) is a book of poetry edited by Hongo. It features the work of dozens of Asian American poets and an introduction by Hongo that details the development of Asian American poetry.

- *Volcano: A Memoir of Hawai'i* (1995), an autobiographical work by Hongo, is a detailed and beautifully written account of the people and places that have touched the poet's imagination.

- *The Woman Warrior* (1976) is Maxine Hong Kingston's autobiographical collection of stories about growing up Chinese in America. This book is a classic of Asian American literature.

- *Yellow Light* (1982), Hongo's first book of poetry, introduces Hongo's perspective on the Asian American experience and his rich poetic style.

---

readers' opinions. If writing is at heart communication, it is natural for a writer to want to tell people how the world seems to operate and offer an individual perspective. But readers live in a time when every available space is being used to sell them something, and they are cynical about anything, even a well-meaning poem, that tries too hard to persuade. Sometimes the well-meaning poems can be the most annoying, coming across as pious and condescending.

This is why Hongo's poem "The Legend" is such a remarkable accomplishment. The poem's main focus is an ordinary man who is going about his mundane business, leaving a laundromat with just-washed clothes, when a gunman fleeing a holdup shoots him dead. The man is so ordinary that he does not have a name: he has no identity other than being the victim of this brief event. In the hands of another poet, this situation could be used to emphasize the writer's extra-large ability to empathize with a hapless victim and to point out the obvious unfairness of a man's being killed while minding his own business. When Hongo shifts the focus from the character to the author, though, it is not to give credit to the author for being able to appreciate the fate of a small person who others would have failed to notice; it is instead a lament for his own inability to empathize, even when a situation is so obviously tragic.

Hongo establishes the main character's sympathetic qualities through the use of simple, uncomplicated touches. First, of course, is the main character's anonymity: having no name makes him a kind of everyman, a traditional literary character used for centuries to allow one person to represent the common fate of all humanity. Then there is the murderer, identified by Hongo as "a boy—that's all he was"; the situation is dampened by the fact that the killer is not even particularly evil, just young. The murder is presented as a scene that could take place in any northern city where it snows: even though the first line specifies Chicago as its setting, there is nothing particularly relevant about where it happens. The fact that the man does his laundry at a commercial laundromat indicates something about his economic situation, in that he does not have laundry facilities in his home, just as the fact that he drives a Ford Fairlane, a car that has not been manufactured since 1970, marks him as a salt-of-the-earth guy who is willing or required to struggle to keep an old car running.

There are a few touches to his personality, however, that ought to incline the poem's speaker to bond in empathy with the main character. For one thing, the victim is identified as "Thai or Vietnamese." Readers who know even the least background information about Hongo know that he is Japanese and that his poems frequently muse on his ethnic identity. Writing about an Asian character puts the poet in a unique social position in relation to his character: they are not of the same background, but readers can assume that there is a closer innate bond between them than the poet might feel for a non-Asian. Along these same lines, the poem specifically mentions that the man is carrying, in addition to his laundry, "crinkled paper." The character in the poem is someone who reads or possibly even writes, an endearing trait to writers. The poet can naturally be expected to empathize with another person from his race who shares a similar interest.

The first three stanzas focus on the man and the pointless death he suffers, with snow already covering him as soon as he has fallen, surrounded by people who cannot even understand his final words. In the fourth stanza, though, the focus shifts to the person telling this story. Having established the facts that should make the fallen man sympathetic to all people and to a person like Hongo in particular, the poem becomes an apology for the poet's inability to sympathize.

Intellectual abstraction is presented as the main divider. Hongo's admiration for the French philosopher René Descartes' dictum "I think; therefore I am" and all of the philosophical implications that follow from it leads him to pronounce Descartes as "courageous." Courage, in this case, stems from Descartes' willingness to recognize the fact that we are all ultimately alone, unsure of anything in this world except our individual existence. Hongo realizes that one result of this courageous stance is that he cannot relate to the other man, who by all other indicators he should feel a bond of kinship toward. For feeling so alienated, so "distinct," he admits, "I am ashamed." Another poet might celebrate his ability to empathize as much as he has with the stranger, but Hongo steers the poem away from self-congratulations and toward his own failure. He manages to avoid wallowing in unearned sentiment by admitting that empathy for another person, even when the subject is carefully and fully realized by sharp writing, just might not be possible at all.

If another writer bathed his subject with the glorifying light that Hongo uses to illuminate the man in the poem—from the twilight he steps into to the orange of his cheeks to the "Rembrandt glow on his face" to the darkening night sky that covers him in the end—it might be a matter of painting the lily or gilding gold (as Shakespeare put it), or unnecessarily adding decoration to something, like

> *He manages to avoid wallowing in unearned sentiment by admitting that empathy for another person, even when the subject is carefully and fully realized, just might not be possible at all.*

a flower, that is already beautiful anyway. Hongo avoids this by changing the reader's assumptions. There is no need for a reader to point out that the poet does not really understand the significance of the murdered man's life: he is the first to admit it. The prayer, in the last stanza, that this man should be carried off to heaven, is not an unearned comment on the man's worthiness but rather a wish for his well-being despite all that Hongo is unable to feel about him. It is a prayer for all people, who are helplessly isolated from each other because of the metaphysical limits that Descartes' dictum identifies.

Thus the poem's title, "The Legend," is perfectly appropriate. At first glance, it may seem to anticipate a poem that will talk about a larger-than-life figure, a person who commits amazing feats. After reading the poem, one might take that title to be the sort of praise for the common man that poets, with their attention to fine detail, like to confer upon situations that would slip by the average person's attention. What it really means, though, in the context of this poet's shame, is that a writer is inclined to create a legend around a situation, regardless of whether it actually describes something unusual. This is not a poem about whether or not a stranger deserves to be elevated in status; rather it is about the fact that there is something in us all that is able to recognize others' humanity only from afar, to understand that each person who is a mystery just might deserve to be made into a legend.

Source: David Kelly, Critical Essay on "The Legend," in *Poetry for Students*, Thomson Gale, 2007.

Sheldon Goldfarb

Goldfarb is a published writer with a Ph.D. in English. In the following essay, he explores the themes of alienation and connection in "The Legend."

Hongo, a poet of Asia and America who draws on the heritage of both West and East, begins this poem very much in the West. The setting is Chicago, and the poem's opening seems to echo the attitude of a famous poem in the Western canon, William Wordsworth's "Composed upon Westminster Bridge, September 3, 1802," with its description of the sleepy calm of London as it first awakes, wearing the "beauty of the morning."

Hongo's poem similarly begins with what at least seems to be a quiet, peaceful scene: It is "snowing softly," and a man who at this point is not further described is carrying his laundry to his car and enjoying the feel of the "warm laundry and crinkled paper." It seems a Wordsworthian portrayal of a charming, mundane scene, meant to lift one's spirits through the enjoyment of one of life's everyday moments. Even in the opening lines of Hongo's poem, however, there are hints that all is not well, that there is something ominous lurking in the twilight. For one thing, it is twilight, the symbolic end of the day, not morning as in Wordsworth's poem. Also, it is only "for a moment" that the man enjoys the feel of the laundry. Something is about to happen, and not something good.

That something happens at the end of the second stanza, when the man is shot by a robber fleeing the scene of his crime. Even before that, however, the second stanza introduces a decidedly darker tone than that found at the beginning of the poem. The man turns out to be poor and skinny, wearing rumpled pants and a dingy coat that is too large for him. He seems not to fit his clothes, and perhaps he also does not fit into this urban Chicago landscape. He is Asian, the speaker notes, and has trouble with a slick of ice. In the first stanza, the softly falling snow of the Chicago winter seems almost comforting; now the winter is the source of a difficult patch of ice.

That the man is Asian seems significant. He is a member of a minority; he is Thai or Vietnamese, from a culture different from the majority one in Chicago, a fact brought out in the third stanza when the man falls "babbling" to the ground, uttering sounds that "no one understands." Perhaps this in part simply means that he is making the sounds of death, which living bystanders cannot comprehend. There is also a suggestion, however, that the sounds are Asian words that the bystanders cannot comprehend because they do not know Asian languages. There is a sense of alienation here, of separation between cultures and a lack of connection. It is perhaps significant that the only other individual in the poem, the only other character who takes on an individual existence, is the boy who shoots the victim. Everyone else is just part of the uncomprehending crowd, suggesting that the only connection this poor Asian man can find in Western society is a violent one; he is separated from everyone except for the man who shoots him down.

This might suggest that there is anger in this poem, and, as Barbara Drake notes in her article on Hongo in the *Dictionary of Literary Biography*, there is outrage in some of his works. But there is no outrage here. The attitude in this poem is best expressed by the word Hongo uses to describe the reaction of the Asian man after he is shot. He is "dumbfounded," Hongo's speaker says at the end of the second stanza, and the whole poem seems dumbfounded, taken aback, bewildered by the sudden eruption of violence that takes the life of the innocent Asian man.

In addition to this dumbfounded feeling, there may be a feeling of relief or fear. After describing the death scene of the Asian man, the poem's speaker switches suddenly to talking about himself. In stanza 4, he reports that he has just read about the famous Western philosopher René Descartes. He says that reading about Descartes' philosophical approach of believing in nothing but his own existence led him to feel distinct from the dying Asian man. It is as if the speaker fears suffering the fate of a fellow Asian man—if the speaker is Asian himself, which seems probable because the speaker is the voice representing the Japanese American Hongo. Reading about Descartes allows the speaker to feel his individuality at the expense of his fellow feeling for the Asian victim; it allows the speaker to distance himself from the suffering.

Although this distancing may offer some comfort, it also makes the speaker ashamed. He turns away from this Western philosophy of individualism and instead utters an invocation, calling on the night sky to cover the dying man and then calling on "the weaver girl" to come comfort him or at least "take up his cold hands." The weaver girl is a character in an ancient Chinese myth about a supernatural being (the weaver girl) who falls in love with a mortal. Her union with the mortal displeases the gods, who cause them to be separated and placed as the stars Vega and Altair in the sky, where they are to be perpetually separated by the Milky

Way. However, one concession is offered them: once a year, magpies fly up and create a bridge so that the two lovers can be together.

Alluding to this bridge, Hongo's speaker calls on the weaver girl to "cross the bridge of heaven" and perhaps in some way to create unity or connection instead of separation. The weaver girl myth is about restoring at least some connection in the midst of separation; at the end of this poem about alienation, separation, and death, Hongo seems to be seeking a way to overcome these negative states and to create connection. Of course, in the weaver girl legend, the weaver girl and her lover are not dead, so it is possible to restore a connection. In Hongo's poem, the Asian man is dead or dying. It is harder to see how a connection might be restored. This is perhaps why the ending of the poem has a sighing, elegiac tone, as if after all there is nothing much that can be done. And yet there is also a feeling of hope, or at least wishfulness—a wishing for something better, a yearning for connection. It is a connection the Asian man himself seemed to be trying to make. He was living in America; trying to adjust to an American winter; driving an American car (a Ford Fairlane); and wearing a plaid mackinaw, a coat bearing a North American Indian name and featuring a Scottish pattern.

It seems as if the Asian man was trying to fit into North American society. The message of the poem might be that there should have been some attempt to meet him halfway. Perhaps that is why Hongo ends with an Asian legend. He might be suggesting that Western society needs to turn a bit away from the individualistic philosophy of Descartes in order to adopt a more connecting philosophy, such as the one underlying the tale of the weaver girl. In this connection, it is interesting to consider the other reference in the poem to a major figure in Western cultural history, the reference in the first stanza to the Dutch painter Rembrandt von Rijn. In that stanza, in first describing the Asian man, the speaker says that he has "a Rembrandt glow on his face."

The speaker here is referring to Rembrandt's characteristic technique of singling out certain figures in his paintings by making them seem to glow brightly against a dark background, as if bringing them out of obscurity. In the context of the poem, however, the Asian man is brought out of obscurity only to be killed. In this case, too, the "Rembrandt glow" is associated with the "flash" of sunset that "blazes the storefronts." In other words, the characteristic effect of a famous Western painter is here associated with violence, with a flash and with blazes. Just as the reference to Descartes seems negative in the end, so does the reference to Rembrandt, emphasizing the underlying message of the poem that perhaps it is time to turn to non-Western guides in an effort to escape violence and individualism.

Source: Sheldon Goldfarb, Critical Essay on "The Legend," in *Poetry for Students*, Thomson Gale, 2007.

Suzanne Arakawa

In the following essay excerpt, Arakawa calls attention to the impulse in Hongo's poetry to find individual identity and place it in the context of communion in the common experiences of humanity.

Hongo's poetry and prose are expansive, for they touch upon the personal, social, historical, and philosophical. In fact, his most successful poems contain poignant examinations of people, places, nature, heritage, and history—all under the aegis of what Robert Schultz terms "Hongo's rich vocabulary and undulant syntax [that] hold his stories of loss and remembrance in a secure, distinctive music."

Hongo first achieved success as a writer while founder and artistic director (1975–77) of the Asian Exclusion Act theater group in Seattle, Washington. His play *Nisei Bar and Grill* (1976) looks at Korean War veterans and their postwar struggle. At this time, Hongo collaborated on a poetic volume with Alan Chong Lau and Lawson Fusao Inada entitled *The Buddha Bandits down Highway 99* (1978), in which he contributed the nine-part poem "Cruising 99."

Yellow Light is Hongo's first poetry collection. This volume offers tender homages to Japanese American history and the working class. Mainly, he venerates the laborer—exemplified by Hongo's own grandfather and father and those in poor neighborhoods who struggle daily to maintain dignity. He also records history through illuminating and bracing personal points of views. One poem entitled "Stepchild" highlights how Japanese American historical exclusion from school textbooks and discussions have affected the speaker. This forgetfulness demonstrates that Japanese Americans are misbegotten because America as a whole has not acknowledged them as Americans. The poem establishes that part of the success of the American past can be attributed to Asian laborers, many of whom were used and then ousted from the country when no longer needed. In other poems, Hongo explores our need not only to discern our own essences but also to generate a depth of feeling for humanity. "Roots" encourages the location of the deeper self, the dedication to its discovery, and the knowledge that there is a unique signature to all things animate and inanimate.

The need for shared common experiences and the need for dignity and escape from ridicule are themes carried over to *The River of Heaven* (1988), which won the Lamont Poetry Prize and a nomination for the Pulitzer Prize in poetry. Hongo retrieves memories by reconstructing the past through a collection of viewpoints. He wants to commune with departed elders, and he memorializes those gone by inhabiting specific people and characters in order to tell their stories. As a result, he records their lives so that they may continue to live.

Hongo's use of parallel phrasing can be described at times as Whitmanesque; in his poetic narrative, he carefully layers words and images. Hongo infuses the visual with other sensate details. Also, animal imagery as well as Hawaiian legend inform his poetic impressions. Consequently, memories imbued with cultural and organic resonances display reverence for nature and its power to help people establish their own identities.

Hongo pays mindful consideration to the amplitude of what makes us human and connected to one another, to the past, and to nature. The need to find music in oneself is significant. His poems ask that we reexamine our detachment from ourselves, from our spirits, from each other. In fact, we sense that the soul can reach magnanimous formulations regarding the preciousness of humanity and nature. As Maxine Hong Kingston eloquently states, Hongo "extends splendor—and the sight and voice and concern of American poetry."

Source: Suzanne Arakawa, "On Garrett Hongo's Poetry," in *Encyclopedia of American Literature*, edited by Steven R. Serafin, Continuum Publishing, 1999.

Garrett Hongo and Bill Moyers

In the following interview, Hongo talks with Moyers about the place (and lack of place) of Japanese Americans in U.S. history, the experiences of his own family during World War II, and his poetry as a "conduit" for those vanished lives.

[*Bill Moyers:*] *Why did you decide to write poetry?*

[Garrett Hongo:] I wanted to explore the life of emotions. As a child in Hawai'i I remember not only having emotions, but they seemed authorized by the world and the family surrounding me. As an adolescent growing up in Los Angeles and the public schools there, emotions seemed to be under a tight reign even in sports. People seemed to want to deny them.

I didn't understand that as a Japanese American I was experiencing a social and historical sadness. Because my own family did not suffer relocation, they were trying to live it down and grow out of their own grief. So I had all these feelings which had no form of expression. My brother became a blues guitarist, and at first I was just angry, then I became a poet. Poetry and photography seemed to give me ways to explore and connect with the history that was repressed.

Repressed in what sense?

There wasn't anything in my high school textbooks about Japanese in America. I knew that we weren't there when Lee surrendered to Grant. I knew we weren't there when Washington crossed the Delaware.

Or at the Alamo, on either side.

Yes, and I wanted the words I was reading to belong to me, but there were no words for me, no words for my grandfather, no words for my grandmother. They simply weren't portrayed, so I felt that I didn't have an identity. Then I set about trying to learn that history and to put what did not exist for me on the page. Poetry was almost completely unwilled, I just had to have it.

Were these concerns shared within your family?

With my grandfather, mostly. My own parents were immigrants from Hawai'i to the mainland and they had a lot to do just to survive and to provide for my brother and me. My father was an American soldier at the same time that my grandfather was imprisoned in Hawai'i. My grandfather was born in America in 1899 but was sent back to Japan for his education, so the day after Pearl Harbor he was arrested and taken down for questioning in Honolulu. In a sense he was disappeared for a short time, not an uncommon story among Japanese Americans. My grandfather was a community leader, the president of the Japanese language school, who sponsored Japanese citizens to come over and be schoolteachers in Hawai'i. So of course he was under suspicion. He would sit down after dinner every night with his bourbon and tell me, his oldest grandchild, the story of how he was arrested and questioned by the FBI and how they tried to trick him into betraying his true identity.

They thought he was a spy?

That's right. And he was still angry about it. He'd tell me the story, and no one else would listen, they were embarrassed by his passion and by his giving me a responsibility for this story. I was told that he was senile, but he wasn't. He was obsessed with a wrong that he felt needed to be righted and he was also obsessed that the story had to be told. So he'd tell me the story every night. He said, "You learn the language good"—he spoke broken English, a Hawaiian kind of pidgin English because he was educated in Japan—"Learn speak like white Americans. You tell story." Kids remember that kind of thing. I remembered it.

I share with so many Japanese Americans of my generation a feeling that we have a story to tell, that we have a responsibility to that generation who suffered the humiliation and the loss and who did not have their presence in this country endorsed. I've been interviewing Japanese American lawyers and different people who've worked on redress, which is to say compensation for their relocation, and I've been more and more impressed with how this is a way for us to earn back what we all felt we lost during World War II.

When you were talking about that subject with the young people today, they responded to your poetry but not to your discussion about relocation. They didn't understand what the term means. It's not a part of their experience.

Exactly, and that's why I needed to write the story of relocation into the books. I remember as a student in Los Angeles, we'd study World War II and there would be no mention of the evacuation, no mention of Executive Order 9066 that sent 120,000 Japanese Americans from the West Coast in the United States to the relocation centers all over the barren places of the West and Arkansas. I wasn't angry about it; I just couldn't believe that it wasn't spoken about so I would raise the question. I didn't understand that this caused a great deal of embarrassment to many of my classmates who were mainland Japanese Americans. I didn't understand that even the *nisei*, second generation, didn't wish to bring up the subject. It was very painful to them, and a source of humiliation. Congressman Robert Matsui from California said that when he was in school and World War II came up, he'd pretend to be sick so he didn't have to go. He was ashamed. But that's something I didn't feel myself.

You said a minute ago that you felt sadness.

Yes. I felt everyone was sad, that there was this unspoken sadness all around me. I wanted to understand it and to bring it into language. What inspired me were things I read, like Greek tragedies. Here was Orestes full of action and Antigone standing up for a principle, so I said, "What the hell are we doing? We're not speaking to the issue. We're not articulating our emotions or our beliefs about the dead and about history." I was basically indoctrinated in a Western vision of articulation, of speaking to emotional and historical issues, but my experience was one of repression.

> *I think poetry is about our most familiar need which we deny in order to lead more practical lives, but ultimately these lives are impractical because they do not have such presences in them. I think poetry can bring such presences back."*

You didn't think that you could talk about this?

I didn't feel that others could or would, and that caused a great frustration. And I didn't know it at the time but I think I unconsciously absorbed my grandfather's directive to me. He'd charged me every evening with this responsibility, so I'd bring it up and then it would be sort of silenced. There was a great social dissonance between my inner life and the exterior life, and I needed to make them come together somehow....

You were talking earlier about two generations of your family laboring as field hands on the plantations of Hawai'i to buy your way out. Has poetry helped you to resurrect the images of your ancestors?

Yes, I believe it has. I feel really fortunate that I was allowed to attain this level of literacy and the leisure to explore the development of an ideal of culture in my own education and in my own life. I feel very powerfully that my place in this country was earned by my forebears so that I could become expressive in a civilized way.

What did your forebears do?

They emigrated from Japan, labored as field hands for two generations in Hawai'i, went to war in Italy and France, worked at menial jobs in industry and civil bureaucracy so that I could attain the leisure to be able to contemplate not just the body of knowledge that is literature but also the lives that they led in order to buy my way out of that kind of life. I feel privileged and I feel responsible to them.

Some of my favorite lines are these: "I want the dead beside me when I dance, to help me / flesh the notes of my song, to tell me it's all right." What's all right?

That they *are* the dead. That they're not the living. That these people whom I treasure and these lives which were exemplary and are exemplary to me, these presences which I don't enjoy as I enjoy yours, are still somehow present. It's a magical belief, a primitive religion, but it's something for me as a poet that's crucial. It's not intellectual, it's almost a *need* to believe. Maybe religion is not so much belief, as the *need* to believe.

But given that poetry is so personal and intimate and that your own poetry is a country populated by your own ancestors, people need help entering that country.

I think poetry is about our most familiar need which we deny in order to lead more practical lives, but ultimately these lives are impractical because they do not have such presences in them. I think poetry can bring such presences back, whether they're the dead or evanescent feelings or insinuations, or glimmerings, or vanishings. These are the most essential things, and poetry turns to them in the way that many arts do. So I feel like a conduit for things other than myself—these vanishings, insinuations, glimmerings. I feel they're essential. I can't do without them.

Source: Bill Moyers, "Excerpt from an Interview with Bill Moyers," in *The Language of Life: A Festival of Poets*, Doubleday, 1995.

Phoebe Pettingell

In the following essay, Pettingell focuses on the autobiographical themes of Hongo, who grew up in the United States as the child of Japanese immigrants, in a world between two worlds.

Each year the Academy of American Poets sponsors the publication of the Lamont Selection, a promising writer's second book of verse. The latest to appear is Garrett Hongo's *The River of Heaven* (Knopf, 67 pp., $16.95.) The author, of Japanese descent, was born in Volcano, Hawaii. The exotic places he describes—seedy Chinatowns, Pacific ports with their international jumble of peoples and customs—might sound, in paraphrase, like backdrops for Mr. Moto or Charlie Chan. Yet they are really nothing like that: "I have no story to tell about lacquer shrines / or filial ashes, about a small brass bell, / and incense smoldering in jade bowls." Hongo's tale, in fact, concerns what it feels like to grow up as the child of unassimilated immigrants, to be soaked with values incompatible with those of one's ancestors, yet not fully accepted by the new culture.

Given Hongo's themes, it is understandable that his method has been powerfully shaped by the poetry of Philip Levine. The old saw that imitation is the sincerest form of flattery never seemed more applicable. Not that Hongo lacks a distinct voice. Rather, Levine's style has provided a vehicle for the disciple to release his own pent-up cries of cultural loss and longing, from the opening "Nostalgic Catalogue" of Hawaii's ethnic diversity to the oriental simplicity of the book's final elegy for a victim of random street violence:

> Let the night sky cover him as he dies. Let the weaver
> girl cross the bridge of heaven and take up his
> cold hands

Hongo chooses his memorable images to illustrate the cruel paradox that those outside the mainstream must purchase success at the price of estrangement from their own peoples.

One of the most effective poems here tells of Hongo's experience as a student in a California high school, where he was put in "advanced placement, / segregated from the rest of the student body." He admirably evokes the intellectual ghetto the "AP" system can create, and the ambivalence of the mostly Japanese whiz kids in it toward the casual lives of those tracked for a more limited education. Looking back, Hongo realizes that his fellow students were all, in a sense, losers: " 'Free, white and twenty-one' is the formulaic. / Cynical and exclusive, it doesn't mean / 'Emancipation,' that freedman's word / signifying unlimited potential, an open road / like Whitman saw, a view from the prospect / of Democratic Vistas, a sense of magnificence / and of election." The punks disappeared into the small time criminal world of the West Coast's oriental slums, and even the bright students remained outside the Anglo establishment they had been ostensibly groomed to enter. "There are none of us elect. Jap or Sheenie / hawking rags in the New York streets, / nothing matters under corrosive skies, / the burdened light that bears down on us / with the tremulous weight of guilt and outrage."

Hongo's verses become an elaborate ritual of atonement for leaving behind his culturally ambiguous background. A pair of historical monologues narrate the tragedies of men trapped between two ways of life. "Pinoy at the Coming World," based on a true account, tells of a sugar cane cutter who has risen to plantation bookkeeper. He sets himself above his former fellows, boasting of children "born, not smuggled here." This hubris is punctured when his offspring become victims of the 1919 flu pandemic. An equally sad story belongs to Jigoku, who declaims "on the glamor of Self-Hate." A Japanese-Hawaiian veteran of the Korean War, he returns to a life of gambling and pimping, then emigrates to Japan, hoping "to drift, guiltless, / on the aspic of Tokyo's squalid human sea." Instead, awash with homesickness, he fancies how his drowned corpse might be borne by the current back to "Hilo Bay, / fused in a posture of supplication / . . . as a fan is folded."

Do these two books signal a loss of faith in Whitman's Democratic Vistas? I don't think so. Whitman never claimed that the melting pot had already dissolved every boundary of race or economic class. He did believe that "The United States themselves are essentially the greatest poem," continuously writing itself, resolving its failures along the way to an eventual apotheosis. What could be more truly democratic than to acknowledge shortcomings, while at the same time preserving faith in the Ideal? In this sense, Philip Levine and Garret Hongo prove to be genuine descendants of Tom and Walt.

Source: Phoebe Pettingell, Review of *The River of Heaven*, in *New Leader*, Vol. 71, No. 10, June 13, 1988, p. 16.

Sources

"American Fact Finder," *U.S. Census Bureau*, http://factfinder.census.gov/home/saff/main.html?_lang=en (February 23, 2006).

"Division of Violence Prevention," *National Center for Injury Prevention and Control*, http://www.cdc.gov/ncipc/dvp/dvp.htm (February 21, 2006).

Drake, Barbara, "Garrett Kaoru Hongo," in *Dictionary of Literary Biography*, Vol. 120, *American Poets since World War II, Third Series*, edited by R. S. Gwynn, Gale Research, 1992, pp. 133–36.

Filipelli, Laurie, *Garrett Hongo*, Boise State University Press, 1997, p. 46.

Hongo, Garrett, "Introduction," in *The Open Boat: Poems from Asian America*, edited by Garrett Hongo, Doubleday, 1993, p. xxi.

———, *The River of Heaven*, Knopf, 1988, pp. 62, 66–67.

———, *Volcano: A Memoir of Hawai'i*, Knopf, 1995, pp. 195–96.

Moyers, Bill, *The Language of Life: A Festival of Poets*, Doubleday, 1995, pp. 211–13.

Muratori, Fred, Review of *The River of Heaven*, in *Library Journal*, Vol. 113, May 1, 1988, p. 82.

Review of *The River of Heaven*, in *Publishers Weekly*, Vol. 233, February 12, 1988, p. 81.

Schultz, Robert, "Passionate Virtuosity," in *Hudson Review*, Vol. 42, No. 1, Spring 1989, pp. 151–53.

U.S. Centers for Disease Control and Prevention, *National Vital Statistics Reports*, Vol. 48, No. 11, July 24, 2000.

Wordsworth, William, "Composed upon Westminster Bridge, September 3, 1802," in *The Norton Anthology of English Literature*, 4th ed., Vol. 2, edited by M. H. Abrams, W. W. Norton, 1979, p. 223.

Further Reading

Bulosan, Carlos, *America Is in the Heart: A Personal History*, Harcourt, 1946.
   This is an autobiographical account of the inspiring life of a Filipino American. The author grew up as a

migrant worker in the American West and later became a writer and labor activist.

Hongo, Garrett, ed., *Under Western Eyes: Personal Essays from Asian America*, Anchor/Doubleday, 1995.
   A compilation of essays from many Asian American writers, this book provides a contemporary perspective of Asian America.

Moyers, Bill, *The Language of Life: A Festival of Poets*, Doubleday, 1995.
   This book features many poets talking about their poems, lives, and careers while being skillfully interviewed.

Yamauchi, Wakako, *Songs My Mother Taught Me: Stories, Plays, and Memoir*, Feminist Press at the City University of New York, 1994.
   This collection presents stories, plays, and essays by a Japanese American woman who lived through tumultuous times.

Originally

Carol Ann Duffy
1990

Memories play a significant role in the poetry of Carol Ann Duffy, particularly her recollections of childhood places and events. The poem "Originally," published in *The Other Country* (1990), draws specifically from memories of Duffy's family's move from Scotland to England when she and her siblings were very young. The first-born child, Duffy was just old enough to feel a deep sense of personal loss and fear as she traveled farther and farther away from the only place she had known as "home" and the family neared its alien destination. This sentiment is captured in "Originally," in which it is described in the rich detail and defining language of both the child who has had the experience and the adult who recalls it.

As the title suggests, a major concern of the poem is beginnings—one's roots, birthplace, and homeland. Stanzas 1 and 2 center on the pain of giving up, or being forced to give up, the comfort of a familiar environment and of feeling odd and out of place in a new one. In stanza 3, the final stanza, Duffy does an about-face, describing what it feels like to accept fate, to resign oneself to change and move on. The last line of the poem, however, presents an intriguing conundrum: Has the speaker really learned to forgo originality, or has she not?

In addition to *The Other Country*, "Originally" appears in *The Salmon Carol Ann Duffy: Poems Selected and New 1985–1999* (2000). This book contains works chosen by Duffy specifically for the Salmon Publishing poetry series and includes poems from five of her previous volumes.

Carol Ann Duffy © Colin McPherson/Corbis

Author Biography

Carol Ann Duffy was born on December 23, 1955, in Glasgow, Scotland. When she was about five years old, she moved with her parents and younger brothers to Stafford, England, where her father took a position as a fitter with English Electric. The move to England would prove to have a profound effect on Duffy, who eventually attributed to it her sense of rootless existence and search for a new identity. Duffy's poem "Originally," published in *The Other Country* (1990), explores this theme, although it is only one of many that do.

Duffy attended grammar school in Stafford from 1962 to 1967 and then spent her middle school years at Saint Joseph's, a convent school, where she first learned to love poetry, both reading and writing it. Encouraged by an enthusiastic teacher, Duffy decided at age fourteen that she wanted to be a poet. From 1970 to 1974, she attended Stafford Girls' High School. Duffy's first small collection of poems, *Fleshweathercock, and Other Poems,* was published in 1973.

Duffy graduated from the University of Liverpool in 1977 with a bachelor's degree in philosophy and worked various jobs while continuing to develop her poetry skills and to earn extra income from freelance writing. By 1982, she was working as a writer in residence in London's East End schools, where she was able to offer the same encouragement to young writers that she had been afforded in her middle and high school years. Also during this time, Duffy met Jackie Kay, the poet and writer who would become her life partner.

In 1986, Duffy's first full-length poetry collection, *Standing Female Nude*, won a Book Award from the Scottish Arts Council, and in 1989 Duffy received the Dylan Thomas Award. Throughout the 1990s, Duffy continued to have poetry published and to win awards. In 1995, Duffy gave birth to a daughter, and in 1996 she and Kay moved to Manchester, England, where Duffy accepted a part-time position teaching creative writing at the city's Metropolitan University.

Although she was considered a candidate for British poet laureate in 1999, Duffy was rejected, presumably because of her unconventional lifestyle. As the lesbian daughter of a working-class Scotsman and raising a child with her black partner, Duffy was not quite what British government had in mind for its leading poet. Undaunted by the political snub, Duffy became one of Great Britain's most celebrated feminist poets. Her works include poetry for children as well as for adults. A volume of poetry for adults, *Rapture*, was published in 2005.

Poem Text

We came from our own country in a red room
which fell through the fields, our mother singing
our father's name to the turn of the wheels.
My brothers cried, one of them bawling *Home,
Home*, as the miles rushed back to the city,   5
the street, the house, the vacant rooms
where we didn't live any more. I stared
at the eyes of a blind toy, holding its paw.

All childhood is an emigration. Some are slow,
leaving you standing, resigned, up an avenue   10
where no one you know stays. Others are sudden.
Your accent wrong. Corners, which seem familiar,
leading to unimagined, pebble-dashed estates, big
     boys
eating worms and shouting words you don't
     understand.
My parents' anxiety stirred like a loose tooth   15
in my head. *I want our own country*, I said.

But then you forget, or don't recall, or change,
and, seeing your brother swallow a slug, feel only
a skelf of shame. I remember my tongue
shedding its skin like a snake, my voice   20

in the classroom sounding just like the rest. Do I
    only think
I lost a river, culture, speech, sense of first space
and the right place? Now, *Where do you come
    from?*
strangers ask. *Originally?* And I hesitate.

Poem Summary

Lines 1–3

Lines 1 through 3 of "Originally" establish the personas in the poem, identified by the phrases "our mother" and "our father's." The first word, "We," must refer to a family. These lines also establish the setting of the work and suggest a personal attachment to a place: "our own country." The setting, or place, however, is not stationary; rather, the "red room," most likely a reference to the vehicle in which the family is traveling, appears to rush along, falling "through the fields" that go by in a blur. The phrase "turn of the wheels" further clarifies that the speaker and her family are in a car, but the words that precede it are a bit misleading in the tone they convey: ". . . our mother singing / our father's name to the turn of the wheels" suggests a merrily traveling family, riding lightheartedly down the road. The rest of the poem, however, suggests otherwise.

Lines 4–6

Lines 4 through 6 imply anything but a carefree joyride. The speaker's brothers are distraught, crying, and "one of them bawling *Home, / Home.*" This boy's cries disclose the source of the children's pain and frustration: they want to go home, but home does not exist anymore. Instead, it is only a house with "vacant rooms" back in the city they have left for good.

Lines 7 and 8

Lines 7 and 8, the final two lines of stanza 1, make clear that the family has moved permanently from their previous home. The speaker's mind is still back in her old house as she clutches a toy, "holding its paw," perhaps in the same manner she would like to have her own hand held in an act of comfort during a tumultuous time. Just as she offers solace to the toy, so, too, the toy provides her a measure of security and relief as she silently longs for the place "where we didn't live any more."

Lines 9–11

Lines 9 through 11, the first lines of stanza 2, present a more objective view of the effects on

Media Adaptations

- Trafalgar Square Books produced an audiocassette of Duffy's poetry collection *The World's Wife* in 1999, the year the book was published and considered for a Forward Prize in the collections category. The poems in this volume are written from the perspectives of the female companions of famous males, such as Sigmund Freud, King Kong, and the devil.

children of pulling up roots. The beginning of line 9 is significant: "All childhood is an emigration." The implication is that the simple fact of growing up involves a continuous departure from one moment, one age, and one level of maturity to another. It seems natural enough that children go through a variety of stages on the way to adulthood, but the word Duffy chooses, "emigration," implies a physical progression, a movement from one place to another. The speaker offers scenarios of how emigration might happen. "Some are slow," allowing the child to ponder the situation, perhaps feeling "resigned" to the fact that he or she has wandered into an area "where no one you know stays." Line 11 ends with a kind of emigration that is more pertinent to the poet's own experience: "Others are sudden."

Lines 12–14

Lines 12 through 14 provide details on the kinds of "sudden" changes that can have a profound effect on a child who encounters them. Even though one may speak the same native language as the citizens of a different state or country, there is still the matter of "wrong" accents and longed-for familiar places that turn into "unimagined, pebble-dashed estates." The latter description implies that even the architectural differences between the home place and the new place can be disturbing to a wary child. Odd customs and language barriers are further depicted in the speaker's astonishment over "big boys / eating worms and shouting words" she cannot understand.

Lines 15 and 16

Lines 15 and 16 reflect the speaker's innermost thoughts concerning the family's move to a new land. She senses her "parents' anxiety," which she finds both nagging and worrying. In a moment of explicit candor, the speaker states her single desire: *"I want our own country."*

Line 17

Line 17, the first line of stanza 3, stands out as an abrupt shift in both the poem's message and its tone. The first word, "But," indicates a change in thought, and it is followed by words that appear to negate the overwhelming power of memory expressed in stanzas 1 and 2: "you forget, or don't recall." Perhaps the final word in this line is most indicative of the speaker's own situation. She comes to accept that "change" is inevitable, a change not only in the physical environment but also in one's own heart and mind.

Lines 18–21

Line 18 is a reference to line 14. The speaker's brother begins to behave like the other boys who are eating worms. Seeing him "swallow a slug" does not make the speaker feel as much shame as when the family first arrived in the new country, because she is getting used to the language and customs. However, she uses the Scottish word for "splinter" ("skelf") to describe her feelings. Use of the original language implies that there is still a sense of nostalgia for the old country. The speaker, however, describes losing her native accent like a snake "shedding its skin" until she sounds "just like the rest" of her classmates in her new school. The words that end line 21, "Do I only think," are important in establishing the speaker's continuing fluctuation in her attempt to assess the effect of the childhood move on the rest of her life. She questions whether she really knows the effect or only believes she does.

Lines 22–24

Lines 22 through 24, the final three lines of "Originally," provide insight into what the speaker questions the loss of. From the obviously physical ("a river") to the more personal and intangible ("culture, speech"), the speaker mulls the bygone things of her former life and country. She equates her "first space" with the "right place," implying that there is something wrong with her current place. With her mind full of questions, doubts, and wonder, the speaker finds it difficult to answer a simple question that someone asks her: *"Where do you come from?"* To one who has struggled with a loss of identity, both national and personal, the question may not be so simple. All the speaker can do is "hesitate" as she tries to determine her original home.

Themes

Identity Loss

"Originally" is a poem about a child fearful of losing her identity and the struggle she goes through in an attempt to retain it. The title itself indicates the significance of roots and of having definite origins, something the speaker worries she has lost by being forced to leave her native country at such a young age. The temperament within the family as a whole seems harmonious enough: The mother sings the father's name "to the turn of the wheels," and there is no mention of quarreling among the children. Instead, it is the idea of place, not people, that stirs feelings of apprehension and uncertainty. The boys cry because they know they have lost their familiar environment forever, and one of them leaves no room for doubting the source of his pain as he bawls, *"Home, / Home."*

A strong sense of patriotic pride and nationalism has been a common theme in British poetry for centuries, and many contemporary poets such as Duffy carry on the tradition. As the central theme of this poem indicates, a native land is not only the place where one is born but also one's starting point, the location where an individual life begins, including the emotional, cultural, and spiritual identity. Every minute of every day, however, adults around the world make conscious decisions to move from one place to another, to leave their places of birth far behind, perhaps forever. These people probably do not suffer identity crises when they arrive in a new home. They choose to move. The significant difference in Duffy's poem is that it derives from a child's perspective, a little girl who has not chosen.

Children place a great deal of emphasis on belonging, both on what and whom they belong to and on what belongs to them. Whether possessions are tangible, like a toy, or intangible, like a country, the idea of having something or identifying with something is important. In "Originally," the speaker uses the phrase "our own country" twice: "We came from our own country" (line 1) and "*I want our own country*" (line 16). "Our own" are

Topics For Further Study

- If you moved from one town, state, or country to another when you were very young, write an essay about your experience. Explain what the greatest challenges were, how you adjusted, what significant lifestyle changes you made, and how you feel about the move now.
- Many of Shakespeare's plays are packed with British history. Research a Shakespeare play that pertains to England and Scotland and select a brief section of it to act out in front of the class. Try to select a part of the play that gives a good idea of the relationship between the two nations, whether it is friendly or contentious.
- Prime Minister Tony Blair is struggling to maintain a positive position as the leader of Great Britain. Pretend that you are Blair and give a speech to your class on how the policies you have set and the international role you have taken are beneficial to the British people in general and the Scots in particular, who continue to lobby for greater self-rule.
- Write a poem from the perspective of a speaker who has been forced to move to an environment where the culture is vastly different from his or her original one. You may be a Chinese moving to Brazil, an American moving to Pakistan, a Nigerian moving to Canada, or anyone relocating to an unfamiliar environment anywhere in the world.

---

the most meaningful words, because they imply a feeling and a place with which the speaker identifies. As an adult, the speaker can look back and conclude, "All childhood is an emigration," but to the child who experiences it, the conclusion is one of fear, loss, and resignation.

Cultural Integration

Another considerable theme in "Originally" is cultural integration. The family is moving not simply from one city to another or one state to another but to an entirely different country. One who knows Duffy's background knows that the particular nations are Scotland and England, the poet having moved with her parents and brothers from the former to the latter when the children were very young. Both countries are part of Great Britain, so the experience is not the same as it would be for one who moves, for example, from Scotland to China or from Iran to the United States. The latter type of move involves drastically different languages, writing systems, and cultures, and adapting can be extremely challenging. Duffy shows, however, that even emigrating from one British nation to another presents language and lifestyle obstacles.

Stanza 3 of "Originally" explores the idea of integrating a familiar way of life into a new way. The accent that is "wrong" in line 12 and the boys who shout "words you don't understand" in line 14 are eventually diluted by the need of the human mind to find peace and reconciliation in line 17: "you forget, or don't recall, or change." Before long, the Scottish brothers are swallowing slugs as their English playmates do. The Scottish speaker's "voice / in the classroom" begins to sound like the voices of her English schoolmates. The impression is that the entire family manages to settle into their new lives in England, not completely forgetting their native country but blending the old culture into the new. Perhaps to emphasize that integrating does not imply forgetting, the speaker makes clear in the end that she still must "hesitate" when someone questions where she is from. She may have no problem answering in regard to her current location, but the notion of "*Originally*" stops her cold.

Style

Loose Blank Verse

Traditional blank verse is composed of lines of unrhymed iambic pentameter, which means lines of ten syllables with the accent on the first syllable of each pair of syllables. A common example is the work of Shakespeare, whose plays are written in this form. In the line, "If music be the food of love, play on" (*Twelfth Night*, act 1, scene 1, line 1), note the TA-dum TA-dum TA-dum TA-dum TA-dum rhythm. Defined more loosely, blank verse can mean any unrhymed poetry, only slight attention being given to the structure of iambic pentameter. "Originally" falls into this category.

Less than a third of the lines in "Originally" have exactly ten syllables, most having eleven or twelve. Nonetheless, stanza 1 contains four ten-syllable lines in a row, lines 2 through 5, and the iambic pentameter is readily recognized in "which fell through the fields, our mother singing / our father's name to the turn of the wheels." The construction of the poem, however, does not become bogged down in too much effort to follow a specific metrical form. Instead, the more interesting aspects of the style are the occasional rhymes and near rhymes that pepper the work.

Examples of near rhymes include "fields" in line 2 with "wheels" in line 3, "*Home, / Home*" in lines 4 and 5 with "rooms" in line 6, "more" in line 7 with "paw" in line 8, "understand" in line 14 with "said" in line 16, and "change" in line 17 with "shame" in line 19. The only example of exact rhyme is "space" in line 22 with "place" in line 23. Alliteration, or the repetition of usually initial consonants for poetic effect, also plays a role in the poem's construction. The most obvious examples are in lines 9, 10, and 11 with the *s* sound: ". . . Some are slow, / leaving you standing, resigned . . . / where no one you know stays. Others are sudden." The *s* sound appears again very effectively in stanza 3 in the phrases "seeing your brother swallow a slug"; "a skelf of shame"; "shedding its skin like a snake, my voice"; "classroom sounding just like the rest"; and "I lost a river, culture, speech, sense of first space / and the right place."

The most important aspect of the construction of any loose blank verse poem such as "Originally" is its nonintrusive formality, a style that not only avoids taking away from the message but also may be difficult to recognize on a first reading. Duffy divides the poem into three stanzas of eight lines each, but beyond that the construction is careful and subtle, leaving room for the more important matter of theme to come through.

Historical Context

That Duffy was born in Scotland but grew up in England has inspired much of her creative work on topics of personal and national origins. Especially early in her life, Duffy struggled to answer a basic question about her identity: Is she Scottish or is she English? While the relationship between the two nations spans many centuries, significant changes were taking place during the 1980s and 1990s, when Duffy composed the work that appears in *The Other Country* and it was published.

Scotland is one of four national units, along with England, Northern Ireland, and Wales, that make up the United Kingdom of Great Britain. Throughout the seventeenth and eighteenth centuries, several independent European dynasties formed political unions, and Scotland was among those self-governing nations that relinquished its sovereignty in favor of forming a more powerful union with allied nations. Regardless of what political entities do, the people of individual nations do not readily forsake their native culture, language, customs, and lifestyle—all the things that make them who they are, in this case, the things that make Scots Scottish.

For the first two-thirds of the twentieth century, Scotland followed suit with the conservative government of Great Britain, even though a rogue party called the Scottish National Party sprouted up in the 1930s and quietly gained supporters for Scotland's independence from Great Britain. In the 1960s and 1970s, the Scottish National Party experienced a resurgence of support. For the first time in the twentieth century, the Labour Party became the largest political party in the country, and it has remained so.

During the 1980s, Margaret Thatcher was the highly influential and powerful prime minister of Great Britain. Although she was elected for an unprecedented three terms in office, her conservative government both angered and disillusioned liberal Scots, who were experiencing some of the highest unemployment rates in the United Kingdom. The country's main industries—coal mining, steel making, shipbuilding, and heavy engineering—all suffered under Thatcher's policies of privatization of state-owned companies. As they became increasingly disgruntled with the conservative rule of

Compare & Contrast

- **1980s:** Many Scots grow weary of Great Britain's conservative government, and the Scottish National Party gains momentum. The party wants greater autonomy for Scotland and less ruling by the British government seat in London.

  Today: Although Scotland is still a prominent member of the United Kingdom, the country has its own parliament to run domestic affairs, such as establishing laws and setting taxes. Jack McConnell becomes the first minister of Scotland in 2001.

- **1980s:** Less than 2 percent of the Scottish population can understand Gaelic, the language that prevailed before the British government's push to make English the official language throughout Great Britain. As Scottish-English develops over the centuries, its Gaelic influences decline, and it is hardly recognizable by Scots in the late twentieth century.

  Today: In a move to retain national pride in language, many Scottish educators encourage students to speak in the rich Scottish dialects of old, a daring linguistic move for which students decades earlier would have been punished.

- **1980s:** Despite being Great Britain's longest continuously serving prime minister in the twentieth century, Thatcher begins to lose popularity toward the end of the 1980s and resigns suddenly in 1990 after the controversial introduction of a community charge, or poll tax, to replace property taxes in Scotland in 1989 and in England and Wales in 1990.

  Today: Because of his close relationship with the American president George W. Bush and his unwavering support for the United States–led war in Iraq, among other political issues, Prime Minister Tony Blair, once highly popular across the United Kingdom, faces increasing criticism, and many people demand that he resign.

Great Britain, many Scots called for greater autonomy for their nation.

The Scottish National Party gained more favor during the late 1980s and early 1990s, but the dominant Labour Party began to lobby the government in London for more areas of self-rule, not for total independence. In essence, Scotland wanted to have its own separate legal and educational systems, its own national church, and its own parliament with wide-ranging powers apart from those of Great Britain. While some members of Thatcher's Conservative Party balked at the idea, political factions in the kingdom's overall Labour Party pledged support for Scotland's bid for greater autonomy.

When, in 1989 and 1990, Thatcher's government introduced an unpopular poll tax to replace property taxes, many citizens across Great Britain were infuriated over what they considered excessive and unfair taxation. The discontent escalated to the point that Thatcher resigned suddenly in 1990, and the remaining government, headed by John Major, was forced to revise its tax program.

The transition from a conservative majority to a liberal majority in Great Britain in the 1990s mirrored Scotland's shift in the same direction a few decades earlier. The ultimate payoff for Scotland came in 1997, when Tony Blair was elected prime minister and made greater Scottish autonomy one of the new government's principal objectives. As a result, Scotland eventually established a parliament to govern its own domestic affairs and to elect its own first minister. Jack McConnell was the first to hold that position.

There is an interesting similarity between Duffy's personal struggle with national identity and that of Scotland itself. Although the country is self-governed and reinforces its independent "Scottishness," Scotland is still part of the United Kingdom of Great Britain. The poet may reconcile her personal life in the same manner. She is both Scottish and English, or, perhaps more important, she is a Briton overall.

Critical Overview

Duffy's poetry has received wide critical acclaim since her first full-length collection, *Standing Female Nude*, was published in 1985, and she has been awarded various prizes for her work. Duffy is commonly noted as one of England's strongest poetic voices of the Thatcher years, particularly as a feminist, liberal, and controversial voice for underrepresented people on the fringe of society. Much of Duffy's earliest work, however, can be classified as love poetry, although gender is ambiguous in the first poems. Not until the publication of *Mean Time* in 1993 does Duffy clearly begin to address lesbian love and her own homosexual lifestyle. Whether it involves politics, nationalism, or romance, Duffy's work is generally received with enthusiasm and respect.

The Other Country is one of Duffy's most studied collections among critics, because its subjects are both personal and political, the poems often blurring the line between the two, demonstrating the interconnectedness of national identity and individual identity. This theme is the primary focus of most of the book's critics. In an essay titled "'Me Not Know What These People Mean': Gender and National Identity in Carol Ann Duffy's Poetry," published in *The Poetry of Carol Ann Duffy: "Choosing Tough Words,"* the scholar and critic Angelica Michelis writes, "The theme of 'afterwardsness' is a ubiquitous one in *The Other Country*: the different poems in this volume oscillate thematically between past, present and future interconnecting the personal history of the poet who moved from Scotland to England with that of national history and identity." Michelis points directly to the poem in question in stating, "To define oneself in relation to home, rather than stating a secure and known position, is here developed as a journey in time ('All childhood is an emigration' as Duffy puts it in the poem 'Originally') which propels the subject backwards as much as forwards from a temporal point of view."

In a lecture titled "Notes from the Home Front: Contemporary British Poetry," published in *Essays in Criticism*, the writer and lecturer John Kerrigan addresses the issue of ambiguous identity in Duffy's work when he states

To say that Carol Ann Duffy hales from Scotland or London, however, would hardly be to the point, since she writes about living in Staffordshire and Liverpool, about the anonymity of rented rooms, and implies that, like many of us, she doesn't come from anywhere much, or anywhere, at least, in particular.

Kerrigan's conclusion is likely one of the most apt in capturing the essence of Duffy's message in her poems about emigration and "the other country": "she doesn't come from anywhere much." But that has not kept her from carving her own definite place in contemporary British poetry.

Criticism

Pamela Steed Hill

Hill is the author of a poetry collection and an editor for a university publications department. In the following essay, she examines Duffy's use of physical displacement as a source of lifelong personal uncertainty and hesitation.

Many of Duffy's poems address the issue of national identity and originality, which, in most cases, are synonymous with personal identity and originality. Although it may be an exaggeration to say that the forced move from her native Scotland to England when she was a young child scarred her for life, there is no doubt that being uprooted at such a tender age had a profound effect on Duffy. At five, she was just old enough to grasp the effects. If she had been younger, she would have enjoyed the comfort of not understanding. If she had been older, she may have been able to rationalize her parents' decision and make the most of it. As it was, however, Duffy understood only the facts as she saw them: Everything she knew about the first five years of her life was soon to be gone forever.

"Originally" deals with the topic of displacement head on. The title reflects the heart of the matter. The specific details of the move in stanza 1, the difficulties of adjusting to a new place in stanza 2, and the seeming resignation to change in stanza 3 all come together to make one central point: Displacement hurts, and the traumatic emotional effects of displacement on a child can last a lifetime.

In stanza 1, the speaker describes the actual physical move from one country to another. Her tone is both fearful and sorrowful as she recalls her brothers weeping, one of them especially hard. The boys are younger than the speaker, but they are able to sense what they may not fully comprehend.

"*Home, / Home,*" is the single cry, the single thought that fills their minds. The words "vacant" and "blind" are particularly revealing of the speaker's own thoughts. She equates the move with a feeling of loss and emptiness. No toy with "eyes" can actually see, of course, but the speaker states, "I stared / at the eyes of a blind toy, holding its paw." Because a stuffed animal is sightless, there must be a reason that the speaker chooses to describe it as "blind." In the poem, blindness symbolizes the void, the blankness the speaker senses as the result of losing her home. Blindness also represents the "vacant rooms" back in the house in which the speaker will never live again. In a sense, the toy is a reflection of the speaker herself: empty, lost, in need of comfort.

Stanza 2 of "Originally" focuses on the difficulties that anyone, especially children, may face when moving to a new area with different customs and an unfamiliar form of native language. The speaker's acknowledgment that "All childhood is an emigration" suggests a more mature perspective than that described in stanza 1, but an intellectual stance does little to alleviate the all-consuming sense of strangeness the speaker feels. Regardless of the type of emigration one may experience— "slow" or "sudden," as the speaker distinguishes them—the fears and worries are the same. Both types thrust an unmistakable awareness of self-doubt and insecurity on the one who has emigrated from a beloved homeland to a peculiar new place.

Although the statement "All childhood is an emigration" is philosophical in nature, the speaker gives specific examples of how a forced move can be emotionally disturbing. One may end up standing on a strange "avenue / where no one you know" lives or speaking with a "wrong" accent when everyone else seems to use the right one. Children in a new land may be both astonished and repulsed by some of the native children's customs, such as "big boys / eating worms," and sometimes the language barrier goes beyond odd accents into unfamiliar words altogether, "shouting words you don't understand." The speaker and her brothers endure these difficulties and eventually overcome them, as stanza 3 suggests, but enduring and overcoming the difficulties do not abolish them. For the speaker especially, the hardships remain in her memory. The passage of time may blunt most of the sting, but it does not heal it completely.

Lines 15 and 16 reiterate not only the speaker's but also the entire family's fear of displacement. The speaker's brothers' feelings are already established,

> "*... if the question asked of her were 'Where do you live?' she would likely answer without thinking twice. 'Where do you come from?' brings in new factors, such as national identity, personal identity, roots, ancestry, homeland.*"

and in these lines the speaker reveals her "parents' anxiety," a tension apparently so obvious that it is felt by the speaker herself. Describing the parents' anxiety in physical terms, "like a loose tooth / in my head," demonstrates how strong and how bothersome relocating can be for a child. Anyone who can recall losing his or her baby teeth at the age of five or six may remember the discomfort of having a wobbly tooth in the mouth for days or weeks before it actually comes out. Duffy's careful choice of words implies that the speaker is still very much a little girl, but she is trying to deal with some very grown-up worries and doubts. There is no doubt, however, about her ultimate conclusion: "*I want our own country*, I said."

Line 17, the first line of stanza 3, may be a bit misleading in its suggestion of resignation to childhood emigration: "But then you forget, or don't recall, or change." This notion is brought out further in the speaker's admission that she soon loses her "shame" upon seeing one of her brothers eat a worm as the English boys do and that her Scottish accent soon becomes watered down with an English one like that of her classmates. At this point, it seems that the trauma of moving from one country to another has faded for the children and that their gradual maturity helps ease the initial pain of leaving home. Perhaps they have come to feel at home in England? The end of the poem makes it clear that this is not the case, that the loss of national identity is indeed personal. More specifically, being displaced as a child can lead to a perpetual feeling of displacement as an adult.

What Do I Read Next?

- *Mean Time* (1993) is considered one of Duffy's strongest and most mature collections. Appearing three years after *The Other Country*, this book also addresses themes of place and identity, but the focus is more on relationships, both sexual and social, between people as well as on self-examination and personal insight. This collection won the 1993 Whitbread Award for Poetry.

- The collection *The Adoption Papers* (1991), by poet Jackie Kay, explores themes similar to Duffy's in regard to childhood memories and events. These semiautobiographical poems concern a black baby's adoption by a white family and are written from the perspectives of three persons: the natural mother, the adoptive mother, and the child. Kay and Duffy have been partners for more than twenty years and are raising Duffy's daughter together.

- Hugo Young's *The Iron Lady: A Biography of Margaret Thatcher* (1989) was a bestseller in Great Britain and remains popular among those interested in the dynamic prime minister who became a global leader alongside the American president Ronald Reagan and the Soviet Union's leader Mikhail Gorbachev. Thatcher's years as the British head gave many of the United Kingdom's poets something to write about as she changed the face of the Conservative Party, waged battles with old-guard politicians and trade unions alike, ruled stoically during the Falklands War, and proved to be one of the most productive, though often-criticized, leaders in modern British history. Duffy became one of the kingdom's most popular and prolific poets during this time.

- The Knitting Circle website maintains an up-to-date page on Duffy at http://myweb.lsbu.ac.uk/~stafflag/carolannduffy.html, with links providing extensive information on her life and publications as well as a bibliography of critical material, press clippings, and related websites.

There is an abrupt shift in thought in the final few lines of "Originally," beginning with the question, "Do I only think / I lost a river, culture, speech . . . ?" The speaker has reached adulthood, as the word "Now" in line 23 indicates. She has admitted her acceptance of certain changes in her life, both physical and emotional, and has hardened against the overt fears and worries of childhood insecurity. Nevertheless, she has not shaken the concerns entirely. Her self-doubt is subtler, and her sense of emptiness and loss is more ingrained, more a part of her psyche. As a grown woman capable of thinking profoundly, rationalizing, and philosophizing, the speaker may have abandoned her childish assertion "*I want our own country,*" but she cannot shake the underlying feeling that a part of her has been taken away at a young age and cannot be regained.

One may wonder why answering a simple question like "*Where do you come from?*" would prove so difficult for the speaker in the poem. It is safe to assume that many readers have been asked the same question at some point in their lives and have had no problem responding with the name of a country, a state or province, a city or town, or a community. The chances are, though, that most readers of this poem were not uprooted at five years of age and moved to a new and unfamiliar culture. A sense of displacement is much greater for children who experience this scenario. In Duffy's case, it is great enough to last a lifetime.

The speaker makes it clear that she equates "first space" with "right place," but because she did not get to live in the "right" place for very long, she hesitates when trying to tell someone where she is from. Answering "I was born in Scotland and grew up in England" would seem simple enough but is not necessarily so, especially when the speaker has experienced two very proud, very traditional national identities when she was only a child. The speaker wants to be able to answer the simple question, but what causes her to hesitate is the "originally" factor. In other words, if the question asked of her were

"Where do you live?" she would likely answer without thinking twice. "Where do you come from?" brings in new factors, such as national identity, personal identity, roots, ancestry, homeland. When these fundamentals of a human life are shaken up by displacement at a young age, the effects of insecurity and self-doubt a child displays early on will undoubtedly soften over time. For some, however, the uncertainty never goes away.

Source: Pamela Steed Hill, Critical Essay on "Originally," in *Poetry for Students*, Thomson Gale, 2007.

Thomson Gale

In the following essay, the critic gives an overview of Duffy's work.

Carol Ann Duffy is an award-winning English poet who, according to Danette DiMarco in *Mosaic*, is the poet of "post-post war England: Thatcher's England." Duffy is best known for writing love poems that often take the form of monologues. Her verses, as an *Economist* reviewer described them, are typically "spoken in the voices of the urban disaffected, people on the margins of society who harbour resentments and grudges against the world." Although she knew she was a lesbian since her days at St. Joseph's convent school, her early love poems give no indication of her homosexuality; the object of love in her verses is someone whose gender is not specified. Not until her 1993 collection, *Mean Time*, and 1994's *Selected Poems*, does she begin to write about homosexual love.

Duffy's poetry has always had a strong feminist edge, however. This position is especially well captured in her *Standing Female Nude*, in which the collection's title poem consists of an interior monologue comprising a female model's response to the male artist who is painting her image in a Cubist style. Although at first the conversation seems to indicate the model's acceptance of conventional attitudes about beauty in art—and, by extension, what an ideal woman should be—as the poem progresses Duffy deconstructs these traditional beliefs. Ultimately, the poet expresses that "the model cannot be contained by the visual art that would regulate her," explained DiMarco. "And here the way the poem ends with the model's final comment on the painting 'It does not look like me'—is especially instructive. On the one hand, her response suggests that she is naive and does not understand the nature of Cubist art. On the other hand, however, the comment suggests her own variableness, and challenges traditionalist notions that the naked model can, indeed, be transmogrified into the male artist's representation of her in the nude form. To the model, the painting does not represent either what she understands herself to be or her lifestyle."

Duffy was seriously considered for the position of poet laureate in Britain in 1999. Prime Minister Tony Blair's administration had wanted a poet laureate who exemplified the new "Cool Britannia," not an establishment figure, and Duffy was certainly anything but establishment. She is the Scottish-born lesbian daughter of two Glasgow working-class radicals. Her partner is another poet, a black woman, and the two of them are raising a child together. Duffy has a strong following among young Britons, partially as a result of her poetry collection *Mean Time* being included in Britain's A-level curriculum, but Blair was worried about how "middle England" would react to a lesbian poet laureate. There were also concerns in the administration about what Britain's notorious tabloids would write about her sexuality, and about comments that Duffy had made urging an updated role for the poet laureate. In the end, Blair opted for the safe choice and named Andrew Motion to the post.

After Duffy had been passed over, Katherine Viner wrote in the *Guardian Weekend* that her "poems are accessible and entertaining, yet her form is classical, her technique razor-sharp. She is read by people who don't really read poetry, yet she maintains the respect of her peers. Reviewers praise her touching, sensitive, witty evocations of love, loss, dislocation, nostalgia; fans talk of greeting her at readings 'with claps and cheers that would not sound out of place at a rock concert.'" Viner lamented that Duffy only came to the attention of many people when she was caricatured and rejected as poet laureate. However, the poet got some satisfaction when she earned the National Lottery award of 75,000 pounds, a sum that far exceeded the stipend that poet laureates receive.

After the laureate debacle, Duffy was further vindicated when her next original collection of poems, *The World's Wife*, received high acclaim from critics. In what *Antioch Review* contributor Jane Satterfield called "masterful subversions of myth and history," the poems in this collection are all told from the points of view of the women behind famous male figures, both real and fictional, including the wives and lovers of Aesop, Pontius Pilate, Faust, Tiresius, Herod, Quasimodo, Lazarus, Sisyphus, Freud, Darwin, and even King Kong. Not all the women are wives, however. For example, one poem is told from Medusa's point of view as she expresses her feelings before being slain by Perseus; "Little Red-Cap" takes the story of Little Red Riding Hood to a new level as a teenage girl is seduced by a "wolf-poet." These fresh perspectives allow Duffy to indulge in a great deal of humor and wit as, for example, Mrs. Aesop grows tired of her husband's constant moralizing, Mrs. Freud complains about the great psychologist's obsession with penises, Sisyphus's bride is stuck with a workaholic, and Mrs. Lazarus, after finding a new husband, has her life ruined by the return of her formerly dead husband. There are conflicting emotions as well in such poems as "Mrs. Midas," in which the narrator is disgusted by her husband's greed, but, at the same time, longs for something she can never have: his physical touch." *The World's Wife* appeals and astonishes," said Satterfield. "Duffy's mastery of personae allows for seamless movement through the centuries; in this complementary chorus, there's voice and vision for the coming ones." An *Economist* reviewer felt that the collection "is savage, trenchant, humorous and wonderfully inventive at its best." And Ray Olson, writing in *Booklist*, concluded that "Duffy's takes on the stuff of legends are . . . richly rewarding."

Duffy has also written verses for children, many of which are published in *Meeting Midnight* and *Five Finger-Piglets*. The poems in *Meeting Midnight*, as the title indicates, help children confront their fears by addressing them openly. "They explore the hinterland in a child's imagination where life seems built on quicksand and nameless worries move in and will not leave," explained Kate Kellaway in an *Observer* review. Kellaway also asserted that "these are real poems by one of the best English poets writing at the moment."

In addition to her original poetry, Duffy has edited two anthologies, *I Wouldn't Thank You for a Valentine: Poems for Young Feminists* and *Stopping for Death: Poems of Death and Loss*, and has adapted eight classic Brothers Grimm fairy tales in *Grimm Tales*. Not intended for young children but for older children and young adults in drama and English classes, *Grimm Tales* includes adaptations of such stories as "Hansel and Gretel" and "The Golden Goose," which are rewritten "with a poet's vigor and economy, combining traditions of style with direct, colloquial dialogue," according to Vida Conway in *School Librarian*.

Source: Thomson Gale, "Carol Ann Duffy," in *Contemporary Authors Online*, Thomson Gale, 2006.

Marian Cox and Robert Swan

In the following essay, Cox and Swan note the many-layered social, political, and historical references and the multiplicity of voices in Duffy's poetry.

Duffy's poems are set in a specific historical, political and social milieu. This is important for A-level students because the key assessment objective in both the Edexcel and the AQA specifications for Duffy is AO5 (literary and historical context). Fully to appreciate the subtlety and richness of the poems requires an extensive knowledge of the ideas, references and concerns of these periods and places. Many of the personas in the poems construct their meaning and identity from specific cultural signposts—films and pop songs associated with key events and stages in their lives, such as 'the first chord of A Hard Day's Night'.

Several key themes recur in Duffy's poetry. The precarious journey from childhood to adulthood is at the core of much of her work, as she says in 'Originally' and 'All childhood is an emigration'. Some of her personas fail to make the journey, remaining locked in an inadequate childhood, such as 'The Captain of the 1964 Top of the Form Team' ('I want it back', he says bluntly). Others suffer deracination and alienation through emigration to another culture, as emphasised by the collection title *The Other Country*. Even those for whom the journey has been a reasonable success look back with varying degrees of nostalgia to childhood. Proust-like, Duffy notes the tiny details and associations which encapsulate the most meaningful memories. These are often linked with the pop music, the films or the popular culture of the time and resonate with enormous significance in the psychological development of the personas. The passage of time—'Mean Time'—assumes a profound importance. So many of her characters are, in their secret inner lives, inadequate or failures that this must count as a prominent theme.

Hidden audiences

Virtually all Duffy's poems are narrated by a persona, generally in some form of monologue. Some are wholly internal, non-grammatical stream-of-consciousness sequences of ideas and images. Others are turned and polished, as if for articulation, although not necessarily in public. Most often, it is left to the reader to infer the circumstances of the 'utterance' (if any) of these monologues. Some clearly have no audience. Many are ambiguous, as if a listener might be being addressed, or at least an imaginary listener is in the persona's mind. Even on the rare occasions when there is explicitly an audience ('Weasel Words' and 'Poet for Our Times'), there is no real dialogue; the audience is generally a foil or a device rather than a participant. Some are delivered in real time; many are retrospective, an account or summation of a life's experiences (this is especially true of *The World's Wife* collection).

Prior to *The World's Wife*, the identity of the persona is often unclear, and the gender of the narrator (so important to Duffy) has to be inferred, frequently only by tone or characteristic preoccupations. The ambiguity is, of course, deliberate and is part of Duffy's subtle subversion of reader expectation. A relatively small proportion of Duffy's poems are told in the voice of a conventional third-person narrator, generally identifiable with Duffy herself. These poems tend to be reflective, mellow, melancholy and lyrical, and often deal with love, a rather subdued theme.

A window on the soul

Duffy's personas open a window on their souls. The device allows them to speak with an honesty and openness which they would never employ with an audience; and what we share, overwhelmingly, is sadness, inadequacy or a guilty secret. But another tantalising feature of this style is that there are no guarantees of veracity: these are the internal thoughts of a rich selection of individuals, and in a significant number of cases the reader is required to ask whether these 'confessions' are reliable, or fantasy, or a perplexing mixture of the two.

Duffy seems to be suggesting not only that many people harbour a secret, but that a substantial number of them live, at least to some extent, in a fantasy world. This is not necessarily harmful—the persona of 'Dear Norman' has 'turned the newspaper boy into a diver / for pearls', but he intends him no harm, and the persona of 'Education for Leisure' has such a shaky grip on reality that we cannot be certain of his real intentions when he says (unusually, directly to the reader) 'I get our breadknife and go out . . . I touch your arm'. In other cases, though, the fantasy spills over into action with worrying consequences, particularly for the girl who meets the persona of 'Psychopath'—'She is in the canal'. Duffy's world is peopled with people who are not what they seem.

Whose voice?

The variety of voices is apparent from even a cursory reading. On closer examination, however, the sensitive reader notices something more subtle going on. In addition to providing the window, Duffy is also furnishing the words which the speakers employ. The more illiterate or uneducated the persona, the more difficult this enterprise becomes, and the

> *The precarious journey from childhood to adulthood is at the core of much of her work, as she says in 'Originally' and 'All childhood is an emigration.'*

more dull for the reader. But in fact none of Duffy's personas is inarticulate; they may choose to 'utter' in an ungrammatical, stream-of-consciousness sequence of thoughts and images, but the language register is often, on reflection, implausibly superior to the persona's capabilities. Similarly, the thoughts, perceptions and feelings of the persona seem, at times, to display a level of self-knowledge at odds with the inadequacy which is being described. These are the cases which tantalise the reader. Whose voice is being heard? Whose ideas are being expressed? The persona's, or the poet's—or an impossibly subtle amalgamation of the two? The reader needs constantly to tune in to these inconsistencies in order to appreciate just how Duffy is working, and the fineness of her craft.

A good starting point is 'Model Village', an early poem from the collection *Selling Manhattan*. Duffy adopts the unusual voice (for her) of a naive child, although tellingly she is unable to sustain this for very long: by the end the persona has, without explanation, lost her innocence. The whole poem therefore has a double echo of Blake's, *Songs of Innocence and Experience*: as the child walks around the (literal) model village, noting the outward appearances of the model (in both senses) characters as childish stereotypes, Duffy makes them, one by one, reveal their guilty secrets.

The title is a characteristic Duffy ambiguity. The physical, miniature model village appears to be (is meant to be) a 'model' of how stereotypical village life should be: each eponymous character, like 'Miss Maiden', in her/his place in the happy community. But, of course, in this latter sense Duffy's village is far from model, because all the characters hide guilty secrets (which Duffy would claim is the reality of all real villages, and the concept of a 'model' village would be hypocrisy and humbug).

Miss Maiden has murdered her mother ('I poisoned her, but no one knows.'); the vicar has sadomasochistic schoolboy fantasies ('I shall dress up as a choirboy'); and so on. A child might be taken in, she seems to be saying, but not an adult observer. As if these silent revelations have somehow penetrated the child's consciousness, she (or he?) suddenly becomes knowing in a way she could not have been before: with the benefit of the internal confessions only the reader has heard, she comments 'The Vicar is nervous/of parrots, isn't he?' Although the tone still sounds like the child, this question reveals the transition of voice from the child to Duffy.

Shift of register

This example foregrounds a key question which has to be addressed in many of Duffy's poems: the relationship between the voice of the poet and the voice of the persona. In some cases, such as 'A Healthy Meal', the voice is clearly that of Duffy herself. More often, though, the voice is ostensibly that of the persona, but it becomes clear that the language, vocabulary and perceptions are inconsistent with the character. This subtle blending is what makes Duffy's own position so hard to pin down. To write from within someone else's mind implies a high level of empathy, although not necessarily sympathy. To include perceptions and observations which can only be the poet's muddies the waters. Because of the importance of sensitivity to language and its use in the study of modern poetry, this provides students with both a good reason and an opportunity to analyse language register, syntax and imagery especially thoroughly. Here are two instructive examples:

'Psychopath'

The persona is a semi-literate fairground worker and serial killer whose world has been formed by Hollywood movies. But compare 'These streets are quiet, as if the town has held its breath/to watch the Wheel go round above the dreary homes' with his more typical style: 'I took a swig of whisky from the flask and frenched it/down her throat.'

'Weasel Words'

In this, one of Duffy's subtlest and most overtly political poems, the Weasel narrator is clearly delivering a speech in the House of Commons, as reported in Hansard. He delivers a shallow but persuasive argument, in the typical style of an oily, complacent, Conservative politician, to the effect that Weasels and Ferrets are fundamentally different in nature. But, at the end, the voice imperceptibly changes, and subverts all that has gone before, first by admitting 'Our brown fur coats turn white in winter', and then by acting out the metaphor of the epigram that 'weasel words' have had their 'contents sucked out by a weasel'. Do we really believe that this was said, and publicly performed? Such subtle, ambiguous transitions fascinate, and offer a range of interpretations to, the sensitive reader.

Man and wife

Following the success of her first four collections, all of which cover broadly similar ground, Duffy published *The World's Wife* in 1999, which differs from her previous work in being her first themed collection. It is more consistently and overtly feminist than much of her earlier work. Other themes also achieve a much greater prominence: religion and classical mythology, as well as a number of explicit language games. In the process, though, a central feature of Duffy's earlier work is lost: because the title of every poem names the historical or mythological character whose wife or female counterpart is to be given a voice, the challenge for the reader of identifying the narrating persona is removed. This leads to a certain uniformity, despite Duffy's efforts to achieve variety, and reduces the scope for the kind of ironic ambiguities which abound in her earlier collections.

The title of the collection is itself a clever turning of a well-known phrase, 'the world and his wife', a deeply patronising commonplace which implies that, in all places and all times, only men have been of importance, and that their wives have been mere appendages. Duffy gives a voice to these previously unheard women, both as individuals and, by extension (as 'The World's Wife') as archetypes of how women respond to male domination and male annexation of credit for ideas and acts which may not have been truly theirs.

The tone is also more relentless and uniform. Unapologetically feminist, the poems hammer home again and again the key themes: men are useless, incompetent, arrogant, vain and, ultimately, unnecessary. The personas, all of course women, are contemptuous of the men they have ended up with, who are generally inadequate, self-obsessed and immature. While it may be true that some men are like this, readers might find the onslaught somewhat unrelieved. Women, by contrast, are resourceful, sturdy and above all capable of taking on the roles traditionally ascribed by society to men. This is an important corrective, especially in the historical contexts in which many of the poems are set.

Some poems plausibly represent the likely viewpoint of these unrecorded women; others are overtly counter-factual, such as 'The Kray Sisters'—an alternative version of history (of the 'What if . . .' school). The range of voices is not as strikingly wide as in Duffy's earlier collections. A large majority are told as retrospective narratives, with a considerable time often having intervened, giving a sense of distance rare in earlier poems. A certain mellowness creeps into some of the monologues as a result, perhaps most surprisingly in 'Mrs. Midas' where, having lambasted her husband as 'the fool/who wished for gold', the speaker ends on a surprisingly tender note: 'I miss most, I even now, his hands, his warm hands on my skin, his touch.'

Mythical pasts

An important difference from earlier collections is the proportion of poems set either in a historical past before Duffy's own experience, or in Biblical and mythological times. In this, she picks up a central concern of women writers in the Modernist movement: looking at the role of mythology in establishing the archetypal dominance of males and submission of females. No fewer than 11 of the 30 poems in the collection explicitly involve characters from Greek mythology, some brought into a contemporary setting as archetypes, the majority left in their original setting. Similarly, a higher proportion of the poems than in previous collections deals with Christian themes or characters, although their overall tone is significantly more atheistic than in Duffy's earlier work (see, for example, 'Moments of Grace' or 'Prayer').

Many of the poems take historical or mythological characters and translate them to the present day, with the striking result that they are belittled by the trivial, middle-class existence they are forced to lead. 'Mrs Midas' turns the noble king of Phrygia into a pathetic, avaricious middle-aged man, and 'Mrs Icarus', in a brilliant epigrammatic poem, witheringly dismisses the heroic attempts of the Classical Greek original: 'he's a total, utter, absolute, Grade A pillock'. Fortunately there are some exceptions to the prevailing pattern. 'Anne Hathaway' proves herself to be a poet just as gifted as Shakespeare (is the implication that she actually wrote his works?) and the resulting sonnet is a delightful mixture of affection and linguistic play ('his touch / a verb dancing in the centre of a noun'). 'The Kray Sisters' present a feminist alternative history in Cockney rhyming slang. 'Demeter', the concluding poem, brings us a lyrical vision of how the birth of a daughter can transcend time and culture, 'bringing all spring's flowers/to her mother's house'.

Reversing the streotype

A key and recurring feature of these poems is the reversal of expectations and assumptions. 'Queen Kong' is a remarkably tender giant gorilla, falling in love with 'My little man'. 'Mrs Aesop' dismisses the celebrated fabulist with 'By Christ, he could bore for Purgatory'. 'Mrs Darwin' states that it was actually she who had the idea for the theory of evolution. 'Mrs Faust' does as well out of the deal as Faust does—and proves herself equally brutal and cynical: 'I went my own sweet way'. 'Mrs Faust' also neatly turns the Faust legend: 'I keep Faust's secret still—/the clever, cunning, callous bastard/didn't have a soul to sell.' 'Penelope' is 'most certainly not waiting' for Odysseus to return. 'Mrs Beast' perhaps embodies most clearly the philosophy of the collection: 'words for the lost, the captive beautiful,/the wives, those less fortunate than we.'

The poems which deal with Bible stories are among the most interesting of the reversal poems, if only because in earlier poems Duffy suggested at least an aesthetic sympathy for the Catholicism in which she was brought up. 'Mrs Herod' is warned by Three Queens of the birth of a not-at-all Christlike figure—'Adulterer. Bigamist. /The Wolf.'—and resolves to have him slaughtered to defend her newborn baby daughter from his advances. 'Pilate's Wife' comments: 'Was he God? Of course not. Pilate believed he was.'

Although the variety of voices is narrower than in earlier collections, and there is not the immediacy of the stream-of-consciousness monologues, the speakers of *The World's Wife* are certainly voicing the inner and unspoken secrets of their characters. Duffy acts as a channel between their silent thoughts and the complicit audience. The old uncertainty about where the persona's voice ends and Duffy's begins has now become irrelevant, as these characters are entirely Duffy's inventions, without even a pretence of historical verisimilitude. As they are all her constructs, they are acting as her mouthpieces and we can say with greater confidence than with her earlier work that this is what Duffy has to say, which no doubt explains the clear, some might say jarring, tones in which themes such as feminism, earlier downplayed or merely alluded to, have now reached centre stage.

Source: Marian Cox and Robert Swan, "The Public and the Private: Secret Lives in Carol Ann Duffy's Poems," in *English Review*, Vol. 15, No. 2, November 2004, pp. 14–17.

Angelica Michelis and Antony Rowland

In the following excerpt, Michelis and Rowland examine Duffy's work as poetry more "interested in questions" than in suggesting any "definite answers," a contention stemming from her doubts and questions about self-identity and nationality.

Cultural identities and 'regulatory structures' in *The Other Country* and *Mean Time*

Within Duffy's poetry, the meaning of art is also a construction and is shown to be produced in relationship to economics, the discourse of the body, and the regulatory structures of gender, race, and class.

The Other Country, Duffy's third (major) volume of poetry, published in 1990, is one of her most overtly political collections of poems. In it she explores a wide range of issues of identity, encompassing questions of gender, race, class and national identity. Writing poetry with a political message can be a haphazard enterprise: in the hands of a less talented poet the subject area can take over and eclipse the poetic genre and its formal aspects; the poems gathered in *The Other Country* are never in danger of falling into that particular trap. As David Kennedy points out so aptly, her poetry emerges as an interrogation of the state of contemporary culture by raising questions such as 'how and to whom is it supposed to be sustaining? If this is the surface then what lies beneath? Who owns it? What is the glue that holds all these items together?' Thus, it could be argued that Duffy's poetry is first of all a poetry interested in questions rather than one which advocates definite answers and empirical truths.

The Other Country establishes its interrogative tone by opening with the poem 'Originally' which is discussed in several chapters in this volume. It also introduces the themes of otherness, displacement and foreignness which so many poems collected here are concerned with. Unlike some of the poems in its predecessor *Selling Manhattan*—which are similarly interested in the relationship between centre and margin—in *The Other Country* Duffy focuses on life in Britain itself. 'Originally' traces the move from one part of the country to another, perceived from the perspective of a child. This journey involves more than just a geographical change when the poem insists that this is a move to another country, emphasising the cultural diversity of contemporary Britain and its effect on how identity is experienced. For the child this is predominantly the experience of displacement and loss as the last two lines of the second stanza point out: 'My parents' anxiety stirred like a loose tooth / in my head. *I want our own country*, I said.' But where and what is our own country? How can we lay claim to a cultural and national identity that can be securely known? This seems to be the most pressing issue here, since the poem concludes with a succession of questions: '. . . Do I only think / I lost a river, culture speech, sense of first space and the right place? Now, *Where do you come from?* / strangers ask. *Originally?* And I hesitate.' As Angelica Michelis points out in this book, this tone of hesitancy and pausing becomes a pertinacious feature of this volume, and recurs in poems such as 'Hometown', 'Too Bad', 'We Remember Your Childhood Well', 'Away From Home', 'River', 'The Way My Mother Speaks' and 'In Your Mind', which link the concept of national identity to a more general interrogation of identity as such. In these poems Duffy plays on the theme of displacement, the experience of being an outsider in your own country and culture, presenting alienation as an integral part of lived subjectivity. As Neil Roberts argues when discussing the general trajectory of Duffy's poetic *ouevre*:

> Outsidedness in Duffy's poetry extends far beyond the conventional notion of the outsider as a person set against the norm. Outsidedness is the norm. It is an aesthetic principle in her representation of subjectivity, especially in the dramatic monologue, and radically influences her dealings with language, explicit and implicit.

But it is not only in relation to the question of national identity that Duffy interrogates notions of subjectivity and the experience of the self as informed by cultural contexts. Memory and nostalgia also emerge as consistent subjects of poetic interest and enquiry in *The Other Country*. Very often these themes are intertwined with those dealing with the search for the meaning of home and belonging, but they also crop up in relation to language and the genre of poetry. 'Weasel Words' and 'M-M-Memory' are the most notable examples of where Duffy explores the contingency of linguistic meaning by revealing the 'palimpsest' layering of language as a medium. Here Duffy is able to show off the most idiosyncratic feature of her poetic voice: a witty but nevertheless pertinacious exploration of an image or metaphor which is probed at and illuminated with verve and intellectual curiosity from a variety of perspectives. Lightheartedness and inquisitiveness are always balanced, opening up the structure of the poem to an active and creative reading experience.

However, some of the most poignant poems gathered in *The Other Country* exude a sense of despair and hopelessness when dealing with the state of the nation and its inhabitants. 'Mrs Skinner, North Street','Job Creation' and 'Losers' paint a bleak picture of a country where greed, consumption and moneymaking have become the main signifiers of contemporary culture. It is in particular the northern regions of Britain which emerge as places of cultural and economic dearth with their inhabitants stigmatised by a politics that has no moral qualms to eradicate historical traditions and infrastructures. These are places where people may lose their bearings because 'Britishness' is now conflated with the traditions and lifestyle of the more affluent, southern parts of the country. However, these poems manage successfully to avoid an overall tone of propaganda and moral indignation because of the attention paid to structure and form. Fragmented text, gaps in the semantic weaving and a staccato-like language ask the reader for intellectual participation based on empathy and understanding. Britain emerges here as the other country for a vast part of its subjects but these poems also fire the imagination for the possibilities of another country where national identity is constructed in a different and more inclusive manner.

The Other Country also contains some of the poems which established Duffy's reputation as one of the most innovative voices of contemporary British poetry. 'Translating the English, 1989', 'Poet For Our Times' and 'Making Money' are typical examples for her talent to parody the language of Thatcherite England, investing it with an ironic twist to create a poetry which takes issue with the contemporary culture of the late 1980s and early 1990s. In these poems Britain, and in particular England, is represented as a consumer society where commercialisation has become the major denominator of national culture. Alcoholism, drug culture, soap operas, corrupt politicians and criminality dominate the country in 'Translating the English, 1989', and have an effect on every other aspect of culture by turning Shakespeare, Charles Dickens, Wordsworth and British history and art into commodities, thus brandishing British culture as a market place where the right amount of money can buy you anything. By presenting national culture as a list of merchandise the poem points out the underlying emptiness of life in a country where only the language of monetary exchange provides a grammar and semantics of understanding and

> *Duffy plays on the theme of displacement, the experience of being an outsider in your own country and culture, presenting alienation as an integral part of lived subjectivity."*

intelligibility. The poem is written in a kind of pidgin English, using short sentences and media-speak and parodying the discursive structures of the tabloid press which became so typical for the Britain of the late 1980s. Whereas the linguistic structure of the poem as such is based on monologue and exclusion, dominated by one autocratic voice, the poem emerges as a dialogue, since it demands to have its gaps filled in and its randomness made sense of by the process of reading. By doing so the text makes a strong point about the national identity since, as David Kennedy puts it so aptly, the

> reader, as a consequence, is prompted to consider his or her own relation to and identity in a culture whose confusions, gaps and apparent randomness suggest a debasement or perhaps even total loss of coherent national identity.

However, rather than nostalgically mourning the loss of a coherent national identity which might once have existed and included all inhabitants of the country, the poem develops a rather different trajectory. Culture, it seems to suggest, is never a fixed, historically transcendent entity but always embedded and dialectically connected to political power. Its language of exclusion is never completely successful since its very structure always provides the means for a counter-discourse which works against its presumed intentions. By focusing on language and analysing its intricate relationship to political and social issues, Duffy is able to develop here a poetry which is highly critical of contemporary living, but avoids falling into the trap of nostalgia. As these poems demonstrate, language is for Duffy never a medium that simply represents and reflects reality and subjectivity; on the contrary, her poetry insists on a non-representational status of language with the effect that whatever is signified can only ever be provisional and contingent on the discursive reality of the cultural and political fabric of society. Therefore, one could argue, Duffy's poetry is at its most political when it is, in terms of its content, at its most postmodern.

Source: Angelica Michelis and Antony Rowland, "Introduction," in *The Poetry of Carol Ann Duffy: "Choosing Tough Words,"* edited by Angelica Michelis and Antony Rowland, Manchester University Press, 2003, pp. 1–32.

Sources

Duffy, Carol Ann, "Originally," in *The Other Country*, Anvil Press, 1990, p. 7.

Kerrigan, John, "Notes from the Home Front: Contemporary British Poetry," in *Essays in Criticism*, Vol. 54, No. 2, April 2004, p. 109.

Michelis, Angelica, " 'Me Not Know What These People Mean': Gender and National Identity in Carol Ann Duffy's Poetry," in *The Poetry of Carol Ann Duffy: "Choosing Tough Words,"* edited by Angelica Michelis and Antony Rowland, Manchester University Press, 2003, p. 92.

Further Reading

Dowson, Jane, and Alice Entwistle, *A History of Twentieth-Century British Women's Poetry*, Cambridge University Press, 2005.

This comprehensive review of Great Britain's women poets of the twentieth century is an easy, accessible, and interesting read on this often overlooked group of British writers. The entire book is an excellent overview of the cultural, literary, political, and personal events that shaped the poets' work. Section 10, "Dialogic Politics in Carol Ann Duffy and Others," highlights Duffy's poetry.

Duffy, Carol Ann, *The Salmon Carol Ann Duffy: Poems Selected and New 1985–1999*, Salmon Publishing, 2000.

This collection is superb for readers interested in gaining a good perspective on Duffy's entire volume of work. It contains poems from *Standing Female Nude* (1985), *Selling Manhattan* (1987), *The Other Country* (1990), *Mean Time* (1993), and *The World's Wife* (1999) along with four poems at the end in a section titled simply "Stray Poems." That Duffy selected all the poems for this collection provides a bit of insight into the work she likes most or finds most important. "Originally" is included.

Rees-Jones, Deryn, *Carol Ann Duffy*, Northcote House, 1999.

This study of Duffy's work from the 1980s and 1990s concentrates on issues of gender and identity in the work but also looks at the development of her love poetry and her use of the dramatic monologue as a style of writing. Rees-Jones makes a strong case for Duffy's innovative attempts at changing typical subjects, themes, and methods of modern British poetry into explicit personal, political, and social commentary.

Smith, Stan, "Suburbs of Dissent: Poetry on the Peripheries," in *Southwest Review*, Vol. 86, No. 4, 2001, pp. 533–51.

This long essay focuses on the works of poets who have moved away from traditional themes of "cozy" nationalism into the realm of contemporary poets who express feelings of disconnection even in the supposedly "safe" suburbs. The section of the article titled "Getting Nowhere" refers to *The Other Country* and the experience of being the type of cultural hybrid Duffy writes about in "Originally."

Rent

Jane Cooper
1984

Jane Cooper's "Rent" first appeared in *Scaffolding*, which was published in England in 1984 and then in the United States in 1993. The poem is addressed to a lover who is coming to share the speaker's apartment, but the speaker wants to be clear that she is more interested in the love relationship than in the shared objects and responsibilities. Cooper herself never married and never had children. Her poetry often explores different kinds of relationships, rather than focusing on the dynamics of traditional families. "Rent" also expresses Cooper's feminist identity, which is less about a political and social agenda and more about integrity and self-expression in daily life. When "Rent" was published in 1984, Cooper was sixty years old, and her identity as a poet and a woman was fully developed. "Rent" also appears in *The Flashboat: Poems Collected and Reclaimed* (2000). These poems were picked by Cooper and collectively offer a thorough overview of her work.

Author Biography

Born in Atlantic City, New Jersey, on October 9, 1924, Jane Cooper is the daughter of Martha (Marvel) Cooper and John Cobb, a writer and legal specialist. Cooper was reared in Jacksonville, Florida, and has lived in New York since 1951. She began her undergraduate work at Vassar College (1942–1944) but had to suspend her studies owing to health problems. With her health improved, she completed a bachelor of arts degree at the University of Wisconsin in 1946. Following graduation, she studied and traveled in postwar Europe, keeping detailed journals that would provide material for her later writing. When she returned from her travels, she took a position as poet in residence at Sarah Lawrence College in New York and began writing in earnest. She went on to teach writing and literature there from 1950 through 1987. She left only briefly, to pursue a master of arts degree at the University of Iowa (which she completed in 1954). At Iowa, she studied with such poet luminaries as Robert Lowell, John Berryman, and the 1995 Pulitzer Prize winner, Philip Levine. At Sarah Lawrence College, she and the poets Grace Paley and Muriel Rukeyser created a writing program that came to be nationally recognized. Although she retired in 1987, she is a professor and poet in residence emerita.

In 1969, when she was forty-four years old, Cooper published her first volume of poetry, *The Weather of Six Mornings*. Since then, she has regularly published and earned awards and fellowships, among them, a Guggenheim Fellowship (1960–1961), the Lamont Poetry Selection Award for *The Weather of Six Mornings* (1968), a National Endowment for the Arts grant (1982), a Maurice English Poetry Award for *Scaffolding* (in which "Rent" appears; 1985), a Radcliffe College Bunting fellowship (1988–1989), an American Academy of Arts and Letters award in literature (1995), and the position of New York State Poet (1996–1997).

Cooper's work reflects many of the same themes and subjects as that of other writers who reached adulthood during the World War II era. She often writes about domestic and personal subjects, the emergence of her individual identity as a woman and as a poet, public and personal conflict, and relationships with other people. Like so many women writers of her generation, she seeks to reveal the truth about womanhood and, in the process, to take down repressive expectations. Cooper frequently relies on symbolism and metaphor as figurative devices in her work, giving depth to her language and content. As she has aged, her poetry has reflected her musings on death and what is lasting.

Poem Text

If you want my apartment, sleep in it
but let's have a clear understanding:
the books are still free agents.

If the rocking chair's arms surround you
they can also let you go, 5
they can shape the air like a body.

I don't want your rent, I want
a radiance of attention
like the candle's flame when we eat,

I mean a kind of awe 10
attending the spaces between us—
Not a roof but a field of stars.

Poem Summary

"Rent" is divided into four three-line strophes, or irregular stanzas. The poem is addressed to a lover who is coming to live with the speaker in her apartment. In the first strophe, the speaker tells the lover that he is welcome to sleep in the apartment but advises him to remember that the books are "still free agents." In the next strophe, she talks about the rocking chair. She says that when he sits in it, he may feel physically embraced by the chair. She cautions him, however, that just as the chair can embrace him, it can also release him. Commenting on the rocking chair's appearance, she says that it can "shape the air like a body," meaning that even with no one sitting in the chair, it retains the shape of a person.

In the third strophe, the speaker turns her focus away from the objects in her apartment and talks about herself and what she wants from the lover. She states boldly, "I don't want your rent," meaning that she is not agreeing to this living arrangement for practical or financial purposes. She makes this decision of her own free will. Still, she does so with certain expectations that are in no way related to the responsibilities of keeping an apartment. She wants her lover's attention. She wants to feel important, and she imagines they eat by candlelight. In the final strophe, she raises her expectations even higher, explaining that by attention, she means "a kind of awe / attending the spaces between us—." She wants more than idle conversation; she wants such a deep connection that awe fills not just the two of them but indeed the very space around them. This connection will be so transcendent that it will seem to them that the roof has become a starry sky.

Themes

Independence

The speaker in "Rent" is an independent woman who has decided to live with a lover. This

Topics For Further Study

- Cooper's "Rent" uses several literary devices, most notably metaphor and simile. Read through the poem with special attention to her use of these techniques and note her underlying meaning in each case. Rewrite the poem without using any literary devices, trying to express the same message in literal language.

- In "Rent," Cooper describes certain objects in an apartment. What items in your room or home have particular meaning or importance? Using photos, drawings, actual objects, or any other kind of visual presentation, create a display, for example, a diorama or short film that tells about yourself through the objects that are meaningful to you.

- Based on your reading of "Rent," what kind of person is the speaker? Write a character sketch about her, drawing from the poem and making educated assumptions about the speaker based on how she presents herself.

- Cooper was born in 1924 and was in her late teens and early twenties during World War II. Research women's experiences before, during, and after this war and write an essay about what a typical woman's life was like, what expectations existed for her, and how strong those expectations were. Then write five journal entries as if you were a woman living in this era who wanted to pursue a path that diverged from the traditional path for women. Your entries may span a week, a month, a year, or any other time period you choose.

---

decision enables the speaker to be deeply involved with the person she loves, while at the same time maintaining that part of her independence that would allow her to leave the relationship at any time. Not only has she chosen to share a home with her lover, but the couple has also decided to live in her apartment. Had she moved into the lover's apartment, she might have risked feeling that she had lost some of her independence because she had physically left her single life. By redefining "her" home as "their" home, however, she gets to stay in her comfort zone and on her own home turf.

The speaker also asserts her independence in the way she addresses her lover in the first two strophes. Rather than begin with flowery declarations of love and commitment like an excited girl, she reminds the lover that there are boundaries in their new home together. The lover may sleep in the apartment but is not necessarily entitled to the books. The lover may feel surrounded by the rocking chair's arms but also risks feeling them let go. The speaker does not immediately surrender her assertiveness to her lover. Although she reveals her romantic side in the second half of the poem, she does so only after making sure the lover knows she has a realistic side, too.

In the third and fourth strophes, the speaker states her expectations for the relationship. She says that she does not want the lover's rent, suggesting that she is financially independent and fully capable of taking care of herself. Any compromise of her independence is done willingly, not desperately. She wants the lover's attention, not the lover's half of the rent. Even in these statements, the speaker continues to assert herself as an independent woman who asks for what she wants and is not afraid to ask a lot of her lover. Her tone matches the boldness of her expectations and indicates that she will be fine on her own again if her lover is unable or unwilling to meet her expectations.

Everyday Joys

In twelve short lines, the speaker reveals much about herself, including the joy she takes in everyday things and experiences. She first talks about her books, which she clearly loves and does not want taken from her too soon. She says that her lover may sleep in her apartment, but the disposition of the books is another matter. That she refers to the books as "free agents" shows that she thinks of books as living things with minds of their own.

She has a genuine love and respect for them, and she needs her lover to understand that they will be a potential battleground should any attempt be made to take any of them. Next, she talks about her rocking chair. Like the books, the chair is given a sort of autonomy and personality. The chair is described as embracing and letting go of those who sit in it. In fact, the chair is so independent that it can actually "shape the air like a body" as if the chair were so self-fulfilled it did not need a person. In both of these cases—the books and the rocking chair—the speaker has fun with the idea that she has perhaps not been living alone prior to her lover's moving in. She takes such joy in her treasured items that she projects personalities onto them.

The speaker also anticipates great joy in the relationship with her lover once they are living together. She envisions candlelit dinners, meaningful discussions, and a deep connection with each other. She does not fantasize about whirlwind trips to Paris, lavish bouquets of exotic flowers, or expensive gifts. Instead, she imagines simple, romantic dinners at home and moments so inspiring that the roof dissolves to become a "field of stars." She can find joy right in her own dining room as long as the relationship is meaningful.

Style

Metaphor as Narrative Device

Cooper is known for her use of metaphor, and in "Rent" she tells her story through metaphor. When the speaker talks about her apartment, she is actually talking about her life. Before her commitment to this lover, she lived happily and independently in her own apartment. Now that she and her lover are ready to merge their lives, she is willing to make her apartment theirs. She gives up part of her independence in giving up part of her apartment, because the apartment represents her single life. The reference to rent, therefore, is a reference not just to money but also to the practical responsibilities of everyday life. While she expects that the lover will uphold part of those responsibilities, what she really wants is the lover.

The speaker warns her lover that the "books are still free agents," meaning that they do not properly belong to anyone yet. She is actually talking about herself. She is not marrying her lover, at least not yet (she uses the word "still"), so she is still a free agent herself. She may choose to stay with the lover, or she may choose to leave at any time. Like the books, she has not yet signed a contract, according to the metaphor, which means she holds on to some of her independence. Similarly, when she talks about the rocking chair, she is talking about herself. When she comments that the chair's arms surround the lover but can also let go, she is asserting the same idea as she did with the books. She loves and chooses to embrace her lover, but she is also still free to let go. The statement "they can shape the air like a body" means that the arms of the chair do not actually need a person to sit between them in order to have the shape of a person. For her, that means that she does not need a lover in her life to be herself. She chooses whom she will embrace and whom she will let go.

The last metaphor characterizes the roof as "a field of stars." In transforming an ordinary roof into a stunning night sky, the metaphor communicates how the speaker anticipates that living with her lover will transform the everyday into the breathtaking. Where her other metaphors were cautionary comments, here the speaker surrenders to the romantic aspirations she holds for the relationship.

Domestic Setting

Much of Cooper's poetry concerns everyday occurrences, feelings, experiences, and musings. In "Rent," the setting is confined to a completely domestic setting, an apartment. From the first phrase ("If you want my apartment") to the last ("Not a roof but a field of stars"), the speaker never strays from the comfortable and familiar setting of her own apartment. In laying down the rules for their living together, the speaker talks to her lover about her books, her rocking chair, and their shared dinners. The context for the relationship is domestic. Within that setting, the speaker is able to discuss ground rules, relationship expectations, and deeply personal hopes.

Historical Context

Feminism

Historians often divide feminism in the United States into two waves, the first including the suffrage movement of the nineteenth and early twentieth centuries and the second encompassing the women's liberation movement of the 1960s. While there is no consensus on the exact dates of either wave, the general division is fairly well defined. Cooper's generation was active during the second wave of feminism, the efforts of which are still

Compare & Contrast

- **1984:** Because the Census Bureau is not yet capturing data on cohabitation, estimates are required to reflect the trend of people living together without being married. This estimate was given the acronym POSSLQ, "Persons of the Opposite Sex Sharing Living Quarters." In 1984, the estimated number of POSSLQs was 2.4 million.

   Today: According to the U.S. Census Bureau, as of the year 2000, more than 11 million unmarried people live with a partner. This represents an increase of 72 percent since 1990 and is ten times the number of people who were cohabitating in 1960. The Centers for Disease Control and Prevention announces in 2002 that 41 percent of women between the ages of fifteen and forty-four have lived with someone at some point in their lives.

- **1984:** The median age for a woman's first marriage is twenty-two, more than a year older than a decade earlier. According to the U.S. Census Bureau, in 1980, 39 percent of American adults are unmarried. This number slowly rises to 41 percent by the end of the decade, indicating an increasing willingness to wait or forgo marriage and an increased acceptance of that decision.

   Today: In 2000, the median age for a woman's first marriage is twenty-five, and 44 percent of American adults are unmarried. As the median age for marrying continues to rise, along with the percentage of adults who remain unmarried, society is increasingly accepting and affirming decisions not to rush into traditional family patterns.

- **1984:** Women's voices in literature are embraced and encouraged. Women's poetry is released by major publishers and reviewed by important journals. In 1983, the *Women's Review of Books* is launched, providing a journal specifically for reviewing writing by and for women. In the preceding ten years, two women won Pulitzer Prizes in Poetry and three women won National Book Awards for poetry.

   Today: Women continue to be major literary figures across genres. Between 1995 and 2005, two women won Pulitzer Prizes in Poetry, and three women won National Book Awards for poetry.

---

under way in the early twenty-first century. In the midst of the Vietnam War, the Civil Rights movement, and social unrest that ensued, many people began to rethink the meaning of democracy and to explore their personal identities. In this context, feminists sought to advance the efforts of the women who had gone before them. Now that they had the vote, women wanted more autonomy and less control by men in their personal and public lives. They wanted equality in other areas of life, including gender roles, career opportunities and pay, and political representation. Unlike the women of the first wave of feminism, the women of this generation had gained more access to educational and workforce opportunities.

Out of the push for equal rights and an end to discrimination against women came the women's liberation movement. No longer satisfied with the roles women had been expected to fulfill in the past, feminists sought to destroy restrictive stereotypes and find the freedom to make decisions about themselves and their futures. Soon, various groups worked to raise consciousness about women's rights in every context, from education to politics to sexuality to family. Some feminists worked within existing groups like churches and neighborhoods, while others considered themselves trailblazers. Their activism not only altered political and professional facets of society but also led to the establishment of child-care facilities, rape crisis centers, and battered women's shelters.

During the late 1960s and early 1970s, women writers found more encouragement and acceptance as they expressed their creativity in new ways. New voices in literature emerged, revealing more complex and varied female experiences. By the mid-1970s, there were about twenty-five feminist presses and close to two hundred feminist journals and periodicals.

Although some historians maintain that the defeat of the Equal Rights Amendment in 1982 brought an end to the second wave, others point to ongoing feminist efforts. In fact, the 1980s brought more breakthroughs for feminists, including the appointment of the first woman to the Supreme Court and the commissioning of the first woman astronaut. In the past, these were careers outside the expectations for women, yet they have become accepted.

World War II Generation

The World War II generation lived through some of the most challenging periods in American history. Its members were born either just before or during the plentiful and generally peaceful 1920s. In the wake of World War I, the United States enjoyed a boom and economic growth. When the Great Depression hit in the 1930s, Americans were unprepared and devastated. Children growing up during the Depression often faced hunger, disease, needing to find work when adults could not, and lack of education when schools were forced to close. Being subjected to such hardships molded these children into adults who had a strong work ethic and took less for granted than other generations did.

Coming out of the Depression, America found itself in another world war in the 1940s. The American people rallied together, fighting abroad and supporting the troops. Women entered the labor force to keep industry going while the men were fighting overseas in Europe and the Pacific. When the men returned after 1945, not all women were content to return to their domestic lives. By 1950, the rate of women entering the workforce was one million per year. Six years later, 35 percent of women were employed outside the home, although the vast majority of the jobs they held were clerical, were on assembly lines, or were service positions.

In the postwar years, women of this generation sought more opportunities to work outside the home, beyond their traditional careers as teachers, nurses, or secretaries. At the same time, the postwar "baby boom" of the late 1940s and early 1950s increased the demands on women as mothers. Education for women took a backseat in the 1950s. As women were torn between traditional roles as wives and mothers and emerging work opportunities that did not require much education, their rate of college enrollment dropped. Many women who did enter college left to marry before they graduated. Also, colleges were more welcoming to veterans, who were pursuing higher education under the benefits of the GI Bill. Media and advertising promoted the traditional image of women as homemakers. Women who had begun to pursue interests outside the home were often blamed for their family's problems.

Critical Overview

Cooper's poetry is generally praised by critics for its consistency in vision and its honest portrayal of a woman's experiences over time. Because Cooper has been publishing poetry since 1969, her writing reflects her own changing perspectives, attitudes, and maturation. "Rent," which first appeared in *Scaffolding* (1984) and was later included in the retrospective anthology *The Flashboat* (1999), portrays domestic life and independence in Cooper's characteristic voice. In *Library Journal*, Lawrence Rungren reviews *Scaffolding*, praising it for its developing feminist voice and insights into relationships. He concludes that the collection "attests to one woman's, and one poet's, courage and perseverance."

The Flashboat contains selections from Cooper's previously published collections, along with unpublished poems she describes as "reclaimed." As a whole, the volume offers an overview of Cooper's career and development as a poet, and critics deem the collection worthy of praise. Commenting on *The Flashboat*, Donna Seaman of *Booklist* calls it a "lustrous collection of a lifetime of poetry." In *Virginia Quarterly Review*, Roberta Silman declares *The Flashboat* a "cause for celebration," adding that Cooper's "work has never gotten the attention it fully deserves." Silman comments that Cooper's lifelong health problems have given the poet a particular perspective on death that is present throughout her poems, from the earliest to the most recent. She further notes, "Yet awareness of death often gives one a heightened mindfulness of the ordinary joys; Cooper's best poems come from her 'radiance of attention,' requested in 'Rent.'" Summarizing the importance of *The Flashboat*, Silman writes,

> If you believe, to return to Keats, that "poetry should be great and unobtrusive, a thing which enters into

one's soul and does not startle or amaze it with itself but its subject," then this collection with its distinctive, strong, dignified voice will continue to engage and surprise and comfort for a long time to come.

Criticism

Jennifer Bussey

Bussey is an independent writer specializing in literature. In the following essay, she explains how the speaker in Cooper's "Rent" is both a feminist and a romantic.

In 1974, Cooper wrote an essay titled "Nothing Has Been Used in the Manufacture of This Poetry That Could Have Been Used in the Manufacture of Bread." This essay appears in the 1993 American edition of *Scaffolding*, along with "Rent." In her essay, Cooper's voice joins many other feminist voices in commenting about unfair expectations of women in American society. Although opportunities had opened up for women and women were making great strides in pursuit of social and political equality, many women still felt compelled to compromise their dreams and ambitions. Sharing her own experiences, Cooper writes about the difficulty of asserting her own creativity and identity in the repressive postwar 1950s. Having never married or had children, she understands that her own experience as an American woman is unique, yet her path did not shield her from the pressures common to women of her era. Still, Cooper was able to discover her true identity and live it fully, unlike so many women she knew and taught in her classes at Sarah Lawrence College.

Cooper's essay, along with many of her poems, reflects the feminist strain in her work. But Cooper has not defined her poetry strictly along feminist lines. Although she supports feminist efforts to liberate women to explore and become their true selves, she writes primarily about her own personal experiences and insights. In "Rent," Cooper reveals both her feminist side and her romantic side in the persona of a woman preparing to live with her lover. (It is assumed for purposes of this discussion that the lover is a man, but it is worth noting that no gender is attributed either to the speaker or to the lover in the poem.) While the poem's speaker is bold in setting certain ground rules and expectations to the man she loves, she is not afraid to reveal her romantic yearnings. In embracing her feminist voice in her relationship, the speaker has not sacrificed the feminine desire for romantic love.

> *It is evidence of Cooper's skill as a poet that the speaker in "Rent" promotes feminism in a nonthreatening way that is free of agenda or artifice."*

It is evidence of Cooper's skill as a poet that the speaker in "Rent" promotes feminism in a nonthreatening way that is free of agenda or artifice. The feminism in "Rent" comes not from the feminist movement but from the personality of the speaker. She is not delivering a message of power and liberation to her lover as a way to empower herself as a woman; she is delivering a message of expectations to her lover because she loves him and wants the relationship to work. She just wants to be sure she lives together with her lover without surrendering too much power to the relationship. This is a voice to which most women can relate, regardless of their political viewpoints or positions on feminist issues. Still, the speaker does express views that are consistent with the feminist perspective, so that feminism is worth examining.

In *The Feminist Poetry Movement*, Kim Whitehead writes that the contemporary feminist poetry movement is as much about social and political progress as it is about unifying women without generalizing their "diverse identities and experiences." She notes:

> At the heart of feminist poetry is still that dictum that drove the early women's movement—"the personal as political"—which means feminist poetics is heavily invested in the details of specific women's lives and simultaneously resisting the gendered oppression of women as a collective in contemporary America and around the world.

By Whitehead's standards, "Rent" can certainly stand as a work of feminist poetry. It involves the details of the speaker's life at a point in which her independence is negotiable. The tone and language of the poem indicate the speaker's awareness of the limits of her own independence, so she shares the collective experience of women in America as described by Whitehead. In the poem,

What Do I Read Next?

- Edited by Taryn Benbow-Pfalzgraf, *American Women Writers: A Critical Reference Guide from Colonial Times to the Present* (2000) profiles thirteen hundred writers, spanning the full history of the United States and including all genres.

- Cooper's first published volume of poems, *The Weather of Six Mornings* (1969), is an award-winning look into the real life of a woman struggling to tell the truth about her experience as a way to liberate herself and others. Although it was Cooper's debut collection, the fact that she was in her forties at the time is reflected in its maturity and thoughtful perspective.

- Susan M. Hartmann's *The Home Front and Beyond: American Women in the 1940s* (1984) examines the lives of women in the World War II era. Unlike many treatments of this topic, however, Hartmann discusses different groups of women based on education, race, class, age, and marital status. The result is a thorough and varied account of women's experiences in this particular chapter of American history.

- Sylvia Plath's Pulitzer Prize–winning *Collected Poems* (1981) offers readers a wide selection of Plath's poetry, along with an introduction by her husband, the writer Ted Hughes. Because Plath and Cooper shared similar life experiences, their writings often invite parallel study.

---

the speaker discusses certain expectations with her lover, who is preparing to move in with her. The couple will live in her apartment, so she is in effect giving up some of her independence and "personal space" for the sake of the relationship. Being mature enough to enter into this arrangement with wisdom and foresight rather than giddy excitement, the speaker welcomes her lover into her apartment, but she also specifies that everything in it is not automatically his. She specifically describes the books and the rocking chair (which are metaphors for herself) to let him know that he does not enter the house as an all-powerful man. Their household will be one of sharing, connection, and love. Because she is an independent-minded woman who is not afraid to assert her will, she can speak to her lover freely in this way. That she does so without fear of rejection suggests that she has partnered with a man who appreciates and respects her.

From a linguistic and thematic point of view, Cooper's poem is in line with Whitehead's description of feminist poetry. Whitehead views feminist poetry as promoting a uniquely feminine expression and existing for the good of the poet and women as a whole. She explains:

> Feminist poets have enlivened the American poetic tradition by rethinking the function of language and poetry, broadening theme and imagery by grounding them in the experiences of women, and developing a formal reorientation based in a feminist consciousness. As women writing with the interests of other women in mind, these women have developed a poetics grounded in women's individual experiences, geared toward women's liberation from gender oppression, and therefore involving the need for both subjective and collective expression.

Although Cooper does not fit neatly into the category of feminist poets that Whitehead goes on to describe in the introductory essay to her book, "Rent" does possess many of the hallmarks of important feminist poetry as laid out in these passages. In its expression by a woman to a man about their new life together, Cooper's poem demonstrates how personal feminism looks in everyday life. This is the heart of feminism, where the freedom gained by women in the social forum is internalized and asserted in one-on-one relationships. Cooper's speaker, however, is not vigilant or demanding. Her voice is completely reasonable and relatable and in no way diminishes the man or the love the two of them share. Indirectly, the speaker advances feminism by detracting from the negative stereotype of feminists as harsh man haters. But the softer side of the speaker of "Rent" goes a little deeper still.

In addition to representing a feminist sensibility, the speaker also represents modern romantic life. Remaining true to herself, she has not sacrificed her romantic ideals to feminism. She understands that the two can coexist and that only when both sides of her personality are given expression can she be truly happy. The first half of the poem is about the apartment itself, but the third strophe begins to blend the feminist with the romantic. When she writes, "I don't want your rent, I want / a radiance of attention," she gives a voice to her deepest desire. It is a romantic expression, but it is delivered boldly and without apology. She wants her lover to understand that he has been invited to share her home not because she needs him but because she wants him. She does not need his financial support or his help with chores. She wants his attention and his love. She wants candlelit dinners that make her feel connected to him. By comparing the attention she wants to the candle's flame, she is letting him know that his affirmation of their love will bring light into her life where there might be darkness or uncertainty. Perhaps the darkness is the loneliness she had been feeling in her apartment. Although she talks about her books and rocking chair as if they were alive, she knows they are merely objects. In this admission to her lover, she reveals her vulnerability to him. If she is apprehensive about revealing it, she does not let on. She seems as bold in asking for what she wants romantically as she is in telling him he cannot assume ownership of the books.

In the last strophe, the speaker continues to uphold her romantic ideal. She specifies that the attention they will give each other will be "a kind of awe" that will turn the ordinary roof into "a field of stars." The image of the starry night relates back to the image of the single candle flame representing the "radiance of attention" she wants from her lover. Now, the single flame has been multiplied in the appearance of a "field of stars." The speaker anticipates that the relationship with her lover will grow until they will feel the same kind of awe that a dark sky bursting with stars gives. At a deeper level, she looks forward to the transformation of the darkness in her life into a million lights.

Cooper makes subtle use of the speaker's references to air. To the speaker, the very air seems infused with her feelings and perceptions. In the second strophe, she claims that the rocking chair's arms can release a person because "they can shape the air like a body." In the fourth strophe, she describes awe "attending the spaces between us." In both cases, the very air is thick with meaning, but in different ways that point to the poem's change in direction as she moves from feminist to romantic. The rocking chair has the ability to form the appearance of a person out of the air because of its intrinsic shape, whether someone is in it or not. It does not need to have the man sitting in it to be what it is. Remember, the rocking chair is a metaphor for the speaker, so what she is really saying is that whether or not he is in her arms, she is still her own person. But when awe attends the spaces between them, a very different idea emerges. She and her lover are not embracing or even touching; after all, there is space between them. But his very presence in the apartment infuses the air with awe. Unlike the rocking chair, the spaces do need him to create the awe.

The two images of the rocking chair and the spaces may seem inconsistent, but Cooper is actually allowing the reader to see how complex the speaker is. Like the rocking chair, she does not need the man. She can continue her life without him if she must, but she would have to do so without the sense of awe his loving presence brings. The two images also tell the reader that the speaker is deeply in love with the man but that she needs to have a certain amount of space. The speaker succeeds in being true to her feminist side and to her romantic side. Cooper has created in twelve short lines a character that is deep, believable, cohesive, and complex. The more the reader gets to know her, the more the reader believes that she will get her lover's "radiance of attention."

Source: Jennifer Bussey, Critical Essay on "Rent," in *Poetry for Students*, Thomson Gale, 2007.

Roberta Silman

In the following essay, Silman praises Cooper's body of work, with special attention to her themes of being true to oneself. Because Cooper chose an unusual path for someone of her generation, her poetry reflects her views of femininity, love, and conformity.

Jane Cooper's latest book is cause for celebration. This new volume includes all of her previously published work as well as poems hitherto not available in book form. Although she has been writing for 50 years and the issuance of this book coincided with her 75th birthday, her work has never gotten the attention it fully deserves; however, with time that will surely come.

Cooper's accomplishments as a poet who could write in the traditional forms were clear with the publication of her first book, *The Weather of*

> "... her delight in her lengthening life allows her to let go, giving us more of herself, her humor, her gift for friendship, her love of architecture and domesticity...."

Six Mornings, (1969) which includes a sestina written on a bet, sonnets, complicated rhyme schemes, a poem that could pass for Yeats, another one for Thomas Hardy. It won the Lamont Prize and announced that here was someone who understood poetry's mysteries: that form keeps emotion manageable and that the flow of the poetic line depends upon its musical cadences, what she calls, so aptly, "the tension between song and speech." Here, as well, was someone safely enough rooted in the world to look not only backward and inward, but also outward, so that in her later years she would write poems as amazing as "The Green Notebook," "My Friend," "Seventeen Questions About King Kong." And, not least, here was a poet who had the courage to wait until the work was right. She addresses this in an essay in her next book, *Maps & Windows*, (1974), called "Nothing Has Been Used in the Manufacture of This Poetry That Could Have Been Used in the Manufacture of Bread," but I am not sure that's the whole story. Cooper sets a very high ethical standard for herself, as poet and human being, and I think she knew, at the deepest level, that she could not publish until she was satisfied with what she had done.

Marching to her own drum was not new to her. Unlike most women from her milieu in the 40's and 50's, she never married, nor had children. She taught fiction, then poetry at Sarah Lawrence, where she was an inspiration to a multitude of devoted students for 37 years. Though a spinster (in the common parlance of those years), she seemed determined "to spin," as a character in an English novel once put it. Poem after poem addresses, fearlessly and with sometimes heartbreaking clarity, the rapture of sexual love and the memories and sorrows that are the aftermath of such love; how such love can nurture and hurt, yet also endow one with insight or wisdom, as in "Obligations,"

> Here where we clasp in a stubble field
> is all the safety either of us hopes for,
> Stubbornly constructing walls of night
> Out of the ordered energies of the sun.
>
> With the same gratitude I feel the hot
> Dazzle on my eyelids and your hand
> Carefully opening my shaded breasts....
>
> ... What extreme
> Unction after love is laid upon us?
> The act itself has built this sphere of anguish
> Which we must now inhabit like our dreams,
> The dark home of our polarities
> And our defense, which we cannot evade.

Since early childhood, Cooper also had to cope with an immune deficiency and was never free of the uncanny sensation that death hovered nearby. She writes about it in her brilliant story, "The Children's Ward," and it runs through poems like "Practicing For Death," "The Faithful," and "The Weather of Six Mornings" to the later, astonishing "The Flashboat" and "The Infusion Room." Yet awareness of death often gives one a heightened mindfulness of the ordinary joys; Cooper's best poems come from her "radiance of attention," requested in "Rent":

> If you want my apartment, sleep in it
> but let's have a clear understanding:
> the books are still free agents...
>
> I don't want your rent, I want
> a radiance of attention
> like the candle's flame when we eat,
>
> I mean a kind of awe
> attending the spaces between us—
> Not a roof but a field of stars.

Thus, she can describe a child furiously building one play house after another with rare sympathy. Or remember her parents with a vivid, poignant exactness, or convey both a marvelous jauntiness and a deep understanding of the ravages of the Depression during her Southern childhood in "Wanda's Blues": "Wanda's daddy was a railroadman, she was his little wife. / Ernest's sister had a baby, she was nobody's wife. / Wanda was the name and wandering, wandering was their way of life." Or suddenly address her mentor, Muriel Rukeyser, juxtapose opposites in "Hotel de Dream": "relish yet redress / my sensuous, precious, upper-class, / unjust white child's past."

By 1984 and her third book, *Scaffolding*, death has been kept at bay for so long that what another poet, Mark Doty, has called the "joy of ongoingness" has taken over. No longer is she, as she describes someone else, "balancing 'herself' like a last glass of water"; her delight in her lengthening life allows her to let go, giving us more of herself, her humor, her gift for friendship, her love of architecture and domesticity, her capacious interest in the world and its literature. And, she takes greater risks. The later poems are less formal, often have longer lines, and address the world with a searing honesty, as in "The Blue Anchor":

> . . . All these years
> I've lived by necessity.
> Now the world shines
> like an empty room
> clean all the way to the rafters . . .
>
> To live in the future
> like a survivor! . . .
>
> —never forgetting
> the wingprint of the mountain
> over the fragile human settlement—

There are many riches here, but for me, the two greatest poems in Cooper's oeuvre are "Threads" and "Vocation: A Life." Here Cooper brings that intensity, which Keats said was "the excellence of every art," to new heights. Based on Rosa Luxemburg's *Prison Letters to Sophie Liebnecht*, Karl Liebnecht's wife, "Threads" evokes the extreme tension between Luxemburg's enforced solitude with her political activism. She consoles herself by reading natural science and making observations of the birds, the plants, the insects, the trees and sky. Woven through these are memories, visions (even of her own death), plans, her ideals, and her bewilderment, as when she says:

> . . . Fragments of the established world
> flame and submerge, they tear away. Day by day
> we witness fresh catastrophes Strange
> how most people see nothing, most people
> feel the earth firm under their feet when it is
> flaming

Here the reader feels, with a painful sharpness, Cooper's love of nature and humanity, and—her own awareness of the inexplicable way time shapes our lives.

When she taught fiction, Cooper told her students that time is the unseen character, and in the longer poems she moves "through time in a way that a lyric cannot do." Nowhere is that more evident than in "Vocation, A Life," subtitled "Suite Based on Four Words from Willa Cather." The four sections, "Desire," "Romance," "Possession," and "Unfurnishing," (the last a reference to Cather's "The Novel Demeuble,") reveal the growth of this wonderful writer by looking at her prose with startling freshness and maturity. So intimate is Cooper's knowledge of this work that one can feel the two women conversing, trying to fathom how one creates art and what such a life is worth:

> When we try to sum up a lifetime, events cease to matter
> just as, in the end, a novel's
> plot does not matter
>
> What we came away with was never written down
> *Vibration, overtone, timbre,* a fragrance as distinct
> as that of an old walled garden . . . *The text is not there—*
> *but something was there, all the same,* some intimacy,
> all that is needed
> in a vigorous, rich speaking voice
>
> 'Your' secret?
> *It is every artist's secret.* Your secret
> was *passion*

Then Cather's words, which express Cooper's striving, as well: *Artistic growth is, more than it is anything else, a refining of the sense of truthfulness.*

If you believe, to return to Keats, that "poetry should be great and unobtrusive, a thing which enters into one's soul and does not startle it or amaze it with itself but with its subject," then this collection with its distinctive, strong, dignified voice will continue to engage and surprise and comfort for a long time to come.

Source: Roberta Silman, "A Radiance of Attention," in *Virginia Quarterly Review*, Vol. 77, No. 4, Autumn 2001, pp. 745–49.

Jane Cooper and Eric Gudas

In the following interview conducted in New York City in July 1994, Cooper discusses her focus on her southern roots and family in her writing, and the importance she places on the "enlargement of the self"—a sense of continuity and history.

[*Eric Gudas:*] Green Notebook, Winter Road *seems to be your most American book so far, in terms of its concerns and even of the forms you've chosen to write in. Do you agree? What do you think has made it possible for you to write, in a way, as a citizen?*

[Jane Cooper:] That's a very complicated question. But yes, you're right, I do think this is my most American book. First of all, it's a book that's very much concerned with history, and how the sense of history extends an individual life, both as you look back and as you look ahead into the future. I used to think that what was most important for Americans was to focus *outward*, to accept internationalism;

> "I've always felt poetry vibrates between the two poles of speech and song, or you could say that the poem has to find itself somewhere between singing and telling."

this was the legacy of World War II for me. At the same time, three-quarters of my ancestors came from what used to be called "old American families," from Georgia, Florida, Tennessee, Delaware. What's changed is that in the "Family Stories" section of *Green Notebook* I've consciously explored that legacy, rather than turning away from it, toward internationalism, as I did earlier. But both these attitudes are aspects of my consciousness of being an American, and of being a citizen, if you will.

Then, I've always been very interested in imagining what the task is for an American writer, an American artist. In this book there are two extended meditations, on Willa Cather and Georgia O'Keeffe, and the American landscapes they chose as their signatures, and that's obviously a very different focus from writing a long poem about Rosa Luxemburg. Cather says at one point—she paraphrases Virgil in *My Ántonia* —"For I shall be the first, if I live, to bring the Muse into my country." Of course she's leaving out the Native Americans, which points to a central flaw in her, but, you know, this too is part of our legacy, that until quite recently someone could still feel that way. . . .

That she could be the first one—

That she could be the first one, that no one had ever written about Nebraska and the Great Plains. Obviously, you're never going to be the first one to write about the South, but still she gave up trying to write like Henry James and decided she could write about Nebraska.

It seems you made a real decision at some point to try and write about the South.

Well, I've always had it in the back of my mind to do. Lately, I've been going through old boxes of poems and poem-drafts with my assistant, Beatrix Gates, and there are a lot of attempts at writing poems about the South, most of them not much good. It's not that I never thought of doing it, but with this book it's as if I'd made a promise to myself.

I'm wondering if you'd talk a little about your family background, to give interested readers an introduction to some of the people they'll meet in the "Family Stories" section of Green Notebook.

I'm half-Southern, by upbringing and inheritance—or, let's say, by geography and inheritance. I spent my childhood in the deep South, until I was ten, and my father's family is Southern from way back. Up till this book I'd written a good deal about my mother, but not about my father, or when I wrote about the Southern part of my life it seemed unsatisfactory. I think now that one reason I didn't write more about my father's family earlier is that they seemed so powerful. I really needed to find out who I was apart from them. I think we know this can be true of boys who have strong paternal figures, but I wonder how much is understood about the effect on young women?

My father, who had been a lawyer in an old family firm in Jacksonville, Florida, became, through a series of surprises, one of the world authorities on aviation and space law—someone who in his fifties began to lead a very international life. And my uncle, his younger brother, Merian C. Cooper, was a pioneer in documentary film-making, and later, for many years, John Ford's partner in Hollywood. He had had a very romantic youth, and was the original genius behind *King Kong*. So as children we breathed the air of romance! And then there was a lot of family mythology, a lot of old stories that we were brought up with. The story told in "How Can I Speak for Her?", for instance, which took place right after the Civil War, was one of the most memorable stories of my childhood. Who knows how much is true?

What seems important to say is that I'm not using family background to create a domestic sense in this book—I'm using it to extend the individual consciousness through history and mythology. And a lot of it is mythology. Also, it was important to me not just to get down the old South in its romantic or terrible aspects, but to get some sense of the honky-tonk South of my childhood during the Depression—that is, the cousin who painted on spider webs and got to the Hobby Lobby of the 1939 World's Fair! And the children in my rural public school—the kind of South that left me with a social conscience. Both those things were very much a part of my life—there was a lot of romantic stuff, and then there was the everyday reality that we lived with, some of which was very funny.

It seems you've been able to get a real mix....

Who knows? I hope so. Marilyn Chin read the manuscript just before it went to press and found a kind of nostalgia—nostalgia for a South of stable families and what she called an "old-fashioned American compassion." That was a shock to me, because the last thing I imagined was that I was feeling nostalgic. But probably there are things here I don't even see yet. I would never underestimate the tremendous charm that the South has for me, the giftedness of many people who come out of that area—and their courage. But it's just such a complicated heritage.

One of the things you really seem to be trying is to balance the complicatedness of the heritage with the charm. Especially in "Hotel de Dream," you get a quite jaunty feeling of being out on the docks....

I wanted to get a jaunty feeling....

But the poem ends by asking a really difficult question—how to "relish yet redress" your "sensuous, precious, upper-class, / unjust white child's past"? How to balance those two verbs against one another...?

The "relish" is also real.

Whereas to just have "redress" would be, in a way, to say, "This is something I'm obligated to do."

That's right....

Your poems have always been concerned with the act of writing itself, and in your new book I see a new concern with the act of narrative. For instance, an early draft of "How Can I Speak for Her?" began with the line, "This is a story I have known all my life, but how can I tell it to you if I don't know whose story it is?" The poems seem to be asking, How does one approach a story? Whose story is it? Who can be spoken for, whose memory? Does this seem accurate to you?

One of the things that always struck me, even as a child, is how the same stories got told differently by different people in the family. When I first was *Roshomon*—this was years before I'd ever heard of deconstruction—I was knocked out by it, because I thought, That's just how it is, each of these people is convinced that the story he or she is telling is *the story*. It was just impossible for me as a child, or even as an adult, to know what was true. My aunt, for instance, always said that my grandfather's grandmother, "the Castilian," had been married off at fourteen, and then her North American husband brought her back to this country and sent her to boarding school. But my father, who was a much more austere storyteller than my aunt, said nonsense, their first child was born before she ever left Cuba. Well, in that case I believe my father's version, but I had originally called *"How Can I Speak for Her?"* "What Each One Saw," and I had wanted to show the same story from three different points of view, starting with my grandfather as a little child, and then his grandmother telling what she saw, and then the black woman. And as I got deeper and deeper into this material, I realized that I simply couldn't do it—I had no right to say what the white woman saw, I couldn't imagine what her life was like, given both the arrogance that she obviously had and the experience of repeated uprootings and suffering that she had. And if I couldn't write about her I certainly couldn't write about the African woman, with her history of slavery, all those years on a plantation, and West Africa before that.... And finally that inability became the point of the story, along with the desire still to bring those women to life somehow.

It was a very important story for me as a child, that that great-great-grandmother knew at least two African tribal dialects, which she had never revealed to her white family. Until that moment—the moment of the poem—they never knew. It was pretty rare, I think, but she had grown up with people who had themselves been taken out of Africa and still spoke those languages, and from the time she was eight she ran the plantation in Cuba, and she knew the languages, I presume, first as a child at the breast, and then as a boss. It was such an evocative story for a kid to hear. Throughout the Southern poems I keep finding little things that are inaccurate, or speculative, and yet I don't think that changes the truthfulness of what I'm trying to do, because I think that those embellishments too have become a part of what happened.

You're seeing the story inside time, as something that's still evolving, that's evolving in your own version of it.

That's probably so. *Time* is very important in this whole book. When I taught fiction writing I used to tell people that time is the unseen character, and part of my wish in writing longer poems is to move through time in a way that the lyric doesn't always do, or doesn't *need* to do in the same way. The Tale of these stories, the meaning of these stories, changes as the generations change.

And you're not trying to deny that as an element in the story itself.

I want not to. I'm sure I fall on my face sometimes, like everybody. But many people read "How Can I Speak for Her?" as it evolved. Jan Heller Levi, for instance, was very helpful to me, because she kept saying, "You can't say that about the African woman, you can't even say 'they embraced,' thinking that the embrace was on her side as well. How do you know how she felt when they embraced?" I was always told the two women embraced, but Jan kept saying, "What does that mean?" And it was out of that question that the title came.

So there's tension between trying to tell a story and not assuming anything about anyone in the story?

I really want to have characters who are not myself, and at the same time not to be any kind of authority over them. It's interesting to try to do that—but it almost drove me crazy!

How do you see relations among the various forms you use in your new book—prose narrative, lyrics in long lines, poems in regular stanzas and even rhyme, blues . . . ? Given the multiplicity of concerns in the book, how conscious was your choice of what forms to work with?

I've always felt poetry vibrates between the two poles of speech and song, or you could say that the poem has to find itself somewhere between singing and telling. Short, regular lyric forms were always fairly easy for me—it took me a long time to learn how to write free verse. This book is different in that I played around with long lines in a number of poems in a way that I had never done before, and I began to explore the use of narratives which aren't in verse at all, but which I certainly think of as poems. Mostly the prose narratives, like "From the Journal Concerning My Father" and "How Can I Speak for Her?", were narratives that contained so much historical detail that a lyric form would have been wrong for them, it would have been impossible. And I wanted the detail, so the form had to be reinvented. I wasn't conscious of varying forms particularly as I went along—the necessity preceded the choice.

Take "From the Journal Concerning My Father," for instance. I had the idea a couple years ago that I wanted to write about my father, and I started putting down a few notes. Then one day I was looking through a box of old drafts, and I found that I had really written most of this poem in the early '80s and forgotten all about it. But what was most interesting was that there were originally three or four separate poems, and the finished piece only came together when I realized that some lines about myself, about saying goodbye to the natural world of my childhood, were intimately connected to what I was saying about him. So it's been an incremental matter for me rather than, most of the time, a deliberate one.

And you wrote a blues poem . . . ?

Yes, "Wanda's Blues." I went to a rural public school outside Jacksonville when I was seven, eight, nine, and many of the kids were the children of shrimp fishermen or white sharecroppers. This was during the Depression, and their poverty seemed bottomless. Later, looking back, I always wanted to write about those children, but I'd lost their language. Somehow the blues form gave me access again to something like the sound of their lives.

What was it like to work in longer lines?

A challenge! The year that I had the Bunting Fellowship I was stuck at one point, and Marie Howe said to me, "I'll give you an assignment. I've just told my freshmen to write a poem in long lines, and so I suggest the same assignment for you, too." And out of her assignment came the elegy called "Long, Disconsolate Lines," which I'd been trying to write in other ways. . . . It's not that I had never used long lines— "Estrangement," written earlier, is in lines that are just as long—but suddenly this became something to really experiment with. I think playing around with long lines then gave me permission to write in prose lines, or speech lines. I like the idea that this whole book is a kind of counterpoint of song and speech, of singing and telling. Musically, I'm always interested in getting different effects and juxtaposing them one with another. I tend to say "compose" rather than "write" when I think of my poems, and in the Willa Cather poem, "Vocation," there's actually a slightly different music for each section. And in the same way in the book as a whole I wanted to keep setting different kinds of tonalities against one other, so that right after "Long, Disconsolate Lines" you have the poem "Bloodroot," which was written the same winter but in very short lines. I didn't want to give up anything.

You were just speaking about thinking of composing rather than writing your poems, and I'm wondering if you feel the same way about putting a book together?

When I say composition, I think both of music and of composing a painting. I had a remarkable painting teacher when I was between the ages of ten and sixteen, and she really taught me more about composition in art than any poetry teacher I ever had. So I still have that sort of spatial sense.

Speaking of music, the four parts of the book really feel like movements to me. Could you talk about what you were thinking of specifically when you put Green Notebook *together?*

I know that this is not going to be an easy book for some readers, because the parts are so different from one another. People are used to books where there's an increasing underlining of a few main themes, and this book really has four very separate sections, so it requires a willingness on the part of the reader to keep starting over. Of course, in the end, for me, everything is related. . . .

The first part, "On the Edge of the Moment," is made up of lyrics that look at friendship, aging, dreams. And there are also poems about my parents in which they're scarcely my literal parents any more, but out of some mythology of parents. I do think that as you get older your parents become almost mythological figures to you. It doesn't mean that you forget who your actual parents were, but if anything they loom even larger than they did when they were alive.

"Family Stories" is the second section, and here there's not only a variety of forms but a variety of different characters as you move back and forth through time. That pleases me very much—I wanted the book to have a more peopled quality than it had in earlier versions before these poems were written. And "Family Stories" is also of course acknowledging what the Southern legacy has meant to someone of my age who then didn't go on to live in the South, who just had that memory.

"Gives Us This Day" concerns illnesses, but specifically what I would call the "culture of illness," that is, the communities that ill people make for themselves and how they think. Incidentally, "The Children's Ward" is the one instance in the book where prose is used as it would be in a short story; this is *not* a non-verse poem—it's too "written out."

And then finally "Vocation: A Life" contains the long sequences on Georgia O'Keeffe and Willa Cather, which are examinations of the experience of an American woman artist at different ages. Age is very important to me, how our experience of the same phenomena changes as we get older—and how it doesn't change. And this is of course another aspect of the fascination with history. I think it's important that in both the "Family Stories" and the "Vocation" sections, the poems keep going back to the nineteenth century and even before that, at the same time that there's a lot of imagery of moving forward into outer space, which is part of the legacy from my father. I really was brought up with questions like what constitutes outer space, and what can we do with it. I had a strange background, I think, in the sense that domestic life in my immediate family was very much what I imagine life in a nineteenth-century family to have been, yet all the time the thinking was extremely pioneering, daring and theoretical. Both Cather and O'Keeffe were born in the nineteenth century—O'Keeffe in the same year as my father, 1887, which I find oddly interesting.

Throughout the book there is that question of the speaking figure being between two eras, of being almost able to touch the nineteenth century and at the same time looking forward to the twenty-first.

I wanted to get that. I wanted to get that enlargement of the self, that sense of continuity. Partly because I think it's what Americans lack right now, a sense of their history, and that gives them a very uncertain sense of destiny. Kids don't study history in school the way they used to, they don't see much that's accurate on television. What do you have to anchor *Star Wars?* I hope I'm not only looking backward, I wanted to be looking forward, too.

Do you feel that there are any other concerns that thread throughout the book's four sections?

Concern with friendship. Concern with solitude—equally. Concern with survival of life on the earth. A sense that our experience includes our dreams as much as our daylight lives.

Have dreams always been a great source for your writing?

Absolutely. I think I use them more freely now, but there have always been dream-poems. Not all dreams make good poems, of course, but periodically there will be a great dream and often I can work that in, and even if it's not the whole poem, if it's only two-and-a-half lines, it's there nevertheless. I like poems that are not just about one thing but that are layering of different parts of my experience. For instance, in the poem "Ordinary Detail," there's a dream in the third stanza about a locked door which was very important to me, and when I had that dream I thought it was going to be a whole poem. Instead it turned out just to be that little sliver—but it certainly changed the poem.

We started talking about larger poems earlier, and maybe we could talk some more at this point.

Basically, I've always thought it was a big mistake for people to think of poems as only, or essentially, lyrics. If you look at the history of literature, the novel doesn't turn up until quite late, and before that it's epic poems, dramatic verse—everything that we consider fiction was originally poetry. And I've always wanted to go beyond the confines of the lyric without losing respect for what the lyric can do. For many years I taught a course called Long Poems. (At one point it was Long Poems and Short Stories! I mean those were my two courses....) What interested me particularly were American long poems, because I've always thought the long poem attempts to put a community on paper and Americans seem to have had an exceptionally hard time doing that. Whitman is the central figure for me here—the Whitman of "Song of Myself." But I also loved teaching the first two books of *Paterson*, and Frost's *North of Boston*, which pretends to be a books of longer poems, but I think it's really a village, and it's as full of solitudes as any village could ever be—nobody can talk to anybody else. Muriel Rukeyser's long poems were very important, and parts of *The Bridge*, and Galway Kinnell's *The Book of Nightmares*, Jean Valentine's "Solitudes." And Adrienne Rich's longer poems and sequences, especially "Twenty-One Love Poems," and the one about pain—"Contradictions: Tracking Poems"—and now, recently, "An Atlas of the Difficult World."

But what about your own practice?

As early as 1953, I was trying to write a longer poem, but I couldn't sustain it yet. I have more luck with sequences. There are three sequences in my first book, *The Weather of Six Mornings,* and another in *Maps & Windows*. Finally, in 1977–78, I wrote a long poem in three parts called "Threads: Rosa Luxemburg from Prison," based on letters Rosa Luxemburg wrote to Sophie Liebknecht when she was a political prisoner in Germany toward the end of World War I. This was very different from anything I'd done before, and I got excited by it—the momentum that builds up as you move through time and yet details, lines, moments of feeling begin to overlap.... The poem is a collage of many of Luxemburg's own images and quotes her actual words, but as I immersed myself in her *Prison Letters*, it was as if I was carrying on a dialogue with her. The Cather and O'Keeffe poems in the new book take the same techniques further, to different ends.

With "Threads," I simply read the *Prison Letters* over and over, and talked to May Stevens who was using the figure of Rosa Luxemburg in collages and paintings, but I didn't read a full-length biography of her till I was through. It took me a year and a half to finish the poem. With "Vocation," I did a great deal of research and it built up incrementally over a period of, finally, ten years! It all started with my realization that for Willa Cather the experience of the Southwest was profoundly connected with declaring herself a writer and nothing else. But to understand her the way I wanted to, I not only read the novels and short stories that deal with New Mexico and the Four Corners region, I read everything she wrote and a good deal that was written about her, especially by contemporaries who had known her personally. No doubt this slowed me up. But the design of the poem is ambitious.

There are four parts, and basically, through Cather, what I wanted to do was explore how a woman artist feels about her art at different ages—in youth, childhood, middle age, and old age. Having been a marvelously vital young woman, Cather became quite an ungenerous person as she grew older, and at one point I began to think I'd never get her through middle age! So this too slowed me up. She really had to face her solitude—the poem has to face it—and what the poem calls "coldness at heart." The O'Keeffe sequence, "The Winter Road," was a kind of spin-off from the Cather, because I had been looking at O'Keeffe's paintings of the Southwest in order to open out my own fairly limited experience of New Mexico. Then, instead of continuing with the Cather poem, I found myself writing the O'Keeffe poems. Originally there were a lot of them—maybe ten or twelve—but I cut down to just four. I think of them as an addendum to the Cather, part of my thinking about the same subject.

Do you see the moving through time in the same way the Cather poem does?

Not really, because they're all old age poems. They move through time a little bit, but all of them bleakly face old age as a kind of abstraction—the abstraction of being very old—which is not something that's much written about but which I feel in O'Keeffe's very late work. And then there are certain things that I personally felt when I was in the Southwest. For instance, I felt that the landscape around Taos, where I was staying, was simply not human-centered. In the Northeast, in New England, everything is more or less human in scale, but then you go to the Southwest and the scale is monumental. I think the Native Americans are related to that landscape because they never tried to possess it, but white people are not particularly related to it. Someone said to me, Every time an Easterner comes here they try and rip us off, take things away, so the poem ends "I was meant to take nothing away." I also felt, profoundly, that this was a landscape that didn't belong to me, it was just there for profound respect, absolute hands-off. So those ideas got into the O'Keeffe, although they are in the background of the Cather, too. A lot of the Cather poem concerns conceptions of property.

The first section of the Cather poem is an evocation of one person's physical experience of a Southwestern landscape. . . .

Right—that's "Desire," the youth section, and it's much the easiest section. I think "Vocation" is a difficult poem for anybody. It's a poem that reads well aloud because it's closely scored musically, but it's hard to follow on the page. And I have no answer to that. Whereas "Threads" is I think a very accessible poem, humanly speaking, even if you don't know much about the actual history. Cather protects herself, she does so even in this poem.

Do you think you were working to protect her, too?

I think she protects herself, I think she's very guarded. In "Threads" what I wanted to explore was the nature of a woman who is a political activist, especially as she grows more and more cut off and vulnerable because she is in prison. I was also very struck by Rosa Luxemburg the scientific thinker, the original ecologist. My Luxemburg probably isn't anyone else's, and she is certainly not a comfortable character. Nor are Willa Cather and Georgia O'Keeffe, who seem to have worked in increasing fame yet isolation. There is a paradox here. These women are absolutely not myself, nor would I have wanted to be any of them. But through them I was able to meditate on some of the themes that most concern me: the survival of the earth, the importance of relationship, the nature of solitude, whether enforced or self-imposed, what it means to grow older, what it means to be a woman who breaks the mold. . . .

In the Foreword to Scaffolding *you wrote of your "urgency to explore a woman's consciousness," specifically in relation to "Threads" and what must have been certain poems from* Green Notebook *still in manuscript. Could you talk about this urgency in relation to your new book?*

I had already started the Willa Cather poem at the time I put *Scaffolding* together, so I was thinking of that, but I believe I've always had an urgency to explore a woman's consciousness. After all, my earliest poems were attempts to write war poems from a woman's point of view. And while I think my definitions of women's roles have changed over the years, I don't think my feeling that I can only write as a woman has ever changed. Maybe it's important to say that the new book is not only full of a woman's consciousness—it's always a female "I" who perceives and puts the individual poems and the book together—but also, there are women characters all the way through. There are friends, like Muriel Rukeyser, there are the various women artists, then there are made-up characters like the young woman in "Ordinary Detail," who's not me and is not anyone I know but is someone that I could imagine quite well, who wants to make everything nice for everybody—her life has come to the point of betraying her. And there's Wanda, Clementene, Maryanne from the Infusion Room, the two women in "How Can I Speak for Her?" Women's lives interest me very much. It's not that men's lives don't interest me—but I feel I can write with some . . . intimacy about the kinds of things that women run into.

I know you've had a long-standing interest in biography. Could you talk a little about that?

Biography and autobiography both attract me because, again, they reveal the intersection of the individual life with history, the way individuals have of being in the world. I think I've said enough about what I wanted to do in "Threads" and what I wanted to do with Cather. Certainly I was influenced by Muriel Rukeyser's concept of the "Lives," both prose and verse, to which she returned throughout her career. But I think this kind of work was important to me even before I read *Willard Gibbs* or "Käthe Kollwitz." The two questions overlap, of long poems and biography, because the long poems I've written turn out, in some real sense, to have been biographies. It's not that I might not write another kind. . . .

But right now . . .

Well, at the moment I'm glad *not* to be writing a long poem!

Could we talk about ways in which you've been able to incorporate awareness of race and class into your new work?

I think you once made the point that I hadn't really dealt with race and class much before, which startled me, because these have always been such passionate concerns. But I was looking back through *Scaffolding,* and I must say I see what you mean. Perhaps the original shape of *Maps & Windows,* my second book, showed a political awareness that is somewhat dissipated now that the poems have a different order in *Scaffolding;* or perhaps some of the still unpublished poems would be revealing. Anyway, there's a small poem from *Maps & Windows* called "A Nightmare of the Suburbs" that you might take a look at. It concerns an upper-middle-class woman in Westchester, time the late '60s—as I imagined her—who thinks there's going to be a black revolution, and so she keeps a pistol in her bedside table. And because she has a pistol, someday she is going to shoot it. I'm convinced, if you have a pistol, you're going to shoot it.... So she's the one who will start the revolution. That is a poem about both race and class, but it's also a poem that was considered racist by several early readers, which was obviously not what I intended—but it was a reading I had to deal with. I think that in *Scaffolding* "The Flashboat" is not only a feminist poem and a poem about work but a poem that is conscious of race and class. At the point in putting *Green Notebook* together when I really set myself to write about the South, I not only had to write about race and class, but also about the sexism and militarism that were endemic in my childhood among people of my generation and of a certain kind of family. I think my father fought all those things as well as anybody ever did, of his age, but they were there, all around us, just the same. And militarism—perhaps people particularly forget to include militarism as somehow part of the whole syndrome.

So it's obviously not a new awareness....

It's not a new awareness, but I do see—in looking back through *Scaffolding*—that the poems might appear to be more limited to the personal than I'd meant. And to be written out of, almost, certain assumptions of how one lives and how one was educated—which I'd rather not feel I was always going to do.

It seems a conscious task of much of this book to get at the root of certain assumptions.

I think that goes back to the ethical idea of whose story is it? Probably it's not quite the same thing, but they are related. Another interesting, related question would be how it's possible in the same book to be writing the Southern poems with their clear social concerns, and writing a poem as inward as "Vocation," which is about an artist who cut herself off increasingly from the daily lives around her. The juxtaposition seems difficult. You asked if I had definite things I wanted to accomplish—and I guess I really needed to do both those things. But even to write about an artist—one doesn't want to be totally self-reflexive.

We've talked about your family and about the South as major presences in the book, and I think a third major presence is that of Muriel Rukeyser.

She was threaded through my life in so many different ways.... She used to ask audiences, "Who was your first living poet?"—by which she meant, At what age did you realize that poems weren't just locked up in books written by dead people, generally men, but that there are living, breathing poets walking the streets around us? And while Allen Tate was the father of one of my schoolmates, and I sort of knew him, Muriel was my first living poet. When I was twelve or fourteen my sister brought back her first two books from college, and I suddenly had the sense that there was this quite young, energetic woman out there in the world writing poems. Of course I didn't understand much of what she was doing, but it was very moving.

And then soon after I went to Sarah Lawrence to teach, in the early '50s, she began to teach there, and we became fast friends—no two people were ever less alike. Her work was important to me, but at the same time it was so different from my own, and especially the work she published before about 1960, that I think I was not much influenced by it and even consciously rejected some aspects of it. Her way of making images flow into one another, for instance, leaving them apparently unfinished, and rushing from one thing to the next, was absolutely what I didn't want to do. I wanted everything I wrote to be very fully fleshed out, very finished and exact—I was still working in another tradition. Eventually, as I've said, I was influenced by the "Lives," and by her concept that this was something poetry could do—work with lives that hadn't been written about before, that had even in some way been "lost."

Recently, I realized something else. You'll remember that in her Preface to the *Collected Poems* she talks about "two kinds of reaching in poetry, one based on document, the evidence itself; the other kind informed by unverifiable fact, as in sex, dream ... where things are shared and we all recognize the secrets." It's taken me till just now to see that the mix I've tried for in *Green Notebook* is, in spirit if not in style, a Rukeyser mix.

And since her death her work has been out of sight, out of print....

Yes—but before I comment on that, let me say that I believe her to be one of the absolutely central figures in twentieth-century American literature. And I'm delighted there is now such a revival of interest in her work. We need her power of making connections, we need her power "to know that I am *it*," her courage, wit, music that comes from writing out of the very center of your body.

All of which makes it seem insane that her *Collected Poems* was allowed to go out of print. And for years she was barely, or badly, anthologized, so it was difficult to teach her work. In any case, she has never been easy to teach. Students often can't deal with the rush of images and the generalizations, though as Jan Heller Levi says in the new *Muriel Rukeyser Reader* (Norton, 1994), it helps if you start at the end, with her last three books, and then work backward.... I used to teach some of her long poems, and always, both at Iowa and Columbia, I had a struggle. I think it would be easier now. I think the world is coming around to her—that people can read her now with pleasure who ten or fifteen years ago might have drawn a blank.

She's in many ways that kind of writer, one who people are just now catching up with.

Well, she really wrote out of what, for her, was the present, which means that she was ahead of most of us. Also, she's a Romantic writer—or, as she would have said, a "poet of possibility." Which doesn't mean that she's eternally optimistic, but does mean that she doesn't give up on salvation. And that's hard for some people to address, especially politically. But what you can't get around is her vitality; there are a lot of more obviously perfect poets who don't give out the same vitality.

It might be important to balance that kind of criticism of her work—that it's not always as perfect as it could be—with a feeling of what it's trying to do in the world.

It's not only a feeling of what it's trying to do in the world, though you're right to bring that up, but it's how the body of poetry and prose adds up, fits together. Here's this enormous body of work, and you can't leave out any of it, if you're really going to do her justice. The more you read of her, the more valuable she becomes. If you simply excerpt a few short poems, you're going to have a hard time, because people are going to see small flaws and think, How did that get there? Why didn't she finish that? Not in every poems—there are some that seem just wonderful from beginning to end. But I think if you think of the *scope* of what she accomplished.... She's an enormous figure. Never having been a writer of a lot of scope myself, I profoundly admire that quality in her.

On the question of scope, you're a writer who, despite a lifelong, passionate commitment to poetry, has published only about a hundred poems in four books. Could you comment on that?

Well, it's true—clearly. I was forty-four before my first book came out, which means I had already been writing seriously for over twenty years when I finally got a book published. So it was in a real sense a "selected poems," and in fact all three books before this one were "selected poems." In going through the boxes of old manuscript that I mentioned earlier, I was startled to find that there are probably a couple of hundred more poems that have never been published. A lot of them *shouldn't* have been published—those decisions were perfectly sound. But some are quite decent, and I don't know what to do about them. It's very odd to consider publishing a *Collected Poems* that would include old poems that have never been seen before! You want to be concerned with what will happen next, not with what you did in some kind of silence twenty or thirty years ago. Still, even I believe that I've made something a bit larger than can be found on the library shelf.

Could you talk about the way the support and guidance of other writers have shaped your work, and your vision of it?

I would be just nowhere as a poet were it not for my friends—that's what I really believe. This book is dedicated to my oldest friends in poetry, who were friends from the early '50s: Muriel Rukeyser; Sally Appleton Weber, a poet with a unique sense of science, theology, and the natural world; and Shirley Eliason Haupt. Shirley, who died in 1988, was primarily a painter, but she was also a very gifted poet. Phil Levine mentions her in his essay, "Mine Own John Berryman," about the Iowa workshop of which we were all three a part. And I'd be glad to dedicate another book to my friends in poetry from the '60s: Grace Paley, Adrienne Rich, and Jean Valentine. I imagine using the same epigraph on the dedication page, from Emily Dickinson, "My friends are my 'estate'." And then there are younger poets who these days are very important to me, including a number of my old students, both graduate and undergraduate. My friends have not only been willing to listen to my endless drafts of poems but have shared their own drafts and shared their lives, and given me extremely good criticism—and have given me patience and fortitude, and put up with the fact that I'm a slow writer and that I keep going back to revise, hoping to make the work more truthful. Of course we've had our disagreements, but that is the breath of life.

Do you think the idea of a writer-mentor is important for younger writers?

Important enough—but not as important as peers. My own experience at Iowa—I really admired the work of both Cal Lowell and John Berryman, who were our teachers, extravagantly, and often they touched me as human beings. But they were not role models for me, nor could they be. Who I learned most from were the other people in the workshop. I had been living in Princeton in the years right after World War II, and there, in order ever to think you could send out a poem to the littlest magazine, you had to believe it was perfect. So I wrote every single day, and never sent out a single poem; writing became my secret life. Then I went to Iowa in 1953, and there were all these young men sending poems out, getting them back, sending them out, getting them back, and it was just a much more daily way to deal with being a poet, a more democratic way. It was a hard time for someone like me to be in a writing class, because there were almost no women. I was lucky to have Shirley. And I don't think I wrote well that year; I got very self-conscious about my work and maybe rather precious. But it was a year that started me writing again, after a painful silence, and started me thinking about my work more professionally, and I believe that came from the workshop members, as it has continued to come from my friends in poetry over these years, all these years in New York.

How have the recent changes in your health affected your work as a writer?

This is a tricky question for me. Probably I need to say, right from the start, that I have primary immune deficiency, and that I've always had it; I lack gamma globulin. But it's not AIDS, thank God, which is an acquired immune deficiency. About five years ago, there was a period when my health began to go downhill, but I got sent to a doctor who pioneered the use of intravenous treatments in this country for people like me, and these treatments have changed my life. Still, what may be most significant for my writing is that I see illness as *ordinary*. I would like to include it within the daily, ordinary world.

"The Children's Ward" is the oldest piece in *Green Notebook,* and it was very important for me to write. I had my life given back when I was five years old, and I never forget that. It's through all my work in various ways. There's a lot of death in my work, but there's also a lot of the opposite—what Mark Doty calls "joy in ongoingness." It was this that I tried hardest to get in "The Children's Ward"—an unexpected vigor and humor that go against everything the story seems to be "about."

In an odd way, I relate "The Children's Ward" to the long prose piece that first appeared in *Maps & Windows* and now is part of *Scaffolding,* "Nothing Has Been Used in the Manufacture of This Poetry That Could Have Been Used in the Manufacture of Bread." In both cases, I felt that I would never be so directly autobiographical unless the material could be useful beyond myself.

I wrote "The Children's Ward" because I wanted people in our relatively protected society to understand how it is for children who know they are dying. We're freaked out by the idea that a child could know he or she is dying. Well, there are a lot of children in the world who do know that. They don't handle it quite the way adults do, of course, but in some ways they handle it better—anyway, remarkably well. For a long time I worried that "The Children's Ward" would seem like a totally separate experience, apart from the rest of the book. But then I wrote the poem "The Infusion Room," which is about the treatment program I'm in now, and I thought, Ah, that too is a culture of illness.

I'm very interested in the people I meet in the real-life Infusion Room, people who also have gamma globulin deficiency and often other serious conditions as well. There are some young children there, too. I have no desire to write a book just about illness; the point is always the people.

The first six months that I had the IV treatments I was very allergic to them, so I would be quite sick. But I would also come home and, you know, rush to write it all down in my journal, because the experience of the Infusion Room seemed so . . . exemplary to me. That poem really came out of my journal entries from the first few months. Even now the people make a strong impression on me, but I no longer have the same clarity. I think with the hospital I was in as a child it was the same thing—I still remember it so vividly.

In introducing your poem "Ordinary Detail" at a reading once, you said that one of the jobs of poetry is to give people the words for what we're feeling at this moment. Could you say more about this?

Poetry gives the poet words, as well as the reader or hearer words. That poems starts out, "I'm trying to write a poem that will alert me to my real life," and I think that's what poetry must do. Too often what we think we feel is what we were taught to feel, or what we felt last year; we click into a familiar complex of feelings. But it's very hard to sit down and think, What is the truth of my life at this actual, passing moment? And if you can do that. . . . It's what you have to try for.

In the jacket copy for the White Pine Press edition of James Wright's Two Citizens, *you wrote of the value you place on "the poetry of renewal."*

Could you say more about how you envision such poetry and why you value it?

Well, what I actually said on the jacket blurb was, "As I get older, it seems what I care most about is the poetry of renewal, or rather, of the gallant effort at self-transcendence." Cather has a line I love—it's quoted in "Vocation"—"Artistic growth is, more that it is anything else, a refining of the sense of truthfulness." And I've always been very interested in people who keep pushing themselves, keep transforming themselves, keep trying to get a little to the truth, and at the same time reach beyond what they have done before. I think Adrienne Rich, for instance, is preeminently this kind of poet. I just think that if you can write so that every stage of your life makes its own contribution, has its own wisdom—that's wonderful, it's a wonderful gift. I would like to be able to do that. I would like to think that I'm writing now things that I couldn't have written any earlier.

Source: Jane Cooper and Eric Gudas, "An Interview with Jane Cooper," in *Iowa Review*, Vol. 25, No. 1, Winter 1995, pp. 90–110.

Bowker Magazine Group

In the following review, the writer finds Cooper's collection a welcome addition to the tradition of women's voices in American poetry. The reviewer praises Cooper's honest content and her skillful style.

Gathering material from two out-of-print collections, as well as new work and early poems, this volume reintroduces an important, and meticulous, poet to a new generation of poetry readers. Born in 1924, Cooper came of age during World War II; as soon as the war ended, middle-class women were expected to begin a family, as she points out in a poignant 1974 essay on poetry and femininity, also included here. It was difficult to take her writing seriously, since "The women poets I read about were generally not known for their rich, stable sexual and family lives." In form, as in content, her poems struggle to break free from the 1950s constraints. Reading these poems now, we have the rare opportunity to watch a female speaker, haunted by dreams and death, progress from self-conscious writing exercises while waiting to meet the right man to the discovery that her body is physically rejecting the status quo. Delicate topics are often couched in symbol or metaphor: the difference between sleeping alone or with a partner is punctuated by her characters' responses to an earthquake, middle age is described as a grey day in which the rain has not yet come. Cooper's *The Weather Of Six Mornings* won the prestigious Lamont Award in 1969.

Source: Bowker Magazine Group, Review of *Scaffolding*, in *Publishers Weekly*, Vol. 240, No. 41, October 11, 1993, p. 82.

Rachel Hadas

In the following essay excerpt, Hadas notes that the title of Cooper's collection Scaffolding *suggests a work of spareness and intensity in progress—which she sees as characteristic of Cooper's "impulse toward self-revision."*

Scaffolding, the title of Jane Cooper's *New and Selected Poems*, suggests a support system, a work in constant progress (scaffolding put up while repairs are made), and also a skeletal, stripped-down intensity—all apt figures for this poet's quest for clarity and impulse toward self-revision. Adrienne Rich refers on the back cover of *Scaffolding* to Cooper's "continuing inner growth," and Cooper herself, in her Foreword, speaks of "the continuous journey the work has been for me all along." Cooper's oeuvre refuses to stand still, which may be one reason critics have tended to detour around it. Nevertheless, the image of scaffolding is more evocative than that of a journey when one considers Cooper's career. It's as if the inner growth Rich mentions is achieved by continually peeling away layer after layer; what once was essential now seems superfluous, and is calmly or exuberantly discarded to make room for the new.

What's that new like? The spareness of Cooper's recent work cuts both ways:

> For the last few years, particularly, we have all lived with the threat of nuclear holocaust. I want just to suggest it through images of all-consuming light, rooms with only a few sticks left in them, and a stripped-down landscape that is both the joyous, essential condition of truth telling and an almost unbearable vision of the future.

(from the Foreword)

So the bright, bare room is both a joyful vision and a frightful glimpse of a bleak wasteland. Once the scaffolding is finally dismantled, we will have arrived at both heaven and hell.

One way to look at Cooper's work as *Scaffolding* presents it is to chart her progress toward that dangerous bright edge. We can note what has happened to the lineation, the prosody, even the punctuation between a poem from *Mercator's World* (1947–51) and one from *The Flashboat* (1975–83).

> Head first, face down, into Mercator's world
> Like an ungainly rocket the child comes,

> "Some other word must be found to convey the finely wrought and modulated character of Cooper's work from first to last, and her unremittingly ardent set of standards for both the style and the substance of her poetry."

Driving dead-reckoned outward through a channel
Where nine months back breath was determined
By love, leaving his watery pen
—That concrete womb with its round concrete walls
Which he could make a globe of all his own—
For flatter, dryer enemies, for home.
(from "For a Boy Born in Wartime"

The future weighs down on me
just like a wall of light!

All these years
I've lived by necessity.
Now the world shines
like an empty room
clean all the way to the rafters.
. . .
To live in the future
like a survivor!
Not the first step up the beach
but the second
then the third

—never forgetting
the wingprint of the mountain
over the human settlement—
(from "The Blue Anchor"

The tightly packed pentameter lines of "For a Boy" tend to split in "The Blue Anchor" into pairs of shorter lines with two or three stresses apiece, creating greater speed even as the syntactical texture is thinned out. The eight quoted lines from "For a Boy" are less than a complete sentence; "Blue Anchor" is almost breathlessly simple by contrast. Alliteration and assonance foster teeming connections within almost every line of "For a Boy" but are sparse in "Anchor," true to the poetics of the empty room. "For a Boy" is altogether more clotted, ponderous, and rich to read; one could liken the very different beauty of "The Blue Anchor" to that paradoxical wall of light, both shining and disembodied.

But careful chronological tracing seems the wrong tactic when we encounter a single (and crucial) poem, "All These Dreams," which is dated 1967–83. How do you disentangle the styles on a palimpsest? And it's also discouraging to an historical approach that Cooper has chosen to put her memorable 1974 essay, "Nothing Has Been Used in the Manufacture of This Poetry That Could Have Been Used in the Manufacture of Bread," between *Mercator's World* and *The Weather of Six Mornings*—that is, between groups of poems dated respectively 1947–51 and 1954–65. Why, for that matter, include an essay at all in a Selected Poems? "Nothing Has Been Used" is less an aesthetic manifesto (if it were, surely it would have been placed first or last in the collection) than an invaluable guide to Cooper's fluid but distinctive sensibility and style. The essay gives us an extended hearing of a voice that is necessarily curtailed in Cooper's usually short poems. Honest, self-critical, vehement without bravado, that voice comes through, for example, when Cooper remembers that

> during one of my interviews [at Sarah Lawrence] I was asked, "And why do you think you can teach poetry?" and I answered, "Because it's the one place where I'd as soon take my own word as anybody else's," though I went on to say that that didn't mean I thought I was always right!

Too shifting to be summarized without distortion, the argument of "Nothing Has Been Used" is faithful to the growth and change that are Cooper's theme. Like Emerson, Cooper is hard to paraphrase, but inspiring to read, and—as she leaps from auto-biographical incident to piercing aphorism—tempting to quote from. Some of the comments about poetry in "Nothing Has Been Used" are worth pondering for any lover of poetry.

> For what poetry must do is alert us to a truth, and it must be necessary; once it exists, we realize how much we needed exactly this.

> A poem uses everything we know, the surprising things we notice, whatever we can't solve that keeps on growing, but it has to reach beyond autobiography even to stay on the page. Autobiography is not true enough . . .

> I have a very old-fashioned idea of what poetry should do. It is the soul's history and whatever troubles the soul is fit material for poetry.

T.S. Eliot long ago pointed out that when poets make general statements about poetry, it is their own work they have in mind. Any reader of these passages can infer that Cooper has a lofty yet grounded notion of the nature and mission of poetry, as derived from facts but needing to transcend them. Despite a protean multiplicity of styles and indeed of subjects ("whatever troubles the soul is fit material"), poetry is marked for her by its high seriousness, its power and obligation to tell the truth.

A problematic part of that truth, for Cooper, is her earlier work. The poems from the 1940s and 1950s may seem to her insufficiently genuine, too influenced by other (and largely male) poets; yet she concludes "Nothing Has Been Used" by saying she has learned to accept those poems "as part of whatever I now am.... For if my poems have always been about survival—and I believe they have been—then survival too keeps revealing itself as an art of the unexpected."

I love the way that sentence twists in one's hands, refusing to end until it has completed its thought in an unexpected way. And the thought, like the entire essay, is complicated. To put it crudely, Cooper is both endorsing and condemning her early work. Her tone seems generous; yet a reader can easily be swayed into agreeing with what is perhaps implied: that the more recent poems are in some way more valuable than the early work. (Or *is* that implied? Cooper's delicacy of tone leaves us room to wonder.)

It is characteristic of Cooper that she relegates a recurrent theme of her work to a subordinate clause. The poems may indeed be about survival. The question, though, is less what Cooper writes about than how she writes. Has her style been crucially changed by the progressive simplifying we can discern between the full lines and complex syntax of "For a Boy Born in Wartime" and the almost hectic immediacy, and greater emphasis on the self, that we see in "The Blue Anchor?"

My answer would be that a family resemblance is discernible between most of the poems in *Scaffolding*, and that the shared features include concision and exactness; careful attention to details both of appearance and of mood; a strong sense of the line, and finally, a rejection of facile endings. These are not easy qualities to describe in literary terms. Grace Paley has well expressed what many of Cooper's admirers must feel: "This is a beautiful and stubborn book of poems. The poems say only what they mean." Is this a negative virtue? It's true that Cooper can be praised in negative terms: She avoids sloppiness, sentimentality, and—perhaps most unusual for a poet of her generation—obscurity. Following her own precept that poetry must go beyond autobiography, she speaks of large matters without sacrificing personal experience or an intimate voice.

In fact, Cooper's voice may be the most distinctive feature of her work. It reminds me of "the low tones that decide" (Emerson's phrase in "Uriel"), and also of the two aunts in *Swann's Way*, helplessly well bred and subtle, who thank M. Swann for his gift of wine in such discreetly veiled terms that no one but their family understands them. Not that Cooper is cryptic; it's just that she's incapable of raising her voice or putting things coarsely, whether she's writing in the forties about World War II or in the seventies about a dream of communality. Words such as "delicate" and "nice" have become terribly suspect: Adrienne Rich has written (and Cooper cites her) of the pressures on women writers of their generation to be "nice." As for "delicate," that adjective was applied to the present writer in a recent magazine article, evoking derision from all kinds of friends and acquaintances. Some other word must be found to convey the finely wrought and modulated character of Cooper's work from first to last, and her unremittingly ardent set of standards for both the style and the substance of her poetry.

An early poem that Cooper includes in *Scaffolding*, "Long View from the Suburbs," is a dramatic monologue in which Cooper attempts to "invent how it might feel to be the old Maud Gonne, whose extraordinary photographs had appeared in *Life* magazine" (from "Nothing Has Been Used"). So much for the poem's provenance; as for its style, Cooper says that "the rhetoric remains heavy (that need to write long lines, to have a battery of sound-effects at my command—like a man?)" She fails to do justice here to the originality and, yes, delicacy of her own effects. Yeats may have contributed to something in the poem's conception, and Auden, surely, to phrases like "A streetlight yielded to the sensual air." But the searchingly quiet mode of the poem is already Cooper's alone:

> Once for instance
> He begged to meet me under an oak
> Outside the city after five o'clock.
> It was early April. I waited there
> Until in the distance
> A streetlight yielded to the sensual air.
>
> Then I walked home again. The next day
> He was touchy and elated
> Because of a new poem which he said
> Marked some advance—perhaps that "honest" style
> Which prostitutes our memories.
> He gave it to me. I said nothing at all
>
> Being weary. It had happened so often.
> He was always deluding himself

> Complaining (honestly) that I spurned his gifts.
> Shall I tell you what gifts are? Although I said
> Nothing at the time
> I still remember evenings when I learned
>
> The tricks of style.

The poem hovers between the figure of Gonne and a probable accumulation of personal experiences as nimbly as its sentences cross stanzas. With a charming authority the tone glides between rueful amusement, amused anger, and weary exasperation at male grandiosity and importunate enthusiasms. Note the eloquent sigh ("it had happened so often") and the barbed parenthetical "honestly." No wonder many poets sacrifice such subtleties for more unmixed rhetorical effects, for reading "Long View" we can neither wholly sympathize with nor wholly condemn the wry and ghostly resonance of a speaking voice that both is and is not a persona. Cooper moves beyond biography here. We don't need to know about Maud Gonne to savor the subtleties and ironies—and the aside (the low voice dropping still lower?) about that "honest" style that prostitutes our memories is surely a reflection of Cooper's own feeling about the kind of desperately autobiographical poetry, exemplified by Lowell and Berryman, that was coming into vogue around the time "Long View" was written.

If the "I" in "Long View" both is and isn't a persona, there is no "I" at all in "For a Boy Born in Wartime." Cooper moves closer, as the years pass, to some center from which that skinny pronoun can authoritatively issue; yet her use of the first person is mostly exploratory; tentative, low-key, until the pivotal "All These Dreams" (dated 1967–83). Even that poem, with its unusual aposiopesis and exclamations, is full of questions.

> Where have I escaped from? What have I escaped to?
> Why has my child no father?
> I must be halfway up the circular stair.
> To shape my own—
> Friends! I hold out my hands
> as all that light pours down, it is pouring down.

In very general terms, the shift of emphasis in Cooper's work is from more public poems (of war) to more private poems (of love, family, dreams, work). Yet one must immediately qualify. The "public" poems were inward in their questing, and the "private" poems open out to speak to concerns as far-flung as nuclear holocaust, or what it means to be a woman, or—in the latest poem here, "Threads,"—what it felt like to be Rosa Luxemburg in prison. Indeed, in "Threads" Cooper presents Luxemburg in a way that forces us to revise any pat notion of this woman as a merely political figure:

> We live in the painfulest moment of evolution,
> the very chapter of change, and you have to ask,
> *What is the meaning of it all?* Listen,
> one day I found a beetle stunned on its back,
> its legs gnawed to stumps by ants; another day
> I clambered to free a peacock butterfly
> battering half dead inside our bathroom pane.
> Locked up myself after six, I lean on the sill.
> The sky's like iron, a heavy rain falls, the nightingale
> sings in the sycamore as if possessed.

Imprisoned for her radical beliefs and opposition to World War I, Luxemburg tries to shed the weight of despair by passionately studying nature, especially birds and geology and insect life. But she cannot help seeing—and mourning—the painful struggles of historical change that have their deadly counterpart in the laws of evolution. Her intervention to save the peacock butterfly comes too late.

But just as Cooper's controlled tone is a pretty dependable constant, so we come to count on the images that surface throughout *Scaffolding*, images that help to shape the soul's troubles into art. One image is clearly signalled by the title of the 1970–73 poems but can also be seen elsewhere: dispossessions. Cooper is working her way toward what, as we've seen, she calls "rooms with only a few sticks left in them . . . a stripped down landscape." We see the inner and outer bareness in the programmatic "All These Dreams:"

> All these dreams, this obsession with bare boards:
> scaffolding, with only a few objects
> in an ecstasy of space, where through the windows
> the scent of pines can blow in . . .
> . . .
> O serenity
> that can live without chairs . . .

It took many readings for me to connect this passage with Thoreau's ecstatically ascetic mysticism, with Andrew Marvell's withdrawing mind in "The Garden," and perhaps also with some of George Herbert's plainly furnished rooms. But "All These Dreams" doesn't feel literary in the way that "Long View" or "For a Boy Born in Wartime" evidently came to feel to Cooper; it is a disembodied vision that is also a joyful *cri de coeur*, as familiar and strange as the dream state it evokes.

Less elated than the vision in "All These Dreams" is this fuller account of the same impulse toward spring-cleaning in "Souvenirs," the second poem in the splendid three-poem title sequence of *Dispossessions*. I quote "Souvenirs" in full:

> Anyway we are always waking
> in bedrooms of the dead, smelling
> musk of their winter jackets, tracking
> prints of their heels across our blurred carpets.
>
> So why hang onto a particular postcard?
> If a child's lock of hair brings back
> the look of that child, shall I
> nevertheless not let it blow away?
>
> Houses, houses, we lodge in such husks!
> inhabit such promises, seeking the unborn
> in a worn-out photograph, hoping to break free
> even of our violent and faithful lives.

Every detail of these expert lines seems to throw poetic light on a domestic dilemma, and vice versa. (The muse as pack rat or housecleaner; as the superego from whom we hope "to break free," or the magical link with the past?) As its title indicates, "Souvenirs" is no mere list of totems but concerns the act of remembering; yet part of the poem's persuasiveness surely derives from the reader's certainty that these carpets, jackets, locks of hair, and postcards are real, that Cooper is writing from abundance, not decorating emptiness with synthetic images.

The emblem of the house full of relics, that postcard especially memorable, reminds me of similar concerns in the work of two of Cooper's contemporaries, Adrienne Rich and James Merrill, whose different approaches to divesting themselves of the weight of the past are discussed in the late David Kalstone's illuminating book *Five Temperaments*. Rich's "Meditation for a Savage Child," writes Kalstone, juxtaposes "indignation [with] a residual attraction to familiar objects and the habit of cherishing." In Merrill's "The Friend of the Fourth Decade," the past is epitomized (as for Cooper in "Souvenirs") by postcards, but throwing them out—or as the friend suggests, rinsing the ink off—doesn't work: "the memories [they] stirred did not elude me." Ruefully Merrill acknowledges the power of what Cooper calls worn-out photographs:

> I put my postcards back upon the shelf.
> Certain things die only with oneself.

One wishes Cooper had found a place among Kalstone's temperaments.

The voice in "Souvenirs" is vehement but not angry. "So why hang onto a particular postcard?" sounds to me like an honest question, not a rhetorical posture; and "shall I / nevertheless not let it blow away?" is similarly a thought, not—or not yet—a dismissal. The same rapt, feeling-its-way intuition toward a desired space makes itself felt in "Rent," from the 1975–83 group *The Flashboat:*

> I don't want your rent, I want
> a radiance of attention
> like the candle's flame when we eat,
>
> I mean a kind of awe
> attending the spaces between us—
> Not a roof but a field of stars.

Notice the poem's rapid zoom from the couple at the candlelit table to the "field of stars"—a change of weather indeed, and scale, and tone, and light.

Such an outdoor space is also the scene of "Praise." The decks have been cleared, and work/play is in progress, beyond the norm:

> Between five and fifty
> most people construct a little lifetime:
> they fall in love, make kids, they suffer
> and pitch the usual tents of understanding.
> But I have built a few unexpected bridges.
> Out of inert stone, with its longing to embrace inert stone,
> I have sent a few vaults into stainless air.
> Is this enough—when I love our poor sister earth?
> Sister earth, I kneel and ask pardon.
> A clod of turf is no less than inert stone.
> Nothing is enough!
> In this field set free for our play
> who could have foretold
> I would live to write at fifty?

Who could have foretold I would set the field free? might be another way of putting it. The poem is a kind of psalm to (re)creation; mere dispossession has yielded both to a more sublime blankness and to a different kind of construction—a creation not of domestic interiors or of kids, but of architecture—more scaffolding! I myself feel more at home with the Cooper of "Souvenirs," but the elation in *The Flashboat* comes from somewhere; it feels honest and earned.

Companion to the successive strippings in Cooper's work is an image a little harder to describe. It might be called recognition, or self-scrutiny, or looking into a mirror, or meeting someone else's eyes—or meeting one's own. The self, after all, cannot be thrown away like a "particular postcard" or a lock of hair; it changes, and we can keep track of the changes by focusing from time to time on the latest manifestation of what we are. As early as "For a Boy Born in Wartime" Cooper refers to "the concrete / Unmalleable mirror world we live in." The mirror slowly clears as the poems continue, but it takes a long time to be able to see oneself.

> Feelings aside I never know my face;
> I comb my hair and what I see is timeless,
> Not a face at all but (besides the hair)

Lips and a pair of eyes, two hands, a body
Pale as a fish imprisoned in the mirror.
(from "The Knowledge That Comes Through Experience"

That fish-pale body is unsettlingly reminiscent of Sylvia Plath's image of a woman looking in a mirror and seeing an old woman rise in it "like a terrible fish," though as we might expect Cooper is more controlled in her distaste for what she sees.

One solution to the problem of appearances, in *The Weather of Six Mornings*, is to address oneself as another. Indeed, the self presented by an old photograph (which has evidently not yet been discarded) *is* another. "Leaving Water Hyacinths" (subtitled "from an old photograph") begins "I see you, child, standing above the river" and moves, at the start of each successive stanza, to a closer identification of speaker with image: "I know—because you become me" and finally "I know—because you contain me."

In two remarkable poems—apparently about her mother but actually, I think, about the double layering of selves (younger and older mother; younger and older daughter)—Cooper is true to the difficulty not only of making images of ourselves, but of reconstructing the appearances even of those we love:

Why can I never when I think about it
See your face tender under the tasseled light
Above a book held in your stubby fingers?
Or catch your tumbling gamecock angers?
Or—as a child once, feverish by night—
Wake to your sleepless, profiled granite?

But I must reconstruct you, feature by feature:
Your sailor's gaze, a visionary blue,
Not stay-at-home but wistful northern eyes;
And the nose Gothic, oversized,
Delicately groined to the eyesockets' shadow,
Proud as a precipice above laughter.

A curious cubism supplies us with more visual details than we can well assimilate; the reconstruction is no more "realistic" than a Picasso portrait, and yet (or therefore) communicates powerfully what struggles to find a niche in memory. These lines, which splendidly render back what the speaker says she can't see, are from a poem entitled "For My Mother in Her First Illness, from a Window Overlooking Notre Dame"; yet at the poem's close it is the daughter who is ill: "Alone and sick, lying in a foreign house, / I try to read. Which one of us is absent?"

A similar pentimento gives an uncanny doubleness to "My Young Mother," quoted here in full.

My young mother, her face narrow
and dark with unresolved wishes
under a hatbrim of the twenties,
stood by my middleaged bed.

Still as a child pretending sleep
to a grownup watchful or calling,
I lay in a corner of my dream
staring at the mole above her lip.

Familiar mole! but that girlish look
as if I had nothing to give her—
Eyes blue—brim dark—
calling me from sleep after decades.

Mother and daughter, past and present: The successive embodiments merge with a fluency reflected in Cooper's supple and sparing use of the first person. A poem about her mother, for example, twists into one about her, rather as a letter that begins by politely eschewing the writer's concerns manages gracefully to arrive at some personal news. Survival, Cooper has said, keeps revealing itself as an art of the unexpected; the unexpectedness of some of Cooper's shifts of emphasis surely has the spryness and resilience necessary for survival.

Cooper is able to invest poems that almost or completely suppress the first person with a searching intimacy that constitutes a kind of mirroring at a remove. "Waiting" and "A Circle, a Square, a Triangle and a Ripple of Water," neighboring poems from *Dispossessions*, look at, and into, not only the eyes but the entire body, both in itself and, especially in "A Circle," in relation to others.

My body knows it will never bear children.
What can I say to my body now,
this used violin?
Every night it cries out strenuously
from its secret cave.
(from "Waiting"

Seemingly untouched she
was the stone at the center of
the pool whose circles
shuddered off around her.
(from "A Circle"

It wouldn't be hard to rewrite this pair of passages so that "Waiting" was in the third person and "A Circle" in the first person, so precise is Cooper's intimacy, and so passionate her observation.

At about the point in Cooper's work where she reaches the ecstasies of empty space, the images of self-searching stop. The overlay of one's parents is, by middle age, a thing of the past—still there, no doubt, but no longer news. And a new kind of mirror can be found in the gaze of like-minded companions and other variants of reflection. In "All These Dreams," there is no mirror—after all there are no rooms, and presumably no walls—but "light poured down through the roof on a circular stair / made of glass." And at the poems's close, which I have quoted earlier but must return to, Cooper interrupts herself in the midst of shaping . . . what?

> I must be halfway up the circular stair.
> To shape my own—

My own image? self? work? Her word does double duty as the object of "to shape" and as a glad apostrophe: "Friends!"

That circular stair is a good emblem for Cooper's work. It may recall Yeats's winding stair, but it has its own radiance; and the poet is halfway up it, not in a dark wood but in a group of friends, laughing. The most rewarding thing about *Scaffolding* is the way Cooper's scrupulous and profoundly serious art moves toward joy.

Source: Rachel Hadas, "An Ecstasy of Space," in *Parnassus*, Vol. 15, No. 1, 1989, pp. 217–39.

Sources

Cooper, Jane, "Rent," in *The Flashboat: Poems Collected and Reclaimed*, W. W. Norton, 2000, p. 154.

"Loving Together, Living Alone: Families and Living Arrangements, 2000," *U.S. Census Bureau*, http://www.census.gov/population/pop-profile/2000/chap05.pdf (March 15, 2006).

Review of *The Flashboat: Poems Collected and Reclaimed*, in *Publishers Weekly*, Vol. 246, No. 39, September 27, 1999, p. 99.

Rungren, Lawrence, Review of *Scaffolding: New and Selected Poems*, in *Library Journal*, Vol. 110, September 1, 1985, p. 202.

Seaman, Donna, Review of *The Flashboat*, in *Booklist*, Vol. 96, No. 4, October 15, 1999, p. 411.

Silman, Roberta, "A Radiance of Attention," in *Virginia Quarterly Review*, Vol. 77, No. 4, Autumn 2001, pp. 745–49.

"Statistics," *Alternatives to Marriage Project*, http://www.unmarried.org/statistics.html (March 15, 2006).

Whitehead, Kim, "Introduction," in *The Feminist Poetry Movement*, University Press of Mississippi, 1996, pp. xi–xxiii.

Further Reading

Cooper, Jane, Gwen Head, and Marcia Southwick, eds., *Extended Outlooks: The "Iowa Review" Collection of Contemporary Women Writers*, Macmillan, 1982.
> Cooper wrote the introduction to this anthology and worked as coeditor. This collection of writings from *Iowa Review*, a literary journal, reflects the wide-ranging styles and subjects of modern women writers.

Kerber, Linda K., and Jane Sherron De Hart, eds., *Women's America: Refocusing the Past*, Oxford University Press, 2003.
> In this widely consulted anthology of women's history in America, the editors offer almost one hundred essays and documents relating the events and experiences of women in America's past. The editors chose selections that give insight into a wide range of experiences from colonial to modern times and include factors such as race and class.

Kooser, Ted, *The Poetry Home Repair Manual: Practical Advice for Beginning Poets*, University of Nebraska Press, 2005.
> Known for his accessible writing style, Kooser has earned a reputation as a poet of stature and, as of 2006, has served two terms as poet laureate of the United States. In this book, he applies his years of experience as a poet to offer easy-to-follow advice for beginners.

Lindenmeyer, Kriste, *The Greatest Generation Grows Up: American Childhood in the 1930s*, Ivan R. Dee, 2005.
> Lindenmeyer takes a look at the childhood experiences of what would become the World War II generation. She explores what it was like to be a child in the wake of the extravagance of the 1920s, to endure the hardship of the Great Depression, and then to face the global turmoil in the events leading up to and culminating in a world war.

The River Mumma Wants Out

Lorna Goodison
2005

Lorna Goodison's "The River Mumma Wants Out," published in 2005, is, on the surface, a lighthearted poem, making fun of people who look for happiness in things that glitter. Below the surface, however, the work is a scathing criticism of a popular culture that fosters insatiable desires, change for change's sake, and a lack of responsibility or spirituality. Goodison has set her poem in her homeland, Jamaica, but the message therein applies to all people everywhere.

Goodison published "River Mumma" at a time when she was equally established in the United States, where she was living with her husband and teaching at the University of Michigan, and in Jamaica, where she would return each summer. Having relationships with both her homeland and a new country provided her with the perspective needed to objectively evaluate each of the two cultures—and indeed, the assessment is fairly depressing. No one, the poem implies, wants to take care of the things that should matter most, such as the environment. Even the most sacred cultural icons have grown tired of living obscure lives with no monetary reward. These guardians, the reader understands, would rather "go clubbing" with glitzy, high-profile celebrities who make large amounts of money.

Although the poem does not present an attractive picture of what this drive for needless change and the associated endless self-absorption result in, such as a polluted Kingston Harbour, the poem could be read as a prayer, a wish, or a hope. In the poem, a speaker asks, "You can't take a hint? You

can't read a sign?" These questions seem to communicate the underlying message. "Wake up and take note," the speaker appears to be shouting. The contention that a mythological creature "wants out" cannot be understood as a good omen.

Author Biography

Born in Kingston, Jamaica, in 1947, Lorna Goodison is reputed to be one of the island nation's favorite poets. She grew up as one of nine children in a family that loved books and writing. However, after comparisons were made (while she was still in public school) between her writing and that of one of her sisters, Goodison chose to keep her poetry to herself. When she published some of her poetry in a Jamaican newspaper while she was in high school, she did so anonymously. This reluctance to identify herself with her writing continued through her studies in art school. At length, as Goodison has stated, her poetry took precedence, almost like a tyrant, over all other forms of creative expression. Although she continues to paint (including the illustrations for her collections), Goodison has found that she best articulates her life experiences through poetry.

Despite her long and loving relationship with the written word, when Goodison graduated from college, her main focus was to find a job that would pay the bills. Hoping that teaching would allow her additional time to continue writing poetry, she found positions at Jamaica College and at a local high school. During this period, Goodison began publishing her poems with her name publicly attached to them. As her reputation grew, she was offered opportunities to travel and to read her poetry in other countries. The more she shared her work, the more she realized that she could finally claim the title of poet.

Not until she reached her early thirties did Goodison see her first collection of poetry, *Tamarind Season* (1980), published. In the twenty-five years that followed, she added nine more collections of verse to her body of work, including *To Us, All Flowers Are Roses* (1995), *Traveling Mercies* (2001), and *Controlling the Silver* (2005), in which "The River Mumma Wants Out" appears. In 1999, she received Jamaica's Musgrave Gold Medal for poetry. She also writes short stories, some of which were collected in *Fool-Fool Rose Is Leaving Labour-in-Vain Savannah* (2005). As of the early twenty-first century, Goodison spent part of each year on the north shore of Jamaica. She has been employed as a professor at various U.S. and Canadian colleges, including Radcliffe, the University of Michigan, and the University of Toronto.

Lorna Goodison   © Ms. Lorna Goodison. Reproduced by permission

Poem Text

You can't hear? Everything here is changing.
The bullrushes on the river banks now want
to be palms in the Kings's garden. (What king?)

The river is ostriching into the sand.
Is that not obvious? the nurse souls ask.   5
You can't take a hint? You can't read a sign?

Mumma no longer wants to be guardian
of our waters. She wants to be Big Mumma,
dancehall queen of the greater Caribbean.

She no longer wants to dispense clean water   10
to baptize and cleanse (at least not gratis).
She does not give a damn about polluted

Kingston Harbour. She must expose her fish
torso, rock the dance fans, go on tour overseas,
go clubbing with P. Diddy, experience snow,   15

shop in those underground multiplex malls,
spending her strong dollars. Go away, she will
not be seeing you, for you have no insurance.

Media Adaptations

- The British Broadcasting Corporation, at http://www.bbc.co.uk/radio4/arts/natpoetday/lorna_goodison.shtml, offers an audio interview with Goodison, who talks about how she came to write poetry.

Poem Summary

Stanza 1

The overall theme of Goodison's poem "The River Mumma Wants Out" is evident in the title. In Jamaican folklore, the River Mumma, or River Maiden, is similar to the mythological mermaid: half human, half fish. Traditionally, the River Mumma lives at the fountainhead of the island's large water channels, acting as protector of the water and of the creatures who live in it. The poem's title declares that the River Mumma would prefer to be absolved of her duties. Another meaning is also suggested by the title: the River Mumma may simply want to emerge from the water or rid herself of her somewhat confining physical form. Whichever of these meanings is implied, the change is in the course of happening.

The poem then begins with a question: "You can't hear?" With these three words, the narrator captures the reader's attention in several ways. First, the narrator's addressing the reader with the second-person pronoun "you" makes the reader a participant in the conversation of the poem. Second, in using the present tense, she invokes an immediacy, luring readers to subconsciously strain their ears, as if they might hear something even as they read. Third, she demands the active consideration of a response to the question. In the second part of the first line, Goodison provides her thematic statement: "Everything here is changing."

In the lines that follow, the narrator employs a personification of nature to characterize the changes that are occurring. "Bullrushes," which are simple, unglamorous, water-loving plants, now "want / to be palms"; the mention of palms, of course, conjures romantic notions of tropical life. Palm trees stretch their long trunks up into the sky and adorn classy gardens, whereas bullrushes are more likely to be completely overlooked. The bullrushes are looking for glory, in other words—what they would imagine to be a better life. They also want to be taken to the "Kings's garden," which desire the narrator mocks by asking, "What king?" No true kings are present on the island. Even the garden's name, the narrator implies, is pompous. Thus, everything would seem to want to be more important than it actually is.

Stanza 2

"The river is ostriching into the sand," reads the opening line of the second stanza, which might be taken in two different ways. Ostriches are known for burying their heads in sand when confronted with danger. This line could suggest that the river, which is perhaps aware that the River Mumma, its protector, wants to leave, is attempting to hide its head in the sand. The statement could also mean that the waters are drying up. Whichever interpretation is made, the river is in trouble. The next line emphasizes this trouble. "Is that not obvious? the nurse souls ask." The nurse souls might be secondary protectors who are aware of the dangerous changes taking place. They are, perhaps, unable to reverse these changes without the River Mumma; they may not have any power if the River Mumma is not involved. But the nurse souls are not hiding their heads in the sand. They are fully aware and appear to be surprised that others are not equally conscious of what is happening: "You can't take a hint? You can't read a sign?" they ask.

Stanza 3

The remainder of the poem enumerates the specific things that the River Mumma wants to do rather than oversee her responsibilities. The first line of stanza 3 reads, "Mumma no longer wants to be guardian / of our waters." From the third stanza on, in fact, the narrator seems to be belittling her own culture, perhaps as a means of criticizing the culture of the world at large. She points out the commercial aspects of society and the people's needs to feed their egos. The River Mumma now "wants to be Big Mumma, / dancehall queen of the greater Caribbean." Thus, she is no longer satisfied living in her hidden places in the mountains. She wants to be noticed, glorified, and popular. She wants to go out and be entertained.

Stanza 4

In the fourth stanza, the reader is told that the River Mumma's cravings go deeper than mere entertainment and ego gratification, as she has also lost her sense of the sacred: "She no longer wants to dispense clean water / to baptize and cleanse (at least not gratis)." That is, she does not care about the health of the water and is no longer concerned with the spiritual practice of cleansing, unless she is being paid to do so. She has lost her desire to do good, to encourage and to nurture her community. She is looking out only for herself. She has retreated from lofty ideals and, like much of the culture around her, now requires some kind of material reward for services rendered. She does not even care that her lack of concern and her shirking of her responsibilities not only damages her immediate surroundings but also spreads pollution many miles beyond her home.

Stanza 5

Whereas the River Mumma used to hide in the mountain waters, she now wants to be "exposed." She wants to be famous the world over; she wants to "go clubbing with P. Diddy," an African American rapper who epitomizes the wealth and celebrity that can be attained through the world of entertainment. She wants to "experience snow," which does not exist in her homeland. In other words, she wants what she does not have, and she is willing to sacrifice everything to get it.

Stanza 6

In the last stanza, the narrator continues listing the outlandish desires of the River Mumma. She persists in wanting to seek out the worst of the commercial environment, such as by visiting the biggest and fanciest of the world's shopping malls and "spending her strong dollars." The use of the word "strong" is worth noting here, as the narrator implies that strength in the commercial world takes precedence over strength in the noncommercial world. The River Mumma is convinced that strength can be obtained only through money, not through the spiritual or mythological. The stories of the past have either failed or bored her. She wants to take part in the new world, the world of money. As such, she will pay no heed to anyone seeking her wisdom or protection—unless, of course, that person has money, which is what provides her with the "insurance" that she will remain strong.

Themes

Commercial World versus Spiritual World

The myths, or folklore, of a people are created to explain things they cannot rationally understand. According to the mythologist Joseph Campbell, spirituality is often centered on these myths. The River Mumma helped the people who believed in her to respect the water and the life that was born in the water. She may have offered these people a sense of security, as they could believe that she would always keep their water flowing and clean. To show their respect, people would bring gifts of food, music, and dance to the River Mumma. Stories about her were told to each succeeding generation, so that children would maintain the practices of respect. As Goodison's poem suggests, however, the culture is changing for the worse.

As presented in the poem, diminishing respect for spirituality is being punctuated by the rise in commercialism. The sense of the spiritual has been corrupted by the commercial world, which emphasizes the immediate gratification of physical needs. The commercial world encourages the acquiring of wealth, often at the expense of nature and with indifference toward the spiritual. In this sense, the spiritual does not refer to the dogma of religion but rather to the idea of the spirits of the culture and of the earth. Under the influence of commercialism, as Goodison asserts through her poem, people ignore the fact that waters are being polluted. The focus is on profits and material goods. As explained by the poem's narrator, the River Mumma "no longer wants to be guardian / of our waters"; rather, she wants to be "Big Mumma." She no longer wants to "baptize and cleanse"; rather, she wants to "go on tour" and to make and spend her "strong dollars." Money is at the heart of everything that the River Mumma now wants to do. She is completely preoccupied with what money can do for her and will pay no attention to anyone who comes to her with nothing but hope and prayers. In stressing the battle between commercialism and spirituality, the narrator sends a warning to her readers, hoping that they might thus see the signs of moral corruption and perhaps hoping that they will help reverse the trend.

Change

"Everything here is changing," the poem's narrator announces in the opening line, and the changes are not toward the good. Indeed, although change is inevitable, the poem asserts that things are changing too fast and in negative ways. Readers can surmise that the changes referred to are happening in Jamaica, where heavy deforestation and water and air pollution are turning what is seen by tourists as a tropical paradise into a potentially devastated piece of real estate. In fact, while tourism fuels Jamaica's economy, the costs of dependence on tourism are

Topics For Further Study

- Research the folklore of the Caribbean. What are some of the stories' main characters? Do similar characters exist in African folklore? Native American folklore? In what ways are the characters alike? Write a paper describing the various characters, the roles that they play, and the lessons that they teach. Were you told similar stories as a child? Discuss some of your personal experiences regarding folklore.

- Find examples of Goodison's artwork (such as on the covers of her poetry collections). Present copies of this artwork to your class, discussing the type of art it represents. Also, compare Goodison's work to that of other artists and discuss whether her work is typical of Jamaican artists.

- Find statistics concerning Jamaica's economic and environmental status. Compare details, such as the cost of housing and the cost of food, to the same costs in your local economy. Specifically, find details regarding literacy, per capita income, death and birth rates, inflation, pollution, deforestation, and the effects of tourism on the general population. In other words, provide an in-depth report on the island, as if you were an investigative reporter or as if your family were planning on living there. Present the report to your class.

- Pretend to be Goodison and paint a picture, in Goodison's style, of what you think the River Mumma would look like. You can use her natural setting by a river as a background or imagine what she would look like, say, as a "dancehall queen."

---

high. The poem suggests that lives that used to be simple, as based on ancient traditions, are being fractured. Tourism brings commercialism to the island, and rather than being satisfied with living off the land, people come to want the glitzy life that they see displayed before them in fancy hotels. Certainly, catering to wealthy people eventually wears on the minds of the local people. Like the River Mumma, they begin to dream about being stars. They become infected by the power of money and want to center their lives on it. Change is also seen in the people's loss of love for their homeland. The people, like the River Mumma, want to move away and forget about responsibilities to the land and to the beliefs of their ancestors. All creatures, including the bullrushes, want to be transformed into something that they are not—something that they perceive as bigger and better than who they are. Change in and of itself is not bad, but as presented in this poem, when people stick their heads in the sand and fail to see the devastation around them, change is indeed bad.

Egocentricity

Another theme expressed in "River Mumma" concerns egocentricity, or thinking of oneself over others. Self-gratification in order to feed the ego is represented in many forms, from the bullrushes wanting to be palm trees to the River Mumma wanting to be a "dancehall queen." In all of the newly developed desires of the River Mumma, the self is emphasized over others. Whereas she used to watch over the waters, she is no longer satisfied with staying in one location high in the mountains, rarely seen by anyone and rarely seeing anything but fish, water, and bullrushes. She has tired of thinking of others, finding little excitement for herself. She may have lost interest in her environment because the people around her have lost interest in her. Regardless of her reasons, the River Mumma's ego has become far more important than even the health of her surroundings. Unlike the river, which is hiding its head in the sand, she wants to do something for herself. She wants to be like everyone else, seeking celebrity at any cost. This state of affairs, one can surmise from the poem, could easily prove to be the downfall of the people on the island.

Lack of Compassion and Responsibility

Compassion and responsibility for the land, the people, and the culture, which were once foremost in the River Mumma's role, have been discarded, according to Goodison's poem. In seeking the material pleasures of life, the River Mumma has forsaken her environment. She "no longer wants to be guardian / of our waters," having grown tired of that role. She no longer has compassion for the people who come to her to be cleansed, either physically or spiritually. Life cannot exist without water, but she no longer cares. She wants to live for the moment and cast off her role of responsibility. "She does not give a damn about polluted / Kingston Harbour" (Kingston is the capital of Jamaica). Her people, her water, and her water creatures will have to survive without her, unless, of course, they can supply her with the pleasures she now seeks. In accentuating this theme, Goodison exposes the concept at the heart of all the commercialism and egocentricity. When one is responsible and compassionate, one will take care of one's neighbors and the environment and will think beyond the immediate moment.

Style

Fantastic Metaphor

"The River Mumma Wants Out" employs metaphors that can be considered fantastic in that they do not present plausible situations. At some points, the fantasy is mildly comedic, as with the bullrushes wanting to be palm trees. The metaphor wherein the "river is ostriching into the sand" presents an image that is essentially impossible to imagine. However, if the poet merely stated that the water was disappearing into the sand, the meaning conveyed would be only that the river is drying up. Thus, by using the fantastic metaphor, a more complex image is provided. A sentiment of fear is attributed to the river and so also to nature, as when an ostrich inserts its head in the sand because it is afraid.

The main metaphor of this poem is that of the River Mumma. As a mythical character, the River Mumma herself can be seen as a metaphor for the spiritual essence of Jamaica. She is half human and half fish, of course, which would make her wanting to do the many things presented in the poem absurd outside the context of a fantastic metaphor. Thus, the River Mumma's desires reflect the waning spirituality of the nation's citizens, perhaps especially the youth, who would be most enamored of the idea of being "dancehall queens" and so forth. In attributing the desires of her nation's citizens to such a revered legendary character, the tragedy of the situation is made clear.

Present Tense and Questions

In using the present tense in her poem, Goodison makes the situation feel immediate. In being told that "everything here is changing," the reader feels the impact of the assertion more acutely because he or she is not being told about something that happened in the past or will happen in the future. Indeed, all that the narrator relates seems to be happening as the poem is being read. In the beginning, she asks, "You can't hear?" By including questions in the present tense, Goodison heightens the intensity of the poem further. Indeed, the narrator both addresses and challenges the reader. "You can't take a hint? You can't read a sign?" she asks, thus questioning the reader's intelligence, insightfulness, credibility, and awareness. This makes the reader want to open his or her senses up more fully to what is happening both in the poem and in the real world. The questions end with the second stanza; Goodison perhaps felt that by this point she had engaged the reader's attention, allowing her thenceforth to share everything she wanted the reader to hear.

Enjambment

Enjambment is the continuation of a clause beyond the end of a line. In "River Mumma," Goodison uses enjambment in several different places. The second and third lines of the first stanza read, "The bullrushes on the river banks now want / to be palms in the Kings's garden." In this example, the poet thus emphasizes the word "want," making the reader wait until the beginning of the third line to discover the object of this wanting. Further into the poem, Goodison uses enjambment somewhat more dramatically: at the end of the fourth stanza, she leaves the sentence open until the beginning of the fifth stanza. "She does not give a damn about polluted," reads the fourth stanza's last line, and only after the stanza break are the words "Kingston Harbour" added to close the sentence. Nowhere else in the poem is a specific place mentioned. A general reference is made to the Caribbean, as the River Mumma wants to be the "dancehall queen of the greater Caribbean," but readers do not know, at this point, from where the River Mumma comes. Once the poet mentions Kingston Harbour, however, the poem is rooted in Jamaica. Through enjambment, here, Goodison gives Kingston Harbour special emphasis.

Historical Context

Jamaican History

Jamaica, a small, mountainous, tropical island slightly smaller than Connecticut, is located south of Cuba in the main shipping lane leading to the Panama Canal. Because of its warm, humid weather and beautiful landscape and seascape, Jamaica is a popular tourist destination. Owing to its strategic location between South America and North America, on the other hand, it is a popular transit station for drug dealers. Both of these elements, in modern times, have contributed to economic growth as well as to an increased crime rate. Jamaica is often advertised as a tropical paradise, but its history is strewn with hardship and violence.

The native Arawak were settled in what is now Jamaica around the year 700, many centuries before Christopher Columbus landed there. The Arawaks, a peaceful people, were all but wiped out by the end of the sixteenth century, owing to pressures caused by the invasion of Spanish settlers. Many were forced into labor, and among those who survived this harsh reality, many more succumbed to the diseases brought by the Europeans.

The Spanish also brought African slaves to the island to work their cattle and pig farms and to raise huge crops of sugarcane. In 1654, the British invaded the poorly protected Spanish settlements and took control of the island. Before slavery was finally abolished in 1834, Jamaica was the scene of waves of bloody rebellions, as slaves occasionally organized themselves into bands that razed plantations and murdered whites. The Europeans, in turn, captured or otherwise tricked the slaves into putting down their arms; they then hung their captives or whipped them into submission. The abolition of slavery did not end the harsh conditions suffered by black people. Wage labor often relegated former slaves to deep poverty, as the wages offered were not enough to account for food and shelter. Jamaica gained independence in 1962, but this change did not end the Jamaicans' struggle against poverty.

Jamaica is ruled by a constitutional parliamentary democracy, with the British monarch acting as chief of state. Percival James Patterson became the island's first black prime minister in 1992. While the government has grown stable in modern times, the economy has not. Jamaica's financial stability is dependent on tourism, which has suffered from domestic problems, such as the rising crime rate and damage caused by hurricanes, as well as international problems, such as terrorism.

The sluggish economy has exacerbated social problems, as almost 20 percent of the people live below the poverty line and 15 percent are unemployed. Drug trafficking is prevalent, as cocaine dealers launder their money in Jamaica and also use the nation as a point of transshipment between South and North America and Europe. Indeed, these factors have all marred the tourism industry and caused domestic instability. Added to this is the pollution of coastal waters by industrial waste and sewage; heavy deforestation; damage to the natural coral reefs surrounding the island; and air pollution in the capital, Kingston. Despite these conditions, according to a 2005 report by the Central Intelligence Agency, Jamaica's economy was projected to rebound by virtue of rises in tourism.

Jamaican Folklore

Jamaican folklore, including stories that have been handed down from generation to generation through an oral tradition, involves several major characters. The River Mumma, invoked in Goodison's poem, is a dominant figure who inspires both fear and awe. The River Mumma was at one time honored with offerings of food and rituals performed at the river's edge in her name. She helped in teaching reverence for the earth. The River Mumma can also be treacherous; according to local beliefs, she does not like to be seen, and if she catches anyone looking at her, that person can expect to be cursed.

People tell stories such as those about the River Mumma to maintain a sense of history and to pass lessons from one generation to the next. Many of the stories in Jamaican folklore were recounted by slaves in attempts to keep African traditions alive. The character Anansi, or Anansy, is a trickster who originated in storytelling in West Africa, especially among the Ashanti people in Ghana. Anansi is a rebel capable of outwitting his suppressors, a theme that was used in Jamaica to empower slaves. Anansi stories encouraged the concept that freedom was worth fighting for.

P. Diddy

Goodison mentions P. Diddy in her poem as a figure of celebrity. Indeed, P. Diddy may well represent the epitome of success and glamour, with respect to both excesses and failures. Born Sean John Combs in Harlem in 1969, he used the names Diddy, Puff Daddy, and Puffy during his rise to fame. He began his career as an intern at Uptown Records and soon afterward founded his own recording label, Bad Boy. In 1993, Combs made his first recording, rapping with the Notorious

Kingston Harbour, Jamaica © Hulton-Deutsch Collection/Corbis

B.I.G., also known as Christopher Wallace, and using the name Puff Daddy. After a series of run-ins with the law and a breakup with the performer Jennifer Lopez, Combs changed his name to P. Diddy. He later created a reality television show called *Making the Band*, started a line of men's clothing, and ran in the New York City Marathon to raise money for the education of New York children. He was once listed in *Fortune* magazine as one of the forty richest men under forty years.

Critical Overview

"The River Mumma Wants Out" was published in Goodison's collection *Controlling the Silver* in 2005. In a review of this collection in the Caribbean arts journal *Calabash*, Michela A. Calderaro notes that previous collections placed Goodison in high standing among Caribbean poets. With *Controlling the Silver*, Goodison takes her readers "on a longer and more complex passage out of the islands and across the wide seas (and back)." Calderaro asserts that the poet's use of language ranks among "the richest and most impressive" of a "number of contemporary Caribbean writers." At the end of the review, Calderaro remarks on *Controlling the Silver*, "If we were to say that it is the finest Caribbean poetry book we've read this year, we'd be limiting its importance. It is, quite clearly, one of the finest books in contemporary world literature, a rich and satisfying feast for the mind."

In a review in the *Weekly Gleaner*, a Jamaican newspaper, Tanya Batson-Savage considers Goodison's art as a poet, as exemplified by this collection: "Goodison's pen slips between the folk and the modern with enviable ease, making space for its own language." Jim Hannan, critiquing an earlier collection of Goodison's poetry in *World Literature Today*, states that her "spiritualism, rendered consistently in strongly earthy images that pay homage to the colors, sights, sounds, and textures of her native Jamaica, frequently predominates, although her political and social consciousness can always be discerned." Hannan adds, "Goodison distills joy and anger through compassion and justice, and through a lyrical intelligence finely observant, rigorous, spiritual, and sensuous." She "avoids fashionable convention," Hannan writes, "and creates a body of work whose clear, uncomplicated free verse, infrequent rhymes, and tactile, precise diction and rhythms perfectly match her vision, her voice, and her sense of vocation." In a review for *Booklist*, Patricia Monaghan describes Goodison's verse as possessing "ripe sensuousness," leading Monaghan to wish that Goodison wrote more often. Monaghan then adds, however, that if Goodison did publish more often, "her delicacy and immense aural power would probably dissipate."

Criticism

Joyce Hart

Hart is a published writer and former teacher. In this essay, she looks beneath the surface of the characters addressed in Goodison's poem to discover implications regarding more complex layers of meaning.

Goodison's poem "The River Mumma Wants Out" mentions three main types of characters. First is the generic "you," as addressed by the narrator; second is the River Mumma, a figure from Jamaican folklore; and third are the nurse souls. Who are these characters, essentially? Who might they represent? Does each represent more than one being? These questions may never be answered exactly as the poet had intended, other than by Goodison herself, but in taking the liberty to explore possibilities, readers might find the poem more enriching.

The River Mumma, with whom most of the poem is concerned, is known to come from stories handed down through the ages to try to explain the unexplainable. Such stories can also help give people a sense of security, which the River Mumma indeed offers in certain ways. She is seen as a guardian of the waters, someone who maintains the health of the rivers, which are the source of the benefits of spiritual and physical cleansing. With her half-fish, half-human body, she is able to live in both worlds—water and earth, or spiritual and physical—taking care of humans and land animals as well as the creatures of her rivers. Yet something dreadful is happening to the River Mumma; after long centuries of watching over the waters, she now "wants out." What could this state of affairs represent?

Indeed, if the story of the River Mumma began as a myth to explain phenomena of the natural world, what might Goodison's revision of the story signify? If the River Mumma represents the guardian of the natural world, particularly the watery environments, the source of life and spiritual cleansing, what would her "wanting out" imply? In essence, who is the River Mumma in this new interpretation? The first image that comes to mind is decay.

The reader can imagine that the River Mumma would suffer physically if she were to follow her dream of touring the world, "clubbing" and dancing all night long. Since the River Mumma is half fish, her body needs water. Thus, in trying to follow the ways of one who is fully human, she would meet her own destruction. In addition, if Kingston Harbour has already become polluted under her watch, what would happen if she were to move away? The result could only be more decay.

Since a myth is not a fact but rather a story used to explain something, readers know that the River Mumma is not real. But the message that a myth attempts to tell *is* real. The original story of the River Mumma might have been told so that people would respect the natural resources around them. The new story has a similar foundation but is instead told as a warning. In Goodison's poem, the River Mumma could represent the conscience of the people, or perhaps their emotions. The River Mumma wants something, Goodison announces in the poem's title, and wants are the direct result of emotions. Goodison might be saying that no one is paying attention to the environment; no one cares about what is happening in the surrounding world. Where is your conscience? she might be asking in the narrator's direct address. Why do you not notice these things? Are you so busy thinking about dancing and hanging out at the malls that you cannot see that the environment around you is dying? If Goodison could stir the people's conscience with her poem, maybe the River Mumma would no longer want out. She would be content where she is, where she belongs. Indeed, perhaps her "wants" would be turned around. Instead of wanting superfluous objects, like those she would find in a glitzy mall, she might want to help clean and therefore save the environment—and likewise, so might readers.

If the reference to the River Mumma is meant to stand as an emotional appeal, then the "you" addressed by the narrator of the poem could be precisely who it seems to be: the reader. Indeed, through this direct address, the narrator pulls any and all readers into her poem. Some of those readers would be the people of Jamaica, certainly, since the environment of that island nation is mentioned in the poem. But Jamaica is not the only place with an environment that is hurting or decaying. Although other countries may not have stories about the River Mumma, they do appear to be sticking their heads in the sand in ignorance, an act mentioned in this poem. Perhaps Goodison believes or hopes that the poem will pull their heads out. "You can't hear?" the narrator asks of everyone who is not paying attention to environmental damage. "You can't take a hint? You can't read a sign?" In directing these questions to the "you" of the poem, the narrator is appealing to the intellect, as if she is trying to shake the sand out of people's eyes and ears. Do you not see what is happening around you? she asks. Be aware of your environment. Do not let your emotions, or your desires for a life of self-gratification, blind you to the consequences of those runaway desires for more and more things. Fun has its place, but in wanting too much or in desiring only to feed the ego, you might be sacrificing more than you can afford. You can live without the glitz. You cannot live without clean water. These are the appeals the narrator is making. In case the more emotional plea made through the figure of the River Mumma proves ineffective, Goodison tries to awaken the reader's intellect. Let me tell you what the River Mumma is doing, the narrator avers. Let me help you to see the danger involved in her frivolity.

So the emotional and the rational pleas have been made. Thus, what is left for the narrator to do? In fact, she might appeal to the spirit or to the soul, which is exactly what she does. The "nurse souls" are brought forth in the second stanza, appearing quite suddenly, without introduction or explanation. They are the voices behind the questions that are asked. As such, they are the ones who are trying to awaken the readers of the poem. They are the ones making a last desperate attempt to turn things around. Without a doubt, the situation is rapidly changing for the worse. If you do not feel it and do not see or understand it, then please just trust us, the nurse souls seem to be saying. "Everything here is changing," the reader is told in the first line, and the nurse souls ask, "Is that not obvious?"

Apparently, nothing is obvious to those who do not care to see or hear. Things have to be pointed out. The emotional and rational elements may be too close to the surface, so the narrator digs down deeper, to the soul. If anywhere, in this spiritual realm, everyone is connected; everyone is made of the same thing. All living creatures are united. As such, the spirit of the water is connected to the spirit of the trees, and the spirit of the trees is connected to the spirit of all human beings. All those wants and desires, all those ego concerns, and even all those rational notions are mere infants in relationship to the longevity and significance of the ancient soul. If hope can be found with respect to turning

> *In appealing to her readers on the three different levels of emotion, intellect, and spirit, Goodison succeeds in driving her point home. In fact, she may drill her message deep inside some readers without their even realizing it."*

negative environmental changes into positives, it will be discovered through appeals to the soul. Possibly in an attempt to emphasize this idea, Goodison refers to spirits as nurse souls. Nurses are helpers and healers. Doctors may diagnose, operate, and prescribe pills, but the nurses are the ones who watch over patients until health is restored. The nurse souls may be acting in this way. They may be attempting to bring health back to the souls of the earth, the water, and the people who are ailing. The nurse souls are the ones who are shouting, Wake up! Look around you! See what is happening before it is too late!

And so, in a simple voice that appears to be telling a simple story about an icon that wishes to go astray, the poet makes a strong appeal to her readers. The elements of the poem seem straightforward at first. It appears to be a whimsical little poem about a character from a story, as told on a small tropical island in the Caribbean. It has nothing to do with me, readers might imagine at first. But the poem haunts them, maybe without their knowing how. Indeed, the poem turns out to be more complex than they might have thought at first, and the poet may be a lot more clever. In appealing to her readers on the three different levels of emotion, intellect, and spirit, Goodison succeeds in driving her point home. In fact, she may drill her message deep inside some readers without their even realizing it.

Source: Joyce Hart, Critical Essay on "The River Mumma Wants Out," in *Poetry for Students*, Thomson Gale, 2007.

What Do I Read Next?

- Donna Hemans's *River Woman* (2002) tells a story about a young mother who waits at the riverside for her own mother to return to her as promised. She does not notice that her own child has wandered into the water until it is too late, and she then has to face some of her worst fears as the women in her village accuse her of drowning her child on purpose.

- *From Behind the Counter: Poems from a Rural Jamaican Experience* (1999) offers readers another view of life in traditional Jamaica. The poet is Easton Lee, a man who grew up holding a pivotal position in his small village: he was the clerk of his father's grocery shop. Lee has a mixed ethnic background, with substantial Chinese ancestry.

- Kwame Dawes edited a collection of interviews with Caribbean poets, including Goodison, called *Talk Yuh Talk: Interviews with Anglophone Caribbean Poets*, published in 2000. Poetry is also included in this collection, covering a wide range of topics and styles, with multiple generations of writers represented. Some of the poems are highly influenced by Caribbean music, while others follow the more classical form of English poetry. The interviews reveal the major themes of the poets' writings.

- One of Goodison's more popular collections is *To Us, All Flowers Are Roses* (1995). In this collection, her sixth, Goodison focuses on the culture and the people of Jamaica. One prominent theme is a plea for the revision of history, to be told anew by the poor people, who could thus relate their struggles for survival and freedom.

- For an overview of Caribbean poetry, *An Introduction to West Indian Poetry* (1998) is a good place to start. This collection features verse written in English by Caribbean poets from the 1920s through the 1980s. The poetry explores the effects of both colonization and decolonization on the region's people and culture.

- In the first half of her 1999 collection *Turn Thanks*, Goodison explores familiar territory, writing about her family. In the second half, she offers a view of her life in North America.

Hugh Hodges

In the following essay excerpt, Hodges notes Goodison's inclination to write poetry of incantation, verbal rituals meant to "cleanse, heal, and strengthen."

Lorna Goodison came to poetic maturity during a period when political violence threatened to destroy Jamaica. At that time, in the early 1980s, she wrote bitterly of "tourist-dream edenism":

> For over all this edenism
> hangs the smell of necromancy
> and each man eats his brother's flesh
> Lord, so much of the cannibal left
> in the jungle on my people's tongues.
>
> We've sacrificed babies
> and burnt our mothers
> as payment to some viridian-eyed God dread
> who works in cocaine under hungry men's heads.

> And mine the task of writing it down
> as I ride in shame round this blood-stained town.
>   ("Jamaica 1980")

Frank Birbalsingh told her, "You are not providing solutions to [the] suffering by writing poetry." She replied, "No, but I feel that where I can talk about it, I should. I think that after 1980, we should have some public grieving, some ceremony, or monument to the fact that over 800 people died. We never really did." *I am Becoming My Mother* and the books that followed became, in a sense, a search for appropriate ceremonies to commemorate not only those who died without monument in 1980, but also those who died in slave ships and barracoons, those who endured and died fighting slavery, oppression, and poverty. Her poems became or sought out rituals to restore hope—Edward Baugh calls them "Rituals of Redemption"—rituals to give glimpses of the true "start-over Eden" that is obscured by tourist-dreams and political necromancy (Goodison, "Never Expect").

These are small rituals. Birbalsingh is right: they are not solutions. But they put something in the universe using the one tool that neither the slaver, nor the politician, nor the International Monetary Fund can steal entirely: the human voice. It may be a soft voice—as Goodison says, Rosa Parks's was a soft voice too ("For Rosa Parks")—but it is the voice of someone traveling, out of Babylon, back to herself.

In her search for rituals—and for the correct ritual language—Goodison draws on the wealth of Jamaica's oral tradition, on mentos, ring tunes, revival hymns, and work songs, on proverbs and Anancy stories, and on the Jamaican traditions of street preaching and prophecy. Her poetry reflects a deep belief in the power of language. "The Living Converter Woman of Green Island," from her recent collection *Travelling Mercies,* speaks of songs that "[s]ound myrhh notes to quell / putrefaction's smell," the putrefaction being both the uneatable contents of the unconverted intestines the singer is turning inside out to clean and the equally indigestible contents of history. In effect, the converter woman's song relies on a kind of sympathetic magic to "[c]leanse the charnel house / of the bloodbath Atlantic." An analogy between tripe and "coiled and sectioned" history becomes an opportunity to work healing on history as the converter woman reads animal intestines as a leaved book

> recording abominable drama in ship's maw
> tragedy of captured and capturer
>
> scenes that [seem] to be calling
> for overdue acts of conversion.

The conversion here is both conversion of the uneatable contents of history into nourishment and conversion of the listener into a believer, and both are converted by song, by words that "bring in / as yet unknown revelation." Goodison's belief in the power of words is rooted in the belief that all things are mystically connected. All things are in all things, so healing in a song puts healing into the world, and the peace within a poem may "stay the devils in our heads" ("Trident"). One of the ways Goodison articulates this sense of unity is through the Rastafarian identification of the Bible as the nexus of history, the point at which past, present, and future meet. "Lush," also from *Travelling Mercies,* speaks of the poet's childhood Jamaica as a "slightly cultivated" garden of Eden, where "Cain and Abel / lived in the village":

> When Abel was slaughtered
> Miss Jamaica paraded the head on a sceptre

> *"In her search for rituals—and for the correct ritual language—Goodison draws on the wealth of Jamaica's oral tradition, on mentos, ring tunes, revival hymns, and work songs, on proverbs and Anancy stories, and on the Jamaican traditions of street preaching and prophecy."*

> as she rode in her win-at-all costs motorcade.
> From his blood sprung a sharp reproach bush
> which drops karma fruit upon sleeping policemen
> to remind them of their grease-palm sins of
> omission.   ("Lush")

Here the mapping of the present onto the biblical past gives life its lushness: its meaningfulness and its capacity for miracles to counterbalance day-to-day brutality. But Goodison's mapping of the present onto the past is not always biblical, and does not generally share Rasta's heavy emphasis on the apocalypse. Partly this is because, as "Jamaica 1980" suggests, Goodison distrusts its promise; Jamaica's modern history is a litany of failed or betrayed revolutions (and revelations). And partly it is because Goodison knows that, with one's eyes firmly fixed on the very end of suffering, one risks missing momentary joy. In some of *Travelling Mercies'* poems, the kaleidoscopic effect of past and present meeting captures a fleeting blissfulness:

> Gypsy man wanders, son of Camargue horse breeders
> tinkers at broken down motor cars, makes them run
> like fiery chariot-wagons over shifting horizon.
>   ("Romany Song")

Without forgetting the hard history of the Romany, "Romany Song" is a celebration of life "that will not settle / into being contained." In part this celebration reflects the fact that Goddison's mysticism, or at least its articulation, has been informed by Sufism. The uncontained experience comes first.

Goodison once said, "What happens to me very often is that I experience these things, or I write them. Then afterwards, I will find a source that will explain them to me" (Birbalsingh 153–54). In Sufism Goodison has found explanations for both her instinctive sense that there is unity in multiplicity and her sense that metaphor and analogy perform a kind of magic. However, the deep source of both instincts is the Jamaica that Goodison grew up with, and grew up within. Sufism has simply been one of the ways she has found of reconnecting with that source.

The purpose of making that connection is always, for Goodison, to heal, and her poetry often becomes the literary equivalent of the Kumina Queen's balm yard. It is a place where herbal remedies are dispensed, prayers offered, and hymns sung; a place of baptism, cleansing, and possession. Very often, even when it is not consciously working from within the balm yard, Goodison's poetry speaks from a place where ritual magic shapes the world. "Turn Thanks to Grandmother Hannah," for example, celebrates the sanctifying vocation of "laundering / the used, soiled vestments of the clergy / into immaculate and unearthly brightness":

> To my grandmother with the cleansing power
> in her hands, my intention here is to give thanks
> on behalf of any who have experienced within
> something like the redemption in her washing.

The discovery of the universal in the most humble domestic activities, indeed uncovering the world-changing potential in any ritual act if it is "correctly and effectively done" ("Angel of Dreamers"), is a recurring theme in Goodison's poetry. Baugh gives an excellent reading of one such domestic ritual in Goodison's "The Domestic Science of Sunday Dinner," in which, he argues, "the articulation of a recipe becomes the enactment of a ritual that subsumes the rituals of love and death" ("Goodison's Rituals" 28). One can also see this kind of metamorphosis in Goodison's poems about painting. A painter herself, Goodison sees in the act of painting a ritual that puts something into the universe. In "Cezanne after Emile Zola," she describes how the artist "painted Mont Saint-Victoire / over and over until [he] drew and coloured / a hard mountain range for a heart." In "Keith Jarrett—Rainmaker" "a painting becomes a / december of sorrel." And in "The Rose Conflagration," the power of the ritual or painting combines with the power of ritually spoken words, to create a sort of Pentecost:

> Last night that gift of roses
> just combusted into flames
> after I shut the blue door
> and recited your names.

> If those without ever imagined
> that the artist of Murray Mountain
> had painted a hill landscape
> that caused a conflagration,
> The inflaming of a rose fire
> in this small rented space [. . .]

This emphasis on ritual has led some commentators to see in Goodison's poetry, particularly her poetry of the late 1980s and early 1990s, a struggle to "subdue the body to the mind" (Webhofer 50). Gudrun Webhofer suggests that "Goodison sometimes sees her role as poet/priestess/healer as conflicting with her libidinal instincts" (51). And Denise deCaires Narain sees Goodison choosing increasingly "not to speak of the body and to articulate a poetic identity which transcends [. . .] particular pain in the projection of a disembodied poetic voice." She adds, "This shift away from the body can be traced in the changing focus of her [first] three collections of poetry [. . .] a shift from a more reproductive/woman-centred delivery of the word to a more asexual/spiritual notion of deliverance via the word" ("Delivering the Word" 432).

There is much to be said for Narain's argument, especially as she has refined it in her more recent criticism. In *Contemporary Caribbean Women's Poetry: Making Style,* Narain suggests that in *Heartease,* the move away from an embodied woman-centered voice reflects the development of "[a] poetic identity [. . .] which is so strongly allied to 'the people' that the individuated poetic voice merges with the collective, so that she becomes the body politic" (161). Narain also argues that Goodison's more recent collections (*To Us All Flowers Are Roses* and *Turn Thanks*) reflect a return to a voice both clearly individuated and embodied (162–63). The trajectory Narain gives Goodison's poetry—from public to increasingly private rituals and from speaking as the people to speaking "about and on behalf of the people" (163)—is, I think, quite right. But I would temper the sense that Narain and Webhofer share, that in *Heartease* Goodison's choice to speak "for and as 'the people'" obliges her to jettison "her embodied woman's self" (162). I also think the reconnection with the body that Narain observes in *Turn Thanks* is not quite such a change in direction as it might seem.

The examples Narain uses to examine Goodison's rejection of an embodied, sexual self are the "Wild Woman" poems in *Heartease.* She argues that they "point to a contradictory pull in Goodison's work between the private and the public; between the 'private' world of female sexuality and her 'public' role as Healer/poet" (436). But it seems to me that Goodison's rejection of the wild woman is not really a rejection of sexuality. The problem with the wild woman is not her sexuality, but her tendency to "succumb to false promise / in the yes of slim dark men" ("Farewell Wild Woman ([I]"). She lacks judgment, lacks the insight that is required if one is to perform life's affirming rituals correctly and effectively. She is chaotic. And she represents a particular kind of creativity that has become less important to Goodison since she started to become her mother and began traveling towards her creative source. The wild woman is a romantic creation, the artist as tortured, convention-defying outcast. Grand-daughter of Baudelaire, she is a Western creation. Goodison has sympathy for her, keeps a room for her. Indeed, Goodison deeply empathizes with all such artists—she has written poems for Don Drummond and Vincent Van Gogh among others—modern Prometheuses destroyed by an egoistic creativity they could not control. Goodison's wild woman risks such self-destruction every time she makes poems of her "worst wounds" ("Some of My Worst Wounds"), every time she admits the King of Swords "who beckons to you with one hand, while he keeps his other hand hidden" (Birbalsingh 158–59). But in *Heartease,* Goodison wrote a "Ceremony for the Banishment of the King of Swords." And as she has become increasingly interested in ritual creativity, the wild woman's tendency to act egoistically, precipitously, and self-destructively has become, if not a liability, then at least an unwanted distraction.

It is important to recognize, however, that Goodison's new focus in *Heartease* and *To Us All Flowers Are Roses* is no less "woman-centred" for that. That is, the identification of a "shift from a more reproductive / woman-centred delivery of the word to a more asexual / spiritual notion of deliverance via the word" risks a rather reductionist understanding of womanhood, especially in the Jamaican context. Goodison has, as Narain observes, begun to explore the role of priestess and healer, but this exploration does not imply a rejection of womanhood, because the Jamaican concept of womanhood comprises, among other things, the role of priestess and healer. With this in mind, it is worth remarking how body-centered, and specifically female-body centered, many spiritual healing rituals are. In-filling in Pentecostalism, possession in Revivalism and Pocomania—they are all intensely physical (and predominantly female) experiences.

They are all also experiences that require a temporary suspension of the ego to allow the Holy Spirit, the Saints, or the ancestors to enter and speak through the body of the celebrant. The prayer-like opening poems of *Heartease* reference these rituals in a number of ways. "Because I Have Been Everything" announces "My heart life is open, transparency / my soul's life in otherworlds" (8); "My Father Always Promised Me" speaks of the receptive being as "wired for sound," "[of] all worlds and a healer / source of mystery"; and "A Forgiveness" draws on the language of the Pentecostal eudemonic, witnessing:

> All changing [. . .]
> is light from within
> . . .
> and that light will draw
> more light to itself
> and that will be light
> enough for a start
> to a new life and a self
> forgiven heart

The rite being prepared for in these poems bears fruit in "Song of Release." Having temporarily given up control of her self, the poet becomes oracle:

> I stand with palms open, salute the sun
> the old ways over. I newborn one.
> . . .
> You sent a message written in
> amharic on the horizon
> I had to read quickly as the sky
> was impatient to be going
> even reading from this distance
> with just opening eyes
> was enough for me, the message
> spelt "free."

Being open to the promptings (and demands) of the spiritual world does not bring about a jettisoning of the body. In fact it is centered in the body and manifests itself in the body sometimes quite painfully. To emphasize this, the poem that follows "Song of Release" likens the experience of being ridden by poetry to the pain of delivery. Sometimes the spirit world treats its messengers brutally, and the prophet says, "I don't want to live like this anymore." It is a sentiment echoed by the prophet Jeremiah in *To Us All Flowers Are Roses.* "Today," he says, "I will not prophesy," but admits:

> If I do not prophesy
> God contends with me,
>
> Turns up a high-marrow deep
> Flame, sealed fire then
> Shut up burning in my bones.

"I did not choose prophecy," he laments, "prophecy chose me." Jeremiah does not want to be the bearer of messages no one wants to hear; he wants to "marry, / Father children and feed them," but he is "used hard" by God. The problem Goodison wrestles with in *Heartease* and *To Us All Flowers Are Roses* is how to remain obedient to her poetic calling as "sojourner poet [. . .] / calling lost souls" without becoming a Jeremiah scorched by his vision. And she seems to have wrestled successfully ("Heartease New England 1985"). As Narain remarks, in recent years "[Goodison's] images of poetry—and the poetic 'calling'—are more often presented in confidently sensual terms, than as a painful wounding" (164). This is not because Goodison has found a way to reconnect with the body—she never really disconnected—but because she has found ways of "delivering the word" that are physically less traumatic than either the possession rites of *Heartease* or the wild woman antics of her earlier poetry. Her love poems, for example, have come increasingly to resemble hymns. Consider "Close to You Now" from the collection *Turn Thanks,* for example; even the title recalls a hymn, "Closer to You My Lord":

> I lie in my bed and cry out to you.
> I cover myself with a humming tune spread
> which says as it weaves itself
> you, you and only you.
> . . .
> I want to walk across this green island
>
> singing like the Guinea woman
> showers, showers of blessing
> until you cover my lips
> and I go silent and still
> and I will see your face
> and want then for nothing.

Given Goodison's engagement with Jamaica's oral traditions, this development should not be surprising—love songs have been an important part of Jamaican religious music since the Great Revival of the 1860s. Ira Sankey's *Gospel Hymns* (a volume so influential that, in Jamaica, hymns are still generically referred to as "sankeys") devotes more hymns to the idea of Jesus as loving and beloved than to any other theme (Sizer 39). What the metaphor of Jesus as lover gives sankeys is a fresh way to speak about salvation. Conversely, for Goodison, the ritualized language of hymn and prayer has become a way of speaking about what is true, upfull, and enlightening in human sexuality.

Significantly, the wild woman has recently begun to reappear in Goodison's poetry, not now as aimless wanton, but as exuberant Revivalist "summoning the freed soul / [. . .] to testify and pray / [t]o wear brimstone red . . . and to move seamlessly/up and down between the worlds of spirit and sense" ("Revival Song of the Wild Woman"). She has become a figure for many intersecting ways of being a Jamaican woman. Not just the "exuberant Revivalist," she is also "the wild heart, the crazy woman, the Accompong Nanny warrior" ("Bringing the Wild Woman Indoors"). But most of all she has become a figure for the capacity to endure or, to use a metaphor Goodison explores in "About the Tamarind," the capacity to bear. The tamarind tree becomes an emblem for Jamaican women because, as the tree says of itself,

> I bear. Not even the salt of the ocean can stunt me.
> Plant me on abiding rock or foaming restless waters.
> Set me in burying grounds, I grow shade for
> ancestors.
> . . .
> I am still here, still bearing after five hundred years.

"Bearing," of course, means both "enduring" and "reproducing," and the two senses of the word are connected. Furthermore, the ability of Jamaican culture to "flourish even in rocky terrain with little or no cultural attention" can be attributed to those who "bear" it. Nourisher, "dwelling place of the spirit of rain," healer, keeper of memory who has "not come to rule over, overpower, / vanquish, conquer or constrain anyone," the tamarind provides a powerful metaphor for the interconnectedness of woman's roles as bearer of children, bearer of culture, and source of strength and healing. Indeed, they are so intimately connected that the distinction between delivery and deliverance becomes almost meaningless. Every delivery—of a baby or a poem—is a sacred act that creates a local miracle, creates possibilities, gives a glimpse of the promise of deliverance. That is, what rituals do (the delivery of a baby is a particularly dramatic example, but they can take the most mundane domestic form) is perform in the same way that songs in Anancy stories perform. They initiate a trick; they announce a possibility that, in the face of all contradiction, becomes a miraculous reality.

Small rituals, but powerful. This was already the message of "For Rosa Parks" in *I Am Becoming My Mother*:

> And how was this soft-voiced woman to know
> that this 'No'
> in answer to the command to rise
> would signal the beginning
> of the time of walking?
> Soft the word
> like the closing of some aweful book—
> a too-long story
> with no pauses for reason
> but yes, an ending
> and the signal to begin the walking.
> . . .
> [saw] a man with no forty acres
> just a mule

riding towards Jerusalem
And the children small somnambulists
moving in the before day morning
And the woman who never raised her voice
never lowered her eyes
just kept walking
leading toward sunrise.

The use of biblical imagery here is rooted in Rastafarianism and Revivalism: the marches that characterized the black liberation movement are imagined as being both figuratively and literally the biblical exodus ("the time of walking"), and the biblical apocalypse ("the closing of some awful book"). And that exodus leads "the children" towards a sunrise that is not just Jerusalem, but also Africa. But the core of the poem comes from further back in Jamaican culture, from Anancy stories. Rosa Parks's "No" is a short but enormously powerful "sing," and it initiates a trick that topples Babylon: by not rising, Rosa Parks rises; by refusing to move, she begins walking. In the Melodians' Rastafarian hymn "Rivers of Babylon," it is Babylon's requirement that the captive children of Israel "sing King Alpha song / In a strange land" that becomes its downfall: the song becomes a chant for freedom. In "For Rosa Parks," Babylon's unwise "command to rise" has the same result. In both cases the oppressed embark on what Goodison, in another early poem, calls "the road of the Dread." There is no sudden deliverance on this road, no apocalypse, no Zion Train. What makes it tolerable is not the promise of the road's imminent end—the promise of apocalypse—but the small miracles on the way that assure one that there is an end no matter how distant:

> [W]hen yu meet another traveller
> who have flour and yu have water and man and man
> make bread together.
> And dem time dey the road run straight and sure
> like a young horse that cant tire
> And yu catch a glimpse of the end
> through the water in yu eye
> I won't tell yu what I spy
> but is fi dat alone I tread this road.
> ("The Road of the Dread")

These small victories against poverty and oppression become an increasingly important focus for Goodison. In "For Rosa Parks," she achieves this focus by framing the grand gesture, the mass marches, with images of the "soft-voiced woman" who began it all. In the end what the poem celebrates most is not the great exodus, but the small personal victory contained in the fact that Rosa Parks "never raised her voice / never lowered her eyes." Such small personal victories are the subject of many of Goodison's poems, particularly those in *To Us All Flowers Are Roses*." October in the Kingdom of the Poor," "Coir," "Nayga Bikkle," and "Bun Down Cross Roads" all celebrate largely symbolic victories over oppression that somehow suggest "a glimpse of the end." . . .

Eden is not the place to which we finally return; it is the place from which we are always beginning. It is the "new garden / of fresh start over" that Goodison gives thanks for in "From the Garden of Women Once Fallen." And for Goodison, it is in Jamaica.

So Jamaica is the land to which Jamaican people must literally and metaphorically return. Redemption means reclaiming Jamaica's history—both its history of pain and its history of healing. It is a process Goodison began for herself in *To Us All Flowers Are Roses*, trying to tell the stories of Jamaican people, "the half that has never been told" ("Mother, the Great Stones Got to Move"): the story of Bag-a-Wire, who betrayed Marcus Garvey, and of Papacita "who always favored a clean merino! over any shirt with collar and sleeves" ("Papacita"); of tenement dwellers who plant "paint pan gardens in the paved yards" ("In City Gardens"); of the sweet vendor Miss Gladys, "the queen of Ptomaine Palace / her flat fritters laying drowsy / with sleeping overnight oil ("Outside the Gates"); and of Anne Pengelly "maidservant, late of the San Fleming Estate" ("Annie Pengelly"), . . .

In "After the Green Gown of My Mother Gone Down," the poem that opens *Turn Thanks*, Goodison recalls the funeral of her mother:

> We laid her down, full of days,
> chant griot from the book of life,
> summon her kin from the longlived
> line of David and Margaret.
> Come Cleodine, Albertha,
> Flavius, Edmund, Howard and Rose,
> Marcus her husband gone before
> come and walk Dear Doris home.

This is the final chapter of life as a journey to meet the ancestors, a return to source. And this journey to the source of self is the final affirmation of the connectedness of all things, the completion of the cycle and entry into the start-over Eden:

> Mama, Aunt Ann says
> that she saw Aunt Rose
> come out of an orchard
> red with ripe fruit
> and called out laughing to you.
> And that you scaled the wall
> like two young girls
> scampering barefoot among
> the lush fruit groves.

Here, perhaps, Goodison has finally found the remedy (part bush tea, part song of conversion) for the "tourist-dream edenism" that "Jamaica 1980" lamented. And the promise of Goodison's poetry in *Travelling Mercies* is that there will always be this start-over—for those traveling; for wild women turned Revivalists; for Jamaica itself. Jamaica will need its healers and shepherds: people who can perform a Nine Night ceremony for those gone down, who can come representing the ancestors, and who know the properties of aloe and peppermint; people who can perform the small rituals that will bring Jamaica back to itself. It will need its griots to sound myrhh notes, shape new psalms and new praise songs; and storytellers, scholars, and bad word merchants to tell the untold half. But it will survive, as long as there are Jamaicans ready to undertake the planting of eve-living healing trees and lush fruit groves, soon come Heartease, "and it reach till / it purge evil from this place / till we start again clean" ("Heartease III").

Source: Hugh Hodges, "Start Over: Possession Rites and Healing Rituals in the Poetry of Lorna Goodison," in *Research in African Literatures*, Vol. 36, No. 2, Summer 2005, pp. 19–32.

Thomson Gale

In the following essay, the critic gives an overview of Goodison's work.

Lorna Goodison is considered one of the most accomplished anglophone Caribbean women writers to emerge in the last quarter of the twentieth century. Goodison's poetry often speaks to women, and she is known for her sympathetic yet unsentimental treatment of the downtrodden. Goodison's appeal both in Jamaica and abroad has many sources, according to Edward Baugh in *Dictionary of Literary Biography*, who wrote: "The appeal of her writing derives from her treatment of themes of gender, class, and race; from the eloquence with which she speaks for the ill-used and disadvantaged; from her blend of earthiness, humor, and spirituality; and from the way in which her poetic idiom combines contemporary Standard English, the traditional languages of religious devotion, and the resourcefulness of Jamaican speech."

Goodison once told *CA*: "My work has always been rooted in Jamaica. My first book, *Tamarind Season*, takes its title from a local phrase synonymous with hard times and referring to the season before the crops have been harvested, when food is scarce. The book includes widely anthologized poems about Jamaica, such as 'The Road of the Dread' and 'For Don Drummond.'" *Tamarind Season* also includes poems of love, both happy, sorrowful, and bitter, poems of friendship, and what Baugh describes as "satiric poems about people who deny their homeplace, their origins, and their color." There are several poems about New York, including "New York Is a Subway Stop-1969" and "Wish You Were Here," that exhibit Goodison's playful sense of humor, and "For My Mother (May I Inherit Half Her Strength)," which also appears in Goodison's second collection, is a poignant tribute to the resilience of all women living in difficult circumstances. In reference to this poem, Baugh wrote, "Like other Goodison poems, it is a grateful recognition of her origins and shows her acceptance of her place in certain cultural traditions even as she sees through the petty bourgeois aspect of them. Goodison is one of a newer generation of West Indian writers whose work suggests a freedom to move beyond the crisis of cultural identity that so preoccupied earlier writers."

"My second book," Goodison told *CA*, "*I Am Becoming My Mother*, bears witness to the experience of women in Jamaica, and indeed throughout the West Indies, and to the heritage of struggle and resistance, of patience and fortitude and independence, which has been an important part of the history of my people since the dislocations and dispossessions of slavery. Poems in this book include 'Nanny,' about the great Jamaican leader Nanny of the Maroons, and a poem 'For My Mother (May I Inherit Half Her Strength)'." *I Am Becoming My Mother* was Goodison's first book to receive a wide distribution and it brought her critical accolades and the Commonwealth Poetry Prize for the Americas Region in 1986. Baugh discerns a musical inflection in many of these poems, some of which, such as "Jah Music" and "Keith Jarrett—Rainmaker," also discuss music thematically. And, like her earlier collection, in *I Am Becoming My Mother* "there are more radiant, large-souled love poems and more poems that speak for the socio-economically disadvantaged," remarked Baugh. As in all her collections, there are numerous poems about women; here, in addition to the piece about Nanny of the Maroons, Goodison treats Winnie Mandela, the leader of the African National Party during her husband's decades-long imprisonment, and Rosa Parks, the black woman whose refusal to give up her seat on the bus to a white sparked the American civil rights movement of the 1950s, as well as numerous nameless women.

Goodison described the subjects of her third collection to *CA*: "*Heartease* continues this preoccupation with the experiences of the Jamaican people, and with the ways in which they are shaped by the places (the title itself refers to a place name in Jamaica) and the possibilities of their land and their ways of life." In Baugh's description, *Heartease* "includes some fine poems about the condition of women, such as 'A Forgiveness,' 'Survivor,' 'Farewell Wild Woman,' and the virtuoso performance of 'Ceremony for the Banishment of the King of Swords,' the poem-for-all-women, which brings a mythopoeic dimension to the theme." But whereas her first two collections are consumed with issues of love and justice, and the necessarily political and well as personal implications of these issues, *Heartease* finds Goodison shifting more toward spiritual concerns. These poems find the author "[working] through and [transcending] the agonies and yearnings of the heart, the tensions and disappointments of personal relationships, the clamors and temptations of the rough world to reach a soul-place she called 'Heartease,' a condition of calm, of grace and healing," summarized Baugh.

Goodison's most recent collection, *To Us, All Flowers Are Roses*, continues the concerns of her earlier works, especially her earliest focus on the people and culture of Jamaica and the West Indies. And, as in her other poetry collections, the sufferings of women are given recounted and thereby some restitution is made. "Taken altogether, these poems reinforce each other's many strengths and constitute a long song of struggle and survival," concluded *Booklist* reviewer Patricia Monaghan.

Goodison is also the author of a collection of short stories, *Baby Mother and the King of Swords*, many of which envision a scenario between a man and a woman in which the former is abusive or takes advantage of the latter. The first term is Jamaican slang for a woman who has a child out of wedlock or who is the victim of incest; the latter term refers to the card in the Tarot deck that features a male figure beckoning with one hand but holding a sword behind his back in the other. Goodison's *Selected Poems* contains poems from each of her previous three collections plus seven new ones. Goodison is also a painter whose works have been exhibited in the United States, Europe, England, and the West Indies. They also grace the covers of all of her books.

Source: Thomson Gale, "Lorna Goodison," in *Contemporary Authors Online*, Thomson Gale, 2005.

Sources

Batson-Savage, Tanya, "A Sunday Morning Serving of Poetry," in the *Weekly Gleaner*, North American ed., October 6–12, 2005, p. 14.

Calderaro, Michela A., "Painting with Words and Make Us See: Lorna Goodison's *Controlling the Silver*," in *Calabash*, Vol. 3, No. 2, Fall–Winter 2005, pp. 167, 170, 172.

Goodison, Lorna, "The River Mumma Wants Out," in *Controlling the Silver*, University of Illinois Press, 2005, p. 54.

Hannan, Jim, Review of *Guinea Woman: New and Selected Poems*, in *World Literature Today*, Vol. 76, No. 2, Spring 2002, pp. 130–31.

Monaghan, Patricia, Review of *Turn Thanks*, in *Booklist*, Vol. 95, June 1, 1999, p. 1774.

Further Reading

Adams, L. Emilie, and Llewelyn Dada Adams, *Understanding Jamaican Patois: An Introduction to Afro-Jamaican Grammar*, LMH Publishers, 1991.

> A unique language has formed in Jamaica, combining English and African lexicons. With the popularity of reggae, Jamaican patois has come to be heard all over the world. This book helps people living outside Jamaica understand some of the popular phrases.

Jekyll, Walter, *Jamaican Song and Story: Annancy Stories, Digging Sings, Ring Tunes, and Dancing Tunes*, Dover Publications, 2005.

> This books provides an overview of some of Jamaica's mythology through stories and songs. Extensive notes and explanations are provided, giving the reader a full understanding of the stories' significance.

Mack, Douglas R. A., *From Babylon to Rastafari: Origin and History of the Rastafarian Movement*, Frontline Distribution International, 1999.

> Much of the poetry of Jamaica is captured in the nation's popular music, much of which expresses the beliefs of the Rastafarian movement. This book was written by a member of that movement, which represents the ongoing struggle for total freedom.

Monteith, Kathleen, and Glen Richards, eds., *Jamaica in Slavery and Freedom: History, Heritage, and Culture*, University of West Indies Press, 2002.

> This text offers a comprehensive overview of the history of Jamaica, from the Arawak to Marcus Garvey to contemporary culture.

Stolzoff, Norman C., *Wake the Town and Tell the People: Dancehall Culture in Jamaica*, Duke University Press, 2000.

> Stolzoff has written a comprehensive study of Jamaican music, addressing its production, its star performers, and its influence on the people. Further, Stolzoff carefully delineates the music's political and cultural influences. Much of Jamaica's poetry is presented through song; within this poetry, the voices of rebellion can still be heard.

Self-Portrait

Adam Zagajewski

1997

Adam Zagajewski came to prominence in his native Poland during the 1960s as his country was suffering under the oppression of the Communist-controlled government. He and other Polish poets spoke out against the totalitarian system through their work, which was eventually censored, forcing many of them to emigrate to the West. As he and other Polish artists worked at a distance to free their country from political oppression, Zagajewski declared that art should focus on social realities rather than lyrical abstractions. Poetry then would be an informative vehicle that could engender change. After Zagajewski immigrated to the West in the late 1970s, however, his artistic attitudes shifted. He no longer believed that poetry should be subordinated to a political agenda and argued that it should instead reflect the individuality of the poet. The finely crafted poem "Self-Portrait," which appears in *Mysticism for Beginners* (1997), reveals the poet's shift in aesthetics in its focus on artistic expression at odds with historical experience. One of the most personal poems in the 1997 collection, "Self-Portrait" shows the difficulties inherent in the struggle to find a clear sense of individuality separate from the external world of experience. As he details the objects in his world and his response to them, the speaker presents a moving portrait of loss and a stubborn insistence on his own distinct voice.

Author Biography

Adam Zagajewski was born to Ludwika and Tadeusz Zagajewski on June 21, 1945, in Lwów, Ukraine, a city that was occupied by and integrated that year into the Soviet Union. The family was forced, along with many others in Lwów, to relocate to Gliwice, a Silesian city that had become part of Poland. Zagajewski's father became a professor at a technical university. In 1963, after Zagajewski graduated from high school, he moved to Kraków, where he studied philosophy and psychology at the Jagiellonian University. In 1968, he was offered a position as a teaching assistant in philosophy at the Academy of Mining and Metallurgy.

In Eastern Europe, Zagajewski encountered much political turmoil, including the Polish student protests against restrictions on free speech in March 1968, the invasion of Czechoslovakia by the Soviet army in August 1968, the anti-Jewish purge of universities in Soviet-controlled countries in 1967, and the suppression of Polish workers' protests over restrictive labor laws in December 1970. Witnessing these events had a profound effect on Zagajewski and on other writers of his generation, who strongly supported the overthrow of the Communist-controlled government in Poland.

In the late 1960s and 1970s, Zagajewski became part of the New Wave poets, or Generation of 1968 poets, who promoted realistic language in their poetry and explored Communist philosophy and its politics in their work. Zagajewski was soon recognized for his involvement in a group called Teraz (Now) in Kraków. Zagajewski's participation in the New Wave movement is illustrated in his first poetry collections, *Komunikat* (The Communiqué, 1972), and *Sklepy mięsne* (Meat Shops, 1975).

Influenced by Czeslaw Milosz, an anti-Communist Polish poet who immigrated to California, Zagajewski became more political in his writings. In 1974, his critical manifesto *Świat nie przedstawiony* (The Unrepresented World) stated that contemporary poetry should have a political focus. During the 1970s, the Polish government censored the New Wave poets under accusations that their works inspired rebelliousness. This criticism and pressure caused Zagajewski and several other poets of his generation to become involved in politically defiant activities, such as protests and underground publications. Zagajewski had his works printed in one such publication, *Zapis* (Record), which first appeared in Warsaw in 1977. In 1978, Zagajewski's poetry collection *List* (A Letter) was published, also by the underground press.

In the late 1970s, Zagajewski's poetic focus shifted from politics to cultural and metaphysical themes. His *Solidarność i samotność* (1986), translated into English as *Solidarity, Solitude* (1990), was a warning against the type of political manifesto that Zagajewski had earlier written. In 1979, Zagajewski moved to Berlin, where he was offered a fellowship by the Internationale Künstlerprogramm. In 1981, he was offered another fellowship, by the MacDowell Colony in Peterborough, New Hampshire. In 1982, Zagajewski immigrated to Paris, where he worked for the journal *Zeszyty Literackie* (Literary Notebooks) and eventually became a member of the editorial board. In 1988, he began teaching a creative writing program one semester a year at the University of Houston, Texas. In 1992, he accepted a fellowship for poetry from the John Simon Guggenheim Memorial Foundation. Zagajewski's collection of poems *Mysticism for Beginners*, which includes "Self-Portrait," was published in 1997 and has become one of his most celebrated works.

Zagajewski's work has been published in English, French, German, Swedish, Norwegian, Italian, Serbo-Croatian, Slovak, Slovenian, Russian, Dutch, and Hungarian. He has received numerous awards and accolades, including the Kurt Tucholsky Prize of the Swedish PEN Club in 1985, the Echoing Green Foundation prize in 1987, the Alfred Jurzykowski Foundation Award in 1989, the Jean Malrieu Prize in 1990, the Vilenica International Literary Prize in 1996, and the Neustadt International Prize for Literature in 2004.

Poem Summary

Lines 1–4

The title of Zagajewski's "Self-Portrait" suggests that the focus of the poem is the speaker's attempt to define himself. In line 1, the speaker identifies himself as a writer, as someone who spends half of his day writing with "a computer, a pencil, and a typewriter." In line 2, he makes a vague reference to time, when he notes, "One day it will be half a century." He does not say whether he means that one day he will be fifty years old, suggesting that he is approaching that milestone, or whether the half a century will mark the period of time that has passed since a particular important event. The event might be the date the speaker left his home and traveled to the first in the series of "strange cities" to which he refers in line 3. The repetition of the word "strange" in lines 3 and 4 implies that the speaker feels alienated in the places in which he now lives, among "strangers" with whom he discusses "matters strange" to him.

Lines 5–11

The speaker listens to music "a lot," and his preference is for classical composers—Bach, Mahler, Chopin, and Shostakovich. Still, the music does not seem to soothe him. The speaker finds weakness, power, and pain to be the main elements of the music. He declares that a fourth element of music is unnamable and turns to his interest in poetry and philosophy. The speaker gains more from poets, from whom he learns "tenacity, faith, and pride." He admits that he has a difficult time understanding the "precious thoughts" of "the great philosophers."

Lines 12–20

In lines 12–20, the speaker moves from descriptions of his personal tastes to descriptions of objects he sees during his walks. Paris is presumably one of the strange cities in which the speaker lives, and he declares that he likes to take long walks on the city's streets. He observes his "fellow creatures" there and determines that they are driven by the emotions of "envy, anger, desire." In lines 14–16, the speaker suggests that these emotions are inspired by materialism as his focus shifts to a "silver coin / passing from hand to hand." He refers to the fading emperor on a silver coin, which may imply that loyalty to country is often supplanted by greed.

In lines 17 and 18, the speaker recognizes the perfection of nature in the form of green trees but suggests that he cannot articulate his relationship to it, because the trees are expressionless and "indifferent." The darker tone of nature emerges in lines 19 and 20, in which the speaker describes black birds pacing "like Spanish widows" waiting for something, possibly death. Zagajewski may be referring to the image of Spanish widows, "waiting patiently" for their sailors to come home from the sea.

Lines 21–30

In lines 21–30, the speaker shifts the focus back to himself. Perhaps thinking of his own death, the speaker notes that he is "no longer young" but then states that others are closer to death than he is. The image of death is carried over into line 22, in which the speaker admits that he enjoys "deep sleep, when I cease to exist." This sense of disconnection from the world is reinforced in lines 23 and 24, in which the speaker expresses fondness for "fast bike rides" on which objects around him disappear "like cumuli [clouds] on sunny days."

The speaker enjoys art, as he does music, poetry, and philosophy, when he feels a connection to it. He notes his love for "gazing at [his] wife's face." In lines 28–30, the speaker expresses loyalty to his father and his friends, although he does not appear to gain pleasure through his contact with them.

Lines 31–39

In the poem's final section, the speaker writes of his feelings about his country. He is probably referring to Poland, Zagajewski's homeland, Communism being the "evil" from which it "freed itself." The speaker hopes for another liberation, without identifying the type, and wonders what his role may be in this process. Refusing to make any commitment, the speaker insists that he is "not a child of the ocean," as Antonio Machado defined himself to be. (Antonio Machado y Ruiz was a Spanish poet and a member of the Generation of 1898 in Spain, a literary group that encouraged a link between politics and poetry, much as the Generation of 1968 had done in Poland.) Zagajewski's later poetry pulled away from the political themes of his earlier works, unlike that of Machado, whose focus was more consistently political. The metaphor of the ocean suggests this consistency. The speaker sees himself as separate from "the ways of the high world" to which Machado belonged. He is instead a combination of "air, mint and cello," objects that reflect a more personal taste. The poem ends with the assertion of the importance of the speaker's sense of individuality.

Themes

Mysticism for Beginners

Mysticism for Beginners, the title of the collection that contains "Self-Portrait," denotes one of the main themes of the poem. As he strives to characterize his relationship with his world, the speaker admits that his immigrant status results in a sense of disconnection and alienation from his adopted, "strange" city. This sense, however, is occasionally alleviated during moments when he is able to connect with the world through art. Music and literature offer him the promise of sublime moments of clarity, during which he can understand the power

Topics For Further Study

- Read another of Zagajewski's poems from *Mysticism for Beginners* and lead a class discussion comparing and contrasting the poem's focus on mysticism to that of "Self-Portrait."

- Choose two New Wave poets and read a poem by each of them. Prepare a computerized slide presentation on their political themes. Give background information on the political topics addressed in the poems.

- Write a poem or short story that could be considered a self-portrait of you.

- Zagajewski outlined his attitude toward individual artistic expression in his collection of essays *Solidarity, Solitude* (1990). Read at least one of these essays and write your own essay summarizing Zagajewski's attitude about artistic expression and relating your conclusions to "Self-Portrait."

---

of pain and faith. His artistic sensibility also enables the speaker to see the "green . . . perfection" of trees, but he has difficulty expressing the true nature of these mystical moments.

The speaker in "Self-Portrait" is able to express articulately a yearning for and lack of mystical connection, as when he notes that there is a fourth element in music that "has no name." Similarly, the green trees impart "nothing" to him but indifference. In this sense, then, the speaker is a beginner in the study of mysticism, focusing on the difficult process of gaining brief moments of transcendent clarity rather than ultimate enlightenment.

Exile

The speaker's sense of exile permeates "Self-Portrait." Throughout most of the poem, he does not identify his homeland or the reason for his emigration. The focus is on his feelings of rootlessness and alienation. The external world is "strange" to him, peopled with "strangers" with whom he fails to connect. His conversations with these people do not help him form new alliances, because what they talk about is "strange" to him.

As he walks the streets of Paris, he observes passersby not as human beings with whom he may eventually feel a sense of solidarity but as "fellow creatures," filled with their own passions. In this state of disconnection, he likens black birds to "Spanish widows" waiting for death, a state the speaker tries to mimic by falling into a "deep sleep" and ceasing to live. Or else he bikes so fast that the images of houses and trees around him "dissolve like cumuli on sunny days."

At the end of the poem, the speaker hints at the reason for his exile and suggests that he will never return home. Perhaps he has left his country to escape artistic censorship, before the country "freed itself from one evil." The speaker says that he does not know whether he will go home to help liberate his country, fearing the loss of his own individuality in the process. As a result, he commits himself to a permanent state of exile, living the life that belongs only to him.

Style

Setting: Public and Private Space

The poem contrasts public and private space to illustrate the details that the speaker considers in creating his self-portrait. He first describes a private space, possibly a home or office, identifying personal objects like "a computer, a pencil, and a typewriter," the necessary tools of his artistic expression. He immediately contrasts this interior world with a more public space when he notes that he lives in "strange cities," suggesting that the external world will also have an impact on how he defines himself. That impact becomes clear in his descriptions of his interaction with the public world. He characterizes himself as an exile, which has produced a sense of disconnection with this public world. His detachment becomes evident when he characterizes those who pass by as "fellow creatures" and admits that he enjoys "dissolving" his surroundings in fast bike rides. He returns to his private space as he listens to music or gazes at his wife's face, which can offer him moments of clarity. By the end of the poem, the speaker appears to have decided that he is defined by interior spaces, not the country that he has left or the new city where he now resides. He has not let the life that "belongs" to him "cross paths" with "the ways of the high world."

Historical Context

Polish New Wave Poets

In the early 1970s, Polish writers who were influenced by the political events in their country in the late 1960s formed a movement called the New Wave. This group was made up of several diverse literary groups, among them, the Poznań group Attempts, which included Stanisław Barańczak and Ryszard Krynicki; the Cracow group Now, which included Zagajewski, Julian Kornhauser, Jerzy Kronhold, and Stanisław Stabro; and the Warsaw and Łódź group Hybrids, which included Krzysztof Karasek, Jarosław Markiewicz, Jacek Bierezin, Zdzisław Jaskuła, and Witold Sulkowski.

The disparate groups came together in a spirit of rebellion against artistic tradition. Tadeusz Witkowski, in the *Slavic and East European Journal*, notes that these poets, who also became known as the Generation of 1968, "rejected the concept of universal poetry, devoid of the concrete 'here and now,' poetry speaking in a highly literary language, exclusively utilizing allusion, metaphors, and abstract symbols." They discarded, according to Witkowski, "the concept of the poet isolated from social realities, the poet escaping from everyday life into a world of myth or even pure metaphysics . . . bypassing in silence the falsity present in the language of mass media." These poets also were united by their anti-Communist sympathies.

The New Wave poets initially had difficulty finding publishers in Communist-ruled Poland and had to turn to underground quarterlies such as *Zapis* and *Puls*, both of which were reprinted in the United States and the United Kingdom. The new poetic theories first appeared in a series of articles that later became collected in Zagajewski's *Świat nie przedstawiony* (Unrepresented World, 1974), written with Julian Kornhauser.

Most of the poets in the New Wave eventually emigrated because of the artistic restrictions they experienced in Poland. As a result, the subject of emigration began to appear in their poetry as they explored themes of alienation and dislocation, loyalty and abandonment. Zagajewski immigrated to Paris and eventually turned away from his previous insistence that contemporary poetry should address political issues. His new attitude toward individual artistic expression is outlined in his collection of essays, *Solidarność i samotność* (*Solidarity, Solitude*, 1990).

Poland and World War II

The world experienced a decade of aggression in the 1930s that culminated in World War II, a war that resulted from the rise of totalitarian regimes in Germany, Italy, and Japan. These powers gained control as a result of the Great Depression of the early 1930s and from the conditions created by the peace settlements that followed World War I. The dictatorships established in each country encouraged expansion into neighboring countries. In March 1938, Germany annexed Austria and in March 1939 occupied Czechoslovakia. On September 1, 1939, one week after Germany and the Soviet Union signed the Molotov-Ribbentrop Pact (also called the Treaty of Nonaggression), Germany invaded Poland, and World War II began.

The Polish people suffered greatly during the war. A large part of the population was massacred, starved, or placed in concentration camps. Approximately six million Poles were killed, and 2.5 million were deported to German camps. Polish Jews were almost eliminated from the country.

Political Turmoil in Postwar Poland

German troops completed their withdrawal from Poland in early 1945, and the socialization of Poland soon began. In 1947, Bolesław Beirut, a Communist Pole and citizen of the Soviet Union, was elected president by the Polish parliament. Soviet Marshall Konstantin Rokossovsky became minister of defense and commander in chief of the Polish army. In 1952, the constitution made Poland a model Soviet republic with a foreign policy identical to that of the Soviet Union. The government subsequently cut off relations with the Vatican, and religious leaders became the chief targets of persecution.

In June 1956, having become increasingly discontent with the Communist-controlled government, students and workers organized mass demonstrations and riots, which forced the government to abandon its more rigid policies. That same year, Władysław Gomułka was elected leader of the Polish United Workers Party and led a revolt against Soviet control of the country. Gomułka eased restrictions on personal freedoms and reestablished ties with the Catholic Church and the West. In the early 1960s, however, Gomułka strengthened his ties with Moscow and began a campaign to return to the restrictive policies of Communism. The student and worker demonstrations and riots that followed again influenced politics in Poland, as Gomułka was ousted and replaced by Edward Gierek, who brought back some of the freedoms enjoyed by the Poles under the early days of Gomułka's rule.

In the late 1970s, poor economic conditions in Poland prompted a series of antigovernment protests, which resulted in the establishment of small independent trade unions that organized strikes throughout the country. One such union, Solidarity, led by Lech Walesa, grew in membership to more than nine million, gaining so much support that the Polish government in 1980 agreed to all of the group's demands. In December 1981, however, the Polish leader Wojciech Jaruzelski reasserted government authority by declaring marshal law and imprisoning Walesa and thousands of other union members, sending Solidarity underground.

By the mid-1980s, after facing the continued passive resistance of the Polish people, the government eased its Communist mandates and started to release members of Solidarity from prison. The last Solidarity members were freed in 1989. Later that year, Solidarity candidates began to win elections for government positions. By the end of 1990, the Communist regime in Poland had crumbled, and Walesa was elected president.

Critical Overview

Adam Kirsch writes in his review of *Mysticism for Beginners* that "the central problem of [Zagajewski's] poetry" is that "the mystical experience is not loquacious" because it is characterized by a "stillness." Kirsch argues, "What yearns to be expressed, rather, is the experience of waiting for the sudden heightening of consciousness; waiting for it, or remembering it, or lacking it." Kirsch determines that Zagajewski's goal is to write poetry "that is a concrete avenue to an invisible reality," requiring him to experiment with "poetic strategies and . . . poetic evasions," which "reveal a great deal about the possibilities of poetry today."

Kirsch concludes that Zagajewski begins to answer the question "how can a poet—an intelligent, serious poet—write mystical verse now," in a modern age when "the presumption, even the suggestion, of a mystical dimension to life can seem anachronistic, an evasion of the real and secular responsibilities of the time?" Kirsch praises the "quick and memorable absurdities" that "temper the darkness" of the poems and Zagajewski's "sophisticated and witty" voice, which expresses "deep feeling lying just beneath the surface." Kirsch concludes that because "the mystic moment is indescribable, incommensurable," Zagajewski, in his search for this moment in his poetry, "is condemned to a kind of eternal recurrence of the same poem."

Jacqueline Osherow, in her assessment of the collection for *Antioch Review*, writes that "it would be impossible to praise this book too highly" and that "the poems seem effortlessly to arrive at the marrow of everything," from "living" to "the intensely experienced present instant." As she reads the poems, Osherow reports that she thinks to herself "so this is what it is to be alive" and "so this is how a person writes a poem." She concludes, "There are no tricks, no gimmicks, no fussiness, no elaborations. The authority of these poems arises from their exquisite accuracy."

John Taylor, in his review for *Poetry*, praises "the engaging movement of these meditative poems, which meander gently toward moments of enlightenment" and concludes that "our lives can briefly crystallize, [Zagajewski] movingly shows, in unexpected plenitude." Taylor finds Zagajewski "a subtle craftsman" who "avoids ostentatious effects," as he "focuses on the deepest meanings." Taylor states that "the path to understanding necessarily remains untrodden; but its first turnings have been glimpsed by the attentive, self-effacing poet."

A reviewer for *Publishers Weekly* writes that the poems in *Mysticism for Beginners* are "mature" and "accessible, written as much for the common reader as for other poets, and treat poetry as a savior, not as a tradition to struggle against." The reviewer finds "most poignant . . . Zagajewski's criticism of his own art and his distrust of its authority" in the poems as well as their expression of a "long[ing] for a speech that can recoup something of the old anxiety and power, the gravity of wholehearted rebellion." In the concluding paragraph, the reviewer states that "this collection reconfirms the international status of a vigorous, ever-questioning voice."

Lech Walesa, leader of the first independent trade union in Poland known as "Solidarity," and first democratically-elected president of Poland after the fall of Communism © Peter Turnley/Corbis

Criticism

Wendy Perkins

Perkins is a professor of American and English literature and film. In this essay, she examines the tensions between private and public, individuality and collectivism in "Self-Portrait."

Zagajewski first gained fame as one of the leading poets of the New Wave movement, established by a group of Polish poets in the late 1960s. Tadeusz Witkowski, in the *Slavic and East European Journal*, notes that these poets were drawn together by a belief that poetry should be written in plain language but, more important, that it should "teach and stimulate thinking" about contemporary "social realities." Zagajewski was one of the most vocal proponents of this poetic manifesto, as outlined in his collection of essays, *Świat nie przedstawiony* (Unrepresented World, 1974) and illustrated in his first collections of poetry, *Komunikat* (The Communiqué, 1972) and *Sklepy mięsne* (Meat Shops, 1975).

After immigrating to Paris, Zagajewski began to question his earlier position on the promotion of poetic didacticism, or poetry that aims to teach a moral, religious, political, or practical lesson. He began to focus instead on the troubling relationship between public and private worlds, between individual experience and history. His later poetry, including the celebrated "Self-Portrait," examines the sense of disconnection between the individual and the collective worlds. In "Self-Portrait," that sense of disconnection is revealed through the speaker's attempts to define and locate himself in relation to the here and now as well as to history.

The speaker identifies himself as a writer in the poem's first lines and focuses on the sense of time passing, suggesting that he feels a sense of creative urgency as he attempts to compose a self-portrait that will delineate his relationship to his world. This relationship is first mapped out in an external sense as the speaker defines himself as an exile who lives "in strange cities" where he "sometimes talk[s] / with strangers about matters strange" to him. The repetition of the word "strange" denotes the speaker's feelings of disconnection and, as a result, a sense of alienation from the place and people with whom he is now in contact.

As he describes his interior space, the speaker suggests that he finds a sense of connection there that he has not been able to establish in his public world. Yet he struggles for a more complete understanding of the things that he values. He listens to music, specifically to Bach, Mahler, Chopin, and Shostakovich. The smooth assonance of the names suggests that the speaker gains comfort from these composers' works, yet he finds contrasting elements of weakness and power along with pain and a fourth element that he cannot name. If he could identify this final element, the speaker could experience the absolute connection, a mystical union between himself and the music. Ultimately unsatisfied, he moves on to poets, who teach him "tenacity, faith, and pride." The speaker finds more connection with poets than with philosophers, whose "precious thoughts" he can only catch in "scraps."

In line 12, the speaker moves back to the exterior world and his relation to it in more specific terms. He identifies Paris as the strange city in which he now finds himself, and his description of Paris embodies the polarities he experiences as he struggles to define himself. An ironic appreciation of Paris emerges as the speaker takes long walks on the streets and watches other inhabitants of the city. He regards them as "fellow *creatures*" [italics added], noting their "envy, / anger, desire" and greed.

The speaker's walks take him past the green perfection of trees. He longs to establish a sympathetic connection with the natural world in all of its multiplicity, as he tries to do with the music he listens to, but ultimately the trees express "nothing." Black birds become "Spanish widows" waiting patiently for news of their drowned husbands, the striking metaphor suggesting the speaker's recognition of nature's more destructive aspect. He links himself to this image of death in line 21 when he admits that he is "no longer young" but finds hope in the realization that "someone else is always older."

In lines 22 to 24, the speaker suggests a world-weariness, almost a death wish that links to the images in the previous lines. He declares that he enjoys sleep so deep that he loses all sense of himself. "Fast bike rides on country roads" allow him to lose a sense of his surroundings as well, when all objects "dissolve like cumuli on sunny days."

The speaker's apparent desire for disconnection from a strange world is interrupted periodically by his visits to museums, where he can occasionally find inspiration from paintings. The paintings "speak to me," he declares, suggesting the possibility of intense moments of clarity, insight into the nature of existence and his relation to it. In these moments, the irony that complicates the speaker's creative vision with its insistent polarities "vanishes," and he can appreciate the beauty of his wife's face. These moments of transcendence are

> *As he describes his interior space, the speaker suggests that he finds a sense of connection there that he has not been able to establish in his public world."*

ephemeral, for soon he must return to the present, where he dutifully calls his father and meets with friends, "proving [his] fidelity" more so than following any natural inclination for solidarity.

In his review of *Mysticism for Beginners*, Adam Kirsch finds Zagajewski "strangely inexplicit" in these intense, transcendent moments that appear through his poetry. Kirsch argues that "we find a longing toward the mystical as the natural consummation of the private, the ahistorical" in his work, but his speakers rarely achieve that state. Zagajewski "remains at the point of hoping that perhaps there is such a truth, though he will probably never comprehend it" or be able to articulate it. Commenting on Zagajewski's focus on the relation between the public and the private, Kirsch writes, "when the collective no longer cares to direct the spirit . . . the individual is thrown back on his own resources, which very often turn out to be inadequate. Zagajewski is the poet of this situation."

In the closing lines of the poem, the speaker reveals that history is the source of his sense of disconnection and his dark vision of the external world. He notes that his home country "freed itself from one evil" but suggests that it is still experiencing another situation from which it must gain "liberation." The speaker never identifies the first evil, but readers can assume, given Zagajewski's own experience, that it is a reference to the totalitarian takeover of Poland after World War II. The second situation is not identified as evil, but it is serious enough to require intervention. Refusing to allow politics to infiltrate his artistic vision, the speaker, and Zagajewski, will not name the evil.

The speaker's sense of dislocation becomes clearer in lines 31 to 39. He suffers the rootlessness

What Do I Read Next?

- Zagajewski expresses his thoughts on politics and art and the tensions between them in his collection of essays *Solidarity, Solitude* (1990), translated by Lillian Vallee.

- Like *Mysticism for Beginners*, Zagajewski's 1985 collection of poetry, *Tremor*, translated by Renata Gorczynski, focuses on the intersection of public and private worlds.

- Timothy Garton Ash's *The Polish Revolution: Solidarity* (2002) presents an absorbing, eye-witness chronicle of the 1980 Polish workers' rebellion against the Communist-controlled government and of the development of the Solidarity movement.

- *The Walls Came Tumbling Down: The Collapse of Communism in Eastern Europe* (1993), by Gale Stokes, is a comparative study of the pressures that led to the fall of Communism in the Soviet Union and Eastern Europe.

- Many of the poems in Czeslaw Milosz's *New and Collected Poems: 1931–2001* (2003) focus on themes similar to those in Zagajewski's poetry, including exile and alienation. Milosz, a Nobel Prize winner, is one of Zagajewski's literary heroes.

---

of exile as well as of the patriot who refuses to return to his home. While recognizing that at home further liberation is necessary, liberation that must be generated by active supporters of freedom, the speaker questions his devotion to the cause. After asking "Could I help in this?" he expresses doubt, admitting that he does not give his work a sense of activism, as others, such as the Spanish poet Antonio Machado, have done. Machado is a "child of the ocean" who has established a political continuity in his work. The speaker is a "child of air, mint, and cello," refusing to devote himself exclusively to any cause. He instead insists on his individuality, his need to follow his own path, which does not cross with "the ways of the high world."

Zagajewski's insistence on the individuality of creative expression generates a complex and often troubling universe for his speaker in "Self-Portrait." As he struggles to understand and express himself in his relation to the external present and historical experience, the speaker faces the inevitable tensions between private and public, individuality and collectivism. Within the darker specter generated by these polarities, the speaker sometimes experiences moments of clarity when he discovers a transcendent connection to his world. Through the voice of his speaker, Zagajewski expresses his belief in the transforming power of artistic vision.

Source: Wendy Perkins, Critical Essay on "Self-Portrait," in *Poetry for Students*, Thomson Gale, 2007.

Magdalena Kay

In the following essay, Kay discusses the idea of journeying in Zagajewski's work and the poet's ability to lift a specific place from the confines of its location and history, investing it with imaginative overtones drawn from imagination.

The poetic masterpiece "Jechac do Lwowa" (To Go to Lvov) occupies a central place in Adam Zagajewski's oeuvre, as it demonstrates the power of the imagination to create its own home and to reveal the nature of the author's feelings of belonging and otherness. A central concern of Zagajewski's poetry is how to keep the historical at bay, how to keep it from establishing sovereignty over one's private world." History is an imperialist force. It is manipulative because it uses ethics to pull the individual into a historical interpretation of events. How can one establish a personal space separate from history? Such a space must be atemporal. "To Go to Lvov" enacts this marvelous feat: it lifts the speaker out of his threatening surroundings and sets him down in a place of rejuvenation. Lvov is both insubstantial, an ethereal vision, and a solid bedrock, the base of artistic creation. It is both a city with a network of streets and a movement, a process of transformation and alliance.

Time is neatly conflated with space in the beginning of the poem: "To go to Lvov. Which station / for Lvov, if not in a dream, at dawn, when dew / gleams on a suitcase, when express trains and bullet trains are being born." The spurious question of which station is immediately confused by talk of dreams and dawn, an in-between time; such confusion lifts the place-name of Lvov out of its literal context into a symbolic realm, where time inevitably influences space. Dawn is the time of birth, when objects are born fresh, coated with a baptismal dew. Dream is a time of separation from the literal world, an unclassifiable realm where the literal and the symbolic elide. They may both be conceived of as temporal "stations," passageways to the imaginary.

If we accept the idea that a journey to a heightened realm is possible, then the title of the poem becomes a question of logistics—how to reach Lvov—instead of ontology—if a journey to Lvov is possible. The poem's breathless hurry compresses time and space into the crowded instant of description. The speaker chooses a moment before he was bore as the temporal center of this poem. Escape from the time span of the speaker's lifetime lifts him out of a stale, processed time into a fresh one. The accumulation of infinitives in the poem sets up an abstract, postulated world, neither proven to exist nor decisively experienced. It contrasts with the detail of the imagery. The infinitive looks forward to what could happen, to the future. These infinitives serve as reminders of the theoretical basis of the poem's actions, but their abstract quality becomes drowned in the exuberant reality of the descriptions. We suspend our doubt that the actions may not be "real." The facts of ontology become divorced from desire.

Desire is a force central to Zagajewski's work. It is the motive for knowledge and for imagination. The desirability of this poem's images makes us assent to them and to our involvement in the world of the poem. We reach its conclusion with a certain shock, though it is the logical endpoint of the journey to Lvov. The poem states, "Lvov is everywhere." It can be conjured every day, at any time and place, because it is a figment. Or rather, the city is a psychological state. It is an imaginative ability, which keeps its peace and purity because of its separation from the actual city of Lvov, which we may have assumed was the subject of the poem.

Our everyday and out dream lives certainly overlap, and the speaker plays with our understanding of the "real" by describing details that could come from memory, only we are told that he wasn't yet born at the "time" the poem describes. This poem shows the prehistory of the self. The boy eyeing a full bucket of raspberries is not a presence but, rather, a center of desire. Just as our desire for the poem's images makes us assent to their reality, so the speaker's desire for Lvov leads him to insert his hunger into the poem as a trace of himself.

The speaker's emotional participation in a constructed world invites us to radically reconsider what is "home." "To Go to Lvov" serves as a beautiful example of the way in which home can be seen as an imaginative (but not wholly imaginary!) construct rather than a material structure. The construct of home answers a deep psychological need. It is both the speaker's origin and the endpoint toward which he travels. The movement of Zagajewski's poem carries us toward this goal. Even if we cannot say that Lvov is Zagajewski's literal home, it is certainly an imaginative one.

We may say that Lvov is an ideal, but ideals are dynamic in Zagajewski's work. "To Go to Lvov" establishes fluidity as a characteristic of the speaker's goal. "Lvov is everywhere." Every location may be part of his ideal. As the speaker constantly gives us fresh images, Lvov becomes dynamic and various. Vision becomes the ability to see the ideal in any available place. This poem shows the imagination's capacity to interact with perception to create an

> "Zagajewski is a master of the precise image. He often lets us watch him chisel a few perfect strokes, turning a shapeless entity into an evocative sculpture. Sometimes the shapes are multiple, and we see a whole gallery of sculptures come into being before our eyes."

emotional reality. The speaker's insistence on Lvov's actuality puts him in a slightly defensive posture—"after all it exists," he asserts at the end of the poem.

Why does he need to defend something he has just celebrated? Much of the poem seems written as if from a child's perspective, and we can hear a childlike persistence in opposition to an imagined adult skepticism. This concluding gesture ("after all") also reveals a split between the reasoning mind (focused on what we call the "real world") and imagination (which creates images based on desire). This split creates a fissure below the structure of the poem. Nevertheless, it doesn't weaken the import of the poem; on the contrary, it is the emotive and intellectual fissures cross-cutting Zagajewski's work that make him such a serious, compelling, and human poet.

The word przeciez, translated as "after all," is a gesture of opposition, but it has a slight quaver of the voice in it; the quaver shows fear that the construction of Lvov isn't sound enough, and the city of dreams may be felled by the axe of reason. It also highlights the fragility of the speaking voice itself. Not only is the speaker's physical situation unstable, but he is himself unstable, uncertain, not a strong presence. The personal self enters this poem as a center of desire, not as someone who possesses this reality. He cannot dominate even his own imaginative space, as history intrudes on the present and the quotidian intrudes on the exalted. The poem's two final images of threatened realities are a jungle and a cathedral: "trees / fell soundlessly, as in a jungle, / and the cathedral trembled." Our belief in these images, in their strength and potency, depends on our belief that natural and human beauty does have spiritual value. We must believe that the human spirit can give meaning to a natural or architectural space. This is a leap of faith. Our acceptance of the poem's imagistic vocabulary depends upon our belief in the potency of spirit, of the imaginative effort. We need to believe that the aesthetic and the spiritual can connect, that desire is a constructive force that leads beyond the sensual at the same time as it celebrates the sensual. The poem reveals an aesthetic program that joins sensual pleasure with a spiritual quest.

The speaker's insistence that Lvov can be found everywhere allows the city to be both transient and eternal. It is the site of momentary delight and it dwells in the realm of eternal ideals. "To Go to Lvov" is a rare case when Zagajewski allows these two worlds to coincide. In his other meditations on the transient and the eternal, the two worlds are opposed. The extraordinary poem "The Gothic" shows us a speaker feeling self-loss and disorientation inside a cathedral. "Who am I, interred in this slim vault, / where is my name, / who's trying to snatch and hurt it away / like wind stealing a cap?" The wind is a force that cannot be situated. The speaker's disorientation becomes stronger when he can't pinpoint who or what is stripping away his identity. The cathedral is not described with the detail in which Lvov is described; perhaps the lack of humanizing detail creates this sense of disorientation.

Zagajewski is a master of the precise image. He often lets us watch him chisel a few perfect strokes, turning a shapeless entity into an evocative sculpture. Sometimes the shapes are multiple, and we see a whole gallery of sculptures come into being before our eyes. Such is the case in "To Go to Lvov." Zagajewski is also adept at evoking disorientation or formlessness, however. If a poem such as "To Go to Lvov" is essentially constructive, presenting a bank of sensual experiences, then a poem such as "The Gothic" is deconstructive, revealing the emptiness that threatens human constructs of place and identity. If a name is like a hat, then it isn't a necessary part of one's identity. However, the threat of removing it creates fear: the speaker repeats the question "Who am I?" with increasing urgency in the first stanza.

A name may be unnecessary, but it is essential for a social existence. The speaker needs a social framework, with its inessential details, to form his sense of self. He instructs himself to reenter a recognizable world: "Go find the height again, and the dark, / where longing, pain, and joy live / and faith in the good God who does / and undoes." Zagajewski establishes the social realm as a place of oppositions, where good and evil exist side by side. The state of not-knowing, of darkness and mystery, is also essential. Someone who is part of the social world can have faith in the presence of others even while he is alone. "The Gothic" ends with the speaker reclaiming the darkness and silence: "I hear / languages, voices, sighs, / the hopeful laments of those who loved / and those who preferred hatred, those who betrayed / and those betrayed. . . . / I feel you, I listen / to your silence."

Silence is no longer absence at the end of the poem, but a cloak thrown over a chorus of other voices. Stillness is a carefully created artifice. I have chosen to set this poem alongside "To Go to Lvov" because of the seeming discrepancy in style and voice between the two poems. In fact, they form a remarkable pair. The speaker of "The Gothic" realizes that human community is necessary for giving the self a shape, a name, and a place. Total abstraction is an unlivable state; that is why the ideal must also be linked to the real. Lvov must be given a name, and it must respond to change, if it is to serve as a workable ideal for the speaker.

The concept of eternity is attractive to most idealists, but Zagajewski counters it with an insistence on the richness of transience. Formlessness and flux are basic human states. There are always elements, in the self and in the world, that one cannot fit into an ordered scheme. Zagajewski has been described by his reviewers as a poet of excess. I would rather describe him as a poet of potentiality, one who does not rest in ready-made formulas but constantly shows us new images and new states of being. If we consider an artist to be someone who takes the raw material of experience and expresses it in a form, then we also assume that experience is capable of being formalized. In other words, we think there must be patterns in experience, and ways of containing it. Zagajewski asks us to reconsider these assumptions. There is always too much for us to have the certitude that we can understand it, much less encompass and formalize it. "To Go to Lvov" is filled with movement. The syntax is breathless. The speaker's restless eye cannot be taken away from its context—the self clings to events and is one with its surroundings. The speaker rarely stands apart from his subject matter in Zagajewski's work but is part of the perceived scene. The self is not always private; a question about the exterior becomes a question about our interior. We are not looking at a solitary, accursed artist figure here but at a speaker who is a specimen of humanity. He is not fully aware of his own potential; the self that becomes visible in these poems is something unfinished—to use Zagajewski's own words, without form. Because it is in flux, its imaginary life is also in flux; this is why every place is capable of being—or, I should say—becoming, home.

Imaginative, social, intellectual, and personal worlds are not opposed in this poetry. Despite Zagajewski's fondness for thinking in oppositions, I believe his poetry is based on unification. Shades of similarity and difference can be hard to perceive: we must accept an idea of "home" that is between belonging and nonbelonging, with no fixed position. The speaker's fight against the domination of history is a fight against forced and inflexible interpretation. Although history has more than one voice, the speaker of these poems feels its pressure as a unified force. We may recall Wallace Stevens's famous definition of the imagination as a force that pushes back against the pressure of external reality. We must see Zagajewski's poetic speaker as one who can bring the imaginary into real life, who can see his mythic Lvov everywhere as a way of defending the strength of the imagination.

Zagajewski is not a thinker who summarily rejects the non-ideal. Rather, he wishes to accept his present state and to create workable ideals that can be realized on this earth. We need to accept a form of idealism that does not crystallize an ideal in a single image but allows for movement and change. A fixed form is as oppressive as a single interpretation. Zagajewski is interested in potentiality, desire, and intention. By means of attentiveness to the present moment, one can arrive at a deep state of awareness, but without imaginative flexibility, one cannot see the full potential of the present moment. Zagajewski allows us to explore this aesthetic in poems that are richly sensual as well as imaginatively original.

Source: Magdalena Kay, "Place and Imagination in the Poetry of Adam Zagajewski," in *World Literature Today*, Vol. 79, No. 2, May–August 2005, pp. 20–22.

Adam Kirsch

In the following review, Kirsch points to the difficulties of writing mystical poetry in the contemporary world and with modern sensibilities. Zagajewski, he says, does not seek another, higher world; he seeks hints of that higher world peeking through the things of this one.

A poetry of mysticism, now? For a mystic of the seventeenth century, for Vaughan or Traherne, the object of mysticism was the old one, the obvious one: God, or Christ. For a Romantic neo-Platonist such as Shelley, the object was less clear, but still plausible: the Idea, the great pattern hidden from human sight. But if Romanticism was spilt religion, today the spill has just about been sopped up; and the presumption, or even the suggestion, of a mystical dimension to life can seem anachronistic, an evasion of the real and secular responsibilities of the time. So how can a poet—an intelligent, serious poet—write mystical verse now? The poetry of Adam Zagajewski provides the beginning of an answer to this question.

Zagajewski is the preeminent Polish poet of his generation. He is a thoroughly contemporary man who aspires, without embarrassment, to a verse that is a concrete avenue to an invisible reality. And the

> "Zagajewski is the preeminent Polish poet of his generation. He is a thoroughly contemporary man who aspires, without embarrassment, to a verse that is a concrete avenue to an invisible reality."

peculiar forms into which this situation forces him, the poetic strategies and the poetic evasions that it requires, reveal a great deal about the possibilities of poetry today.

Zagajewski was born in Lvov, in eastern Poland, in 1945. Within the year his family was transplanted to the western city of Gliwice, victims of the postwar redrawing of Poland's borders. As a student he moved to Cracow, and after several clashes with the authorities emigrated to Paris in 1982. Zagajewski emerged as a prominent poet and polemicist in 1974 with the publication of *The Unrepresented World,* a critical manifesto which, as Stanislaw Baranczak wrote in these pages, "stirred up one of the greatest controversies in postwar Polish culture [by attacking] the noncommittal literature of the previous decades." As Zagajewski ruefully wrote years later, "I took my place among the Catos of this world for a while, among those who know what literature should be and ruthlessly exact these standards from others." Of this phase of his career, English-readers have nothing—his first book published in English, *Tremor,* dates from 1985, well into his Paris period. Yet it is crucial for understanding his later development, since the poet whom we know from his five American books is in full flight from this politically engaged view of poetry. Indeed, the antinomy between politics and poetry—or between history and art, or between the collective and the private—is the main argument of his mature work.

This flight from history was a product of history, specifically the history of Communism in Poland. After the Solidarity movement rose to prominence in 1980, Zagajewski sensed that Communism in Poland was in retreat. Not defeated, of course—Solidarity was driven underground by the proclamation of martial law in 1981—but beginning its decline; within ten years it would be dead. Zagajewski's poems and essays of the 1980s—collected in *Tremor* and *Solidarity, Solitude*—look forward quite consciously to a life after totalitarianism, in which "antitotalitarianism" will no longer be a sufficient worldview. Zagajewski in this phase is preparing the ground for post-Communist Polish intellectual life. He points insistently to a world beyond the old definitions of good and evil, a world in which a truly private mental existence, unfettered but also unenergized by the struggle with communism, will have to find other reasons for being.

These concerns are announced in the title of *Solidarity, Solitude,* the remarkable collection of essays that appeared in 1990. As he writes in the preface to that book: "The word 'Solidarity' on the jacket of this book stands mostly for the Solidarity, a dynamic, robust, political and social movement in Poland. . . . Solitude stands for literature, art, meditation, for immobility." Zagajewski is not for solitude and against Solidarity, or solidarity; a concern for public justice is rather a kind of precondition, a given, for men of good will. But neither is he for solidarity at the expense of solitude, which gives access to another realm: the world of art, beauty, epiphanous experience. As he writes in the title essay of *Two Cities*:

> The piercing sense of community, intimacy, of possessing something elusive—that half-legendary country of Poland. . . . An even more important ingredient of this philosophy was a thesis I knew well . . . that all is social, common, and collective.
>
> I did not know how to formulate my opposition, I did not have the appropriate arguments at my disposal; but I did feel that not everything belonged to everybody. We are different and we also experience things which social groups will never know.

Zagajewski's difficulty, as a poet in a time of national crisis, was that these two realms are, strictly speaking, incommensurable: art (that is, art which is truly and only art) does not get the tanks off the streets, and mass movements do not write poems.

The dilemma of solidarity and solitude is unfamiliar to an American, and it may be difficult for an American to enter into it fully. Here poetry is such a minor, sidelined pursuit that its practitioners by and large never even think of using their art to serve a larger cause. (The few writers who do make poems into polemics, such as Adrienne Rich or

Audre Lorde, generally fail at both.) For some critics—George Steiner most egregiously—this amounts to a complacency that diminishes American art. On this view, the moral crisis of Eastern Europe gives poetry an urgency and a public stature that it can never have in the United States, where it is largely a hobby confined to writing workshops.

Zagajewski's work is important for its rejection of this view. His writing, in poetry and in prose, is in part an attempt to diagnose the deformities of a poetry under too much public pressure, a poetry that feels a duty to participate in politics. As a poet who feels poetry to be a calling in an older, more Romantic sense, Zagajewski knows well that there is a zone of solitude, of "immobility," which is necessary for writing perfectly achieved poetry. Indeed, Zagajewski parodies the Steiner view quite devastatingly in "Central Europe," a short sketch from *Two Cities:*

> He was an unremarkable, tiny man with dark greasy hair combed flat across his head who, without waiting for permission, joined my table. It was clear he was dying to talk. He would have exchanged half his life for a moment of conversation. "Where are you from?" he asked. "From Poland," I said. "Ah, how lucky, how lucky you are!" he exclaimed, overcome by genuine Mediterranean enthusiasm. "Mourning! Long live mourning! ... You are a lucky man." "Why lucky?" "Force. Force of conviction. Categorical feelings. Moral integrity. A literature that is not alienated from the polis. You have not experienced that alarming split. ... I always felt in you the desire for unity, the Greek dream of combining emotion and courage. ..."

This Westerner is using Poland just as generations of modern Westerners have used Greece, or the Renaissance, or the Middle Ages: as an imagined ideal, an instrument of vicarious living, a name for a condition of spiritual wholeness. He values the mournful country for its solidarity. He even envies it.

In Zagajewski's view, however, solidarity is not a mode in which the poet—or, indeed, any reflective person—can come to rest. Rather, he sees solidarity as the antithesis that arises in opposition to the thesis of totalitarianism: "Totalitarians have their own primitive seal, which they stamp onto the wax of reality. Antitotalitarians have fashioned their own seal. And it, too, shapes the wax.... Poor wax, lashed by seals!" Solidarity is something with which Zagajewski would like to dispense, in the way that one puts away a tool that has served its purpose. Scorn, hatred, loathing for totalitarianism is everywhere in his work; but so is a distrust of antitotalitarianism, the other seal that disfigures the wax of reality.

Solidarity, Solitude, then, is a manifesto, but not of the kind that Zagajewski produced in *The Unrepresented World.* It is a manifesto against manifestos, a warning against too much solidarity, written at a time when solidarity was both a necessary stance and a kind of moral intoxicant. Zagajewski reminds his countrymen that "we have to conquer totalitarianism in passing, on our way to greater things, in the direction of this or that reality, even though we may be unable to say exactly what reality is." When one considers how tempting solidarity can be, and how difficult and lonely a private definition of reality is, the real nobility of such a statement begins to emerge. At a time when collective thought and collective identity came under the seductive sign of liberation, Zagajewski was self-possessed enough to remain wary of history.

But once Zagajewski has made his choice for privacy, for the inner life, he is faced with a more difficult problem, and one which is less specific to Poland. To write against the public and historical life, and in favor of the private and individual life, is still to be conditioned by the public, even if one's response to it is a negative one. In *Solidarity, Solitude* Zagajewski turns his back on one definition of life and of its purpose, but it is not yet clear what he has turned toward. What is the inner life? And it is here that Zagajewski becomes, not only a Polish poet, but to a great extent a representative poet of our time.

When Zagajewski begins to write about things not conditioned by history—and, in his books, this is clearly the role set aside for poetry, as opposed to prose—we find him strangely inexplicit. Zagajewski is, in some sense, a mystic; the title of his new book is *Mysticism for Beginners,* and throughout his poetry we find a longing toward the mystical as the natural consummation of the private, the ahistorical. But he is certainly not a mystic in the sense that Yeats was a mystic. He doesn't have a doctrine or a system or a single truth; he remains at the point of hoping that perhaps there is such a truth, though he will probably never comprehend it.

In this paradoxical way, Zagajewski is representative: he is a mystical poet of the liberal imagination. He cannot abide oppression of the spirit, even when it comes wearing the friendly face of the Solidarity movement; he insists on solitude, on the freedom to go where his thoughts lead him. But then he finds that they lead him to no place in particular. One (admittedly narrow) definition of liberalism is neutrality; but what happens when the collective no longer cares to direct the spirit? The individual is thrown back on his own resources, which very often turn out to be inadequate. Zagajewski is the poet of this situation, which is responsible both for the universality of his appeal and for the important restrictions of his poetry.

One of those restrictions, of course, lies not in the poems, but in ourselves: almost no American reader will be able to read these poems in the original. How much is really lost in translation is a constant question; but it is likely to be closer to everything than to nothing. And the difficulty with Zagajewski's poetry is the greater because he is, in Schiller's sense, a sentimental poet: he writes about a feeling rather than from within a feeling, and writing about delicate emotions is perhaps the most difficult thing to do in poetry without sounding ridiculous. It is much easier successfully to write a clever line, or a sounding line, than a tender line. And the margin between the touching and the maudlin is inevitably blurred in translation.

Typically, Zagajewski reaches sentiment through the maze of irony, thus justifying the reward by the difficulty of the quest. His characteristic voice is sophisticated and witty, with deep feeling lying just beneath the surface. But occasionally he will write a poem, usually a short one, that is pure sentiment:

> Anecdote of Rain
> I was strolling under the tents of trees and raindrops occasionally reached me as though asking: Is your desire to suffer, to sob?
> Soft air, wet leaves;—the scent was spring, the scent sorrow.

This poem is like one of those sweet, sad lyrics of Eichendorff or Heine that Schumann set to music—not just because of the concision and the directness of the sentiment, but also because of the English speaker's sense that something is missing. It is a beautiful poem, but beautiful in a way that no one writing in English could manage without embarrassment. Reading Zagajewski is, in part, a continual negotiation with this embarrassment, an attempt to recognize that what's missing is just what could redeem the poems from excess of sentiment.

But this is a technical problem, which most likely arises from our ignorance of Polish. There is also a deeper sentiment here, which is not accidental but essential. It is attached to the subject of mystical experience, which for Zagajewski is a constant, tantalizing possibility, if one which is seldom attained. In *Solidarity, Solitude,* the poet insisted that the most important events are private, not public; and in his poetry, we see that these important events are often mystical, which is privacy carried to the point of incommunicability.

In fact, they become more explicitly mystical as Zagajewski's work progresses. In *Tremor,* his first American book, we already see that what matters most to Zagajewski is the transitory feeling of completion, of clarity, which is the hallmark of mystical experience. This feeling comes up in poem after poem, sometimes tinged with wit, sometimes given directly:

> Don't allow the lucid moment to dissolve Let the radiant thought last in stillness though the page is almost filled and the flame flickers....

> At night, an invisible bonfire blazes, the fire which, burning, doesn't destroy but creates, as if it wanted to restore in one moment all that was ravished by flames on various continents....

> The quest for perfection will find fulfillment casually, it will bypass all obstacles just as the Germans learned how to bypass the Maginot Line....

> ... there was so much of the world that it had to do encores over and over, the audience was in frenzy and didn't want to leave the house.

These are all descriptions of a single feeling, in various manifestations. And it is characteristic of this mystical feeling that it is transitory and incomplete:

> The earth won't open up, a thunderbolt won't burn fiery letters on the sky's pelt. Did we deserve a sign so distinct, we who talk too loudly and can't listen? A train pulls out when the stationmaster raises his arm, but a waterfall doesn't wait for a signal. A leaf will sway, a drop of water will glisten.

Or again:

> Clear moments are so short. There is much more darkness. More ocean than firm land. More shadow than form.

Such "clear moments" become more common in his later books of poetry, *Canvas* (1991) and now *Mysticism for Beginners.* In these later books, there is a growing sense that the instant of rapt attention to the world is the center of life, and the proper subject for poetry. These poems are shot through with intimations of immortality:

> So what if Pharaoh's armies pursue you, when eternity is woven through the days of the week like moss in the chinks of a cabin?

> Turn off the glaring sun, listen to the tale of the seed of a poppy. A fence. Chestnut trees. Bindweed. God.

A moment of quiet covenant in the Egyptian museum in Turin.... Here the mysticism is reminiscent of Rilke, at a lower pitch. Zagajewski's litany ("A fence. Chestnut trees. Bindweed. God.") recalls the litany in the *Duino Elegies:*

> Maybe we're here only to say: house, bridge, well, gate, jug, olive tree, window—at most: pillar, tower . . .

Like Rilke, Zagajewski is overcome at times by a powerful sense that the singular being of objects conceals some higher truth. For him, too, things are the sites of illumination.

But for Zagajewski these intimations remain intimations, not explanations or descriptions. And here we are faced with the central problem of his poetry, which is the problem of poetry in the face of the mystical: the mystical experience is not loquacious. The poet may seek "the still point of the turning world," but stillness writes no poetry. What yearns to be expressed, rather, is the experience of waiting for the sudden heightening of consciousness; waiting for it, or remembering it, or lacking it. These are situations of pathos; and the main colors in Zagajewski's palette are loss, longing, and awe, lightened from time to time with shades of wit.

And there is a further problem with mysticism as a subject for poetry: it does not admit of much variation. Poetry thrives on themes that are at the same time simple and fertile: thus Shakespeare can write 154 sonnets about love, and Tennyson can write hundreds of stanzas on mourning, because the subject is at the same time universal enough to compel our interest and general enough to admit of new situations, new shadings. But the mystic moment is indescribable, incommensurable: that is why it is so longed for. Thus Zagajewski, as a poet of the mystical, is condemned to a kind of eternal recurrence of the same poem. To look at the ends of the poems in *Mysticism for Beginners* is to see his predicament: I've taken long walks, craving one thing only: lightning, transformation, you.

> I don't know how—the palm trees opened up my greedy heart.
>
> . . . take me to Tierra del Fuego, take me where the rivers flow straight up, horizontal rivers flowing up and down.

This moment, mortal as you or I, was full of boundless, senseless, silly joy, as if it knew something we didn't. The destination of these poems is usually the same: the moment of opening out to the insensible object of the soul's yearning, whether it is described as "silly joy" or allegorized as "Tierra del Fuego." The poem wants to get to this point, and whatever it describes is a means to an end, not an end in itself.

Zagajewski himself describes this phenomenon in one of the aphoristic essays in *Two Cities,* "The Untold Cynicism of Poetry": "The inner world, which is the absolute kingdom of poetry, is characterized by its inexpressibility. . . . What then does this inner world accomplish if in spite of its inexpressibility it wants more than anything to express itself? It uses cunning. It pretends that it is interested, oh yes, very interested, in external reality." What we have here, perhaps, is the natural evolution of Zagajewski's praise of solitude. In his earlier work, solitude stood in opposition to the collective and the public; and it was good. But now solitude and inwardness are considered in themselves, and they are difficult things. They verge on inexpressibility. As Zagajewski writes in "Lecture on Mystery":

> We do not know what poetry is. We do not know what suffering is. We do not know what death is. We do know what mystery is. Even if we allow that this is true, it still leaves two possibilities for poetry. One is to make poetry describe its subject as attentively as possible: thus Shakespeare's sonnets do not tell us "what love is," but they bring us closer to such an understanding. The other possibility is to stand scrupulously back from the subject, honoring its inexpressibility. In this case, the ostensible subject of the poem—love, death, suffering—is no longer the real subject; rather, the subject is the author's consciousness in the face of this ultimate limitation.

This is the kind of poetry Zagajewski writes. It is poetry that threatens to lead to silence.

But Zagajewski is in no danger of falling silent. He is not an otherworldly or ascetic mystic, who feels driven from this world by hints of another. His alienation is not radical, it is occasional. And in this, too, he is a poet of the liberal imagination: his vision of the mystical does not put everything at stake. Not for him wagers or leaps; he is content to see the lineaments of something higher peeking through the things of this world, without forcing it to reveal itself as a coherent structure.

The clearest sign of Zagajewski's attachment to the world is his wit. Mysticism and humor do not usually go together. But quick and memorable absurdities temper the darkness of much of Zagajewski's poetry: Practicing elocution like a timid Demosthenes, the Danube flows over flat stones.

> What are baroque churches? Deluxe health clubs for athletic saints.
>
> Now rain dictates a long, tedious lecture. . . .

Sometimes Zagajewski is simply funny, as in the title of one poem: "Franz Schubert: A Press Conference." ("No, I'm not familiar with Wagner's music.") But more often his wit is employed to intimate a darkness without stating it, as in this miniature theodicy:

> At the Orthodox church in Paris, the last White gray-haired Russians pray to God, who is centuries younger than they and equally helpless.

Or this, about Stalinism:

> One day apes made their grab for power. Gold seal-rings, starched shirts, aromatic Havanas, feet squashed into patent leather.

Wit is even more evident in Zagajewski's prose. His most important achievement in prose is the development of a kind of very short essay, occasionally shrinking to aphorism, in which wit and irony can flourish. This is the style of "The Little Larousse," from *Solidarity, Solitude* and "The New Little Larousse," from *Two Cities*. Here Zagajewski is very often brilliant:

> [The Poles] write books as if they were to be documents considered during a future peace conference that will decide the fate of Europe.

> Territorial conquests are not just changes in boundaries and the imposition of an unwanted government. They are also detectable when we cease to see the earth.

The adjective is the indispensable guarantor of the individuality of people and things. I see a pile of melons at a fruit stand. For an opponent of adjectives, this matter presents no difficulty: "Melons are piled on the fruit stand." Meanwhile, one melon is as sallow as Talleyrand's complexion when he addressed the Congress of Vienna . . . another has sunken cheeks, and is lost in a deep, mournful silence, as if it could not bear to part with the fields of Provence. This side of Zagajewski's sensibility seems far removed from the yearning mystic. Indeed, it is what can make him attractive even to those readers who have little patience for epiphany; it gives evidence of an unconstrained, undogmatic intelligence. With its rapid and unlikely juxtapositions, wit tends to undermine certainty. When you begin to see God as an old Russian exile, or commissars as cigar-smoking apes, you have stolen their old authority; a doubleness of perspective has set in.

In this respect, wit is intimately bound up with the liberal imagination, and with sentimental poetry. In *Solidarity, Solitude,* Zagajewski writes that "one must think against oneself . . . otherwise one is not free." But what is implied by this is that freedom of thought is more important than thinking rightly. Once the thinker becomes more devoted to his thinking than to his thought, dogma is impossible. And clearly the importance of thinking against oneself was brought home to Zagajewski living in a totalitarian state, where the stupidity and cruelty of the prevailing dogmas was plain.

What is left, then, is not correctness of thought, but nimbleness of thought. The Danube is not the Danube but Demosthenes; the rain is not the rain but a tedious professor. And the mystical is, perhaps, not the mystical at all, but merely a moment of contentment, a feeling, a shadow. This possibility hovers around the title poem of *Mysticism for Beginners,* itself a fine example of Zagajewski's philosophical wit:

> The day was mild, the light was generous. The German on the cafe terrace held a small book on his lap. I caught sight of the title: *Mysticism for Beginners.* Suddenly I understood that the swallows patrolling the streets of Montepulciano with their shrill whistles . . . and the dusk, slow and systematic, erasing the outlines of medieval houses, and olive trees on little hills . . . and any journey, any kind of trip, are only mysticism for beginners, the elementary course, prelude to a test that's been postponed.

Zagajewski does not disavow mysticism in this poem, but he makes it the subject of a melancholy lightness, and thus puts it at an immense remove from belief. It is the same thing that happens when Donne begins a poem about the Judgment Day with "At the round earth's imagined corners, blow/Your trumpets, angels": since we know that there are no corners, we start to question whether there are angels. Similarly, in Zagajewski, the unlikeliness of mysticism "for beginners," as if it were a hobby like woodworking, makes us wonder about mysticism itself. The test has been postponed. Or has it been cancelled? Perhaps the test was never scheduled at all.

And so the mystical for Zagajewski is never free from doubt. The last poem in his new book is a touching example of this:

> I walked through the medieval town in the evening or at dawn, I was very young or rather old. I didn't have a watch or a calendar, only my stubborn blood measured the endless expanse. I could begin life, mine or not mine, over, everything seemed easy, apartment windows were partway open, other fates ajar. It was spring or early summer, warm walls, air soft as an orange rind; I was very young or rather old, I could choose, I could live.

This is the emotional ground out of which mysticism grows; but here the poet sticks to what is empirical and indisputable, to the emotion itself. The ability of the man who aspires to certainty to stop short of certainty: this is the hallmark of the liberal intelligence. The "thinking against oneself" which gives rise to wit also gives rise to hesitancy in the face of the absolute and the infinite, even when they are devoutly desired. And for this reason, Zagajewski's verse is unsettled and unsettling. He puts the matter perfectly:

> Two contradictory elements meet in poetry: ecstasy and irony. The ecstatic element is tied to an unconditional acceptance of the world, including even what is cruel and absurd. Irony, in contrast, is the artistic representation of thought, criticism, doubt. Ecstasy is ready to accept the entire world; irony, following in the steps of thought, questions everything, asks tendentious questions, doubts the meaning of poetry and even of itself. Irony knows that the world is tragic and sad.

That two such vastly different elements shape poetry is astounding and even compromising. No wonder almost no one reads poems.

Source: Adam Kirsch, Review of *Mysticism for Beginners*, in *New Republic*, Vol. 218, No. 12, March 23, 1998, pp. 36–40.

John Taylor

In the following review, Taylor speaks of the uprooted and nomadic nature of Zagajewski's own life as a Polish exile and how it has influenced these meditative poems, which seek a spiritual security and illumination.

"Suddenly you see the world lit differently," writes the Polish poet Adam Zagajewski in *Mysticism for Beginners*, his third translated collection. This declaration sums up well the engaging movement of these meditative poems, which meander gently toward moments of enlightenment. Informed by exile and travel (Zagajewski divides his time between Paris and Houston), as well as by respect for everyday life, his longer poems especially search not so much for severed Polish roots as for insight and wisdom—wherever he is. In "Letter from a Reader," which seemingly defines his own aims, he tells himself to attend to "the endless patience / of the light." Metaphors involving light and darkness (or shadow) indeed appear frequently, with the hope tendered that this miraculous light can sometimes—as he remarks apropos of Vermeer's "Little Girl"—inhabit a work of art.

Contemporary lives, suggests Zagajewski, are only rarely rooted, stable, spiritually secure, let alone illuminated. We experience "travel instead of remembrance"; we write "quick poem[s]" instead of "hymn[s]." Yet for all its sad tonalities, his verse shows that an existence marked by mobility and ontological doubt need not eventually bog down into anguish—the paralyzing predicament of many modern writers. Despair can depend on our view of our earliest years—from which we may be brutally separated. Yet "why is childhood," asks the poet, "our only origin, our only longing?"

Zagajewski grapples with this key question. Typically, he studies the present and looks forward, though elegiac images do arise and give pause. "It was a gray landscape," he solemnly recalls, "houses small / as Tartar ponies, concrete high-rises, / massive, stillborn; uniforms everywhere, rain, / drowsy rivers not knowing where to flow, / dust, Soviet gods with swollen eyelids." Another compelling poem likewise mourns his mother and meditates on memory. Yet moving away from the post-war Poland in which he grew up, he more often readies himself for encounters with uplifting transcendence (amidst the flat dehumanizing drabness of modern societies, little matter the political regime). Near-prayers can result, such as is expressed by his wish to see "Tierra del Fuego, / . . . where the rivers / flow straight up."

Our lives can briefly crystalize, he movingly shows, in unexpected plenitude. After leaving a Romanesque church, for example, he marvels at how a mere moment miraculously enters "the timid grass," inhabits "stems and genes, / the pupils of our eyes" and conveys its "boundless, senseless, / silly joy." Tellingly, however, these moments "know something" we cannot grasp. Aspiring to such mysteries, Zagajewski realizes that he must eschew irony, become completely sincere, turn poetry into a means of exploration, not an end in itself. Some poems reflect his struggles to do so. A subtle craftsman, he avoids ostentatious effects, focuses on the deepest meanings. The title poem revealingly equates even our finest perceptions with only an "elementary course" in mysticism. The path to understanding necessarily remains untrodden; but its first turnings have been glimpsed by the attentive, self-effacing poet.

Source: John Taylor, Review of *Mysticism for Beginners*, in *Poetry*, Vol. 173, No. 2, December 1998, p. 185.

Sources

Kirsch, Adam, "The Lucid Moment," in the *New Republic*, March 23, 1998, pp. 36, 38–40.

Osherow, Jacqueline, "Books: Poetry Collections," in *Antioch Review*, Vol. 56, No. 4, Fall 1998, p. 500.

Review of *Mysticism for Beginners*, in *Publishers Weekly*, December 22, 1997, pp. 55–56.

Taylor, John, "Short Reviews," in *Poetry*, Vol. 173, No. 2, December 1998, pp. 185–86.

Witkowski, Tadeusz, "The Poets of the New Wave in Exile," in *Slavic and East European Journal*, Vol. 33, No. 2, Summer 1989, pp. 204–205.

Zagajewski, Adam, "Self-Portrait," in *Mysticism for Beginners*, Farrar, Straus and Giroux, 1999, pp. 35–36.

Further Reading

Hawkins, Gary, "Between the Quotidian and the Transcendent," in *World Literature Today*, Vol. 79, No. 2, August 2005, pp. 23–26.

In this essay, Hawkins applies Zagajewski's literary theories to his poetry, specifically his thoughts on irony.

Hong, Anna Maria, "Adam Zagajewski on the Power to Restore Beauty and Advice for Beginning Mystics," in *Poets and Writers*, August 13, 2004, available online at http://www.pw.org/mag/dq_zagajewski.htm.

In this interview, Zagajewski discusses his views of the relationship between poetry and the world.

Shallcross, Bozena, "The Divining Moment: Adam Zagajewski's Aesthetics of Epiphany," in *Slavic and East European Journal*, Vol. 44, No. 2, Summer 2000, pp. 234–52.

Shallcross examines the sudden, intense experiences sparked by art in Zagajewski's poetry.

Witkowski, Tadeusz, "Between Poetry and Politics: Two Generations," in *Periphery: Journal of Polish Affairs*, Vol. 2, 1996, pp. 38–43, available online at http://www.personal.engin.umich.edu/~zbigniew/Periphery/No2/witkowski.html.

Witkowski traces the development of Zagajewski's poetics, from his early days in the New Wave to his later years as an exile.

Supernatural Love

Gjertrud Schnackenberg
1985

In the 1980s, a number of young American poets, Gjertrud Schnackenberg among them, began writing poetry in rhyme and meter rather than in the free verse that had dominated the American poetry scene since the late 1950s. Schnackenberg's "Supernatural Love" is written in iambic pentameter, a meter of five two-syllable feet with the first syllable accented and the second unaccented; it is divided into tercets, or triplets—three-line stanzas in which the last word of each line rhymes with the other two. Thematically, the poem explores the relationship between the history and definitions of certain words and Christian theological doctrine, weaving these elements into a touching anecdote about the relationship between a four-year-old girl and her father.

"Supernatural Love," was first published in Schnackenberg's second collection of poetry, *The Lamplit Answer*, in 1985. It subsequently has been reprinted in many poetry anthologies, including the second edition of the *Norton Anthology of Modern Poetry* (1996). *The Lamplit Answer* was so well received by critics that during the 1980s Schnackenberg was considered one of the outstanding young poets writing in America. Her later publications have solidified her reputation. Much of her work is difficult, but "Supernatural Love" is one of her most accessible poems.

Author Biography

Gjertrud Schnackenberg was born on August 27, 1953, in Tacoma, Washington. Her Lutheran family was of Norwegian descent. Her father, Walter Charles Schnackenberg, taught at Pacific Lutheran University in Tacoma, a college that was founded by Norwegian immigrants. As Schnackenberg grew up, she enjoyed a very close relationship with her father, and his early death in 1973 affected her profoundly. At the time, she was an undergraduate student at Mount Holyoke College, from which she graduated summa cum laude with a bachelor of arts degree in 1975. At Mount Holyoke, students and professors alike were aware of her remarkable talent, and in 1973 and 1974 she won the prestigious Glascock Prize for poetry. This recognition brought her work to the attention of influential poets. Her first published collection, *Portraits and Elegies* (1982), was enthusiastically received by critics and established her as one of the foremost young poets in America. Many of the poems in the collection were tributes to her late father, recalling the times she had spent with him. In "Nightfishing," for example, she remembers a predawn fishing trip they made together; in "Returning North," she describes a trip to Norway they took when she was ten years old.

During the 1980s, Schnackenberg won many awards, including the Lavan Younger Poets Award from the Academy of American Poets (1983), the Rome Prize in Literature (1983–1984) from the American Academy and Institute of Arts and Letters, and an Amy Lowell Traveling Prize (1984–1985), which enabled her to spend two years in Italy. She was also awarded an honorary doctorate from Mount Holyoke College in 1985, the same year in which her second collection, *The Lamplit Answer*, was published. This collection contains the poem "Supernatural Love."

Schnackenberg has published her poetry infrequently. It was seven years before her third collection, *A Gilded Lapse of Time*, appeared in 1992. *The Throne of Labdacus*, poems based on the Oedipus legend, followed in 2000. In the same year, *Supernatural Love: Poems 1976–1992* was published, containing selections from her previously published work.

Schnackenberg's first marriage, to Paul Smyth, ended in divorce. She married Robert Nozick, a Harvard philosophy professor, in 1987. They had met after Nozick read *The Lamplit Answer* in the Harvard bookstore in 1985 and decided that he wanted to meet the author. They shared a life of art, philosophy, writing, and travel until Nozick's death from cancer in 2002.

Poem Summary

Stanzas 1–4

In "Supernatural Love," the speaker tells of an incident that involved herself and her father when she was four years old. The poem is set in a dimly lit study in which father and daughter are present. The father is at a dictionary stand, consulting a dictionary, which is illumined by a lamp. He holds a magnifying glass in his hand and scans the dictionary, running his finger down the page in order to find the word he is looking for. Then he holds the magnifying glass still above the definition of the word *carnation*. He bends closer to the dictionary and puts his finger on the page and reads the definition. The definition of one word seems to help him make some kind of as yet unspecified connection with something much larger.

Stanzas 5–8

The child, who is doing cross-stitch on a needlework sampler, imitates her father by bringing her sewing needle to her eye, which allows her to see her father through the eye of the needle "as through a lens ground for a butterfly" (stanza 4). It is likely that she is sitting very near him, to be close to the light; as she looks up at him, she sees his eyes "magnified and blurred" (stanza 3) through the lens of his magnifying glass. The poet then compares the girl looking through the needle's eye to a butterfly probing a flower ("flower-hallways") with its long, tubelike mouth in order to suck up the nectar it needs. Perhaps the nectar is located in the "room / shadowed and fathomed" within the flower, to which the "hallways" lead. These rooms are imagined by the poet to be as dark as the dimly lit study in which the girl sits. Another simile follows, in which the father, poring over a dictionary and reading the Latin derivation of the word he is looking up ("Latin blossom"), is compared to a scholar bending over a tomb to read the inscription on it.

The four-year-old girl then spills her pins and needles on the floor as she tries "to stitch the word 'Beloved' " (stanza 8) in her sampler, cross-stitch by cross-stitch. Although she cannot read, she feels connected by her needle to the word. She refers to her needle as dangerous for reasons that will become apparent later in the poem.

Stanzas 9–13

The girl's father is looking up the word *carnation* in the dictionary to find out why his daughter calls carnations "Christ's flowers." He knows that she can give no explanation for this other than to say "Because." All she knows (the adult speaker's voice explains) is that for some reason, the root meanings of words convey a silent, preverbal message to her, just as the threads at the back of her sampler (themselves like roots) contribute in an unseen way to the word "beloved" she is trying to create, which has as its root the word *love*.

Her father then reads out the definition of *carnation* in the dictionary. It is a pink variety of clove, from the Latin root *carnatio*, meaning flesh. The adult speaker's voice suggests that it is as if the essential oils of the flower are sending the fragrance of Christ through the room. When the girl hears this definition, the odor of carnations floats up to her, and she imagines the stems of the flowers squeaking in her scissors as they are cut. With that cut, the stems seem to speak, or at least a voice is heard, saying, *"Child, it's me"* (stanza 13).

Stanzas 14–16

Her father then turns the pages of the dictionary to the word *clove* and reads the definition aloud to her. The clove is a spice dried from a flower bud. He reads further that the word is from the French word, *clou*, meaning "a nail." Twice he rereads the information, as if he has not understood it the first time. Then he gazes, standing completely still, contemplating. He again mulls over the fact that clove, *clou*, means "a nail."

The girl continues stitching "beloved." Then the girl's needle catches within the threads. An italicized phrase follows, *"Thy blood so dearly bought"* (stanza 16), which is a reference to the doctrine that Christ's blood bought salvation for all. The relevance of this becomes apparent in the first line of the next stanza.

Stanzas 17–19

As she tries to free the needle from the thread in which it has been caught up, the girl accidentally pricks her finger with the needle. It cuts to the bone. She lifts her hand and sees that she has actually driven the needle through her own flesh ("it is myself I've sewn"). Now the threads she sees are threads of her own blood as it trickles down her hand. Startled and in pain, she lifts her hand and calls out for her father, "Daddy daddy."

Her father touches her injured finger lightly, as "lightly as he touched the page" (stanza 19) of the dictionary just a few moments earlier. The poem ends with a reiteration of the significance of the definitions of the words he looked up: the French and Latin roots of the words *carnation* and *clove* explain why the four-year-old child was correct in her association of carnations with Christ.

Themes

Poetic Symbolism and Theological Doctrine

The theme of supernatural love, the love of God for humans, is emphasized by the activity of both father and daughter. The father investigates the root meanings of words and discovers why the carnation is a perfect symbol for the incarnation and crucifixion of Christ, since *carnation* comes from the Latin root meaning "flesh" and a carnation is a type of clove, which comes from the French word *clou*, meaning "nail." Thus a kind of poetic shorthand symbolizing a central Christian doctrine is set up, in which flesh equals incarnation and nail equals crucifixion. In Christian theology, Jesus Christ is the son of God, sent by God to save humankind from sin. By dying on the Cross, Christ redeemed humans from the curse of the Original Sin committed by Adam and Eve in the Garden of Eden. Christ was wholly divine but was born into human flesh and was therefore fully human too.

The activity of the four-year-old girl as she stitches "Beloved" in her needlework sampler suggests the inner meaning of the incarnation, death, and resurrection of Christ. "Beloved" is a reference to Christ, especially to the passage in the Gospels that follows Christ's baptism. A voice from heaven is heard saying, "This is my beloved Son, with whom I am well pleased" (Matthew 3:17). The incarnation of Christ is a demonstration of God's love for the world, since he sent his only son, whom he loved, to redeem it. The girl's cross-stitches in her sampler, indicated in the poem by the letter *X* (stanza 8), graphically suggest the cross on which Christ was crucified. Thus, just as her father, in his investigation in the dictionary, unearths a link between incarnation and crucifixion, so does the girl, in her needlework, stumble upon a link between supernatural love (the significance of the word *beloved* when applied to Christ) and the crucifixion.

Finally, the poem brings father and daughter together in a small but symbolic interaction that not only establishes their close relationship but also echoes the relationship between God and his son Christ in Christian theology. When the girl pricks herself with the needle and bleeds, she re-creates

Topics For Further Study

- Write an essay in which you compare and contrast "Supernatural Love" with Sylvia Plath's poem "Daddy," from her collection *Ariel*, or Andrew Hudgins's poem "Elegy for My Father, Who Is Not Dead," in Hudgins's collection *The Never-Ending* (1991). What does each poem reveal about the relationship between son or daughter and father?

- Write a short poem on any topic in metered verse that rhymes. Try to introduce variations in the meter, so that the poem does not sound monotonous. Then take the same theme and write the poem in free verse. Write a separate brief essay in which you state which is the better poem and why and which was easier to write.

- Make a class presentation in which you discuss the question of whether poetry has any relevance for modern life. What do poetry and other forms of literature add to life that cannot be gained from business, science, or technology? Why are the arts needed at all?

- Consider whether popular song lyrics, for example, rap or country-and-western songs, can be thought of as poetry. What poetic techniques do these songs use and why? Are some advertising jingles poetry? What poetic techniques do they use and why? Make a class presentation, using examples from CDs or music videos to illustrate your points.

---

within herself in miniature the drama of the crucifixion, when the nails pierced Christ's flesh. Her call, "Daddy daddy—" (stanza 18) is an echo of the cry of Jesus to his father on the cross: "My God, my God, why hast thou forsaken me?" (Matthew 27:46). Resurrection and salvation are implied at the end of the poem when the girl's father, now also identified with the heavenly father, touches her lightly to heal her. In a theological context, this suggests the absolute human dependence on God for salvation.

The theological framework of the poem is reinforced by clusters of images. After the girl pricks her finger with the needle, she says, "the threads of blood my own" (stanza 17), which suggests the relevance of the crucifixion to her own experience and also links her stitching of the word *beloved* to the crucifixion, since the threads she is using are now stained with her blood and the blood associated with Christ's saving death has just been mentioned, in stanza 16 ("*Thy blood so dearly bought*"). Further, the blood-thread image is linked to the incarnation of Christ, in the words "my threads like stems" (stanza 16), meaning the stems of carnations. In this way, the images all weave together to create a tapestry of meaning that reinforces the theme of supernatural love manifesting through the incarnation and crucifixion of Christ. The child speaker, who intuits much more than she understands intellectually, is used by the poet to create and communicate poetic symbolism through the interplay between the root meanings of the words the child's father looks up and theological concepts.

Style

Variations in Rhyme

The poem is written in tercets, which are stanzas of three lines that contain a single rhyme. In other words, the endings of all three lines rhyme. In stanza 1, for example, "dictionary-stand," "understand," and "hand" all rhyme; in stanza 2, "lens," "suspends," and "bends" all rhyme; and so on. In some stanzas, the rhymes are approximate rather than exact, and these are known as off rhymes, near rhymes, or imperfect rhymes. Stanza 10, ending with "because," "messages," and "does," is an example in which the vowel sounds are different in each word.

Stanza 11 contains an example of what is called eye rhyme, in which the endings of words are spelled the same and thus look as if they rhyme, but they are pronounced differently. These words are "move," "love," and "clove." In stanza 15, all three lines end in the word "nail," an example of what is called identical rhyme or tautological rhyme. When a rhymed word at the end of a line falls on a stressed syllable, it is known as a masculine rhyme. Examples of masculine rhymes occur in stanza 3 with "blurred," "word," and "heard"; in stanza 4 with "string," "thing," and "bring"; in stanza 6 with "room," "gloom," and "tomb"; and in stanza 7 with "pore," "four," and "floor." When a rhymed word at the end of the line falls on an unstressed syllable, it is known as a feminine rhyme. An example occurs in stanza 18 with "agony," "daddy," and "injury."

Variations in Meter

The overall meter of the poem is iambic pentameter. Meter is the rhythm of stressed and unstressed syllables in a poetic foot. A foot consists of a combination of stressed and unstressed syllables (sometimes called strong stresses and weak, or light, stresses). An iambic foot (or, in its noun form, an iamb) is an unstressed syllable followed by a stressed syllable. Iambic pentameter is made up of five iambic feet to a line. One of the clearest examples of iambic pentameter in the poem is in stanza 14: "He turns the page to 'Clove' and reads aloud." Another line in which the iambic meter is especially clear is in stanza 10: "The way the thread behind my sampler does."

Poets make subtle alterations to the meter of their poems. These alterations keep the poems from becoming monotonous and sing-song. Often the alterations are used to bring sharper attention to a word or concept. A common variation in iambic pentameter is to invert the first foot in a line. In "Supernatural Love," stanza 1 begins not with an iamb but with a trochee, "Touches," in which a stressed syllable is followed by an unstressed one. Other examples of an inverted first iambic foot (or a trochaic foot, to use the adjective form of *trochee*), in which the variation stands out against the basic metrical rhythm, occur in stanza 6 ("Shadowed"), stanza 8 ("trying"), and stanza 12 ("Christ's fra-"). In stanza 10, there is another kind of variation in the first foot, a spondee, "Word-root," in which both syllables are stressed. This spondaic foot (the adjective form of *spondee*) is then followed by another metrical variation, a trochee ("blossom") rather than an iamb.

Caesura

A caesura is a pause within the line, often indicated by a comma or a period. Poets will use caesura to create emphasis and variety in a line of verse. In stanza 7, there is a caesura: "Over the Latin blossom. I am four." Stanza 15 contains two caesuras, the second longer than the first: "He gazes, motionless. 'Meaning a nail.'" The caesuras, which slow the poem down, express the sense of stillness conveyed by the meaning of the words. The caesuras in the last lines of stanza 2 ("Above the word 'Carnation.' Then he bends") and stanza 4 ("That's smaller than the 'universe.' I bring") help illustrate another technique the poet uses. The placing of the period near the end of the line ensures that the sentence that follows it carries over to the next stanza. This is known as a run-on line, in which the end of the line does not correspond with a completed unit of meaning. Schnackenberg makes frequent use of run-on lines in this poem, especially in the last lines of the stanzas.

Historical Context

The New Formalism

In the 1960s and 1970s, most poets in America wrote in free verse, which paid no attention to rhyme or meter or traditional poetic form. The predominant form was the personal lyric. During the 1980s, this started to change, and a movement emerged known as the New Formalism, in which poets returned to writing verse in traditional forms. The trend is noted by the poet and critic Dana Gioia in his 1987 essay "Notes on the New Formalism." He points out that two of the most impressive first poetry volumes of the decade are Brad Leithauser's *Hundreds of Fireflies* (1983) and Vikram Seth's *The Golden Gate* (1986), both of which were written entirely in formal verse. He might well have added Schnackenberg's *Portraits and Elegies* (1982) and *The Lamplit Answer* (1985), since she, too, was a poet working exclusively with traditional poetic forms. Gioia's own first collection of poetry, *Daily Horoscope* (1986), is also a contribution to the new movement.

Gioia notes that the new development is quite radical because, in 1980, most young poets had been trained so exclusively on free verse that they were unable to write poems in traditional meters. The literary culture in which they were raised emphasized the visual (sight) rather than the aural (sound), and poems were seen as words on a page

Compare & Contrast

- **1980s:** The emergence of New Formalism in American poetry challenges the dominance of free verse.

    Today: The coexistence of free verse and formalism in contemporary poetry creates a highly diverse literary culture.

- **1980s:** The poetry slam is invented in a jazz club in Chicago in 1986. It treats poetry as a competition, with cash prizes for the winner. Poetry slams spread to other major cities in the United States and attract large audiences, showing that poetry can still be popular.

    Today: Poetry slams continue to flourish nationwide. The National Slam attracts teams from all over the United States, Canada, and other countries. Academic credentials are unimportant for success in poetry slams. Performers must be able to project their poetry to an audience, and showmanship counts as much as poetic skill. The vocal delivery of successful poetry slam performers is similar to hip-hop music.

- **1980s:** In a decade of political and cultural conservatism, momentum builds for large budget cuts in federal subsidies for the arts, including the National Endowment for the Arts (NEA) and the National Endowment for the Humanities (NEH). This is, in part, because several controversial artists supported by NEA grants produce work that offends mainstream religious sensibilities.

    Today: After the 1990s, in which some Republican congressmen called for the abolition of the NEA and the NEA budget was cut by 40 percent, the NEA and NEH receive relatively favorable treatment from the administration of George W. Bush. At a time of budget cuts, both endowments remain stable in the allocation of federal funds. In 2005, for financial year 2006, Congress approves an increase of $4.4 million for the NEA.

---

rather than something to be read out loud. "Literary journalism has long declared it [traditional form] defunct, and most current anthologies present no work in traditional forms by Americans written after 1960," writes Gioia. He argues that the New Formalism, which was a revival not only of rhyme and meter but also of narrative poetry (that is, poetry that tells a story) came about as a reaction to the fact that poetry had lost its broad popular audience. It had become overly intellectualized, and poets were mostly confined to the academy, where they wrote poems that were read only by a small coterie of other poets, graduate students in creative writing, editors of poetry magazines and small presses, and grant-giving organizations. New Formalists, on the other hand, saw themselves as populists, which means in this context that they wrote for people who were not necessarily highly educated. Many of the New Formalists also worked outside the university setting. Gioia, for example, made his living as a businessman. Other poets associated with New Formalism in the 1980s included Marilyn Hacker, William Logan, Timothy Steele, Robert McDowell, Mark Jarman, and Mary Jo Salter.

The New Formalism was greeted with some hostility by poets and critics who preferred free verse to traditional forms. The term *New Formalism* itself was coined by hostile critics, who believed that traditional poetic forms were artificial and elitist and stifled free expression. In his essay "What's New about the New Formalism," Robert McPhillips describes the attack on the new movement by critics who "labeled these new formal poems as the products of 'yuppie' poets for whom a poem is mere artifice, something to be valued as a material object; or, more perniciously, as the product of a neoconservative *Zeitgeist*." (*Zeitgeist* is a German word that can be translated as "spirit of the times.") The argument is that there was nothing new about New Formalism, that it was merely a throwback to what was regarded as the dry, academic poetry of the

1950s, against which free verse was a welcome revolution. McPhillips argues that this is untrue. He believes that the New Formalists' "attention to form has allowed a significant number of younger poets to think and communicate clearly about their sense of what is of most human value—love, beauty, mortality."

Sometimes the New Formalism has been referred to as the Expansive Movement, meaning that poetry was being expanded in terms of the number of forms that were considered acceptable. This term included the attempt to revive narrative and dramatic verse, in what was sometimes called the New Narrative.

Critical Overview

When "Supernatural Love" was first published in *The Lamplit Answer*, Rosetta Cohen, reviewing the book for *The Nation*, picked it out for appreciative comment: "Through the rigid symmetries of the tercets, Schnackenberg conflates the love of parent with the love of Christ, and the simplest actions—the child embroidering, the father searching out the Latin root of a word—become transcendent by way of the child's sudden, tiny self-inflicted wound." Since publication, the poem has often been reprinted in poetry anthologies and has been posted and discussed on various Internet poetry forums. When it was included in the selection of Schnackenberg's poems published under the title *Supernatural Love: Poems 1976–1992*, it attracted more favorable comment from reviewers. In *Poetry*, Christian Wiman declares it to be finest poem in the book and places it with some of Schnackenberg's other poems of the period as "a substantial and rare accomplishment. I think people will be reading some of these poems for a long time." Wiman adds, in a comment that could certainly apply to "Supernatural Love," " Schnackenberg's particular gift is for a kind of clear density, for making many different strands of experience part of a single, deceptively simple weave. Difficulty dissolves into the fluent lines and surprising rhymes of the finished poem."

In the *New York Review of Books*, Daniel Mendelsohn has similar praise for "Supernatural Love" as "thematically ambitious . . . an intricately achieved meditation on poetry, time, love, and faith." Adam Kirsch, in the *New York Times Book Review*, also admires Schnackenberg for the ambitious nature of her poetry and comments in words that might well apply to "Supernatural Love": "Her verse is strong, dense and musical, anchored in the pentameter even when it veers into irregularity; behind it are formidable masters, Robert Lowell most notably, but also Yeats and Auden."

Criticism

Bryan Aubrey

Aubrey holds a Ph.D. in English and has published many articles on twentieth-century poetry. In this essay, he discusses "Supernatural Love" in the context of the acrimonious debate in the 1980s over the respective merits of free and formal verse.

In the 1980s, a virtual civil war broke out in America among those whose job it was to write and discuss poetry. The free-verse movement, which had gathered strength in the late 1950s as a rebellion against what it perceived as the lifeless academic poetry of the literary establishment, now felt compelled, having become an establishment itself, to defend its turf against the New Formalists. The acrimonious debate between those who favored "open" or "closed" poetic forms had political overtones. In a decade that was dominated politically by conservatism (the Reagan era), some advocates of free verse denounced the New Formalists as cultural and political conservatives.

In an essay published in *Writer's Chronicle* in 1984, Ariel Dawson refers to the New Formalists as yuppies intent on reviving elitist traditions. (*Yuppie* was a term used in the 1980s to describe young, high-earning urban or suburban professionals.) In "The New Conservatism in American Poetry," a notorious essay published in 1986, the poet Diane Wakoski, whose work was heavily influenced by the free verse of Allen Ginsberg and William Carlos Williams, argues for the centrality of Walt Whitman and Williams to American poetry. She attacks John Hollander, a poet who writes in traditional forms and who defended the new movement, and she insists that it is un-American to write in traditional forms. Dana Gioia responds by suggesting that Wakoski's position is the literary equivalent of "the quest for pure Germanic culture led by the late Joseph Goebbels" (quoted by Robert McPhillips in "Reading the New Formalists").

In the midst of these blistering accusations and counter-accusations—neutral onlookers were no doubt surprised to see people who happened to prefer one type of poetry over another denounce one

> "English is not a language rich in rhymes, and a stanza that calls for three rhyming words will tax the ingenuity of the best of poets."

another as Fascists or Nazis—some New Formalists took to defending their poetic practice by appealing to their understanding of human physiology and biology. In their 1985 essay "The Neural Lyre: Poetic Meter, the Brain, and Time," Frederick Turner and Ernst Pöppel use the latest scientific knowledge about how the human brain works to shed light on what they regard as the universal pleasurable appeal of poetic meter. They argue that in numerous cultures in the world, the most common unit of poetry is a metrical line that takes about three seconds to recite. This corresponds to the three-second rhythm of the human information-processing system; in other words, it is how the brain best processes information. Metrical variations, the authors argue, also encourage whole-brain functioning, uniting the linguistic powers of the left hemisphere with the musical and pictorial powers of the right hemisphere. They claim that poetic meter produces positive subjective sensations, such as "a profound muscular relaxation yet an intense alertness and concentration" that can produce an "avalanche of vigorous thought, in which new connections are made." Turner and Pöppel also claim that metered verse may promote "biophysiological stress-reduction (peace) and social solidarity (love)." In a swipe at their opponents, the authors insist that free verse does not engage the whole brain and produces none of these benefits. Free verse suits the needs of a bureaucratic and even totalitarian state, because it tends to restrict poetry to a narrow range of personal lyric descriptions that do not threaten existing power structures.

In his 1988 essay "Strict Wildness: The Biology of Poetry," the poet Peter Viereck argues in similar fashion that the iambic or trochaic foot, with its two beats, corresponds to various biological processes and is therefore fundamental to human life. The heart beats to an iambic rhythm, and the inhaling and exhaling of the lungs is iambic, as is "the open-shut of nerve synapse, the alternating current of electric shock, the ebb-flow of the moon-leashed tides." Viereck also contends that even the pentameter line (containing five feet of two beats each) corresponds to a physiological rhythm, since the inhale-exhale of the lungs takes five times as long as two heartbeats (the systole and diastole) of the heart; there are five heartbeats per breath. Thus, in a sense, the iambic pentameter is in our pulse and our breath. Viereck uses these and many more examples drawn from natural processes to proclaim the necessity of metered rather than free verse. He does not denounce all free verse but advocates what he calls a "strict wildness" in poetry, which he defines as "a living, biological, content-expressing form," and he names Schnackenberg, among others, as a poet who exemplifies this ideal.

Schnackenberg herself took no part in the polemics that flew back and forth regarding the claims of formal or free verse. She preferred to let her poetry, itself consistently formal, speak for itself. But others drew her into the dispute. The critic Vernon Shetley, in his book *After the Death of Poetry: Poet and Audience in Contemporary America* (1993), argues that the New Formalists were wrong to believe that "poetry can stand aside from the general tide of culture and restore an earlier form of community by resurrecting earlier poetic forms." He singles out Schnackenberg's "Supernatural Love," a poem praised by so many, for stinging criticism. Taking up one of the common complaints about the New Formalism, he claims that the poem exhibits metrical monotony.

In particular, he quotes the last four stanzas and argues that they are especially marked by lack of metrical variation. He points out that all the lines are perfect pentameters, with "largely unadventurous" variations. The accented syllables in the lines are very close to each other in the degree of stress they are given. The lines are also made up mostly of monosyllables, meaning that boundaries of words and feet coincide. Finally, Shetley states that there is little variety in the placement of the caesuras, which in these lines occur after the fourth, fifth, and sixth syllables. His conclusion is that this "repetitious line structure" gives the "impression of stiffness and monotony in the handling of meter." Readers may judge for themselves whether Shetley's criticisms are valid. It should be noted, however, that the earlier part of the poem, which Shetley does not quote, shows considerably more metrical variety as well as more variety in the placing of the caesuras.

Meter, of course, is only one aspect of the formal structure of "Supernatural Love." Many readers

What Do I Read Next?

- Schnackenberg's first book, *Portraits and Elegies* (1982), marked her emergence as a poet who had mastered a wide variety of types of formal verse. Reviewers hailed this collection as evidence of an exciting new voice in American poetry. Many of the poems in this collection are more accessible for the general reader than some of Schnackenberg's complex later work.

- *Rebel Angels: 25 Poets of the New Formalism* (1996), edited by Mark Jarman and David Mason, is an anthology that brings together most of the major poets of the New Formalism. Curiously, the editors omit Schnackenberg. The poets represented include Tom Disch, Timothy Steele, Mary Jo Salter, Brad Leithauser, Marilyn Hacker, Molly Peacock, Sydney Lea, Dana Gioia, and Andrew Hudgins.

- In his introduction to *The Direction of Poetry: An Anthology of Rhymed and Metered Verse Written in the English Language since 1975* (1988), Robert Richman describes this collection as a celebration of a particular group of poets whose work is marked by their use of rhyme and meter. This is an important anthology that marked the rise of New Formalism in the 1980s. Seventy-six poets are represented, including Schnackenberg.

- *Poetry after Modernism* (1998), edited by Robert McDowell, is a collection of fourteen essays by poet-critics who discuss contemporary poetry from a variety of points of view. The poets write for the general reader, without indulging in obscure critical jargon. Many of them are associated with New Formalism.

---

may feel that Schnackenberg deserves plaudits for the skill with which she handles the demands for triple rhymes that her chosen stanza, the tercet, places on her. English is not a language rich in rhymes, and a stanza that calls for three rhyming words will tax the ingenuity of the best of poets. There surely cannot be many (or perhaps any) poems of this length in the English language that consist solely of tercets. (A tercet, in which all the lines of the stanza rhyme, is distinguished from the more common *terza rima* used by poets such as John Milton, Percy Bysshe Shelley, Lord Byron, W. H. Auden, and T. S. Eliot, in which only the first and third lines of the three-line stanza rhyme.) Examples of poems written in tercets include Robert Herrick's "Upon Julia's Clothes," and, among modern poems, Louis Untermeyer's "Long Feud" and Alfred Kreymborg's "The Ditty the City Sang." John Masefield's "A Consecration" is also written in tercets, with the exception of the final stanza. None of these poems is more than six tercets in length, however, and all employ perfect rhyme, unlike Schnackenberg's, which contains many imperfect rhymes.

Schnackenberg's achievement in "Supernatural Love" is to work within the strict formal structure of tercets in iambic pentameter, whether lacking variety or not, while maintaining the naturalness of the speaker's tone as she tells her anecdote of what happened when she was four years old. This impression of relaxed naturalness in the midst of great artifice is a sure sign of a poet who is fully in command of her demanding craft.

Source: Bryan Aubrey, Critical Essay on "Supernatural Love," in *Poetry for Students*, Thomson Gale, 2007.

Glyn Maxwell

In the following review of the poetry of Schnackenberg, Maxwell notes that she is a poet who is attuned to the "white space" of the poem, which he likens to a kind of soil in which the language of the poem grows. The "sustained dignity" and "tuned quality" of her poems derive, he notes, from her ability to counterpoise light against dark, "utterance," and "nothing."

How good is any verse? What is going to be good enough, strong enough? When the anthologies of fifty years hence fall into the hands of the few of us still present, Time, to paraphrase Auden's useful acknowledgment of uselessness, will say

> "The changes that Schnackenberg has wrought upon the shapes of her verse over the years attest to an essential struggle with the nature of form itself, of art and artifice, resulting in a sort of flowering through anxiety."

nothing but that it told us so. Well, whatever it told us it told us very quietly, and we didn't quite catch it. Critics claim they did, but no two transcripts are the same. What will tell us now how good any verse is? Science has not cracked it. Higher education seems no longer even to believe in the question. Linguistics has come up with verse that is rigorously theoretical and looks as if a child arranged it on the door of the refrigerator. Popularity, insofar as there exist instruments that can pick up the noise of verse in America at all, tells us nothing, except perhaps that the best new poetry is written by people who are famous.

Here is a suggestion. It might be a hairsbreadth easier to tell worthwhile verse from worthless verse if, instead of the negative reproduction that is observed in every book—the convention of black markings on white—the words were accorded shades that more accurately represented them. Namely, the reverse: white for the words, black for the paper. Pale for the sound, dark for the silence. Coherent signals across crackling space. Lamps in the windows of inhabited houses. The lines would end in darkness, hush, terror of cold—not in what so many contemporary poets mistake for blankness, carte blanche, and an open invitation to keep going.

For it is hard to keep going. It is sometimes wrong to keep going. There is often nothing to say, or nothing to say yet. Blackness would remind one of that, and would be a friend to do so. Blackness would push against the line, lean hard against it, make it warm itself to survive, make the dash to the next line vital, a dodge, bring a gasp to the breath. The chill of the leapt darkness would enliven us, make us shiver. We would think we were in the arms of somebody who could hold us, who could swipe a meaningful light through the gloom. We would think we were in a world where we needed holding and light, which is indeed where we are.

If this sounds peculiar, try copying out Frost's "Acquainted with the Night" in white chalk on a blackboard. This is an act of restoration. Or the death-row speech of Claudio in *Measure for Measure:* "Ay, but to die, and go we know not where!" The edges that you come to will feel like they did on the day they were made. When Edward Thomas ends "Old Man" with the line "Only an avenue, dark, nameless, without end," one feels almost compelled to put one's fingers to the black words, as if they were twigs in the snow, some last vestige of life. To reverse the white and the black would at least remind us that the words are lamps in the night, and may mean a place to stay.

Vitality in poetry consists in a marshalling of the two elements that the eye can see: something and nothing. The ear, too, at the deepest level, contributes only something or nothing. The poet's ancestor is the man outside the cave on guard, and these words were his only essential tools—What do you see? Nothing. What do you hear? Nothing; or as Frost, our chief cave-guard of recent times, reported: "For once, then, something." He, who wrote of verse as the overhearing of a muffled conversation in the next room, meant that the ear could register all manner of human feeling in little more than something or nothing.

Most verse falls short of being poetry because it is incapable of hearing or seeing nothing, so it is hearing with one ear, it is one-eyed, it is building with one hand. A poet must see and hear the white space for nothing, for cold, for the end, for the before-us and the after-us, for the people who will never know or care that we existed. Otherwise that space misleads. It says anything is next. Free verse says that, too. Free verse says: So what's next? You are! Verse without form says that whatever is next is whatever you think. What is there but what you think? White space, which it thinks is nothing.

But what you think is going to have to grow in soil other than you, and so it is going to have to have what is needed. Language grows its own flowers, and a black cold air around the bed of the line will either make its flowers die or force them to be stronger than death. That will be verse that outlives the gardener, and Time, at least in this eavesdropper's opinion, is mumbling something along those lines. In the meantime, white paper and free verse and the frictionless rapidity of the word processor continue to turn most American verse into badly paid prose.

The poetry of Gjertrud Schnackenberg has always seemed to be written white-on-black, not only because her lines have the tuned quality of work that has absorbed how sheer is the drop from white to black, from utterance to nothing, but also because the wellsprings of her art seem connected at some profound level to the witnessing of light against dark or dark against light. These two factors are both the cause and the effect of the work's sustained dignity and strength.

The changes that Schnackenberg has wrought upon the shapes of her verse over the years attest to an essential struggle with the nature of form itself, of art and artifice, resulting in a sort of flowering through anxiety. Each book, from the confident young display of *Portraits and Elegies* to the tremulous, fractured repetitions of *The Throne of Labdacus*, seems to indicate a changed attitude to the art itself, a genuine pause for thought in the silence between volumes. This is rare, for most contemporary poets take as few breaths between books as they do between lines. But Schnackenberg's aesthetic remains constant: after twenty-five years of published work, she is still gazing from darkness into lamplight and giving voice to those whom she imagines are warmed by it.

Though her first book, *Portraits and Elegies,* appeared in 1982, the two long sequences that comprised much of it ("19 Hadley Street" and "Laughing With One Eye"), and are now included in *Supernatural Love,* were written in 1976 and 1977. Those years were not particularly receptive to the wielding of a heavy, decorous pentameter in the hubbub of American verse, which was in large measure splashing in still-fresh delusions of liberty and rebellion. But any young poet who has placed faith in form at the outset of a career is merely doing what sprinters do: looking ahead up the lane, never across. That lane connects one to both the distant past and the distant future, and in the confines of our language those poles of time become the same: Lowell's work may stand in both places for Schnackenberg, where she has come from and where she is trying to get to; so may Auden's, or Donne's. The young poet who makes rhymes and stanzas because she must—not because she thinks that she ought to make them, or because she thinks that it is time poetry did again—is in the eyeline of all the other poets who ever had to make them, who were ever moved in utter stillness and anonymity to make sounding shapes. This is why the humility of the best poets is commonly mistaken for arrogance by the rest. Schnackenberg has rarely seemed to be in dialogue with any contemporary, and perhaps for this reason she is one of the few American poets whose voice one might recognize in a line.

Portraits and elegies showed a young poet still enthralled by her newfound ability. It has the successes and the failures of early work—the freshness and the impact, along with the overgrown lines ("We'd hear jazz sprouting thistles of desire") and hasty closures, often in the sequence of poems to the poet's father, as if the packed and polished squares of verse were not quite ready to open further, to expose or to be wounded. In retrospect, it is not Schnackenberg's facility with forms that is striking in her early work (for one can sometimes sense promise as keenly in a failed line as in a finished one), but rather the high quality of her attention. This is what enables her to prevail in the territories of the freeversifier. "Inhaled smoke illuminates his nerves" is a line of extraordinary precision, but it needs no formal context to bolster it. She feels the candy-box vertigo of America's "Halloween": "Out of his bag of sweets he plucks the world." She can already laugh in form, as when she has the elderly Darwin yearn "to immerse/Himself in tales where he could be the man/In once upon a time there was a man." In "A Dream," she writes of her father with a sorrow that is all the richer for being unsparing, firm: "And marveling, I watch the face you wear,/Hardened into remote indifference,/Become my own."

Whatever stillness or darkness Schnackenberg happens upon, whether an empty house, a death, or a daguerrotype, the need to light it and to animate it is irresistible. It is the nature of her force. She fills a home, "19 Hadley Street," with two centuries of recorded inhabitants, until the rooms, and the mind, are teeming with lives. She both inhabits and observes the schoolgirl alone in a bedroom with a ravenous imagination; she places herself as a bookish child marching alongside her father, wondering anxiously what he's thinking of: "Turks in Vienna? Luther on Christian love?" This plays comically—the poet as exasperating co-ed; but it speaks more broadly of the early Schnackenberg, rummaging for subjects, never staying long in the moment, her satchel bursting with both textbooks and fairy tales.

A poem such as "Bavaria" exemplifies it all: Schnackenberg's eye tracks rapidly across history, like the old camera-trick of taking us miles by way of an accelerating blur, but again it is the still eye and the fine ear that rescue the poem from that blur:

> A small eraser rubs a list of names
> To rubber bits; now, as the Fuhrer naps,
> Dreaming of Wild Westerns in his chair
> Till early morning, now, in North Berlin,
> An apartment building shatters from within,
> And, like a tooth, a bathtub dangles there.

Nobody who has read Auden's "The Shield of Achilles," or Anthony Hecht's poems in *The Hard Hours*—or Gloucester's blinding, for that matter—can still peddle the old nonsense that there is some innate consolation to poetic form. "Bavaria," in contrast to Auden's featureless dystopian plain seen far away, simply goes in close (and not appropriatingly close, as Plath did in "Daddy"). It may take the innocence or the bravado of a young poet to throw open the door of the bunker, or to write pentameters such as "The burning baby carriages of Jews"; but this is material for poetry, because how we cope with knowing it is material for poetry.

The Lamplit Answer appeared in 1985, which was the last time Schnackenberg published a collection of poems, as opposed to a book-length poem. The unresting animator is at work again, notably in the sequence about Chopin in Paris called "Kremlin of Smoke," which is typically ornate but also more guarded, straining less for immediate significance:

> At which high-sign the grand piano is rolled in,
> Its curving wing unfolded, like a great black butterfly
> That slowly sails toward charades by candlelight
> Across the polished chasm of parquet.

The lines are slightly plainer than before, more patient, more intelligently withholding, but the book shows the poet already sailing outwards into uncharted waters.

The "Two Tales of Clumsy," for example, suddenly drain away all reference and echo—not an easy thing to do, if you have hitherto sought them so assiduously—and play on a weirdly blank canvas, ending up as scarifying oddities in the domestic-Gothic strain of Auden's "Victor" or Edward Gorey. This tentative journey reaches its destination in the very good "Imaginary Prisons," a compassionate and genuinely funny pan around the hapless statues of Sleeping Beauty's frozen castle:

> The kitchen boy distracted by a quarrel
> Is dreaming that he opens up a box
> Of banished knives blinding even at twilight
> And this way makes his adversary cower,
> But ducks in fact before the furnace-stoker
> Around whose lifted shovel embers sparkle
> And hang like bumblebees around a flower.
> And though you laugh, to them it greatly matters....

Too much can be in motion sometimes; but success in Schnackenberg is all about finding focus, and this poem works so well because she is keeping some things still, so that her eye can work on them there, rather than sweeping past a stanza with a turn of the head and a skip across the centuries. The last line quoted above has absorbed the authentic lightness of Frost, whose favorite line in Shakespeare was "So have I heard and do in part believe it." Sometimes the comic velocity sounds like Pope trapped in the modern world, a wasp in a glass: "Assigned to live next door because he's silent,/Though under lock and key, because he's mad...."

The sequence "Sonata," meditating on unrequited love inside a musical structure, seems a kind of superfluous doodling, which at some level all love poetry is, except that in this case the wrong thing—the poet—is being kept still. The logic of unrequited love demands of the poet a false pose of adequate consolation, and it seldom rings true for longer than a sonnet. Still, among the shorter poems in *The Lamplit Answer* are three of Schnackenberg's finest early lyrics, which is to say three of America's finest lyrics from the last twenty years. "The Heavenly Feast" threads itself beautifully around Simone Weil, expiring in wartime in an English sanatorium: "To sing you in their way,/I swear I can hear the words,/Send it to them, they say,/Send it to them, it is theirs." "Supernatural Love" is the best of Schnackenberg's poems about her father: it might be prescribed to students as an antidote to the ubiquitous "Daddy." And "Advent Calendar" returns to Schnackenberg's primary scene of a child gazing into light from shadow, but deepens and widens until the child is the watcher of all, and the images behind the little cardboard windows seem to be both Bethlehem under the star and a late nineteenth-century Austrian town oblivious to its own new arrival.

A poet's apprenticeship is about finding the right bandwidth, the distance from objects at which her senses act most vitally. Schnackenberg seems to have started with a sense of herself as a panoramic poet, a conductor of allusion and historical echo. This is evident in early poems such as "Bavaria" and "There Are No Dead," and it reaches its apogee in *A Gilded Lapse of Time*; but much of her best work, even in the poems that most obviously manifest such width and perspective, is in the exquisite accuracy with which she beholds details, as if the bright child did her true apprenticeship not in the beam of the study lamp, but in the glow of the dollhouse windows.

A Gilded Lapse of Time, which takes up the last third of *Supernatural Love,* appeared as a book in 1992. It is a winding odyssey through the tombs, the monuments, and the galleries of the ancient world, drifting in and around historical facts and legends pertaining to Dante, the Crucifixion, and Mandelstam. It is extremely allusive, in that it rarely steps far without the clank of footnotes. Yet it is more difficult and more ambitious than what went before. In the work of poets still learning their trade, the word "ambitious" is associated with arrogance, but in truth the undertaking of a poem such as *A Gilded Lapse of Time* is an act of homage, and therefore an act of humility. And the greater the figure to whom homage is being done, the deeper the humility.

If one loves Dante, writing at length about him is not a literary gesture or a professional ambition: it is a creative compulsion. But in a culture that has slid so far toward a leveling of art and a rejection of the possibility that aesthetic endeavor creates a hierarchy, trying hardest to grow is routinely mistaken for strutting one's stuff. The humility of voice in this poem—which risks at times tugging the verse below audibility as verse at all—is a rare sound indeed in contemporary poetry. Homage is no more arrogance than confessional poetry is humility.

Schnackenberg seems to have felt the need to set her work alongside the most astonishing things that she so far knew—Dante, the Gospels, a great poet who died for ridiculing Stalin—and then to quiet it to a hush among them by jettisoning the very things that had hitherto come most easily. Whether in homage or in fear or in uncertainty, she seems to have approached *A Gilded Lapse of Time* almost mute with reverence. She relinquishes rhyme at the outer gate. The forms in which she has attained such facility, the pentameters and the tetrameters, are beaten out into a miscellaneous, often awkward jumble of lengths. Some of the verse sounds almost left in its note form, still chatting with prose out of politeness. She writes of her own work after reading Dante's, both describing and enacting the kind of genuflection that ensues:

> . . . a glimpse of that sound,
> After which everything I had scribbled
> In my own hand came to a weightless bundle,
> But what foundered beyond the page was more
> Than I could lift, more than could be enshadowed
> Even in a private script in the margins—

Still, at several points, by way of reticence, Schnackenberg reaches further heights. This contemplation of Dante's death-mask, as well as being a simile of genius, reminds one of her acute sensitivity to light falling on faces. It also shows metrical precision so considerable that it can stand back and seem to have departed: "The likeness of a man who, closing his eyes,/Holds still in order to discern/A very faint sound."

And not all of the poem is so hushed. Flaring up through almost penitent passages are moments of formidable power, as when she feels a star sweep past her, each of its points a sulphurous whiff of the letter "p":

> Only a raindrop
> On my lashes into which
> I look in time to see
> A black star drawing near
> Plunge past my peripheral sight,
> And disappear.

The variations of speed and scale in these lines put one in mind of an example given by Mandelstam in his "Conversation About Dante": "Of all our arts only painting, and at that only modern French painting, still has an ear for Dante. This is the painting which elongates the bodies of the horses approaching the finish line at the race track."

Schnackenberg's quest for Dante becomes a wiping away of palimpsests: of her own voice, of the places as they look now, of the paving stones or the rotting wall behind which Alighieri (it is said) hid the last cantos of *Paradiso,* of the volumes of footnotes, of Eliot's fragments; and what she reaches beneath them is not *The Divine Comedy* at all, but the lonely figure of Osip Mandelstam. The final section of the poem, "A Monument in Utopia," is devoted to him.

Nobody who has read "Conversation About Dante" can help but feel themselves brought nearer to the gates of *The Divine Comedy,* if only to vow silence; or to the gates of all creative impulse, if only to vow infinite pains. Mandelstam's burning intelligence seems to shrivel away the barriers of three languages, largely because it moves by glittering crystals of revelatory metaphor, touching only on things that lie beyond language or before it: stone, weather, water, flight. And Schnackenberg reaches Mandelstam; she doesn't just choose to go there next. Searching for the great poet who wrote of Hell, she finds naturally enough a great poet who also lived and died in it. Long before we reach the sanctuary of Mandelstam's desk in a Paris to which he fictionally escapes, he is a presence in Schnackenberg's poem. But then, of all the prematurely dead poets of the last century, he is the best to have been, as it were, sacrificed to its inferno. To where but a utopia would the consolation of the dead poet's living work drive a living poet?

> It will have evaporated,
> That whiff of the scaffold, the siege tower,
> Of vaults sealed so long that no one
> Would wish to break them,
> That sense that a bone is being broken
> Somewhere in the world,
> That one's number is called out.

Mandelstam, in a way, saves *A Gilded Lapse of Time.* For all the many moments of beauty and power in the first two sections, Schnackenberg is playing to her weakness for rapid allusiveness and shifting viewpoint, and her thirst for the next image hauls us away before we have absorbed the last. Until "A Monument in Utopia," we lack the fixed point we tend to need in her work, because as a host she is an ethereal presence, liable to disappear down a tunnel and find a library at the end. We may have to leaf to the notes to find her. And we drift too, particularly in the central "biblical" section, from legend to landscape to invention to fact; and the effect is unsettling, centrifugal. There are so many monumental creatures through whom our eyes are flashing, angels and emperors, painters and poets—often we have to stop for breath in the heat, like tourists.

These sections are so heavily footnoted that when one finds that a certain legend ("When they met face-to-face, both/God and the worm laughed") has been untraceable, one feels the poem itself deflate. The poems are still drinking from their sources when we reach them. The Mandelstam sections are footnoted, too—but usefully rather than essentially. What the Russian poet's presence gives Schnackenberg is the constant of physical space. The most exquisite passage of all floats in through the window of his imagined Paris apartment, takes in the old man at his desk, then departs again, now tethered loosely to a single created consciousness that can illuminate all detail:

> And through the streets of the city, the cold pink cliff
> Of afternoon's glacier will press its path,
> Dropping at its forefront the crumbling
> Particles of twilight's mauve, pushing past
> The momentarily lustrous glass panes
> Of eternity where you had laid
> The humid whorls of childhood's breath.

Those hoping for a return to the jaunty elegance of the younger Schnackenberg will not find it in *The Throne of Labdacus,* in which her style is pared down to a flinty austerity of foreshortened rhymeless couplets, stalling and reiterating. Cold air is blowing in. At times it could be the bone-dry mutter of Ted Hughes in his very late *Alcestis*—a comparison that speaks to the sheer distance Schnackenberg makes herself travel in search of apposite sound. Unlike *A Gilded Lapse of Time* or the early lyrics, the new work is without passages of quotable, haunt-the-mind beauty—it is, arguably, shunning them; but it has the quality of that work's best sections, which is a rootedness in the notions or the actions of a single figure, in this case Apollo. That stability works against Schnackenberg's appetite for cascades of allusion, and the cold air of quickly recurring stanza-breaks holds things still, lets them shine, or speak, or expire:

> And, stalled in his crimson wooden cart,
> He peered ahead, vexed,
> At the narrow, sun-dazzled road
> Where a pedestrian,
> Double-striking and deadly-footed,
> Raised his walking-stick and struck him
> In the skull, too soon, too soon—

Experiment with form is one method of curbing one's habits and developing new ones, but a more important method here is narrational: Schnackenberg's sense of how a god, existing outside of time, would experience chronology. (Set against the many poets who these days feel they have the right to experiment with narrative virtually from the cradle—often prior to having a narrative with which to experiment—Schnackenberg's endeavor seems profoundly considered.) This aspect of the poem explains its repetitions and its uncanny sense of being motionless. Not that nothing happens: it is the Oedipus story that Apollo is contemplating; and we know what always happens. What matters in Schnackenberg's poem, rather, is the curious feeling that nothing ever has happened—or if anything has, it has happened only in language. And language, in the stillness, is suffering a sea-change, or a sand-change, into something interestingly altered, a medium of faded significance but heightened tactility:

> Things done blindly, things, things
> Done on earth; human things; with a gap
> Between what is done and what is seen,
> What is seen and what is known,
> Whereas, in the gods' reality
> The same things are done, but with
> open eyes—
> With open eyes they fasten on what is.

Nearly all these words and phrases have been and come back again in the work, particularly the word "things," like a touchstone one's hand just passes through. The italics give the sense of vainly trying to make words have edges. Again, Schnackenberg has traveled the whole way to the point. She has earned the right to make a word, for once, do nothing. There are young writers in America who begin there and it turns them to stone.

Where language is being set difficult questions, the most vexatious interrogator in literature cannot be far away. The Sphinx's riddles here are characterized by language that barely holds its head above the surface of babble: "If you acquire an aura, an oracle, a horror, a laurel,/For Apollo as if an oracle were an inherited jewel...." The surface is unruffled. Moments drift by unanchored: "The god's face/Is a gray windblown room which no one enters/ And no one answers the door/Though the heart pounds and pounds—" Whose room? Whose heart? Rumors pass through Thebes: "Somebody heard that somebody heard/That somebody heard that such-and-such happened...." And, perhaps inevitably, the poem, the poet, Apollo, and we meet an entity even stranger than the Sphinx—someone else's alphabet, and the arbitrariness of its sudden appearance is finely judged, bleak, unsparing:

> Into OI?I1/2OY.... : the Greek letters,
> Waiting in silence to be rearranged
> Into comedies and tragedies,
> Waiting to turn the people into gods
> Who gaze at things tied
> Into sequences of knots....

If *The Throne of Labdacus* is Schnackenberg's most black-on-white book, composed as it is of two-line stumps in the hot shimmering noon of the ancient world, it is not without abrupt splashes of color. The gong that begins the premiere of Oedipus Tyrannus "[turns] the wind red," which is magnificent. The diadem of Laius "darkens.... As if gold were a flame that could go out." That latter transmutation speaks to a sense of fragility and replaceability that informs what is, paradoxically, the poet's harshest, most unyielding work to date.

Lightning is black in the poem, "dirtied, dark." Its shape is made by the meeting of two broken halves of a prophecy. One departs *The Throne of Labdacus* with a sense that this outstanding poet of lamplight-in-darkness has reached a kind of antipodes of bleakness and intractability. Looking for enlightenment and finding the word "things"—things—Schnackenberg has reached a point beyond which lies silence, a silence littered with the wreckage of numberless futile experiments, and her only way back to us may be to hold a flame to the things and begin naming them again. In the meantime the quiet will matter to the poet; and what comes of her quiet ought to matter to poetry.

Source: Glyn Maxwell, "Things Done on Earth," in *New Republic*, Vol. 225, November 12, 2001, p. 53.

Rosetta Cohen

In the following review, Cohen praises Schnackenberg for broadening her range of subject matter while, at the same time, keeping it within the context of her usual ordered and detailed universe.

Gjertrud Schnackenberg's *The Lamplit Answer* is the first full-length collection by a young poet whose work has appeared widely in recent months and who has been much praised as a gifted stylist since the publication, in 1982, of her chapbook *Portraits and Elegies*. Tightly formal and consistently elegiac in tone, Schnackenberg's earlier collection showed her to be a poet of enormous control, capable of working small miracles with cadence and rhyme. In this recent volume Schnackenberg seems to have made an attempt to move beyond the limits of subject and style on which her reputation is based. A number of long poems appear here, including a historical portrait in free verse and a lengthy fairy-tale parable. The selection also contains a beautiful elegy to the poet's father, a pair of humorous pieces and a series of light, less successful, love poems.

But despite the broadened range of subject the essence of a good Schnackenberg poem is still quite the opposite of far-reaching. In fact, much of the delight one derives from her work comes from its capacity to create a limited, ordered universe that transcends, by way of intricate detail, the larger context of the subject itself. The most imposing historical figures—Chopin or Darwin—are reduced to the domestic intimacies of tea sets, backgammon and naps "beneath a London Daily tent."

It is this talent for creating small, intricate worlds that seems to place Schnackenberg within a tradition that has less to do with a particular poetic mode than it does with the nineteenth-century novel. There is a Jamesian pre-occupation here with the nuances of small gestures and quiet moments. And the parallels to James or Austen or Eliot are reinforced by the numerous nineteenth-century settings in which her dramas are played out: the salon, the garden, the gentleman's study.

Nowhere is the novelistic quality of Schnackenberg's work better exemplified than in the most successful poem in the book, "Kremlin of Smoke." The poem is composed of a series of fictional frames from the life of Frederic Chopin. Using fragments from the composer's letters and journals, Schnackenberg creates eight subtly cadenced "etudes" in which we see Chopin alternately as a young child and as a 20-year-old exile from Warsaw during the Russian invasion of 1831. The opening poem in the series is set in the Faubourg Saint-Germain, where the protege holds court amid the beau monde:

> The swan's neck of the teacup, her black vizard
> Plunged underwing, conceals her face like a modest

cocotte Who can't bring herself to look up at the honored guest, As the silver hammer of the tea service practices Chings in runs of triplets, and the tea steam hangs Phantom chrysanthemums on long, evaporating stems In the air of the winter apartment. The guests, Having gathered for games, for mimicries, For gossp's intricate, expensive inventions, Crowd toward the pianist who, leaning forward, Clasps his hands, like a child's prison for butterflies, To begin a tale, perfected in his room, of his Reception on a tour in the South, where they had hired A sedan chair with servants to bear him to the theater, "Like a captured king from a remote, Saxon metropolis," And then killed him in the reviews—a smashing joke, and his hostess snaps her fan shut when she laughs, In the city of slaves to mirrors, of rivalries Championed for less than a day by charlatans, Of politics lending heat to the rented rooms Of exiled virtuosos, and of cholera warnings affixed To the posts of the streetlamps, whose heads Flare with fever from here to the outermost districts.

The catalogue of ironic detail here, most of it rendered in a single breathless sentence tied together with internal rhymes, is wonderfully effective at conjuring up Chopin's own imagined ambivalence to the scene—a mixture of egocentric pleasure and quiet unease.

Schnackenberg's novelistic style also works well with more personal, lyrical subjects. In the last poem of the collection, "Supernatural Love," she deflates her perspective literally to the nearness of a magnifying lens:

> My father at the dictionary-stand Touches the page to fully understand The lamplit answer, tilting in his hand His slowly scanning magnifying lens, A blurry, glistening circle he suspends Above the word "Carnation." Then he bends So near his eyes are magnified and blurred, One finger on the miniature word, As if he touched a single key and heard A distant, plucked, infinitesimal string, "The obligation due to every thing That's smaller than the universe." I bring My sewing needle close enough that I Can watch my father through the needle's eye, As through a lens ground for a butterfly.

Through the rigid symmetries of the tercets, Schnackenberg conflates the love of parent with the love of Christ, and the simplest actions—the child embroidering, the father searching out the Latin root of a word—become transcendent by way of the child's sudden, tiny self-inflicted wound:

> I twist my threads like stems into a knot And smooth "Beloved," but my needle caught Within the threads, Thy blood so dearly bought, The needle strikes my finger to the bone. I lift my hand, it is myself I've sewn, The flesh laid bare, the threads of blood my own, I lift my hand in startled agony And call upon his name, "Daddy daddy"—My father's hand touches the injury As lightly as he touched the page before, Where incarnation bloomed from roots that bore The flowers I called Christ's when I was four.

Almost all the best poems in *The Lamplit Answer* deal in one way or another with this kind of intense scrutiny. There is a piece about the artist Ivan Generalic, for example, whose painting style is characterized by the tight, hard-edged precision of the miniaturist. Another shows an aging Darwin, weary at last of a lifetime spent looking into "beetle-jaws" and "bivalve hinges." Unfortunately, however, the collection is not entirely devoted to poems at close range such as these. One whole section of the book, which includes mainly love poems, falls flat. Here, the rhymes suddenly become predictable, and the glorious detail is replaced by bathos or coy banter:

> Dear love, though I'm a hopeless correspondent, I found your letter habits lacking too Till I received your card from H.-lulu. It made me more-than-slightly-less despondent To see how you transformed your ocean swim Among dumb bubble-blowers ito meters And daffy rhymes about exotic tweeters Beyond your balcony at 2 a.m.

One can only wonder at the inclusion of these pieces: They have a certain scraped-together quality and make for a strange contrast to the rest of this soberly disciplined volume.

Source: Rosetta Cohen, Review of *The Lamplit Answer*, in *Nation*, Vol. 241, December 7, 1985, pp. 621–23.

Phoebe Pettingell

In the following review, Pettingell cites Schnackenberg's gift of absorbing herself in contemplation and her use of rhyme and pattern to heighten emotional complexity in her poems.

Like Clampitt, Schnackenberg has a religious, metaphysical mind, but she is more of a formalist. Rhyme comes so naturally to her that you would hardly be surprised to find she converses in it. Even in the new volume's opening sequence, "Kremlin of Smoke," a fictional portrait of Chopin, blank verse keeps breaking into rhyme. Most often, as in the conclusion to "Darwin in 1881," she employs it unaffectedly:

> He lies down on the quilt,
> He lies down like a fabulous headed
> Fossil in a vanished riverbed,
> In ocean drifts, in canyon floors, in silt,
> In lime, in deepening blue ice,
> In cliffs obscured as clouds gather and float;
> He lies down in his boots and overcoat,
> And shuts his eyes.

How simply, how humorously she summarizes the geologic records that buttressed Darwin's evolutionary arguments.

Patterns symbolize emotional complexity for Schnackenberg. "Love Letter," about the comic, heartbreaking indignities of being a slave to one's feelings, uses the jaunty rhyme royal of Byron's "Don Juan"—an ironic yet rueful commentary on the same subject. Musing on the impulse to distance ourselves from those we love, she observes: "Tonight the giant galaxies outside/Are tiny, tiny on my window pane."

"Paper Cities" concerns intersections between life and art, and the way they intensify under the pressure of powerful emotions. The poet, reading a collection of Flaubert's letters, identifies her own lover's withdrawal with Flaubert's treatment of Louise, the mistress he neglected for his writing. She envisions Louise raising her eyes from one of the letters to watch clouds that soon float into the poet's world. "My books are towers," she says, "Rooms, dreams whose scenes tangle." Later, while she is reading a fairy tale, a goose feather plucked by a weeping kitchen maid also drifts into the poet's surroundings. Afraid that misery may be destroying her sanity, she picks King Lear off the shelf and imagines him as he "sits in his jail, cut to the brains' by his own reverses:

> He spreads his drenched map
> And waits till it dries,
> Then folds it into a pointed hat,
> And the faded countries wave in his hair
> Like tattered butterflies.

The images of "Paper Cities" poignantly demonstrate how grief can suppress all other feelings: Everything serves to remind the sufferer of despair.

Schnackenberg possesses a child's ability to wholly absorb herself in whatever she contemplates. "Advent Calendar" revives a girlhood memory of paper representations designed to teach children the meaning of this Christian season of anticipation: "Picture boxes in the stars/Open up like cupboard doors/In a cabinet Jesus built," she marvels. The secrets to be revealed behind each door, though, cannot live up to the excitement of expectation. Drawings of ordinary toys, "Wooden soldier, wooden sword.... Hints of something bought and sold,/Hints of murder in the stars" lead the child to a darker religious mystery—the revelation of a suffering world.

Schnackenberg and Clampitt represent a change in current poetic style. They both recognize a universe of ideas outside their own personal impressions and treat form as an enhancement and delight, rather than a trap. This is not backsliding toward the Modernism that dominated the first decades of the 20th century. These women are true Romantics. But the battles fought by poets in the '50s and '60s against Modernist values need not be taken up again by writers in the '80s. Amy Clampitt and Gjertrud Schnackenberg are two outstanding members of a growing poetic movement devoted to both sound and sense.

Source: Phoebe Pettingell, Review of *The Lamplit Answer*, in *New Leader*, Vol. 68, No. 15, September 23, 1985, p. 15.

Sources

Cohen, Rosetta, Review of *The Lamplit Answer*, in the *Nation*, December 7, 1985, p. 621.

Dawson, Ariel, "The Yuppie Poet," in *Writer's Chronicle*, Vol. 14, No. 5, 1984.

Gioia, Dana, "Notes on the New Formalism," in *Expansive Poetry: Essays on the New Narrative & the New Formalism*, edited by Frederick Feirstein, Story Line Press, 1989, p. 164; originally published in the *Hudson Review*, Autumn 1987.

Kirsch, Adam, "All Eyes on the Snow Globe," in *New York Times Book Review*, October 29, 2000, p. 27.

McPhillips, Robert, "Reading the New Formalists," in *Sewanee Review*, Vol. 97, Winter 1989, p. 75.

———, "What's New about the New Formalism?" in *Expansive Poetry: Essays on the New Narrative & the New Formalism*, edited by Frederick Feirstein, Story Line Press, 1989, pp. 195, 207; originally published in *Crosscurrents*, Vol. 8, No. 2, 1988.

Mendelsohn, Daniel, "Breaking Out," in the *New York Review of Books*, March 29, 2001, p. 39.

Schnackenberg, Gjertrud, "Supernatural Love," *The Lamplit Answer*, Farrar, Straus and Giroux, 1985, pp. 81–83.

Shetley, Vernon, *After the Death of Poetry: Poet and Audience in Contemporary America*, Duke University Press, 1993, pp. 157, 190.

Turner, Frederick, and Ernst Pöppel, "The Neural Lyre: Poetic Meter, the Brain, and Time," in *Expansive Poetry: Essays on the New Narrative & the New Formalism*, edited by Frederick Feirstein, Story Line Press, 1989, pp. 240, 241, 249.

Viereck, Peter, "Strict Wildness: The Biology of Poetry," in *Poets & Writers Magazine*, Vol. 16, No. 3, May–June 1988, pp. 8, 11.

Wakoski, Diane, "The New Conservatism in American Poetry," in *American Book Review*, Vol. 8, No. 4, May–June 1986.

Wiman, Christian, Review of *Supernatural Love: Poems, 1976–1992*, in *Poetry*, Vol. 179, No. 2, November 2001, p. 91.

Further Reading

Finch, Annie, ed., *After New Formalism: Poets on Form, Narrative and Tradition*, Story Line Press, 1999.
   This collection of twenty-four essays explores the formal possibilities of contemporary poetry and the implications of formalism for poetic history, practice,

and theory. Contributors include Dana Gioia, Mark Jarman, David Mason, Marilyn Nelson, Molly Peacock, Adrienne Rich, and others.

Lake, Paul, "Return to Metaphor: From Deep Imagist to New Formalist," in *Southwest Review*, Vol. 74, Fall 1989, pp. 515–29.

> Lake explores the different use of figurative language between the so-called deep image poets of the 1960s and 1970s and the New Formalists. He includes an analysis of Schnackenberg's poem "The Paperweight," from *Portraits and Elegies*.

McPhillips, Robert, *The New Formalism: A Critical Introduction*, Textos Books, 2005.

> This study of New Formalist poetry and poetics includes chapters on Schnackenberg ("Gjertrud Schnackenberg and the High Style"), Dana Gioia, Timothy Steele, and the verse satire of Tom Disch, R. S. Gwynn, and Charles Martin. There is also a comprehensive bibliography.

Schnackenberg, Gjertrud, "The Epistle of Paul the Apostle to the Colossians," in *Incarnation: Contemporary Writers on the New Testament*, edited by Alfred Corn, Penguin, 1990, pp. 189–211.

> In this engaging, elegantly written essay, Schnackenberg discusses the historical and theological aspects of Paul's letter to the Colossians. The book as a whole includes similar essays by other writers and poets, including Dana Gioia, Amy Clampitt, John Updike, and Annie Dillard, in which they give their personal responses to other New Testament books.

Shapiro, Alan, "The New Formalism," in *Critical Inquiry*, Vol. 14, No. 1, Autumn 1987, pp. 200–13.

> Shapiro argues that much of the poetry written by the New Formalists is metrically monotonous.

View

Marvin Bell
2004

Marvin Bell's poem "View," from his 2004 collection *Rampant*, is a work that addresses the anxieties of the contemporary world in the wake of the terrorist attacks of September 11, 2001, without ever referring to specific events or political trends. While many contemporary poets have focused on expressing their emotions, Bell has purposely focused on the world outside the individual, using the details of reality to make points that would lack impact if they were simply stated as opinions. With the experience of more than forty years of writing and teaching, Bell has honed his craft to an advanced level of subtlety, allowing him to address the major anxieties of our time with the calm assurance that even the things that seem most overturned are normal.

In "View," Bell sets his thoughts in a real-life, everyday situation, describing the common longing that people have to look out at large bodies of water, snatching what glimpses they can from afar or driving to the shore to just sit in a car, look, and wonder. The poem points to a truism that is often overlooked: that the trees that might obscure one's view, the air itself, and even the person doing the looking are all made mostly of water. Bell then compares this unity to the nature of modern warfare, implying that the enemies are no longer, like oceans, large and obvious, as were many of the armies of earlier eras; instead, wars are fought by individuals who move through society undistinguishable from other ordinary citizens, as prevalent as the molecules of water that exist unseen throughout the world.

Marvin Bell Photograph By Tom Jorgensen. Reproduced by permission of the author and photographer

he also held several visiting professorships at other universities, including Saint Mary's College of California, the University of Hawaii, Birmingham-Southern College, and Pacific Lutheran University.

Bell is one of the most well-respected and oft-published poets of his generation. He is the author of sixteen books of poetry, the most famous being the two books constituting his "Dead Man" series: *The Book of the Dead Man* (1995) and *Ardor: The Book of the Dead Man, Volume 2* (1997). He also published a collection of essays and interviews called *Old Snow Melting*, and his work has been included in hundreds of anthologies of literature. From 1975 to 1978 and again from 1990 to 1993, he contributed a regular column to the *American Poetry Review*, called "Homage to the Runner." The many honors accorded Bell over the course of his long writing career have included fellowships from the Guggenheim Foundation and the National Endowment for the Arts, an American Academy of Arts and Letters Award in Literature, and senior Fulbright appointments to Yugoslavia and Australia. In 2000, he was appointed the first poet laureate of the state of Iowa, a position that he held for two terms.

Author Biography

Marvin Bell was born on August 3, 1937, in New York City, to a Jewish family that had emigrated from the Ukraine, and he grew up in a rural section of Long Island, New York. His childhood in a small town among farms would heavily influence his poetic vision. He attended Alfred University, in western New York, earning a bachelor of arts degree in 1958, the same year as his first, short-lived marriage. He then attended Syracuse University and then earned a master of arts degree from the University of Chicago in 1961. In Chicago, Bell took a class given by John Logan, a poet who inspired him to write poetry seriously and to join an informal group called the Poetry Seminar. He was so inspired by this group that he enrolled in the Writers' Workshop program at the University of Iowa, where he was awarded a master of fine arts degree in 1963. Bell would be associated with the University of Iowa throughout most of his adult life: he was a visiting professor in 1965, an assistant professor from 1965 to 1967, an associate professor from 1967 to 1975, and a full professor thereafter, retiring in 2004 with the position of Flannery O'Connor Professor of Letters. Over the course of his decades at Iowa,

Poem Text

When you look through the window in Sag Harbor
 and see
 the trees, and you think they are blocking your
  view, you
 are looking, even then, at the water.
Those leaves are mainly water, the air between you
  and them
 mainly water.   5
The distance, as the bird flies or the squirrel
  scampers,
 mainly water.
You yourself are a kind of flooded hollow hull.
On the bays, on land that was water, on back roads
  that float
 in floodplains, you bob like a log separated   10
  from its boom.
And when the bodies fall from shrapnel or direct
  hits, they fall
 so far they begin to dissolve.
Interred as flesh, they become air, leaving a chart
  of bones.
You think you can't see the current war and don't
  want to, but
 the war is in the trees.   15
The leaves fall, and there it is.
The branches of the evergreen sway to one side,
  and you see it.
It is the ocean between us that makes others seem
  so far away.

In Sag Harbor, a slight seacoast breeze at forty
    degrees can
        shave your skin.   20
So people stay in their cars to sit by the docks.
It's a busy day when looking out to sea is the one
    thing one
        has to do in the dark before going home to
            sleep.
People who never travel otherwise think they can
    see England.
Not so much see it with their own eyes as with   25
    their
        imaginations.
Their idea of Europe extends beyond their line of
    sight.
The morning papers will carry the battle reports.
The gossip from the front lines is that the enemy
    has
        melted away.   30
We hear the eyes in the sky can find only civilians
    now.
We want justice, not just a momentary view of
    justice.
A black cloud has blocked the dawn.
We know it is morning by the dew and the frost on
    the
        windowpanes.   35

Media Adaptations

- Bell was recorded discussing and reading poetry for the *New Letters on the Air* radio program in November 1984. A cassette recording of this performance was released by the University of Missouri Press in 1990.

- The speech Bell gave upon becoming the first poet laureate of the state of Iowa is available on-line at http://www.uiowa.edu/~humiowa/marvinbspeech.htm and includes the text of "White Clover," a gentle nature poem that exemplifies the tone of his kinder works.

Poem Summary

Lines 1–7

Sag Harbor, mentioned in the first line of "View," is a town at the end of Long Island, New York, not far from where Bell grew up. It has a long history as a seaport, primarily for whaling vessels, with European settlers arriving in the late 1600s. The village is a well-known tourist destination. In the beginning lines of this poem, the speaker presents a character (referred to as "you") who is interested, like many tourists, in a view of the water. The narrator explains that the trees that come between "you" and the harbor are not actually blocking the view, because they are made of water themselves. In fact, both the leaves of the trees and the air are said to be composed mainly of water. Even "the distance, as the bird flies or the squirrel scampers," is identified as something composed of water.

Lines 8–10

In the eighth line, the poem turns more personal, noting that even the person being addressed is composed of water, specifically, "a kind of flooded hollow hull," such as that of a capsized boat. This draws a connection between the physical nature of humans and the rest of the physical world. The poem then mentions other places where water can be found. It refers to bays and to "land that was water," continuing with the conceit that everything, no matter how apparently solid, is made of water; this latter reference may be to bodies of water that have dried up. The wandering human being, meanwhile, is compared to "a log separated from its boom," where a boom is a barrier of logs chained in place to prevent other logs cut by foresters from floating away. An implication may be that when individuals are disconnected from their community, the community can no longer adequately serve its function, as a disjointed boom might allow other logs to float away.

Lines 11–13

In these lines, Bell drastically shifts focus, conjuring images of people being killed during wartime. The poem mentions death by "shrapnel" as well as by "direct hit," perhaps to highlight the fact that, despite the inclination to examine the sublime distinctions, any cause of death ends with the same result. The process of dying is presented as an exceptionally long fall, and the process of human decay is presented as "dissolving," as objects do in water. When the fleshy, or watery, parts of the body dissolve and "become air," all that is left is the bone structure, which line 13 refers to as a "chart."

Lines 14–18

Line 14, which reintroduces the person whom the poem is addressing, mentions "the current war," accusing the addressee of not wanting to see the war and of believing that he indeed cannot. Whether this person does not wish to see the war because he is indifferent or because he would be overwhelmed by the enormity and sorrow of war news is unclear. Likewise, whether the person believes he cannot see the war because it is too far away or because it in no way affects him is also unclear. The narrator then asserts that the poem's addressee is deceived, as "the war is in the trees." Given that the narrator earlier equated trees with water and water with everything, the inference here may be that the war, also, is like water, perhaps in its unseen ubiquity. Line 16, "The leaves fall, and there it is," likely conjures in the reader's mind an image of the leaves of the trees that otherwise obscure the sight of the water falling; thus, one sees the water; given line 15, the "it" in question would seem to be "the war." Line 17 mentions swaying evergreen trees, which likewise, in moving aside, reveal the water behind. Line 18 refers to the expanse of water—and perhaps of war—as an "ocean between us" that serves to make all others seem especially distant.

Lines 19–23

In coastal locations like Sag Harbor, the humidity-laden air often feels colder than dry air of the same temperature would feel. A breeze intensifies this coldness, making the sting of the air even more bitter, an effect that the poem refers to as shaving one's skin. The narrator points out how the human fascination with water brings onlookers to the shore even when the air is too uncomfortably cold for them to stand outside; thus, they park their cars and stay inside them, separated from the natural world by the car's windshield. One might imagine that a person who has the time to go to the harbor and park for a few minutes, watching the water, has ample time on his hands; yet the narrator remarks, "It's a busy day" when watching the water is the one thing to be done in the dark before bedtime. This may be a sarcastic statement, or it may be forthright, if the person in question does not have the time to watch the water during the day.

Lines 24–27

The poem next addresses the concept of distance, specifically in the minds of Americans who "never travel otherwise," with reference to the effect that looking out at the wide open water has on the human imagination. That is, people imagine that "they can see England." Line 27 reads, "Their idea of Europe extends beyond their line of sight." Perhaps noteworthy is the fact that the place people imagine they see is another segment of the Western world, with which they conceive of some connection even over the vast ocean.

Lines 28–32

The narrator next returns to discussion regarding the ongoing war. He refers to "gossip," which can be considered commonly accepted but insubstantial truth, such as, perhaps, the distinction between solid objects and water, or the concept of distance itself. The enemy has supposedly "melted away," acting as water, but the reader may understand that this "gossip" is in effect untrue; the water, or war, that has melted or even evaporated is still present, only in an altered physical state, such as that of vapor. The "eyes in the sky" of line 31 would, during an actual war, indicate government surveillance tools, such as satellite cameras; here, they may also indicate the version of reality that is most widely accepted. The fact that these means of observation do not see enemies, only "civilians," means that the conflict, between America and the enemy or between existence and dissolution, has not actually ended but has shifted form. Line 32 reads, "We want justice, not just a momentary view of justice." Thus, perhaps, people understand that the change in the form of the conflict does not indicate that it has actually ended; in the same way in which they know what is beyond the harbor, they know what justice in a universal sense must be like, and they know that it has not yet been established.

Lines 33–35

In the closing lines, water imagery is reintroduced. A "black cloud," which is of course made of water, is mentioned; just as the trees supposedly blocked the sight of the harbor, so the cloud blocks the view of the dawn. The narrator then asserts that only the dew and frost, which are both the condensation of water out of the air, indicate the presence of a new morning. Though "frost on the windowpanes" indicates an unpleasant coldness, the coming of a new day may be understood as a universal sign of hope.

Themes

Space

In line 6 of "View," after Bell's narrator has pointed out that the trees separating the viewer from the sea are actually made of water themselves, he

Topics For Further Study

- Create a chart that shows the water content of different objects mentioned in the poem, such as the human body, trees, clouds, and air. Explain the scientific principles that allow the objects on your chart to keep their separate identities without dissolving into puddles.

- This poem specifically mentions Sag Harbor as a place where people go when they want to look out at water and imagine the world. Identify a place near where you live where people go to reflect, such as a body of water, a forest, an airfield, or a tall building. Write a poem about what you think an ordinary person might ponder there.

- Bell makes a distinction between "justice" and "a momentary view of justice." Using examples from books and the Internet, write an extended definition, several paragraphs in length, that explains the complexity of the abstract concept of justice.

- Divide students into two panels to debate opposing perspectives about how much the war in Iraq affects the daily lives of Americans, including students, using examples from your surroundings to illustrate both sides.

- Would people from previous eras understand this poem's message that "the war is in the trees?" Pick a war from America's history, such as the Revolutionary War, the Civil War, or the Vietnam War, and write a letter from the perspective of one of the citizens who lived through it, explaining what she or he would understand about spies and terrorism.

---

claims that the distance is also made of water. This description leads to a significant philosophical issue: by pointing out that the person and the sea are made of the same water that constitutes the air between them, Bell questions whether the distance exists at all. Things are ordinarily thought to be separated by space, but this poem erases that separation by positing the idea that all physical matter exists continuously. The space between the two objects is not empty but is in fact made of the same substance that the objects are made of; thus the two are connected.

This idea is explored further later in the poem, in line 18. Having described the distance between things as being composed of water, the poem refers to this separation as "the ocean between us." This is consistent with the scene that is described, with people lined up along Sag Harbor and looking out to sea. The narrator then notes that this ocean makes people "seem" far away. The implication here is that they are not really an ocean away; in other words, the space between them is an illusion. The poem completes this train of thought in lines 24–27. Here, the space between Europe and America is negated by the imagination. People looking out across the water, or through the water that composes the air, are able to "see" across 3,400 miles. In emphasizing the imagination, Bell further negates space, reducing distance not just to water but even to nothing more than a state of mind.

Sense Perception

"View" raises questions about the ways in which people generally perceive the world. The revelation that the trees are mostly made up of water is not a fantasy but a reminder of a simple botanical fact. Similarly, the statement that "the distance ... [is] mainly water" is true, if one bears in mind the humidity content of the air that fills that distance. Indeed, one can view the world as a continuum of water, not just in the seas and oceans but on the land and in the skies as well.

Another matter raised in the poem that stands as a matter of perception appears in lines 14–15: "You think you can't see the current war and don't want to, but / the war is in the trees." The traditional perception of war has been of a series of battles between two defined armies, taking place at defined places and times. For Americans, since 1865, wars have taken place exclusively in foreign locations and have therefore been experienced only through news reports. Since the destruction of the World Trade Center on September 11, 2001, however, the American perception of war has changed. Citizens have tried to absorb the notion that "war" can be something that is around them, as ubiquitous as trees and as systematic in its methods as the process of trees shedding their leaves.

War

The perspective of this poem may be less a reaction to a specific war than a commentary on the way Americans perceive the idea of war in the twenty-first century. The poem's final lines explain the complexity of this idea, as in lieu of enemy soldiers, "only civilians" can be found; one cannot clearly determine who is to be fought or where danger will come from, because "the enemy has / melted away." This statement does not imply that the world has become free from danger; rather, it implies that the modern enemy is scattered and always present, like water.

One of the poem's most powerful statements is found in line 32, with its demand for justice and the distinction that it makes for permanent, not temporary, justice. On one level, this can be read as a response to the United States–led 2003 invasion of Iraq, whereby the conflict was temporary in the sense that it lasted for just two months but was followed by years of hostility between American forces and insurgents. In a larger sense, this line may refer to the temporal nature of all wars, which offer a "momentary view of justice" because they take place only for a specific duration, even when they do not achieve their stated goals of settling the injustices that began them.

Style

Unified Imagery

Throughout "View," Bell uses the image of water symbolically in various ways, each having its own significance while also adding to the poem's overall meaning. Images of actual water include Sag Harbor, the waterways used to transport logs, the dark cloud, and the dew and frost. More obliquely, water is explained as the base constitutional element in the air, in plants, and in human bodies, which dissolve upon death. Since the poem focuses on the interconnectedness of life and the widespread impact of war and terrorism, these variations on the properties of water are appropriate. The water imagery remains a consistent mirror of elements of society throughout the entire poem.

Incidental Enjambment

The term *enjambment* refers to the poetic practice of breaking a line in a place where there is no punctuation or other natural pause between the words in question. The term comes from the French word for "straddling." Bell organizes his poem in complete sentences, always ending these sentences at the ends of lines. For example, the end of the first sentence occurs at the end of the third line. A poet who was not employing enjambment might break this sentence more frequently, where natural pauses already exist, such as after "trees," "view," or "looking." Intentional enjambment can help a poet call attention to a word or phrase that would not otherwise be emphasized; that is, the words at the ends of lines are especially noticeable: if they are not followed by punctuation, readers are left to muse about why the poet wanted them to be noticed. The lines of "View," on the other hand, extend as far as the right margin, except when punctuated with periods. Thus, the line breaks seem to be merely incidental, as dictated by the limits of space. As such, the poem puts equal stress on each sentence, deemphasizing the visible structure.

Historical Context

The War on Terror

Antipathy toward the United States among Middle Eastern extremists was well known throughout the 1980s and 1990s. Various incidents offered warnings: New York's World Trade Center was targeted by a car bomb that was meant to topple the taller of its twin towers on February 26, 1993. An Algerian man was caught trying to cross the border from Canada with explosives in December 1999, with the plan to destroy the Los Angeles International Airport during the millennial New Year's Eve observance. A boat carrying operatives from the al Qaeda terrorist organization exploded alongside the navy ship USS *Cole* in the harbor of Aden, Yemen, on October 12, 2000. Despite these incidents, Americans paid little attention to the threat posed by terrorism until after the morning of September 11, 2001. That day, members of al Qaeda hijacked four airplanes simultaneously. One was flown into the Pentagon, in Washington, D.C.; two were flown into the towers of the World Trade Center; and one was grounded in a field in Pennsylvania after passengers fought back against the hijackers. The sight of the collapse of the two towers of the World Trade Center, which had ranked among the tallest buildings in the world and had essentially defined the skyline of America's busiest city, immediately made the growing threat of terrorist organizations a priority in the mind of the public. Similar attacks against a nightclub in Bali in 2002, the Madrid subway system in 2004, and the London transit system in 2005 served to remind people that the unseen threat of terrorism exists throughout the world.

Investigations of the September 11 attacks soon showed that al Qaeda had been given support from the Taliban party that then ruled Afghanistan. On October 7, 2001, a small coalition of international forces, led by the United States, initiated air strikes against Afghanistan. Resistance to the coalition was weak but managed to persist, fighting city by city, for almost three years before the country's first democratic election occurred in October 2004. Still, as coalition forces withdrew, terrorist activities in Afghanistan were rumored to again be increasing.

Beyond the direct assault against the country that had harbored the terrorists behind the September 11 attacks, the U.S. government took further steps to establish an ongoing "war on terror." One of the most significant domestic events was the passage of the Patriot Act. This bill swept through Congress within a month after September 11, giving broad powers to the executive branch to investigate and detain individuals suspected of terrorist activities who might have been able to elude justice under earlier laws. Civil liberties groups opposed the powers that the Patriot Act allowed the government, but many Americans supported the expansion of federal authority as an acceptable trade-off for security against terrorism.

Invasion of Iraq

One tangible aspect of the war on terror was the invasion of Iraq by coalition forces. After the September 11 terrorist attacks, the U.S. government pursued an atypically aggressive course of military action, expressing a willingness to strike first against countries deemed dangerous, regardless of whether those countries had staged any attacks themselves. In his State of the Union speech in January 2002, President George W. Bush identified three countries—Iran, Iraq, and North Korea—as being particularly dangerous, dubbing them the "Axis of Evil." In the following months, the U.S. government built a coalition of countries willing to invade Iraq, which had refused to allow weapons inspectors from the United Nations to perform tests to determine whether Saddam Hussein's regime was producing nuclear or chemical weapons.

Evidence was presented to Congress and the American people to demonstrate that an invasion was necessary, though evidence also suggested that Iraq had in fact abandoned its weapons programs more than a decade earlier, as it claimed. A full-scale invasion began on March 19, 2003, and the Iraqi military quickly crumbled. By May 1, the United States declared an end to major combat operations. In the following months and years, the public was made aware that the suspicions that Iraq was building and hiding weapons of mass destruction had been exaggerated, as no such weapons were ever used or found.

Indeed, the end of formal combat operations against Iraq did not mark the end of conflict there. U.S. and coalition forces, which were charged with policing the country once its government had been vanquished, found themselves under constant threat of attack from insurgents, many of whom were presumed to be aligned with al Qaeda and other terrorist organizations. During the following years' sustained hostilities, several times more coalition soldiers died from suicide bombings and homemade explosives than died during the two-month-long invasion, and tens of thousands of Iraqi citizens were injured or killed. With the formal Iraqi army disbanded, the U.S. military encountered extreme difficulty in identifying the enemy; as phrased by Bell in "View," "the eyes in the sky can find only civilians now."

Critical Overview

By the time "View" was published in Bell's collection *Rampant*, the author was recognized as one of America's foremost poets, having built a distinguished career over the course of forty years of publication. Reviewers generally greeted this book, his first collection of new works since his signature "Dead Man" series, with enthusiasm. A reviewer for the *Seattle Post-Intelligencer* lauded *Rampant* as "a lucid and affecting collection of real world poems, often enlivened by wisdom and humor." *Publishers Weekly* quoted extensively from "View" in its short review, illustrating the point that "Bell's speaker looks at the world as if through a microscope . . . and the truths he extracts and extrapolates

The start of the "Shock and Awe" campaign in Iraq on the second day of war, showing heavy bombing in Baghdad © Olivier Coret/In Visu/Corbis

are cynical." Further, the reviewer notes, "Bell's empathy for inanimate objects can be disingenuous, but it is also often felicitous and funny."

James Parker, writing about *Rampant* in the *New York Times Book Review*, calls the work an "excellent new collection," later referring to what he called "Bell's territory": "echo, aftermath, a looking backward through the veil of things." The poet's focus on consciousness is particularly well handled, in Parker's opinion, making Bell "a less sleek Wallace Stevens," in reference to one of the poetic masters of the twentieth century. Barbara Hoffert and Mirela Roncevic, reviewing *Rampant* in the *Library Journal* in July 2004, found the book to be "a brief but inspired collection that describes the 'rampant' nature of the human condition. Often equally amusing and perceptive, the seemingly quaint verse oozes with a kind of timeless quality."

One of the few reviews clouded with anything short of absolute praise for *Rampant* was published in the *Seattle Times*, where Rick Wakefield notes that the book "sometimes sounds like the work of a poet writing for poets." Wakefield explains, "The style is straightforward, even swaggering in its self-assurance, and then, as if to be too easily understood would somehow damage his credentials as a Serious Poet, along comes a turn that seems willfully obscure." Wakefield does remark that this effect occurred to him seldom: "Far more often, however, these poems make eloquent connections, and their difficulty, such as it is, is a way of soliciting our awareness, our participation."

Criticism

David Kelly

Kelly is an instructor of creative writing and literature. In this essay, he examines the way that Bell links water and war throughout the poem, only to offer a negation of that connection in the end.

Bell has distinguished himself from other contemporary poets through his focus on a broad view of the human situation, rather than on the events of individual lives. In the poem "View," for instance, Bell discusses trends, not moments. Such a position is a difficult one for a poem to take, given that individual moments tend to pack more emotional impact, but Bell has always managed to involve readers in social trends by linking them to tangible symbols that reach into their real lives. In the case of "View," the symbol is water, and the social aspect is the danger posed by terrorism that has come to dominate American political discourse. The poem examines the ubiquitous nature of water, which can indeed be found everywhere, and it talks about war, which in the twenty-first century often means the fight against stealth attacks. Readers might be inclined to link the two, to take from the poem the message that war, like water, is everywhere and must be accepted as a condition of modern life. A more correct interpretation would hold that "View" manages, without overt discussion, to draw the distinction between eternal war and eternal vigilance.

After the high-profile terrorist attacks in New York; Washington, D.C.; and Pennsylvania on September 11, 2001, Americans shifted their understanding of what the word *war* means. The traditional meaning of the word implies a defined conflict against defined enemies, which ends when one side is defeated and announces surrender or a truce, signaling to all combatants to lay down their weapons. Beginning with President Lyndon Johnson's announcement of a "War on Poverty" in his 1964 State of the Union address, however, the word began to take on a more general meaning. With the attacks of September 11, the U.S. government reacted in two ways. The first was to engage in conventional military action—initially by invading Afghanistan, whose government was considered to have aided the people who had perpetrated the September 11 attacks, and then, later, by invading Iraq, which was identified as having a pro-terrorist, anti-American government. The second was to announce the inception of a "Global War on Terror," a title that was to change several times over the coming years, with variations including the "Global Struggle against Violent Extremism" and "The Long War."

What any of these new uses of the term *war* failed to provide, as they drifted further and further away from the traditional understanding, was their own clear definition. The enemy was now identified as those who wished law-abiding citizens harm, but that definition only helped identify such people after the fact, once they had proved their malice. Without a defined enemy, how could one know when victory had been achieved? And without knowing what would constitute victory, how could the situation be called a *war*? Twenty-first-century meanings of the word drifted so far from the traditional definition that they hardly seemed related.

> *If everything is war, then the word war means nothing in particular; much more useful would be to say that everything has war in it, just as the poem points out that just about everything, noticeably or not, contains water."*

These alterations of meaning are implicit in "View." Indeed, the definition of the word, according to Bell's usage, is no more clear than it is when "war" is talked of as an ongoing struggle against an undefined enemy; what is clear is that his use of the word draws it away from being a mere call for perpetual fear. The war referred to in "View" may be open-ended, but Bell presents it as a natural fact of life, not as a call to arms. He uses the laws of the natural world to illustrate his point: the central conceit of the poem is that water exists just about everywhere in the physical world. Bell offers a range of places and objects that are made of water, from the obvious to the unusual to the barely credible. The different levels cover just about all possible situations.

The first and most compelling idea put forward in "View," in its opening lines, is that humans possess an innate urge to look out across bodies of water. Bell names Sag Harbor specifically, but this is clearly just one example to represent all. The urge to look out across expansive seascapes is so strong, according to the poem, that people find themselves straining to catch glimpses of the water through the trees that stand in their way; it is so strong that people will drive to the water's edge at the end of a long hard day just to gaze out and dream.

This observation about human nature would in itself be a solid enough basis for a good, strong poem. Bell adds another level, though, when he brings up, without any preparation, images of death resulting from war, in particular, from "this war." Of course, this draws readers' attention; war always does. It is as compelling to the human imagination

What Do I Read Next?

- Of the many poetry collections that Bell has published over the years, the most controversial and widely praised is *The Book of the Dead Man* (1994). The poems in this book, told in a dry, anesthetized voice, examine life's most basic elements. This book and its sequel, *Ardor: The Book of the Dead Man, Volume 2* (1997), are available from Copper Canyon Press.

- In the 1980s, Bell and the equally celebrated poet William Stafford corresponded with each other in poetry, each using the poem most recently received as the basis for a responding poem. The result is a book of solid poetry and also an instructive look at the creative process. *Segues: A Correspondence in Poetry* is out of print but easily available through libraries and used-book outlets. It was published in 1983 by David R. Godine Publishers.

- Bell's poetry has been likened to that of the Pulitzer Prize–winning writer Jorie Graham, with whom he taught at the Iowa Writers' Workshop. In particular, Graham's poem "Philosopher's Stone" seems to mirror the skepticism and wonder of "View." This poem, as well as Graham's other works in her 2003 collection *Never*, complement Bell's work in capturing the tone of the new millennium.

- "View" relies on readers' understanding of the metaphoric significance of water and of war. George Lakoff and Mark Johnson's *Metaphors We Live By* is a well-respected polemic on the use and significance of metaphors. First published in 1980, a second edition was produced by the University of Chicago Press in 2003.

- Another poet associated with the Iowa Writers' Workshop, James Galvin, published his collection *X* in 2003; like *Rampant*, it was recognized by the Lannan Foundation with a Literary Award.

---

as open water, drawing the mind beyond itself, out into a larger scale of things. With the introduction of war into the poem, Bell merges nature with human nature and the physical with the psychological, meanwhile retaining an outsider's perspective on everything.

In raising the ideas that compel human imagination, Bell turns to aspects that are not open to full view. Regarding water, he discusses the way it is hidden within physical objects. By the second line, the poem draws attention to the way that the very trees are composed of water, and it goes on to point out other places where intellect tells us that water resides. While common language defines water only as the wet, clear liquid in the bay, the poem reminds us that squirrels, flesh, and leaves are all just variations on the theme of water.

As obvious as these notions are, they are quite discomforting when applied to modern warfare. Bell handles these main ideas in a way that implies that war, like water, can be found in the most unobvious places and is in fact present almost all of the time. This idea would have been remote to Americans before the September 11 attacks; they may have been able to articulate the notion if asked, but its impact would have been theoretical, not deeply felt, just as the notion that solid objects are composed of water is too abstract to hold as an emotional truth.

Even after moving the poem away from the types of immediate emotional experiences that poetry usually relies on, Bell goes one step further: visible, solid objects are made of water, the poem tells us, and water hides from view in the transparent air. This idea about water can be correlated to war, too: it is, in fact, the poem's most controversial implication. Bell implies not only that war is drawing us to it, or that it is all around us, but also that war is itself the basis of reality, the core element of everything that is and ever will be, observed or not.

If the poem solely delineated the parallels between war and water, then its overall message would be that war could be seen, as water sometimes is, as ylem, which is a term that physicists use to describe a primordial substance from which all matter derives. Plenty of evidence supports this notion. A line about people imagining England, of all places, could be interpreted as a hint at the way the British empire was tricked by their optimism into denying the reality of war until Germany invaded Poland in 1939; a line like "the war is in the trees" could be read as a warning of the danger that lurks underneath all. In this way, "View" can be seen as tilting toward the same sort of verbal dissolution as the phrase "war on terror," actually losing relevance by trying to account for too many variables at once. If everything is war, then the word *war* means nothing in particular; much more useful would be to say that everything has war *in* it, just as the poem points out that just about everything, noticeably or not, contains water.

At the end of the poem, Bell makes clear that his view of the war is, in fact, limited, not limitless. For one thing, the mention of "morning" in the last line implies the passage of time, a sense of things coming around again, in contrast to the notion of some eternal reality. Here, water is again recognized as being separate from the observer, appearing as a black cloud and as dew and frost. Bell has presented the enemy's defeat as just "gossip," replacing them in the search for enemies with civilians; this could mean that the enemy hides within the hearts of civilians, which is indeed a belief that permeates a society ever on the defense against terrorism. Still, it could also mean that, given a choice, one could define others not as the enemy but as citizens like oneself.

The poem's key phrase, and the one that keeps it from being a justification for a life of constant fear, is its distinction between "justice" and "a momentary view of justice." This statement raises, without further explanation, the notion that an innate sense of justice, not war, permeates our sensibilities in the way that water permeates the physical world. The problem is that this notion is presented as an unsupported assertion: throughout the poem, "war" is repeatedly touched on and connected with the ubiquitous nature of water, but the idea of justice is not explored, only mentioned. This is the poet's right: it puts the responsibility on the reader to determine independently exactly how justice fits into the grand scheme of things, rather than explaining how. Readers either get the point or they do not. While war has been explored throughout the poem, justice is presented as a grander concept, one far beyond the need for explanation.

"View" is a risky poem, because it leads readers in one direction for most of its unbroken length only to change the terms of its understanding in the last few lines. In this sense, it fits well with the sensibilities of America after the events that brought terrorism into the public discourse. In a flash, the expectation of violent attack went from being an abstract possibility to a fact of modern life, and this poem acknowledges that. At the same time, it directs readers toward the horizon, raising, though not fully establishing, the idea that even more universal than the narrow concept of war is the concept of justice.

Source: David Kelly, Critical Essay on "View," in *Poetry for Students*, Thomson Gale, 2007.

Michael Allen Holmes

Holmes is a freelance writer and editor. In this essay, he contends that in "View," one of Bell's intentions is to subtly awaken the consciences of his readers.

Different poets certainly write for different reasons. Some may write exclusively for themselves, to channel and express their innermost thoughts, with total disregard for the effects borne on any audience, perhaps neglecting even to attempt to publish their work. Others may prize the emotional connection they can develop with their readers, presenting either their own or fictionalized experiences in ways that stir sentiments perhaps previously unknown to those readers. Still other poets may go beyond that bare emotional connection to prod their audience not only to feel but also to think—to consider particular concepts and perhaps reflect on the relevance of those concepts to their own lives. Bell may indeed be considered a member of this last group, intentionally taking advantage of the poetic format to allow his readers to learn and understand more than can be learned and understood through functional prose. In fact, given his subtlety, his readers may not even be aware of what they are absorbing.

In an interview with Martin Blackman for *Copper Canyon Press*, Bell remarked, "I confess that, for me, poetry has philosophic import, and I believe it is to be valued, not only for itself, but as a manifestation of deeper things." He also stated, "A poetic image is not just a thing but a wedding of inner feeling with outer perception." Thus, the reader might expect his poems to bear meanings more profound than those evoked in the course of first readings. In "View," the emphasis seems to lie in the comparison drawn between water and war,

> *In fact, the poet effectively focuses on the notion that for most Americans, their "view" is simply that: only a view. Rather than participating or engaging in debate regarding world events, they are merely watching."*

both of which can be construed as ubiquitous. On a less apparent level, Bell may be highlighting the lack of worldly awareness of the average American.

The primary setting of "View" is Sag Harbor, which is mentioned twice by name; in line 19, Bell may have more simply written "In the harbor," effectively reestablishing the setting, but he chose to again present the proper name in full. As such, Sag Harbor should probably be considered to represent more than simply any and all harbors. Indeed, Sag Harbor is something of a resort village on Long Island. Those visiting its waters, at least as represented in the poem, might be expected to have a fair amount of leisure time at their disposal and, more generally, to be relatively idle people. The name of the harbor would seem to underscore this point, conjuring images of things, or perhaps people, that are no longer as firm or taut as they used to be. Those staying at the harbor's resorts may be sagging both mentally and physically.

Line 8 depicts the person being addressed by the poem, "you," as "a kind of flooded hollow hull." The use of the second person is itself indicative of Bell's intent to fully engage his readers. This line may even be seen as something of an affront. To reduce humans in general to their physical components might be seen as strictly scientific, but the term "hollow hull" connotes a regrettable emptiness. If the hull in question is that of a seed, its being hollow indicates that nothing exists inside it to one day produce growth; the seed will come to naught. If the hull is that of a ship, and it is flooded, it will certainly sink. Line 10, meanwhile, reads, "you bob like a log separated from its boom."

A "boom" is a mass of floating logs used as a barrier. A log set adrift from a boom is purposeless; also, in bobbing, it is simply carried along by the water and can in no way control its course. Thus, aside from establishing humans as largely aqueous, Bell is construing them, the reader included, as empty and purposeless.

Lines 11 through 13 offer a vivid description of bodies that first "fall from shrapnel," then "dissolve," and then are "interred as flesh," leaving behind only "a chart of bones." Bell further dehumanizes the human, somewhat unexpectedly, given the pacific nature of the first ten lines, perhaps in an effort to jolt his readers. In line 14, he declares that his reader wishes not to see the "current war" at all; to a philosophic poet such as Bell, for whom ideas and understanding would be revered, an accusation of willful ignorance must be taken as a serious charge. In line 18, he offers a reason for this ignorance: "It is the ocean between us that makes others seem so far away." But especially in the twenty-first century, the world is indeed a small one, and even those that "seem" far away are neighbors in a global sense; the plights of all should be considered, especially by those who are comfortable. Bell highlights the level of comfort of the denizens of Sag Harbor in noting that they stay in their cars because the "slight seacoast breeze at forty degrees can shave your skin." This comment may be sarcastic; in light of the horrors of war and the possibility of death, one perhaps ought to at least briefly cherish, not seek shelter from, a bracing sea breeze. Lines 22 and 23 seem more pointedly sarcastic; if one has only one thing to do "in the dark before going home to sleep," especially if at the time residing in the resort town of Sag Harbor, that person is probably not "busy."

Lines 24 through 27 make reference to England and Europe, another seeming departure from the content of the poem thus far. The "current war," given the poem's 2004 publication, must be the conflict between American troops and insurgents taking place in Iraq. Aside from the recent Balkan conflicts, Europe, perhaps especially England, America's primary national ancestor, is likely seen by Americans as a place of peace. The denizens of Sag Harbor, then, are again construed as somewhat willfully ignorant in seeing, whether with their eyes or their imaginations, only that continent of similar culture and peace; the Middle East, on the contrary, is not a place that comfortable Americans generally try to "see." The poem concludes with further references to perspective. The dawn is obscured by a "black cloud," which may be taken to represent the war in question or, more broadly, injustice. Given the absence of light, "we" are only aware that morning has come by virtue of "the dew and the frost on the windowpanes." With the image of frost, Bell further portrays Americans as having their view of the world obscured. That frost might be interpreted as the news of death that would come in the "morning papers" referred to in line 28.

In sum, Bell seems to have taken several opportunities to very subtly question the perspectives of Americans. In fact, the poet effectively focuses on the notion that for most Americans, their "view" is simply that: only a view. Rather than participating or engaging in debate regarding world events, they are merely watching. In the aforementioned interview, Bell declared that he is affected by his "view of the human condition, by the swirl of the arts, and of course by the news." Perhaps, then, he believes that the average American is not affected by the news, in particular, nearly enough. Regarding the poems found in *Rampant*, he refers to them as "sewn, sometimes tightly," with any given poem something like "a single ball of twine you can hold in one hand." Indeed, in "View," he has quite meticulously woven together several different strands of thought, regarding, water, war, and Sag Harbor, into a powerful coherent unit. That power may not be especially obvious to the casual reader. A last quote from Bell may account for that fact: "I think complexity gets lost in overstatement. The wholeness of poetry only happens inside a reader or listener who leans forward to take part." Thus, Bell would not wish to make any sort of overt statement regarding the intent of his poem; he would not admonish the reader to pay more attention to the news and demonstrate more compassion for those living elsewhere in the world. Rather, through a number of statements that at times seem disjointed, he manages to unite those concepts in the minds of his readers, and whether they are aware of the fact or not, they will have developed a more profound understanding of the far-reaching relevance of war.

Source: Michael Allen Holmes, Critical Essay on "View," in *Poetry for Students*, Thomson Gale, 2007.

Richard Jackson

In the following review, Jackson describes Bell's poems as gems of "associative thinking," linking past, present, and future in a way that reimagines them all.

In answering objections that the poems of Horace and Goethe seem to break off in many directions, Schopenhauer writes: "But here the logical sequence is intentionally neglected, in order that the unity of the fundamental sensation and mood expressed in them may take its place; and precisely in this way does this unity stand out more clearly, since it runs like a thread through the separate pearls, and brings about the rapid change of the objects of contemplation." What he is talking about is the nature of perception, a poetic logic, the kind of associative thinking Marvin Bell has perfected in his famous "Dead Man" poems and evident here in poems like "View," a poem structured by its images' relationships to water. As with those Dead Man poems and several others in this astonishingly smart and evocative book, each line of the poem is a sentence: the result is a vision that gives each image its own authority and yet ties it into the inevitable movement of the whole poem. The effect is a poetry of process that informs the entire book, a sense of the poet creating a representation of the world in order to understand what the world is supposed to represent in the first place, as Schopenhauer would have it. In "Meditation" Bell describes how one creates a room from "bare" essentials:

> You do this
> solely by the power of your inner eye.
> Project, also, on the wall, one owl,
> at times wise and penitential on a branch,
> at others calculating the swoop to home
> while a young rabbit drips from its talons.

For Schopenhauer, each poem uncovers a logic of its own, a logic not aimed at a final result as much as the process of uncovering itself. It is an endless process, as Bell suggests in "Ashes Poetica":

> Corpuscles of light descend from darkness, randomly, quietly,
> and are able to penetrate the exposed eye
> where they fall into bits and pieces, trying to form
> a picture.

In "Persistent Memory," for example, the poem moves from a "greasy spoon" to a bookstore, Martin Luther, Noah, a garage full of dolls, a memory of a boy on a trampoline and other associations that are juxtaposed like the boy who is "up in the air / and won't come down." Playing off Dali's famous title, the poem suggests a weave of associations that is always provisional, and indeed the whole book, as it moves geographically and historically, echoes that weave. Perhaps the central image for this sophisticated sense of the poem is Gaudi's unfinished cathedral ("Winter in Stiges").

The result, as Bell describes it in the "Coda" to the long poem that ends this book, is a "metaphysical

> "... each line of the poem is a sentence: the result is a vision that gives each image its own authority and yet ties it into the inevitable movement of the whole poem."

seesaw," what Schopenhauer called "a mingled state of mind." "Which is the happy light, dawn or dusk," the poet asks in one poem. And so the book is filled with images of edges, reversals, approaches, thresholds, everyday images that become loaded with metaphysical freight. In "He Sees Himself" the speaker confronts a mirror and "the front of himself but not the back" which is seen by the "other" in which the speaker exists like a dream, and, in a reversal of perspective, "he sees my back reflected in the glass. / As if I were moving away as I came closer." In "The New World" this seesaw effect extends to time: the poem begins with a description of classical Greek ships approaching and ends with two contemporary boys taking a boat to "set out for the horizon." Another poem, "The Castle," is set in the Prague of the distant past of "jesters" and magic, the "tanks" of a more recent time and the present as the speaker who is "slumping / into a doze." An extension of this sort of perception leads to a number of poems that deal with the relationship between art and reality. In "Nature Morte" the poet hears a plane too low, one that shakes the houses, but at the same time the moment is suspended: "Some thought a crash was coming / and still do." But for the poet there is also another possibility:

> Others said Aristotle was wrong
> and art doesn't imitate nature because
> art stops the plane before we can tell
> and hangs cotton in the air that sought
> the peace of landing.

Even a description of a schoolyard becomes an occasion for a meditation on the intertwinings of inside and outside.

> There is an outside beyond the farthest
> thing we can imagine. There is a schoolyard
> with a fence around it to keep out bad ideas
> just up the street from the bus station.

Here the furthest distance becomes a matter of imagination, representation, and the enclosed inner world is threatened by the outside, by an image of distancing, the "bus station."

Of course there is also a political dimension to all this, and it plays an important role throughout the book. In "Boys Walking" two boys in the Sudan of 1988 start walking, are joined by others, setting a course to food and a better life by "constellations." But "Who cared?" the speaker asks, before associating the march with Stalingrad, Bataan, "Man's thousand miles,"—all ending, as this one, with "the bodies / found hundreds of miles from home." This political orientation is evident from the opening poem, "In Beruit, at the Worst of It." Here four young men play Russian roulette in a "derelict" car, handing the gun around "with figs and an apple." After four clicks, they hesitate, and then one grabs it—"My turn." The ending of the poem, with its image of their feeble hope at the end, suggests the endlessness on a metaphysical level is manifest on a political and social level, too, and this is one of the great powers of the book:

> He has woken from fever to find a cold hell.
> There are burns behind the forehead that do not smoke.
> While the talk continues, one of them from a napkin
> makes a bird you can make the tail wave on.

The irony here is almost unbearable: the seesaw effect becomes a game of chance and chance replaces political, moral and ethical order. Suddenly poetics become a matter of ethics.

The last poem in the book, the ten part "Journal of the Posthumous Present," collects perspectives from Seurat, Salome, the poet's own past, the film "Dancer in the Dark," in order to build a sense of the complexity of the moment. Building on the point counterpoint structure of the two-part dead man poems, this poem works by statement and qualification upon qualification, context upon context, gathering all the perspectives suggested in earlier poems, especially that of the doubleness of the moment:

> We who are old cannot return to childhood,
> unreal gathering of the flock before shearing.
> So we must go back to these pictures of times before
> we came to be.

But the past, as we reexamine it, reconstitute it, is always something about to be discovered, something in the future. In fact, the moment is always futural; the present as such is thus always posthumous. "I found that I was at home in the future, not in the present," he says. The edge becomes the window through which the "history of this moment lengthens into shadow." Seeing becomes not so much a matter of perception but of imagination, of representation. In order to see this way, the poet abandons typical structures of perception, and finds ways of perceiving the world away from the usual paths: "There are whole sections of brain without road traffic. / Domains where the mind is but a knapsack." What it carries are the associations radiating out on all levels so that, for instance, Salome can be seen as "the one we die for," as "Helen" of Troy was, and so also "the power to change the world."

In the end, this is what *Rampant* is out to do, not in any direct way, but by giving us a fresh way to perceive and connect. If the title suggests a certain rage for a new order, it also suggests an unbridled conquest and the stabilizing order of a heraldic emblem at once. "Write a poem that doesn't sound like a poem," Marvin Bell once quipped to a group of students. Good advice, to be sure, for it suggests how every good poem is an innovation, an experiment, and it also suggests how every good poem is subversive of the current views of the writer as well as the reader. In this, his best book, a major contribution to our poetry, he is continually remaking himself and the world all the better to imagine them both. It is a book that is an imaginary lamp and not a mirror of realism, a book of truly visionary sweep:

> I have not wanted a watchtower, a lighthouse, an overlook.
> I am something of a miner who has turned off his headlamp.
> To better see in the dark, if you can believe it.
>   ("Eyelashes, Doorknob and Pen")

Source: Richard Jackson, Review of *Rampant*, in *Prairie Schooner*, Vol. 79, No. 2, Summer 2005, pp. 193–96.

Bowker Magazine Group

In the following review, the writer notes Bell's close scrutiny of the world and his "stream-of-consciousness" style, calling the poems in this collection both "cynical" and "funny."

A resurgent lyric voice marks Bell's first all-new collection since the "Dead Man" persona poems of the 1990s, pitched toward action and reaction: a twisted rope, when released, will "spring back / toward its most direct shape," just as "the molecules of a husband align themselves / with those of a wife." Bell's speaker looks at the world as if through a microscope: ("Those leaves are mainly water, the air between you and them mainly water"), and the troths he extracts and extrapolates are cynical: "You yourself are a kind of flooded hollow hull." The prosaic lists that dominated the Dead Man's doings persist in "Journal of the Posthumous Present," a laborious meditation that ponders Seurat, Salome and the film *Dancer in the Dark* until this dead man finally "blows a kiss through the wispy curtain of closure." Stream-of-consciousness by design, the poems move through settings from Beirut to Amsterdam to the Homeric Mediterranean. When successful, they stitch one thread of imagery through digressive meditation, as in "Resolving the Gold" and "Another Primer about the Flag," while a sweaty pair of shoes forms the backbone of "Ashes Poetica," a poem about futility. Bell's empathy for inanimate objects can be disingenuous, but it is also often felicitous and funny, as when "The boats were at their moorings, / applauding the good wood." At such moments, Bell's speaker pulls himself up into a high, dim realm of intelligence, hard to paraphrase and willfully poetical.

Source: Bowker Magazine Group, Review of *Rampant*, in *Publishers Weekly*, Vol. 251, No. 12, March 22, 2004, pp. 81–82.

Julianne Hill

In the following essay, Hill describes Bell's long history with the Iowa Writers' Workshop and discusses his theories about teaching and publication.

Poet Marvin Bell believes that "a good [writers] workshop continually signals that we are all in this together, teacher too."

As a professor at the University of Iowa's fabled Iowa Writers' Workshop, Bell should know. During his tenure dating back to 1965, he's written such acclaimed poems as "To Dorothy" and The Dead Man series, earning him the spot as Iowa's poet laureate.

"There are two rules for the workshop. No. 1: No one has to write a good poem. No. 2: Teacher has to do all the assignments, too."

The workshop, where Bell has helped spawn the careers of John Irving, Lee Blessing, Patricia Hampl and James Tate, is a graduate program of 12 or 13 self-motivated people. "These writers are very far along. They have written and read quite a lot."

Degrees are offered in both fiction and poetry, each taking about two years to earn. In addition to traditional courses, many professors offer seminars, which meet weekly for group discussions of student writing.

Bell also conferences informally with students by request. "Some people will want to meet a lot;

others will not want a conference at all," he says. "The odd thing is, they don't have to write. There are no requirements except their thesis and an MFA exam."

During workshops, Bell asks students to read their poems aloud, then asks what they like about their work. He also takes note of which poets each student has read. But the bulk of Bell's role involves his critiques of student work.

"I fill their heads with possibilities. My job is giving them permission to go new directions," he says. "They're encouraged to surrender themselves, let their writing lead them."

Talking to Bell is a seminar in itself. His conversation is peppered with excerpts from his "32 Statements About Writing Poetry," an original creed which guides both his writing and his teaching. Point No. 1: "Every poet is an experimentalist."

Bell's interest in poetry came after pursuing other arts, such as photography and jazz. It wasn't until he started on a master's degree in journalism at Syracuse University in 1958 that he became influenced by the Beat poets Jack Kerouac and Allen Ginsberg.

He shifted gears, heading to the University of Chicago the next year for a master's in literature. There he enrolled in a poetry writing class taught by John Logan, a poet who would become the first of several mentors.

Logan took an interest in Bell and asked him to join a poetry seminar that he led. The group fueled Bell's passion for poetry. Soon Logan led Bell to the Iowa Writers' Workshop, where he met Donald Justice, a graduate poetry workshop professor.

"If you're going to be serious about any art form, sooner or later, you have to run into a great teacher," he says. Justice became another mentor for Bell, who felt at home at the workshop, surrounded by others who shared his passion for poetry.

After graduating from the workshop in 1963, Bell spent the following year serving in the U.S. Army. But by 1965, Bell was back in Iowa City as a workshop professor, passing on his love of writing and sharing the gifts his mentors had given him.

Although his works have been widely published, Bell tries to impress upon his students that writing is important all on its own.

"Writing is getting in motion. What is very important about writing is writing. Being published and getting recognition is secondary."

Source: Julianne Hill, "Marvin Bell: Professor of Poetry and Poet Laureate," in *Writers Digest*, Vol. 83, No. 3, March 2003, p. 55.

Sources

Bell, Marvin, "View," in *Rampant*, Copper Canyon Press, 2004, pp. 47–48.

Bell, Marvin, and Martin Blackman, "An Interview with Marvin Bell," in *Copper Canyon Press*, October 1, 2004, available online at http://www.coppercanyonpress.org/poemsAloud/paAuthor/dsp_paAuthorInterview.cfm?PASeries_ID=3&Author_ID=9007.

Hoffert, Barbara, and Mirela Roncevic, "Poetry: A Seasonal Roundup," in *Library Journal*, Vol. 129, No. 12, July 15, 2004, p. 87.

"Northwest Bookshelf," What's Happening, in the *Seattle Post-Intelligencer*, April 30, 2004, p. 25.

Parker, James, "The Ocean in the Head," in the *New York Times Book Review*, April 18, 2004, sect. 7, p. 28.

Review of *Rampant*, in *Publishers Weekly*, Vol. 251, No. 12, March 22, 2004, pp. 81–82.

Wakefield, Richard, Review of *Rampant*, in the *Seattle Times*, July 18, 2004, sect. L, p. 9.

Further Reading

Behn, Robin, *The Practice of Poetry: Writing Exercises from Poets Who Teach*, Collins, 1992.
    Bell is one of the dozens of writing teachers featured in this book, which can be useful in helping readers understand how a poem like "View" is put together.

Emoto, Masaru, *The Hidden Message of Water*, translated by David A. Thayne, Beyond Words Publishing, 2004.
    Emoto is a Japanese philosopher and motivational speaker whose theory of hope, based on the fact that the common element of water transmits emotions and ideas, has become the center of international attention, in part because his photographs of water were featured in the 2004 film *What the Bleep Do We Know!?*

Feinstein, Sascha, and Yusef Komunyakaa, eds., *The Jazz Poetry Anthology*, Indiana University Press, 1991–1996.
    Although the style of "View" is Bell's alone, he is often grouped with poets from the "jazz poetry" tradition. This two-volume work explains jazz poetry and includes Bell's poem "The Fifties" as an example.

Schneier, Bruce, *Beyond Fear: Thinking Sensibly about Security in an Uncertain World*, Springer Press, 2003.
    This book looks at American society's insecurity regarding possible attacks, the various threats faced in the modern world, and how fear can be stirred up and manipulated.

Virtue

**George Herbert
1633**

"Virtue" is one of the poems in a collection of verse called *The Temple* (1633), which George Herbert wrote during the last three years of his life. By then, he had taken holy orders in the Anglican Church and become rector in Bemerton, England, near Salisbury. Herbert's poems are lyrical and harmonious, reflecting the gentle voice of a country parson spreading the Christian message. He appreciates the beauty of creation not only for its own sake but also because he sees it as a mirror of the goodness of the Creator. Yet, despite Herbert's sense of the world's loveliness, his poems often reflect the transience of that beauty and the folly of investing it with any real value. In "Virtue," he presents a vision of an eternal world beyond the one available to sense perception.

Implicit in "Virtue" is a delicately expressed struggle between rebellion and obedience. The understated conflict lies between the desire to experience worldly pleasures and the desire—or as Herbert would insist, the need—to surrender to the will of God. The battle waged between rebellion and obedience can be seen more clearly in one of the best-known poems in *The Temple*, "The Collar." Therein, the poet "raves" against the yoke of submission that he must bear until he hears the voice of God call him "child"; then, he submissively yields, as the poem ends with the invocation "My Lord!" This conclusion indicates that what the narrator feels about the experience of the natural world is of less authenticity than an inner voice of authority that directs him toward God.

George Herbert Engraving by E. Smith. © Getty Images

Herbert's poetry displays a conjunction of intellect and emotion. Carefully crafted structures, like the first three quatrains, or four-line stanzas, of "Virtue," all of which are similarly formed, contain sensuously perceived content, like depictions of daytime, nightfall, a rose, and spring. Such a combination of intellect and emotion, in which the two forces, expressed in bold metaphors and colloquial language, struggle with and illuminate each other, is most apparent in the poetry of one of Herbert's contemporaries, John Donne, and is called metaphysical poetry. In "Virtue," an example of this combination of the intellectual and the sensuous can be seen in the second line of the third quatrain, when the spring is compared to a box of compressed sweets.

In "Virtue," which comprises four quatrains altogether, Herbert reflects on the loveliness of the living world but also on the reality of death. Building momentum by moving from the glory of a day to the beauty of a rose to the richness of springtime, while reiterating at the end of each quatrain that everything "must die," Herbert leads the reader to the last, slightly varied quatrain. There, the cherished thing is not a tangible manifestation of nature but the intangible substance of "a sweet and virtuous soul." When all else succumbs to death, the soul "then chiefly lives." Not through argument but through an accumulation of imagery, Herbert contrasts the passing glories of the mortal world with the eternal glory of the immortal soul and thereby distinguishes between momentary and eternal value.

"Virtue" and many other poems from *The Temple* can be found in *Seventeenth-Century Prose and Poetry*, edited by Alexander M. Witherspoon and Frank J. Warnke and published by Harcourt, Brace & World, in 1963.

Author Biography

George Herbert was born into a wealthy and titled family at Montgomery Castle, in Wales, on April 3, 1593, as one of nine children. His father, Sir Richard Herbert, died in 1596, when George was three years old. His mother, Lady Magdalen Newport Herbert, was a patron of the poet and clergyman John Donne, who presided at her funeral when she died in 1627. Herbert was educated privately until 1605, when he attended the prestigious Westminster School as a King's Scholar. In 1609, he entered Trinity College, Cambridge, earning his bachelor's degree in 1613 and a master's in 1616. Two years later, he became a teacher, with the title of "reader in rhetoric," at Trinity, and a year later, in 1619, he was appointed orator for the university, a post that he held until 1628. In this capacity, he represented the university on public occasions, such as by delivering the welcoming addresses when King James I visited Cambridge. In this way, Herbert became known to the King, who, delighted by his performances, awarded him a yearly stipend.

Herbert's first poems were Latin sonnets that he wrote for his mother. In them, he argued that a more fitting subject for poetry than love for a woman was love for God. His first published verses appeared in 1612. They were two poems, also in Latin, written in memory of King James's son Prince Henry, who had died that year. In 1624 and 1625, Herbert was elected to Parliament to represent Montgomery. However, rather than pursuing a career in politics or as a courtier, which had been his intention, after the death of King James, he devoted himself to the priesthood. In 1630, Herbert took holy orders in the Church of England and became the rector of Bemerton, near Salisbury. He married Jane Danvers, the cousin of his mother's second husband, in 1629. During his three years as a priest, Herbert wrote *A Priest to the Temple; or, The Country Parson, His Character, and Rule of Holy Life*, in which he set forth a guide for pastors in caring for their parishioners and in developing their own spirituality.

On March 1, 1633, Herbert died of tuberculosis. He had always been sickly, and one of his reasons for not pursuing an academic career at Trinity College after graduation had been the taxing effect of study upon his unsturdy constitution. From his deathbed, he sent a manuscript of poems called *The Temple*, in which is included the poem "Virtue," to his friend Nicholas Ferrar, a fellow clergyman, asking him to publish them if he thought they were worthy and would contribute to people's spiritual advancement. Ferrar indeed published the poems that year, and by 1680 the collection had gone through thirteen printings.

By all accounts, Herbert was a gentle and pious person with a sweet and generous nature. He helped rebuild the decaying church at Bemerton with his own money and was loved and esteemed by his parishioners, whom he cared for spiritually and, when necessary, by sharing in their labor or giving them money. Izaak Walton, his first biographer, wrote of him, "Lowly was Mr. George Herbert in his own eyes, thus lovely in the eyes of others."

Poem Text

Sweet day, so cool, so calm, so bright,
The bridal of the earth and sky;
The dew shall weep thy fall tonight,
For thou must die.
Sweet rose, whose hue, angry and brave,   5
Bids the rash gazer wipe his eye;
Thy root is ever in its grave,
And thou must die.
Sweet spring, full of sweet days and roses,
A box where sweets compacted lie;   10
My music shows ye have your closes,
And all must die.
Only a sweet and virtuous soul
Like seasoned timber, never gives;
But though the whole world turn to coal,   15
Then chiefly lives.

Poem Summary

Lines 1–4

Herbert begins "Virtue" with an apostrophe, or invocation. That is, here, he starts with a direct rhetorical address to a personified thing: as if speaking to the day, the narrator says, "Sweet day" and then characterizes the day as "cool," "calm," and "bright." Thus, for one noun, "day," he provides four adjectives. The rest of the line is made up of the adverbial "so," signifying intensity, repeated three times. Herbert is presenting a fairly generic image, without any action, as no verb appears among these eight words. Nor can a verb be found in the next line, which is a kind of appositive, or a noun phrase placed beside the noun that it describes. "The bridal of the earth and sky," which describes the "day," indicates no action, instead merely illustrating and amplifying the conditions depicted in the first line. That is, the "sweet day" is the bridal—the marriage, conjunction, or union—of the earth and the sky. In sum, Herbert presents a serene yet invigorating day and locates the reader in the celestial and terrestrial realms simultaneously, for the day in its loveliness brings them together.

Day, however, gives way to night, just as life gives way to death: "The dew shall weep thy fall tonight," the narrator asserts, turning a daily natural event, nightfall, into a metaphor. Beyond death, the line also suggests grief at the loss of paradise on Earth, the Fall, which is the original cause of death in the Judeo-Christian story of the Creation. The evening dew, invested with emotion and made to represent grief, is equated with tears, which are shed at nightfall over the Fall, the sin that brought death into the world.

Lines 5–8

In beginning the second quatrain with the word "sweet," Herbert continues to connect the beauty of nature with impermanence, as any "sweet" thing must, over time, lose its sweetness. Like the day, the rose is an emblem of earthly splendor. It is "sweet" like the day, saturated with color, and graced with magnificence. (*Angry* and *brave* are complex words in Herbert's usage, as aspects of their meanings have all but passed from English. *Angry*, in the seventeenth century, could signify "inflamed," while *brave* could signify "having a fine or splendid appearance." The suggestions of wrath and courage carried by these words also reinforce the rose's magnificence, as it is characterized thus as standing knowingly in the prospect of doom.) So magnificent is the rose that Herbert calls one who looks at it a "rash gazer." Here, "rash" suggests a lack of necessary caution in taking in a sight so dazzling that the gazer is moved to "wipe," or rub, "his eye," as one does in wonder. Also, a warning may be understood to be present in the word "rash": one who beholds the rose is in danger of desiring its seductive but transitory beauty over the sweetness of what endures in eternity, the soul itself.

As with the day, so with the rose: despite its living splendor, death awaits. "Thy root," buried in the earth, as it must be if the rose is to flourish, "is ever in its grave." Thus, life and death are entwined, and death is an ever-present aspect of life. Indeed, by emphasizing the common ground shared by the root, the source of life, and the grave, the receptacle for death, Herbert evokes two Christian lessons: first, that life contains elements of death and must inevitably give way to death and, second, that death is not finality but part of the continuum of existence. In awareness of death, one realizes the true meaning and purpose of life and will thus prepare his or her soul, through the exercise of virtue, for eternity.

Lines 9–12

The word "sweet" begins the third quatrain as well, now describing the spring, which is subsequently characterized as "full of sweet days and roses." As such, the delights presented in the first two quatrains are contained in the third, and the narrator solidifies his suggestion of the earth's rich bounty. In the second line of the quatrain, spring is likened to "a box where sweets compacted lie." Then, as in the previous quatrains, the third line iterates the transience of earthly delights: "My music shows ye have your closes." Through this line, the narrator offers the poem itself as proof of his argument regarding the impermanence of things. By "my music," the narrator refers to the very verse being read, this poem. "Close" is a technical term in music indicating the resolution of a musical phrase. Thus, the poetic verse, like everything else the narrator has so far depicted, must come to an end, as it temporarily does with the four stressed and conclusive beats of the twelfth line: "And all must die."

Lines 13–16

Breaking the pattern established in the previous three quatrains, the final quatrain begins not with the word "sweet" but with a limiting expression: "Only a." The reader has been told that the "sweet day," the "sweet rose," and the "sweet spring" all "must die." In contrast to them is the soul: "Only a sweet and virtuous soul / . . . never gives." "Sweet" is no longer used to denote an aesthetic quality, nor is the word sufficient to stand alone anymore; in fact, in being yoked with "virtuous," it is invested with a moral and spiritual dimension. The soul that is sweet and virtuous, unlike the spring, the rose, and the day, "never gives," that is, it never gives way to death, instead ever enduring. Such a sweet soul, disciplined by virtue like wood that has been seasoned, is fully strengthened. Lumber that has been seasoned, aged, and dried is more suitable for use in construction than is fresh lumber; "seasoned timber" is sturdy and enduring. The conflagration suggested in line 15 by the image of "the whole world turn[ing] to coal" alludes to chapter 3, verse 10, of 2 Peter, in the New Testament, where Peter speaks of "the day of the Lord," the judgment day when "the elements shall melt with fervent heat" and "the earth also and the works that are therein shall be burned up."

Thus, the first three quatrains present images of earthly beauty, but each ends with the word "die." The last quatrain presents images of an eternal soul and of a conflagration that turns the whole world, except that virtuous soul, to blackened coal, and its last line ends with the word "live." As such, the entire poem, which all along warned of death, shows the way in which Herbert believes that he and his readers may achieve eternal life: by shunning transient glory and humbly embracing virtue.

Themes

The Transience of Earthly Beauty

Repeatedly, throughout the sixteen lines of "Virtue," Herbert asserts beauty's transitory nature. His warning is not that people themselves must die but that the things that delight people while they are alive must pass away. The word "thou," repeated in the last line of each of the first three stanzas, serves as an address to each of the day, the rose, and the spring. The word does not refer to the poet himself or to the reader, even if one hears associative and suggestive echoes in those directions. Consequently, Herbert's poem does not assume the character of a threat. It serves, rather, as an instrument devised to wean both poet and reader off dependence on the visible world for joy and spiritual nourishment in order to redirect both poet and reader to the inner cultivation of virtue.

The Interconnection of Life and Death

Besides expressing the impermanence of natural phenomena in "Virtue," Herbert also reveals the interconnection of the realms of life and death. The earth, which represents impermanence, and the sky, which represents eternity, are joined (by the day) in union in the second line of the poem. Similarly, the seventh line shows that a root, a source of life, and a grave, a tomb for life, share the earth as a common

Topics For Further Study

- In an essay, discuss whether Herbert's "Virtue" is or is not significant in the twenty-first century.

- Virtually all religions present some idea of what happens to people after they die. In an essay, consider the following questions: If you are religious, what are the teachings of your religion about what happens after death? If you are not religious, what ideas have been taught to you about what happens after death? What are your own beliefs about what happens after death? Are they in accord with what you have been taught, or have you developed other ideas? Is death a serious concern to you, or is it something you do not think about? Fully explain all of your responses.

- Consider a loss you have suffered. In an essay, discuss the nature of the loss, how it affected you, and how you coped with it. Then conduct interviews with six people regarding loss and coping with it. Present your results to your class, analyzing the responses and comparing and contrasting the nature of the responses with consideration for the age of the respondents.

- Write a dialogue in which two characters, one a believer in God and one a nonbeliever, discuss Herbert's poem "Virtue."

- In "Virtue," Herbert focuses on the transience of the delights of the natural world. Rewrite the poem using products of technology instead of natural phenomena.

---

location. In the Christian story, Jesus's temporary journey into earthly death assures humankind of the existence of a way into eternal life.

The Power of Christian Virtue to Overcome Mortality

The last stanza reverses the despair built up in the first three, by expressing the notion that salvation is achieved through the cultivation of a "sweet and virtuous soul." Such a soul is formed, Herbert suggests, through appreciation of the beauty of nature, with the understanding that those natural objects, which indeed exercise a positive influence on the soul, must perish. The soul that is shaped by the appreciation of the sweetness of natural beauty—as long as that beauty is seen to be transient—can itself become sweet by refocusing its appreciation on the beauty of virtue, sacrifice, and the eternal afterlife.

Nature

Despite his poem's focus on the transience of earthly beauty and of the experience of earthly rapture, Herbert delights in the depiction of nature and natural phenomena. He brings the reader into the English countryside in springtime, to be dazzled by the light of day, the hue of a rose, the scent of the earth, and the dew-covered fields at evening, as well as by the music of the poet's appreciation of these things. Herbert introduces natural images into his verse not as ends in themselves but as a means of carrying out the religious instruction to which the poem is devoted.

Faith

An implicit theme of "Virtue" is faith. Although what is visible to humankind in the poem is the transience of earthly delight and the decay of nature, the poem ultimately conveys what cannot be seen and must instead be felt: the existence of a quality, the soul, which exists in eternal delight in a dimension other than the one in which our bodies live. The first three quatrains show what the poet can actually see; the fourth refers to what he knows by virtue of the vision granted to him by his Christian faith. Faith allows him to see what is invisible to the eye.

Style

Anaphora

Much of the force and grace of "Virtue" come from the device of anaphora, which gives the poem

Compare & Contrast

- **1630s:** Most of England was made up of cities and villages that were integrated with the natural world depicted in Herbert's "Virtue."

    Today: After the Industrial Revolution of the nineteenth century and urban development of the twentieth, England is no longer the green, open country it was in Herbert's time. However, through concerted conservation efforts much of the nation's forest land has been restored.

- **1630s:** Universities like Cambridge were dedicated primarily to educating young men to serve in the priesthood and thus focused on divinity studies.

    Today: The great English universities provide secular education in the sciences, social sciences, and humanities to male and female students alike.

- **1630s:** The English monarchy was the central governing power.

    Today: England is a constitutional monarchy in which the government is made up of an elected prime minister, an elected House of Commons, and a House of Lords, some of whose members are elected and some of whom hold hereditary positions. The monarchy has no real governing power and as such is rather a symbolic institution providing England with a cultural identity.

---

its orderly and predictable structure and endows it with a soothing and even hypnotic quality. *Anaphora* is the repetition of words and patterns for poetic effect. This device is immediately apparent in the first line, with the triple repetition of the word "so." Moreover, the same poetic structure governs each of the first three stanzas, while the fourth stanza is shaped by a slight variation of this structure. Each of the first three stanzas begins with the word "sweet" and ends with the word "die." The second line of each stanza presents an image reflecting nature's splendor, while the third line of each stanza offers a diminution, or lessening, of that splendor. Each of the fourth lines contains four one-syllable words, with these four words nearly identical from stanza to stanza. The effect of anaphora is to make an argument by means of a pattern of language, as the use of anaphora suggests that in several different instances, the same laws apply. Finally, the variation allowed by the last stanza breaks the tension built up by the repetition, offering a solution, the practice of virtue, to a problem that had seemed unsolvable, transience.

Apostrophe

In poetry, *apostrophe* is the technique of calling upon or addressing a particular person or thing. In the first three stanzas of "Virtue," Herbert indirectly addresses the reader of the poem by directly addressing the day, a rose, and the spring. In the fourth stanza, he does not address the soul but instead talks about it. Thus, he differentiates his relationship to the eternal world of the soul from his relationship to the natural world. Also, he thus puts himself in the role of a teacher and a preacher, conveying a message about the natural world and its impermanence.

Historical Context

Lyric Poetry

Originally, a *lyric* poem was one sung to the accompaniment of a lyre, a small stringed instrument resembling a harp. In time, a lyric poem became such a poem that might be so accompanied even if it actually was not. Lyric poetry is characterized by the poet's giving intimate expression to his innermost thoughts and feelings, in a way that he could not simply by, say, telling a story. Herbert's "Virtue" reflects his inner delight at the loveliness of nature as well as his meditation in response to nature. Rather than telling a story,

"Virtue" reveals an internal mood. In part because of the value given to human perception by the Renaissance, lyric poetry flourished during the late sixteenth and early seventeenth centuries in England.

Metaphysical Poetry

Metaphysical poetry is the name given to the poetry written by a loose collection of seventeenth-century poets, including John Donne foremost as well as George Herbert, Henry Vaughan, Abraham Cowley, Richard Crashaw, and John Cleveland. Metaphysical poetry is characterized by intellectual argument expressed in sensual imagery and a colloquial, or everyday, style of writing. (Writing that was colloquial in the seventeenth-century, of course, would not seem so in the twenty-first.) Sentence structure is often complex, and metaphors bring together images that might not at first seem appropriate, as Herbert does in "Virtue" when he speaks of the spring as "a box" in which "sweets compacted lie."

Devotional Poetry

While verse may be classified as metaphysical poetry based on formal, technical, and stylistic aspects, verse may be classified as devotional poetry based on the content and intention of the work. Devotional poetry is exactly what its name implies: poetry written, and intended to be read, as an act and expression of devotion to the Deity, as is all of Herbert's verse. Like metaphysical poetry, devotional poetry was especially prevalent in the seventeenth century, when the intersection of religion and politics dominated intellectual discussions; in fact, many of the authors of metaphysical poetry, including Donne, Vaughan, and Crashaw, are also renowned for their devotional poetry. In "Virtue," Herbert praises the virtue of the Creator by praising the beauty of the creation. Beyond that, he intuits from that beauty a dimension of existence attainable only through faith in and devotion to the Creator, not merely through what he has created.

Critical Overview

Next to his great contemporary John Donne, who was a family friend, fellow poet, and fellow churchman, Herbert is regarded as the foremost among the seventeenth-century metaphysical poets. His book of verse, *The Temple*, in which "Virtue" is included, enjoyed immense popularity throughout the seventeenth century in part because of the devotional aspect of his poetry and in part because of his reputation for having a character marked by gentleness and saintliness. His poetry remained popular despite the disfavor his religion, his family, and his allegiance to the monarchy earned him as a result of the displacement of the monarchy by the government of Oliver Cromwell between 1640 and 1660.

The great American intellectual Ralph Waldo Emerson, discussing Herbert's verse in his lecture "English Literature: Ben Jonson, Herrick, Herbert, Wooton," remarks that Herbert was "not content with the obvious properties of natural objects but delights in discovering abstruser relations between them and the subject of his thought." Emerson adds that Herbert's "thought is often recondite and far fetched yet the language is always simple and chaste" and that he demonstrated "the power of exalted thought to melt and bend language." In his essay "The Metaphysical Poets," T. S. Eliot comments, "In the verse of George Herbert . . . simplicity is carried as far as it can go." Russell Fraser, in an essay titled "George Herbert's Poetry," writes that "among makers of the short poem in English Herbert's peers are Yeats, Frost, Donne and Jonson, and Shakespeare at sonnets." This is high praise.

Criticism of "Virtue" is usually of the exegetical type, as it might be for scripture; *exegesis* is a type of critical investigation that sets out to clarify and explore the meaning of images of and allusions to objects like "dew" and "seasoned timber." For the general reader, such criticism can tend to be obscure and to make a poem seem more convoluted than it first appears. Nevertheless, when a reader can connect, for example, "dew" with Christ's grace or a "rose" with his simultaneous presence and departure, "Virtue" gains added breadth.

Criticism

Neil Heims

Heims is a writer and teacher living in Paris. In this essay, he attempts to show how a contemporary reader might approach Herbert's early-seventeenth-century poem "Virtue."

If poetry that is nearly four centuries old, like Herbert's lyric poem "Virtue," is to be meaningful to contemporary readers, something within that poetry must transcend its own time, bridging the distance between history and experience. If a poem cannot do these things, then it is only a museum

> "Somewhat paradoxically, while 'Virtue' warns against attending to day, rose, and spring as if they were permanent, it demands the reader's lingering attention to itself."

piece—an artifact, a remnant of the past. Such a poem may be interesting to the general reader as a curiosity, for the glimpse it gives of another time; otherwise, it may be interesting to specialists and scholars as material to put under the microscope and dissect, allowing them to track down learned allusions and write largely unread scholarly articles. What, then, does "Virtue" have to offer a contemporary, common reader, rather than a scholar?

"Virtue" was written by a priest of the Church of England in a rural district of England sometime between 1630 and 1633, nearly a decade before Oliver Cromwell's Puritan Revolution and the beheading of King Charles I. Following in the tradition of "warning" verse, which reminds readers of the transience of the temporal world, however beautiful, and of the possible perils of the world to come, the poem appears on first reading to be lovely in a genteel sort of way and certainly transient itself. It is a poem of sixteen brief, alternately rhymed lines, made up of ninety-eight words in all, with the word "sweet" appearing six times and the word "die" three times. In addition, the word "die," which appears at the end of the fourth, eighth, and twelfth lines, dictates the rhymes of the preceding second, sixth, and tenth lines; the sounds of the first words of the seventh and eleventh lines, "thy" and "my," respectively, also accord with this rhyme scheme. The poem is not only brief, therefore, but also concentrated. It is composed of four stanzas and is structured anaphorically, meaning that each of the first three stanzas repeats the same established pattern, while the fourth offers a slight, and meaningful, variation of that pattern.

Each of the first three stanzas begins with an invocation, or an address: to the "day," to a "rose," and to the "spring." Each is called "sweet." The third line of each stanza reiterates the message of transience: day will fall; the earth that nourishes also serves as a grave; and musical phrases come to an end. The fourth lines of the three stanzas present similar warnings in almost identical words: "For thou must die," "And thou must die," and "And all must die." The last stanza offers what must be seen as a moral: While all the lovely delights of Earth will perish, the soul that has devoted itself to becoming "sweet and virtuous" will live.

"Virtue" is thus an instruction not only in how we must look at life but also in faith itself. Presenting what is clearly visible to the human eye in the first three stanzas, that is, impermanent earthly delights, the poem moves in the fourth stanza to what is invisible and is thus apparent only to the faithful: the permanence of the eternal life that follows death for the soul that is "sweet and virtuous." Herbert attempts to make his argument more convincing by setting up a tension in the first three stanzas that he resolves in the fourth. Indeed, each of the first three stanzas ends in frustration, and through that frustration Herbert instills a longing in the reader. By heralding day, rose, and spring as desirable and then devaluing them in demonstrating their impermanence, Herbert fosters in the reader a desire for something worthy and permanent. Thus, by breaking, in the fourth stanza, the pattern that governed the first line of each of the first three stanzas, beginning with the word "only," Herbert resolves his poem's tension. The structure of his rhetoric naturally wins the reader to his position, even if only momentarily.

When he composed "Virtue," Herbert was writing for a like-minded audience. He was a pastor, and he was communicating a common belief among his followers, in a form intended to delight them and reaffirm what they knew. He was speaking not only to those in his small village, who could hear him preach his sermons on Sundays, but, indeed, to members of his religion throughout England. The poems in *The Temple*, of which "Virtue" is but one of many, are sermons, or lessons for the faithful. They are designed to strengthen faith by addressing resistance and celebrating acquiescence. This sort of verse is called "devotional poetry." For the poet, the verse exists as a testament of his faith; for faithful readers, it sings of their spiritual condition and offers the lyrical pleasure of dwelling in a familiar abode, as comforted by the reiteration of a common belief.

What, then, does "Virtue" offer to readers nearly four centuries later? The answer seems self-evident.

What Do I Read Next?

- "Life," available in Alexander Witherspoon and Frank Warnke's *Seventeenth-Century Prose and Poetry* (1963), is another poem of Herbert's from *The Temple*. Like "Virtue," it focuses on how nature's products die off and thereby reveal the fate of humankind.

- In "On My First Son," a lyric written in 1603, also available in Witherspoon and Warnke's *Seventeenth-Century Prose and Poetry* (1963), Ben Jonson laments the death of his son at the age of seven years. Jonson tries to balance his profound grief with the consolation that death has put his beloved child in a state he ought to envy rather than regret, in removing him from earthly care.

- In act 4, scene 2, of his play *Cymbeline* (c. 1612), William Shakespeare introduces a funereal lament, "Fear No More the Heat of the Sun," in which the singers console themselves over the fact of death by accepting its inevitability and its power as liberator from the cares of the world.

- Robert Herrick's "To the Virgins, to Make Much of Time" (1648), found in *The Works of Robert Herrick* (1823), like Herbert's "Virtue," contemplates the impermanence of time. Rather than offering the alternative of an eternal afterlife, however, Herrick advises that a fitting course of action is to seize the day before it departs and enjoy to the fullest what is offered on Earth.

- The second poem in A. E. Houseman's cycle *A Shropshire Lad* (1896), "Loveliest of Trees," is a brief lyric in which the poet contemplates the beauty of nature with an awareness that he, not nature, will pass away.

- In "Spring and Fall to a Young Child" (1880), found in *Poems of Gerard Manley Hopkins* (1931), Hopkins considers the transience of life and nature from the point of view of an older man reflecting on a girl's experience of autumn.

- In "Do Not Go Gentle into That Good Night" (c. 1945), found in *The Poems of Dylan Thomas* (1952), the Welsh poet celebrates fiercely holding onto life, despite the inevitability of death, to the very end.

For readers who share Herbert's belief, "Virtue" simply reinforces what they already feel and, as it did centuries ago, offers the consolation of a familiar and fundamental belief sweetly restated. For readers who do not share Herbert's belief, "Virtue" can be dismissed as old-fashioned piety not to their taste, or it can, perhaps, be enjoyed and esteemed as an aesthetic object. In either case, the apparent simplicity of the poem may present the greatest difficulty to contemporary readers of whatever persuasion. Whether read by those who agree with it or by those who do not, "Virtue" can be given a cursory glance and dismissed as a pretty set of verses. Scholars, certainly, can offer plenteous evidence to the contrary. They can show the poem's complexity and resonance through analyses of terms like "dew," "fall," and "seasoned timber." Dew can signify the presence of Christ. The word "fall" invokes the biblical story of the Fall of humankind in the Garden of Eden. "Seasoned timber" may suggest the soul that has been cured of its naive and youthful devotion to the manifestations of divinity in nature, allowing it to focus its devotion on divinity itself. The term may also refer, perhaps, to the cross upon which Christ was crucified. Such extensive analyses, however, do not make "Virtue" any more striking as a poem, rather making it only more doctrinal or obscure than it first appears.

The demands that "Virtue" makes on a twenty-first-century reader are different from the demands it made on seventeenth-century ones. In essence, it demands an aesthetic readjustment, which a responsible reading of the poem will help foster. That is, for the contemporary reader, "Virtue" is less about faith in a world hereafter than about the quiet contemplation of the present world in a gentle and penetrating spirit. Herbert's original intention, as revealed in the poem, was to show the impermanence of earthly delight. As the poem highlights the melancholy aspect of earthly experience by dwelling upon what is disappearing, it compels the reader to in turn dwell upon the words of the poem. This compulsion comes about not because the words are complex or have scriptural resonance but because their pace is one of rhythmic slowness. For the contemporary reader, "Virtue" is as much about embedding oneself in the poem's present as it is about the deceptiveness of temporality.

After the image of the "sweet day" is first invoked in the poem's opening, it is extended by the languorous triple modification, "so cool, so calm, so bright." Implicit in the repetition is a rhythmic instruction to the reader: read this slowly. The tempo is adagio—leisurely, contemplative, slow, and balanced. As the short line proceeds, this implicit tempo marking is reinforced by the hard *k* sounds of "cool" and "calm" and by the opening and closing consonants of "bright." The opening *b* of "bright" prevents any elision, or sliding together of sounds, with the *o* of the preceding "so," which an opening vowel would have allowed. Similarly, the *t* at the end of "bright" forces the reader to stop, making the line a self-contained unit despite the lack of a verb. Only with a new intake and release of breath can the reader attack the second line's first word, "the," which is followed with another *b* barrier, in the word "bridal."

This pattern of forced retardation continues in the third line and recurs in the succeeding stanzas. In the first line of the second stanza, "sweet rose" forces the reader to negotiate the trill between the two words. Following immediately is the hurdle of *h*'s presented by "whose hue"; the reiterated *oo* sound also delays the reading. At its end, the line skids to a halt with the *v* sound in "brave." Over the next lines, many of the same sounds from the first stanza are employed, like the *b* of "bids" and the *th* of "thy." Even when new sounds are introduced, they have the same effect of keeping the tempo of the poem slow.

Only in the final stanza does the rhythmic pattern change. The opening vowel of "only" begins what in the context of "Virtue" is a forward tumble of sounds: The reader is propelled by the easy connection between the *t* of "sweet" and the succeeding "and," as well as by the elision of "virtuous" and "soul," through the blending of the final *s* of "virtuous" and the initial *s* of "soul." The second line of the fourth stanza, unlike lines 2, 6, and 10, presents no pause, instead offering a continuation of the first line: "Only a sweet and virtuous soul / Like seasoned timber." The *l* of "soul," with which the first line terminates, reappears immediately as the initial sound in the first word of the second line, "like." Similarly, the *d* of "seasoned" merges with the *t* of "timber."

This kind of minute examination of the most basic elements of "Virtue," the individual letters of individual words, illuminates the way in which Herbert achieved certain aesthetic effects. Indeed, simply undertaking such an examination disciplines the reader to pay attention to the smallest details of objects of the senses and to the process of perception itself. Thus, while the primary notion expressed in the poem is that the phenomena of the natural world are transient and ought not distract one from the eternity of the supernatural world, the poem itself contradicts that notion by demanding a focused and steady attention to its most minute details and, consequently, to its mechanics and to the images represented within it.

Thus, in a sense, "Virtue" seems to be separated from its author's apparent intention: rather than warning a reader not to become fixated on the created world, it stands as a work of human creation demanding absorbed attention. The poem itself is not transient but endures as an object worthy of contemplation across the boundaries of time, as confirmed by succeeding eras. Somewhat paradoxically, while "Virtue" warns against attending to day, rose, and spring as if they were permanent, it demands the reader's lingering attention to itself. Yet, in truth, no contradiction exists. At the core of this earthly, aesthetic object, a mortal creation, is what Herbert believed to be an immortal truth; indeed, "Virtue" instructs the reader in Christian dogma. Moreover, in contemplating the poem, the reader is not truly contemplating that transient something, essentially an artifact of nature. Rather, the reader is contemplating the transformation, by the poet's art, of the transient into the permanent, as the poem itself tempers the way in which the reader perceives the world. What makes something eternal is not only its duration in time but also the depth of people's consciousness, their perception, of it. In this respect, intensity is as much a dimension as time. When it succeeds, that is, when a reader yields to its demands, "Virtue" acts as a vehicle for the expression of the eternal. The poem also compels the reader to reside in and as such create an aspect of permanence, rather than allowing that reader to yield to the hurry and inattentiveness that endow an experience with an aspect of transience.

Source: Neil Heims, Critical Essay on "Virtue," in *Poetry for Students*, Thomson Gale, 2007.

Suzanne McDonald

In the following essay, McDonald argues that "Virtue" is an Easter poem celebrating the dual nature of Christ, as both a temporal and an eternal figure.

At the literal level, George Herbert's lyric poem "Vertue" has a self-evident and incontrovertible meaning: it juxtaposes earthly transience and mutability with the immortality of the true Christian soul. In addition, though, there seems to be both internal and external evidence to suggest an added dimension concerned with the dual nature of Christ, both mortal and divine, as we encounter this paradox through the events of Easter. This should not altogether surprise us. As one commentator has remarked, "a glance at Herbert's table of contents will show how many of his poems are subsumed under the series Advent, Nativity, Ash Wednesday and Lent, Holy Week, Easter, Ascension, Whitsun, and some special days like Trinity Sunday and All Saints; also, many more of the poems are Lenten or Holy Week poems than we have recognized." External evidence for this surmise is provided by implicit biblical allusions incorporating imagery which has fixed meanings outside the immediate context of the poem, while internal evidence is provided by the strategic choice of these images in "Vertue," and the occurrence of similar words and images throughout the fabric of *The Temple*. The literal and metaphoric modes are not, of course, mutually exclusive, since both views derive from the same source: it is the Fall which brings the decay of nature and of earthly beauty, and hence the need for Christ to assume flesh and to die. If we see the poem in the light of Christ's death and resurrection, rather than viewing it merely as an account of nature's corruption and the survival of the upright soul, then some of its perceived difficulties and peculiarities will disappear, and its richness and pathos will be enhanced.

The poem's most suggestive line is the second, where the day is described as "the bridall of the earth and skie" (l. 2). The implications of this are clear: the earth and sky are united by the day, and not, as has been suggested, that the stanza depicts

> *The equation of Christ with the rose of the second stanza of 'Vertue' provides a more plangent explanation of the second line, where the sight of the crucified Christ is more likely to move the gazer to tears than the commonplace... representation of a beauty which must fade."*

the deflowering of an innocent bride. Rather, it is the concept of marriage itself which is present: it is in the day itself that the earth and sky are joined. There is little to hinder the natural extension of this image to include the person of Christ, who, in spite of his divinity, assumes man's flesh, accomplishing in himself that which Herbert attributes to the day: the union of heaven and earth. The scriptural and patristic resonance which surrounds the notion of "bridall" is strong, including such universal commonplaces as the marriage of both the earthly church and the individual soul to Christ the divine bridegroom. That the day represents Christ is likewise a commonplace, since the sun, by its perpetual rise and fall, is a constant symbol of Christ's birth, death and resurrection, a topic most famously explored and developed in Donne's "Good Friday, 1613. Riding Westward" and Milton's "Nativity Ode." The first stanza may therefore contain an implicit suggestion of the Easter pattern inherent in the concept of the fall of the day and of the sun.

Other poems in *The Temple*, and the structure of the work itself, support this approach. "Vertue," for instance, is immediately preceded by "Lent," a fact to which I shall have occasion to return. Looking further afield, however, other poems in *The Temple* employ the same vocabulary and imagery to focus on the central paradox of the Easter celebration. "Sunday," for instance, which has for one of its major themes the significance of Sunday in the Easter cycle ("This day my Saviour rose" [l. 36]) opens with a line comparable to the first line of "Vertue") "O Day most calm, most bright") and Sunday is presented as "Th' indorsement of supreme delight, / Writ by a friend, and with his bloud" (ll. 3–4). Moreover, Christ is again depicted as a source of light: "The week were dark, but for thy light: / Thy torch doth show the way" (ll. 6–7). "Sunday" is concerned most centrally with the Resurrection. By implicitly invoking its first line, "Vertue" maintains the association, but shifts it from the triumph of Easter Sunday to the pathos and paradox of Good Friday. "Self-condemnation," another poem which deals with the events surrounding the Passion, sees Herbert prefiguring "the last great day" (l. 19) when the light of truth and justice "shines bright and cleare" (l. 23). In "The British church" the Word made flesh is described as "sweet and bright" (l. 3), and again, in the alchemical poem "The Elixir," God is the tincture who will make all things like unto himself, "bright and clean" (l. 16).

Following this apparent equation of Christ with the day comes the reference to dew, another scripturally charged image, in part because in the Old Testament divine visitations can be in the form of dew, a concept utilized in the celebrated anonymous fifteenth-century lyric "I sing of a maiden . . ." In the Bible, dew is evidence of God's grace and blessing in such texts as Genesis 27:28 ("God give thee of the dew of heaven, and the fatness of the earth") and Deuteronomy 33:13 ("Blessed of the Lord be his land, for the precious things of heaven, for the dew . . ."), a correspondence which Herbert invokes in the third stanza of "Grace." Dew is the manifestation of God's word in Deuteronomy 32:2) "My doctrine shall drop as the rain, my speech shall distil as the dew") but, most significantly, it is associated with types of Christ and with prophecy concerning his death and resurrection. Gideon learns that he is to save Israel, just as his antitype, Christ, will save mankind, when God directs the dew to cover, and then avoid, the fleece (Judges 6:36–40). In Isaiah 26:19, revitalizing dew is directly associated with the resurrection of the dead: "Thy dead men shall live, together with my dead body shall they arise. Awake and sing, ye that dwell in dust: for thy dew is as the dew of herbs . . ." Similarly, in Hosea 14:5–7, "I will be as the dew unto Israel: he shall grow. . . . They that dwell under his shadow shall return; they shall revive as the corn." And in Micah 5:7, "the remnant of Jacob shall be in the midst of many people as a dew from the Lord, as the showers upon the grass. . . ." However, the dew in "Vertue" is not simply a possible representation of God's Word made man, or of God's blessing contained within Christ's death. The most appropriate of all biblical references is Psalms 133:3) "As the dew of Hermon, and as the dew that descended upon the mountains of Zion: for there the Lord commanded the blessing, even life for evermore") where the dew of Hermon is conventionally glossed as the community of saints. Here, almost certainly, is the dew which weeps for the death of Christ, who, as the second Adam, must suffer his own "fall" in order that mankind may be saved from the consequences of the first Fall.

Having used the day as one trope for Christ, Herbert employs a second in the "sweet rose" whose hue is "angrie and brave" (l. 5), a conjunction of adjectives which has perplexed and irritated many commentators. How can the reader reconcile sweetness, anger, and bravery in a flower which should represent, in the conventional interpretation of the poem, the transience of earthly beauty? I would suggest that, as with the earth and the sky, these adjectives meet in the person of Christ and his sacrifice. Although, admittedly, the majority of allusions to roses in *The Temple* suggest the deceptiveness of worldly beauty and its temptations, other forms of denotation are also present. "Church-rents and schismes," for instance, opens with the phrase "Brave rose" to describe the Church, Christ's bride and the antitype of the rose of Sharon (Song of Solomon 2:1). In lines 12–13 it is Christ's blood which is specifically stated to have given the rose its hue, in keeping with the traditional iconography in which the rose is not only the flower of the Virgin Mary, but also of the martyrs. At the poem's conclusion Herbert, sorrowing over a falling Church, desires "to lick up all the dew, / Which falls by night, and poure it out for you!" (ll. 29–30).

"Angrie" and "brave" are not unprecedented adjectives in *The Temple*. "Angrie," aside from its common dialect meaning of "inflamed," is not, perhaps, readily associated with Christ and the New Law, but Herbert employs it in "Bitter-sweet") "Ah my deare angrie Lord, / Since thou dost love, yet strike" (ll. 1–2). The "brave rose" of "Church-rents and schismes" is paralleled by an early version of "Easter" in the Williams MS, where Herbert writes that "The Sunn arising in the East. . . . Can not make up so brave a feast / As thy discoverie presents" (ll. 23–26), a poem which, in addition to presenting Christ as a "brave feast," reiterates, in its first stanza, the importance of the Christ/day relationship. The equation of Christ with the rose of the second stanza of "Vertue" provides a more plangent explanation of the second line, where the sight of the crucified Christ is more likely to move the gazer to tears than the commonplace (and conventionally amorous) representation of a beauty which must fade.

The emblem of the rose whose "root is ever in its grave," usually interpreted as further suggesting the inevitable decline of natural beauty, lends itself equally well to the notion of Christ's ordained destiny on earth to fulfil the predictions of the prophets, a destiny which necessarily involves his own death. Apart from the fact that Christ is conventionally the Root of Jesse and the Root of David, biblical images of the root are frequently associated with the resurrection of the dead, since, for example, though it "wax old in the earth, and the stock thereof die in the ground; Yet . . . it will bud, and bring forth boughs like a plant," just as "man lieth down" until "the heavens be no more . . ." (Job 14:8–12). Herbert expresses similar sentiments in his poem "The Flower," where the "shrivel'd heart," renewed by grace, is likened to the flower and its root.

> Who would have thought my shrivel'd heart
> Could have recover'd greennesse? It was gone
> Quite under ground; as flowers depart
> To see their mother-root, when they have blown;
> Where they together
> All the hard weather,
> Dead to the world, keep house unknown.
>
> (ll. 8–14)

Here the heart, having suffered its own death, experiences its own resurrection, while in "Vertue" the type of this process is implied in the depiction of the Christ-rose which, its root in the grave, encompasses not only the sorrow of Christ's inevitable sacrifice, but the joy of the equally inevitable resurrection to follow.

After the "sweet day" and the "sweet rose" have exemplified Christ, and been described in suggestive detail, both are subsumed into the "sweet spring, full of sweet dayes and roses" (l. 9). At the beginning of this interpretation, I pointed out the significance of the placement of "Vertue," immediately following the poem "Lent." Lines 25–27 of the latter poem clearly indicate that, whatever connotations spring may carry of a natural beauty which fades, its ecclesiastical significance is highly pertinent.

> Then those same pendant profits, which the spring
> And Easter intimate, enlarge the thing,
> And goodnesse of the deed.
>
> (ll. 25–27)

Just as the spring marks the Annunciation and the Passion, the key images of the dew and the rose possess a dual function in designating aspects both of the Virgin Mary and the Annunciation, and of Christ himself, bringing into one nexus spring, Easter, Annunciation, and Passion.

Following this series of liturgical and biblical images, however, Herbert unsettles the reader by relating spring, days, and roses to the vexed "box where sweets compacted lie." Despite critical attempts to equate this mysterious box with a box of perfumes or an anachronistic musical box, its true identity almost certainly lies within *The Temple* itself, this time in the poem "Ungratefulness." Here Herbert describes "two rare cabinets full of treasure" (l. 7), the first being the Trinity (the "statelier cabinet"). More importantly, though,

> all thy sweets are packt up in the other
> Thy mercies thither flock and flow:
> That as the first affrights,
> This may allure us with delights;
> Because this box we know.
>
> (ll. 19–23)

This other box is the Incarnation. I would suggest, moreover, that in "Vertue" it also signifies, by analogy, the box which contains the Communion host, types of which are the Ark of the Covenant and, in particular, the sepulchre of Christ. If this is so, then the introduction of the Eucharist) the sharing by all of the results of Christ's sacrifice) marks a shift in the poem from the specific to the general. The specific is represented by a preponderance of demonstratives ("the bridall," "the dew," "the gazer") which imply the particular ("sweet day," "sweet rose"), as do the possessives ("thy fall," "thy root"). The general, though, is inaugurated by "*a* box" (italics added), the introduction of the poet himself ("my musick") and the corresponding change in the refrain. Even though all must die, the reference to the Eucharist, which brings about this change, lessens potential sorrow, since, as the final stanza indicates, it also represents a release from death.

Even in Herbert's music, references to Christ's suffering and resurrection are inescapable in yet another commonplace, the comparison of the tortured Christ on the cross to a musical instrument, emitting divine melody at the hands of his tormentors, an allusion which Donne incorporates in the first stanza of "Hymne to God My God, in My Sicknesse." In "Easter" Herbert sings the praises of the risen Lord, whose "crosse taught all wood to resound his name" (l. 9), and whose "stretched sinews taught all strings, what key / Is best to celebrate this most high day" (ll. 11–12). Moreover, "since all musick is but three parts vied / And multiplied" (ll. 15–16), in the context of the poem Herbert asks the risen Christ) his "blessed Spirit") to join his "sweet art" to the music of Herbert's awakened and consorted lute and heart. "Easter" is one of several poems relevant to "Vertue" to make significant use of the word "sweet," repeated here in reference to Christ's entrance into Jerusalem on Palm Sunday: "But thou wast up by break of day, / And brought'st thy sweets along with thee" (ll. 21–22). Likewise, in "The Sacrifice," Christ comments that the ointment was "not half so sweet as my sweet sacrifice" (l. 19), and in "The Flower" the Lord's "Returns" are "sweet and clean . . . as the flowers in spring" (ll. 1–2). In "Faith" the incarnate Christ "sweetly took / Our flesh and frailtie, death and danger" (ll. 23–24), and, as already indicated above, the Incarnation becomes a box of sweets in "Ungratefulness." Especially remarkable, however, are "The Odour" and "The Banquet"; the most cursory reading reveals the complete domination which "sweetness" holds over them. The former is based upon 2 Corinthians 2:15–16) "For we are unto God a sweet savour of Christ, in them that are saved, and in them that perish: To the one we are the savour of death unto death; and to the other the savour of life unto life." Although "sweet" appears only once in the biblical text which I have proposed as central to "Vertue," it is the basis of Herbert's entire poem, as adjective, adverb, and noun, with various guises and significations. In "The Banquet," which has for its subject the bread and wine of the Eucharist (a motif clearly important for "Vertue" as an Easter poem), Herbert employs "sweet" and "sweetnesse" as part of the structural development of the first three stanzas, compares the sweetness of flowers to that of Christ's sacrifice, and dwells on the sweet taste of the Communion wine.

In the final stanza, images of Christ's Incarnation and death are replaced by the knowledge not only of his resurrection, but, with the continuation of the new suggestion of community which surfaced in the preceding stanza, with the guaranteed resurrection of all Christian souls. Christ's resurrection and its consequences are implicit in the entire image skein) in the day, the dew, the root, and the rose. For the country parson, the rose is a purge, one of the "home-bred medecines," in contrast to exotic spices, which he "condemns for vanities, and so shuts them out of his family." In an analogous sense, in "Providence" the "rose, besides his beautie, is a cure" (l. 78), and in its figurative sense in "Vertue," Christ's cure for the primordial sin of Adam and the contagion of eternal death. The images of the first two stanzas hence unite the whole preordained cycle of Christ's life) Annunciation, Passion, Resurrection) and the perpetual significance of his life and sacrifice is contained in the diurnal cycle and the atemporal "gazer."

The "season'd timber" of this final stanza is therefore an unmistakable reference) one is tempted to say the most explicit of the entire poem) to the cross as a synecdoche for the crucifixion and its consequences, a mercy which never fails or "gives." Moreover, it is the type of the Christian soul, tempered by suffering, which remains upright until its ultimate vindication, when the final result of Christ's suffering is made apparent and "the whole world turn[s] to coal" (l. 15).

Source: Suzanne McDonald, "George Herbert's 'Vertue': An Easter Poem?" in *George Herbert Journal*, Vol. 17, No. 1, Fall 1993, pp. 61–69.

Kathleen M. Swaim

In the following essay, Swaim argues that the "season'd timber" of "Virtue" is a reference to charcoal and in opposition to the coal mentioned in the poem's penultimate line.

George Herbert's much anthologized and annotated "Vertue" has been generally recognized as what Arnold Stein labels it, "one of the purest lyrics in the language," and as "Herbert's poetry at its best" in the words of Louis L. Martz. Its deliberate architecture has been much praised. For M. M. Mahood its form of three statements plus a counterstatement makes it "essentially a poem in which anticipation dominates over discovery, in which our pleasure is to find all so well expressed"; for M. L. Rosenthal and A. J. M. Smith "its four tiny prophecies" are founded upon a "process of elimination"; and more recently Barbara H. Smith has called attention to the poem's architecture as modifying the norms of closure in favor of a fourth stanza which "has the effect, entirely appropriate to its theme, of a revelation—that which is known beyond what can be demonstrated logically."

There is an exquisite shapeliness to the art and thought of this lyric, in its progression from "thou" to "all" and from "die" to "lives"; in its shift from the diurnal rhythm of stanza 1—day/night—to the eternity of its conclusion; in the major imagery development of vegetative context (earth, sun, dew), to rose (singular) and root, to roses (plural), both sweetly growing and sweetly compacted or preserved for later seasons, and to the larger vegetative category of trees, this too plural and this too preserved in the form of usable timber; and in the secondary imagery of the third lines of the stanzas, especially the "weep" and "fall" of stanza 1, the "root" and "grave" of stanza 2, the "closes" both musical and mortal of stanza 3, and the apocalyptic transformation and reversal of stanza 4. The development of size and range and the reversal of stanza 4 fill out the poem's shape. My purpose in this note is to enhance our appreciation of both Herbert's metaphysics and his graceful artistry by closely attending to the concluding conceit.

The climactic stanza of "Vertue" reads thus:

> Onely a sweet and vertuous soul,
> Like season'd timber, never gives;
> But though the whole world turn to coal,
> Then chiefly lives.

F. E. Hutchinson paraphrases the meaning thus: "While the day and the rose and the spring come to a natural end, virtue alone survives the general conflagration at the end of the world, which reduces all else to 'coal' (i.e. cinder, ashes)." Several anthologists supplement this usual gloss of "coal" with a citation of II Peter 3:10, which reads in the King James Version:

> But the day of the Lord will come as a thief in the night; in the which the heavens shall pass away with a great noise, and the elements shall melt with fervent heat, the earth also and the works that are therein shall be burned up.

"Coal" is sometimes amplified to "glowing coal" or "red-hot coal" or attention is called to man as "a quick coal / Of mortall fire" in Herbert's "Employment."

"Season'd timber" too has come in for a share of special attention, most frequently as a unit in the artistic structure, as for example a confined resemblance that becomes a wide-ranging metaphor or as "an arbitrary symbol" in contrast to the images of the other stanzas. In the most fully developed study of the poem, Arnold Stein reads "season'd timber" as a natural object that "achieves its purpose after death—not as a tree but as wood"; for him it is a deliberate illustrative comparison, a simile, a product of human creation, in contrast to the symbols of the earlier stanzas, but a notably limited comparison which will barely allow us to stretch our imaginations to include the possibility that "seasoned timber burns well and has a kind of second life in its coals." Such glosses on the final stanza do not allow the full meaning and thus the full shape of the poem to emerge. In the words of Helen Vendler, "The real question is not what

> *The vocabularies of economics, chemistry, and physics all illuminate the rightness and richness of Herbert's chosen image of 'season'd timber.'..."*

accommodations we can make *post-hoc* to the image but what made Herbert think of seasoned timber in the first place, and what effect this note, sounded at this point in the poem, has on the poem as a whole."

The limitation of the verbal glosses on the fourth stanza of "Vertue" is that, although they recognize some of the meanings of coal, they do not recognize that coal may also include "charcoal," and that coal thus contains the contrast between that which fire destroys and that which fire purifies or creates. For the most part Herbert's "coal" is black carbon fuel, the non-renewable resource deposited in earth strata. Such *OED* meanings of "coal" as "a piece of carbon glowing without flame" and "a piece of burnt wood, etc., that still retains sufficient carbon to be capable of further combustion without flame; a charred remnant" are not wrong; they are merely not sufficient for Herbert's range of meaning. His larger climax requires a contrast with "season'd timber."

"Charcoal" captures that greater range. Charcoal too is a carbon residue resulting from the imperfect combustion of animal or vegetable matter. It is, in the *OED*'s fourth meaning of "coal," "Fuel prepared from wood by a process of smothered combustion or 'dry distillation,' whereby the volatile constituents are driven off, and the substance reduced to a more or less pure carbon." The chief difference between "cinder" and "charcoal" is in use or intention. A cinder or ember is an accidental residue of a completed or nearly completed process, still retaining some of the heat of its combustion, but waning toward cold ashes. Charcoal, on the other hand, has been deliberately prepared through the manufacture of its imperfect combustion in order that its impurities may be removed and it may be ready to fulfill its larger destiny, of burning with not waning but enhanced intensity. Some etymologies of "charcoal" emphasize the work invested in its preparation, noting that its first syllable echoes "chore" or "char" (as in "charwoman"). Even when we turn to a strictly technical account of charcoal the details suggest meanings we may employ to explicate the spiritual thrust of Herbert's lyric. Thus before modern technology, charcoal was normally manufactured in kilns or by placing a quantity of wood upright with bottom air vents and a central air shaft, then covering the whole with moistened earth, and igniting it at the bottom. Depending upon the rate of combustion, the process reduces the wood in the ratio of two to one or even four to one, and the product itself burns at between 300 and 700 degrees, thus generating very high heats for use in metallurgy.

The vocabularies of economics, chemistry, and physics all illuminate the rightness and richness of Herbert's chosen image of "season'd timber," and the fusion of multiple layers of meaning generates and reinforces the powerfully felt climax of "Vertue." Along with distinctions of combustion, the melting away of the elements with fervent heat from II Peter 3:10 and the burning up there of the earth and human works certainly contribute to the meaning of Herbert's stanza. In the final total conflagration, only the properly prepared soul shall survive. Purified by fire, the soul's sweetness and virtue not merely survive the destruction of earthly matter, but are intensified to the point of transcendence. Then, though the whole world turn to "coal" in the sense of cinders, the soul will turn to "coal" in the sense of charcoal—then chiefly living.

Source: Kathleen M. Swaim, "The 'Season'd Timber' of Herbert's 'Vertue,'" in *George Herbert Journal*, Vol. 6, No. 1, Fall 1982, pp. 21–25.

Helen Vendler

In the following essay, Vendler compares "Virtue" with other poets' rewrites of Herbert's original and analyzes the original in an effort to understand the pattern of Herbert's thought in writing it.

Vertue

Sweet day, so cool, so calm, so bright,
The bridall of the earth and skie:
The dew shall weep thy fall tonight,
For thou must die.

Sweet rose, whose hue, angrie and brave,
Bids the rash gazer wipe his eye:
Thy root is ever in its grave,
And thou must die.

Sweet spring, full of sweet dayes and roses,
A box where sweets compacted lie;
My musick shows ye have your closes,
And all must die.

Onely a sweet and vertuous soul,
Like season'd timber, never gives;
But though the whole world turn to coal,
Then chiefly lives.

For at least one of Herbert's critics, the poem 'Vertue' is the touchstone by which one enters into Herbert's feelings and truly senses his poetry; anthologists (following Coleridge's taste) have felt the poem to be peculiarly expressive of Herbert's spirit; John Wesley adapted it for the common Christian worshipper to sing at services. Though it seems an 'easy' poem, I do not find it easy to reconstruct Herbert's process of thought in writing it. Almost every line in it surprises expectation, though few poems in English seem to unfold themselves with more impersonality, simplicity, and plainness.

When a reader attempts to imagine himself composing the poem, suddenly he finds his confidence in its simplicity quite gone. What, he wonders, led the poet to see the day as a bridal, and call the rose's hue an angry one; why did the poet gratuitously introduce a rash gazer; why should the music of the poet himself (since he has so far maintained his anonymity) provide the conclusive proof of the necessary ending of spring; and finally (a problem which has been reluctantly taken on by every critic of the poem) how did the seasoned timber make its appearance? There are other difficulties, but these perhaps first strike a reader trying to reconstruct the creation of the poem.

Critics have reached two extremes in accounting for the surprising elements in conceits. One is expressed by Dr Johnson in his suspicion that metaphysical poets were simply striving for effect, while the sympathetic extreme, in Rosemond Tuve for instance, finds conceits often appropriate granted certain special canons of decorum (the grotesque, for example, can be in certain contexts 'decorous'). But both of these solutions seem inapplicable here. The poem is really anything but flashy, so little do its rather startling conceits disturb its harmonies of tone; and since the decorum ought to be one of praise (of the limited sweetness of nature and the unlimited sweetness and virtue of the soul), that decorum supports with difficulty either the angry hue of the rose or timber-like qualities of the soul, the latter seeming so awkward in its modification of something 'sweet' as well as virtuous.

There have been some *post-hoc* attempts to get round the seasoned timber: Arnold Stein has insisted on the formal nature of the simile, '*like* season'd timber', by which, he argues, the quality compared in soul and wood is strictly limited to a fugitive resemblance, and Joseph Summers makes somewhat the same point in speaking of the 'limitation' of conceits: "'Season'd timber" is limited to its one point of resemblance of the "vertuous soul" that it "never gives".' This seems a weak acquiescence to the famous stanza. The real question is not what accommodations we can make *post-hoc* to the image but what made Herbert think of seasoned timber in the first place, and what effect this note, sounded at this point in the poem, has on the poem as a whole. I believe that Herbert is not arbitrary or wilful in his comparisons, that they rather tend to arise from a motive appearing perhaps *sotto-voce* in the development of the poem, but which helps to guide the poem from the beginning.

Mary Ellen Rickey has remarked that 'Vertue' is a *carpe diem* poem in reverse, quoting the precedent that A. Davenport has shown in Ovid for a conclusion in praise of virtue rather than in praise of seizing the day. However, the difference in tone between this poem and its erotic predecessors (a difference occurring not only at the end, as we shall see) seems to remove the poem almost entirely from its parent genre. That is, we would, if we were sufficiently responsive, sense from the beginning that this poem could not possibly end with a call to gather the roses of today, any more than it could end, as the passage in the *Ars Amatoria* does, with a total rejection of all natural solace.

The high resignation of the first stanza of 'Vertue' sets the initial theme, which, though it is ostensibly the death of a day, seems rather, metaphorically speaking, to be the immortal theme of the death of a maiden, etherealized into a virginal day. Herbert is struck, not by the sunny, earthly beauty, of the day, but by its remoteness, its spiritual stillness; it is so cool, so calm, that it seems more heavenly than earthly, an appearance which engenders Herbert's metaphor making the day a bridge to the skies; it is, in short, the most innocent and celestial of earthly beauties. We can scarcely doubt that 'bright' suggested 'bride': the Spenserian adjectives—'so cool, so calm, so bright'—could only suggest a bride, but the suggestion is abstracted into a bridal, presumably to avoid confusion of the fall of night with the marriage-bed. But the weeping dew (it is of course the falling dew, or the night-fall, which led to Herbert's invention of day-fall) reminds us of what is usually meant by the 'fall' of something innocent to which we respond by weeping—a fall into corruption, which is a premonition of the fall to death. A stanza, then, which is apparently about Time's destruction of a day is, by virtue of its metaphors, a stanza about the fall of bridal innocence. This fall has not very much to do with Time, but everything to do with intrinsic corruptibility or, to use theological terms, with sin. Herbert has seen this day-fall before, and so his verb is prophetic, not factual (a tone later imitated by Hopkins in 'Spring and Fall', with a sister-recognition of the intrinsic (and not caused by time) nature of the 'fall' we weep for). The dew is the elegist of the day, the witness and mourner of its fall in an unmixed sympathy, and therefore stands as Herbert's representative in the stanza, a helpless and grieving spectator, dwelling 'a weeping Hermit, there'. The emotions here are very pure and unalloyed, since the apparently 'natural' character of the day-fall clears the day of any logical 'guilt' in its descent into night.

If Herbert's representative in the first stanza feels only grief at vanished innocence, his representative in the second stanza is suffering from the smart of the sensual world. The hue of the rose, on which he has so rashly gazed (not glanced), irritates his tender senses and brings involuntary tears to his eye. The beauty of the rose (as Herbert will say explicitly in his poem of that name) is accompanied by qualities that make the flower physically harmful and therefore, in the emblematic universe of this poem, morally inimical to man. The weeping dew is rather a female figure, appropriate attendant to the bridal day, but the rash gazer is clearly masculine, and so is the rose, angry in hue. It is a small duel they engage in, in which the rose pricks the eye of the one

> "*In 'Vertue' the sweetness of the soul is not immediate or felt, but only remembered or inferred, and this memory or inference creates the pathos of the poem. It is a poem of faith, not of love.*"

so rash as to approach him. The mutually symmetrical relations between nature and the spectator in the first stanza (the falling day, the falling dew, the clear day, the clear dew) become, then, mutually antagonistic ones after a seductive beginning in the gazer's rash love; and though on the surface the hostility is quickly passed by, it is nevertheless present in the little drama of the flaunting rose, the gazer's love, and the rose's retort. Herbert immediately takes revenge on the rose in a chilling statement, not of prophecy as with the day, but of fact, in which he insists, in an image which has nothing temporal about it at all, on the simultaneous death-in-life of the rose, which is, in a sense, as much dead as alive, since its root is *ever* in its grave.

The Book of Thel and 'The Sick Rose' are the Blakean parallels to the first and second stanzas of 'Vertue', and we may say that Herbert's feelings are considerably more mixed in respect to aggressive passion than in respect to necessarily-vanished innocence. Or we may say that he prefers the more feminine manifestations of nature (including his own nature) to the more thorny masculine ones. There was no need to make the rose masculine (its Romance predecessors having been by gender feminine) except to insist on the principle of aggression and unexpected harm in the encounter with passion. In fact, the real question raised by the second stanza is why the rose is called 'sweet' at all. If a reader, unacquainted with the poem, were to be shown the stanza, with the first word missing ('———rose, whose hue, angry and brave', etc.) and asked to supply a plausible first word, the last adjective to come to mind, I presume, would be 'sweet'. Nothing else in the stanza supports the initial epithet, a fact especially striking because the sweetness of the 'sweet day' is so wholly borne out by the succeeding adjectives. Is, in fact, Herbert's rose sweet at all? Not, certainly by its angry hue, which is only a superior (because mobile) sort of thorn; not, certainly, by its entombed root; by its bravery, perhaps? But 'sweetness', in the conventional sense established by earlier poems on the sweet rose, and by the 'sweet' day and the 'sweet' spring here in the poem, is almost antithetical to 'bravery' in Herbert's sense. We are left with the notoriously unmentioned sweetness of the rose's perfume or nectar, what Herbert calls in another poem 'hony of roses'. No doubt this aspect of the rose is what Herbert includes in the next stanza with its 'chest of sweets', but all mention of perfume, the only thing that could make the epithet 'sweet' seem plausible, is suppressed in this second stanza. The rose, in short, is not praised as the day was.

Let us, in an apologetic experiment, rewrite the second stanza so that it becomes a 'praise' like the first, expanding its first epithet logically:

Sweet rose, whose hue, so gently brave,
Delights the gazer's tender eye,
Thy root, alas, is in the grave,
And thou must die.

The first thing necessary, in such a rewriting, is to change Herbert's bold rhythm (so noticeable after the placid sweetness in the rhythmic conduct of the first stanza, with its perfect and famous partition of stress among all the words of its first line, and its subsequent iambic regularity). The markedly irregular rhythm of Herbert's first two lines about the rose mimics the encounter of rose and rash gazer, with two head-on shocks 'hue: angry' and 'brave: bids') and one slighter one ('rash: gazer'): the subsidence of this stanza into iambic rhythm can occur only after the duel of hue and eye has ceased.

The third stanza, with its feminine rhymes, is always breaking into a dance meter, and here there is no difficulty at all about the initial epithet. Spring is indeed not only sweet but the quintessence of sweetness, at once its expansion and contraction, and Herbert's rush of responsive feeling betrays the passion underlying the poem, hitherto kept at an impersonal distance. For the first time Herbert himself enters the poem, and again he denies, as he had in the stanza on the rose, that dissolution is basically a temporal event. With the rose, death was co-temporal with life; with the spring, we discover that ending is, on this earth, of one essence with existing. It is not because music exists in time that it 'has its closes'; it is rather because the beginning seeks the end, and makes no sense without it. All unities are also separations from other things, and therefore all earthly essences, whether in life or in art, have limits.

Because 'Vertue' has been seen so often as a poem contrasting the corruptibility of the natural order with the incorruptibility of the soul, and, consequently, as a poem about nature's subjection to Time, it is worth remarking on the fate attending each of Herbert's instances. The lovely day will 'fall'—almost a gravitational matter coinciding with the setting of the sun, and implying no real change occurring in the essence of the day itself; the passionate rose lives in its own grave, and comes closest, but certainly not by a Time-process, to 'death' in our usual sense; the spring, like music, comes to a close in a 'horizontal' ending that implies neither a burial nor a fall from a height. In fact, 'death' is thrice defined in the poem, and the only grisly death (like the only equivocal 'sweetness') belongs to the rose. The day dies intact, as effortlessly as it has lived; spring, like music, has a dying fall; but these declensions are sweet ones. The poem is not occupied chiefly with the *corruption* of nature by Time, only with the eventual (and philosophically necessary) *cessation* of nature.

Similarly, though the temporal question can hardly be excluded from the poem (given the presence of some temporal words like 'tonight' or 'spring'—I except the words 'ever' and 'never' as being eternal rather than temporal), the subject of each stanza, as it appears in the two initial lines, is conceived of not temporally, but solely in spatial or visual terms. The day is a span between earth and sky; the rose sends forth its pricking hue to the gazer through the ether; the spring is a box full of days and roses. The word 'day', itself, normally a temporal one, is transformed into a spatial unit by its alliance with the word 'roses' in the phrase, 'Spring, full of . . . days and roses'; the oddity of the link is not seen until we create a similar pair, say, 'full of weeks and oranges', or something similar. An addition of dissimilar things tends to assimilate one of the pair to the other, and here 'day' is clearly assimilated to 'rose', since both are, in the poem, things that can be put into a box of compacted sweets. We might say, given the visual stress, that these are objects which vanish rather than events which end; the poem, once again, is concerned not with time but with cessation.

When we reach the famous final stanza, we realize that there has been an abrupt break in format. The principle of inertial movement, transferred to poetry, suggests that Herbert might have continued the poem in the strict framework of its repeated construction: 'Sweet——, thou must (or shall——'. The frame is one of direct address, coupled with prophetic statement about the future destiny of the thing addressed. If I may be forgiven another rewriting, a fourth stanza resembling the first three in syntactic form would give us something like:

> Sweet soul, thy vertue cannot rust,
> Like timber aged thou dost not give,
> And when the world will turn to dust,
> Thou'lt chiefly live.

The question I want to raise by this affront to the poem is not one of worth, but one of procedure. Why did Herbert depart from his 'Sweet X' format and his direct address? and why did he not put the future of the soul in the future tense? But I defer answers here in order to put another question.

If Herbert wanted to say that the soul was better than natural things, why did he not say that though natural things were sweet the soul was still sweeter? I again rewrite the final stanza:

> Only the sweet and vertuous soul,
> A honey'd spring perpetual gives,
> And when the whole world turns to coal,
> Then chiefly lives.

It is of course clear at once that the rewritten 'sweet' last stanza like the rewritten 'sweet' stanza on the rose earlier, is insipid in conception, and we must conclude that the smarting gazer, the angry-hued rose, and the seasoned timber have some common stiffening function in the poem. That stiffening function lies behind the pun present in the title of the poem: the rose has 'vertue' in the sense of power, and the soul must be given at least as much resistance as the world has power. The poem, then, centres on both power and sweetness.

The customary Christian view is that to the seducing sweetness of the world must be opposed a stern and resistant power of the soul. Herbert is not unwilling to see the truth of this view, but he does not wish to adopt it at the cost of placing the order of nature and the order of spirit in radical opposition to each other. He wants to attribute to the soul a sweetness too. But as we might have asked what justification there was for the epithet 'sweet' applied to the armed rose, so we may well ask what justification is offered us for calling the soul sweet. The only things we are told about it are that it 'never gives' and that it lives now but 'chiefly lives' after the Last Day. There are rather colourless phrases. Are we to conclude that Herbert is illegitimately counting on our extra-poetic assent to the soul's sweetness because we are good Anglicans? The sweetness of the rose, after all, is at least justified later in the poem by its implicit inclusion in the 'chest of sweets' of the elegiac third stanza, a ceremonial farewell to beauty paralleling the lines in 'The Forerunners':

> Lovely enchanting language, sugar cane,
> Hony of roses, whither wilt thou fly?

The soul, we think, needs its sweetness defined even more desperately, because it seems in so many ways opposed to the previous sweetness, of day, rose, and spring, found in the poem.

The soul, linked by the epithet which it shares with the other self-evidently sweet things, seems to be included as one member of the class of 'sweets'. However, it would be fatal to describe it, as I have done in rewriting the stanza, in terms of the sweetness of nectar, light, or perfume: it would then be in a natural subclass along with the day, the rose, and the spring. George Herbert Palmer, in his beautiful but sometimes misleading edition of Herbert, represents the subject of 'Vertue' as 'the perpetuity of goodness', and he adds that goodness is 'bright as the day, sweet as the rose, lovely as the spring, but excels them all in never fading'. Surely the emphasis of this paraphrase is mistaken: Herbert's poem is not one which says, 'O Vertue, thou art beautiful as the day' in the first stanza, and 'O Vertue, thou art lovely as the rose' in the second stanza, and then 'O Vertue, thou art sweet as the spring' in the third stanza. If the poem had done this, we should have no trouble in believing in the sweetness of the soul; it would have been demonstrated for us thrice over. Herbert, on the contrary, establishes first the absolute priority (in the development of the poem) of the sweetness of nature, allowing for the bitter-sweetness of the rose, and only then begins to talk of the soul. We cannot presume, as Palmer seems to do, a knowledge of the end of the poem in reading the first stanza.

The sweetness of the soul, then, is not precisely the sweetness of air, of perfume, or of nectar. What, then, is it? It is not the experienced sweetness of the felt ecstasy of the soul. That, for Herbert, is represented in 'The Banquet', where indeed the soul, to express its ecstasy, resorts to metaphors of melted sugar, sweetened wine, and the fragrance of 'flowers, and gummes, and powders', but with the qualification:

> Doubtless, neither starre nor flower
> Hath the power
> Such a sweetness to impart;
> Only God, who gives perfumes,
> Flesh assumes,
> And with it perfumes my heart.

In 'Vertue' the sweetness of the soul is not immediate or felt, but only remembered or inferred, and this memory or inference creates the pathos of the poem. It is a poem of faith, not of love. Therefore Herbert cannot *say* anything sweet *about* the soul (as Palmer implies he does): he can only say that it *is* sweet, and trust us to believe that he knows whereof he speaks, having so elaborately assumed his credentials as a connoisseur of sweetness by the first three stanzas. He then, without any elaboration of the adjective 'sweet', immediately begins to illustrate the virtue of the soul—the Holdfast, the staunchness, the unyieldingness of it. The anchor and the optick of 'Hope' are the emblems of this poem too, and having said so much, we are tempted once again to think that while the poem succeeds very well in realizing the beauties of spring, it succeeds less well in realizing their brother-and-antithesis, the staunch soul.

The answer to this problem lies partially in the second stanza, where a type of sweetness is shown to give a sudden smart in the 'tasting' (a meditation continued, as stated above, in 'The Rose'). Our relishing of the day and the spring is impeded only philosophically, by reflection on their brevity, but the relish of the rose is physically impeded by the after-smart—it 'biteth in the close', either visually or physiologically. If things which seem sweet are not, then things which seem not may be. If the soul is sweet, it is with a hidden sweetness rather resembling the hidden smart in the rose, an 'aftertaste' in the soul which comes on the Last Day.

In most *carpe diem* poems, the direct address is made by the lover to his mistress (or he may address himself and her together, as in 'To His Coy Mistress' and 'Corinna's Going A-Maying'). If instances of natural brevity are given as proof of mortality, they are given in the third person. This convention is so strong, that the *thing addressed* (in a poem reminding us, as 'Vertue' does, of the *carpe diem* genre) unconsciously becomes, whatever its logical function, the poet's 'mistress' and by extension himself, since *carpe diem* poems addressed to a mistress are likewise, as Marvell and Herrick saw, equally *carpe diem* poems addressed to oneself; the poet wants his mistress to seize the day because without her compliance he cannot seize it himself. (In the special case of the elder poet counselling the younger, the elder is regretting his own lost opportunities and therefore symbolically and *a posteriori* addressing himself.) In a *carpe diem* poem, in short, the poet might say, 'O Rose, thou shalt die', but he would be including himself or his mistress (his other self) implicitly in the statement: 'Since *we* are but decaying,' says Herrick. The profound object of commiseration is always really the poet himself.

The day, the rose, and the spring, then, are all figures which, to the extent to which he uses the tradition of direct address, Herbert means to represent himself: this seemingly so impersonal poem is in fact a miniature autobiography, which witnesses to the necessary cessation, in the order of Nature, of Herbert's original innocence, 'brave' passion, and rapturous youth. However, from the very beginning of the poem, the poet is also implicitly set against nature, not identifying himself *in toto* with it, though he certainly identifies elements of himself—his youth, his aggression, his passion—with it. The pathos of the poem comes as a result of this partial identification of himself with nature, but the strength of the poem comes from the means by which Herbert distinguishes other elements of himself from mortal nature. The day dies—but the dew of tears remains behind (with Herbert) to mourn its fall; the rose's root is in the grave even while it sends forth its angry dart—but the rash gazer, wiping his eye, remains behind (with Herbert) the wiser perhaps for his experience, to moralize on the eventual powerlessness of the rose's power; the spring dies—but Herbert's music remains behind (with Herbert) to exemplify the years that bring the philosophic mind. In each stanza, then, someone or something—the weeping dew, the rash gazer wiping his eye, a strain of music—stands outside the pictured death of nature, just as Herbert's voice, tender but stern in its prophecies, stands outside the events it foretells. This is a voice which 'never gives'. Though it yields to its own passion of regret in the rush of sensibility betrayed in 'Sweet spring, full of sweet dayes and roses, / A box where sweets compacted lie', it checks itself, recovers its equilibrium, and reverts, with the gravity of the seasoned soul, to the undeniable necessity for musical closes.

It is truly the voice of the sweet and virtuous soul which has been speaking to us all through the poem—sweet in its instant emotion of kinship towards all other sweet things (even to the point of being hurt by its own precipitancy) and virtuous in its response to the encounters with sweetness. It loves other beings of innocent sweetness and weeps their disappearance; it chastises itself for rashness after an encounter with the bitter sweetness of passion; and it acknowledges the philosophical necessity for all sweetness' coming to an end. The sweetness of the soul, however, is rather baffled by the end of the poem. It has watched the day die, the rose wound, and the spring disappear, and has reacted virtuously; but what to do with its sweetness when the whole world turns to coal? There is nothing left for the natural sweetness of the soul to turn congenially to; springs, days, and roses are gone; it is time for it to call on its other qualities, and to be staunch, to be stoic, to be seasoned timber. No image of sweetness would do in this all-consuming end. There can be no natural appeal to sweetness in the fire which 'solvet saeclum in favilla'.

Why this energetic holocaust at the end? Herbert is perhaps cavalier, we may think, in his oversevere 'punishment' of the beautiful, in burning up, in his penultimate line, the 'little world' of his poem. It is his day and his rose and his spring which he burns to coal, deliberately. His conflagration raises the very old question of the possibility of 'natural' virtue. Is unreflecting virtue, 'innate' virtue, we might say, virtue at all? As Newman put it later on, what has gentlemanliness, or sweetness, to do with holiness? What is the relation between natural virtue and 'real' virtue? Is it possible to do good without the intention of doing good? (Such is the 'virtue' that goes forth from herbs.) Shakespeare thought a flower could be said to be, in this sense, all unconsciously 'vertuous':

> The summer's flower is to the summer sweet,
> Though to itself it only live and die.

The notorious ambiguity and bitterness that surround this statement in the *Sonnets* betray the difficulties of founding an ethic on beauty or sweetness or 'vertue' of the natural sort.

A possible stiffening, Shakespeare thought, can be added to sweetness by way of truth:

> O how much more doth beauty beauteous seem
> By that sweet ornament which truth doth give!

Herbert hints at the deceptiveness of beauty in the 'untruth' of the rose, with its root hidden in death (though it is uninvaded by Shakespeare's canker or Blake's worm). But it is not deceptiveness in worldly beauty which is Herbert's main difficulty. The day he gives us is pure truth (unlike Shakespeare's 'glorious morning' which turns false under the 'basest cloud'), and Herbert's spring is a quintessence of pure sweetness with no lilies which fester in it. For Herbert, then, beauty does not so much need the complement of truth since it is so often of itself 'true'. It rather needs two other things: strength and usefulness. Beauty, for all Herbert's passionate sensibility, seemed frail to him; its action was no stronger than a flower, a 'momentarie bloom'. It needed some admixture of the masculine. When God first poured out his blessings on man, according to 'The Pulley',' Strength *first* made a way; / *Then* beautie flow'd, then wisdom, honor, pleasure'. Perhaps this list represents Herbert's own scale of worth.

Are we convinced, then, by the end of 'Vertue', of the necessity of adding strength to sweetness, and if so, how? Herbert has regretted, in the poem, the perishing of his innocence and his passion, the passing of his springtime. If the selves of spring—the innocent self, the importunate self, the self full of 'compacted' potential—are gone, who is the Herbert who is left, and does he have any continuity with these vanished selves? The problem is one we generally think of as Wordsworthian, but it is first of all a human problem, and certainly antedated Wordsworth. Is there a natural piety binding together the past and present selves of Herbert?

The word 'sweet', applied to the soul, is the only verbal sign of identity between the later and the earlier selves. That identity is partly submerged by the dominant duties or possibilities of middle age: to be staunch, not to give in, to be useful. In youth one is beautiful, innocent, energetic, ravishing; in middle age one is to be a support, a piece of seasoned timber supporting the fabric of the world, like the just Sundays in Herbert's poem of that name:

> Sundaies the pillars are,
> On which heav'ns palace arched lies;
> The other dayes fill up the spare
> And hollow room with vanities.
> They [i.e. Sundays] are the fruitfull beds and borders
> In Gods rich garden: that is bare
> Which parts their ranks and orders.

Pillars are here identified with the fruit which follows the springtime of blossoms; to be useful or fruitful is the function of the seasoned soul. But as it would be presumptuous to attribute fruit to oneself, Herbert forbears to attribute to himself in 'Vertue' anything but staunchness.

Two things survive Herbert's holocaust of his blossoms and his spring days: the 'vertuous soul', of course, exemplified not only in the last stanza but in the voice which speaks the entire poem and expresses its final attitudes toward day, rose, and spring; but also, the order of music, which Herbert distinctly separates from the perishing order of natural decay. Its logical function is superior to the function of natural order, and its harmony allows it a spirituality near to the soul's own. 'My music'—it is all that the speaker of the poem tells about his present self, that he has music. Each purely natural element in the poem is characterized by one death-like attributed noun: the day by 'thy fall'; the rose by 'thy root . . . in its grave'; the spring by 'your closes'. The poet alone has a 'living' attributed noun: 'my music'. That music is part of the continuity of sweetness, contributing its sweetness to the virtuous soul, linking age and youth, and binding each to each.

If we now return to the earlier question of direct address, we realize that Herbert's delicacy forbids his making a blunt apostrophe to the virtuous soul. 'But thou, O soul'—it would seem his own soul he was invoking, and though he can tell us he has music, he will not tell us that he has a virtuous soul. On the other hand, neither will he use the usual form for abstract philosophical generalization: he will not say 'Onely *the* sweet and vertuous soul . . . never gives.' It seems that the indefinite article in such a case points usually to the speaker's having a particular case potentially in mind: that the indefinite article, in brief, attributes a superior reality-value to the illustration. The reality-value of the soul is also increased by the reiteration of the epithet 'sweet', which links it to those supremely real examples of sweetness we have already been given in the poem, and which compares the soul, under that rubric, with the day, the rose, and the spring. It is true that the poem exists primarily to differentiate the soul from these, that the poem is, as Rosemond Tuve says, a 'definition by differences'—but the soul would not need differentiation unless at first blush it looked to belong to the same order as the day, the rose, and the spring. What do we use differentia for if not to distinguish similar things? For this reason the soul must co-exist with its companions. It may indeed *chiefly* live after the last Day, but it certainly also lives a life of sweetness, like its companions, now. When Wesley rewrote the poem into a hymn, he not only effaced Herbert's metaphor of timber, with its attributions of staunchness and usefulness, but he also virtually effaced the soul from existence in natural life, as Elsie Leach has remarked, quoting Wesley's final stanza:

> Only a sweet and virtuous soul,
> When nature all in ruins lies,
> When earth and heaven a period find,
> Begins a life that never dies.

The firmness of the soul which, though subjected to the hammer-blows of life and death, never gives, is marked by Herbert's strong reversion to trochaic meter in his last stanza. If we cut the feet in iambics, the sense is badly served: 'A sweet / and ver- / tuous soul / like sea- / son'd tim- / ber nev- / er gives.' The more 'natural' way to read these lines is in trochaics, where the words fit easily into the feet: 'Onely a / sweet and / vertuous / soul like / season'd / timber / never / gives.' The repeated strokes and lifts show the firmness of the staunch soul under attack. The tone in Herbert's last stanza, then, is not triumphant as we might have expected, but rather grave and judicious, largely on account of the limiting word 'chiefly'. Wesley's version is a far more triumphant 'religious' paean, and shows us strongly, by its contrast with Herbert, how careful Herbert was to express dogma only in so far as he could make it real in his own feelings and therefore in a poem. The distinction between the hymn writer, versifying doctrine, and the poet, expressing feeling, is nowhere clearer than in Wesley's revisions of Herbert.

'Vertue' does not go on to the time when the intrinsic sweetness of the soul, so followed in life by the natural sweetness which it must see die around it, will find a correspondence in heavenly sweetness. We end in the deprivations of judgement, with the soul sternly more alive, but lonely in its solitary immunity to fire, its strength taking precedence, visibly, over its sweetness. We are accustomed to poems ending in stoicism; we know them well in Wordsworth. What Wordsworth could not write of was the recovered sweetness of the redeemed soul. Herbert could not write of it in this poem, either, but he is the author of the most exquisite poem in English expressing the state in which faith and hope, the necessary virtues of middle and old age, are dissolved, and pure sweetness returns and remains: 'Love bade me enter. . . . So I did sit and eat.' To write of the hoped-for future in the past tense, as Herbert does in 'Love', is only possible to a poet of a changeable temperament, who has already had the experience which he hopes to have again. If Herbert had not known so naturally the sweetness of the day, the rose, and the spring, and the different-but-similar sweetness of his own music and his own soul, he could not have imagined, in 'Love', the sweetness which, after the fire of the Last Day, should incorporate them all in a final banquet.

Source: Helen Vendler, "George Herbert's 'Vertue,'" in *Ariel*, Vol. 1, No. 2, 1970, pp. 54–70.

Sources

Eliot, T. S. "The Metaphysical Poets," in *Seventeenth-Century Prose and Poetry*, 2d ed., edited by Alexander M. Witherspoon and Frank J. Warnke, Harcourt, Brace & World, 1963, p. 1062.

Emerson, Ralph Waldo, "English Literature: Ben Jonson, Herrick, Herbert, Wooton," in *The Early Lectures of Ralph Waldo Emerson: 1833–1836*, Vol. 1, edited by Stephen E. Whicher and Robert E. Spiller, Harvard University Press, 1959, p. 337.

Fraser, Russell, "George Herbert's Poetry," in *Sewanee Review*, Vol. 95, No. 4, Fall 1987, p. 560.

Herbert, George, "The Collar," in *Seventeenth-Century Prose and Poetry*, 2d ed., edited by Alexander M. Witherspoon and Frank J. Warnke, Harcourt, Brace & World, 1963, p. 857.

———, "Virtue," in *Seventeenth-Century Prose and Poetry*, 2d ed., edited by Alexander M. Witherspoon and Frank J. Warnke, Harcourt, Brace & World, 1963, p. 852.

Walton, Izaak, "The Life of Mr. George Herbert," in *Seventeenth-Century Prose and Poetry*, 2d ed., edited by Alexander M. Witherspoon and Frank J. Warnke, Harcourt, Brace & World, 1963, p. 281.

Further Reading

Dreiser, Theodore, *An American Tragedy*, Signet Classic, 2000.
   Dreiser's 1925 novel, which traces the rise and fall of a poor boy striving to attain a position in the upper reaches of society, shows the struggle between the dazzling effects of transitory things upon the character of a young man who has lost a sense of eternally determined virtue.

Kushner, Tony, *Angels in America: A Gay Fantasia on National Themes*, Theatre Communications Group, 1993–1994.
   In his two-part, six-hour-long drama, Kushner shows the effect of AIDS on his characters' sense of the value of the transient world: AIDS makes that world more desirable and natural phenomena all the more ravishing. He also confronts a search for an eternal meaning beyond transitory experience, with insight into the value of life itself.

Ruskin, John, "The White-Thorn Blossom," in *The Genius of John Ruskin*, edited by John D. Rosenberg, Houghton Mifflin, 1963.
   Ruskin's essay, written in 1871, discusses the destruction of England's green world, which he sees as representing the permanence of natural values, by the overwhelming force of the Industrial Revolution.

Tolstoy, Leo, *Anna Karenina*, translated by Joel Carmichael, Bantam Books, 1978.
   Tolstoy's great nineteenth-century Russian novel, which first appeared in its completed form in 1878, counterpoises a consciousness of the world's attractions with a sense of their inadequacy and an intimation of something eternal.

Wilder, Thornton, *Our Town*, in *A Treasury of the Theatre: From Henrik Ibsen to Eugene Ionesco*, 3d college ed., edited by John Gassner, Simon and Schuster, 1960.
   In this play, set in a small New Hampshire town in the early twentieth century, Wilder focuses on the value of transient experiences, the futility of trying to hold on to these experiences, and the importance of living life to the fullest.

Whoso List to Hunt

Thomas Wyatt

1557

"Whoso List to Hunt" is one of thirty sonnets written by Sir Thomas Wyatt. Although Wyatt never published his poems, several, including "Whoso List to Hunt," appeared in the 1557 edition of the printer Richard Tottel's *Songs and Sonnets written by the Right Honorable Lord Henry Howard late Earl of Surrey and other*, more briefly referred to as *Tottel's Miscellany*.

"Whoso List to Hunt" is held to be Wyatt's imitation of "Rime 190," written by Petrarch, a fourteenth-century Italian poet and scholar. In "Whoso List to Hunt," Wyatt describes a hunt wherein a deer is pursued and ultimately owned by the royal who owns the land. Scholars generally believe that the poem is an allegory referring to Anne Boleyn's courtship by King Henry VIII, such that when Wyatt speaks of the deer as royal property not to be hunted by others, he is acknowledging that Anne has become the property of the King alone. Wyatt was said to have been interested in Anne—and may have been her lover—but would have withdrawn as a suitor after the King made clear his wish to claim her.

Wyatt introduced the sonnet, a fourteen-line poem with a fixed format and rhyme scheme, to England. Despite not publishing his poetry, Wyatt would have made his poems readily available to others. During the Elizabethan period, poets passed their work around in aristocratic circles, in what has been described as a sort of game of one-upmanship: each poet's work inspired his readers to create something comparable or better. Wyatt

chose the Petrarchan sonnet as his inspiration. The Petrarchan sonnet is a fourteen-line poem in which the first eight lines, the octave, present a problem, which is resolved by the final six lines, the sestet. Wyatt altered the Petrarchan formula, ending the sestet with two lines, a couplet, that rhyme. As such, he set a precedent for later poets, many of whom further altered the sonnet formula. Also, in focusing on a hunting allegory in "Whoso List to Hunt," Wyatt demonstrated that sonnets could explore more than unrequited love, on which Petrarch had focused. Wyatt's poem is frequently found in literature anthologies, as well as in several editions of his own poetry, including *Sir Thomas Wyatt: Collected Poems* (1975), edited by Joost Daalder.

Author Biography

Sir Thomas Wyatt is thought to have been born in about 1503 at Allington Castle, in Kent, England. Wyatt's father, Henry Wyatt, was a powerful and wealthy member of the Privy Council under two kings, Henry VII and Henry VIII. Henry Wyatt's influence was such that his young son Thomas was allowed to be an honorary attendant at the christening of Princess Mary in 1516. Some scholars assume that Thomas Wyatt was educated at Cambridge, since young men of his rank commonly attended that institution. In 1520, Wyatt married Elizabeth Brooke; their son, also named Thomas, who would later be known as Sir Thomas Wyatt the Younger, was born in 1521. The elder Wyatt's marriage had apparently ended by 1525, when he charged his wife with adultery and ceased to live with her.

Wyatt's political career advanced quickly. Initially, he served in minor clerical roles in the royal court, such as clerk of the king's jewels. In 1525, Wyatt was part of an official delegation to the French court, and the following year he accompanied a legation to the papal court in Rome, where he apparently became acquainted with the poetry of Petrarch, a fourteenth-century Italian. After his return to England, Wyatt began translating Petrarch's poems, becoming the first Englishman to compose a sonnet, a fourteen-line poem with a specific format. Wyatt's primary focus, however, was his life as a courtly gentleman. By 1532, he had found a political patron, Thomas Cromwell, who was secretary and adviser on religious matters for Henry VIII. By 1535, Wyatt had been knighted and awarded considerable property and men to command in Kent. The following year, Elizabeth Darrell became Wyatt's mistress, which she would remain until his death.

Thomas Wyatt Drawing by J.Thurston, engraving by W. H. Worthington. The Library of Congress

Wyatt was imprisoned several times, once after being accused of being one of the lovers of Anne Boleyn, who became the second wife of Henry VIII; Wyatt was able to watch Boleyn's execution in 1536 from his prison cell in the Tower of London. Within months, he had been cleared of charges and was freed. In 1540, Wyatt's patron, Cromwell, was executed, and the following year Wyatt was arrested yet again. Nevertheless, he once again found favor in the court. Although Wyatt was a knight with considerable courtly importance, he is best known as a poet. He made translations of Petrarch popular in England and also created his own sonnets. No precise date has been attributed to his poem "Whoso List to Hunt," but scholars generally assume that it was written sometime in the late 1520s or early 1530s, as the subject of the poem is thought to be Anne Boleyn, who was then being courted by Henry VIII. As was common during this period, Wyatt never published his works; indeed, he had no financial incentive to do so. Poetry was a diversion, not a vocation. Sir Thomas Wyatt died in Sherborne, England, in the fall of 1542.

Poem Text

Whoso list to hunt: I know where is an hind.
But as for me, alas I may no more:
The vain travail hath weariest me so sore,
I am of them that farthest cometh behind.
Yet may I by no means my wearied mind   5
Draw from the deer, but as she fleeth afore
Fainting I follow. I leave off therefore,
Sithens in a net I seek to hold the wind.
Who list her hunt, I put him out of doubt,
As well as I may spend his time in vain,   10
And graven with diamonds in letters plain
There is written her fair neck round about:
'*Noli me tangere*, for Caesar's I am,
And wild for to hold, though I seem tame.'

Media Adaptations

- Four of Wyatt's poems were adapted by Thea Musgrave and recorded in 1953 as *Four Madrigals*, published by Chester Music. The songs are eight minutes in length and are sung by an unaccompanied chorus.

Poem Summary

Lines 1–4

In line 1 of "Whoso List to Hunt," the narrator states that for those who wish to hunt, he knows of a particular hind, a female deer. The narrator himself is trying to abandon the hunt, acknowledging in line 2 that this hind is beyond his reach. Indeed, he is "wearied" from the "vain travail," the useless work, of the hunt; he has begun to recognize the futility of the pursuit. He laments in the fourth line that he is the last of the pursuers, the one "that farthest cometh behind."

Lines 5–8

In the second stanza, the narrator states that he cannot take his "wearied mind . . . from the deer." When she flees, he proclaims, "Fainting I follow." Nevertheless, he is ultimately forced to indeed abandon the chase, as she is too fast and all that he can catch is the wind that rises after she passes. In sum, the first eight lines, the octave, state the problem of the writer's wasted hunt.

Lines 9–14

In the closing sestet, the invitation initially offered by the narrator to whoever wishes to hunt this particular hind is partly rescinded; in line 9, the narrator states that he will remove any doubt about the wisdom of doing so. Just as his hunt was in vain, so would be those of other hunters, as the hind wears a diamond collar around her neck proclaiming her ownership by another. The concluding couplet notes that the collar reads "*Noli me tangere*," or "Touch me not" in Latin. Thus, the first part of the warning is "Touch me not, for Caesar's I am." According to legend, long after the ancient Roman emperor Caesar's death, white stags were found wearing collars on which were inscribed the words "*Noli me tangere; Caesaris sum*," or "Touch me not; I am Caesar's." The first part of that phrase, "*Noli me tangere*," is also a quotation from the Vulgate Bible, from John 20:17, when Christ tells Mary Magdalene, "Do not touch me, for I have not yet ascended to my Father." In the final line, the warning on the collar continues: the deer herself declares that while she appears tame, holding her is dangerous, as she is wild.

Themes

Courtly Love

Traditionally, early English sonnets focused on romantic and idealized love, as did the Petrarchan sonnets that inspired the English to adopt the format. The love sonnet often celebrated the woman's beauty, comparing in great detail the features of her face and body to forms in nature. For example, a poet might compare a woman's cheeks to roses in bloom. In "Whoso List to Hunt," Wyatt deviates from the typical love sonnet and casts the woman as a deer, who is pursued in an evidently ardent fashion. In being not an inanimate object of the suitor's affection but a wild animal in flight, the female has more personality than the typical subject of a courtly love poem. While she does not speak, she holds a sort of dialogue with the narrator through her actions and through the display of her collar. Thus, Wyatt shifts the perspective on courtly love to focus on the ideas of masculine desire and ownership.

Topics For Further Study

- Select at least two additional sonnets by other sixteenth-century poets, such as William Shakespeare or Sir Philip Sidney, to read alongside Wyatt's "Whoso List to Hunt" and the Petrarchan sonnet that inspired Wyatt, "Rime 190." Write an essay in which you compare and contrast the rhyme and meter of these four sonnets as well as the manner in which the English poets use the sonnet to explore different topics of Elizabethan life. Discuss what your findings suggest about the evolution of the sonnet form and about the interests and abilities of each poet.

- The court of King Henry VIII was filled with gaiety and spectacle. Henry was himself well known for his elaborate clothing, and he encouraged his courtiers to dress for "show" as well. Research the garments characteristic of the Tudor court and create a poster presentation of your findings, using illustrations to help explain the nature and purpose of the various articles. Explain what these clothes reveal about the Tudor court and especially about what the people valued.

- Watch one of the film versions of the life of Henry VIII and his six wives and compare the film to what you have discovered through research about the real six wives of Henry VIII. Create an individual "biography" for each wife that will function as a comparative study guide; then, after watching the film, make a poster or graph for each wife's comparison. Discuss the changes that the film's actors and director made to the actual personages and events and why those changes might have been made.

- A feminist study of Wyatt's poem "Whoso List to Hunt" might focus on the objectification of the woman prey, who is hunted as if she were a forest animal. Research the roles of women in sixteenth-century English society, paying particular attention to how women acted as daughters, wives, and mothers. Write a report that examines the following issues: Consider how wealth or poverty affected women's roles. How much control did women have over their bodies and their property? Discuss women's legal rights, if any, and what they might have done if they chose not to marry. Evaluate the lives of these women in relation to the lives of women in modern society. Finally, considering the role that you might have played as either a man or a woman, explain whether or not you would have enjoyed living in this time period.

- Using the fourteen-line format, write your own love sonnet. You might employ one of the customary rhyme schemes of Elizabethan poets, or you can create your own rhyme scheme; regardless, a clear pattern must be present. Your topic can be any kind of love—love for a pet, a parent, a grandparent, a friend, or even an object like a car. Then write a one-page critique of your poem. What do you consider your poem's strengths and weaknesses? Explain why you chose your rhyme scheme and whether adhering to it was difficult or easy. Discuss why you chose your particular topic and how you approached the actual writing of the sonnet.

Divine Right of Kings

The doctrine of the "divine right of kings" held that kings were God's representatives on earth and that all of the king's subjects were, in fact, his property. The final lines of the sonnet, when it is revealed that the hind's collar declares her to be the property of Caesar alone, allude to this doctrine. The royal ruler supposedly had the right to possess this female, regardless of her wishes or the desires of any other suitors. While he courted Anne Boleyn, Henry VIII gave her many gifts, which established that he was serious about her. These gifts also served to warn other suitors that the object of the King's desire was not available to other men. Although Anne Boleyn did not wear a collar inscribed with the King's name, she wore jewels and other gifts that he supplied. As king, Henry VIII would have believed in his divine right to possess his subjects, and he would not have been shy about seizing whomever he desired.

Obsession

In Wyatt's sonnet, the hunter can be said to be obsessed with possessing his prey. He describes himself as "wearied" twice, in lines 3 and 5. In line 7, he refers to himself as "fainting" as he continues to follow the hind, even as she flees him. The pursuit is dangerous, as the deer is labeled as royal property, but the hunter follows anyway. When a desire is so intense that it cannot be ignored, even when danger is present, it might be labeled an obsession; mere reasoning is not enough to rid the obsessed lover of his desire.

Sexism

The object of the hunt in Wyatt's sonnet is a hind, a female deer, which is held to represent the person of Anne Boleyn. The deer is hunted as prey and wears a collar that proclaims her ruler's ownership over her. This portrayal of a woman as a forest animal to be hunted and possessed reflects the low esteem with which women were often viewed in Elizabethan society. In this allegory, courtship and wooing have no role in the relationship between hunter and hunted, and the female cannot escape the fact that she is a royal possession.

Style

Allegory

In literature, an allegory is an extended metaphor in which objects and events hold symbolic meanings outside of the literal meanings made explicit in the narrative. In Wyatt's sonnet, the hunter's pursuit of the hind can be held to represent Wyatt's pursuit of Anne Boleyn, and the hind's being the property of Caesar can represent the "ownership" of Anne Boleyn by King Henry VIII. All of the accompanying descriptions of the hunt and the hunter's emotions, then, can be applied to this actual romantic situation.

Petrarchan Sonnet

The Petrarchan sonnet, also known as the Italian sonnet, consists of two separate sections. The first part is the octave, an eight-line stanza, wherein a problem or issue is put forth. The second part is the sestet, wherein some resolution to the problem is provided. In "Whoso List to Hunt," the octave describes the futile pursuit of the hind, while the sestet explains why the hunter cannot capture his prey: she is the property of her royal master, and to capture her would endanger both the hind and the hunter. More specifically, Wyatt's sestet consists of a quatrain (four lines) and a couplet (two lines), as can be seen in examining the rhyme scheme. Petrarch divided his sonnets into octaves of *abbaabba* and sestets of various rhyme schemes, usually *cdecde* or *cdcdcd*. Wyatt's rhyme scheme is slightly different: *abbaabba, cddc, ee*. Within such structures, certain rhymes may be somewhat irregular, particularly in that certain words may have been pronounced differently in Elizabethan times. In Wyatt's sonnet, *wind*, as in "breeze," with a short *i* sound, is held to rhyme with the long *i* of *hind, behind*, and *mind*. Similarly, in the last couplet, the long *a* of *tame* is held to rhyme with the short *a* of *am*. In reading that couplet aloud, one might distort the sounds of either or both of those words in order to approximate a rhyme. In ending with a couplet, Wyatt puts emphasis on both of the last two lines; in contrast, the Petrarchan form places more emphasis on the last line of the octave and the last line of the sestet.

Pentameter

The most common meter of the Elizabethan period was pentameter, wherein a line of verse contains five measures, or feet. If each foot contains two syllables—such as with an iamb, where the second syllable is stressed—each line will contain a total of ten syllables. The resulting rhythm can heighten the reader's aesthetic appreciation of and emotional response to the poem. The best way to understand iambic pentameter is to read a poem aloud, paying close attention to the sounds of the stressed and unstressed syllables. Wyatt's use of iambic pentameter was irregular; in fact, when some of his poems were included in *Tottel's Miscellany*, the printer revised and smoothed out the meter. In "Whoso List to Hunt," lines 1, 4, 6, and 8 contain eleven syllables, and line 14 contains only nine syllables; the remaining lines all contain the expected ten syllables. With respect to the measures, or feet, line 10, for example, can be read as a sequence of five iambs; in line 5, on the other hand, only the last two feet are true iambs, while the first three are either trochees, with the first of two syllables stressed, or spondees, with the first and second syllables both stressed. Wyatt used meter and measure irregularly to create his own style.

Visual Imagery

Within a poem, the relationships between images can suggest important meanings. Line 3, "The vain travail hath wearied me so sore," calls to mind the image of a hunter weary with a chase; in being aware of the poem's allegory, the reader will associate this image with a suitor who has exhausted himself in trying to court the object of his affection. Throughout the poem, then, images of the active hunt are associated with the romantic situation in question, endowing it with a degree of excitement that might not otherwise be present. Indeed, effective visual imagery allows the reader to experience a poem in a heightened fashion.

Historical Context

The Court of Henry VIII

Wyatt created his sonnets during a period of sweeping artistic and cultural change, in the beginning of an era known as the English Renaissance. The English Renaissance was dominated by literature, whereas much of the continental European Renaissance was dominated by art and architecture. By the latter part of the sixteenth century, English literature was characterized by Christian beliefs; in particular, the conflicts created by the dissolving of the Roman Catholic Church and the establishment of the Anglican Church by Henry VIII received much focus. Wyatt's poetry predates this focus on Christianity, instead showing the influence of the Italian Renaissance and the work of Petrarch.

Wyatt was a courtier and diplomat in the court of Henry VIII, who was immediately popular upon becoming king in 1509. He was tall and handsome, with the stature of an athlete, and the people loved him. As Henry VII was dying, he urged his son to marry Catherine of Aragon, who had been engaged to Henry's older brother, Arthur, before his death. Marrying Catherine would maintain the nation's alliance with Spain, which was politically important to England's security. Indeed, six weeks after his father's death, Henry VIII married Catherine, who became queen.

Early in his reign, the young Henry VIII became a patron of the arts, encouraging music and literature in his court, such that Wyatt would have certainly felt comfortable as both courtier and poet. Henry was intelligent and well educated. He spoke French, Spanish, and Latin, and he composed music and wrote books, in addition to spending much time hunting and playing tennis. His interest in the joust and other acts of knightly pageantry extended to the field of conflict. He enjoyed displays of power, especially his own. He held large banquets, balls, and jousts, including a joust between the kings of England and France. Overall, the court of King Henry VIII was focused on theatrical displays and diplomacy and on seizing the pleasure of the moment.

Religion and Royal Marriage

As a young man and new husband, Henry VIII was very religious. He wrote and published a very popular book, *Defence of the Seven Sacraments*, defending the Roman Catholic Church and attacking Martin Luther. Luther was a German Augustinian monk who in 1517 challenged the excesses and abuses of the Roman Catholic Church by nailing ninety-five theses to the door of the Wittenberg Cathedral. Luther's actions led to the Protestant Reformation. The attack on Luther by Henry VIII was very successful and went through several printings. In response, Pope Leo X rewarded the King with the title "Defender of the Faith" in 1521.

Later, however, Henry VIII would come to regret some of his defense of papal authority when his desire for a son began to outweigh his devotion to the Catholic Church. Although Catherine gave birth to a son in 1511, he did not survive. After a series of miscarriages and stillbirths, Princess Mary was born in 1516. Although the child was healthy, Henry wanted a son, and he soon began to think that he had offended God by marrying his older brother's intended wife. Henry VIII was only the second Tudor king, and he was concerned that not leaving a male heir would put the Tudor dynasty at risk. He became convinced that his marriage to Catherine was unlawful in God's eyes and that he needed to divorce Catherine and find a new queen, who would provide him with a son. Thomas Cardinal Wolsey tried for five years to persuade Pope Clement VII to annul Henry's marriage to Catherine, but he was unsuccessful.

The King's desire to divorce Catherine preceded his love of Anne Boleyn. By 1527, Henry VIII was indeed in love with Anne and wanted to marry her, and as Wyatt's poem attests, Henry's courtship of Anne was no secret. She was beautiful and more flamboyant and glamorous than Catherine, and Henry loved displays of beauty. By January 1533, Anne was pregnant, and she and Henry were secretly married. That year, too, Henry persuaded Thomas Cranmer, the archbishop of Canterbury, to annul his marriage to Catherine. By 1534, a series of parliamentary actions had reduced the pope's authority in England, and the pope responded by excommunicating Henry. The English clergy and members of the court were then forced to choose between Henry and the pope; those who chose the pope were executed, and Henry also dissolved the monasteries and

Compare & Contrast

- **1500s:** Henry VIII receives the title "Defender of the Faith" from Pope Leo X for his opposition to Martin Luther, who is condemned as a heretic and excommunicated. After Luther's death, Pope Paul urges Emperor Charles V of Spain to go to war in Europe in an effort to eliminate Protestantism and reunite the Roman Catholic Church. The Church supplies both money and troops for this war.

    Today: Religion still plays a substantial role in international politics, but conflicts take place more explicitly between governments, rather than between religious denominations. In some cases, however, fundamentalism and religious fanaticism are linked to terrorism, which has led to the deaths of many innocent people around the globe.

- **1500s:** Henry VIII requires all of his noblemen to swear an oath acknowledging that he is the head of the Church of England. Sir Thomas More, Henry's good friend and the lord chancellor, is arrested and later executed when, as a devout Catholic, he refuses to take the oath demanded by Henry VIII.

    Today: The Queen of England, Elizabeth II, remains the titular head of the Church of England, but an oath acknowledging the monarch as head of the church is no longer required. The Catholic traditions for which Sir Thomas More gave his life remain in place.

- **1500s:** During the long reign of Henry VIII, he married six times. He divorced two of his wives and had two others beheaded for adultery. One wife died in childbirth, and the last wife outlived Henry and even remarried after his death. Marriage was complicated for monarchs during this period, since diplomatic treaties played important roles in marriage arrangements.

    Today: The situation surrounding the divorce of England's Prince Charles from Princess Diana illustrates how much royal marriage has changed. While the infidelity of both partners embarrassed the monarchy, Diana was not arrested, tried for treason, or beheaded. What has not changed since the sixteenth century is the public fascination with the marital choices of the royals.

---

seized their land and goods. The romance with Anne Boleyn resulted in the English Protestant Reformation, which, in turn, more than doubled the King's revenues. Indeed, King Henry VIII was supreme in his own country, and he demanded that his subjects support his decisions. Those who did not were arrested, tried for treason, and executed. Wyatt's poem suggests that hunting royal property could be dangerous; he could not have foreseen that such danger could arise not only from the pursuit of the King's "hind" but also from religious and political actions.

Critical Overview

Wyatt is considered the first of the great Elizabethan poets. His experiments with new formats, especially regarding meter and measure, were very influential in inspiring the great English poets who followed later in the sixteenth century, such as Sir Philip Sidney, Edmund Spenser, and, of course, William Shakespeare. Wyatt did not publish his poems, but he did circulate them within the Tudor court, where they were read and enjoyed. As a reflection of Wyatt's importance in the English literary canon, several new editions of his poetry were published in the last thirty years of the twentieth century, offering important insight into his work. Among the best are *Collected Poems of Sir Thomas Wyatt*, edited by Kenneth Muir and Patricia Thomson (1969); *Sir Thomas Wyatt: Collected Poems*, edited by Joost Daalder (1975); and *Sir Thomas Wyatt: The Complete Poems*, edited by Ronald A. Rebholz (1981).

In the introduction to his edition of Wyatt's poems, Joost Daalder observes that "Wyatt's poems now enjoy greater critical esteem than at almost any time since his death." Daalder recognizes that in the past Wyatt was often "severely attacked for his supposed lack of prosodic skill," but that is no longer the case. Indeed, much of that earlier criticism was directed at Wyatt's lack of smoothness in his use of iambic pentameter, but Daalder explains that Wyatt was striving not for smoothness but for originality. Regarding the criticism that Wyatt only imitated other poets, notably Petrarch, or was just a translator of poems into English, Daalder notes that Wyatt was a poet "whose style bears the stamp of his own personality." Even in his translations, Wyatt demonstrates a uniqueness that reflects his experience as a courtier and diplomat. Further, Daalder suggests that "originality is perhaps overvalued in our age"; that is, the translation of any literature into English was much valued in Wyatt's time, and so he did not need to perceive himself as an "original poet" in the same way that modern poets might. Daalder also mentions that some critics fault Wyatt because the actual phrasing in some of his poems lacks originality, but, according to Daalder, "we should not admire something because it is new or old, but because it is intrinsically important and appealing."

In the first chapter of *Imitating the Italians: Wyatt, Spenser, Synge, Pound, Joyce*, Reed Way Dasenbrock refers to Wyatt as the "first great English Petrarchan," conveying how important he was in influencing other poets, especially the greatest poets of the English Renaissance. According to Dasenbrock, Wyatt deserves greater admiration than has been forthcoming from literary scholars; he argues that Wyatt's "translations and imitations of Petrarch created a tradition of (and a form and language for) writing love sonnets in English, which later culminated in the great sonnet sequences of Sidney, Spenser, and Shakespeare." That is, Dasenbrock sees Wyatt's imitations of Petrarch as critical contributions to Elizabethan poetry. Indeed, in the early sixteenth century, poets were expected to imitate the great masters of the past "in accordance with the Italian Renaissance canons of imitation that Petrarch himself established." Dasenbrock perceives that in altering the sonnet format, Wyatt "transforms all of these poems into his own highly personal poems of lament and reproach," and as a result "these poems of Wyatt have great intensity and power." He asserts that Wyatt's "interest in and work with Petrarch's poetry, in short, was one of the seeds of the English Renaissance."

Anne Boleyn Bettmann/Corbis

Criticism

Sheri Metzger Karmiol

Metzger Karmiol has a doctorate in English Renaissance literature and teaches literature and drama at the University of New Mexico. In this essay, she discusses Wyatt's representation of the hind and argues that Wyatt's depiction of a hunted woman as an animal parallels the very real risk that women faced in a society in which they held no power.

In early-sixteenth-century England, women had little identity that was their own to possess. Women were governed by fathers, brothers, and husbands, belonging to these men in a very literal sense, as property. Women were expected to be chaste and to present themselves in a manner that would not elicit gossip or in any way diminish the reputations of their male "owners." Women's lack of power in this society provides an important framework in which to examine Wyatt's sonnet "Whoso List to Hunt." The hind's status in the poem as the property of a royal owner makes her too dangerous for the narrator to hunt, and she is also herself at risk in being the property of a powerful man. The hind's seeming inability to recognize this danger, as a mere animal, adds to the

> "Although women readers should acknowledge Wyatt's trivialization of the feminine, the poem still stands as a historical and cultural representation of the way in which courtship and politics could be intermingled by the poet."

complexity of the narrative, especially when the cultural and historical realities of the Tudor court are considered. Wyatt disguises the real-life female subject of the poem as a hind not because her identity is unimportant but because naming her would have created gossip that would endanger both poet and woman.

Hunting the hind is evidently a familiar activity for the narrator. The sonnet begins with the narrator stating, "I know where is an hind." He does not say that he knows where there *are* hinds; he knows where there *is* a specific hind. Thus, he immediately establishes that he has hunted *her* before, and the choice of animal is not random. The hunter admits that he cannot possess the hind and eventually warns off other hunters. Feminists might argue that Wyatt trivializes women in reducing the female subject to prey being chased through the forest by an eager hunter, but such an assessment limits the poem's possibilities. Within the language of poetry, an author can obfuscate meaning and deny intent by claiming that the reader has misread the text; in his sonnet, Wyatt clouds his meaning through the creation of the hind.

In *Renaissance Self-Fashioning: From More to Shakespeare*, a book that examines the interplay between culture and certain poets' identities, the critic Stephen Greenblatt discusses Wyatt's caution in choosing the right words for his sonnet and the way in which he uses his language to disguise meaning. Greenblatt suggests that a cultural and historical reading of the poem might focus on Wyatt's experience as a diplomat when Henry VIII was negotiating treaties with the French and Spanish. Wyatt was conversant in several languages and certainly understood how the precise meanings of words could be crucial in diplomacy. According to Greenblatt, Wyatt was

> highly conscious of the potential shifts in meaning as words pass from one language to another, and this sensitivity intersects with an acute awareness of the way conventions of courtesy and friendliness may conceal hostility and aggression, on the one hand, or weakness and anxiety, on the other.

As Wyatt's poem makes clear, the hunter recognizes that there is real risk for whoever pursues this hind. In the penultimate line of his sonnet, Wyatt writes, "*Noli me tangere*, for Caesar's I am." The Latin phrase on the collar, "Touch me not," makes clear that she is owned by another man. This is a deliberate divergence from the original Petrarchan sonnet, in which the hind explains that the collar is meant to free her, even from Caesar's ownership. In line 11 of Petrarch's "Rime 190," the collar of the doe explains, "It pleased my Caesar to create me free." Caesar was often identified as a god to Roman citizens, and so this line suggests that a god has set the hind free. In Wyatt's sonnet, the collar signifies not freedom but ownership. The hunt is abandoned not because the hind is meant to be free but because she is the property of a powerful owner. Greenblatt points out that "the collar stops the hunt, transforms the hind from prey to pet or possession," although she does not behave as a possession. Indeed, Greenblatt explains that the collar itself is a "manifest sign of her wildness." Its presence implies that she is otherwise impossible to grasp (note the line "wild for to hold"), just as the narrator states in line 8 that he is essentially seeking to capture the wind. With respect to the poem's allegory, the woman in question is wild in that society cannot tame or control her. This is especially relevant in the patriarchal society of sixteenth-century England, in which women were to be controlled, first by fathers and brothers and later by husbands.

One might easily study this poem and focus on what is missing—a clear feminine identity with which modern readers can identify. According to Marguerite Waller, the poem holds nothing for the female reader. In Waller's essay, "The Empire's New Clothes: Refashioning the Renaissance," she points out that Wyatt's poem is about a man, the hunter. Waller notes that the poem was created for male readers, which is of course historically true, as the predominately English poets of the Renaissance would have passed their poems around only to their male friends. Since women had so little poetic voice

What Do I Read Next?

- To better understand the sonnet tradition, consider *The Penguin Book of the Sonnet: 500 Years of a Classic Tradition in English* (2001), edited by Phillis Levin. This book begins with the sonnets of Petrarch and Chaucer and has representative sonnets from each century since, including a good selection of twentieth-century poets. Five of Wyatt's poems are reprinted in this book, including "Whoso List to Hunt."

- *Sir Philip Sidney: The Major Works* (2002), edited by Katherine Duncan-Jones, provides a selection of texts by one of the sixteenth century's most important poets. His sonnets were influenced by both Petrarch and Wyatt.

- *Edmund Spenser's Poetry: Authoritative Texts, Criticism* (1993) takes a critical look at the work of another poet who was influenced by Wyatt.

- A good source for sixteenth-century love sonnets is *The Sonnets: Poems of Love* (1980), by William Shakespeare.

- To hear William Shakespeare's sonnets read aloud, listen to *Sonnets CD* (1996), narrated by Sir John Gielgud.

- Elizabeth Barrett Browning's *Sonnets from the Portuguese: A Celebration of Love* (1986) presents love sonnets written with a woman's voice.

---

early in the sixteenth century as to be essentially nonexistent, women's lack of real identity as the subjects of men's poems is unsurprising. But this lack of identity limits only the woman reader who chooses to ignore the poem's historical and social context. When Waller asserts that women readers "contemplate an image of their own nonidentity or noncoincidence with themselves when they try to read themselves as readers of this poem," she is trying to amend a cultural injustice that cannot be changed. Waller points out that a feminine presence cannot be found in Wyatt's poem, such that a woman instead "comes face to face with a kind of 'nonbeing' when she tries to read herself in the story of the hunter."

Indeed, "Whoso List to Hunt" is a text in which the reader is meant to identify with the male hunter. However, to argue that there is no feminine identity ignores the implied presence of Anne Boleyn, whose story can be understood as a clear warning of the dangers that result when women are appropriated as property by rich and powerful males. Waller claims that the hunt "casts the poet in the role of aristocratic hunter and the beloved in the role of an animal to be hunted" as well as that the "poet's superior social status and the inferior status of the woman" are not challenged. But again, Waller is discounting historical reality. In sixteenth-century England, women were judged to be inferior—even women such as Anne Boleyn, who perhaps had more notoriety than most. Although women readers should acknowledge Wyatt's trivialization of the feminine, the poem still stands as a historical and cultural representation of the way in which courtship and politics could be intermingled by the poet. Henry's court, of which Wyatt was a member, would not have separated love from politics.

All of the Tudor court—including Wyatt, according to gossip—was obsessed with Anne. In that Anne was later executed for adultery, her story and the importance of an unsullied reputation add another layer of complexity to the sonnet. In *An Ordered Society: Gender and Class in Early Modern England*, Susan Dwyer Amussen proposes that "women's reputations were more easily threatened than were men's." In many cases, vague allegations were enough to prove hazardous to women, and as a possession of the King, Anne would have been especially vulnerable to gossip involving infidelity. In "The Fall of Anne Boleyn," G. W. Bernard assesses the evidence against Anne in an effort to determine whether the charges of infidelity were true or just gossip. Ultimately, Bernard decides that Anne was executed because she really did commit adultery, perhaps in an effort to become pregnant and supply Henry with a male heir or perhaps because Henry was unfaithful and she was jealous.

As Amussen suggests in her discussion of challenges to social order, "The primary challenge to social expectations within marriage arose when women interpreted gender in ways that differed from the prescriptions of social theory." Anne's mistake, then, was in not recognizing that the rules for women were different than those for men. As Bernard observes, her downfall might have been "a defiant resentment of the double standard which allowed that freedom [infidelity] to men but not to women." In evaluating historical documents and what is known about Anne's reputation, Bernard notes that, according to rumors, before Henry was to marry Anne, "he asked Wyatt what he thought of her: Wyatt had told the King not to marry her because she was a bad woman." In response, Henry banished Wyatt from the court for two years as punishment. Later, after Anne was arrested for adultery and just days before she was to be executed, Wyatt was also arrested. Bernard notes that, again according to rumor, Wyatt "wrote to Henry, reminding him of what he had said, and adding that he knew what Anne was like, because she had been willing, many years ago, to kiss him." This is supposition, as no real records prove either why Wyatt was arrested or why he was released, but this possible episode offers one way to evaluate the last line of Wyatt's sonnet.

One might posit that within Wyatt's poem, the hunter is even less powerful than the hind. Although women had no power in this period, neither did men when confronted with the King's desires. Greenblatt suggests that the intensity of the hunter's grief at the loss of the hind means that "neither audience nor poet is permitted to stand at a comfortable distance from the speaker." Greenblatt contends that Wyatt's poem is not merely a monologue; the readers are participants. The hunter longs for the woman, and this passion draws the reader into the poem and forces a response. The fact that the woman is depicted as a wild animal should be irrelevant, as the discerning reader understands that the poem offers layers of complexity and disguise regarding the hunter's unabated desire, which is leashed only because the risk is too great. The lesson for female readers is not that there is no feminine identity; it is that the expression of the feminine entails risk, especially in a society in which women lack power.

Source: Sheri Metzger Karmiol, Critical Essay on "Whoso List to Hunt," in *Poetry for Students*, Thomson Gale, 2007.

Ellen C. Caldwell

In the following essay, Caldwell gives a critical analysis of Thomas Wyatt's life and work.

No poet represents the complexities of the court of Henry VIII better than Sir Thomas Wyatt. Skilled in international diplomacy, imprisoned without charges, at ease jousting in tournaments, and adept at writing courtly poetry, Wyatt was admired and envied by his contemporaries. The distinction between his public and private life was not always clearly marked, for he spent his life at various courts, where he wrote for a predominantly aristocratic audience who shared common interests. Through and in this milieu he created a new English poetics by experimenting with meter and voice and by grafting Continental and classical forms and ideas to English traditions. Wyatt wrote the first English sonnets and true satires, projecting through them the most important political issues of the period: the Protestant Reformation and the centralization of state power under the reigns of the Tudors. For this combination of formalistic innovation and historical reflection, he is today considered the most important poet of the first half of the sixteenth century. Living and writing dangerously in an era of national and international, religious and secular transformations, Wyatt was the Henrician Renaissance man, and his poetry was the soul of his age.

Wyatt's position, attitudes, character, and fortunes were formed at the courts of the first two Tudor monarchs. One of the most important issues in scholarship on Wyatt remains the relationship between his poetry and his life as a Henrician courtier. With its extensive reproduction of primary sources, the best biography of Wyatt is still Kenneth Muir's *Life and Letters of Sir Thomas Wyatt* (1963). All letters and documents are quoted from this edition, while all poetry is cited from *Sir Thomas Wyatt: The Complete Poems* (1978).

Born around 1503 at Allington Castle in Kent, Thomas was the son of Sir Henry Wyatt of Yorkshire and Anne Skinner Wyatt of Surrey. Imprisoned more than once by Richard III, Sir Henry had become under Henry VII a powerful, wealthy privy councillor, and he remained so after Henry VIII's accession. In 1516 his son Thomas served as an honorary attendant at Princess Mary's christening. John Leland writes that Thomas attended Cambridge, and although there is no record to confirm the statement, it seems plausible that he did. It is often assumed that in 1516 he entered Saint John's College, Cambridge, but his name may have been confused with another Wyatt matriculating there. After marriage to Elizabeth Brooke, daughter of Thomas, Lord Cobham, in 1520 and the birth of a son in 1521, Wyatt progressed in his career at court, as esquire of the king's body and clerk of the king's jewels (1524). He probably acquired these posts through a combination of innate abilities and his father's influence. Stephen Miriam Foley suggests in *Sir Thomas Wyatt* (1990) that the positions were more significant than their titles might imply, for they helped to entrench him in the king's household. Members of that household sought power, struggling with the king's councillors to influence the king.

Sometime after the birth of his son, perhaps around 1525, Wyatt seems to have become estranged from his wife; all editors and biographers assume the reason to be her infidelity, for such were the rumors during his life. The *Spanish Calendar*, for instance, gives this detail: "Wyatt had cast [his wife] away on account of adultery." It is certain that in 1526, when Sir Thomas Cheney embarked for the French court on an official delegation, Wyatt accompanied him. There he may have met Clément Marot, whose poetry influenced his own work and whose epigram "Frere Thibault" is copied into the Egerton manuscript of Wyatt's poetry. In 1527 Wyatt asked for and was granted permission to attend Sir John Russell on his legation to Rome. On this journey he became acquainted with Continental political affairs and the methods of persuasive diplomacy, for when Russell was injured, Wyatt accomplished one part of the mission alone. He was briefly imprisoned by Spanish imperial forces, but he and Russell left Rome shortly before it was taken by the emperor's army.

Around 1527 Queen Catherine of Aragon, first wife of Henry VIII, asked Wyatt to translate Petrarch's *De remediis utriusque fortunae*. Wyatt translated in its place a piece he found less tedious, Guillaume Budé's Latin version of Plutarch's *De tranquillitate et securitate animi*. It was soon published by Richard Pynson as *The Quiet of Mind* (1528), and as several scholars have pointed out, the echoes of "quiet mind" in Wyatt's poetry indicate that the piece continued to hold philosophical importance for him. From around 1528 or 1529 to November 1530, Wyatt held the post of high marshal of Calais, and in 1532 he became commissioner of the peace in Essex. From this time forward he was under the patronage of Thomas Cromwell, Henry VIII's secretary and adviser on religious matters, one of the most powerful men in the kingdom.

> *Although it has been widely debated, a poem historically thought to indicate Wyatt's loss of Boleyn to Henry is the sonnet "Whoso list to hunt, I know where is an hind"* (no. 11)."

In 1533 Wyatt served for his father at the coronation of Anne Boleyn. Although in 1534 he was imprisoned in the Fleet for what was recorded as his involvement in a "great affray" in which a sergeant of London was slain, his rapid success as a courtier dates from this period. Also in 1534 he was given "command of all men able for war in the seven hundreds" and in various parishes of the county of Kent, and license "to have twenty men in his livery." He is thought to have been knighted in 1535. Around 1536 Wyatt formed an attachment to Elizabeth Darrell, who became his mistress for life. Some of his poems, such as "A face that should content me wondrous well" and "So feeble is the thread," almost surely allude to this relationship.

The woman with whom Wyatt has been notoriously associated, however, is Anne Boleyn, second queen of Henry VIII. Careful scholars acknowledge that although Wyatt's poetry is suggestive, the hard evidence for his role as Boleyn's lover, or scorned lover, is so bedeviled by legend and rumor as to affect even the most cautious statements. One poem long considered to allude to Boleyn is the riddle "What word is that that changeth not" (no. 54), for its solution (*anna*) is penned above the poem in the Egerton manuscript (though not in Wyatt's or the scribe's hand and, it seems, after the poem was copied there.) The third line of the poem puns on the solution: "It is mine answer" (*mine Anne, sir*). There is nothing, however, to indicate that the poem is about any specific Anne. Although anecdotes have circulated of the rivalry between Wyatt and Henry, it is very difficult and perhaps even impossible to gauge the extent of Wyatt's relationship with Boleyn, especially when Henry decided to divorce Catherine and marry her.

Henry's doing so resulted in the Act of Supremacy (1534), whereby he broke from the hegemony of the pope and the Catholic church and proclaimed himself head of the church in England. This move had severe domestic and international consequences, in which Wyatt was implicated.

Although it has been widely debated, a poem historically thought to indicate Wyatt's loss of Boleyn to Henry is the sonnet "Whoso list to hunt, I know where is an hind" (no. 11). Wyatt altered the original poem, Petrarch's *Rime* 190, "Una candida cerva sopra l'erba," to center on the "chase," a courtly sport that provides an apt metaphor for the pursuit of love and power at Henry's court, as several scholars have acknowledged. In Wyatt's sonnet the speaker advises other suitors that they may pursue the hind/lady as vainly as he has and give her up with as much difficulty. The poem concludes that the chase should be given over, for the motto on the hind's collar suggests that although she has been claimed by someone more powerful than they, she will not be constrained by anyone:

> And graven with diamonds in letters plain
> There is written her fair neck round about:
> *'Noli me tangere* for Caesar's I am,
> And wild for to hold though I seem tame.'

Julius Caesar's deer are reported to have worn this motto on their collars. Wyatt's decision to retain the term *Caesar* from the Italian poem does suggest that the speaker or poet alludes to a royal master with powerful edicts, such as Henry VIII. Although the hind/lady might topically designate any one of several women, it could appropriately refer to Boleyn. To describe a lady of the court as an object of prey, bound by words or laws to a ruler absolute in name if not in reality, is to flatter neither the lady, who is seen to be promiscuous or at least willful, nor "Caesar," who is seen to be unsuccessful in his attempt to "own" her with his inscription. In another sonnet also thought to refer to Boleyn in her role as court star, reformer, and the catalyst behind Henry's divorce, "If waker care, if sudden pale color" (no. 28), the speaker claims he has replaced his former love with another. The poem is found in the Egerton manuscript, where the line "Her that did set our country in a roar," so suggestive of Boleyn, has been revised, in Wyatt's hand, to "Brunet that set my wealth in such a roar."

The execution of Boleyn and her alleged lovers is one of the more sordid episodes of Henry's turbulent reign and has attracted a great deal of prurient interest. The episode does, however, indicate the violence attendant upon the very structure of dynastic succession and illustrates the instability of fortunes in a Renaissance court. Readers should consult the most reliable biographies and remember that theories about Wyatt's attachment to Boleyn involve the consideration not only of his life but also of the very densely recorded lives of Henry VIII and Boleyn. In 1536 Wyatt was arrested a few days after the arrests of Anne and five men alleged to have been her lovers. Most speculations about his relationship with Anne center on his arrest and imprisonment at this time. Muir gives three independent, sixteenth-century accounts, all of uncertain authority, which claim that before Henry married Boleyn, Wyatt told either Henry or his Council that she was not fit to become queen because she had been Wyatt's lover; but Muir adds that these anecdotes could have been devised to explain why Wyatt was not executed with the five men accused of adultery. Whatever the actions of Anne may have been, after she gave birth to Princess Elizabeth and then miscarried a second child, she lost Henry's favor; desperate for a male heir, he had already begun to look for her replacement. Cromwell is said to have instigated a plot to remove her by accusing her of adultery and therefore treason. A court musician, Mark Smeaton, was tortured and produced the names of four other men, some of them Wyatt's friends. Anne's brother, Thomas Boleyn, Viscount Rochford, was charged with incest, and Henry himself claimed that "more than a hundred had to do with her." There were no official charges against Wyatt, who in 1541 declared that his court enemy, Charles Brandon, Duke of Suffolk, was responsible: "My Lord of Suffolk himself can tell that I imputed it to him, and not only at the beginning but even the very night before my apprehension now last." A letter of petition from Wyatt's father to Cromwell does not reveal the nature of the charges beyond "the displeasure that [Wyatt] hath done to god otherwise."

One poem that seems to date from this period of imprisonment (no. 123) is headed *V. Innocentia / Veritas Viat Fides / Circumdederunt me inimici mei*. If one accepts that Viat indicates Wyatt, then the heading reads, "Innocence, Truth, Wyatt, Faith; my enemies have surrounded me." Editors have suggested that innocence, truth, and faith "surround" Wyatt's name in contradistinction to his enemies. The speaker asks that anyone "Who list his wealth and ease retain" should strive to live a private life, for there is danger, or "thunder," around seats of power. The refrain of the poem is *circa Regna tonat*, a phrase from Seneca's *Phaedra*, in which Jupiter "thunders about thrones." The opening line of the third stanza, "These bloody days have broken my heart," may refer to the fall of Anne and her courtiers. Even more powerful is the image Wyatt paints of the speaker in his cell, witnessing through its window grating what may have been Anne's execution:

> The bell tower showed me such sight
> That in my head sticks day and night.
> There did I learn out of a grate,
> For all favor, glory, or might,
> That yet *circa Regna tonat*.

In the last stanza the speaker learns that the wit to plead one's case or one's innocence is not always useful. This poem does not apologize for the speaker's conduct or his situation or the system in which he must live; rather, it vividly demonstrates the well-known fact that proximity to the king could be fatal. An elegy for Anne's putative lovers, "In mourning wise since daily I increase" (no. 197) is also dated to this period. The poem devotes a stanza to each man executed, naming him (Lord Rochford, Sir Henry Norris, Sir Francis Weston, Sir William Brereton, and Smeaton), acknowledging his guilt, yet mourning his death. This poem, which appears in one manuscript only, has not always been attributed to Wyatt.

After the executions of Anne and her alleged lovers, Wyatt was soon restored to favor, made sheriff of Kent, and asked to muster men and to attend on Henry VIII. In November 1536 his father died, and in 1537 he once again undertook a diplomatic mission, this time as ambassador to the court of Emperor Charles V. On his journey Wyatt wrote to his son, advising him to emulate the exemplary life of Sir Henry Wyatt rather than Wyatt's own: "And of myself I may be a near example unto you of my folly and unthriftness that hath as I well deserved brought me into a thousand dangers and hazards, enmities, hatreds, prisonments, despites, and indignations." He further admonished his son to "make God and goodness" his "foundations." An epigram in Wyatt's hand in the Egerton manuscript, "Of Carthage he, that worthy warrior," ends with a reference to Spain: "At Monzòn thus I restless rest in Spain" (no. 46). Henry VIII wished to prevent Charles V from forming what would amount to a Catholic alliance with Francis I and thus to prevent a concerted attack on England. Wyatt returned home in mid 1538; but when Charles and Francis, without Henry, reached a separate accord at Nice, the danger of an attack against England grew more grave. Wyatt's poem in ottava rima, "Tagus, farewell" (no. 60), probably dates from this period. With this poem, as with the letter to his son, scholars have tried to establish Wyatt's character. Despite his sufferings and despite his criticisms of the king and his court, he was a loyal servant to Henry VIII. In the last lines the speaker looks forward to returning to London: "My king, my country, alone for whom I live, / Of mighty love the wings for this me give."

Once more ambassador to the emperor in 1539, Wyatt was to watch his movements through France and to ascertain his intentions regarding England. But by mid 1540, after Henry VIII's marriage to Anne of Cleves threatened to create a Protestant league, and in the event of growing distrust between Charles and Francis, the danger of an attack against England was no longer imminent, so Wyatt returned home. On 28 July his patron, Cromwell, was executed. Historians attribute Cromwell's fall in part to factional resistance to his foreign and religious policies and in part to Henry's severe dislike of Anne of Cleves. He had married her sight unseen and claimed that descriptions of her beauty were untrue (historian John Guy notes that he called her "the Flanders mare"). An account found in the Spanish chronicle claims that at the execution Cromwell asked Wyatt to pray for him but that Wyatt was so overcome by tears he could not speak. It is thought that the sonnet Richard Tottel entitles "The lover laments the death of his love" refers instead to Wyatt's loss of his friend and patron, for it imitates Petrarch's *Rime* 269, *"Rotta è l'alta colonna e 'l verde lauro,"* an elegy on the occasion of his patron's death, as well as the death of Laura. Wyatt's poem (no. 29) begins:

> The pillar perished is whereto I leant,
> The strongest stay of mine unquiet mind;
> The like of it no man again can find—
> From east to west still seeking though he went.

The "pillar" could easily designate Cromwell. The reference to an "unquiet mind" echoes Wyatt's translation of Plutarch and suggests an attempt to find some sort of relief from the uncertainties of life under Henry VIII. Cromwell's papers were investigated after his execution, and in 1541 Wyatt was arrested and imprisoned on the weight of old allegations that he had met with the traitor Reginald Pole and had otherwise misrepresented the king's interests. Wyatt had been cleared of those charges in 1538, but Cromwell's death left him open to further attack from his court enemies.

A poem addressed to Sir Francis Brian (no. 62) has traditionally been dated to this last period of incarceration:

> Sighs are my food, drink are my tears;
> Clinking of fetters such music would crave.

Stink and close air away my life wears.
Innocency is all the hope I have.

Besides its graphic depiction of the speaker's suffering and humiliation—"this wound shall heal again / But yet, alas, the scar shall still remain"—this poem echoes "Who list his wealth and ease retain" in its claim of the speaker's innocence. Wyatt had in 1536 suffered imprisonment in the Tower and, if scholarly dating is correct, had written of it. "Sighs are my food," though shorter, is more bitter in tone than the earlier poem. When commanded to answer in writing the accusations against him, Wyatt provided a declaration of his innocence. He insisted that "for my part I declare affirmingly, at all proofs whereby a Christian man may be tried, that in my life in crime toward the Majesty of the King my master or any his issue, in deed, word, writing or wish I never offended, I never committed malice or offense, or (as I have presently said before you) done thing wherein my thought could accuse my conscience." He then prepared a lengthy, sharply worded defense of his actions, turning the case against his accusers. At its end he declares: "Thus much I thought to say unto you afore both God and man to discharge me, that I seem not to perish in my own fault, for lack of declaring my truth; and afore God and all these men I charge you with my innocent truth that in case, as God defend, you be guilty of mine innocent blood, that you before his tribunal shall be inexcusable." No evidence of a trial survives; but the Privy Council later mentioned Wyatt's confession and pardon, both of which may have been wrought from this defense. At the time, the pardon was believed to have been urged by Queen Catherine Howard and to have rested on the removal of Elizabeth Darrell and the reinstatement of Wyatt's wife. In 1541 Wyatt made his will, providing for Darrell and their son, Francis, and for his legitimate son, Thomas. There are indications that Wyatt was restored to favor, for later in 1541 he received some of the awards of Thomas Culpepper, who was charged with adultery with Queen Catherine Howard, and made an advantageous exchange of property with Henry VIII. Early in 1542 Wyatt was probably member of Parliament for Kent, and it is possible that he was to be made vice admiral of a fleet. On 11 October 1542, on his way to Falmouth to meet and escort to London the Spanish envoy, he died of a fever at the home of Sir John Horsey at Sherborne in Dorset.

It is clear, then, that although the records of Wyatt's life are not always reliable, they are numerous. Besides details in official records, in foreign chronicles, letters, and memoirs, there are letters in his hand, which help to establish his own concerns as a courtier and the demands placed on him by others. His letters to Cromwell and the king reveal a command of detail and dialogue as well as a sensitivity to delicate national and international issues. The two letters to his son have long been used to establish Wyatt's forthright character. His defense in 1541 demonstrates his acuity and his ability to outmaneuver his enemies. For Wyatt's poetry perhaps the most salient features of his life are his worldliness and his wavering fortunes as a courtier. Despite his imprisonments, which must surely have made him aware of the precariousness of his position, Wyatt remained a courtier and accepted diplomatic missions. Those years as ambassador must also have made him aware that diplomacy is a game of negotiation and refusal, that international alliances are quickly and of necessity broken with the changing expectations of new governments and the shifting needs of the state or the monarch. Wyatt's courtly poetry, then, transcribes, whether explicitly or obliquely, his life as a courtier.

Every aspect of Wyatt's poetry has been widely debated: the canon, the texts, the prosody, the occasion, the personae or voices, the significance of French and Italian influences, and the representation of court life. Wyatt's poems circulated widely among various members of Henry's court, and some may first have been published in a miscellany or verse anthology, *The Court of Venus*, of which three fragments survive. They were edited in 1955 by Russell A. Fraser, who dates the first fragment (Douce) to 1535–1539, the second (Stark) to 1547–1549, and the third (Folger) to 1561–1564, the subtitle of the Stark fragment running *A Book of Ballets*. Five of the poems in these fragments are Wyatt's, and others are thought to be his as well. The Douce fragment is, in fact, the earliest known printed miscellany in England. By far the most important of the miscellanies, however, is that compiled and edited in 1557 by Tottel: *Songs and Sonnets*, better known as *Tottel's Miscellany*. This collection of various verse forms and types, from the sonnet to satire, went through at least nine editions in thirty years. Intended to honor and represent "English eloquence," it is arranged by author, Wyatt being the best represented. Tottel or his editors exercised a great deal of license in altering Wyatt's poetry, omitting lines, rearranging the poems to resemble sonnets, regularizing the meter, smoothing out the irony, and giving them titles that prescribe their meanings. This collection includes about one-third of Wyatt's canon, concentrating on his lyrics and his adaptations from Italian sources, such as Petrarch and Serafino d'Aquilano. It is clear that Tottel thought this collection to represent the best of the courtly tradition and the best of Continental imitations, and although it is uneven in quality, it remains one of the most important publications of the sixteenth century.

Since Tottel's 1557 *Miscellany*, Wyatt's name has been coupled with that of a younger poet, another translator of Petrarch: Henry Howard, Earl of Surrey. The work of both poets is presented by Tottel, but Wyatt's metrical forms, rugged and experimental in the manuscripts, have been regularized into more-fluid and more-recognizably iambic-pentameter lines. Through George F. Nott's edition (1816) of the poems from manuscripts, it became apparent that Tottel had altered the poems, and Wyatt's prosody began to be studied independently of Surrey's. Wyatt both experiments with metrical forms and writes poems in various recognizable meters, but there is much disagreement over his facility in writing iambic pentameter. One view is that in his difficult lines the four-stress pull of the Anglo-Saxon line competes with pentameter. A common opinion in the twentieth century, however, is that although these lines are basically iambic pentameter, the language wrenches the meter to produce a more forceful and expressive line. For three centuries Surrey was generally considered the more aristocratic, harmonious, and therefore superior poet; but in recent times Wyatt has been judged the more individualistic, original, and complex of the two.

Despite the significance of *Tottel's Miscellany* as an influential text for later poets of the sixteenth century, any serious discussion of Wyatt's poetry must be grounded in his work as it is preserved in various manuscripts. The primary manuscript, British Library Egerton 2711, has been treated almost as if it were an "edition" of the poems, for it was certainly Wyatt's own book and contains poems in several hands, including his own, as can be ascertained from his autograph letters. It also contains poems with corrections and alterations (some in his hand) and some poems ascribed to him by the markers "Tho" or "Wyat." Several theories have been advanced to account for the chronology of the poems in this manuscript, but no firm conclusions have been reached. The poems need not have been copied in the order they were composed, and although a few can be dated, most editors do not think that poems following those datable were necessarily composed after them. One glance at the Egerton manuscript reveals some of the obstacles in deciding the texts of the poems: they are written in several hands and different inks, and the manuscript is scribbled over, having served its later owners as a commonplace book and calculation sheet. Peter Beal (1980) states that Egerton features copies of 107 poems by Wyatt, his paraphrase of the Penitential Psalms, two letters to his son (not in his hand), and three other poems that are not his. The first poem in the manuscript, "Behold, Love, thy power how she despiseth," imitates a poem by Petrarch. The poems in Wyatt's handwriting include *"Of Carthage he, that worthy warrior," "Tagus, farewell,"* and *"What rage is this?"* Some of Wyatt's better-known poems in this manuscript, although not in his hand, are *"The long love that in my thought doth harbor," "Whoso list to hunt, I know where is an hind," "Farewell, Love, and all thy laws forever," "I find no peace and all my war is done," "My galley charged with forgetfulness," "They flee from me that sometime did me seek," "My mother's maids,"* and *"A spending hand."*

While Egerton is acknowledged to be the primary manuscript of Wyatt's poetry, the significance of the Blage, Devonshire, and Arundel Harington manuscripts, to mention only the major ones, in determining Wyatt's canon is contested. The 1969 Muir-Thomson edition of the poems may have conflated the canon by including doubtful poems from these manuscripts. The Blage manuscript, compiled during the 1530s and 1540s and once owned by Wyatt's close friend Sir George Blage, is a collection of various types of poems, eighty-five of which have been attributed to Wyatt. It circulated among members of the court and, according to Ronald A. Rebholz, presents "versions" of poems earlier than those in Egerton. He claims the same dating for the Devonshire manuscript, also a verse collection, which circulated especially among members of the Howard family and which contains the largest collection of Wyatt's love lyrics. The poems in Devonshire, 122 of which have been attributed to Wyatt, are written in the hands of Margaret Howard, Mary Fitzroy (Surrey's sister), and Mary Shelton. The Arundel Harington manuscript, yet another verse miscellany, was written by or for John Harington and is generally considered later than the Egerton. It contains the Penitential Psalms plus fifty-five other poems that have been attributed to Wyatt.

Although the canon is to this day disputed, it has in the past generally been decided with the following logic and hierarchy, according to Rebholz: certainly canonical are those Egerton poems in Wyatt's hand; those Egerton poems in the hand of a scribe but corrected in Wyatt's hand; those Egerton poems in various hands but designated "Tho." or "Tho"; those Egerton poems in various hands but designated "Wyat"; and those ninety-seven poems attributed to Wyatt by Tottel, fifteen without manuscript sources. Less certainly canonical are those poems found in Blage, Devonshire, or Arundel Harington, among poems known to be Wyatt's or ascribed to him. The extent of the controversy over canonical and textual problems is best illustrated by the fact that since 1969 four independent editions of the poems and one book-length critique of one of those editions have been published. While the Muir-Thomson *Collected Poems* (1969), with its lengthy notes and full texts of many original sources, is still considered to be the standard edition, Rebholz's *Complete Poems* (1978) is often cited as standard because of its accuracy in transcription, its modern spelling, and its comprehensive notes. The Oxford edition by Joost Daalder (1975) is also well regarded. H. A. Mason's *Editing Wyatt* (1972) prints tables of errors in transcriptions for the Muir-Thomson edition. Editors of Wyatt differ sharply over editorial principles and the hierarchy of the manuscripts, one of the most serious debates being whether, given various and varied copies, the poems should be transcribed or reconstructed, and on what grounds (for instance, metrical and stylistic) emendation should proceed.

Dating the poetry also raises serious problems. Editors can place a few poems with some degree of accuracy, according either to the dates of their sources or to genuine allusions to topical events. For example, the three epistolary satires were composed after 1532-1533, the publication date of the *Opere Toscane*, by Luigi Alamanni, whose tenth satire provides the source for Wyatt's *"Mine own John Poyntz"* and, it is thought, the terza-rima form for his three satires and his paraphrases of the Penitential Psalms. A few poems contain references to Spain, which date them during or after Wyatt's visit there from 1537 to 1539.

In most of his poetry Wyatt worked both with English models, notably Geoffrey Chaucer, and Continental sources. This combination gives his poems their peculiar characteristic of following the conventions of *amour courtois* yet implicitly rejecting those conventions at the same time. His canon falls into two subgenres: courtly poetry and religious poetry. The courtly poetry may be divided, with some difficulty, between the love poems and the satiric poems. The love poetry predominates and includes work in several forms, such as sonnets, epigrams, and what have traditionally been called songs. Many of Wyatt's Petrarchan sources had been set to music by the early sixteenth century, but recent scholars have doubted whether he wrote his poems for musical accompaniment.

Since the publication of Raymond Southall's *The Courtly Maker: An Essay on the Poetry of Wyatt and His Contemporaries* (1964), most scholars have recognized the importance of the "courtly" context for Wyatt's oeuvre. According to Southall, the love complaints, besides being personal expressions of love or pain, may also be stylized verses designed to win the favor of court ladies who could offer political advancement to a courtier. Southall notes that many of Wyatt's poems repeatedly stress the insecurity of a man's fortunes, an attitude consistent with the realities of court life. Others have suggested that love poetry masks the pursuit of power at court, and it now seems clear that Wyatt's metaphors serve a double purpose. This courtly context has been filled in by historicist scholars, who have more thoroughly explored the role-playing, submission to authority, and engaging in intrigue required for success at Henry VIII's court.

In the love lyrics, or "amorous" poetry, the lover complains of lost or unrequited love and begs the beloved for favor or mercy, as in the Egerton poem of four stanzas, corrected in Wyatt's hand (no. 106):

> Though I cannot your cruelty constrain
> For my goodwill to favor me again,
> Though my true and faithful love
> Have no power your heart to move,
>   Yet rue upon my pain.

The same complaint, with variation and in several verse forms, may be found in many of Wyatt's poems. In the following doubled sonnet (no. 34), the lover's pain of rejection is expressed by his tears, sighs, moans, and, of course, his love poetry:

> The flaming sighs that boil within my breast
> Sometime break forth and they can well declare
> The heart's unrest and how that it doth fare,
> The pain thereof, the grief, and all the rest.

The eloquence of these sighs and complaints is counterbalanced by the pain they cause the lover. In much of Wyatt's love poetry, it is characteristic for the lover to protest his loyalty despite all odds against him and, further, despite the beloved's scorn and rejection of his suit, as here (no. 110):

> I have sought long with steadfastness
> To have had some ease of my great smart
> But naught availeth faithfulness
> To grave within your stony heart.

Although these courtly love poems lament personal loss or suffering, they take on added meaning read in the light of Southall's claim that such lyrics were often addressed to women of rank who could offer a courtier advancement. Southall notes that the vocabulary of Wyatt's love poetry often includes words that recall the patron/client relationship: *service, desert, suit, hope, reward, promise, fortune, grant*—a vocabulary suggesting that the dependency of the underling parallels the dependency of the lover. In a canzone that again boasts of the lover's steadfastness (no. 78), the refrain claims that the lover will "serve" the beloved, despite his "reward" of cruelty:

> Though for goodwill I find but hate
> And cruelty my life to waste
> And though that still a wretched state
> Should pine my days unto the last,
> Yet I profess it willingly
> To serve and suffer patiently.

This attitude of resignation, though traditional in courtly love poetry, has been seen by many scholars over the centuries as unseemly, and the poems themselves as slight. Read in the context of competition for preferment at court, for offices and awards, or for access to them, the poems reveal the courtier's relative lack of power. In the sonnet "My heart I gave thee, not to do it pain" (no. 14), the language of courtly love is barely distinguishable from the language of aristocratic patronage. The lover admits that he has entered a servant/mistress relationship, in which he expects to be remunerated for faithful service:

> I served thee, not to be forsaken,
> But that I should be rewarded again.
> I was content thy servant to remain
> But not to be paid under this fashion.

The speaker is so frustrated by his treatment that he rejects the lady as she has rejected him, acknowledging the hopelessness of receiving any gain for his service to her. In this and other love poems, Wyatt is distinguished by expressing anger over losing what he sees as his due by right and in questioning the codes of courtly love. This anger and contempt find their most sustained outlet in his satires of court life.

One of Wyatt's greatest poetic achievements is his adaptation of the sonnet form into English. Although he has been criticized by modern scholars for imitating the self-conscious conceits (extended comparisons) and oxymora (oppositions such as "ice / fire") of his sources, such language and sentiments would have found an appreciative audience at the time. A clear example of this type of sonnet is his translation of Petrarch's *Rime* 134, "*Pace non trovo e non ho da far guerra.*" Wyatt's poem (no. 17) begins:

> I find no peace and all my war is done.
> I fear and hope, I burn and freeze like ice.
> I fly above the wind yet can I not arise.
> And naught I have and all the world I seize on.

Each succeeding line expresses a contradiction in the lover's situation: he feels both freedom and constraint; he wishes both life and death; he is both blind and seeing, mute and complaining, loving another and hating himself, sorrowful and joyful. The last line of this poem is typical of Wyatt in indicating that such internal divisions derive from the beloved: his "delight is causer of this strife."

Leonard Forster, in *The Icy Fire: Five Studies in European Petrarchism* (1969), reasons that because such devices are highly rhetorical and easily imitable, early English poets imitated them. Most of Wyatt's adaptations, however, express a highly dramatic situation and seem the overwrought outpourings of severe and personal pain, not the static result of artifice. Thus, even close translations often result in original beauty. Although it has not always been appreciated, an often-anthologized and haunting sonnet is *"My galley charged with forgetfulness"* (no. 19), a translation of Petrarch's *Rime* 189, "*Passa la nave mia colma d'oblio.*" Here the comparison the speaker makes between a ship and love is not merely an exercise in sustained allegory but with its unexpected phrases and halting meter—"Thorough sharp seas in winter nights doth pass"—expresses the lover's inability to recover from his loss. The cause of his suffering is described with effective simplicity—"The stars be hid that led me to this pain"—and the couplet evokes a sense of true despair, for the lover knows he is beyond recovery precisely because love is not rational: "Drowned is reason that should me comfort / And I remain despairing of the port."

Perennially fascinated by Wyatt's use of French and Italian sources, scholars have continued to debate the significance of his Petrarchism. There is scholarly concern over what is meant by translation; Wyatt's tendency to imitate rather than transliterate has been widely discussed. Some take it as an indication that he adopted the principles for translation that Continental poets themselves used in turning classical poetry into the vernacular; therefore, Wyatt brought Renaissance humanism to England. Some scholars argue that he translated the Italian texts into an essentially English context or that he personalized that context, while others argue that many of the translations falter.

By far the most widely held view is that when Wyatt's poetry defies the beloved and denounces the game of love, or rejects the devotion to love found in his models, it approaches the anti-Petrarchism of the sort evident later in Elizabethan poetry. His sonnet beginning "Was I never yet of your love grieved / Nor never shall while that my life doth last" (no. 12), a translation of Petrarch's *Rime 82*, *"Io non fu' d' amar voi lassato unqu' anco,"* declares that "of hating myself that date is past" and ends with the lines that project the speaker's disdain:

> If otherwise ye seek for to fulfill
> Your disdain, ye err and shall not as ye ween,
> And ye yourself the cause thereof hath been.

If this frustration of the beloved's satisfaction seems vengeful and petty, one must remember that it is bred by a system that seems arbitrary in its delegation of power and responsibility but is in fact closed and dependent on personal loyalties.

A sonnet often cited as an example of Wyatt's anti-Petrarchism is one for which no source has yet been found, *"Farewell, Love, and all thy laws forever"* (no. 31). As the first line indicates, the speaker has renounced love; he will replace it with the philosophy of Seneca and Plato and adopt a more Stoic attitude toward love. He decides to set no more store by such "trifles" and bids love "Go trouble younger hearts." The rejection of love as a waste of one's time and a sure means to suffer is complete in the couplet: "For hitherto though I have lost all my time, / Me lusteth no longer rotten boughs to climb." A similar theme is sounded in another poem whose source is likewise unknown, *"There was never file half so well filed"* (no. 32). Here the speaker intends to abandon the passion or "folly" of youthful love for the "reason" of maturity. Expressing regret for wasted time and wasted trust, the poem ends by claiming that one who deceives should not complain of being deceived in return but should receive the "reward" of "little trust forever." Both these poems are more severely critical views of the artificiality and duplicity of courtly life than the one to be found in a translation such as "I find no peace and all my war is done"; and yet its juxtapositions of opposites may also indicate the underlying insecurity of that life.

Some of Wyatt's sourceless poems that are not sonnets, such as *"My lute, awake"* (no. 109), also convey a markedly anti-Petrarchan attitude. The several copies of this eight-stanza song, including those in the Stark and Folger fragments of *The Court of Venus*, suggest the extent of its popularity. It begins with the standard lover's complaint but then abandons the courtly love game and pronounces what amounts to a curse on the beloved:

> Vengeance shall fall on thy disdain
> That makest but game on earnest pain.
> Think not alone under the sun
> Unquit to cause thy lovers plain
> Although my lute and I have done.
>
> May chance thee lie withered and old
> The winter nights that are so cold,
> Plaining in vain unto the moon.
> Thy wishes then dare not be told
> Care then who list for I have done.

It is unclear whether the poem's bitter tone is a projection by Wyatt or by the speaker; and although its message may be traditional, it is a stark reminder of the importance of youth in Henry's court. These poems have an edge to them that jars with the very concept of courtly love poetry but that matches the tone of traditional court satire from other sources, including earlier English poets. This rejection or theme of lost beauty is carried to a misogynistic extreme in another of Wyatt's better-known poems, *"Ye old mule"* (no. 7). Here the faded beauty is compared to a worn-out beast of burden: she can no longer choose her lovers but must buy what is available.

In these and later anti-Petrarchan poems in English, the lover's pain is blamed on the beloved's artifice, guile, deceit, dissembling, fickleness, and hard-heartedness; in Wyatt's poems the lover's constancy is repeatedly compared to the beloved's lack of faith. In *"Thou hast no faith of him that hath none"* (no. 6), the lover, rather than begging for mercy or favor, is angered at having been betrayed:

> I thought thee true without exception.
> But I perceive I lacked discretion
> To fashion faith to words mutable:
> Thy thought is too light and variable.
> To change so oft without occasion,
>   Thou hast no faith.

Many of Wyatt's poems treat mutability as an undesirable characteristic for a lover, a servant, a patron, or a king; changefulness or betrayal is his common theme. It is not always clear, however, whether in these poems Wyatt speaks in his own voice or creates various personae. Some of the poems project a great deal of venom over personal and political events and seem to reveal an intelligent courtier struggling to define himself against a political structure he both criticizes and enjoys. Some scholars thus see Wyatt as a rebellious figure in a corrupt and corrupting system; others see him as hopelessly caught in that system and its dynastic concerns.

The poem that best illustrates these issues is *"They flee from me"* (no. 80), which combines eroticism with a contempt for the beloved's changefulness. This three-stanza poem, or ballade, moves between dreaming and waking, fantastic and realistic states of consciousness. It owes something to the amorous poetry of Ovid, perhaps something to Petrarch's sonnets, and much to Chaucer. The poem opens with the speaker remembering former love(s): "They flee from me that sometime did me seek / With naked foot stalking in my chamber." The poem's first few lines recall "Whoso list to hunt" in claiming that those who once sought the speaker were tamed but "now are wild"; further, "now they range / Busily seeking with a continual change" that the speaker finds problematic. In the second stanza the speaker recalls a time when the beloved caught him in her arms, kissed him, and asked, "'Dear heart, how like you this?'" The poem shifts abruptly to the present and to reality: "It was no dream: I lay broad waking." Despite the lover's "gentleness" or "gentility," he has been rejected, and his loss leaves him, if not vengeful, at least sardonic:

> And I have leave to go of her goodness
> And she also to use newfangleness.
> But since that I so kindly am served
> I would fain know what she hath deserved.

"They flee from me," a poem of betrayal and remembrance, may be the definitive expression of Wyatt's attitude toward courtly love: it is a game that can cause real pain, and one in which the players are only half-aware of their own complicity.

Wyatt's Italian sources range beyond Petrarch. The epigrams, many of them based on the *strambotti* of Serafino d'Aquilano, also comment on the uncertainties of court life. Several are written in ottava rima, and many, like some of the classical epigrams of Martial, are biting. In a court where *"none is worse than is a friendly foe"* (no. 52), dissembling is common: *"But well to say and so to mean— / That sweet accord is seldom seen"* (no. 70). In *"Lucks, my fair falcon"* (no. 68), a poem most editors date to the period of Cromwell's execution and Wyatt's second imprisonment in the Tower, the speaker notes that he has few friends in adversity. In fact, some of the epigrams do mark Wyatt as a Stoic, such as the translation from Seneca's *Thyestes*, which describes the court as a dangerous and even foul place (no. 49):

> Stand whoso list upon the slipper top
> Of court's estates, and let me here rejoice
> And use me quiet without let or stop,
> Unknown in court that hath such brackish joys.

The poem suggests that life at court is uncertain if not dangerous, and again the word *quiet* marks the speaker's anxiety. While one must remember that anticourt satire is conventional, Wyatt's descriptions in this poem go beyond the original: Rebholz notes that "brackish joys" is Wyatt's own addition to Seneca's Latin. The speaker asks to be allowed to live away from the court and die among common men, for those who are well known often die ignominious deaths: "That is much known of other, and of himself, alas, / Doth die unknown, dazed, with dreadful face." The last phrase, again Wyatt's own addition, personalizes the translation. The common thread running through Wyatt's poetry—that the glitter of court life has a darker side, that court service has a "bitter taste" (no. 71)—is congruent with his experiences as a courtier.

Wyatt's most sustained and effective criticism of the court is to be found in what are commonly known as his "epistolary satires." Once again their immediate source is Italian, but their tone is definitely Horatian, thus marking them as humanist pieces. Although there is a known point after which the poems must have been written—the publication date of Alamanni's *Opere Toscane*, the source of the first satire—scholars disagree on the date of their composition in relation to the Penitential Psalms. In the first satire, *"Mine own John Poyntz"* (no. 149), addressed to a friend of Wyatt, the speaker explains that because he cannot meet the courtly requirements of duplicity, dissembling, and fraud, he has withdrawn to the country. The hundred-plus-line poem begins with a disclaimer: the speaker does not mock those whom Fortune has made rulers. Although the speaker at one time sought glory, he cannot now obtain it because he is unable to lie, to praise those who do not deserve it, to honor those who prey on others, to dissemble, to call deceit strategy, to gain profit from bending laws, to say that people have accomplishments that they have not, to cloak vice with virtue, to claim "tyranny / To be the right of a prince's reign," or to seem rather than to be. Rebholz notes that the polished Italian is often translated into homespun English proverbs, as if to underscore the speaker's inability to frame fair words to foul practices. Many scholars date this poem to the period of Wyatt's enforced exile in Kent in 1536; some argue that if he could, the speaker, whom they read as Wyatt, would be in the midst of that court, despite its demands and dangers, for he valued the active life.

The second satire, *"My mother's maids"* (no. 150), retells Aesop's fable of the country mouse and the city mouse, a story Wyatt could have taken from many sources, including Horace. Wyatt's version differs radically from most others in which the city mouse tempts the country mouse by describing the splendors of city life, criticizing country life, and inviting her to the city. The country mouse, after tasting the dangers of city life, returns home convinced of her error. Wyatt's country mouse, however, is described as living in desperate and destitute conditions, which she herself attempts to better by visiting her sister. This city mouse is frightened by the very noise the country mouse makes on her arrival. When a cat attacks the two mice, the city mouse escapes, but the country mouse is restrained by the cat and perhaps killed. The satire then offers a long moral on the best means to attain "quiet of mind," for "each kind of life hath with him his disease." The speaker counsels contentment with one's allotted life:

> Then seek no more out of thyself to find
> The thing that thou hast sought so long before,
> For thou shalt feel it sitting in thy mind.

The poem's attitude of mental resignation to adversity is consistent with Wyatt's Stoicism. The poem ends with characteristic Wyattian disdain at those who stray from Virtue (here personified); the speaker hopes they will look behind them and "fret inward for losing such a loss."

Wyatt's third satire, *"A spending hand"* (no. 151), is a dialogue between the speaker and Sir Francis Brian, a courtier whom the speaker cynically advises to adopt the methods of flattery and fraud to obtain riches. Brian should learn to fawn, for then he "shall purchase friends where truth shall but offend." His best strategy is to seek out a rich old man to cozen; but if this does not work, he may marry the man's rich widow, no matter how old and unpleasant she might be, and still sleep with whom he pleases. To further his profit he may pander his own female relatives to his superiors. In the poem Brian ignores this advice, this "thrifty jest," because it would compromise his honor, and thus he seems to be the poem's ideal, although scholars have continued to debate Brian's historical appropriateness as an ideal. The poem, modeled roughly on Horace's *Satire* 2.5, takes on a life of its own, using proverbs, of which Brian was a collector, and examples appropriate to Henry's court. (Wyatt once lent money to Brian, but the extent or nature of their relationship is unknown.)

Although many have argued that Wyatt's Penitential Psalms were written before his satires (considered the better poems), the psalms deserve attention apart from the courtly poetry in part because they help to establish Wyatt as a poet of the Reformation. They are also written and corrected in his hand in Egerton, thus providing editors with an unparalleled instance of the poet at work. Published in 1549, the poems were composed sometime after the publication date of their most important sources: the paraphrase of the Penitential Psalms by Pietro Aretino (1534), another paraphrase by Joannis Campensis (1532), printed again in 1533 with a Latin translation by Ulrich Zwingli, and English translations of the latter two in 1534 and 1535. The Vulgate is evident in Wyatt's version, and paraphrases by other writers have also been cited as minor sources. The seven Penitential Psalms, used as a group in the medieval church, center on King David's repentance, after his denunciation by Nathan, for sending Uriah, husband of Bathsheba, to his death in battle. Wyatt, following Aretino's paraphrase, provides a prologue and narrative sequences between the psalms.

As with Wyatt's other poems, there is controversy over the date and meanings of these paraphrases. Some scholars link them to his 1536 or 1541 imprisonment. Others see the poems as unconnected to Wyatt's biography; instead, they are a psychological drama in which David does or does not progress. Several scholars think Wyatt's deviation from his sources may indicate his intention to present David as a "Reformed Christian," whose despair and suffering lead to permanent penitence. Or, the poems may constitute a transcription of Henry VIII into God the absolute ruler, who demands and obtains the complete submission of his "servant" (no. 152), or into David himself, whose adultery has brought hardships to the kingdom; David may also be read as a figure for Wyatt, whose poems acknowledge his own complicity, as psalmist, in the situation he describes. Wyatt seems to have been capable of projecting whatever persona he wished, but he was not blind to the political, national, and personal politics of the Reformation in England: neither should be the interpreters of his religious poetry. The prologue begins as an amorous poem in which David desires Bathsheba and sends Uriah to his death. After his crime is discovered, David removes himself to a cave, takes up his harp, and sings. The paraphrases explore themes common to all Wyatt's poetry: betrayal, loyalty, truth, submission, and particularly "the chastisings of sin . . . that never suffer rest unto the mind" (no. 152).

Those who wish to study Wyatt beyond his poems might begin by reading his letters, edited by

Muir (1963). Wyatt's critical fortunes should also be explored through Patricia Thomson's *Wyatt: The Critical Heritage* (1974). This book begins with the preface to the first edition of *The Quiet of Mind* (1528) and ends with an excerpt from C. S. Lewis, who named Wyatt the father of Drab (as opposed to Golden) Age verse and who made the famous pronouncement that "poor Wyatt seems to be always in love with women he dislikes." In 1542 John Leland published a set of elegies extravagant in their praise of Wyatt's eloquence and forthright character. His paraphrases of the Penitential Psalms were highly regarded in the sixteenth century and, after the publication of *Tottel's Miscellany*, so were his courtly poems. In the seventeenth and much of the eighteenth century, Wyatt and other writers of Henry VIII's reign were eclipsed by the Elizabethans and later poets; when he again received critical attention, by Thomas Warton in 1781, it was as a satirist of "spirited and manly reflections," not a love poet, that he was admired. Nott first used Wyatt's manuscripts to edit the poetry and, although he is somewhat more generous, comes to much the same conclusions as Warton—that Surrey, the nobleman, is the better poet. Not until E. M. W. Tillyard published his edition in 1929 were the lyrics appreciated, and then because they represented what has come to be known as "the native English tradition." Wyatt's Petrarchan translations and imitations have not, since the sixteenth century, been generally admired, even by those who have studied the sources. H. A. Mason, in much of his work, has insisted that Wyatt is best in his "serious" poetry, especially the satires. Since Stephen Greenblatt's *Renaissance Self-Fashioning: From More to Shakespeare* (1980), most critical attention afforded Wyatt has been linked, once again, to his biography, to his struggle not merely to survive but to succeed as a courtier in a social order under stress. The latest study, Foley's excellent *Sir Thomas Wyatt* (1990), continues in this vein.

Until recently many critics have found it instructive to return to the first literary biographies of Wyatt, to learn from his contemporaries what they thought admirable about him. One of his earliest literary biographers was Surrey, whose reputation has fallen not only because he is now considered to be a more facile and less ambiguous poet than Wyatt, but also, perhaps, because he was an aristocrat whose family was involved in court intrigues throughout Henry's reign. Unlike Wyatt, Surrey *was* executed by his king; one might therefore expect to find in the work of the poet who managed not to be executed, despite his imprisonments and expected death, greater ambiguities than one finds in the work of the poet who was killed. In one of his poems on the occasion of Wyatt's death, "Wyatt resteth here, that quick could never rest," Surrey writes a *blason*, or stylized description of various parts of the body, in which he extols Wyatt's virtues and denounces his enemies; he also explains the conditions under which Wyatt wrote and the value of the work he produced. While the elegy is conventionally epideictic, praising its subject and blaming his detractors, it is clear that Wyatt saw his world in terms of this duality, both in his poems and in his defense (1541).

In the *blason* proper, Surrey describes "a head, where wisdom mysteries did frame," or an intelligent courtier who incessantly worked for his country's good, an ambassador whose "tongue ... served in foreign realms his king." Unlike the courtiers he describes in his satires, Wyatt had "a visage, stern and mild," which condemned vice and praised virtue; his mind was "void of guile." In the midst of his discussion of Wyatt as a courtier, Surrey praises his craft as a poet: "A hand, that taught what might be said in rime; / That reft Chaucer the glory of his wit." It is no coincidence that Wyatt's success as a poet is associated with his work as an ambassador, for his contact with French and Italian cultures must have inspired him to imitate Continental poetry. The eighth stanza is the antecedent for all those critical analyses aimed at describing Wyatt's attempt to define himself against the change, chance, and uncertainty of life at court. Surrey's premise is that the more Wyatt was envied, the better his life and works became; he was a singular man in a compromised world:

> A valiant corps, where force and beauty met,
> Happy, alas! too happy, but for foes,
> Lived, and ran the race that nature set;
> Of manhood's shape, where she the mold did lose.

The loss or the individuality lies in the power of Wyatt's poetry to evoke that precarious and ceremonialized life.

Source: Ellen C. Caldwell, "Thomas Wyatt," in *Dictionary of Literary Biography*, Vol. 132, *Sixteenth-Century British Nondramatic Writers, First Series*, edited by David A. Richardson, Gale Research, 1993, pp. 346–363.

Reed Way Dasenbrock

In the following essay, Dasenbrock establishes that Wyatt's use of Petrarch was new and inventive and that Wyatt laid the groundwork for later poets who built upon his work with the sonnet format. Dasenbrock believes that Wyatt has not received the

> *... Wyatt also translates Petrarch so as to establish a difference as well as a kinship. This is all part of the process of imitation in the Renaissance, in which one defines one's identity as a poet by engaging in the play of resemblance and difference known as imitation."*

credit that he deserves as an imitator and translator of Petrarch's poetry.

Perhaps the biggest barrier to a proper understanding and appreciation of older works of art is our tendency to place them in our categories and judge them accordingly. Nowhere is this more true than in the consideration of works of art whose origins lie partly in other works. Ever since the Romantics, originality has been privileged over imitation, and this has relegated the once honorable activity of translation to a secondary place. In this view, the great writer works *sui generis*; only the second-rate proceed by imitating and translating the work of others. We can date the birth of this categorical distinction historically, but we have nevertheless tended to apply it to much earlier works.

An outstanding casualty of this approach has been Sir Thomas Wyatt. Wyatt has had the misfortune of being known primarily as an imitator and translator, as the first English Petrarchan. Except for Chaucer's translation of one of Petrarch's sonnets into three stanzas of *Troilus and Criseide*, he was the first translator of Petrarch's lyrics into English and he translated more of Petrarch's lyrics than anyone before the nineteenth century. He introduced the sonnet and the strambotto into English, tried somewhat less successfully to find an English equivalent for the canzone, and translated poems by a number of other Italian Petrarchans, most notably Serafino. Most importantly, his translations and imitations of Petrarch created a tradition of (and a form and language for) writing love sonnets in English that later culminated in the great sonnet sequences of Sidney, Spenser, and Shakespeare. Wyatt's interest in and work with Petrarch's poetry, in short, was one of the seeds of the English Renaissance. But in the cultural horizon provided by the opposition between originality and imitation, our understanding of the seminal role played by Wyatt has not enhanced our opinion of him. Wyatt is still a comparatively little-read and regarded figure. We may praise him for translating Petrarch, for paving the way for later poets, but that is damning praise that prevents us from praising him for being a fine (and indeed original) poet.

The purpose of this essay is to describe the fundamental mistake we have been making in our approach to Wyatt's translations and imitations of Petrarch. We have concentrated on their origins as poems by Petrarch, not on their identity as poems by Wyatt. As a result, Wyatt scholarship has tended to categorize his translations according to the degree of faithfulness they bear towards their Petrarchan originals. I hope to show, however, that this approach fails to make sense either of Wyatt's interest in Petrarch or of the poems that result. Only by considering his versions of Petrarch in his or Petrarch's framework can we avoid the false dichotomy that has prevented us from understanding this crucial and seminal poetic relationship.

Many leading Wyatt critics have found his interest in Petrarch utterly inexplicable....

Hallett Smith in 1946 was the first modern critic to find Wyatt's interest in Petrarch understandable, as he recognizes that "Wyatt must have seen something more in these sonnets [of Petrarch] than merely 14-line poems with certain rhyme schemes." But he examines only one of Wyatt's translations, "The longe love that in my thought doeth harbour," and the point of his discussion is that Wyatt's translation is a better poem than Surrey's version of the same Petrarch original.

J. W. Lever's 1956 discussion of Wyatt is the first of a number of detailed discussions of Wyatt's versions of Petrarch. But his discussion is hampered by his acceptance of a dichotomy between translation and original work. Lever therefore claims that Wyatt matures as a poet by moving in effect from translation to original composition. In Lever's account, Wyatt began translating Petrarch in a respectful and faithful fashion, but then, repudiating Petrarch's values, he thereafter began to handle his Petrarchan originals in a "cynical and rebellious" fashion. His mature, most successful work is so free with the original that Lever calls it original composition, not translation, and this independence for Lever is something to praise. But this analysis cannot account for Wyatt's own perspective. If the degree of merit of a Wyatt poem is to be equated with the degree of independence it shows from its Petrarch original, why would Wyatt be interested in translating so many poems of Petrarch? Moreover, our knowledge of the chronology of Wyatt's poems is so sketchy that Lever's construction of a strict temporal sequence for these poems is problematic. Finally, and most tellingly, Lever cannot make his discussion consistent. The next to last sonnet he discusses, "The pillar pearisht is wheartoo I lent," which he praises highly and justly, is far closer to its Petrarchan source than the poems he presents as Wyatt's breakthrough into independence from Petrarch. In short, Wyatt's best poems are not necessarily his most original, nor does "originality" seem to have been his prime concern. . . .

Thus none of these prominent Wyatt critics who have concerned themselves with his translations from Petrarch can understand Wyatt's interest in Petrarch, and this failure indicates a more fundamental failure to understand Wyatt's own categories for an activity like translating Petrarch. . . .

Donald Guss in 1964 was the first to suggest that what Wyatt is doing with Petrarch is far more coherent and purposeful than these source studies indicate: "Throughout, Wyatt's poems reveal themselves to be his, not Petrarch's." Guss's central intuition is that Wyatt transforms his Petrarchan originals in one consistent direction, and that the rationale for this seemingly roundabout method of writing one's own poetry is to be found in Renaissance notions of imitation. Placing Wyatt's translations of Petrarch, in short, in *their* contemporary context makes it far easier to see why Wyatt would transform Petrarch and how he does so.

Thomas M. Greene has included a chapter on Wyatt in his study of Renaissance notions of imitation, *The Light in Troy*, and his analysis confirms Guss's pioneering notion that we need to recover the Renaissance idea of imitation in order to see why Wyatt would translate so much of Petrarch. As Greene has made clear, a central notion in Renaissance humanism, stemming largely from Petrarch himself, was that one forms an identity, a personal voice, precisely through the imitation of models. Petrarch's discussions of imitation are to be found in his letters, and in those discussions he always criticizes those who simply borrow or translate uncreatively. . . . Imitation is the transformation of a model which establishes a relation to that past model yet allows the later writer creative freedom. . . .

This quick summary of the Renaissance notion of imitation should provide a context in which Wyatt's work with Petrarchan models can be understood. Wyatt imitates Petrarch partly because he is imitable and partly because he is inimitable. Something of the model can be brought over and that something creates the family resemblance that enables us to call Wyatt's poetry Petrarchan. But the resemblance does not have to be exact and in this case it isn't: Wyatt also translates Petrarch so as to establish a difference as well as a kinship. This is all part of the process of imitation in the Renaissance, in which one defines one's identity as a poet by engaging in the play of resemblance and difference known as imitation. Each poet transforms his model and in that transformation creates his own distinctive and individual style. Originality, in short, is born from imitation. . . .

Complaint is a central theme in Wyatt's poetry and we can see Wyatt transforming . . . poems of Petrarch in which a lady is not so much as mentioned into similar poems of complaint. Petrarch's sonnet, "Vinse Anibàl, et non seppe usar poi," is a poem addressed to Petrarch's friend and patron, Stefano Colonna. It alludes to Hannibal's inaction after victory as a way to warn his friend not to do the same thing. Petrarch assumes that Colonna will heed his advice and that therefore the comparison will ultimately be a contrast. And he concludes as usual by moving away from the situation at hand and by assuring Colonna that his fame will last for thousands of years.

Wyatt turns this poem into an eight line strambotto about himself, "Off Cartage he that worthie warier," and he assumes a parallel—not a contrast—between himself and Hannibal: Hannibal failed and so did I. And in the conclusion which introduces two Petrarchan antitheses not in the original, he brings everything back to the situation at hand:

> so hangith in balaunce
> off warr my pees/ reward of all my payne
> At Mountzon thus I restles rest in spayne.

Petrarch generalizes and praises his friend, whereas Wyatt tells us where he is and how unhappy he is. Thus, though Wyatt is here translating quite a different kind of Petrarch poem than "S' i' 'l dissi mai," he takes it to exactly the same place, creating another highly personal and specific poem of lament and complaint.

Wyatt procedes in the same way in "Though I my self be bridilled of my mynde". This is a translation of Petrarch's "Orso, al vostro destrier si po ben porre" (*Canzoniere* 98). Petrarch writes to his friend, Orso, who has to be absent from a tournament, and who is disappointed because he will miss the opportunity of seeing his Lady there. Wyatt again changes this second-person poem into a first-person poem, and writes about his own situation. He is away from his Lady on duty, and his poem is a fine lament about this.

It is completely characteristic that Wyatt, having a Lady, would have to leave her. But this can be put another way: he would not have thought of writing poems about her until he was away from her or unless he had something else to complain about. Petrarch's situation in love was no more satisfactory than Wyatt's, but his poems about Laura are nonetheless almost always in praise of her. In contrast to Petrarch's "stile de la loda," or praise-style, Wyatt's should be called a blame-style or a complaint-style. Wyatt's poems characteristically move towards a complaint for which someone specific is to blame. And these freer translations we have been examining are so free because Wyatt must rework Petrarch's poems rather extensively to replace Petrarch's praise and compensations with his own uncompensated blaming and complaints.

What I am suggesting is that the degree of freedom of a Wyatt translation is a function, not of Wyatt's degree of independence or rebelliousness, but of the distance the poem must travel to become a poem by Wyatt....

A poem like "Passa la nave mia colma d'oblio" is a straightforward piece of personal complaint, so Wyatt translates it into English (in "My galy charged with forgetfulnes,") almost without modification. He removes a mythological allusion in line 3 and heightens the sense of despair at the close by changing the original "i' 'ncomincio a desperar" ("I begin to despair") into "I remain dispering." Otherwise, this is a faithful translation, but paradoxically *only because* Petrarch's poem lacks his usual compensations in vision, religion, or the possibility of generalizing from and out of his personal experience.

Wyatt, in short, translates Petrarch much more faithfully here because Petrarch's poem is more like one of Wyatt's....

In conclusion, Guss and Greene are correct in placing Wyatt in the Renaissance tradition of imitation, but how he imitates Petrarch has not yet been correctly defined. In brief, what Wyatt does to Petrarch's original poems varies because they vary, not because Wyatt does. Our division of Wyatt's poems into various groups according to their distance from their Petrarchan models (imitations, free and close translations) obscures their essential similarity. As we have seen in an examination of approximately one third of Wyatt's translations of Petrarch, his translations are sometimes quite faithful, sometimes quite free; and what determines this is the distance he needs to take the poem in order to transform it into his kind of poem. Petrarch can be addressing friends or Love or Laura; his theme can be politics or love or religion; but Wyatt transforms all of these poems into his own highly personal poems of lament and reproach. The difference in treatment is a function of Petrarch's variety, since Wyatt's poems are all in the style of which Wyatt is the great master, the blame- or complaint-style. Wyatt is simply not interested in arriving at a faithful—or even at an unfaithful—translation of his model; those categories are not his categories but ours. What he is interested in is writing poems by Wyatt, and what he does with all of the poems by Petrarch that he translates—to put it simply—is to transform them all into poems by Wyatt.

Hence, Wyatt did—according to the Renaissance notion of imitation—find his own identity as a poet through his struggle with his model. And the firmness of that identity is shown when we can say that Petrarch in "Cesare, poi," for example, is proceeding in a way atypical of him, but very typical of Wyatt. Wyatt found this typical manner, in all likelihood, by translating poems such as these in the *Canzoniere,* but his "pervasive transformation" of Petrarch, to use Guss's phrase, allowed him to make that manner his own. Wyatt therefore is not necessarily being cynical or rebellious or anti-Petrarchan when he translates Petrarch freely. He is simply transforming his model in accordance with the canons of imitation of which Petrarch himself approved. Moreover, his transformation of Petrarch in a more realistic, personal, and self-centered direction is as important for the later, greater sonneteers of the English Renaissance as his introduction of the form of the sonnet. The English sonneteers—except for Spenser, as I have argued elsewhere—lack Petrarch's patience and his consolations in philosophy and religion. Their model in this, the typical English Petrarchan divergence from Petrarch, is Sir Thomas Wyatt.

Source: Reed Way Dasenbrock, "Wyatt's Transformation of Petrarch," in *Comparative Literature*, Vol. 40, No. 2, Spring 1988, pp. 122–33.

Sources

Amussen, Susan Dwyer, "Gender Order in Families and Villages," in *An Ordered Society: Gender and Class in Early Modern England*, Columbia University Press, 1988, pp. 103, 117.

Bernard, G. W., "The Fall of Anne Boleyn," in the *English Historical Review*, Vol. 106, No. 420, July 1991, pp. 607, 609.

Daalder, Joost, "Introduction," in *Sir Thomas Wyatt: Collected Poems*, edited by Joost Daalder, Oxford University Press, 1975, pp. xi–xiii.

Dasenbrock, Reed Way, "Understanding Renaissance Imitation: The Example of Wyatt," in *Imitating the Italians: Wyatt, Spenser, Synge, Pound, Joyce*, Johns Hopkins University Press, 1991, pp. 19, 30, 31.

Greenblatt, Stephen, "Power, Sexuality, and Inwardness in Wyatt's Poetry," in *Renaissance Self-Fashioning: From More to Shakespeare*, University of Chicago Press, 1980, pp. 145–48, 152.

Petrarca, Francesco, "Rime 190," in *The Poetry of Petrarch*, translated by David Young, Farrar, Straus, and Giroux, 2004, p. 144.

Waller, Marguerite, "The Empire's New Clothes: Refashioning the Renaissance," in *Seeking the Woman in Late Medieval and Renaissance Writings*, edited by Sheila Fisher and Janet E. Halley, University of Tennessee Press, 1989, pp. 169, 173.

Wyatt, Thomas, Sir, "Whoso List to Hunt," in *Sir Thomas Wyatt: Collected Poems*, edited by Joost Daalder, Oxford University Press, 1975, p. 7.

Further Reading

Fraser, Antonia, ed., *The Lives of the Kings and Queens of England*, University of California Press, 1998.

> Fraser's book is a large coffee-table book filled with many color portraits and copies of early English documents. She provides a concise biography of the kings and queens of England, presented in an easy-to-grasp narrative style and arranged chronologically. This book is very useful for digesting basic information about the British royalty.

Guy, John, *Tudor England*, Oxford, 1990.

> This book, written in clear narrative prose, gives a historical account of the religious and political events of the Tudor reign. Guy includes discussion of economic and social conditions that were affected by the Protestant Reformation.

Jardine, Lisa, *Worldly Goods: A New History of the Renaissance*, W. W. Norton, 1996.

> Jardine looks at the Renaissance as a source not only of great cultural achievement but also of accomplishments in commerce. During the Renaissance, the acquisition of property became an important way to define success; Jardine examines the kinds of property that were acquired—including jewels, rich fabrics, tapestries, and art—and discusses the significance of the accumulation of goods.

Rose, Mary Beth, ed., *Women in the Middle Ages and the Renaissance*, Syracuse University Press, 1985.

> This book remains a good source for understanding the diversity of women's lives during the period in which Wyatt was writing. The essays included by Rose explore women's education, women's roles in the church, and women as the subject of men's writing.

Schama, Simon, *A History of Britain*, 3 Vols., Hyperion, 2000–2002.

> Schama's three volumes contain many maps, illustrations, and photos as well as a very readable history of Britain; Schama is often described as a storyteller. There is a great deal of information about both the obscure legends of Britain and the better-documented events. Schama includes information about the earliest chronicles of British history, the traditions that govern the nation, and the wars and monarchs that have defined it.

Singman, Jeffery L., *Daily Life in Elizabethan England*, Greenwood Press, 1995.

> This book provides many small details about life in sixteenth-century England, explaining how people lived, the clothes they wore, what they ate, and the kinds of jobs they held.

Weir, Alison, *Henry VIII: The King and His Court*, Ballantine Books, 2001.

> This is a very readable biography with a great deal of information about the Tudor court and the people who inhabited it. Weir includes several interesting pieces of information about Wyatt's role within the court, making her book an especially good read for fans of Wyatt's work.

Glossary of Literary Terms

A

Abstract: Used as a noun, the term refers to a short summary or outline of a longer work. As an adjective applied to writing or literary works, abstract refers to words or phrases that name things not knowable through the five senses.

Accent: The emphasis or stress placed on a syllable in poetry. Traditional poetry commonly uses patterns of accented and unaccented syllables (known as feet) that create distinct rhythms. Much modern poetry uses less formal arrangements that create a sense of freedom and spontaneity.

Aestheticism: A literary and artistic movement of the nineteenth century. Followers of the movement believed that art should not be mixed with social, political, or moral teaching. The statement "art for art's sake" is a good summary of aestheticism. The movement had its roots in France, but it gained widespread importance in England in the last half of the nineteenth century, where it helped change the Victorian practice of including moral lessons in literature.

Affective Fallacy: An error in judging the merits or faults of a work of literature. The "error" results from stressing the importance of the work's effect upon the reader—that is, how it makes a reader "feel" emotionally, what it does as a literary work—instead of stressing its inner qualities as a created object, or what it "is."

Age of Johnson: The period in English literature between 1750 and 1798, named after the most prominent literary figure of the age, Samuel Johnson. Works written during this time are noted for their emphasis on "sensibility," or emotional quality. These works formed a transition between the rational works of the Age of Reason, or Neoclassical period, and the emphasis on individual feelings and responses of the Romantic period.

Age of Reason: See *Neoclassicism*

Age of Sensibility: See *Age of Johnson*

Agrarians: A group of Southern American writers of the 1930s and 1940s who fostered an economic and cultural program for the South based on agriculture, in opposition to the industrial society of the North. The term can refer to any group that promotes the value of farm life and agricultural society.

Alexandrine Meter: See *Meter*

Allegory: A narrative technique in which characters representing things or abstract ideas are used to convey a message or teach a lesson. Allegory is typically used to teach moral, ethical, or religious lessons but is sometimes used for satiric or political purposes.

Alliteration: A poetic device where the first consonant sounds or any vowel sounds in words or syllables are repeated.

Allusion: A reference to a familiar literary or historical person or event, used to make an idea more easily understood.

Amerind Literature: The writing and oral traditions of Native Americans. Native American literature was originally passed on by word of mouth, so it consisted largely of stories and events that were easily memorized. Amerind prose is often rhythmic like poetry because it was recited to the beat of a ceremonial drum.

Analogy: A comparison of two things made to explain something unfamiliar through its similarities to something familiar, or to prove one point based on the acceptedness of another. Similes and metaphors are types of analogies.

Anapest: See *Foot*

Angry Young Men: A group of British writers of the 1950s whose work expressed bitterness and disillusionment with society. Common to their work is an antihero who rebels against a corrupt social order and strives for personal integrity.

Anthropomorphism: The presentation of animals or objects in human shape or with human characteristics. The term is derived from the Greek word for "human form."

Antimasque: See *Masque*

Antithesis: The antithesis of something is its direct opposite. In literature, the use of antithesis as a figure of speech results in two statements that show a contrast through the balancing of two opposite ideas. Technically, it is the second portion of the statement that is defined as the "antithesis"; the first portion is the "thesis."

Apocrypha: Writings tentatively attributed to an author but not proven or universally accepted to be their works. The term was originally applied to certain books of the Bible that were not considered inspired and so were not included in the "sacred canon."

Apollonian and Dionysian: The two impulses believed to guide authors of dramatic tragedy. The Apollonian impulse is named after Apollo, the Greek god of light and beauty and the symbol of intellectual order. The Dionysian impulse is named after Dionysus, the Greek god of wine and the symbol of the unrestrained forces of nature. The Apollonian impulse is to create a rational, harmonious world, while the Dionysian is to express the irrational forces of personality.

Apostrophe: A statement, question, or request addressed to an inanimate object or concept or to a nonexistent or absent person.

Archetype: The word archetype is commonly used to describe an original pattern or model from which all other things of the same kind are made. This term was introduced to literary criticism from the psychology of Carl Jung. It expresses Jung's theory that behind every person's "unconscious," or repressed memories of the past, lies the "collective unconscious" of the human race: memories of the countless typical experiences of our ancestors. These memories are said to prompt illogical associations that trigger powerful emotions in the reader. Often, the emotional process is primitive, even primordial. Archetypes are the literary images that grow out of the "collective unconscious." They appear in literature as incidents and plots that repeat basic patterns of life. They may also appear as stereotyped characters.

Argument: The argument of a work is the author's subject matter or principal idea.

Art for Art's Sake: See *Aestheticism*

Assonance: The repetition of similar vowel sounds in poetry.

Audience: The people for whom a piece of literature is written. Authors usually write with a certain audience in mind, for example, children, members of a religious or ethnic group, or colleagues in a professional field. The term "audience" also applies to the people who gather to see or hear any performance, including plays, poetry readings, speeches, and concerts.

Automatic Writing: Writing carried out without a preconceived plan in an effort to capture every random thought. Authors who engage in automatic writing typically do not revise their work, preferring instead to preserve the revealed truth and beauty of spontaneous expression.

Avant-garde: A French term meaning "vanguard." It is used in literary criticism to describe new writing that rejects traditional approaches to literature in favor of innovations in style or content.

B

Ballad: A short poem that tells a simple story and has a repeated refrain. Ballads were originally intended to be sung. Early ballads, known as folk ballads, were passed down through generations, so their authors are often unknown. Later ballads composed by known authors are called literary ballads.

Baroque: A term used in literary criticism to describe literature that is complex or ornate in style or diction. Baroque works typically express tension, anxiety, and violent emotion. The term "Baroque Age" designates a period in Western European literature beginning in the late sixteenth century and ending about one hundred years later.

Works of this period often mirror the qualities of works more generally associated with the label "baroque" and sometimes feature elaborate conceits.

Baroque Age: See *Baroque*

Baroque Period: See *Baroque*

Beat Generation: See *Beat Movement*

Beat Movement: A period featuring a group of American poets and novelists of the 1950s and 1960s—including Jack Kerouac, Allen Ginsberg, Gregory Corso, William S. Burroughs, and Lawrence Ferlinghetti—who rejected established social and literary values. Using such techniques as stream-of-consciousness writing and jazz-influenced free verse and focusing on unusual or abnormal states of mind—generated by religious ecstasy or the use of drugs—the Beat writers aimed to create works that were unconventional in both form and subject matter.

Beat Poets: See *Beat Movement*

Beats, The: See *Beat Movement*

Belles-lettres: A French term meaning "fine letters" or "beautiful writing." It is often used as a synonym for literature, typically referring to imaginative and artistic rather than scientific or expository writing. Current usage sometimes restricts the meaning to light or humorous writing and appreciative essays about literature.

Black Aesthetic Movement: A period of artistic and literary development among African Americans in the 1960s and early 1970s. This was the first major African American artistic movement since the Harlem Renaissance and was closely paralleled by the civil rights and black power movements. The black aesthetic writers attempted to produce works of art that would be meaningful to the black masses. Key figures in black aesthetics included one of its founders, poet and playwright Amiri Baraka, formerly known as LeRoi Jones; poet and essayist Haki R. Madhubuti, formerly Don L. Lee; poet and playwright Sonia Sanchez; and dramatist Ed Bullins.

Black Arts Movement: See *Black Aesthetic Movement*

Black Comedy: See *Black Humor*

Black Humor: Writing that places grotesque elements side by side with humorous ones in an attempt to shock the reader, forcing him or her to laugh at the horrifying reality of a disordered world.

Black Mountain School: Black Mountain College and three of its instructors—Robert Creeley, Robert Duncan, and Charles Olson—were all influential in projective verse. Today poets working in projective verse are referred to as members of the Black Mountain school.

Blank Verse: Loosely, any unrhymed poetry, but more generally, unrhymed iambic pentameter verse (composed of lines of five two-syllable feet with the first syllable accented, the second unaccented). Blank verse has been used by poets since the Renaissance for its flexibility and its graceful, dignified tone.

Bloomsbury Group: A group of English writers, artists, and intellectuals who held informal artistic and philosophical discussions in Bloomsbury, a district of London, from around 1907 to the early 1930s. The Bloomsbury Group held no uniform philosophical beliefs but did commonly express an aversion to moral prudery and a desire for greater social tolerance.

Bon Mot: A French term meaning "good word." A *bon mot* is a witty remark or clever observation.

Breath Verse: See *Projective Verse*

Burlesque: Any literary work that uses exaggeration to make its subject appear ridiculous, either by treating a trivial subject with profound seriousness or by treating a dignified subject frivolously. The word "burlesque" may also be used as an adjective, as in "burlesque show," to mean "striptease act."

C

Cadence: The natural rhythm of language caused by the alternation of accented and unaccented syllables. Much modern poetry—notably free verse—deliberately manipulates cadence to create complex rhythmic effects.

Caesura: A pause in a line of poetry, usually occurring near the middle. It typically corresponds to a break in the natural rhythm or sense of the line but is sometimes shifted to create special meanings or rhythmic effects.

Canzone: A short Italian or Provencal lyric poem, commonly about love and often set to music. The *canzone* has no set form but typically contains five or six stanzas made up of seven to twenty lines of eleven syllables each. A shorter, five- to ten-line "envoy," or concluding stanza, completes the poem.

Carpe Diem: A Latin term meaning "seize the day." This is a traditional theme of poetry, especially lyrics. A *carpe diem* poem advises the reader or the person it addresses to live for today and enjoy the pleasures of the moment.

Catharsis: The release or purging of unwanted emotions—specifically fear and pity—brought about by exposure to art. The term was first used by the Greek philosopher Aristotle in his *Poetics* to refer to the desired effect of tragedy on spectators.

Celtic Renaissance: A period of Irish literary and cultural history at the end of the nineteenth century. Followers of the movement aimed to create a romantic vision of Celtic myth and legend. The most significant works of the Celtic Renaissance typically present a dreamy, unreal world, usually in reaction against the reality of contemporary problems.

Celtic Twilight: See *Celtic Renaissance*

Character: Broadly speaking, a person in a literary work. The actions of characters are what constitute the plot of a story, novel, or poem. There are numerous types of characters, ranging from simple, stereotypical figures to intricate, multifaceted ones. In the techniques of anthropomorphism and personification, animals—and even places or things—can assume aspects of character. "Characterization" is the process by which an author creates vivid, believable characters in a work of art. This may be done in a variety of ways, including (1) direct description of the character by the narrator; (2) the direct presentation of the speech, thoughts, or actions of the character; and (3) the responses of other characters to the character. The term "character" also refers to a form originated by the ancient Greek writer Theophrastus that later became popular in the seventeenth and eighteenth centuries. It is a short essay or sketch of a person who prominently displays a specific attribute or quality, such as miserliness or ambition.

Characterization: See *Character*

Classical: In its strictest definition in literary criticism, classicism refers to works of ancient Greek or Roman literature. The term may also be used to describe a literary work of recognized importance (a "classic") from any time period or literature that exhibits the traits of classicism.

Classicism: A term used in literary criticism to describe critical doctrines that have their roots in ancient Greek and Roman literature, philosophy, and art. Works associated with classicism typically exhibit restraint on the part of the author, unity of design and purpose, clarity, simplicity, logical organization, and respect for tradition.

Colloquialism: A word, phrase, or form of pronunciation that is acceptable in casual conversation but not in formal, written communication. It is considered more acceptable than slang.

Complaint: A lyric poem, popular in the Renaissance, in which the speaker expresses sorrow about his or her condition. Typically, the speaker's sadness is caused by an unresponsive lover, but some complaints cite other sources of unhappiness, such as poverty or fate.

Conceit: A clever and fanciful metaphor, usually expressed through elaborate and extended comparison, that presents a striking parallel between two seemingly dissimilar things—for example, elaborately comparing a beautiful woman to an object like a garden or the sun. The conceit was a popular device throughout the Elizabethan Age and Baroque Age and was the principal technique of the seventeenth-century English metaphysical poets. This usage of the word conceit is unrelated to the best-known definition of conceit as an arrogant attitude or behavior.

Concrete: Concrete is the opposite of abstract, and refers to a thing that actually exists or a description that allows the reader to experience an object or concept with the senses.

Concrete Poetry: Poetry in which visual elements play a large part in the poetic effect. Punctuation marks, letters, or words are arranged on a page to form a visual design: a cross, for example, or a bumblebee.

Confessional Poetry: A form of poetry in which the poet reveals very personal, intimate, sometimes shocking information about himself or herself.

Connotation: The impression that a word gives beyond its defined meaning. Connotations may be universally understood or may be significant only to a certain group.

Consonance: Consonance occurs in poetry when words appearing at the ends of two or more verses have similar final consonant sounds but have final vowel sounds that differ, as with "stuff" and "off."

Convention: Any widely accepted literary device, style, or form.

Corrido: A Mexican ballad.

Couplet: Two lines of poetry with the same rhyme and meter, often expressing a complete and self-contained thought.

Criticism: The systematic study and evaluation of literary works, usually based on a specific method or set of principles. An important part of literary studies since ancient times, the practice of criticism has given rise to numerous theories, methods, and "schools," sometimes producing conflicting, even contradictory, interpretations of literature in general as well as of individual works. Even such basic issues as what constitutes a poem or a novel have been the subject of much criticism over the centuries.

D

Dactyl: See *Foot*

Dadaism: A protest movement in art and literature founded by Tristan Tzara in 1916. Followers of the movement expressed their outrage at the destruction brought about by World War I by revolting against numerous forms of social convention. The Dadaists presented works marked by calculated madness and flamboyant nonsense. They stressed total freedom of expression, commonly through primitive displays of emotion and illogical, often senseless, poetry. The movement ended shortly after the war, when it was replaced by surrealism.

Decadent: See *Decadents*

Decadents: The followers of a nineteenth-century literary movement that had its beginnings in French aestheticism. Decadent literature displays a fascination with perverse and morbid states; a search for novelty and sensation—the "new thrill"; a preoccupation with mysticism; and a belief in the senselessness of human existence. The movement is closely associated with the doctrine Art for Art's Sake. The term "decadence" is sometimes used to denote a decline in the quality of art or literature following a period of greatness.

Deconstruction: A method of literary criticism developed by Jacques Derrida and characterized by multiple conflicting interpretations of a given work. Deconstructionists consider the impact of the language of a work and suggest that the true meaning of the work is not necessarily the meaning that the author intended.

Deduction: The process of reaching a conclusion through reasoning from general premises to a specific premise.

Denotation: The definition of a word, apart from the impressions or feelings it creates in the reader.

Diction: The selection and arrangement of words in a literary work. Either or both may vary depending on the desired effect. There are four general types of diction: "formal," used in scholarly or lofty writing; "informal," used in relaxed but educated conversation; "colloquial," used in everyday speech; and "slang," containing newly coined words and other terms not accepted in formal usage.

Didactic: A term used to describe works of literature that aim to teach some moral, religious, political, or practical lesson. Although didactic elements are often found in artistically pleasing works, the term "didactic" usually refers to literature in which the message is more important than the form. The term may also be used to criticize a work that the critic finds "overly didactic," that is, heavy-handed in its delivery of a lesson.

Dimeter: See *Meter*

Dionysian: See *Apollonian and Dionysian*

Discordia concours: A Latin phrase meaning "discord in harmony." The term was coined by the eighteenth-century English writer Samuel Johnson to describe "a combination of dissimilar images or discovery of occult resemblances in things apparently unlike." Johnson created the expression by reversing a phrase by the Latin poet Horace.

Dissonance: A combination of harsh or jarring sounds, especially in poetry. Although such combinations may be accidental, poets sometimes intentionally make them to achieve particular effects. Dissonance is also sometimes used to refer to close but not identical rhymes. When this is the case, the word functions as a synonym for consonance.

Double Entendre: A corruption of a French phrase meaning "double meaning." The term is used to indicate a word or phrase that is deliberately ambiguous, especially when one of the meanings is risque or improper.

Draft: Any preliminary version of a written work. An author may write dozens of drafts which are revised to form the final work, or he or she may write only one, with few or no revisions.

Dramatic Monologue: See *Monologue*

Dramatic Poetry: Any lyric work that employs elements of drama such as dialogue, conflict, or characterization, but excluding works that are intended for stage presentation.

Dream Allegory: See *Dream Vision*

Dream Vision: A literary convention, chiefly of the Middle Ages. In a dream vision a story is presented as a literal dream of the narrator. This device was commonly used to teach moral and religious lessons.

E

Eclogue: In classical literature, a poem featuring rural themes and structured as a dialogue among shepherds. Eclogues often took specific poetic forms, such as elegies or love poems. Some were written as the soliloquy of a shepherd. In later centuries, "eclogue" came to refer to any poem that was in the pastoral tradition or that had a dialogue or monologue structure.

Edwardian: Describes cultural conventions identified with the period of the reign of Edward VII of England (1901–1910). Writers of the Edwardian Age typically displayed a strong reaction against the propriety and conservatism of the Victorian Age. Their work often exhibits distrust of authority in religion, politics, and art and expresses strong doubts about the soundness of conventional values.

Edwardian Age: See *Edwardian*

Electra Complex: A daughter's amorous obsession with her father.

Elegy: A lyric poem that laments the death of a person or the eventual death of all people. In a conventional elegy, set in a classical world, the poet and subject are spoken of as shepherds. In modern criticism, the word elegy is often used to refer to a poem that is melancholy or mournfully contemplative.

Elizabethan Age: A period of great economic growth, religious controversy, and nationalism closely associated with the reign of Elizabeth I of England (1558–1603). The Elizabethan Age is considered a part of the general renaissance—that is, the flowering of arts and literature—that took place in Europe during the fourteenth through sixteenth centuries. The era is considered the golden age of English literature. The most important dramas in English and a great deal of lyric poetry were produced during this period, and modern English criticism began around this time.

Empathy: A sense of shared experience, including emotional and physical feelings, with someone or something other than oneself. Empathy is often used to describe the response of a reader to a literary character.

English Sonnet: See *Sonnet*

Enjambment: The running over of the sense and structure of a line of verse or a couplet into the following verse or couplet.

Enlightenment, The: An eighteenth-century philosophical movement. It began in France but had a wide impact throughout Europe and America. Thinkers of the Enlightenment valued reason and believed that both the individual and society could achieve a state of perfection. Corresponding to this essentially humanist vision was a resistance to religious authority.

Epic: A long narrative poem about the adventures of a hero of great historic or legendary importance. The setting is vast and the action is often given cosmic significance through the intervention of supernatural forces such as gods, angels, or demons. Epics are typically written in a classical style of grand simplicity with elaborate metaphors and allusions that enhance the symbolic importance of a hero's adventures.

Epic Simile: See *Homeric Simile*

Epigram: A saying that makes the speaker's point quickly and concisely.

Epilogue: A concluding statement or section of a literary work. In dramas, particularly those of the seventeenth and eighteenth centuries, the epilogue is a closing speech, often in verse, delivered by an actor at the end of a play and spoken directly to the audience.

Epiphany: A sudden revelation of truth inspired by a seemingly trivial incident.

Epitaph: An inscription on a tomb or tombstone, or a verse written on the occasion of a person's death. Epitaphs may be serious or humorous.

Epithalamion: A song or poem written to honor and commemorate a marriage ceremony.

Epithalamium: See *Epithalamion*

Epithet: A word or phrase, often disparaging or abusive, that expresses a character trait of someone or something.

Erziehungsroman: See *Bildungsroman*

Essay: A prose composition with a focused subject of discussion. The term was coined by Michel de Montaigne to describe his 1580 collection of brief, informal reflections on himself and on various topics relating to human nature. An essay can also be a long, systematic discourse.

Existentialism: A predominantly twentieth-century philosophy concerned with the nature and perception of human existence. There are two major strains of existentialist thought: atheistic and Christian. Followers of atheistic existentialism believe that the individual is alone in a godless universe and that the basic human condition is one of suffering and loneliness. Nevertheless, because there are no fixed values, individuals can create their own characters—indeed, they can shape themselves—through the exercise of free will. The atheistic strain culminates in and is popularly associated with the works of Jean-Paul Sartre. The Christian existentialists, on the other hand, believe that only in God may people find freedom from life's anguish. The two strains hold certain beliefs in common: that existence cannot be fully understood or described through empirical effort; that anguish is a universal element of life; that individuals must bear responsibility for their actions; and that there is no common standard of behavior or perception for religious and ethical matters.

Expatriates: See *Expatriatism*

Expatriatism: The practice of leaving one's country to live for an extended period in another country.

Exposition: Writing intended to explain the nature of an idea, thing, or theme. Expository writing is often combined with description, narration, or argument. In dramatic writing, the exposition is the introductory material which presents the characters, setting, and tone of the play.

Expressionism: An indistinct literary term, originally used to describe an early twentieth-century school of German painting. The term applies to almost any mode of unconventional, highly subjective writing that distorts reality in some way.

Extended Monologue: See *Monologue*

F

Feet: See *Foot*

Feminine Rhyme: See *Rhyme*

Fiction: Any story that is the product of imagination rather than a documentation of fact. Characters and events in such narratives may be based in real life but their ultimate form and configuration is a creation of the author.

Figurative Language: A technique in writing in which the author temporarily interrupts the order, construction, or meaning of the writing for a particular effect. This interruption takes the form of one or more figures of speech such as hyperbole, irony, or simile. Figurative language is the opposite of literal language, in which every word is truthful, accurate, and free of exaggeration or embellishment.

Figures of Speech: Writing that differs from customary conventions for construction, meaning, order, or significance for the purpose of a special meaning or effect. There are two major types of figures of speech: rhetorical figures, which do not make changes in the meaning of the words; and tropes, which do.

Fin de siecle: A French term meaning "end of the century." The term is used to denote the last decade of the nineteenth century, a transition period when writers and other artists abandoned old conventions and looked for new techniques and objectives.

First Person: See *Point of View*

Folk Ballad: See *Ballad*

Folklore: Traditions and myths preserved in a culture or group of people. Typically, these are passed on by word of mouth in various forms—such as legends, songs, and proverbs—or preserved in customs and ceremonies. This term was first used by W. J. Thoms in 1846.

Folktale: A story originating in oral tradition. Folktales fall into a variety of categories, including legends, ghost stories, fairy tales, fables, and anecdotes based on historical figures and events.

Foot: The smallest unit of rhythm in a line of poetry. In English-language poetry, a foot is typically one accented syllable combined with one or two unaccented syllables.

Form: The pattern or construction of a work which identifies its genre and distinguishes it from other genres.

Formalism: In literary criticism, the belief that literature should follow prescribed rules of construction, such as those that govern the sonnet form.

Fourteener Meter: See *Meter*

Free Verse: Poetry that lacks regular metrical and rhyme patterns but that tries to capture the cadences of everyday speech. The form allows a poet to exploit a variety of rhythmical effects within a single poem.

Futurism: A flamboyant literary and artistic movement that developed in France, Italy, and Russia from 1908 through the 1920s. Futurist theater and poetry abandoned traditional literary forms. In their place, followers of the movement attempted to achieve total freedom of expression through bizarre imagery and deformed or newly invented words. The Futurists were self-consciously modern artists who attempted to incorporate the appearances and sounds of modern life into their work.

G

Genre: A category of literary work. In critical theory, genre may refer to both the content of a given work—tragedy, comedy, pastoral—and to its form, such as poetry, novel, or drama.

Genteel Tradition: A term coined by critic George Santayana to describe the literary practice of certain late nineteenth-century American writers, especially New Englanders. Followers of the Genteel

Tradition emphasized conventionality in social, religious, moral, and literary standards.

Georgian Age: See *Georgian Poets*

Georgian Period: See *Georgian Poets*

Georgian Poets: A loose grouping of English poets during the years 1912–1922. The Georgians reacted against certain literary schools and practices, especially Victorian wordiness, turn-of-the-century aestheticism, and contemporary urban realism. In their place, the Georgians embraced the nineteenth-century poetic practices of William Wordsworth and the other Lake Poets.

Georgic: A poem about farming and the farmer's way of life, named from Virgil's *Georgics*.

Gilded Age: A period in American history during the 1870s characterized by political corruption and materialism. A number of important novels of social and political criticism were written during this time.

Gothic: See *Gothicism*

Gothicism: In literary criticism, works characterized by a taste for the medieval or morbidly attractive. A gothic novel prominently features elements of horror, the supernatural, gloom, and violence: clanking chains, terror, charnel houses, ghosts, medieval castles, and mysteriously slamming doors. The term "gothic novel" is also applied to novels that lack elements of the traditional Gothic setting but that create a similar atmosphere of terror or dread.

Graveyard School: A group of eighteenth-century English poets who wrote long, picturesque meditations on death. Their works were designed to cause the reader to ponder immortality.

Great Chain of Being: The belief that all things and creatures in nature are organized in a hierarchy from inanimate objects at the bottom to God at the top. This system of belief was popular in the seventeenth and eighteenth centuries.

Grotesque: In literary criticism, the subject matter of a work or a style of expression characterized by exaggeration, deformity, freakishness, and disorder. The grotesque often includes an element of comic absurdity.

H

Haiku: The shortest form of Japanese poetry, constructed in three lines of five, seven, and five syllables respectively. The message of a *haiku* poem usually centers on some aspect of spirituality and provokes an emotional response in the reader.

Half Rhyme: See *Consonance*

Harlem Renaissance: The Harlem Renaissance of the 1920s is generally considered the first significant movement of black writers and artists in the United States. During this period, new and established black writers published more fiction and poetry than ever before, the first influential black literary journals were established, and black authors and artists received their first widespread recognition and serious critical appraisal. Among the major writers associated with this period are Claude McKay, Jean Toomer, Countee Cullen, Langston Hughes, Arna Bontemps, Nella Larsen, and Zora Neale Hurston.

Hellenism: Imitation of ancient Greek thought or styles. Also, an approach to life that focuses on the growth and development of the intellect. "Hellenism" is sometimes used to refer to the belief that reason can be applied to examine all human experience.

Heptameter: See *Meter*

Hero/Heroine: The principal sympathetic character (male or female) in a literary work. Heroes and heroines typically exhibit admirable traits: idealism, courage, and integrity, for example.

Heroic Couplet: A rhyming couplet written in iambic pentameter (a verse with five iambic feet).

Heroic Line: The meter and length of a line of verse in epic or heroic poetry. This varies by language and time period.

Heroine: See *Hero/Heroine*

Hexameter: See *Meter*

Historical Criticism: The study of a work based on its impact on the world of the time period in which it was written.

Hokku: See *Haiku*

Holocaust: See *Holocaust Literature*

Holocaust Literature: Literature influenced by or written about the Holocaust of World War II. Such literature includes true stories of survival in concentration camps, escape, and life after the war, as well as fictional works and poetry.

Homeric Simile: An elaborate, detailed comparison written as a simile many lines in length.

Horatian Satire: See *Satire*

Humanism: A philosophy that places faith in the dignity of humankind and rejects the medieval perception of the individual as a weak, fallen creature. "Humanists" typically believe in the perfectibility of human nature and view reason and education as the means to that end.

Humors: Mentions of the humors refer to the ancient Greek theory that a person's health and personality were determined by the balance of four basic fluids in the body: blood, phlegm, yellow bile, and black bile. A dominance of any fluid would cause extremes in behavior. An excess of blood created a sanguine person who was joyful, aggressive, and passionate; a phlegmatic person was shy, fearful, and sluggish; too much yellow bile led to a choleric temperament characterized by impatience, anger, bitterness, and stubbornness; and excessive black bile created melancholy, a state of laziness, gluttony, and lack of motivation.

Humours: See *Humors*

Hyperbole: In literary criticism, deliberate exaggeration used to achieve an effect.

I

Iamb: See *Foot*

Idiom: A word construction or verbal expression closely associated with a given language.

Image: A concrete representation of an object or sensory experience. Typically, such a representation helps evoke the feelings associated with the object or experience itself. Images are either "literal" or "figurative." Literal images are especially concrete and involve little or no extension of the obvious meaning of the words used to express them. Figurative images do not follow the literal meaning of the words exactly. Images in literature are usually visual, but the term "image" can also refer to the representation of any sensory experience.

Imagery: The array of images in a literary work. Also, figurative language.

Imagism: An English and American poetry movement that flourished between 1908 and 1917. The Imagists used precise, clearly presented images in their works. They also used common, everyday speech and aimed for conciseness, concrete imagery, and the creation of new rhythms.

In medias res: A Latin term meaning "in the middle of things." It refers to the technique of beginning a story at its midpoint and then using various flashback devices to reveal previous action.

Induction: The process of reaching a conclusion by reasoning from specific premises to form a general premise. Also, an introductory portion of a work of literature, especially a play.

Intentional Fallacy: The belief that judgments of a literary work based solely on an author's stated or implied intentions are false and misleading. Critics who believe in the concept of the intentional fallacy typically argue that the work itself is sufficient matter for interpretation, even though they may concede that an author's statement of purpose can be useful.

Interior Monologue: A narrative technique in which characters' thoughts are revealed in a way that appears to be uncontrolled by the author. The interior monologue typically aims to reveal the inner self of a character. It portrays emotional experiences as they occur at both a conscious and unconscious level. Images are often used to represent sensations or emotions.

Internal Rhyme: Rhyme that occurs within a single line of verse.

Irish Literary Renaissance: A late nineteenth- and early twentieth-century movement in Irish literature. Members of the movement aimed to reduce the influence of British culture in Ireland and create an Irish national literature.

Irony: In literary criticism, the effect of language in which the intended meaning is the opposite of what is stated.

Italian Sonnet: See *Sonnet*

J

Jacobean Age: The period of the reign of James I of England (1603–1625). The early literature of this period reflected the worldview of the Elizabethan Age, but a darker, more cynical attitude steadily grew in the art and literature of the Jacobean Age. This was an important time for English drama and poetry.

Jargon: Language that is used or understood only by a select group of people. Jargon may refer to terminology used in a certain profession, such as computer jargon, or it may refer to any nonsensical language that is not understood by most people.

Journalism: Writing intended for publication in a newspaper or magazine, or for broadcast on a radio or television program featuring news, sports, entertainment, or other timely material.

K

Knickerbocker Group: A somewhat indistinct group of New York writers of the first half of the nineteenth century. Members of the group were linked only by location and a common theme: New York life.

Kunstlerroman: See *Bildungsroman*

L

Lais: See *Lay*

Lake Poets: See *Lake School*

Lake School: These poets all lived in the Lake District of England at the turn of the nineteenth century. As a group, they followed no single "school" of thought or literary practice, although their works were uniformly disparaged by the *Edinburgh Review.*

Lay: A song or simple narrative poem. The form originated in medieval France. Early French *lais* were often based on the Celtic legends and other tales sung by Breton minstrels—thus the name of the "Breton lay." In fourteenth-century England, the term "lay" was used to describe short narratives written in imitation of the Breton lays.

Leitmotiv: See *Motif*

Literal Language: An author uses literal language when he or she writes without exaggerating or embellishing the subject matter and without any tools of figurative language.

Literary Ballad: See *Ballad*

Literature: Literature is broadly defined as any written or spoken material, but the term most often refers to creative works.

Lost Generation: A term first used by Gertrude Stein to describe the post-World War I generation of American writers: men and women haunted by a sense of betrayal and emptiness brought about by the destructiveness of the war.

Lyric Poetry: A poem expressing the subjective feelings and personal emotions of the poet. Such poetry is melodic, since it was originally accompanied by a lyre in recitals. Most Western poetry in the twentieth century may be classified as lyrical.

M

Mannerism: Exaggerated, artificial adherence to a literary manner or style. Also, a popular style of the visual arts of late sixteenth-century Europe that was marked by elongation of the human form and by intentional spatial distortion. Literary works that are self-consciously high-toned and artistic are often said to be "mannered."

Masculine Rhyme: See *Rhyme*

Measure: The foot, verse, or time sequence used in a literary work, especially a poem. Measure is often used somewhat incorrectly as a synonym for meter.

Metaphor: A figure of speech that expresses an idea through the image of another object. Metaphors suggest the essence of the first object by identifying it with certain qualities of the second object.

Metaphysical Conceit: See *Conceit*

Metaphysical Poetry: The body of poetry produced by a group of seventeenth-century English writers called the "Metaphysical Poets." The group includes John Donne and Andrew Marvell. The Metaphysical Poets made use of everyday speech, intellectual analysis, and unique imagery. They aimed to portray the ordinary conflicts and contradictions of life. Their poems often took the form of an argument, and many of them emphasize physical and religious love as well as the fleeting nature of life. Elaborate conceits are typical in metaphysical poetry.

Metaphysical Poets: See *Metaphysical Poetry*

Meter: In literary criticism, the repetition of sound patterns that creates a rhythm in poetry. The patterns are based on the number of syllables and the presence and absence of accents. The unit of rhythm in a line is called a foot. Types of meter are classified according to the number of feet in a line. These are the standard English lines: Monometer, one foot; Dimeter, two feet; Trimeter, three feet; Tetrameter, four feet; Pentameter, five feet; Hexameter, six feet (also called the Alexandrine); Heptameter, seven feet (also called the "Fourteener" when the feet are iambic).

Modernism: Modern literary practices. Also, the principles of a literary school that lasted from roughly the beginning of the twentieth century until the end of World War II. Modernism is defined by its rejection of the literary conventions of the nineteenth century and by its opposition to conventional morality, taste, traditions, and economic values.

Monologue: A composition, written or oral, by a single individual. More specifically, a speech given by a single individual in a drama or other public entertainment. It has no set length, although it is usually several or more lines long.

Monometer: See *Meter*

Mood: The prevailing emotions of a work or of the author in his or her creation of the work. The mood of a work is not always what might be expected based on its subject matter.

Motif: A theme, character type, image, metaphor, or other verbal element that recurs throughout a single work of literature or occurs in a number of different works over a period of time.

***Motiv*:** See *Motif*

Muckrakers: An early twentieth-century group of American writers. Typically, their works exposed the wrongdoings of big business and government in the United States.

Muses: Nine Greek mythological goddesses, the daughters of Zeus and Mnemosyne (Memory). Each muse patronized a specific area of the liberal arts and sciences. Calliope presided over epic poetry, Clio over history, Erato over love poetry, Euterpe over music or lyric poetry, Melpomene over tragedy, Polyhymnia over hymns to the gods, Terpsichore over dance, Thalia over comedy, and Urania over astronomy. Poets and writers traditionally made appeals to the Muses for inspiration in their work.

Myth: An anonymous tale emerging from the traditional beliefs of a culture or social unit. Myths use supernatural explanations for natural phenomena. They may also explain cosmic issues like creation and death. Collections of myths, known as mythologies, are common to all cultures and nations, but the best-known myths belong to the Norse, Roman, and Greek mythologies.

N

Narration: The telling of a series of events, real or invented. A narration may be either a simple narrative, in which the events are recounted chronologically, or a narrative with a plot, in which the account is given in a style reflecting the author's artistic concept of the story. Narration is sometimes used as a synonym for "storyline."

Narrative: A verse or prose accounting of an event or sequence of events, real or invented. The term is also used as an adjective in the sense "method of narration." For example, in literary criticism, the expression "narrative technique" usually refers to the way the author structures and presents his or her story.

Narrative Poetry: A nondramatic poem in which the author tells a story. Such poems may be of any length or level of complexity.

Narrator: The teller of a story. The narrator may be the author or a character in the story through whom the author speaks.

Naturalism: A literary movement of the late nineteenth and early twentieth centuries. The movement's major theorist, French novelist Emile Zola, envisioned a type of fiction that would examine human life with the objectivity of scientific inquiry. The Naturalists typically viewed human beings as either the products of "biological determinism," ruled by hereditary instincts and engaged in an endless struggle for survival, or as the products of "socioeconomic determinism," ruled by social and economic forces beyond their control. In their works, the Naturalists generally ignored the highest levels of society and focused on degradation: poverty, alcoholism, prostitution, insanity, and disease.

Negritude: A literary movement based on the concept of a shared cultural bond on the part of black Africans, wherever they may be in the world. It traces its origins to the former French colonies of Africa and the Caribbean. Negritude poets, novelists, and essayists generally stress four points in their writings: One, black alienation from traditional African culture can lead to feelings of inferiority. Two, European colonialism and Western education should be resisted. Three, black Africans should seek to affirm and define their own identity. Four, African culture can and should be reclaimed. Many Negritude writers also claim that blacks can make unique contributions to the world, based on a heightened appreciation of nature, rhythm, and human emotions—aspects of life they say are not so highly valued in the materialistic and rationalistic West.

Negro Renaissance: See *Harlem Renaissance*

Neoclassical Period: See *Neoclassicism*

Neoclassicism: In literary criticism, this term refers to the revival of the attitudes and styles of expression of classical literature. It is generally used to describe a period in European history beginning in the late seventeenth century and lasting until about 1800. In its purest form, Neoclassicism marked a return to order, proportion, restraint, logic, accuracy, and decorum. In England, where Neoclassicism perhaps was most popular, it reflected the influence of seventeenth-century French writers, especially dramatists. Neoclassical writers typically reacted against the intensity and enthusiasm of the Renaissance period. They wrote works that appealed to the intellect, using elevated language and classical literary forms such as satire and the ode. Neoclassical works were often governed by the classical goal of instruction.

Neoclassicists: See *Neoclassicism*

New Criticism: A movement in literary criticism, dating from the late 1920s, that stressed close textual analysis in the interpretation of works of literature. The New Critics saw little merit in historical and biographical analysis. Rather, they aimed to examine the text alone, free from the question of how external events—biographical or otherwise—may have helped shape it.

New Journalism: A type of writing in which the journalist presents factual information in a form usually used in fiction. New journalism emphasizes description, narration, and character development to bring readers closer to the human element of the story, and is often used in personality profiles and in-depth feature articles. It is not compatible with "straight" or "hard" newswriting, which is generally composed in a brief, fact-based style.

New Journalists: See *New Journalism*

New Negro Movement: See *Harlem Renaissance*

Noble Savage: The idea that primitive man is noble and good but becomes evil and corrupted as he becomes civilized. The concept of the noble savage originated in the Renaissance period but is more closely identified with such later writers as Jean-Jacques Rousseau and Aphra Behn.

O

Objective Correlative: An outward set of objects, a situation, or a chain of events corresponding to an inward experience and evoking this experience in the reader. The term frequently appears in modern criticism in discussions of authors' intended effects on the emotional responses of readers.

Objectivity: A quality in writing characterized by the absence of the author's opinion or feeling about the subject matter. Objectivity is an important factor in criticism.

Occasional Verse: Poetry written on the occasion of a significant historical or personal event. *Vers de societe* is sometimes called occasional verse although it is of a less serious nature.

Octave: A poem or stanza composed of eight lines. The term octave most often represents the first eight lines of a Petrarchan sonnet.

Ode: Name given to an extended lyric poem characterized by exalted emotion and dignified style. An ode usually concerns a single, serious theme. Most odes, but not all, are addressed to an object or individual. Odes are distinguished from other lyric poetic forms by their complex rhythmic and stanzaic patterns.

Oedipus Complex: A son's amorous obsession with his mother. The phrase is derived from the story of the ancient Theban hero Oedipus, who unknowingly killed his father and married his mother.

Omniscience: See *Point of View*

Onomatopoeia: The use of words whose sounds express or suggest their meaning. In its simplest sense, onomatopoeia may be represented by words that mimic the sounds they denote such as "hiss" or "meow." At a more subtle level, the pattern and rhythm of sounds and rhymes of a line or poem may be onomatopoeic.

Oral Tradition: See *Oral Transmission*

Oral Transmission: A process by which songs, ballads, folklore, and other material are transmitted by word of mouth. The tradition of oral transmission predates the written record systems of literate society. Oral transmission preserves material sometimes over generations, although often with variations. Memory plays a large part in the recitation and preservation of orally transmitted material.

Ottava Rima: An eight-line stanza of poetry composed in iambic pentameter (a five-foot line in which each foot consists of an unaccented syllable followed by an accented syllable), following the *abababcc* rhyme scheme.

Oxymoron: A phrase combining two contradictory terms. Oxymorons may be intentional or unintentional.

P

Pantheism: The idea that all things are both a manifestation or revelation of God and a part of God at the same time. Pantheism was a common attitude in the early societies of Egypt, India, and Greece—the term derives from the Greek *pan* meaning "all" and *theos* meaning "deity." It later became a significant part of the Christian faith.

Parable: A story intended to teach a moral lesson or answer an ethical question.

Paradox: A statement that appears illogical or contradictory at first, but may actually point to an underlying truth.

Parallelism: A method of comparison of two ideas in which each is developed in the same grammatical structure.

Parnassianism: A mid nineteenth-century movement in French literature. Followers of the movement stressed adherence to well-defined artistic forms as a reaction against the often chaotic expression of the artist's ego that dominated the work of the Romantics. The Parnassians also rejected the moral, ethical, and social themes exhibited in the works of French Romantics such as Victor Hugo. The aesthetic doctrines of the Parnassians strongly influenced the later symbolist and decadent movements.

Parody: In literary criticism, this term refers to an imitation of a serious literary work or the signature style of a particular author in a ridiculous manner. A typical parody adopts the style of the original and applies it to an inappropriate subject for humorous effect. Parody is a form of satire and could be considered the literary equivalent of a caricature or cartoon.

Pastoral: A term derived from the Latin word "pastor," meaning shepherd. A pastoral is a literary composition on a rural theme. The conventions of the pastoral were originated by the third-century Greek poet Theocritus, who wrote about the experiences, love affairs, and pastimes of Sicilian shepherds. In a pastoral, characters and language of a courtly nature are often placed in a simple setting. The term pastoral is also used to classify dramas, elegies, and lyrics that exhibit the use of country settings and shepherd characters.

Pathetic Fallacy: A term coined by English critic John Ruskin to identify writing that falsely endows nonhuman things with human intentions and feelings, such as "angry clouds" and "sad trees."

Pen Name: See *Pseudonym*

Pentameter: See *Meter*

Persona: A Latin term meaning "mask." *Personae* are the characters in a fictional work of literature. The *persona* generally functions as a mask through which the author tells a story in a voice other than his or her own. A *persona* is usually either a character in a story who acts as a narrator or an "implied author," a voice created by the author to act as the narrator for himself or herself.

Personae: See *Persona*

Personal Point of View: See *Point of View*

Personification: A figure of speech that gives human qualities to abstract ideas, animals, and inanimate objects.

Petrarchan Sonnet: See *Sonnet*

Phenomenology: A method of literary criticism based on the belief that things have no existence outside of human consciousness or awareness. Proponents of this theory believe that art is a process that takes place in the mind of the observer as he or she contemplates an object rather than a quality of the object itself.

Plagiarism: Claiming another person's written material as one's own. Plagiarism can take the form of direct, word-for-word copying or the theft of the substance or idea of the work.

Platonic Criticism: A form of criticism that stresses an artistic work's usefulness as an agent of social engineering rather than any quality or value of the work itself.

Platonism: The embracing of the doctrines of the philosopher Plato, popular among the poets of the Renaissance and the Romantic period. Platonism is more flexible than Aristotelian Criticism and places more emphasis on the supernatural and unknown aspects of life.

Plot: In literary criticism, this term refers to the pattern of events in a narrative or drama. In its simplest sense, the plot guides the author in composing the work and helps the reader follow the work. Typically, plots exhibit causality and unity and have a beginning, a middle, and an end. Sometimes, however, a plot may consist of a series of disconnected events, in which case it is known as an "episodic plot."

Poem: In its broadest sense, a composition utilizing rhyme, meter, concrete detail, and expressive language to create a literary experience with emotional and aesthetic appeal.

Poet: An author who writes poetry or verse. The term is also used to refer to an artist or writer who has an exceptional gift for expression, imagination, and energy in the making of art in any form.

Poete maudit: A term derived from Paul Verlaine's *Les poetes maudits* (*The Accursed Poets*), a collection of essays on the French symbolist writers Stephane Mallarme, Arthur Rimbaud, and Tristan Corbiere. In the sense intended by Verlaine, the poet is "accursed" for choosing to explore extremes of human experience outside of middle-class society.

Poetic Fallacy: See *Pathetic Fallacy*

Poetic Justice: An outcome in a literary work, not necessarily a poem, in which the good are rewarded and the evil are punished, especially in ways that particularly fit their virtues or crimes.

Poetic License: Distortions of fact and literary convention made by a writer—not always a poet—for the sake of the effect gained. Poetic license is closely related to the concept of "artistic freedom."

Poetics: This term has two closely related meanings. It denotes (1) an aesthetic theory in literary criticism about the essence of poetry or (2) rules prescribing the proper methods, content, style, or diction of poetry. The term poetics may also refer to theories about literature in general, not just poetry.

Poetry: In its broadest sense, writing that aims to present ideas and evoke an emotional experience in the reader through the use of meter, imagery, connotative and concrete words, and a carefully constructed structure based on rhythmic patterns. Poetry typically relies on words and expressions that have several layers of meaning. It also makes use of the effects of regular rhythm on the ear and may make a strong appeal to the senses through the use of imagery.

Point of View: The narrative perspective from which a literary work is presented to the reader. There are four traditional points of view. The "third person omniscient" gives the reader a "godlike" perspective, unrestricted by time or place, from which to see actions and look into the minds of characters. This allows the author to comment openly on characters and events in the work. The "third-person" point of view presents the events of the story from outside of any single character's perception, much like the omniscient point of view, but the reader must understand the action as it takes place and without any special insight into characters' minds or motivations. The "first person" or "personal" point of view relates events as they are perceived by a single character. The main character "tells" the story and may offer opinions about the action and characters which differ from those of the author. Much less common than omniscient, third person, and first person is the "second-person" point of view, wherein the author tells the story as if it is happening to the reader.

Polemic: A work in which the author takes a stand on a controversial subject, such as abortion or religion. Such works are often extremely argumentative or provocative.

Pornography: Writing intended to provoke feelings of lust in the reader. Such works are often condemned by critics and teachers, but those which can be shown to have literary value are viewed less harshly.

Post-Aesthetic Movement: An artistic response made by African Americans to the black aesthetic movement of the 1960s and early 1970s. Writers since that time have adopted a somewhat different tone in their work, with less emphasis placed on the disparity between black and white in the United States. In the words of post-aesthetic authors such as Toni Morrison, John Edgar Wideman, and Kristin Hunter, African Americans are portrayed as looking inward for answers to their own questions, rather than always looking to the outside world.

Postmodernism: Writing from the 1960s forward characterized by experimentation and continuing to apply some of the fundamentals of modernism, which included existentialism and alienation. Postmodernists have gone a step further in the rejection of tradition begun with the modernists by also rejecting traditional forms, preferring the antinovel over the novel and the antihero over the hero.

Pre-Raphaelites: A circle of writers and artists in mid nineteenth-century England. Valuing the pre-Renaissance artistic qualities of religious symbolism, lavish pictorialism, and natural sensuousness, the Pre-Raphaelites cultivated a sense of mystery and melancholy that influenced later writers associated with the Symbolist and Decadent movements.

Primitivism: The belief that primitive peoples were nobler and less flawed than civilized peoples because they had not been subjected to the corrupt influence of society.

Projective Verse: A form of free verse in which the poet's breathing pattern determines the lines of the poem. Poets who advocate projective verse are against all formal structures in writing, including meter and form.

Prologue: An introductory section of a literary work. It often contains information establishing the situation of the characters or presents information about the setting, time period, or action. In drama, the prologue is spoken by a chorus or by one of the principal characters.

Prose: A literary medium that attempts to mirror the language of everyday speech. It is distinguished from poetry by its use of unmetered, unrhymed language consisting of logically related sentences. Prose is usually grouped into paragraphs that form a cohesive whole such as an essay or a novel.

Prosopopoeia: See *Personification*

Protagonist: The central character of a story who serves as a focus for its themes and incidents and as the principal rationale for its development. The protagonist is sometimes referred to in discussions of modern literature as the hero or antihero.

Proverb: A brief, sage saying that expresses a truth about life in a striking manner.

Pseudonym: A name assumed by a writer, most often intended to prevent his or her identification as the author of a work. Two or more authors may work together under one pseudonym, or an author may use a different name for each genre he or she publishes in. Some publishing companies maintain "house pseudonyms," under which any number of authors may write installations in a series. Some authors also choose a pseudonym over their real names the way an actor may use a stage name.

Pun: A play on words that have similar sounds but different meanings.

Pure Poetry: poetry written without instructional intent or moral purpose that aims only to please a reader by its imagery or musical flow. The term pure poetry is used as the antonym of the term "didacticism."

Q

Quatrain: A four-line stanza of a poem or an entire poem consisting of four lines.

R

Realism: A nineteenth-century European literary movement that sought to portray familiar characters, situations, and settings in a realistic manner. This was done primarily by using an objective narrative point of view and through the buildup of accurate detail. The standard for success of any realistic work depends on how faithfully it transfers common experience into fictional forms. The realistic method may be altered or extended, as in stream of consciousness writing, to record highly subjective experience.

Refrain: A phrase repeated at intervals throughout a poem. A refrain may appear at the end of each stanza or at less regular intervals. It may be altered slightly at each appearance.

Renaissance: The period in European history that marked the end of the Middle Ages. It began in Italy in the late fourteenth century. In broad terms, it is usually seen as spanning the fourteenth, fifteenth, and sixteenth centuries, although it did not reach Great Britain, for example, until the 1480s or so. The Renaissance saw an awakening in almost every sphere of human activity, especially science, philosophy, and the arts. The period is best defined by the emergence of a general philosophy that emphasized the importance of the intellect, the individual, and world affairs. It contrasts strongly with the medieval worldview, characterized by the dominant concerns of faith, the social collective, and spiritual salvation.

Repartee: Conversation featuring snappy retorts and witticisms.

Restoration: See *Restoration Age*

Restoration Age: A period in English literature beginning with the crowning of Charles II in 1660 and running to about 1700. The era, which was characterized by a reaction against Puritanism, was the first great age of the comedy of manners. The finest literature of the era is typically witty and urbane, and often lewd.

Rhetoric: In literary criticism, this term denotes the art of ethical persuasion. In its strictest sense, rhetoric adheres to various principles developed since classical times for arranging facts and ideas in a clear, persuasive, appealing manner. The term is also used to refer to effective prose in general and theories of or methods for composing effective prose.

Rhetorical Question: A question intended to provoke thought, but not an expressed answer, in the reader. It is most commonly used in oratory and other persuasive genres.

Rhyme: When used as a noun in literary criticism, this term generally refers to a poem in which words sound identical or very similar and appear in parallel positions in two or more lines. Rhymes are classified into different types according to where they fall in a line or stanza or according to the degree of similarity they exhibit in their spellings and sounds. Some major types of rhyme are "masculine" rhyme, "feminine" rhyme, and "triple" rhyme. In a masculine rhyme, the rhyming sound falls in a single accented syllable, as with "heat" and "eat." Feminine rhyme is a rhyme of two syllables, one stressed and one unstressed, as with "merry" and "tarry." Triple rhyme matches the sound of the accented syllable and the two unaccented syllables that follow: "narrative" and "declarative."

Rhyme Royal: A stanza of seven lines composed in iambic pentameter and rhymed *ababbcc*. The name is said to be a tribute to King James I of Scotland, who made much use of the form in his poetry.

Rhyme Scheme: See *Rhyme*

Rhythm: A regular pattern of sound, time intervals, or events occurring in writing, most often and most discernably in poetry. Regular, reliable rhythm is known to be soothing to humans, while interrupted, unpredictable, or rapidly changing rhythm is disturbing. These effects are known to authors, who use them to produce a desired reaction in the reader.

Rococo: A style of European architecture that flourished in the eighteenth century, especially in

France. The most notable features of *rococo* are its extensive use of ornamentation and its themes of lightness, gaiety, and intimacy. In literary criticism, the term is often used disparagingly to refer to a decadent or overly ornamental style.

Romance: A broad term, usually denoting a narrative with exotic, exaggerated, often idealized characters, scenes, and themes.

Romantic Age: See *Romanticism*

Romanticism: This term has two widely accepted meanings. In historical criticism, it refers to a European intellectual and artistic movement of the late eighteenth and early nineteenth centuries that sought greater freedom of personal expression than that allowed by the strict rules of literary form and logic of the eighteenth-century Neoclassicists. The Romantics preferred emotional and imaginative expression to rational analysis. They considered the individual to be at the center of all experience and so placed him or her at the center of their art. The Romantics believed that the creative imagination reveals nobler truths—unique feelings and attitudes—than those that could be discovered by logic or by scientific examination. Both the natural world and the state of childhood were important sources for revelations of "eternal truths." "Romanticism" is also used as a general term to refer to a type of sensibility found in all periods of literary history and usually considered to be in opposition to the principles of classicism. In this sense, Romanticism signifies any work or philosophy in which the exotic or dreamlike figure strongly, or that is devoted to individualistic expression, self-analysis, or a pursuit of a higher realm of knowledge than can be discovered by human reason.

Romantics: See *Romanticism*

Russian Symbolism: A Russian poetic movement, derived from French symbolism, that flourished between 1894 and 1910. While some Russian Symbolists continued in the French tradition, stressing aestheticism and the importance of suggestion above didactic intent, others saw their craft as a form of mystical worship, and themselves as mediators between the supernatural and the mundane.

S

Satire: A work that uses ridicule, humor, and wit to criticize and provoke change in human nature and institutions. There are two major types of satire: "formal" or "direct" satire speaks directly to the reader or to a character in the work; "indirect" satire relies upon the ridiculous behavior of its characters to make its point. Formal satire is further divided into two manners: the "Horatian," which ridicules gently, and the "Juvenalian," which derides its subjects harshly and bitterly.

Scansion: The analysis or "scanning" of a poem to determine its meter and often its rhyme scheme. The most common system of scansion uses accents (slanted lines drawn above syllables) to show stressed syllables, breves (curved lines drawn above syllables) to show unstressed syllables, and vertical lines to separate each foot.

Second Person: See *Point of View*

Semiotics: The study of how literary forms and conventions affect the meaning of language.

Sestet: Any six-line poem or stanza.

Setting: The time, place, and culture in which the action of a narrative takes place. The elements of setting may include geographic location, characters' physical and mental environments, prevailing cultural attitudes, or the historical time in which the action takes place.

Shakespearean Sonnet: See *Sonnet*

Signifying Monkey: A popular trickster figure in black folklore, with hundreds of tales about this character documented since the nineteenth century.

Simile: A comparison, usually using "like" or "as," of two essentially dissimilar things, as in "coffee as cold as ice" or "He sounded like a broken record."

Slang: A type of informal verbal communication that is generally unacceptable for formal writing. Slang words and phrases are often colorful exaggerations used to emphasize the speaker's point; they may also be shortened versions of an often-used word or phrase.

Slant Rhyme: See *Consonance*

Slave Narrative: Autobiographical accounts of American slave life as told by escaped slaves. These works first appeared during the abolition movement of the 1830s through the 1850s.

Social Realism: See *Socialist Realism*

Socialist Realism: The Socialist Realism school of literary theory was proposed by Maxim Gorky and established as a dogma by the first Soviet Congress of Writers. It demanded adherence to a communist worldview in works of literature. Its doctrines required an objective viewpoint comprehensible to the working classes and themes of social struggle featuring strong proletarian heroes.

Soliloquy: A monologue in a drama used to give the audience information and to develop the speaker's character. It is typically a projection of the speaker's innermost thoughts. Usually delivered while the speaker is alone on stage, a soliloquy is intended to present an illusion of unspoken reflection.

Sonnet: A fourteen-line poem, usually composed in iambic pentameter, employing one of several rhyme schemes. There are three major types of sonnets, upon which all other variations of the form are based: the "Petrarchan" or "Italian" sonnet, the "Shakespearean" or "English" sonnet, and the "Spenserian" sonnet. A Petrarchan sonnet consists of an octave rhymed *abbaabba* and a "sestet" rhymed either *cdecde, cdccdc,* or *cdedce.* The octave poses a question or problem, relates a narrative, or puts forth a proposition; the sestet presents a solution to the problem, comments upon the narrative, or applies the proposition put forth in the octave. The Shakespearean sonnet is divided into three quatrains and a couplet rhymed *abab cdcd efef gg.* The couplet provides an epigrammatic comment on the narrative or problem put forth in the quatrains. The Spenserian sonnet uses three quatrains and a couplet like the Shakespearean, but links their three rhyme schemes in this way: *abab bcbc cdcd ee.* The Spenserian sonnet develops its theme in two parts like the Petrarchan, its final six lines resolving a problem, analyzing a narrative, or applying a proposition put forth in its first eight lines.

Spenserian Sonnet: See *Sonnet*

Spenserian Stanza: A nine-line stanza having eight verses in iambic pentameter, its ninth verse in iambic hexameter, and the rhyme scheme *ababbcbcc.*

Spondee: In poetry meter, a foot consisting of two long or stressed syllables occurring together. This form is quite rare in English verse, and is usually composed of two monosyllabic words.

Sprung Rhythm: Versification using a specific number of accented syllables per line but disregarding the number of unaccented syllables that fall in each line, producing an irregular rhythm in the poem.

Stanza: A subdivision of a poem consisting of lines grouped together, often in recurring patterns of rhyme, line length, and meter. Stanzas may also serve as units of thought in a poem much like paragraphs in prose.

Stereotype: A stereotype was originally the name for a duplication made during the printing process; this led to its modern definition as a person or thing that is (or is assumed to be) the same as all others of its type.

Stream of Consciousness: A narrative technique for rendering the inward experience of a character. This technique is designed to give the impression of an ever-changing series of thoughts, emotions, images, and memories in the spontaneous and seemingly illogical order that they occur in life.

Structuralism: A twentieth-century movement in literary criticism that examines how literary texts arrive at their meanings, rather than the meanings themselves. There are two major types of structuralist analysis: one examines the way patterns of linguistic structures unify a specific text and emphasize certain elements of that text, and the other interprets the way literary forms and conventions affect the meaning of language itself.

Structure: The form taken by a piece of literature. The structure may be made obvious for ease of understanding, as in nonfiction works, or may obscured for artistic purposes, as in some poetry or seemingly "unstructured" prose.

Sturm und Drang: A German term meaning "storm and stress." It refers to a German literary movement of the 1770s and 1780s that reacted against the order and rationalism of the enlightenment, focusing instead on the intense experience of extraordinary individuals.

Style: A writer's distinctive manner of arranging words to suit his or her ideas and purpose in writing. The unique imprint of the author's personality upon his or her writing, style is the product of an author's way of arranging ideas and his or her use of diction, different sentence structures, rhythm, figures of speech, rhetorical principles, and other elements of composition.

Subject: The person, event, or theme at the center of a work of literature. A work may have one or more subjects of each type, with shorter works tending to have fewer and longer works tending to have more.

Subjectivity: Writing that expresses the author's personal feelings about his subject, and which may or may not include factual information about the subject.

Surrealism: A term introduced to criticism by Guillaume Apollinaire and later adopted by Andre Breton. It refers to a French literary and artistic movement founded in the 1920s. The Surrealists sought to express unconscious thoughts and feelings in their works. The best-known technique used for achieving this aim was automatic writing—transcriptions of spontaneous outpourings from the unconscious. The Surrealists proposed to unify the contrary levels of conscious and unconscious, dream and reality, objectivity and subjectivity into a new level of "super-realism."

Suspense: A literary device in which the author maintains the audience's attention through the buildup of events, the outcome of which will soon be revealed.

Syllogism: A method of presenting a logical argument. In its most basic form, the syllogism consists of a major premise, a minor premise, and a conclusion.

Symbol: Something that suggests or stands for something else without losing its original identity. In literature, symbols combine their literal meaning with the suggestion of an abstract concept. Literary symbols are of two types: those that carry complex associations of meaning no matter what their contexts, and those that derive their suggestive meaning from their functions in specific literary works.

Symbolism: This term has two widely accepted meanings. In historical criticism, it denotes an early modernist literary movement initiated in France during the nineteenth century that reacted against the prevailing standards of realism. Writers in this movement aimed to evoke, indirectly and symbolically, an order of being beyond the material world of the five senses. Poetic expression of personal emotion figured strongly in the movement, typically by means of a private set of symbols uniquely identifiable with the individual poet. The principal aim of the Symbolists was to express in words the highly complex feelings that grew out of everyday contact with the world. In a broader sense, the term "symbolism" refers to the use of one object to represent another.

Symbolist: See *Symbolism*

Symbolist Movement: See *Symbolism*

Sympathetic Fallacy: See *Affective Fallacy*

T

Tanka: A form of Japanese poetry similar to *haiku*. A *tanka* is five lines long, with the lines containing five, seven, five, seven, and seven syllables respectively.

Terza Rima: A three-line stanza form in poetry in which the rhymes are made on the last word of each line in the following manner: the first and third lines of the first stanza, then the second line of the first stanza and the first and third lines of the second stanza, and so on with the middle line of any stanza rhyming with the first and third lines of the following stanza.

Tetrameter: See *Meter*

Textual Criticism: A branch of literary criticism that seeks to establish the authoritative text of a literary work. Textual critics typically compare all known manuscripts or printings of a single work in order to assess the meanings of differences and revisions. This procedure allows them to arrive at a definitive version that (supposedly) corresponds to the author's original intention.

Theme: The main point of a work of literature. The term is used interchangeably with thesis.

Thesis: A thesis is both an essay and the point argued in the essay. Thesis novels and thesis plays share the quality of containing a thesis which is supported through the action of the story.

Third Person: See *Point of View*

Tone: The author's attitude toward his or her audience may be deduced from the tone of the work. A formal tone may create distance or convey politeness, while an informal tone may encourage a friendly, intimate, or intrusive feeling in the reader. The author's attitude toward his or her subject matter may also be deduced from the tone of the words he or she uses in discussing it.

Tragedy: A drama in prose or poetry about a noble, courageous hero of excellent character who, because of some tragic character flaw or *hamartia*, brings ruin upon him- or herself. Tragedy treats its subjects in a dignified and serious manner, using poetic language to help evoke pity and fear and bring about catharsis, a purging of these emotions. The tragic form was practiced extensively by the ancient Greeks. In the Middle Ages, when classical works were virtually unknown, tragedy came to denote any works about the fall of persons from exalted to low conditions due to any reason: fate, vice, weakness, etc. According to the classical definition of tragedy, such works present the "pathetic"—that which evokes pity—rather than the tragic. The classical form of tragedy was revived in the sixteenth century; it flourished especially on the Elizabethan stage. In modern times, dramatists have attempted to adapt the form to the needs of modern society by drawing their heroes from the ranks of ordinary men and women and defining the nobility of these heroes in terms of spirit rather than exalted social standing.

Tragic Flaw: In a tragedy, the quality within the hero or heroine which leads to his or her downfall.

Transcendentalism: An American philosophical and religious movement, based in New England from around 1835 until the Civil War. Transcendentalism was a form of American romanticism that had its roots abroad in the works of Thomas Carlyle, Samuel Coleridge, and Johann Wolfgang von Goethe. The Transcendentalists stressed the importance of intuition and subjective experience in communication with God. They rejected religious dogma and texts in favor of mysticism and scientific naturalism. They pursued truths that lie beyond the "colorless" realms perceived by reason and the senses and were active social reformers in public education, women's rights, and the abolition of slavery.

Trickster: A character or figure common in Native American and African literature who uses his ingenuity to defeat enemies and escape difficult situations. Tricksters are most often animals, such as the spider, hare, or coyote, although they may take the form of humans as well.

Trimeter: See *Meter*

Triple Rhyme: See *Rhyme*

Trochee: See *Foot*

U

Understatement: See *Irony*

Unities: Strict rules of dramatic structure, formulated by Italian and French critics of the Renaissance and based loosely on the principles of drama discussed by Aristotle in his *Poetics*. Foremost among these rules were the three unities of action, time, and place that compelled a dramatist to: (1) construct a single plot with a beginning, middle, and end that details the causal relationships of action and character; (2) restrict the action to the events of a single day; and (3) limit the scene to a single place or city. The unities were observed faithfully by continental European writers until the Romantic Age, but they were never regularly observed in English drama. Modern dramatists are typically more concerned with a unity of impression or emotional effect than with any of the classical unities.

Urban Realism: A branch of realist writing that attempts to accurately reflect the often harsh facts of modern urban existence.

Utopia: A fictional perfect place, such as "paradise" or "heaven."

Utopian: See *Utopia*

Utopianism: See *Utopia*

V

Verisimilitude: Literally, the appearance of truth. In literary criticism, the term refers to aspects of a work of literature that seem true to the reader.

Vers de societe: See *Occasional Verse*

Vers libre: See *Free Verse*

Verse: A line of metered language, a line of a poem, or any work written in verse.

Versification: The writing of verse. Versification may also refer to the meter, rhyme, and other mechanical components of a poem.

Victorian: Refers broadly to the reign of Queen Victoria of England (1837–1901) and to anything with qualities typical of that era. For example, the qualities of smug narrowmindedness, bourgeois materialism, faith in social progress, and priggish morality are often considered Victorian. This stereotype is contradicted by such dramatic intellectual developments as the theories of Charles Darwin, Karl Marx, and Sigmund Freud (which stirred strong debates in England) and the critical attitudes of serious Victorian writers like Charles Dickens and George Eliot. In literature, the Victorian Period was the great age of the English novel, and the latter part of the era saw the rise of movements such as decadence and symbolism.

Victorian Age: See *Victorian*

Victorian Period: See *Victorian*

W

Weltanschauung: A German term referring to a person's worldview or philosophy.

Weltschmerz: A German term meaning "world pain." It describes a sense of anguish about the nature of existence, usually associated with a melancholy, pessimistic attitude.

Z

Zarzuela: A type of Spanish operetta.

Zeitgeist: A German term meaning "spirit of the time." It refers to the moral and intellectual trends of a given era.

Cumulative Author/Title Index

A

Accounting (Alegría): V21
Ackerman, Diane
  On Location in the Loire Valley: V19
Acosta, Teresa Palomo
  My Mother Pieced Quilts: V12
Addonizio, Kim
  Knowledge: V25
Address to the Angels (Kumin): V18
The Afterlife (Collins): V18
An African Elegy (Duncan): V13
Ah, Are You Digging on My Grave? (Hardy): V4
Ai
  Reunions with a Ghost: V16
Aiken, Conrad
  The Room: V24
Air for Mercury (Hillman): V20
Akhmatova, Anna
  Midnight Verses: V18
Alabama Centennial (Madgett): V10
The Alchemy of Day (Hébert): V20
Alegría, Claribel
  Accounting: V21
Alexander, Elizabeth
  The Toni Morrison Dreams: V22
All I Was Doing Was Breathing (Mirabai): V24
All It Takes (Phillips): V23
Allegory (Bang): V23
Always (Apollinaire): V24
American Poetry (Simpson): V7
Amichai, Yehuda
  Not like a Cypress: V24
Ammons, A. R.
  The City Limits: V19
An Arundel Tomb (Larkin): V12
Anasazi (Snyder): V9
And What If I Spoke of Despair (Bass): V19
Angelou, Maya
  Harlem Hopscotch: V2
  On the Pulse of Morning: V3
Angle of Geese (Momaday): V2
Annabel Lee (Poe): V9
Anniversary (Harjo): V15
Anonymous
  Barbara Allan: V7
  Go Down, Moses: V11
  Lord Randal: V6
  The Seafarer: V8
  Sir Patrick Spens: V4
  Swing Low Sweet Chariot: V1
Anorexic (Boland): V12
Answers to Letters (Tranströmer): V21
Any Human to Another (Cullen): V3
A Pièd (McElroy): V3
Apollinaire, Guillaume
  Always: V24
Apple sauce for Eve (Piercy): V22
Arnold, Matthew
  Dover Beach: V2
Ars Poetica (MacLeish): V5
The Arsenal at Springfield (Longfellow): V17
The Art of the Novel (Sajé): V23
Art Thou the Thing I Wanted (Fulton): V25
Arvio, Sarah
  Memory: V21
As I Walked Out One Evening (Auden): V4
Ashbery, John
  Paradoxes and Oxymorons: V11
Astonishment (Szymborska): V15
At the Bomb Testing Site (Stafford): V8
At the Cancer Clinic (Kooser): V24
Atwood, Margaret
  Siren Song: V7
Auden, W. H.
  As I Walked Out One Evening: V4
  Funeral Blues: V10
  Musée des Beaux Arts: V1
  The Unknown Citizen: V3
Aurora Leigh (Browning): V23
Auto Wreck (Shapiro): V3
Autumn Begins in Martins Ferry, Ohio (Wright): V8

B

Ballad of Orange and Grape (Rukeyser): V10
Baraka, Amiri
  In Memory of Radio: V9
Barbara Allan (Anonymous): V7
Barbie Doll (Piercy): V9
Ballad of Birmingham (Randall): V5
Bang, Mary Jo
  Allegory: V23
Barot, Rick
  Bonnard's Garden: V25
Barrett, Elizabeth
  Sonnet 43: V2
The Base Stealer (Francis): V12
Bashō, Matsuo
  Falling Upon Earth: V2
  The Moon Glows the Same: V7
  Temple Bells Die Out: V18

Bass, Ellen
    And What If I Spoke of Despair: V19
Baudelaire, Charles
    Hymn to Beauty: V21
The Bean Eaters (Brooks): V2
Because I Could Not Stop for Death (Dickinson): V2
Bedtime Story (MacBeth): V8
Behn, Robin
    Ten Years after Your Deliberate Drowning: V21
Bell, Marvin
    View: V25
La Belle Dame sans Merci (Keats): V17
The Bells (Poe): V3
Beowulf (Wilbur): V11
Beware: Do Not Read This Poem (Reed): V6
Beware of Ruins (Hope): V8
Bialosky, Jill
    Seven Seeds: V19
Bidwell Ghost (Erdrich): V14
Biele, Joelle
    Rapture: V21
Birch Canoe (Revard): V5
Birches (Frost): V13
Birney, Earle
    Vancouver Lights: V8
A Birthday (Rossetti): V10
Bishop, Elizabeth
    Brazil, January 1, 1502: V6
    Filling Station: V12
Blackberrying (Plath): V15
Black Zodiac (Wright): V10
Blake, William
    The Lamb: V12
    A Poison Tree: V24
    The Tyger: V2
A Blessing (Wright): V7
Blood Oranges (Mueller): V13
The Blue Rim of Memory (Levertov): V17
Blumenthal, Michael
    Inventors: V7
Bly, Robert
    Come with Me: V6
    Driving to Town Late to Mail a Letter: V17
Bogan, Louise
    Words for Departure: V21
Boland, Eavan
    Anorexic: V12
    It's a Woman's World: V22
Bonnard's Garden (Barot): V25
The Boy (Hacker): V19
Bradstreet, Anne
    To My Dear and Loving Husband: V6
Brazil, January 1, 1502 (Bishop): V6
Bright Star! Would I Were Steadfast as Thou Art (Keats): V9

Brooke, Rupert
    The Soldier: V7
Brooks, Gwendolyn
    The Bean Eaters: V2
    The Sonnet-Ballad: V1
    Strong Men, Riding Horses: V4
    We Real Cool: V6
Brouwer, Joel
    Last Request: V14
Browning, Elizabeth Barrett
    Aurora Leigh: V23
    Sonnet 43: V2
    Sonnet XXIX: V16
Browning, Robert
    My Last Duchess: V1
    Porphyria's Lover: V15
Burns, Robert
    A Red, Red Rose: V8
Business (Cruz): V16
The Bustle in a House (Dickinson): V10
But Perhaps God Needs the Longing (Sachs): V20
Butcher Shop (Simic): V7
Byrne, Elena Karina
    In Particular: V20
Byron, Lord
    The Destruction of Sennacherib: V1
    She Walks in Beauty: V14

C

The Canterbury Tales (Chaucer): V14
Cargoes (Masefield): V5
Carroll, Lewis
    Jabberwocky: V11
Carson, Anne
    New Rule: V18
Carver, Raymond
    The Cobweb: V17
Casey at the Bat (Thayer): V5
Castillo, Ana
    While I Was Gone a War Began: V21
Cavafy, C. P.
    Ithaka: V19
Cavalry Crossing a Ford (Whitman): V13
Celan, Paul
    Late and Deep: V21
The Chambered Nautilus (Holmes): V24
The Charge of the Light Brigade (Tennyson): V1
Chaucer, Geoffrey
    The Canterbury Tales: V14
Chicago (Sandburg): V3
Childhood (Rilke): V19
Chocolates (Simpson): V11
Chorale (Young): V25
The Cinnamon Peeler (Ondaatje): V19

Cisneros, Sandra
    Once Again I Prove the Theory of Relativity: V19
The City Limits (Ammons): V19
Clifton, Lucille
    Climbing: V14
    Miss Rosie: V1
Climbing (Clifton): V14
The Cobweb (Carver): V17
Coleridge, Samuel Taylor
    Kubla Khan: V5
    The Rime of the Ancient Mariner: V4
Colibrí (Espada): V16
Collins, Billy
    The Afterlife: V18
Come with Me (Bly): V6
The Constellation Orion (Kooser): V8
Concord Hymn (Emerson): V4
The Conquerors (McGinley): V13
The Continuous Life (Strand): V18
Cool Tombs (Sandburg): V6
Cooper, Jane
    Rent: V25
The Cossacks (Pastan): V25
The Country Without a Post Office (Shahid Ali): V18
Courage (Sexton): V14
The Courage That My Mother Had (Millay): V3
Crane, Stephen
    War Is Kind: V9
The Creation (Johnson): V1
Creeley, Robert
    Fading Light: V21
The Cremation of Sam McGee (Service): V10
The Crime Was in Granada (Machado): V23
Cruz, Victor Hernandez
    Business: V16
Cullen, Countee
    Any Human to Another: V3
cummings, e. e.
    i was sitting in mcsorley's: V13
    l(a: V1
    maggie and milly and molly and may: V12
    old age sticks: V3
    somewhere i have never travelled,gladly beyond: V19
The Czar's Last Christmas Letter. A Barn in the Urals (Dubie): V12

D

The Darkling Thrush (Hardy): V18
Darwin in 1881 (Schnackenberg): V13
Daughter-Mother-Maya-Seeta (Vazirani): V25

Dawe, Bruce
  Drifters: V10
Daylights (Warren): V13
Dear Reader (Tate): V10
The Death of the Ball Turret Gunner (Jarrell): V2
The Death of the Hired Man (Frost): V4
Death Sentences (Lazić): V22
Deep Woods (Nemerov): V14
Dennis, Carl
  The God Who Loves You: V20
The Destruction of Sennacherib (Byron): V1
Dickey, James
  The Heaven of Animals: V6
  The Hospital Window: V11
Dickinson, Emily
  Because I Could Not Stop for Death: V2
  The Bustle in a House: V10
  "Hope" Is the Thing with Feathers: V3
  I felt a Funeral, in my Brain: V13
  I Heard a Fly Buzz—When I Died—: V5
  Much Madness Is Divinest Sense: V16
  My Life Closed Twice Before Its Close: V8
  A Narrow Fellow in the Grass: V11
  The Soul Selects Her Own Society: V1
  There's a Certain Slant of Light: V6
  This Is My Letter to the World: V4
Digging (Heaney): V5
Dobyns, Stephen
  It's like This: V23
Do Not Go Gentle into that Good Night (Thomas): V1
Donne, John
  Holy Sonnet 10: V2
  A Valediction: Forbidding Mourning: V11
Dove, Rita
  Geometry: V15
  This Life: V1
Dover Beach (Arnold): V2
Dream Variations (Hughes): V15
Drifters (Dawe): V10
A Drink of Water (Heaney): V8
Drinking Alone Beneath the Moon (Po): V20
Driving to Town Late to Mail a Letter (Bly): V17
Drought Year (Wright): V8
Dubie, Norman
  The Czar's Last Christmas Letter. A Barn in the Urals: V12
Du Bois, W. E. B.
  The Song of the Smoke: V13

Duffy, Carol Ann
  Originally: V25
Dugan, Alan
  How We Heard the Name: V10
Dulce et Decorum Est (Owen): V10
Duncan, Robert
  An African Elegy: V13
Dunn, Stephen
  The Reverse Side: V21
Duration (Paz): V18

E

The Eagle (Tennyson): V11
Early in the Morning (Lee): V17
Easter 1916 (Yeats): V5
Eating Poetry (Strand): V9
Elegy for My Father, Who is Not Dead (Hudgins): V14
Elegy Written in a Country Churchyard (Gray): V9
An Elementary School Classroom in a Slum (Spender): V23
Eliot, T. S.
  Journey of the Magi: V7
  The Love Song of J. Alfred Prufrock: V1
  The Waste Land: V20
Emerson, Ralph Waldo
  Concord Hymn: V4
  The Rhodora: V17
Erdrich, Louise
  Bidwell Ghost: V14
Espada, Martín
  Colibrí: V16
  We Live by What We See at Night: V13
Ethics (Pastan): V8
The Exhibit (Mueller): V9

F

Facing It (Komunyakaa): V5
Fading Light (Creeley): V21
Falling Upon Earth (Bashō): V2
A Far Cry from Africa (Walcott): V6
A Farewell to English (Hartnett): V10
Farrokhzaad, Faroogh
  A Rebirth: V21
Fenton, James
  The Milkfish Gatherers: V11
Fern Hill (Thomas): V3
Fiddler Crab (Jacobsen): V23
Fifteen (Stafford): V2
Filling Station (Bishop): V12
Fire and Ice (Frost): V7
The Fish (Moore): V14
For a New Citizen of These United States (Lee): V15
For An Assyrian Frieze (Viereck): V9
For Jean Vincent D'abbadie, Baron St.-Castin (Nowlan): V12

For Jennifer, 6, on the Teton (Hugo): V17
For the Sake of Strangers (Laux): V24
For the Union Dead (Lowell): V7
For the White poets who would be Indian (Rose): V13
The Force That Through the Green Fuse Drives the Flower (Thomas): V8
Forché, Carolyn
  The Garden Shukkei-en: V18
The Forest (Stewart): V22
Four Mountain Wolves (Silko): V9
Francis, Robert
  The Base Stealer: V12
Frost, Robert
  Birches: V13
  The Death of the Hired Man: V4
  Fire and Ice: V7
  Mending Wall: V5
  Nothing Gold Can Stay: V3
  Out, Out—: V10
  The Road Not Taken: V2
  Stopping by Woods on a Snowy Evening: V1
  The Wood-Pile: V6
Fulton, Alice
  Art Thou the Thing I Wanted: V25
Funeral Blues (Auden): V10

G

Gacela of the Dark Death (García Lorca): V20
Gallagher, Tess
  I Stop Writing the Poem: V16
García Lorca, Federico
  Gacela of the Dark Death: V20
The Garden Shukkei-en (Forché): V18
Geometry (Dove): V15
Ghazal (Spires): V21
Ginsberg, Allen
  A Supermarket in California: V5
Gioia, Dana
  The Litany: V24
Giovanni, Nikki
  Knoxville, Tennessee: V17
Glück, Louise
  The Gold Lily: V5
  The Mystery: V15
Go Down, Moses (Anonymous): V11
The God Who Loves You (Dennis): V20
The Gold Lily (Glück): V5
Goodison, Lorna
  The River Mumma Wants Out: V25
A Grafted Tongue (Montague): V12
Graham, Jorie
  The Hiding Place: V10
  Mind: V17

Gray, Thomas
   Elegy Written in a Country Churchyard: V9
The Greatest Grandeur (Rogers): V18
Gregg, Linda
   A Thirst Against: V20
Grennan, Eamon
   Station: V21
Gunn, Thom
   The Missing: V9

H

H.D.
   Helen: V6
Hacker, Marilyn
   The Boy: V19
Hahn, Kimiko
   Pine: V23
Hall, Donald
   Names of Horses: V8
Hardy, Thomas
   Ah, Are You Digging on My Grave?: V4
   The Darkling Thrush: V18
   The Man He Killed: V3
Harjo, Joy
   Anniversary: V15
Harlem (Hughes): V1
Harlem Hopscotch (Angelou): V2
Hartnett, Michael
   A Farewell to English: V10
Hashimoto, Sharon
   What I Would Ask My Husband's Dead Father: V22
Having a Coke with You (O'Hara): V12
Having it Out with Melancholy (Kenyon): V17
Hawk Roosting (Hughes): V4
Hayden, Robert
   Those Winter Sundays: V1
Heaney, Seamus
   Digging: V5
   A Drink of Water: V8
   Midnight: V2
   The Singer's House: V17
Hébert, Anne
   The Alchemy of Day: V20
Hecht, Anthony
   "More Light! More Light!": V6
The Heaven of Animals (Dickey): V6
Helen (H.D.): V6
Herbert, George
   Virtue: V25
Herbert, Zbigniew
   Why The Classics: V22
Herrick, Robert
   To the Virgins, to Make Much of Time: V13
The Hiding Place (Graham): V10
High Windows (Larkin): V3
The Highwayman (Noyes): V4

Hillman, Brenda
   Air for Mercury: V20
Hirsch, Edward
   Omen: V22
Hirshfield, Jane
   Three Times My Life Has Opened: V16
His Speed and Strength (Ostriker): V19
Hoagland, Tony
   Social Life: V19
Holmes, Oliver Wendell
   The Chambered Nautilus: V24
   Old Ironsides: V9
Holy Sonnet 10 (Donne): V2
Hongo, Garrett
   The Legend: V25
Hope, A. D.
   Beware of Ruins: V8
Hope Is a Tattered Flag (Sandburg): V12
"Hope" Is the Thing with Feathers (Dickinson): V3
The Horizons of Rooms (Merwin): V15
The Hospital Window (Dickey): V11
Housman, A. E.
   To an Athlete Dying Young: V7
   When I Was One-and-Twenty: V4
How We Heard the Name (Dugan): V10
Howe, Marie
   What Belongs to Us: V15
Hudgins, Andrew
   Elegy for My Father, Who is Not Dead: V14
Hugh Selwyn Mauberley (Pound): V16
Hughes, Langston
   Dream Variations: V15
   Harlem: V1
   Mother to Son: V3
   The Negro Speaks of Rivers: V10
   Theme for English B: V6
Hughes, Ted
   Hawk Roosting: V4
   Perfect Light: V19
Hugo, Richard
   For Jennifer, 6, on the Teton: V17
Hum (Lauterbach): V25
Hunger in New York City (Ortiz): V4
Huong, Ho Xuan
   Spring-Watching Pavilion: V18
Hurt Hawks (Jeffers): V3
Hymn to Aphrodite (Sappho): V20
Hymn to Beauty (Baudelaire): V21

I

I felt a Funeral, in my Brain (Dickinson): V13
I Go Back to May 1937 (Olds): V17
I Hear America Singing (Whitman): V3
I Heard a Fly Buzz—When I Died— (Dickinson): V5
I Stop Writing the Poem (Gallagher): V16
i was sitting in mcsorley's (cummings): V13
The Idea of Order at Key West (Stevens): V13
If (Kipling): V22
In a Station of the Metro (Pound): V2
In Flanders Fields (McCrae): V5
In Memory of Radio (Baraka): V9
In Particular (Byrne): V20
In the Land of Shinar (Levertov): V7
In the Suburbs (Simpson): V14
Incident in a Rose Garden (Justice): V14
Inventors (Blumentha): V7
An Irish Airman Foresees His Death (Yeats): V1
Island of the Three Marias (Ríos): V11
Ithaka (Cavafy): V19
It's a Woman's World (Boland): V22
It's like This (Dobyns): V23

J

Jabberwocky (Carroll): V11
Jacobsen, Josephine
   Fiddler Crab: V23
Jarrell, Randall
   The Death of the Ball Turret Gunner: V2
Jeffers, Robinson
   Hurt Hawks: V3
   Shine Perishing Republic: V4
Johnson, James Weldon
   The Creation: V1
Jonson, Ben
   Song: To Celia: V23
Journey of the Magi (Eliot): V7
Justice, Donald
   Incident in a Rose Garden: V14

K

Keats, John
   La Belle Dame sans Merci: V17
   Bright Star! Would I Were Steadfast as Thou Art: V9
   Ode on a Grecian Urn: V1
   Ode to a Nightingale: V3
   When I Have Fears that I May Cease to Be: V2
Kelly, Brigit Pegeen
   The Satyr's Heart: V22
Kenyon, Jane
   Having it Out with Melancholy: V17
   "Trouble with Math in a One-Room Country School": V9

Kilroy (Viereck): V14
Kim, Sue (Suji) Kwock
　Monologue for an Onion: V24
Kindness (Nye): V24
King James Bible
　Psalm 8: V9
　Psalm 23: V4
Kinnell, Galway
　Saint Francis and the Sow: V9
Kipling, Rudyard
　If: V22
Kizer, Carolyn
　To an Unknown Poet: V18
Knowledge (Addonizio): V25
Knoxville, Tennessee (Giovanni): V17
Koch, Kenneth
　Paradiso: V20
Komunyakaa, Yusef
　Facing It: V5
　Ode to a Drum: V20
Kooser, Ted
　At the Cancer Clinic: V24
　The Constellation Orion: V8
Kubla Khan (Coleridge): V5
Kumin, Maxine
　Address to the Angels: V18
Kunitz, Stanley
　The War Against the Trees: V11
Kyger, Joanne
　September: V23

L

l(a (cummings): V1
The Lady of Shalott (Tennyson): V15
Lake (Warren): V23
The Lake Isle of Innisfree (Yeats): V15
The Lamb (Blake): V12
Lament for the Dorsets (Purdy): V5
Landscape with Tractor (Taylor): V10
Lanier, Sidney
　Song of the Chattahoochee: V14
Larkin, Philip
　An Arundel Tomb: V12
　High Windows: V3
　Toads: V4
The Last Question (Parker): V18
Last Request (Brouwer): V14
Late and Deep (Celan): V21
Lauterbach, Ann
　Hum: V25
Laux, Dorianne
　For the Sake of Strangers: V24
Lawrence, D. H.
　Piano: V6
Layton, Irving
　A Tall Man Executes a Jig: V12
Lazić, Radmila
　Death Sentences: V22
Leda and the Swan (Yeats): V13

Lee, Li-Young
　Early in the Morning: V17
　For a New Citizen of These United States: V15
　The Weight of Sweetness: V11
The Legend (Hongo): V25
Lepidopterology (Svenbro): V23
Levertov, Denise
　The Blue Rim of Memory: V17
　In the Land of Shinar: V7
Leviathan (Merwin): V5
Levine, Philip
　Starlight: V8
The Litany (Gioia): V24
Longfellow, Henry Wadsworth
　The Arsenal at Springfield: V17
　Paul Revere's Ride: V2
　A Psalm of Life: V7
Lord Randal (Anonymous): V6
Lorde, Audre
　What My Child Learns of the Sea: V16
Lost in Translation (Merrill): V23
Lost Sister (Song): V5
The Love Song of J. Alfred Prufrock (Eliot): V1
Lowell, Robert
　For the Union Dead: V7
　The Quaker Graveyard in Nantucket: V6
Loy, Mina
　Moreover, the Moon: V20

M

MacBeth, George
　Bedtime Story: V8
Machado, Antonio
　The Crime Was in Granada: V23
MacLeish, Archibald
　Ars Poetica: V5
Madgett, Naomi Long
　Alabama Centennial: V10
maggie and milly and molly and may (cummings): V12
Malroux, Claire
　Morning Walk: V21
The Man He Killed (Hardy): V3
Marlowe, Christopher
　The Passionate Shepherd to His Love: V22
A Martian Sends a Postcard Home (Raine): V7
Marvell, Andrew
　To His Coy Mistress: V5
Masefield, John
　Cargoes: V5
Maternity (Swir): V21
Matsuo Bashō
　Falling Upon Earth: V2
　The Moon Glows the Same: V7
　Temple Bells Die Out: V18

Maxwell, Glyn
　The Nerve: V23
McCrae, John
　In Flanders Fields: V5
McElroy, Colleen
　A Pièd: V3
McGinley, Phyllis
　The Conquerors: V13
　Reactionary Essay on Applied Science: V9
McHugh, Heather
　Three To's and an Oi: V24
McKay, Claude
　The Tropics in New York: V4
Meeting the British (Muldoon): V7
Memoir (Van Duyn): V20
Memory (Arvio): V21
Mending Wall (Frost): V5
Merlin Enthralled (Wilbur): V16
Merriam, Eve
　Onomatopoeia: V6
Merrill, James
　Lost in Translation: V23
Merwin, W. S.
　The Horizons of Rooms: V15
　Leviathan: V5
Metamorphoses (Ovid): V22
Midnight (Heaney): V2
Midnight Verses (Akhmatova): V18
The Milkfish Gatherers (Fenton): V11
Millay, Edna St. Vincent
　The Courage That My Mother Had: V3
　Wild Swans: V17
Milosz, Czeslaw
　Song of a Citizen: V16
Milton, John
　[On His Blindness] Sonnet 16: V3
　On His Having Arrived at the Age of Twenty-Three: V17
Mind (Graham): V17
Mirabai
　All I Was Doing Was Breathing: V24
Mirror (Plath): V1
Miss Rosie (Clifton): V1
The Missing (Gunn): V9
Momaday, N. Scott
　Angle of Geese: V2
　To a Child Running With Outstretched Arms in Canyon de Chelly: V11
Monologue for an Onion (Kim): V24
Montague, John
　A Grafted Tongue: V12
Montale, Eugenio
　On the Threshold: V22
The Moon Glows the Same (Bashō): V7
Moore, Marianne
　The Fish: V14
　Poetry: V17
"More Light! More Light!" (Hecht): V6

Moreover, the Moon (Loy): V20
Morning Walk (Malroux): V21
Mother to Son (Hughes): V3
Much Madness Is Divinest Sense (Dickinson): V16
Muldoon, Paul
   Meeting the British: V7
   Pineapples and Pomegranates: V22
Mueller, Lisel
   Blood Oranges: V13
   The Exhibit: V9
Musée des Beaux Arts (Auden): V1
Music Lessons (Oliver): V8
Muske-Dukes, Carol
   Our Side: V24
My Father's Song (Ortiz): V16
My Last Duchess (Browning): V1
My Life Closed Twice Before Its Close (Dickinson): V8
My Mother Pieced Quilts (Acosta): V12
My Papa's Waltz (Roethke): V3
The Mystery (Glück): V15

N

Names of Horses (Hall): V8
A Narrow Fellow in the Grass (Dickinson): V11
The Negro Speaks of Rivers (Hughes): V10
Nemerov, Howard
   Deep Woods: V14
   The Phoenix: V10
Neruda, Pablo
   Tonight I Can Write: V11
The Nerve (Maxwell): V23
New Rule (Carson): V18
Not like a Cypress (Amichai): V24
Not Waving but Drowning (Smith): V3
Nothing Gold Can Stay (Frost): V3
Nowlan, Alden
   For Jean Vincent D'abbadie, Baron St.-Castin: V12
Noyes, Alfred
   The Highwayman: V4
Nye, Naomi Shihab
   Kindness: V24
The Nymph's Reply to the Shepherd (Raleigh): V14

O

O Captain! My Captain! (Whitman): V2
Ode on a Grecian Urn (Keats): V1
Ode to a Drum (Komunyakaa): V20
Ode to a Nightingale (Keats): V3
Ode to the West Wind (Shelley): V2
O'Hara, Frank
   Having a Coke with You: V12
   Why I Am Not a Painter: V8

old age sticks (cummings): V3
Old Ironsides (Holmes): V9
Olds, Sharon
   I Go Back to May 1937: V17
Oliver, Mary
   Music Lessons: V8
   Wild Geese: V15
Omen (Hirsch): V22
On Freedom's Ground (Wilbur): V12
[On His Blindness] Sonnet 16 (Milton): V3
On His Having Arrived at the Age of Twenty-Three (Milton): V17
On Location in the Loire Valley (Ackerman): V19
On the Pulse of Morning (Angelou): V3
On the Threshold (Montale): V22
Once Again I Prove the Theory of Relativity (Cisneros): V19
Ondaatje, Michael
   The Cinnamon Peeler: V19
   To a Sad Daughter: V8
One Is One (Ponsot): V24
Onomatopoeia (Merriam): V6
Ordinary Words (Stone): V19
Originally (Duffy): V25
Ortiz, Simon
   Hunger in New York City: V4
   My Father's Song: V16
Ostriker, Alicia
   His Speed and Strength: V19
Our Side (Muske-Dukes): V24
Out, Out— (Frost): V10
Overture to a Dance of Locomotives (Williams): V11
Ovid, (Naso, Publius Ovidius)
   Metamorphoses: V22
Owen, Wilfred
   Dulce et Decorum Est: V10
Oysters (Sexton): V4

P

Paradiso (Koch): V20
Paradoxes and Oxymorons (Ashbery): V11
Parker, Dorothy
   The Last Question: V18
The Passionate Shepherd to His Love (Marlowe): V22
Pastan, Linda
   The Cossacks: V25
   Ethics: V8
Paul Revere's Ride (Longfellow): V2
Pavese, Cesare
   Two Poems for T.: V20
Paz, Octavio
   Duration: V18
Perfect Light (Hughes): V19
Phillips, Carl
   All It Takes: V23
The Phoenix (Nemerov): V10

Piano (Lawrence): V6
Piercy, Marge
   Apple sauce for Eve: V22
   Barbie Doll: V9
Pine (Hahn): V23
Pineapples and Pomegranates (Muldoon): V22
Pinsky, Robert
   Song of Reasons: V18
Plath, Sylvia
   Blackberrying: V15
   Mirror: V1
A Psalm of Life (Longfellow): V7
Po, Li
   Drinking Alone Beneath the Moon: V20
Poe, Edgar Allan
   Annabel Lee: V9
   The Bells: V3
   The Raven: V1
Poetry (Moore): V17
A Poison Tree (Blake): V24
Ponsot, Marie
   One Is One: V24
Pope, Alexander
   The Rape of the Lock: V12
Porphyria's Lover (Browning): V15
Portrait of a Couple at Century's End (Santos): V24
Pound, Ezra
   Hugh Selwyn Mauberley: V16
   In a Station of the Metro: V2
   The River-Merchant's Wife: A Letter: V8
Practice (Voigt): V23
Proem (Tennyson): V19
Psalm 8 (King James Bible): V9
Psalm 23 (King James Bible): V4
Purdy, Al
   Lament for the Dorsets: V5
   Wilderness Gothic: V12

Q

The Quaker Graveyard in Nantucket (Lowell): V6
Queen-Ann's-Lace (Williams): V6

R

Raine, Craig
   A Martian Sends a Postcard Home: V7
Raleigh, Walter, Sir
   The Nymph's Reply to the Shepherd: V14
Randall, Dudley
   Ballad of Birmingham: V5
The Rape of the Lock (Pope): V12
Rapture (Biele): V21
The Raven (Poe): V1
Reactionary Essay on Applied Science (McGinley): V9

A Rebirth (Farrokhzaad): V21
A Red, Red Rose (Burns): V8
The Red Wheelbarrow (Williams): V1
Reed, Ishmael
   Beware: Do Not Read This Poem: V6
Remember (Rossetti): V14
Rent (Cooper): V25
Reunions with a Ghost (Ai): V16
Revard, Carter
   Birch Canoe: V5
The Reverse Side (Dunn): V21
The Rhodora (Emerson): V17
Rich, Adrienne
   Rusted Legacy: V15
Richard Cory (Robinson): V4
Rilke, Rainer Maria
   Childhood: V19
The Rime of the Ancient Mariner (Coleridge): V4
Ríos, Alberto
   Island of the Three Marias: V11
The River-Merchant's Wife: A Letter (Pound): V8
The River Mumma Wants Out (Goodison): V25
The Road Not Taken (Frost): V2
Robinson, E. A.
   Richard Cory: V4
Roethke, Theodore
   My Papa's Waltz: V3
Rogers, Pattiann
   The Greatest Grandeur: V18
The Room (Aiken): V24
Rose, Wendy
   For the White poets who would be Indian: V13
Rossetti, Christina
   A Birthday: V10
   Remember: V14
Rukeyser, Muriel
   Ballad of Orange and Grape: V10
Rusted Legacy (Rich): V15

S

Sachs, Nelly
   But Perhaps God Needs the Longing: V20
Sailing to Byzantium (Yeats): V2
Saint Francis and the Sow (Kinnell): V9
Sajé, Natasha
   The Art of the Novel: V23
Salter, Mary Jo
   Trompe l'Oeil: V22
Sandburg, Carl
   Chicago: V3
   Cool Tombs: V6
   Hope Is a Tattered Flag: V12
Santos, Sherod
   Portrait of a Couple at Century's End: V24

Sappho
   Hymn to Aphrodite: V20
The Satyr's Heart (Kelly): V22
Schnackenberg, Gjertrud
   Darwin in 1881: V13
   Supernatural Love: V25
The Seafarer (Anonymous): V8
The Second Coming (Yeats): V7
Seeing You (Valentine): V24
Self-Portrait (Zagajewski): V25
September (Kyger): V23
Service, Robert W.
   The Cremation of Sam McGee: V10
Seven Seeds (Bialosky): V19
Sexton, Anne
   Courage: V14
   Oysters: V4
Shahid Ali, Agha
   The Country Without a Post Office: V18
Shakespeare, William
   Sonnet 18: V2
   Sonnet 19: V9
   Sonnet 29: V8
   Sonnet 30: V4
   Sonnet 55: V5
   Sonnet 116: V3
   Sonnet 130: V1
Shapiro, Karl
   Auto Wreck: V3
She Walks in Beauty (Byron): V14
Shelley, Percy Bysshe
   Ode to the West Wind: V2
Shine, Perishing Republic (Jeffers): V4
Silko, Leslie Marmon
   Four Mountain Wolves: V9
   Story from Bear Country: V16
Simic, Charles
   Butcher Shop: V7
Simpson, Louis
   American Poetry: V7
   Chocolates: V11
   In the Suburbs: V14
The Singer's House (Heaney): V17
Sir Patrick Spens (Anonymous): V4
Siren Song (Atwood): V7
60 (Tagore): V18
Small Town with One Road (Soto): V7
Smart and Final Iris (Tate): V15
Smith, Stevie
   Not Waving but Drowning: V3
Snyder, Gary
   Anasazi: V9
   True Night: V19
Social Life (Hoagland): V19
The Soldier (Brooke): V7
somewhere i have never travelled,gladly beyond (cummings): V19
Song, Cathy
   Lost Sister: V5

Song of a Citizen (Milosz): V16
Song of Reasons (Pinsky): V18
Song of the Chattahoochee (Lanier): V14
The Song of the Smoke (Du Bois): V13
Song: To Celia (Jonson): V23
Sonnet 16 [On His Blindness] (Milton): V3
Sonnet 18 (Shakespeare): V2
Sonnet 19 (Shakespeare): V9
Sonnet 30 (Shakespeare): V4
Sonnet 29 (Shakespeare): V8
Sonnet XXIX (Browning): V16
Sonnet 43 (Browning): V2
Sonnet 55 (Shakespeare): V5
Sonnet 116 (Shakespeare): V3
Sonnet 130 (Shakespeare): V1
The Sonnet-Ballad (Brooks): V1
Soto, Gary
   Small Town with One Road: V7
The Soul Selects Her Own Society (Dickinson): V1
Southbound on the Freeway (Swenson): V16
Spender, Stephen
   An Elementary School Classroom in a Slum: V23
Spires, Elizabeth
   Ghazal: V21
Spring-Watching Pavilion (Huong): V18
Stafford, William
   At the Bomb Testing Site: V8
   Fifteen: V2
   Ways to Live: V16
Starlight (Levine): V8
Station (Grennan): V21
Stevens, Wallace
   The Idea of Order at Key West: V13
   Sunday Morning: V16
Stewart, Susan
   The Forest: V22
Stone, Ruth
   Ordinary Words: V19
Stopping by Woods on a Snowy Evening (Frost): V1
Story from Bear Country (Silko): V16
Strand, Mark
   The Continuous Life: V18
   Eating Poetry: V9
Strong Men, Riding Horses (Brooks): V4
Sunday Morning (Stevens): V16
A Supermarket in California (Ginsberg): V5
Supernatural Love (Schnackenberg): V25
Svenbro, Jesper
   Lepidopterology: V23
Swenson, May
   Southbound on the Freeway: V16

Swing Low Sweet Chariot
    (Anonymous): V1
Swir, Anna
    Maternity: V21
Szymborska, Wislawa
    Astonishment: V15

T

Tagore, Rabindranath
    60: V18
A Tall Man Executes a Jig (Layton):
    V12
Tate, James
    Dear Reader: V10
    Smart and Final Iris: V15
Taylor, Henry
    Landscape with Tractor: V10
Tears, Idle Tears (Tennyson): V4
Teasdale, Sara
    There Will Come Soft Rains:
        V14
Temple Bells Die Out (Bashō): V18
*Ten Years after Your Deliberate
    Drowning* (Behn): V21
Tennyson, Alfred, Lord
    The Charge of the Light Brigade:
        V1
    The Eagle. V11
    The Lady of Shalott: V15
    Proem: V19
    Tears, Idle Tears: V4
    Ulysses: V2
Thayer, Ernest Lawrence
    Casey at the Bat: V5
Theme for English B (Hughes): V6
There's a Certain Slant of Light
    (Dickinson): V6
There Will Come Soft Rains
    (Teasdale): V14
A Thirst Against (Gregg): V20
This Life (Dove): V1
Thomas, Dylan
    *Do Not Go Gentle into that Good
        Night:* V1
    Fern Hill: V3
    *The Force That Through the
        Green Fuse Drives the
        Flower:* V8
Those Winter Sundays (Hayden): V1
Three Times My Life Has Opened
    (Hirshfield): V16
Three To's and an Oi (McHugh):
    V24
Tintern Abbey (Wordsworth): V2
*To a Child Running With
    Outstretched Arms in Canyon
    de Chelly* (Momaday): V11
To a Sad Daughter (Ondaatje): V8
To an Athlete Dying Young
    (Housman): V7
To an Unknown Poet (Kizer): V18
To His Coy Mistress (Marvell): V5

*To His Excellency General
    Washington* (Wheatley): V13
To My Dear and Loving Husband
    (Bradstreet): V6
*To the Virgins, to Make Much of
    Time* (Herrick): V13
Toads (Larkin): V4
Tonight I Can Write (Neruda): V11
The Toni Morrison Dreams
    (Alexander): V22
Tranströmer, Tomas
    Answers to Letters: V21
Trompe l'Oeil (Salter): V22
The Tropics in New York (McKay):
    V4
True Night (Snyder): V19
Two Poems for T. (Pavese): V20
The Tyger (Blake): V2

U

Ulysses (Tennyson): V2
Ungaretti, Giuseppe
    Variations on Nothing: V20
The Unknown Citizen (Auden): V3

V

A Valediction: Forbidding Mourning
    (Donne): V11
Valentine, Jean
    Seeing You: V24
Van Duyn, Mona
    Memoir: V20
Vancouver Lights (Birney): V8
Variations on Nothing (Ungaretti):
    V20
Vazirani, Reetika
    Daughter-Mother-Maya-Seeta:
        V25
Viereck, Peter
    For An Assyrian Frieze: V9
    Kilroy: V14
View (Bell): V25
Virtue (Herbert): V25
Voigt, Ellen Bryant
    Practice: V23

W

Walcott, Derek
    A Far Cry from Africa: V6
The War Against the Trees (Kunitz):
    V11
War Is Kind (Crane): V9
Warren, Rosanna
    Daylights: V13
    Lake: V23
The Waste Land (Eliot): V20
Ways to Live (Stafford): V16
We Live by What We See at Night
    (Espada): V13

We Real Cool (Brooks): V6
The Weight of Sweetness (Lee): V11
What Belongs to Us (Howe): V15
*What I Would Ask My Husband's
    Dead Father* (Hashimoto):
    V22
What My Child Learns of the Sea
    (Lorde): V16
Wheatley, Phillis
    *To His Excellency General
        Washington:* V13
*When I Have Fears That I May
    Cease to Be* (Keats): V2
*When I Heard the Learn'd
    Astronomer* (Whitman): V22
When I Was One-and-Twenty
    (Housman): V4
While I Was Gone a War Began
    (Castillo): V21
Whitman, Walt
    Cavalry Crossing a Ford: V13
    I Hear America Singing: V3
    O Captain! My Captain!: V2
    *When I Heard the Learn'd
        Astronomer:* V22
Whoso List to Hunt (Wyatt): V25
Why I Am Not a Painter (O'Hara):
    V8
Why The Classics (Herbert): V22
Wilbur, Richard
    Beowulf: V11
    Merlin Enthralled: V16
    On Freedom's Ground: V12
Wild Geese (Oliver): V15
Wild Swans (Millay): V17
Wilderness Gothic (Purdy): V12
Williams, William Carlos
    *Overture to a Dance of
        Locomotives:* V11
    Queen-Ann's-Lace: V6
    The Red Wheelbarrow: V1
The Wood-Pile (Frost): V6
Words for Departure (Bogan): V21
Wordsworth, William
    *Lines Composed a Few Miles
        above Tintern Abbey:* V2
Wright, Charles
    Black Zodiac: V10
Wright, James
    A Blessing: V7
    *Autumn Begins in Martins Ferry,
        Ohio:* V8
Wright, Judith
    Drought Year: V8
Wyatt, Thomas
    Whoso List to Hunt: V25

Y

Yeats, William Butler
    Easter 1916: V5
    *An Irish Airman Foresees His
        Death:* V1

The Lake Isle of Innisfree: V15
Leda and the Swan: V13
Sailing to Byzantium: V2
The Second Coming: V7
Young, Kevin
   Chorale: V25

Z

Zagajewski, Adam
   Self-Portrait: V25

Cumulative Nationality/Ethnicity Index

Acoma Pueblo
Ortiz, Simon
  Hunger in New York City: V4
  My Father's Song: V16

African American
Ai
  Reunions with a Ghost: V16
Angelou, Maya
  Harlem Hopscotch: V2
  On the Pulse of Morning: V3
Baraka, Amiri
  In Memory of Radio: V9
Brooks, Gwendolyn
  The Bean Eaters: V2
  The Sonnet-Ballad: V1
  Strong Men, Riding Horses: V4
  We Real Cool: V6
Clifton, Lucille
  Climbing: V14
  Miss Rosie: V1
Cullen, Countee
  Any Human to Another: V3
Dove, Rita
  Geometry: V15
  This Life: V1
Giovanni, Nikki
  Knoxville, Tennessee: V17
Hayden, Robert
  Those Winter Sundays: V1
Hughes, Langston
  Dream Variations: V15
  Harlem: V1
  Mother to Son: V3
  The Negro Speaks of Rivers: V10
  Theme for English B: V6

Johnson, James Weldon
  The Creation: V1
Komunyakaa, Yusef
  Facing It: V5
  Ode to a Drum: V20
Lorde, Audre
  What My Child Learns of the Sea: V16
Madgett, Naomi Long
  Alabama Centennial: V10
McElroy, Colleen
  A Pièd: V3
Phillips, Carl
  All It Takes: V23
Randall, Dudley
  Ballad of Birmingham: V5
Reed, Ishmael
  Beware: Do Not Read This Poem: V6

American
Ackerman, Diane
  On Location in the Loire Valley: V19
Acosta, Teresa Palomo
  My Mother Pieced Quilts: V12
Addonizio, Kim
  Knowledge: V25
Ai
  Reunions with a Ghost: V16
Aiken, Conrad
  The Room: V24
Alegría, Claribel
  Accounting: V21
Alexander, Elizabeth
  The Toni Morrison Dreams: V22

Ammons, A. R.
  The City Limits: V19
Angelou, Maya
  Harlem Hopscotch: V2
  On the Pulse of Morning: V3
Ashbery, John
  Paradoxes and Oxymorons: V11
Arvio, Sarah
  Memory: V21
Auden, W. H.
  As I Walked Out One Evening: V4
  Musée des Beaux Arts: V1
  The Unknown Citizen: V3
Bang, Mary Jo
  Allegory: V23
Barot, Rick
  Bonnard's Garden: V25
Bass, Ellen
  And What If I Spoke of Despair: V19
Behn, Robin
  Ten Years after Your Deliberate Drowning: V21
Bell, Marvin
  View: V25
Bialosky, Jill
  Seven Seeds: V19
Biele, Joelle
  Rapture: V21
Bishop, Elizabeth
  Brazil, January 1, 1502: V6
  Filling Station: V12
Blumenthal, Michael
  Inventors: V7
Bly, Robert
  Come with Me: V6
  Driving to Town Late to Mail a Letter: V17

Bogan, Louise
    Words for Departure: V21
Bradstreet, Anne
    To My Dear and Loving Husband: V6
Brooks, Gwendolyn
    The Bean Eaters: V2
    The Sonnet-Ballad: V1
    Strong Men, Riding Horses: V4
    We Real Cool: V6
Brouwer, Joel
    Last Request: V14
Byrne, Elena Karina
    In Particular: V20
Carver, Raymond
    The Cobweb: V17
Castillo, Ana
    While I Was Gone a War Began: V21
Cisneros, Sandra
    Once Again I Prove the Theory of Relativity: V19
Clifton, Lucille
    Climbing: V14
    Miss Rosie: V1
Collins, Billy
    The Afterlife: V18
Cooper, Jane
    Rent: V25
Crane, Stephen
    War Is Kind: V9
Creeley, Robert
    Fading Light: V21
Cruz, Victor Hernandez
    Business: V16
Cullen, Countee
    Any Human to Another: V3
cummings, e. e.
    i was sitting in mcsorley's: V13
    l(a: V1
    maggie and milly and molly and may: V12
    old age sticks: V3
    somewhere i have never travelled,gladly beyond: V19
Dennis, Carl
    The God Who Loves You: V20
Dickey, James
    The Heaven of Animals: V6
    The Hospital Window: V11
Dickinson, Emily
    Because I Could Not Stop for Death: V2
    The Bustle in a House: V10
    "Hope" Is the Thing with Feathers: V3
    I felt a Funeral, in my Brain: V13
    I Heard a Fly Buzz—When I Died—: V5
    Much Madness Is Divinest Sense: V16
    My Life Closed Twice Before Its Close: V8
    A Narrow Fellow in the Grass: V11
    The Soul Selects Her Own Society: V1
    There's a Certain Slant of Light: V6
    This Is My Letter to the World: V4
Dobyns, Stephen
    It's like This: V23
Dove, Rita
    Geometry: V15
    This Life: V1
Dubie, Norman
    The Czar's Last Christmas Letter. A Barn in the Urals: V12
Du Bois, W. E. B.
    The Song of the Smoke: V13
Dugan, Alan
    How We Heard the Name: V10
Duncan, Robert
    An African Elegy: V13
Dunn, Stephen
    The Reverse Side: V21
Eliot, T. S.
    Journey of the Magi: V7
    The Love Song of J. Alfred Prufrock: V1
Emerson, Ralph Waldo
    Concord Hymn: V4
    The Rhodora: V17
Erdrich, Louise
    Bidwell Ghost: V14
Espada, Martín
    Colibrí: V16
    We Live by What We See at Night: V13
Forché, Carolyn
    The Garden Shukkei-En: V18
Francis, Robert
    The Base Stealer: V12
Frost, Robert
    Birches: V13
    The Death of the Hired Man: V4
    Fire and Ice: V7
    Mending Wall: V5
    Nothing Gold Can Stay: V3
    Out, Out—: V10
    The Road Not Taken: V2
    Stopping by Woods on a Snowy Evening: V1
    The Wood-Pile: V6
Fulton, Alice
    Art Thou the Thing I Wanted: V25
Gallagher, Tess
    I Stop Writing the Poem: V16
Ginsberg, Allen
    A Supermarket in California: V5
Gioia, Dana
    The Litany: V24
Giovanni, Nikki
    Knoxville, Tennessee: V17
Glück, Louise
    The Gold Lily: V5
    The Mystery: V15
Graham, Jorie
    The Hiding Place: V10
    Mind: V17
Gregg, Linda
    A Thirst Against: V20
Gunn, Thom
    The Missing: V9
H.D.
    Helen: V6
Hacker, Marilyn
    The Boy: V19
Hahn, Kimiko
    Pine: V23
Hall, Donald
    Names of Horses: V8
Harjo, Joy
    Anniversary: V15
Hashimoto, Sharon
    What I Would Ask My Husband's Dead Father: V22
Hayden, Robert
    Those Winter Sundays: V1
Hecht, Anthony
    "More Light! More Light!": V6
Hillman, Brenda
    Air for Mercury: V20
Hirsch, Edward
    Omen: V22
Hirshfield, Jane
    Three Times My Life Has Opened: V16
Hoagland, Tony
    Social Life: V19
Holmes, Oliver Wendell
    The Chambered Nautilus: V24
    Old Ironsides: V9
Hongo, Garrett
    The Legend: V25
Howe, Marie
    What Belongs to Us: V15
Hudgins, Andrew
    Elegy for My Father, Who is Not Dead: V14
Hughes, Langston
    Dream Variations: V15
    Harlem: V1
    Mother to Son: V3
    The Negro Speaks of Rivers: V10
    Theme for English B: V6
Hugo, Richard
    For Jennifer, 6, on the Teton: V17
Jarrell, Randall
    The Death of the Ball Turret Gunner: V2
Jeffers, Robinson
    Hurt Hawks: V3
    Shine, Perishing Republic: V4
Johnson, James Weldon
    The Creation: V1

Justice, Donald
    Incident in a Rose Garden: V14
Kelly, Brigit Pegeen
    The Satyr's Heart: V22
Kenyon, Jane
    Having it Out with Melancholy: V17
    "Trouble with Math in a One-Room Country School": V9
Kim, Sue (Suji) Kwock
    Monologue for an Onion: V24
Kinnell, Galway
    Saint Francis and the Sow: V9
Kizer, Carolyn
    To An Unknown Poet: V18
Koch, Kenneth
    Paradiso: V20
Komunyakaa, Yusef
    Facing It: V5
    Ode to a Drum: V20
Kooser, Ted
    At the Cancer Clinic: V24
    The Constellation Orion: V8
Kumin, Maxine
    Address to the Angels: V18
Kunitz, Stanley
    The War Against the Trees: V11
Kyger, Joanne
    September: V23
Lanier, Sidney
    Song of the Chattahoochee: V14
Lauterbach, Ann
    Hum: V25
Laux, Dorianne
    For the Sake of Strangers: V24
Lee, Li-Young
    Early in the Morning: V17
    For a New Citizen of These United States: V15
    The Weight of Sweetness: V11
Levertov, Denise
    The Blue Rim of Memory: V17
    In the Land of Shinar: V7
Levine, Philip
    Starlight: V8
Longfellow, Henry Wadsworth
    The Arsenal at Springfield: V17
    Paul Revere's Ride: V2
    A Psalm of Life: V7
Lorde, Audre
    What My Child Learns of the Sea: V16
Lowell, Robert
    For the Union Dead: V7
    The Quaker Graveyard in Nantucket: V6
Loy, Mina
    Moreover, the Moon: V20
MacLeish, Archibald
    Ars Poetica: V5
Madgett, Naomi Long
    Alabama Centennial: V10
McElroy, Colleen
    A Pièd: V3

McGinley, Phyllis
    The Conquerors: V13
    Reactionary Essay on Applied Science: V9
McHugh, Heather
    Three To's and an Oi: V24
McKay, Claude
    The Tropics in New York: V4
Merriam, Eve
    Onomatopoeia: V6
Merrill, James
    Lost in Translation: V23
Merwin, W. S.
    The Horizons of Rooms: V15
    Leviathan: V5
Millay, Edna St. Vincent
    The Courage that My Mother Had: V3
    Wild Swans: V17
Momaday, N. Scott
    Angle of Geese: V2
    To a Child Running With Outstretched Arms in Canyon de Chelly: V11
Montague, John
    A Grafted Tongue: V12
Moore, Marianne
    The Fish: V14
    Poetry: V17
Mueller, Lisel
    The Exhibit: V9
Muske-Dukes, Carol
    Our Side: V24
Nemerov, Howard
    Deep Woods: V14
    The Phoenix: V10
Nye, Naomi Shihab
    Kindness: V24
O'Hara, Frank
    Having a Coke with You: V12
    Why I Am Not a Painter: V8
Olds, Sharon
    I Go Back to May 1937: V17
Oliver, Mary
    Music Lessons: V8
    Wild Geese: V15
Ortiz, Simon
    Hunger in New York City: V4
    My Father's Song: V16
Ostriker, Alicia
    His Speed and Strength: V19
Parker, Dorothy
    The Last Question: V18
Pastan, Linda
    The Cossacks: V25
    Ethics: V8
Phillips, Carl
    All It Takes: V23
Piercy, Marge
    Apple sauce for Eve: V22
    Barbie Doll: V9
Pinsky, Robert
    Song of Reasons: V18

Plath, Sylvia
    Blackberrying: V15
    Mirror: V1
Poe, Edgar Allan
    Annabel Lee: V9
    The Bells: V3
    The Raven: V1
Ponsot, Marie
    One Is One: V24
Pound, Ezra
    Hugh Selwyn Mauberley: V16
    In a Station of the Metro: V2
    The River-Merchant's Wife: A Letter: V8
Randall, Dudley
    Ballad of Birmingham: V5
Reed, Ishmael
    Beware: Do Not Read This Poem: V6
Revard, Carter
    Birch Canoe: V5
Rich, Adrienne
    Rusted Legacy: V15
Ríos, Alberto
    Island of the Three Marias: V11
Robinson, E. A.
    Richard Cory: V4
Roethke, Theodore
    My Papa's Waltz: V3
Rogers, Pattiann
    The Greatest Grandeur: V18
Rose, Wendy
    For the White poets who would be Indian: V13
Rukeyser, Muriel
    Ballad of Orange and Grape: V10
Salter, Mary Jo
    Trompe l'Oeil: V22
Sandburg, Carl
    Chicago: V3
    Cool Tombs: V6
    Hope Is a Tattered Flag: V12
Santos, Sherod
    Portrait of a Couple at Century's End: V24
Schnackenberg, Gjertrud
    Darwin in 1881: V13
    Supernatural Love: V25
Sexton, Anne
    Courage: V14
    Oysters: V4
Shapiro, Karl
    Auto Wreck: V3
Silko, Leslie Marmon
    Four Mountain Wolves: V9
    Story from Bear Country: V16
Simic, Charles
    Butcher Shop: V7
Simpson, Louis
    American Poetry: V7
    Chocolates: V11
    In the Suburbs: V14

Snyder, Gary
  Anasazi: V9
  True Night: V19
Song, Cathy
  Lost Sister: V5
Soto, Gary
  Small Town with One Road: V7
Spires, Elizabeth
  Ghazal: V21
Stafford, William
  At the Bomb Testing Site: V8
  Fifteen: V2
  Ways to Live: V16
Stevens, Wallace
  The Idea of Order at Key West: V13
  Sunday Morning: V16
Stewart, Susan
  The Forest: V22
Stone, Ruth
  Ordinary Words: V19
Strand, Mark
  The Continuous Life: V18
Swenson, May
  Southbound on the Freeway: V16
Tate, James
  Dear Reader: V10
  Smart and Final Iris: V15
Taylor, Henry
  Landscape with Tractor: V10
Teasdale, Sara
  There Will Come Soft Rains: V14
Thayer, Ernest Lawrence
  Casey at the Bat: V5
Valentine, Jean
  Seeing You: V24
Van Duyn, Mona
  Memoir: V20
Vazirani, Reetika
  Daughter-Mother-Maya-Seeta: V25
Viereck, Peter
  For An Assyrian Frieze: V9
  Kilroy: V14
Voigt, Ellen Bryant
  Practice: V23
Warren, Rosanna
  Daylights: V13
  Lake: V23
Wheatley, Phillis
  To His Excellency General Washington: V13
Whitman, Walt
  Cavalry Crossing a Ford: V13
  I Hear America Singing: V3
  O Captain! My Captain!: V2
  When I Heard the Learn'd Astronomer: V22
Wilbur, Richard
  Beowulf: V11
  Merlin Enthralled: V16
  On Freedom's Ground: V12
Williams, William Carlos
  Overture to a Dance of Locomotives: V11
  Queen-Ann's-Lace: V6
  The Red Wheelbarrow: V1
Wright, Charles
  Black Zodiac: V10
Wright, James
  A Blessing: V7
  Autumn Begins in Martins Ferry, Ohio: V8
Young, Kevin
  Chorale: V25

Asian American
Hahn, Kimiko
  Pine: V23
Hashimoto, Sharon
  What I Would Ask My Husband's Dead Father: V22
Hongo, Garrett
  The Legend: V25
Kim, Sue (Suji) Kwok
  Monologue for an Onion: V24

Australian
Dawe, Bruce
  Drifters: V10
Hope, A. D.
  Beware of Ruins: V8
Wright, Judith
  Drought Year: V8

Canadian
Atwood, Margaret
  Siren Song: V7
Birney, Earle
  Vancouver Lights: V8
Carson, Anne
  New Rule: V18
Hébert, Anne
  The Alchemy of Day: V20
Jacobsen, Josephine
  Fiddler Crab: V23
Layton, Irving
  A Tall Man Executes a Jig: V12
McCrae, John
  In Flanders Fields: V5
Nowlan, Alden
  For Jean Vincent D'abbadie, Baron St.-Castin: V12
Purdy, Al
  Lament for the Dorsets: V5
  Wilderness Gothic: V12
Strand, Mark
  Eating Poetry: V9

Canadian, Sri Lankan
Ondaatje, Michael
  The Cinnamon Peeler: V19
  To a Sad Daughter: V8

Chilean
Neruda, Pablo
  Tonight I Can Write: V11

Chinese
Po, Li
  Drinking Alone Beneath the Moon: V20

Egyptian
Cavafy, C. P.
  Ithaka: V19

English
Alleyn, Ellen
  A Birthday: V10
Arnold, Matthew
  Dover Beach: V2
Auden, W. H.
  As I Walked Out One Evening: V4
  Funeral Blues: V10
  Musée des Beaux Arts: V1
  The Unknown Citizen: V3
Blake, William
  The Lamb: V12
  A Poison Tree: V24
  The Tyger: V2
Bradstreet, Anne
  To My Dear and Loving Husband: V6
Brooke, Rupert
  The Soldier: V7
Browning, Elizabeth Barrett
  Aurora Leigh: V23
  Sonnet XXIX: V16
  Sonnet 43: V2
Browning, Robert
  My Last Duchess: V1
  Porphyria's Lover: V15
Byron, Lord
  The Destruction of Sennacherib: V1
  She Walks in Beauty: V14
Carroll, Lewis
  Jabberwocky: V11
Chaucer, Geoffrey
  The Canterbury Tales: V14
Coleridge, Samuel Taylor
  Kubla Khan: V5
  The Rime of the Ancient Mariner: V4
Donne, John
  Holy Sonnet 10: V2
  A Valediction: Forbidding Mourning: V11
Eliot, T. S.
  Journey of the Magi: V7
  The Love Song of J. Alfred Prufrock: V1

The Waste Land: V20
Fenton, James
   The Milkfish Gatherers: V11
Gray, Thomas
   Elegy Written in a Country Churchyard: V9
Gunn, Thom
   The Missing: V9
Hardy, Thomas
   Ah, Are You Digging on My Grave?: V4
   The Darkling Thrush: V18
   The Man He Killed: V3
Herbert, George
   Virtue: V25
Herrick, Robert
   To the Virgins, to Make Much of Time: V13
Housman, A. E.
   To an Athlete Dying Young: V7
   When I Was One-and-Twenty: V4
Hughes, Ted
   Hawk Roosting: V4
   Perfect Light: V19
Jonson, Ben
   Song: To Celia: V23
Keats, John
   La Belle Dame sans Merci: V17
   Bright Star! Would I Were Steadfast as Thou Art: V9
   Ode on a Grecian Urn: V1
   Ode to a Nightingale: V3
   When I Have Fears that I May Cease to Be: V2
Kipling, Rudyard
   If: V22
Larkin, Philip
   An Arundel Tomb: V12
   High Windows: V3
   Toads: V4
Lawrence, D. H.
   Piano: V6
Levertov, Denise
   The Blue Rim of Memory: V17
Loy, Mina
   Moreover, the Moon: V20
Marlowe, Christopher
   The Passionate Shepherd to His Love: V22
Marvell, Andrew
   To His Coy Mistress: V5
Masefield, John
   Cargoes: V5
Maxwell, Glyn
   The Nerve: V23
Milton, John
   [On His Blindness] Sonnet 16: V3
   On His Having Arrived at the Age of Twenty-Three: V17
Noyes, Alfred
   The Highwayman: V4
Owen, Wilfred
   Dulce et Decorum Est: V10
Pope, Alexander
   The Rape of the Lock: V12
Raine, Craig
   A Martian Sends a Postcard Home: V7
Raleigh, Walter, Sir
   The Nymph's Reply to the Shepherd: V14
Rossetti, Christina
   A Birthday: V10
   Remember: V14
Service, Robert W.
   The Cremation of Sam McGee: V10
Shakespeare, William
   Sonnet 18: V2
   Sonnet 19: V9
   Sonnet 30: V4
   Sonnet 29: V8
   Sonnet 55: V5
   Sonnet 116: V3
   Sonnet 130: V1
Shelley, Percy Bysshe
   Ode to the West Wind: V2
Smith, Stevie
   Not Waving but Drowning: V3
Spender, Stephen
   An Elementary School Classroom in a Slum: V23
Tennyson, Alfred, Lord
   The Charge of the Light Brigade: V1
   The Eagle: V11
   The Lady of Shalott: V15
   Proem: V19
   Tears, Idle Tears: V4
   Ulysses: V2
Williams, William Carlos
   Queen-Ann's-Lace: V6
   The Red Wheelbarrow: V1
Wordsworth, William
   Lines Composed a Few Miles above Tintern Abbey: V2
Wyatt, Thomas
   Whoso List to Hunt: V25
Yeats, W. B.
   Easter 1916: V5
   An Irish Airman Forsees His Death: V1
   The Lake Isle of Innisfree: V15
   Leda and the Swan: V13
   Sailing to Byzantium: V2
   The Second Coming: V7

French

Apollinaire, Guillaume
   Always: V24
Baudelaire, Charles
   Hymn to Beauty: V21
Malroux, Claire
   Morning Walk: V21

German

Amichai, Yehuda
   Not like a Cypress: V24
Blumenthal, Michael
   Inventors: V7
Erdrich, Louise
   Bidwell Ghost: V14
Mueller, Lisel
   Blood Oranges: V13
   The Exhibit: V9
Rilke, Rainer Maria
   Childhood: V19
Roethke, Theodore
   My Papa's Waltz: V3
Sachs, Nelly
   But Perhaps God Needs the Longing: V20
Sajé, Natasha
   The Art of the Novel: V23

Ghanaian

Du Bois, W. E. B.
   The Song of the Smoke: V13

Greek

Cavafy, C. P.
   Ithaka: V19
Sappho
   Hymn to Aphrodite: V20

Hispanic

Castillo, Ana
   While I Was Gone a War Began: V21
Cruz, Victor Hernandez
   Business: V16
Espada, Martín
   Colibrí: V16

Indian

Mirabai
   All I Was Doing Was Breathing: V24
Shahid Ali, Agha
   Country Without a Post Office: V18
Tagore, Rabindranath
   60: V18
Vazirani, Reetika
   Daughter-Mother-Maya-Seeta: V25

Indonesian

Lee, Li-Young
   Early in the Morning: V17
   For a New Citizen of These United States: V15
   The Weight of Sweetness: V11

Iranian

Farrokhzaad, Faroogh
  A Rebirth: V21

Irish

Boland, Eavan
  Anorexic: V12
  It's a Woman's World: V22
Grennan, Eamon
  Station: V21
Hartnett, Michael
  A Farewell to English: V10
Heaney, Seamus
  Digging: V5
  A Drink of Water: V8
  Midnight: V2
  The Singer's House: V17
Muldoon, Paul
  Meeting the British: V7
  Pineapples and Pomegranates: V22
Yeats, William Butler
  Easter 1916: V5
  An Irish Airman Foresees His Death: V1
  The Lake Isle of Innisfree: V15
  Leda and the Swan: V13
  Sailing to Byzantium: V2
  The Second Coming: V7

Israeli

Amichai, Yehuda
  Not like a Cypress: V24

Italian

Apollinaire, Guillaume
  Always: V24
Montale, Eugenio
  On the Threshold: V22
Pavese, Cesare
  Two Poems for T.: V20
Ungaretti, Giuseppe
  Variations on Nothing: V20

Jamaican

Goodison, Lorna
  The River Mumma Wants Out: V25
McKay, Claude
  The Tropics in New York: V4
Simpson, Louis
  In the Suburbs: V14

Japanese

Ai
  Reunions with a Ghost: V16
Bashō, Matsuo
  Falling Upon Earth: V2
  The Moon Glows the Same: V7
  Temple Bells Die Out: V18

Jewish

Bell, Marvin
  View: V25
Blumenthal, Michael
  Inventors: V7
Espada, Martín
  Colibrí: V16
  We Live by What We See at Night: V13
Hirsch, Edward
  Omen: V22
Piercy, Marge
  Apple sauce for Eve: V22
  Barbie Doll: V9
Sachs, Nelly
  But Perhaps God Needs the Longing: V20
Shapiro, Karl
  Auto Wreck: V3

Kiowa

Momaday, N. Scott
  Angle of Geese: V2
  To a Child Running With Outstretched Arms in Canyon de Chelly: V11

Lithuanian

Milosz, Czeslaw
  Song of a Citizen: V16

Mexican

Paz, Octavio
  Duration: V18
Soto, Gary
  Small Town with One Road: V7

Native American

Ai
  Reunions with a Ghost: V16
Erdrich, Louise
  Bidwell Ghost: V14
Harjo, Joy
  Anniversary: V15
Momaday, N. Scott
  Angle of Geese: V2
  To a Child Running With Outstretched Arms in Canyon de Chelly: V11
Ortiz, Simon
  Hunger in New York City: V4
  My Father's Song: V16
Revard, Carter
  Birch Canoe: V5
Rose, Wendy
  For the White poets who would be Indian: V13
Silko, Leslie Marmon
  Four Mountain Wolves: V9
  Story from Bear Country: V16

Osage

Revard, Carter
  Birch Canoe: V5

Philippine

Barot, Rick
  Bonnard's Garden: V25

Polish

Herbert, Zbigniew
  Why The Classics: V22
Milosz, Czeslaw
  Song of a Citizen: V16
Swir, Anna
  Maternity: V21
Szymborska, Wislawa
  Astonishment: V15
Zagajewski, Adam
  Self-Portrait: V25

Roman

Ovid (Naso, Publius Ovidius)
  Metamorphoses: V22

Romanian

Celan, Paul
  Late and Deep: V21

Russian

Akhmatova, Anna
  Midnight Verses: V18
Levertov, Denise
  In the Land of Shinar: V7
Merriam, Eve
  Onomatopoeia: V6
Shapiro, Karl
  Auto Wreck: V3

St. Lucian

Walcott, Derek
  A Far Cry from Africa: V6

Scottish

Burns, Robert
  A Red, Red Rose: V8

Byron, Lord
 The Destruction of Sennacherib: V1
Duffy, Carol Ann
 Originally: V25
MacBeth, George
 Bedtime Story: V8

Senegalese

Wheatley, Phillis
 To His Excellency General Washington: V13

Serbian

Lazić, Radmila
 Death Sentences: V22

Spanish

García Lorca, Federico
 Gacela of the Dark Death: V20
Machado, Antonio
 The Crime Was in Granada: V23
Williams, William Carlos
 The Red Wheelbarrow: V1

Swedish

Sandburg, Carl
 Chicago: V3
Svenbro, Jesper
 Lepidopterology: V23
Tranströmer, Tomas
 Answers to Letters: V21

Vietnamese

Huong, Ho Xuan
 Spring-Watching Pavilion: V18

Welsh

Levertov, Denise
 In the Land of Shinar: V7
Thomas, Dylan
 Do Not Go Gentle into that Good Night: V1
 Fern Hill: V3
 The Force That Through the Green Fuse Drives the Flower: V8

Yugoslavian

Lazić, Radmila
 Death Sentences: V22

Subject/Theme Index

A

Acceptance
　Art Thou the Thing I Wanted: 5
Adultery
　Whoso List to Hunt: 293–296, 298, 304
Adulthood
　Rent: 167–168
Air and Sky
　Hum: 100
Alienation
　The Legend: 129
　Originally: 160–161
Allegory
　Whoso List to Hunt: 284–285, 288
American Midwest
　View: 259–260
American Northeast
　Hum: 97–98, 100–103
American South
　Rent: 174, 177, 179
Anger
　Virtue: 276–279, 281
　Whoso List to Hunt: 301–302
Anonymity
　The Legend: 130
Art
　Bonnard's Garden: 36
Atonement
　The River Mumma Wants Out: 200, 202, 205

B

Beauty
　Art Thou the Thing I Wanted: 12–13, 15, 18
　Bonnard's Garden: 32, 36–38, 41, 43–44
　Hum: 97–106
　Virtue: 261–267, 271–274, 277–282
　Whoso List to Hunt: 297, 301–302, 305
Betrayal
　Whoso List to Hunt: 296, 302–304
Biography
　Whoso List to Hunt: 294–296, 304–305

C

Change
　The River Mumma Wants Out: 193
Childhood
　Originally: 145, 147–149, 152, 156–158
　Rent: 174, 176, 178, 180
Christianity
　Supernatural Love: 227, 229, 233
Classicism
　Whoso List to Hunt: 294, 301, 303
Commercial World Versus Spiritual World
　The River Mumma Wants Out: 193
Communism
　Self-Portrait: 208, 210, 212–213
Couplet
　Whoso List to Hunt: 285–286, 288
Courage
　Virtue: 272, 276, 278, 280
Courtly Love
　Whoso List to Hunt: 286
Crime and Criminals
　Whoso List to Hunt: 297–298, 303–304
Cruelty
　Knowledge: 112, 114–116, 118
　The Legend: 127, 131, 133
Cultural Integration
　Originally: 149
Cynicism
　The Cossacks: 68, 70–71
　Knowledge: 114–117

D

Dance
　The River Mumma Wants Out: 192–195
Death
　The Cossacks: 68–73, 75–77
　Hum: 99–103
　Knowledge: 112, 116, 118
　The Legend: 138–139
　The River Mumma Wants Out: 200–202, 205
　Supernatural Love: 228–231, 233, 236–237, 239
　View: 247, 250–251
　Virtue: 262–266, 268, 271–274, 276–283
　Whoso List to Hunt: 286, 289–291, 297–298, 300–301, 303–305
Deceit
　Whoso List to Hunt: 302–303, 305

Description
  The Legend: 128, 130–131
Dialect
  Chorale: 56
Discomfort
  Art Thou the Thing I Wanted: 6
Discrimination
  Daughter-Mother-Maya-Seeta: 85
Disintegration
  Hum: 101
Divine Right of Kings
  Whoso List to Hunt: 287
Divorce
  Whoso List to Hunt: 289–290
Dreams and Visions
  Rent: 177, 180, 183, 185–186, 188
  Self-Portrait: 216–218

E

Ecology
  The River Mumma Wants Out: 190, 193, 195–196
Egocentricity
  The River Mumma Wants Out: 194
Emotions
  Art Thou the Thing I Wanted: 1, 7–11, 14, 21
  Bonnard's Garden: 35–37, 42, 47–48
  Chorale: 53, 56, 59–61, 64, 67
  The Cossacks: 71, 73, 75–76, 78, 80
  Daughter-Mother-Maya-Seeta: 84, 86, 89, 91–94
  Hum: 102
  Knowledge: 119–125
  The Legend: 130–131, 134–135, 140–141
  Originally: 148, 152–154, 156
  Rent: 172
  The River Mumma Wants Out: 198–199
  Self-Portrait: 210, 217–218, 221–222, 224
  Supernatural Love: 242–243
  View: 245, 252, 254
  Virtue: 277, 281
  Whoso List to Hunt: 288
Envy
  Daughter-Mother-Maya-Seeta: 85–86
Eternity
  Art Thou the Thing I Wanted: 28, 30
  Virtue: 261–262, 264–266, 268, 270, 272, 274
Europe
  Art Thou the Thing I Wanted: 27, 29–30
  Knowledge: 118
  Originally: 145, 149–155, 160–161
  Rent: 174, 178–179
  Self-Portrait: 208, 210, 212–213, 220–221, 224
  View: 248–249, 251
  Virtue: 261, 266–267
  Whoso List to Hunt: 284, 289–290, 295–298, 300–301, 304
Everyday Joys
  Rent: 165
Evil
  Knowledge: 114–116, 119–120
  The River Mumma Wants Out: 206
Execution
  Supernatural Love: 229–230
  Whoso List to Hunt: 296–297, 303
Exile
  Self-Portrait: 211
Expressionism
  Hum: 97, 99, 101

F

Faith
  Virtue: 265
Farm and Rural Life
  Art Thou the Thing I Wanted: 5–6, 8
Fate and Chance
  Art Thou the Thing I Wanted: 19, 21–22, 24–26
  Bonnard's Garden: 44–47, 49
  Chorale: 51–53
  The Cossacks: 78–80
  Rent: 174–175, 177–179, 181–182
  View: 257–258
  Virtue: 273
Fear
  Knowledge: 115
Fear and Terror
  Art Thou the Thing I Wanted: 20–21, 23–24
  The Cossacks: 68, 70–73, 75–77
  Knowledge: 115–121
  Supernatural Love: 236–237, 239, 241
Feminism
  Art Thou the Thing I Wanted: 20, 23, 26
  Rent: 163, 166–171
Folklore
  Originally: 156, 159
  The River Mumma Wants Out: 192–193, 196
  Supernatural Love: 237
Freedom
  Daughter-Mother-Maya-Seeta: 84–87

G

Gender Roles
  Rent: 167

Ghost
  Art Thou the Thing I Wanted: 27–28
God
  Chorale: 57–58
  Daughter-Mother-Maya-Seeta: 84–86, 88
  Self-Portrait: 219, 222–224
  Supernatural Love: 229–230
  Virtue: 261, 266–267, 271–272, 274
  Whoso List to Hunt: 296–298, 304
Goodness
  Knowledge: 114–116
Grief and Sorrow
  Art Thou the Thing I Wanted: 27–28
  Hum: 97, 99–104, 106
  Self-Portrait: 221–224
  Whoso List to Hunt: 297, 300–302
Guilt
  Whoso List to Hunt: 296–298, 303–304

H

Happiness and Gaiety
  Daughter-Mother-Maya-Seeta: 82, 84–85
  Rent: 165–166, 168, 183, 186, 189
  Self-Portrait: 223, 225
  Whoso List to Hunt: 301, 303, 305
Hatred
  View: 245, 248, 250–251, 253, 255
  Whoso List to Hunt: 295–298, 300–303, 305
Heaven
  Chorale: 57
  Virtue: 271–272
History
  The Legend: 130–133
  Originally: 152
  Rent: 166, 168, 173–175, 177, 179
  The River Mumma Wants Out: 201, 205
  Self-Portrait: 220–221
  Supernatural Love: 227
Homosexuality
  Originally: 155
Honor
  Whoso List to Hunt: 298, 303–304
Hope
  Bonnard's Garden: 41–42
  Chorale: 52–54
  The Cossacks: 70–71
  Knowledge: 115–116

Human Condition
 Daughter-Mother-Maya-Seeta: 82
Humiliation and Degradation
 The Legend: 130–131, 134–135
Humility
 Supernatural Love: 237, 239
Humor
 Art Thou the Thing I Wanted: 19, 21, 25
 Chorale: 64–65

I

Identity
 The Legend: 130
Identity Loss
 Originally: 148
Ignorance
 Whoso List to Hunt: 302–304
Imagery and Symbolism
 Art Thou the Thing I Wanted: 6–7, 9, 12–17, 23
 Bonnard's Garden: 32, 36–37
 The Cossacks: 69, 72–73
 Daughter-Mother-Maya-Seeta: 84, 86–87
 Hum: 99, 101–102, 108, 110
 Rent: 166, 170–171
 The River Mumma Wants Out: 195, 202, 204–205
 Self-Portrait: 217
 View: 248, 250
 Virtue: 262–263, 266–267, 274–275, 277, 280, 282
 Whoso List to Hunt: 288–289
Imagination
 Art Thou the Thing I Wanted: 11–14, 18
 Self-Portrait: 216–219
Immigrants and Immigration
 Daughter-Mother-Maya-Seeta: 84, 87–88, 91–92
 Self-Portrait: 208, 210, 212
Independence
 Rent: 164
Innocence
 Knowledge: 115
The Interconnection of Life and Death
 Virtue: 264
Irony
 Self-Portrait: 222, 224–225

J

Judaism
 The Cossacks: 68, 71, 73

K

Killers and Killing
 Knowledge: 114, 117, 119, 121
 Whoso List to Hunt: 295, 304–305

Knowledge
 Art Thou the Thing I Wanted: 13

L

Lack of Compassion and Responsibility
 The River Mumma Wants Out: 194
Lamentation
 Hum: 101
Landscape
 Hum: 108–110
 Rent: 183–184, 186–188
 The River Mumma Wants Out: 192–200, 202, 204–206
 View: 245, 247–249, 251
Law and Order
 View: 248, 250–251
 Whoso List to Hunt: 294–305
Limitations and Opportunities
 Hum: 108–110
 Virtue: 276–278, 280, 282
Literary Terms
 Rent: 185
Loneliness
 Self-Portrait: 212, 221
Love
 Knowledge: 116
Love and Passion
 Art Thou the Thing I Wanted: 3–6, 8–10, 21, 23, 25–30
 Bonnard's Garden: 41–45, 48
 Chorale: 59–62
 Daughter-Mother-Maya-Seeta: 82, 85–87
 Knowledge: 112, 116, 118, 125
 Originally: 155
 Rent: 163–166, 169–173, 184–188
 The River Mumma Wants Out: 202, 204
 Supernatural Love: 228–231, 233, 241–242
 Virtue: 272–274, 277–278, 280–281, 283
 Whoso List to Hunt: 284–289, 291–297, 299–305
Loyalty
 Self-Portrait: 210, 212
 Virtue: 265, 267–269
 Whoso List to Hunt: 297, 300–302, 304

M

Marriage
 Whoso List to Hunt: 289–290, 294–295, 297
Memory and Reminiscence
 Art Thou the Thing I Wanted: 11–14, 17
Metaphysical Poetry
 Virtue: 262, 267

Middle East
 Daughter-Mother-Maya-Seeta: 84–85, 87–88, 95–96
 Knowledge: 117–118
 View: 250–251
Mixing of Eastern and Western Cultures
 The Legend: 130
Modernism
 Art Thou the Thing I Wanted: 7–8
 Hum: 101–102
Monarchy
 The River Mumma Wants Out: 192, 194–196
 Virtue: 266–267
 Whoso List to Hunt: 284, 287–290, 294–298, 302–305
Money and Economics
 The River Mumma Wants Out: 190, 193–197
Monologue
 Chorale: 64–65
 Originally: 156, 159
Mood
 Hum: 101–103
Morals and Morality
 Virtue: 262, 264–267, 276–277, 280–282
 Whoso List to Hunt: 298, 300–301, 303–305
Motherhood
 Daughter-Mother-Maya-Seeta: 89–90
Mother's Love
 Daughter-Mother-Maya-Seeta: 85
Murder
 Knowledge: 119
Music
 Art Thou the Thing I Wanted: 18, 22–25
 Bonnard's Garden: 38–39
 Chorale: 50, 53–56, 59–62, 66
 Hum: 101–102
 Rent: 174, 176, 178–180
 The River Mumma Wants Out: 193, 201–207
 Self-Portrait: 210–212
 Supernatural Love: 236–238
 Virtue: 264–266, 272–274, 276, 278–279, 281–283
 Whoso List to Hunt: 296–297, 300, 302, 304
Mystery and Intrigue
 Originally: 156–157, 159
Mysticism
 Self-Portrait: 219, 222–224
Mysticism for Beginners
 Self-Portrait: 210
Myths and Legends
 Art Thou the Thing I Wanted: 12, 15–17
 Bonnard's Garden: 40–42
 The Legend: 127, 129–131, 133–135, 138–139

Originally: 155–156, 158–159
Rent: 174, 177–178
The River Mumma Wants Out: 191–193, 195
Supernatural Love: 238–241

N

Narration
Art Thou the Thing I Wanted: 3–7, 9–11, 28
Bonnard's Garden: 34–36, 41–42, 46
Chorale: 51–53
Hum: 98–102, 104–106
Knowledge: 112, 114–115, 117, 123–125
The Legend: 127–131, 133–135
Originally: 157–159
Rent: 176
The River Mumma Wants Out: 192–193, 195, 198–199
Supernatural Love: 232–233
View: 247–249
Virtue: 261, 263–264
Whoso List to Hunt: 286, 288, 291–292

Nature
Art Thou the Thing I Wanted: 4, 9, 13, 15, 17
Bonnard's Garden: 32, 35–37, 39
Hum: 102–103
Rent: 185–186
The River Mumma Wants Out: 192–193, 195
Self-Portrait: 210–211
Supernatural Love: 236–237
View: 245, 247, 250, 252
Virtue: 262–266, 271, 276–282
Whoso List to Hunt: 286

1980s
Originally: 150–151

North America
Daughter-Mother-Maya-Seeta: 84–85, 87–88, 91–92
The Legend: 131–132
View: 250–251

O

Obsession
Whoso List to Hunt: 288

P

Painting
Art Thou the Thing I Wanted: 26–27, 29
Bonnard's Garden: 32, 34–39, 41, 43
Chorale: 63–65
Hum: 97, 101–102, 109
The Legend: 128, 130–131, 139
Rent: 174, 176, 178, 181
The River Mumma Wants Out: 202–203, 205

Passage of Time
Hum: 99

Perception
The Cossacks: 71–74
Knowledge: 114–118
The River Mumma Wants Out: 192, 194–195, 197
View: 249–252

Permanence
Art Thou the Thing I Wanted: 27–28, 30
Virtue: 264, 268, 270–271

Persecution
The Legend: 136

Personal Identity
The Legend: 127–128, 130–131
Originally: 148, 150–153, 155, 160–161
Whoso List to Hunt: 291–294

Personification
Art Thou the Thing I Wanted: 14–16
The River Mumma Wants Out: 202

Pessimism
The Cossacks: 71

Plants
Bonnard's Garden: 32, 34–36
View: 245, 247–250

Plot
Chorale: 64–65

Poetic Symbolism and Theological Doctrine
Supernatural Love: 229

Poetry
Art Thou the Thing I Wanted: 1, 3–30
Bonnard's Garden: 32, 35–49
Chorale: 50–57, 59–67
The Cossacks: 68–73, 75–81
Daughter-Mother-Maya-Seeta: 82, 84–95
Hum: 97–99, 101–110
Knowledge: 112–125
The Legend: 127–131, 133–142
Originally: 145, 147–152, 155–162
Rent: 163–189
The River Mumma Wants Out: 190, 192–206
Self-Portrait: 208–225
Supernatural Love: 227–242
View: 245, 247–260
Virtue: 261–262, 264–283
Whoso List to Hunt: 284–286, 288–308

Point of View
Rent: 186, 188

Politicians
Originally: 150–151
Self-Portrait: 212–213

Politics
Chorale: 59–60
The Cossacks: 73–74
Originally: 150–152
The River Mumma Wants Out: 196–197
Self-Portrait: 208, 210, 212–213, 220–221, 224
View: 245, 248, 251
Virtue: 266–267
Whoso List to Hunt: 289–291, 294–295, 298, 300, 302, 304

Postmodernism
Art Thou the Thing I Wanted: 7–8
Hum: 97, 102–103

The Power of Christian Virtue To Overcome Mortality
Virtue: 265

Pride
Daughter-Mother-Maya-Seeta: 82, 85, 87

Prophecy
The River Mumma Wants Out: 201, 203

Protestantism
Whoso List to Hunt: 289–290

Psalm
Whoso List to Hunt: 299–300, 303–305

Psychology and the Human Mind
Art Thou the Thing I Wanted: 11–14, 16
Originally: 154

R

Race
Daughter-Mother-Maya-Seeta: 84
The Legend: 127, 129, 131–133

Racism and Prejudice
Daughter-Mother-Maya-Seeta: 82, 85–88

Religion and Religious Thought
Chorale: 50, 52–53, 56–57, 59–60
The Cossacks: 73–74
The River Mumma Wants Out: 204
Self-Portrait: 219
Supernatural Love: 232, 240–241
Virtue: 261, 263, 265, 267–268, 272–273, 279, 282
Whoso List to Hunt: 289–290, 294–295, 297, 300, 304

The Renaissance
Whoso List to Hunt: 306–308

Revenge
Whoso List to Hunt: 302–303

Roman Catholicism
Whoso List to Hunt: 289–290

S

Sadness
Chorale: 53

Salvation
Supernatural Love: 229–230
Satire
Whoso List to Hunt: 294, 298, 300–305
Science and Technology
Art Thou the Thing I Wanted: 12–14, 18, 20–21, 24, 26
Virtue: 275–276
Search for Knowledge
Rent: 167–168
Sense Perception
View: 249
Setting
The Legend: 128–129, 134
Originally: 147, 151
Rent: 166
Sexism
Whoso List to Hunt: 288
Shame
The Legend: 131
Sin
Chorale: 58
The River Mumma Wants Out: 201
Virtue: 277–278
Whoso List to Hunt: 302–304
Slavery
The River Mumma Wants Out: 196
Social Masks
The Cossacks: 71
Social Order
Daughter-Mother-Maya-Seeta: 85, 87–88
Solitude
Chorale: 51, 53
Rent: 177–179
Self-Portrait: 220–221, 223
Sonnet
Whoso List to Hunt: 284–289, 291–298, 300–303, 306–308
Soul
Chorale: 53, 55–56
Virtue: 262, 264–266, 268–270, 276–283
Space
View: 248

Spiritual Leaders
Whoso List to Hunt: 289–290
Spirituality
Chorale: 51–54, 56–60
The River Mumma Wants Out: 190, 193, 195–196
Virtue: 268–270, 277, 280, 282–283
Whoso List to Hunt: 296, 302
Sports and the Sporting Life
Whoso List to Hunt: 285–286, 288–290, 292–294
Spring
Bonnard's Garden: 35
Storms and Weather Conditions
Hum: 97–102
Stream of Consciousness
Originally: 156–157, 159
Strength
Virtue: 281, 283
Structure
Art Thou the Thing I Wanted: 14, 21–22, 26
Daughter-Mother-Maya-Seeta: 93–94
Knowledge: 123–125
Originally: 161
Supernatural Love: 234–235
Virtue: 266–267

T

Time and Change
Art Thou the Thing I Wanted: 27
Virtue: 263–266, 268, 270–271, 273
Tone
Art Thou the Thing I Wanted: 12, 14
Knowledge: 124
The Legend: 129, 131
Originally: 157–161
Rent: 185–187
Virtue: 276–277, 282
Whoso List to Hunt: 298, 302–303
Totalitarianism
Self-Portrait: 220–221, 224

Tragedy
Hum: 98, 100–101, 103–106
The Transience of Earthly Beauty
Virtue: 264
Trust
Virtue: 268
Whoso List to Hunt: 300–302, 306, 308

U

Understanding
Art Thou the Thing I Wanted: 14–15, 17–18
Knowledge: 112–113, 116–117
Upper Class
Whoso List to Hunt: 284, 287–288, 290, 294, 296, 299, 301, 305

W

Wanting
Art Thou the Thing I Wanted: 5
War
View: 250
War, the Military, and Soldier Life
Art Thou the Thing I Wanted: 20
The Cossacks: 73–74
Hum: 104–105
Rent: 174, 178–180, 182, 184–186
View: 245, 247–251, 253–257
Whoso List to Hunt: 295, 301–303
Wildlife
Bonnard's Garden: 32, 34, 36
Daughter-Mother-Maya-Seeta: 84, 87
Self-Portrait: 221, 224
Whoso List to Hunt: 284, 286, 288
World War II
The Legend: 131–133, 141

Y

Yearning
Self-Portrait: 221, 223–224

Cumulative Index of First Lines

1

1. Mother I was born under the mudbank (Seeing You) V24:244–245

A

A brackish reach of shoal off Madaket,— (The Quaker Graveyard in Nantucket) V6:158
"A cold coming we had of it (Journey of the Magi) V7:110
A few minutes ago, I stepped onto the deck (The Cobweb) V17:50
A gentle spring evening arrives (Spring-Watching Pavilion) V18:198
A line in long array where they wind betwixt green islands, (Cavalry Crossing a Ford) V13:50
A narrow Fellow in the grass (A Narrow Fellow in the Grass) V11:127
A pine box for me. I mean it. (Last Request) V14: 231
A poem should be palpable and mute (Ars Poetica) V5:2
A stone from the depths that has witnessed the seas drying up (Song of a Citizen) V16:125
A tourist came in from Orbitville, (Southbound on the Freeway) V16:158
A wind is ruffling the tawny pelt (A Far Cry from Africa) V6:60
a woman precedes me up the long rope, (Climbing) V14:113
About me the night moonless wimples the mountains (Vancouver Lights) V8:245
About suffering they were never wrong (Musée des Beaux Arts) V1:148
Across Roblin Lake, two shores away, (Wilderness Gothic) V12:241
After the double party (Air for Mercury) V20:2–3
After the party ends another party begins (Social Life) V19:251
After you finish your work (Ballad of Orange and Grape) V10:17
Again I've returned to this country (The Country Without a Post Office) V18:64
"Ah, are you digging on my grave (Ah, Are You Digging on My Grave?) V4:2
All Greece hates (Helen) V6:92
All my existence is a dark sign a dark (A Rebirth) V21:193–194
All night long the hockey pictures (To a Sad Daughter) V8:230
All over Genoa (Trompe l'Oeil) V22:216
All winter your brute shoulders strained against collars, padding (Names of Horses) V8:141
Also Ulysses once—that other war. (Kilroy) V14:213
Always (Always) V24:15
Among the blossoms, a single jar of wine. (Drinking Alone Beneath the Moon) V20:59–60
Anasazi (Anasazi) V9:2
"And do we remember our living lives?" (Memory) V21:156
And God stepped out on space (The Creation) V1:19
And what if I spoke of despair—who doesn't (And What If I Spoke of Despair) V19:2
Animal bones and some mossy tent rings (Lament for the Dorsets) V5:190
Any force— (All It Takes) V23:15
April is the cruellest month, breeding (The Waste Land) V20:248–252
As I perceive (The Gold Lily) V5:127
As I walked out one evening (As I Walked Out One Evening) V4:15
As in an illuminated page, whose busy edges (Bonnard's Garden) V25:33
As virtuous men pass mildly away (A Valediction: Forbidding Mourning) V11:201
As you set out for Ithaka (Ithaka) V19:114

At noon in the desert a panting lizard (At the Bomb Testing Site) V8:2
Ay, tear her tattered ensign down! (Old Ironsides) V9:172

B

Back then, before we came (On Freedom's Ground) V12:186
Bananas ripe and green, and ginger-root (The Tropics in New York) V4:255
Because I could not stop for Death— (Because I Could Not Stop for Death) V2:27
Before the indifferent beak could let her drop? (Leda and the Swan) V13:182
Before you know what kindness really is (Kindness) V24:84–85
Be happy if the wind inside the orchard (On the Threshold) V22:128
Bent double, like old beggars under slacks, (Dulce et Decorum Est) V10:109
Between my finger and my thumb (Digging) V5:70
Beware of ruins: they have a treacherous charm (Beware of Ruins) V8:43
Bright star! would I were steadfast as thou art— (Bright Star! Would I Were Steadfast as Thou Art) V9:44
But perhaps God needs the longing, wherever else should it dwell, (But Perhaps God Needs the Longing) V20:41
By the rude bridge that arched the flood (Concord Hymn) V4:30
By way of a vanished bridge we cross this river (The Garden Shukkei-en) V18:107

C

Cassandra's kind of crying was (Three To's and an Oi) V24:264
Celestial choir! enthron'd in realms of light, (To His Excellency General Washington V13:212
Come with me into those things that have felt his despair for so long— (Come with Me) V6:31
Complacencies of the peignoir, and late (Sunday Morning) V16:189
Composed in the Tower, before his execution ("More Light! More Light!") V6:119

D

Darkened by time, the masters, like our memories, mix (Black Zodiac) V10:46
Death, be not proud, though some have called thee (Holy Sonnet 10) V2:103
Devouring Time, blunt thou the lion's paws (Sonnet 19) V9:210
Disoriented, the newly dead try to turn back, (Our Side) V24:177
Do not go gentle into that good night (Do Not Go Gentle into that Good Night) V1:51
Do not weep, maiden, for war is kind (War Is Kind) V9:252
Don Arturo says: (Business) V16:2
Drink to me only with thine eyes, (Song: To Celia) V23:270–271
(Dumb, (A Grafted Tongue) V12:92

E

Each day the shadow swings (In the Land of Shinar) V7:83
Each morning the man rises from bed because the invisible (It's like This) V23:138–139
Each night she waits by the road (Bidwell Ghost) V14:2
Even when you know what people are capable of, (Knowledge) V25:113

F

Face of the skies (Moreover, the Moon) V20:153
Falling upon earth (Falling Upon Earth) V2:64
Far far from gusty waves these children's faces. (An Elementary School Classroom in a Slum) V23:88–89
Five years have past; five summers, with the length (Tintern Abbey) V2:249
Flesh is heretic. (Anorexic) V12:2
For a long time the butterfly held a prominent place in psychology (Lepidopterology) V23:171–172
For Jews, the Cossacks are always coming. (The Cossacks) V25:70
For three years, out of key with his time, (Hugh Selwyn Mauberley) V16:26
Forgive me for thinking I saw (For a New Citizen of These United States) V15:55
From my mother's sleep I fell into the State (The Death of the Ball Turret Gunner) V2:41

G

Gardener: Sir, I encountered Death (Incident in a Rose Garden) V14:190
Gather ye Rose-buds while ye may, (To the Virgins, to Make Much of Time) V13:226
Gazelle, I killed you (Ode to a Drum) V20:172–173
Go down, Moses (Go Down, Moses) V11:42
Gray mist wolf (Four Mountain Wolves) V9:131

H

"Had he and I but met (The Man He Killed) V3:167
Had we but world enough, and time (To His Coy Mistress) V5:276
Half a league, half a league (The Charge of the Light Brigade) V1:2
Having a Coke with You (Having a Coke with You) V12:105
He clasps the crag with crooked hands (The Eagle) V11:30
He was found by the Bureau of Statistics to be (The Unknown Citizen) V3:302
He was seen, surrounded by rifles, (The Crime Was in Granada) V23:55–56
Hear the sledges with the bells— (The Bells) V3:46
Heart, you bully, you punk, I'm wrecked, I'm shocked (One Is One) V24:158
Her body is not so white as (Queen-Ann's-Lace) V6:179

Her eyes were coins of porter and her West (A Farewell to English) V10:126
Here they are. The soft eyes open (The Heaven of Animals) V6:75
His speed and strength, which is the strength of ten (His Speed and Strength) V19:96
Hog Butcher for the World (Chicago) V3:61
Hold fast to dreams (Dream Variations) V15:42
Hope is a tattered flag and a dream out of time. (Hope is a Tattered Flag) V12:120
"Hope" is the thing with feathers— (Hope Is the Thing with Feathers) V3:123
How do I love thee? Let me count the ways (Sonnet 43) V2:236
How shall we adorn (Angle of Geese) V2:2
How soon hath Time, the subtle thief of youth, (On His Having Arrived at the Age of Twenty-Three) V17:159
How would it be if you took yourself off (Landscape with Tractor) V10:182
Hunger crawls into you (Hunger in New York City) V4:79

I

I am not a painter, I am a poet (Why I Am Not a Painter) V8:258
I am the Smoke King (The Song of the Smoke) V13:196
I am silver and exact. I have no preconceptions (Mirror) V1:116
I am trying to pry open your casket (Dear Reader) V10:85
I became a creature of light (The Mystery) V15:137
I cannot love the Brothers Wright (Reactionary Essay on Applied Science) V9:199
I don't mean to make you cry. (Monologue for an Onion) V24:120–121
I felt a Funeral, in my Brain, (I felt a Funeral in my Brain) V13:137
I gave birth to life. (Maternity) V21:142–143
I have just come down from my father (The Hospital Window) V11:58
I have met them at close of day (Easter 1916) V5:91
I haven't the heart to say (To an Unknown Poet) V18:221
I hear America singing, the varied carols I hear (I Hear America Singing) V3:152
I heard a Fly buzz—when I died— (I Heard a Fly Buzz—When I Died—) V5:140
I know that I shall meet my fate (An Irish Airman Foresees His Death) V1:76
I leant upon a coppice gate (The Darkling Thrush) V18:74
I lie down on my side in the moist grass (Omen) v22:107
I looked in my heart while the wild swans went over. (Wild Swans) V17:221
I prove a theorem and the house expands: (Geometry) V15:68
I see them standing at the formal gates of their colleges, (I go Back to May 1937) V17:112
I sit in the top of the wood, my eyes closed (Hawk Roosting) V4:55
I thought wearing an evergreen dress (Pine) V23:223–224
I'm delighted to see you (The Constellation Orion) V8:53
I've known rivers; (The Negro Speaks of Rivers) V10:197
I was angry with my friend; (A Poison Tree) V24:195–196
I was born too late and I am much too old, (Death Sentences) V22:23
I was born under the mudbank (Seeing You) V24:244–245
I was sitting in mcsorley's. outside it was New York and beautifully snowing. (i was sitting in mcsorley's) V13:151
I will arise and go now, and go to Innisfree, (The Lake Isle of Innisfree) V15:121
If all the world and love were young, (The Nymph's Reply to the Shepard) V14:241
If ever two were one, then surely we (To My Dear and Loving Husband) V6:228
If I should die, think only this of me (The Soldier) V7:218
If you can keep your head when all about you (If) V22:54–55
If you want my apartment, sleep in it (Rent) V25:164
"Imagine being the first to say: *surveillance*," (Inventors) V7:97
Impatient for home, (Portrait of a Couple at Century's End) V24:214–215
In 1790 a woman could die by falling (The Art of the Novel) V23:29
In 1936, a child (Blood Oranges) V13:34
In a while they rose and went out aimlessly riding, (Merlin Enthralled) V16:72
In China (Lost Sister) V5:216
In ethics class so many years ago (Ethics) V8:88
In Flanders fields the poppies blow (In Flanders Fields) V5:155
In India in their lives they happen (Ways to Live) V16:228
In May, when sea-winds pierced our solitudes, (The Rhodora) V17:191
In the bottom drawer of my desk . . . (Answers to Letters) V21:30–31
In the groves of Africa from their natural wonder (An African Elegy) V13:3
In the Shreve High football stadium (Autumn Begins in Martins Ferry, Ohio) V8:17
In the sixty-eight years (Accounting) V21:2–3
In Xanadu did Kubla Khan (Kubla Khan) V5:172
Ink runs from the corners of my mouth (Eating Poetry) V9:60
Is it the boy in me who's looking out (The Boy) V19:14
It is a cold and snowy night. The main street is deserted. (Driving to Town Late to Mail a Letter) V17:63
It is an ancient Mariner (The Rime of the Ancient Mariner) V4:127
It is in the small things we see it. (Courage) V14:125
It little profits that an idle king (Ulysses) V2:278
It looked extremely rocky for the Mudville nine that day (Casey at the Bat) V5:57
It must be troubling for the god who loves you (The God Who Loves You) V20:88
It seems vainglorious and proud (The Conquerors) V13:67
It starts with a low rumbling, white static, (Rapture) V21:181
It was in and about the Martinmas time (Barbara Allan) V7:10
It was many and many a year ago (Annabel Lee) V9:14
Its quick soft silver bell beating, beating (Auto Wreck) V3:31

J

Januaries, Nature greets our eyes (Brazil, January 1, 1502) V6:15
Just off the highway to Rochester, Minnesota (A Blessing) V7:24
just once (For the White poets who would be Indian) V13:112

L

l(a (l(a) V1:85
Let me not to the marriage of true minds (Sonnet 116) V3:288
Let us console you. (Allegory) V23:2–3
Listen, my children, and you shall hear (Paul Revere's Ride) V2:178
Little Lamb, who made thee? (The Lamb) V12:134
Long long ago when the world was a wild place (Bedtime Story) V8:32

M

maggie and milly and molly and may (maggie & milly & molly & may) V12:149
Mary sat musing on the lamp-flame at the table (The Death of the Hired Man) V4:42
Men with picked voices chant the names (Overture to a Dance of Locomotives) V11:143
"Mother dear, may I go downtown (Ballad of Birmingham) V5:17
Much Madness is divinest Sense— (Much Madness is Divinest Sense) V16:86
My black face fades (Facing It) V5:109
My father stands in the warm evening (Starlight) V8:213
My heart aches, and a drowsy numbness pains (Ode to a Nightingale) V3:228
My heart is like a singing bird (A Birthday) V10:33
My life closed twice before its close— (My Life Closed Twice Before Its Close) V8:127
My mistress' eyes are nothing like the sun (Sonnet 130) V1:247
My uncle in East Germany (The Exhibit) V9:107

N

Nature's first green is gold (Nothing Gold Can Stay) V3:203
No easy thing to bear, the weight of sweetness (The Weight of Sweetness) V11:230
Nobody heard him, the dead man (Not Waving but Drowning) V3:216
Not like a cypress, (Not like a Cypress) V24:135
Not marble nor the gilded monuments (Sonnet 55) V5:246
Not the memorized phone numbers. (What Belongs to Us) V15:196
Now as I was young and easy under the apple boughs (Fern Hill) V3:92
Now as I watch the progress of the plague (The Missing) V9:158
Now I rest my head on the satyr's carved chest, (The Satyr's Heart) V22:187
Now one might catch it see it (Fading Light) V21:49

O

O Captain! my Captain, our fearful trip is done (O Captain! My Captain!) V2:146
O Lord our Lord, how excellent is thy name in all the earth! who hast set thy glory above the heavens (Psalm 8) V9:182
O my Luve's like a red, red rose (A Red, Red Rose) V8:152
O what can ail thee, knight-at-arms, (La Belle Dame sans Merci) V17:18
"O where ha' you been, Lord Randal, my son? (Lord Randal) V6:105
O wild West Wind, thou breath of Autumn's being (Ode to the West Wind) V2:163
Oh, but it is dirty! (Filling Station) V12:57
old age sticks (old age sticks) V3:246
On either side the river lie (The Lady of Shalott) V15:95
On the seashore of endless worlds children meet. The infinite (60) V18:3
Once upon a midnight dreary, while I pondered, weak and weary (The Raven) V1:200
Once some people were visiting Chekhov (Chocolates) V11:17
One day I'll lift the telephone (Elegy for My Father, Who Is Not Dead) V14:154
One foot down, then hop! It's hot (Harlem Hopscotch) V2:93
one shoe on the roadway presents (A Piéd) V3:16
Out of the hills of Habersham, (Song of the Chattahoochee) V14:283
Out walking in the frozen swamp one gray day (The Wood-Pile) V6:251
Oysters we ate (Oysters) V4:91

P

Pentagon code (Smart and Final Iris) V15:183
Poised between going on and back, pulled (The Base Stealer) V12:30

Q

Quinquireme of Nineveh from distant Ophir (Cargoes) V5:44
Quite difficult, belief. (Chorale) V25:51

R

Recognition in the body (In Particular) V20:125
Red men embraced my body's whiteness (Birch Canoe) V5:31
Remember me when I am gone away (Remember) V14:255

S

Shall I compare thee to a Summer's day? (Sonnet 18) V2:222
She came every morning to draw water (A Drink of Water) V8:66
She sang beyond the genius of the sea. (The Idea of Order at Key West) V13:164

She walks in beauty, like the night (She Walks in Beauty) V14:268
Side by side, their faces blurred, (An Arundel Tomb) V12:17
Since the professional wars— (Midnight) V2:130
Since then, I work at night. (Ten Years after Your Deliberate Drowning) V21:240
S'io credesse che mia risposta fosse (The Love Song of J. Alfred Prufrock) V1:97
Sky black (Duration) V18:93
Sleepless as Prospero back in his bedroom (Darwin in 1881) V13:83
so much depends (The Red Wheelbarrow) V1:219
So the man spread his blanket on the field (A Tall Man Executes a Jig) V12:228
So the sky wounded you, jagged at the heart, (Daylights) V13:101
Softly, in the dark, a woman is singing to me (Piano) V6:145
Some say it's in the reptilian dance (The Greatest Grandeur) V18:119
Some say the world will end in fire (Fire and Ice) V7:57
Something there is that doesn't love a wall (Mending Wall) V5:231
Sometimes walking late at night (Butcher Shop) V7:43
Sometimes, a lion with a prophet's beard (For An Assyrian Frieze) V9:120
Sometimes, in the middle of the lesson (Music Lessons) V8:117
somewhere i have never travelled,gladly beyond (somewhere i have never travelled,gladly beyond) V19:265
South of the bridge on Seventeenth (Fifteen) V2:78
Stop all the clocks, cut off the telephone, (Funeral Blues) V10:139
Strong Men, riding horses. In the West (Strong Men, Riding Horses) V4:209
Such places are too still for history, (Deep Woods) V14:138
Sundays too my father got up early (Those Winter Sundays) V1:300
Sweet day, so cool, so calm, so bright, (Virtue) V25:263
Swing low sweet chariot (Swing Low Sweet Chariot) V1:283

T

Take heart, monsieur, four-fifths of this province (For Jean Vincent D'abbadie, Baron St.-Castin) V12:78
Tears, idle tears, I know not what they mean (Tears, Idle Tears) V4:220
Tell me not, in mournful numbers (A Psalm of Life) V7:165
Temple bells die out. (Temple Bells Die Out) V18:210
That is no country for old men. The young (Sailing to Byzantium) V2:207
That negligible bit of sand which slides (Variations on Nothing) V20:234
That time of drought the embered air (Drought Year) V8:78
That's my last Duchess painted on the wall (My Last Duchess) V1:165
The apparition of these faces in the crowd (In a Station of the Metro) V2:116

The Assyrian came down like the wolf on the fold (The Destruction of Sennacherib) V1:38
The broken pillar of the wing jags from the clotted shoulder (Hurt Hawks) V3:138
The bud (Saint Francis and the Sow) V9:222
The Bustle in a House (The Bustle in a House) V10:62
The buzz saw snarled and rattled in the yard (Out, Out—) V10:212
The courage that my mother had (The Courage that My Mother Had) V3:79
The Curfew tolls the knell of parting day (Elegy Written in a Country Churchyard) V9:73
The fiddler crab fiddles, glides and dithers, (Fiddler Crab) V23:111–112
The force that through the green fuse drives the flower (The Force That Through the Green Fuse Drives the Flower) V8:101
The grasses are light brown (September) V23:258–259
The green lamp flares on the table (This Life) V1:293
The ills I sorrow at (Any Human to Another) V3:2
The instructor said (Theme for English B) V6:194
The king sits in Dumferling toune (Sir Patrick Spens) V4:177
The land was overmuch like scenery (Beowulf) V11:2
The last time I saw it was 1968. (The Hiding Place) V10:152
The Lord is my shepherd; I shall not want (Psalm 23) V4:103
The man who sold his lawn to standard oil (The War Against the Trees) V11:215
The moon glows the same (The Moon Glows the Same) V7:152
The old South Boston Aquarium stands (For the Union Dead) V7:67
The others bent their heads and started in ("Trouble with Math in a One-Room Country School") V9:238
The pale nuns of St. Joseph are here (Island of Three Marias) V11:79
The Phoenix comes of flame and dust (The Phoenix) V10:226
The plants of the lake (Two Poems for T.) V20:218
The rain set early in to-night: (Porphyria's Lover) V15:151
The river brought down (How We Heard the Name) V10:167
The rusty spigot (Onomatopoeia) V6:133
The sea is calm tonight (Dover Beach) V2:52
The sea sounds insincere (The Milkfish Gatherers) V11:111
The slow overture of rain, (Mind) V17:145
The Soul selects her own Society—(The Soul Selects Her Own Society) V1:259
The time you won your town the race (To an Athlete Dying Young) V7:230
The way sorrow enters the bone (The Blue Rim of Memory) V17:38
The whiskey on your breath (My Papa's Waltz) V3:191
The white ocean in which birds swim (Morning Walk) V21:167
The wind was a torrent of darkness among the gusty trees (The Highwayman) V4:66
There are strange things done in the midnight sun (The Cremation of Sam McGee) V10:75
There have been rooms for such a short time (The Horizons of Rooms) V15:79

There is a hunger for order, (A Thirst Against) V20:205
There is no way not to be excited (Paradiso) V20:190–191
There is the one song everyone (Siren Song) V7:196
There's a Certain Slant of Light (There's a Certain Slant of Light) V6:211
There's no way out. (In the Suburbs) V14:201
There will come soft rains and the smell of the ground, (There Will Come Soft Rains) V14:301
There you are, in all your innocence, (Perfect Light) V19:187
These open years, the river (For Jennifer, 6, on the Teton) V17:86
These unprepossessing sunsets (Art Thou the Thing I Wanted) V25:2–3
They eat beans mostly, this old yellow pair (The Bean Eaters) V2:16
they were just meant as covers (My Mother Pieced Quilts) V12:169
They said, "Wait." Well, I waited. (Alabama Centennial) V10:2
This girlchild was: born as usual (Barbie Doll) V9:33
This is a litany of lost things, (The Litany) V24:101–102
This is my letter to the World (This Is My Letter to the World) V4:233
This is the Arsenal. From floor to ceiling, (The Arsenal at Springfield) V17:2
This is the black sea-brute bulling through wave-wrack (Leviathan) V5:203
This is the ship of pearl, which, poets feign, (The Chambered Nautilus) V24:52–53
This poem is concerned with language on a very plain level (Paradoxes and Oxymorons) V11:162
This tale is true, and mine. It tells (The Seafarer) V8:177
Thou still unravish'd bride of quietness (Ode on a Grecian Urn) V1:179
Three times my life has opened. (Three Times My Life Has Opened) V16:213
Time in school drags along with so much worry, (Childhood) V19:29
to fold the clothes. No matter who lives (I Stop Writimg the Poem) V16:58
To replay errors (Daughter-Mother-Maya-Seeta) V25:83
To weep unbidden, to wake (Practice) V23:240
Tonight I can write the saddest lines (Tonight I Can Write) V11:187
Toni Morrison despises (The Toni Morrison Dreams) V22:202–203
tonite, *thriller* was (Beware: Do Not Read This Poem) V6:3
Turning and turning in the widening gyre (The Second Coming) V7:179
'Twas brillig, and the slithy toves (Jabberwocky) V11:91
Two roads diverged in a yellow wood (The Road Not Taken) V2:195
Tyger! Tyger! burning bright (The Tyger) V2:263

W

wade (The Fish) V14:171
Wanting to say things, (My Father's Song) V16:102
We are saying goodbye (Station) V21:226–227
We came from our own country in a red room (Originally) V25:146–147
We could be here. This is the valley (Small Town with One Road) V7:207
We met the British in the dead of winter (Meeting the British) V7:138
We real cool. We (We Real Cool) V6:242
Well, son, I'll tell you (Mother to Son) V3:178
What dire offense from amorous causes springs, (The Rape of the Lock) V12:202
What happens to a dream deferred? (Harlem) V1:63
What of the neighborhood homes awash (The Continuous Life) V18:51
What thoughts I have of you tonight, Walt Whitman, for I walked down the sidestreets under the trees with a headache self-conscious looking at the full moon (A Supermarket in California) V5:261
Whatever it is, it must have (American Poetry) V7:2
When Abraham Lincoln was shoveled into the tombs, he forgot the copperheads, and the assassin . . . in the dust, in the cool tombs (Cool Tombs) V6:45
When I consider how my light is spent ([On His Blindness] Sonnet 16) V3:262
When I have fears that I may cease to be (When I Have Fears that I May Cease to Be) V2:295
When I heard the learn'd astronomer, (When I Heard the Learn'd Astronomer) V22:244
When I see a couple of kids (High Windows) V3:108
When I see birches bend to left and right (Birches) V13:14
When I was born, you waited (Having it Out with Melancholy) V17:98
When I was one-and-twenty (When I Was One-and-Twenty) V4:268
When I watch you (Miss Rosie) V1:133
When, in disgrace with Fortune and men's eyes (Sonnet 29) V8:198
When the mountains of Puerto Rico (We Live by What We See at Night) V13:240
When the world was created wasn't it like this? (Anniversary) V15:2
When they said *Carrickfergus* I could hear (The Singer's House) V17:205
When you consider the radiance, that it does not withhold (The City Limits) V19:78
When you look through the window in Sag Harbor and see (View) V25:246–247
Whenever Richard Cory went down town (Richard Cory) V4:116
While I was gone a war began. (While I Was Gone a War Began) V21:253–254
While my hair was still cut straight across my forehead (The River-Merchant's Wife: A Letter) V8:164
While the long grain is softening (Early in the Morning) V17:75
While this America settles in the mould of its vulgarity, heavily thickening to empire (Shine, Perishing Republic) V4:161
While you are preparing for sleep, brushing your teeth, (The Afterlife) V18:39
Who has ever stopped to think of the divinity of Lamont Cranston? (In Memory of Radio) V9:144
Whose woods these are I think I know (Stopping by Woods on a Snowy Evening) V1:272

Whoso list to hunt: I know where is an hind. (Whoso List to Hunt) V25:286
Why should I let the toad *work* (Toads) V4:244

Y

You are small and intense (To a Child Running With Out-stretched Arms in Canyon de Chelly) V11:173

You can't hear? Everything here is changing. (The River Mumma Wants Out) V25:191
You do not have to be good. (Wild Geese) V15:207
You should lie down now and remember the forest, (The Forest) V22:36–37
You stood thigh-deep in water and green light glanced (Lake) V23:158
You were never told, Mother, how old Illya was drunk (The Czar's Last Christmas Letter) V12:44

Cumulative Index of Last Lines

A

. . . a capital T in the endless mass of the text. (Answers to Letters) V21:30–31
a fleck of foam. (Accounting) V21:2–3
A heart that will one day beat you to death. (Monologue for an Onion) V24:120–121
A heart whose love is innocent! (She Walks in Beauty) V14:268
a man then suddenly stops running (Island of Three Marias) V11:80
A perfect evening! (Temple Bells Die Out) V18:210
a space in the lives of their friends (Beware: Do Not Read This Poem) V6:3
A sudden blow: the great wings beating still (Leda and the Swan) V13:181
A terrible beauty is born (Easter 1916) V5:91
About my big, new, automatically defrosting refrigerator with the built-in electric eye (Reactionary Essay on Applied Science) V9:199
about the tall mounds of termites. (Song of a Citizen) V16:126
Across the expedient and wicked stones (Auto Wreck) V3:31
affirming its brilliant and dizzying love. (Lepidopterology) V23:171
Ah, dear father, graybeard, lonely old courage-teacher, what America did you have when Charon quit poling his ferry and you got out on a smoking bank and stood watching the boat disappear on the black waters of Lethe? (A Supermarket in California) V5:261
All losses are restored and sorrows end (Sonnet 30) V4:192
Amen. Amen (The Creation) V1:20
Anasazi (Anasazi) V9:3
and all beyond saving by children (Ethics) V8:88
and all the richer for it. (Mind) V17:146
And all we need of hell (My Life Closed Twice Before Its Close) V8:127
And, being heard, doesn't vanish in the dark. (Variations on Nothing) V20:234
and changed, back to the class ("Trouble with Math in a One-Room Country School") V9:238
And Death shall be no more: Death, thou shalt die (Holy Sonnet 10) V2:103
and destruction. (Allegory) V23:2–3
And drunk the milk of Paradise (Kubla Khan) V5:172
and fear lit by the breadth of such calmly turns to praise. (The City Limits) V19:78
And Finished knowing—then— (I Felt a Funeral in My Brain) V13:137
And gallop terribly against each other's bodies (Autumn Begins in Martins Ferry, Ohio) V8:17
and go back. (For the White poets who would be Indian) V13:112
And handled with a Chain—(Much Madness is Divinest Sense) V16:86
And has not begun to grow a manly smile. (Deep Woods) V14:139
And his own Word (The Phoenix) V10:226
And I am Nicholas. (The Czar's Last Christmas Letter) V12:45
And I was unaware. (The Darkling Thrush) V18:74
And in the suburbs Can't sat down and cried. (Kilroy) V14:213
And it's been years. (Anniversary) V15:3
and joy may come, and make its test of us. (One Is One) V24:158
and leaving essence to the inner eye. (Memory) V21:156
And life for me ain't been no crystal stair (Mother to Son) V3:179
And like a thunderbolt he falls (The Eagle) V11:30
And makes me end where I begun (A Valediction: Forbidding Mourning) V11:202

And 'midst the stars inscribe Belinda's name. (The Rape of the Lock) V12:209
And miles to go before I sleep (Stopping by Woods on a Snowy Evening) V1:272
and my father saying things. (My Father's Song) V16:102
And no birds sing. (La Belle Dame sans Merci) V17:18
And not waving but drowning (Not Waving but Drowning) V3:216
And oh, 'tis true, 'tis true (When I Was One-and-Twenty) V4:268
And reach for your scalping knife. (For Jean Vincent D'abbadie, Baron St.-Castin) V12:78
and retreating, always retreating, behind it (Brazil, January 1, 1502) V6:16
And settled upon his eyes in a black soot ("More Light! More Light!") V6:120
And shuts his eyes. (Darwin in 1881) V13: 84
And so live ever—or else swoon to death (Bright Star! Would I Were Steadfast as Thou Art) V9:44
and strange and loud was the dingoes' cry (Drought Year) V8:78
and stride out. (Courage) V14:126
and sweat and fat and greed. (Anorexic) V12:3
And that has made all the difference (The Road Not Taken) V2:195
And the deep river ran on (As I Walked Out One Evening) V4:16
And the midnight message of Paul Revere (Paul Revere's Ride) V2:180
And the mome raths outgrabe (Jabberwocky) V11:91
And the Salvation Army singing God loves us. . . . (Hope is a Tattered Flag) V12:120
and these the last verses that I write for her (Tonight I Can Write) V11:187
and thickly wooded country; the moon. (The Art of the Novel) V23:29
And those roads in South Dakota that feel around in the darkness . . . (Come with Me) V6:31
and to know she will stay in the field till you die? (Landscape with Tractor) V10:183
and two blankets embroidered with smallpox (Meeting the British) V7:138
and waving, shouting, *Welcome back*. (Elegy for My Father, Who Is Not Dead) V14:154
And—which is more—you'll be a Man, my son! (If) V22:54–55
and whose skin is made dusky by stars. (September) V23:258–259
And wild for to hold, though I seem tame.' (Whoso List to Hunt) V25:286
And would suffice (Fire and Ice) V7:57
And yet God has not said a word! (Porphyria's Lover) V15:151
and you spread un the thin halo of night mist. (Ways to Live) V16:229
And Zero at the Bone— (A Narrow Fellow in the Grass) V11:127
(answer with a tower of birds) (Duration) V18:93
Around us already perhaps future moons, suns and stars blaze in a fiery wreath. (But Perhaps God Needs the Longing) V20:41
As any She belied with false compare (Sonnet 130) V1:248
As ever in my great Task-Master's eye. (On His Having Arrived at the Age of Twenty-Three) V17:160
As far as Cho-fu-Sa (The River-Merchant's Wife: A Letter) V8:165
As the contagion of those molten eyes (For An Assyrian Frieze) V9:120
As they lean over the beans in their rented back room that is full of beads and receipts and dolls and clothes, tobacco crumbs, vases and fringes (The Bean Eaters) V2:16
aspired to become lighter than air (Blood Oranges) V13:34
at home in the fish's fallen heaven (Birch Canoe) V5:31
away, pedaling hard, rocket and pilot. (His Speed and Strength) V19:96

B

Back to the play of constant give and change (The Missing) V9:158
Before it was quite unsheathed from reality (Hurt Hawks) V3:138
before we're even able to name them. (Station) V21:226–227
behind us and all our shining ambivalent love airborne there before us. (Our Side) V24:177
Black like me. (Dream Variations) V15:42
Bless me (Hunger in New York City) V4:79
bombs scandalizing the sanctity of night. (While I Was Gone a War Began) V21:253–254
But, baby, where are you?" (Ballad of Birmingham) V5:17
But be (Ars Poetica) V5:3
but it works every time (Siren Song) V7:196
but the truth is, it is, lost to us now. (The Forest) V22:36–37
But there is no joy in Mudville—mighty Casey has "Struck Out." (Casey at the Bat) V5:58
But we hold our course, and the wind is with us. (On Freedom's Ground) V12:187
by a beeswax candle pooling beside their dinnerware. (Portrait of a Couple at Century's End) V24:214–215
by good fortune (The Horizons of Rooms) V15:80

C

Calls through the valleys of Hall. (Song of the Chattahoochee) V14:284
chickens (The Red Wheelbarrow) V1:219
clear water dashes (Onomatopoeia) V6:133
Columbia. (Kindness) V24:84–85
come to life and burn? (Bidwell Ghost) V14:2
Comin' for to carry me home (Swing Low Sweet Chariot) V1:284
crossed the water. (All It Takes) V23:15

D

Dare frame thy fearful symmetry? (The Tyger) V2:263
"Dead," was all he answered (The Death of the Hired Man) V4:44
deep in the deepest one, tributaries burn. (For Jennifer, 6, on the Teton) V17:86

Delicate, delicate, delicate, delicate—now! (The Base Stealer) V12:30
Die soon (We Real Cool) V6:242
Do what you are going to do, I will tell about it. (I go Back to May 1937) V17:113
Down in the flood of remembrance, I weep like a child for the past (Piano) V6:145
Downward to darkness, on extended wings. (Sunday Morning) V16:190
Driving around, I will waste more time. (Driving to Town Late to Mail a Letter) V17:63
dry wells that fill so easily now (The Exhibit) V9:107
dust rises in many myriads of grains. (Not like a Cypress) V24:135
dusty as miners, into the restored volumes. (Bonnard's Garden) V25:33

E

endless worlds is the great meeting of children. (60) V18:3
Eternal, unchanging creator of earth. Amen (The Seafarer) V8:178
Eternity of your arms around my neck. (Death Sentences) V22:23
even as it vanishes—were not our life. (The Litany) V24:101–102
every branch traced with the ghost writing of snow. (The Afterlife) V18:39

F

fall upon us, the dwellers in shadow (In the Land of Shinar) V7:84
Fallen cold and dead (O Captain! My Captain!) V2:147
filled, never. (The Greatest Grandeur) V18:119
Firewood, iron-ware, and cheap tin trays (Cargoes) V5:44
Fled is that music:—Do I wake or sleep? (Ode to a Nightingale) V3:229
For I'm sick at the heart, and I fain wad lie down." (Lord Randal) V6:105
For nothing now can ever come to any good. (Funeral Blues) V10:139
forget me as fast as you can. (Last Request) V14:231
from one kiss (A Rebirth) V21:193–194

G

going where? Where? (Childhood) V19:29

H

Had anything been wrong, we should certainly have heard (The Unknown Citizen) V3:303
Had somewhere to get to and sailed calmly on (Mus,e des Beaux Arts) V1:148
half eaten by the moon. (Dear Reader) V10:85
hand over hungry hand. (Climbing) V14:113
Happen on a red tongue (Small Town with One Road) V7:207
Has no more need of, and I have (The Courage that My Mother Had) V3:80
Hath melted like snow in the glance of the Lord! (The Destruction of Sennacherib) V1:39
He rose the morrow morn (The Rime of the Ancient Mariner) V4:132
He says again, "Good fences make good neighbors." (Mending Wall) V5:232
He writes down something that he crosses out. (The Boy) V19:14
here; passion will save you. (Air for Mercury) V20:2–3
Has set me softly down beside you. The Poem is you (Paradoxes and Oxymorons) V11:162
History theirs whose languages is the sun. (An Elementary School Classroom in a Slum) V23:88–89
How at my sheet goes the same crooked worm (The Force That Through the Green Fuse Drives the Flower) V8:101
How can I turn from Africa and live? (A Far Cry from Africa) V6:61
How sad then is even the marvelous! (An African Elegy) V13:4

I

I am black. (The Song of the Smoke) V13:197
I am going to keep things like this (Hawk Roosting) V4:55
I am not brave at all (Strong Men, Riding Horses) V4:209
I could not see to see— (I Heard a Fly Buzz—When I Died—) V5:140
I didn't want to put them down. (And What If I Spoke of Despair) V19:2
I have just come down from my father (The Hospital Window) V11:58
I cremated Sam McGee (The Cremation of Sam McGee) V10:76
I hear it in the deep heart's core. (The Lake Isle of Innisfree) V15:121
I never writ, nor no man ever loved (Sonnet 116) V3:288
I romp with joy in the bookish dark (Eating Poetry) V9:61
I see Mike's painting, called SARDINES (Why I Am Not a Painter) V8:259
I shall but love thee better after death (Sonnet 43) V2:236
I should be glad of another death (Journey of the Magi) V7:110
I stand up (Miss Rosie) V1:133
I stood there, fifteen (Fifteen) V2:78
I take it you are he? (Incident in a Rose Garden) V14:191
I turned aside and bowed my head and wept (The Tropics in New York) V4:255
I'll be gone from here. (The Cobweb) V17:51
I'll dig with it (Digging) V5:71
If Winter comes, can Spring be far behind? (Ode to the West Wind) V2:163
In a convulsive misery (The Milkfish Gatherers) V11:112
In balance with this life, this death (An Irish Airman Foresees His Death) V1:76
in earth's gasp, ocean's yawn. (Lake) V23:158
In Flanders fields (In Flanders Fields) V5:155
In ghostlier demarcations, keener sounds. (The Idea of Order at Key West) V13:164
In hearts at peace, under an English heaven (The Soldier) V7:218
In her tomb by the side of the sea (Annabel Lee) V9:14
in the family of things. (Wild Geese) V15:208

in the grit gray light of day. (Daylights) V13:102
In the rear-view mirrors of the passing cars (The War Against the Trees) V11:216
In these Chicago avenues. (A Thirst Against) V20:205
in this bastion of culture. (To an Unknown Poet) V18:221
iness (l(a) V1:85
Into blossom (A Blessing) V7:24
Is Come, my love is come to me. (A Birthday) V10:34
is love—that's all. (Two Poems for T.) V20:218
is safe is what you said. (Practice) V23:240
is still warm (Lament for the Dorsets) V5:191
It asked a crumb—of Me (Hope Is the Thing with Feathers) V3:123
It is our god. (Fiddler Crab) V23:111–112
it is the bell to awaken God that we've heard ringing. (The Garden Shukkei-en) V18:107
It rains as I write this. Mad heart, be brave. (The Country Without a Post Office) V18:64
It was your resting place." (Ah, Are You Digging on My Grave?) V4:2
it's always ourselves we find in the sea (maggie & milly & molly & may) V12:150
its bright, unequivocal eye. (Having it Out with Melancholy) V17:99
It's the fall through wind lifting white leaves. (Rapture) V21:181
its youth. The sea grows old in it. (The Fish) V14:172

J

Judge tenderly—of Me (This Is My Letter to the World) V4:233
Just imagine it (Inventors) V7:97

L

Laughing the stormy, husky, brawling laughter of Youth, half-naked, sweating, proud to be Hog Butcher, Tool Maker, Stacker of Wheat, Player with Railroads and Freight Handler to the Nation (Chicago) V3:61
Learn to labor and to wait (A Psalm of Life) V7:165
Leashed in my throat (Midnight) V2:131
Leaving thine outgrown shell by life's un-resting sea (The Chambered Nautilus) V24:52–53
Let my people go (Go Down, Moses) V11:43
life, our life and its forgetting. (For a New Citizen of These United States) V15:55
Life to Victory (Always) V24:15
like a shadow or a friend. *Colombia.* (Kindness) V24:84–85
Like Stone— (The Soul Selects Her Own Society) V1:259
Little Lamb, God bless thee. (The Lamb) V12:135
Look'd up in perfect silence at the stars. (When I Heard the Learn'd Astronomer) V22:244
love (The Toni Morrison Dreams) V22:202–203

M

'Make a wish, Tom, make a wish.' (Drifters) V10: 98
make it seem to change (The Moon Glows the Same) V7:152
midnight-oiled in the metric laws? (A Farewell to English) V10:126
Monkey business (Business) V16:2
More dear, both for themselves and for thy sake! (Tintern Abbey) V2:250
My foe outstretchd beneath the tree. (A Poison Tree) V24:195–196
My love shall in my verse ever live young (Sonnet 19) V9:211
My soul has grown deep like the rivers. (The Negro Speaks of Rivers) V10:198

N

never to waken in that world again (Starlight) V8:213
newness comes into the world (Daughter-Mother-Maya-Seeta) V25:83
Nirvana is here, nine times out of ten. (Spring-Watching Pavilion) V18:198
No, she's brushing a boy's hair (Facing It) V5:110
no—tell them *no*— (The Hiding Place) V10:153
Noble six hundred! (The Charge of the Light Brigade) V1:3
nobody,not even the rain,has such small hands (somewhere i have never travelled,gladly beyond) V19:265
Not a roof but a field of stars. (Rent) V25:164
not be seeing you, for you have no insurance. (The River Mumma Wants Out) V25:191
Not even the blisters. Look. (What Belongs to Us) V15:196
Not of itself, but thee. (Song: To Celia) V23:270–271
Nothing gold can stay (Nothing Gold Can Stay) V3:203
Nothing, and is nowhere, and is endless (High Windows) V3:108
Now! (Alabama Centennial) V10:2
nursing the tough skin of figs (This Life) V1:293

O

O Death in Life, the days that are no more! (Tears, Idle Tears) V4:220
O Lord our Lord, how excellent is thy name in all the earth! (Psalm 8) V9:182
O Roger, Mackerel, Riley, Ned, Nellie, Chester, Lady Ghost (Names of Horses) V8:142
Of all our joys, this must be the deepest. (Drinking Alone Beneath the Moon) V20:59–60
of blood and ignorance. (Art Thou the Thing I Wanted) V25:2–3
of gentleness (To a Sad Daughter) V8:231
of love's austere and lonely offices? (Those Winter Sundays) V1:300
of peaches (The Weight of Sweetness) V11:230
Of the camellia (Falling Upon Earth) V2:64
Of the Creator. And he waits for the world to begin (Leviathan) V5:204
Of what is past, or passing, or to come (Sailing to Byzantium) V2:207
Oh that was the garden of abundance, seeing you. (Seeing You) V24:244–245
Old Ryan, not yours (The Constellation Orion) V8:53
On the dark distant flurry (Angle of Geese) V2:2
on the frosty autumn air. (The Cossacks) V25:70

On the look of Death— (There's a Certain Slant of Light) V6:212
On your head like a crown (Any Human to Another) V3:2
One could do worse that be a swinger of birches. (Birches) V13:15
Or does it explode? (Harlem) V1:63
Or help to half-a-crown." (The Man He Killed) V3:167
or last time, we look. (In Particular) V20:125
or nothing (Queen-Ann's-Lace) V6:179
or the one red leaf the snow releases in March. (Three Times My Life Has Opened) V16:213
ORANGE forever. (Ballad of Orange and Grape) V10:18
our every corpuscle become an elf. (Moreover, the Moon) V20:153
outside. (it was New York and beautifully, snowing . . . (i was sitting in mcsorley's) V13:152
owing old (old age sticks) V3:246

P

patient in mind remembers the time. (Fading Light) V21:49
Perhaps he will fall. (Wilderness Gothic) V12:242
Petals on a wet, black bough (In a Station of the Metro) V2:116
Plaiting a dark red love-knot into her long black hair (The Highwayman) V4:68
Powerless, I drown. (Maternity) V21:142–143
Pro patria mori. (Dulce et Decorum Est) V10:110

R

Rage, rage against the dying of the light (Do Not Go Gentle into that Good Night) V1:51
Raise it again, man. We still believe what we hear. (The Singer's House) V17:206
Remember the Giver fading off the lip (A Drink of Water) V8:66
rise & walk away like a panther. (Ode to a Drum) V20:172–173
Rises toward her day after day, like a terrible fish (Mirror) V1:116

S

Shall be lifted—nevermore! (The Raven) V1:202
Shantih shantih shantih (The Waste Land) V20:248–252
share my shivering bed. (Chorale) V25:51
Shuddering with rain, coming down around me. (Omen) v22:107
Simply melted into the perfect light. (Perfect Light) V19:187
Singing of him what they could understand (Beowulf) V11:3
Singing with open mouths their strong melodious songs (I Hear America Singing) V3:152
slides by on grease (For the Union Dead) V7:67
Slouches towards Bethlehem to be born? (The Second Coming) V7:179
So long lives this, and this gives life to thee (Sonnet 18) V2:222
So prick my skin. (Pine) V23:223–224

Somebody loves us all. (Filling Station) V12:57
spill darker kissmarks on that dark. (Ten Years after Your Deliberate Drowning) V21:240
Stand still, yet we will make him run (To His Coy Mistress) V5:277
startled into eternity (Four Mountain Wolves) V9:132
Still clinging to your shirt (My Papa's Waltz) V3:192
Stood up, coiled above his head, transforming all. (A Tall Man Executes a Jig) V12:229
strangers ask. *Originally?* And I hesitate. (Originally) V25:146–147
Surely goodness and mercy shall follow me all the days of my life: and I will dwell in the house of the Lord for ever (Psalm 23) V4:103
syllables of an old order. (A Grafted Tongue) V12:93

T

Take any streetful of people buying clothes and groceries, cheering a hero or throwing confetti and blowing tin horns . . . tell me if the lovers are losers . . . tell me if any get more than the lovers . . . in the dust . . . in the cool tombs (Cool Tombs) V6:46
Than from everything else life promised that you could do? (Paradiso) V20:190–191
Than that you should remember and be sad. (Remember) V14:255
That then I scorn to change my state with Kings (Sonnet 29) V8:198
that there is more to know, that one day you will know it. (Knowledge) V25:113
That when we live no more, we may live ever (To My Dear and Loving Husband) V6:228
That's the word. (Black Zodiac) V10:47
the bigger it gets. (Smart and Final Iris) V15:183
The bosom of his Father and his God (Elegy Written in a Country Churchyard) V9:74
the bow toward torrents of *veyz mir.* (Three To's and an Oi) V24:264
The crime was in Granada, his Granada. (The Crime Was in Granada) V23:55–56
The dance is sure (Overture to a Dance of Locomotives) V11:143
The eyes turn topaz. (Hugh Selwyn Mauberley) V16:30
The garland briefer than a girl's (To an Athlete Dying Young) V7:230
The guidon flags flutter gayly in the wind. (Cavalry Crossing a Ford) V13:50
The hands gripped hard on the desert (At the Bomb Testing Site) V8:3
The holy melodies of love arise. (The Arsenal at Springfield) V17:3
the knife at the throat, the death in the metronome (Music Lessons) V8:117
The Lady of Shalott." (The Lady of Shalott) V15:97
The lightning and the gale! (Old Ironsides) V9:172
the long, perfect loveliness of sow (Saint Francis and the Sow) V9:222
The Lord survives the rainbow of His will (The Quaker Graveyard in Nantucket) V6:159
The man I was when I was part of it (Beware of Ruins) V8:43

the quilts sing on (My Mother Pieced Quilts) V12:169
The red rose and the brier (Barbara Allan) V7:11
The self-same Power that brought me there brought you. (The Rhodora) V17:191
The shaft we raise to them and thee (Concord Hymn) V4:30
The sky became a still and woven blue. (Merlin Enthralled) V16:73
The spirit of this place (To a Child Running With Outstretched Arms in Canyon de Chelly) V11:173
The town again, trailing your legs and crying! (Wild Swans) V17:221
the unremitting space of your rebellion (Lost Sister) V5:217
The woman won (Oysters) V4:91
their guts or their brains? (Southbound on the Freeway) V16:158
their dinnerware. (Portrait of a Couple at Century's End) V24:214–215
Then chiefly lives. (Virtue) V25:263
There is the trap that catches noblest spirits, that caught— they say—God, when he walked on earth (Shine, Perishing Republic) V4:162
there was light (Vancouver Lights) V8:246
They also serve who only stand and wait." ([On His Blindness] Sonnet 16) V3:262
They are going to some point true and unproven. (Geometry) V15:68
They rise, they walk again (The Heaven of Animals) V6:76
They think I lost. I think I won (Harlem Hopscotch) V2:93
This is my page for English B (Theme for English B) V6:194
This Love (In Memory of Radio) V9:145
Tho' it were ten thousand mile! (A Red, Red Rose) V8:152
Though I sang in my chains like the sea (Fern Hill) V3:92
Till human voices wake us, and we drown (The Love Song of J. Alfred Prufrock) V1:99
Till Love and Fame to nothingness do sink (When I Have Fears that I May Cease to Be) V2:295
To every woman a happy ending (Barbie Doll) V9:33
to glow at midnight. (The Blue Rim of Memory) V17:39
to its owner or what horror has befallen the other shoe (A Piéd) V3:16
To live with thee and be thy love. (The Nymph's Reply to the Shepherd) V14:241
To strive, to seek, to find, and not to yield (Ulysses) V2:279
To the moaning and the groaning of the bells (The Bells) V3:47
To the temple, singing. (In the Suburbs) V14:201

U

Undeniable selves, into your days, and beyond. (The Continuous Life) V18:51
until at last I lift you up and wrap you within me. (It's like This) V23:138–139
Until Eternity. (The Bustle in a House) V10:62
unusual conservation (Chocolates) V11:17
Uttering cries that are almost human (American Poetry) V7:2

W

War is kind (War Is Kind) V9:253
watching to see how it's done. (I Stop Writing the Poem) V16:58
Went home and put a bullet through his head (Richard Cory) V4:117
Were not the one dead, turned to their affairs. (Out, Out—) V10:213
Were toward Eternity— (Because I Could Not Stop for Death) V2:27
What will survive of us is love. (An Arundel Tomb) V12:18
When I died they washed me out of the turret with a hose (The Death of the Ball Turret Gunner) V2:41
when they untie them in the evening. (Early in the Morning) V17:75
when you are at a party. (Social Life) V19:251
When you have both (Toads) V4:244
Where deep in the night I hear a voice (Butcher Shop) V7:43
Where ignorant armies clash by night (Dover Beach) V2:52
Which Claus of Innsbruck cast in bronze for me! (My Last Duchess) V1:166
Which for all you know is the life you've chosen. (The God Who Loves You) V20:88
which is not going to go wasted on me which is why I'm telling you about it (Having a Coke with You) V12:106
which only looks like an *l*, and is silent. (Trompe l'Oeil) V22:216
white ash amid funereal cypresses (Helen) V6:92
Who are you and what is your purpose? (The Mystery) V15:138
Wi' the Scots lords at his feit (Sir Patrick Spens) V4:177
Will always be ready to bless the day (Morning Walk) V21:167
will be easy, my rancor less bitter . . . (On the Threshold) V22:128
Will hear of as a god." (How we Heard the Name) V10:167
Wind, like the dodo's (Bedtime Story) V8:33
windowpanes. (View) V25:246–247
With gold unfading, WASHINGTON! be thine. (To His Excellency General Washington) V13:213
with my eyes closed. (We Live by What We See at Night) V13:240
With the slow smokeless burning of decay (The Wood-Pile) V6:252
With what they had to go on. (The Conquerors) V13:67
Without cease or doubt sew the sweet sad earth. (The Satyr's Heart) V22:187
Would scarcely know that we were gone. (There Will Come Soft Rains) V14:301

Y

Ye know on earth, and all ye need to know (Ode on a Grecian Urn) V1:180
You live in this, and dwell in lovers' eyes (Sonnet 55) V5:246

You may for ever tarry. (To the Virgins, to Make Much
  of Time) V13:226
you who raised me? (The Gold Lily) V5:127
you'll have understood by then what these Ithakas mean.
  (Ithaka) V19:114